INTRODUCTI
TO THE GRA
OF ENGLISH

RODNEY HUDDLESTON

DEPARTMENT OF ENGLISH
UNIVERSITY OF QUEENSLAND

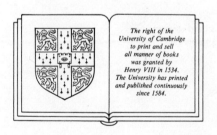

*The right of the
University of Cambridge
to print and sell
all manner of books
was granted by
Henry VIII in 1534.
The University has printed
and published continuously
since 1584.*

CAMBRIDGE UNIVERSITY PRESS

CAMBRIDGE

LONDON   NEW YORK   NEW ROCHELLE

MELBOURNE   SYDNEY

Published by the Press Syndicate of the University of Cambridge
The Pitt Building, Trumpington Street, Cambridge CB2 1RP
32 East 57th Street, New York, NY 10022, USA
10 Stamford Road, Oakleigh, Melbourne 3166, Australia

First published 1984

Printed in Great Britain at the Bath Press, Avon
Reprinted 1985, 1986

Library of Congress catalogue card number: 84–3191

British Library Cataloguing in Publication Data
Huddleston, Rodney
Introduction to the grammar of English. –
(Cambridge textbooks in linguistics)
1. English language – Grammar – 1950–
I. Title
428.2   PE1112

ISBN 0 521 22893 X hard covers
ISBN 0 521 29704 4 paperback

PP

CAMBRIDGE TEXTBOOKS IN LINGUISTICS

General Editors: B. COMRIE, C. J. FILLMORE, R. LASS, R. B. LE PAGE,
J. LYONS, P. H. MATTHEWS, F. R. PALMER, R. POSNER, S. ROMAINE,
N. V. SMITH, A. ZWICKY

INTRODUCTION TO THE GRAMMAR OF ENGLISH

For Cheryll

CONTENTS

Contents

PREFACE

This book is written primarily for students of linguistics in universities and other tertiary institutions. It assumes no previous knowledge of linguistics: the first three chapters introduce the theoretical concepts and methodological principles needed to follow the later descriptive chapters. I have likewise made minimal assumptions about the reader's familiarity with 'traditional grammar' – all terms borrowed from the traditional repertoire, such as 'noun', 'transitive verb', 'relative clause', and so on, are fully explained. Although the book covers a fair amount of the grammar, it is not simply a short grammar of English, inasmuch as it devotes a good deal of attention to the problem of justifying the analysis proposed (where, for example, it differs from the traditional analysis) or of choosing between alternative analyses – it is in this sense that it is directed towards the student of linguistics. It does not, however, attempt to formalise the grammar: it is not 'generative' – and it is not written within the framework or model of any particular contemporary school of linguistics such as 'transformational grammar', 'systemic grammar', 'functional grammar' or the like. It follows, rather, a 'structural' approach, in a very broad understanding of that term, one where the grammatical categories postulated derive from a study of the combinational and contrastive relationships the words and other forms enter into. The aim is to give a reasonably careful and precise account of major areas of English grammar that will provide a foundation for more advanced work in theoretical linguistics.

For practical reasons I have confined my attention to Standard English; there is, of course, a good deal of regional variation within Standard English: I have drawn attention to such variation in a number of places but have not attempted to give a systematic description of it. Also for practical reasons I have been highly selective in the references given at the end of each chapter under the heading 'Further reading': I have very often mentioned only relatively recent works, but the reader who follows up these references will of course generally find there details of earlier works on the topics concerned.

I would like to express my gratitude to Frank Palmer, of the Editorial Board, for his support, advice and comments on draft chapters. A number of other friends and colleagues were good enough to give their time to read all or part of the book in draft form: my thanks are due to Barry Blake, Bob Cochrane, Peter Collins, Bob Dixon, Dick Hudson, Steve Johnson, Hank Kylstra, David Lee, Jeff Pittam and Neil Smith for their comments on particular chapters, and especially to Peter Matthews, Bernard Comrie, Sidney Greenbaum and Graham Mallinson for numerous constructive suggestions on the whole book at various stages of writing – but they are not of course to blame for the weaknesses that remain. I would also like to thank Deborah McNeill for the marvellous job she made of typing a long and complex manuscript – and for her stoicism in the face of repeated and often massive revision. Finally my greatest debt is to my wife Cheryll; much of the book has been written at weekends: I thank her for putting up with the long period of neglect that this has necessitated, and for her constant support and encouragement.

TABLE OF SYMBOLS AND NOTATIONAL CONVENTIONS

Bold face italics indicate lexemes (see 1.1).

Ordinary italics are used for citing sentences, words and other forms (in orthographic representation).

<u>*Underlined italics*</u> indicate location of sentence stress in cited examples.

/ /	obliques enclose phonological representations of forms.
/	oblique is used to abbreviate examples: *He can/will go* is an abbreviation of *He can go* and *He will go*.
( )	parentheses enclose optional elements: *He spent the money (that) you gave him* indicates that the *that* may be present, *He spent the money that you gave him*, or absent, *He spent the money you gave him*.
[ ]	square brackets enclose relevant context for an example: *[Nobody] I know [thinks that]* represents the form *I know* considered as occurring in the context '*Nobody ____ thinks that*'.
⟨ ⟩	angle brackets enclose letters representing different speakers: ⟨A⟩ *What are you doing?* – ⟨B⟩ *Reading the paper* cites an exchange where *What are you doing?* is uttered by one speaker, *Reading the paper* by another.
*	asterisk indicates that what follows is ungrammatical – at least in the construal under consideration.
?	indicates that the grammaticality (or, if followed by *, the ungrammaticality) of what follows is questionable.
†	indicates a hypothetical form from which some actual form is transformationally derived (see 1.4).

Subscripts distinguish different words or lexemes (**bottle**$_N$ vs **bottle**$_V$); superscript descriptive terms distinguish different uses of a single word or lexeme (*what* ^{interrogative} vs *what* ^{relative}), while superscript numerals distinguish lexical homonyms (**bat**^{1} vs **bat**^{2}) – see 3.2.

ROMAN SMALL CAPITALS	are used for emphasis.
Roman bold face	is used for important technical terms when explained.
' '	single quotation marks are used for quotations and as 'scare quotes', e.g. for technical terms not yet explained.
" "	double quotation marks are used to represent meanings.
{ }	braces are used within double quotation marks to indicate semantic constituent structure.

The following abbreviations are used for syntactic classes, functions and other categories:

A	adjunct	O	object
Adj	adjective	O^d	direct object
AdjP	adjective phrase	O^i	indirect object
Adv	adverb	P	predicator
AdvP	adverb phrase	PC	predicative complement
Art	article	PC^o	objective predicative complement
Aux	auxiliary verb	PC^s	subjective predicative complement
C	complement	pers	person
Comp	complement	pl	plural
Detnr	determiner	PossP	possessive phrase
Detve	determinative	PP	preposition phrase
EVP	extended verb phrase	Prep	preposition
Mod	modal auxiliary	S	subject
MV	main verb	sg	singular
N	noun	V	verb
NP	noun phrase	VP	verb phrase

Phonological symbols:

Consonant phonemes

/p/	as in *pie*	/v/	as in *view*	/n/	as in *no*
/t/	*tie*	/θ/	*thigh*	/ŋ/	*wing*
/d/	*die*	/ð/	*thy*	/l/	*lie*
/k/	*car*	/s/	*see*	/r/	*row*
/g/	*go*	/z/	*zoo*	/j/	*you*
/tʃ/	*chew*	/ʃ/	*shy*	/w/	*we*
/dʒ/	*jaw*	/h/	*high*		
/f/	*few*	/m/	*my*		

Vowel phonemes

/iː/ as in *peat*	/ʌ/ as in *putt*	/ɛə/ as in *paired*
/ɪ/ *pit*	/əʊ/ *pole*	/ʊə/ *poor*
/e/ *pet*	/aɪ/ *pile*	/ə/ *sofa*
/æ/ *pat*	/aʊ/ *pout*	

' precedes accented syllable in the word, as in '*photo*, a'*fraid*.

↓ indicates intonation with falling terminal, ↑ with rising terminal

I
Basic concepts in grammar

The term 'grammar' is used in a number of different senses – the grammar of a language may be understood to be a full description of the form and meaning of the sentences of the language or else it may cover only certain, variously delimited, parts of such a description. Here we shall use it in one of these narrower senses, embracing **syntax** and **morphology**. Syntax is concerned with the way words combine to form sentences, while morphology is concerned with the form of words. We will launch without delay into a discussion of basic concepts in syntax and morphology, returning in §8 to the distinction between grammar in this sense and various other components of a full description and to the basis for dividing grammar into syntactic and morphological subcomponents. The only terms that we shall need to anticipate are 'phonology' and 'semantics': phonology deals with the sound system, with the pronunciation of words and sentences, semantics deals with meaning.

1.1 **Words and lexemes**

Syntax deals with combinations of words, we have said, morphology with the form of words. But again the term 'word' has been used in a variety of senses. For our immediate purposes it will suffice to draw just one distinction, which we can approach by considering the relation between, say, *tooth* and *teeth*: are they different words or the same word? From one point of view they are clearly different words: they are pronounced and spelt differently, they differ in meaning, and they occur in different positions in sentences (so that we could not, for example, replace *tooth* by *teeth* in *This tooth is loose* or *teeth* by *tooth* in *These teeth are loose*, and so on). Yet they are also traditionally said to be different forms of the same word. This is a more abstract sense: we abstract away the differences between them to isolate what is common to both. It will be helpful to distinguish both terminologically and notationally between these two senses. I shall use **word** for the less abstract concept, **lexeme** for the more abstract one, and I shall cite words in ordinary italics, lexemes in bold face italics. We accordingly say that *tooth* and *teeth* are different words, but **forms** of the same lexeme ***tooth***.

More specifically, we will say that *tooth* is the 'singular' form of **tooth** and that *teeth* is its 'plural' form. The words *tooth* and *teeth* are thus each analysed into two components, the abstract lexeme and what we shall call an **inflectional property**. These properties are relevant to both the morphological and syntactic components of the grammar (and for this reason are commonly referred to also as 'morphosyntactic properties'). The morphology will include rules for deriving the various inflectional forms of a lexeme from the 'lexical stem', while the syntax will include rules specifying under what conditions a lexeme may or must carry a given inflectional property. Thus it is a fact of morphology that the plural of **tooth** is *teeth*, whereas it is a fact of syntax that if **tooth** enters into construction with **this** there must be 'agreement' in number, i.e. both must carry the singular inflection or both the plural. Similarly, the morphology will tell us that the 'past participle' of the verb **see** is *seen*, whereas the syntax will say that a past participle is required in the 'passive' construction, as in *He was seen by the caretaker*.

Not all words enter into inflectional contrasts such as we find between *tooth* and *teeth*, *this* and *these*, or *see*, *sees*, *saw*, *seeing* and *seen*. Usually, as with words like *because*, *of*, *however*, *besides*, this is because there is simply no inflectional property present at all – and, precisely because there is no inflectional property to abstract away, the concept of lexeme will be inapplicable in such cases. Thus *because* is a word that is not a form of any lexeme. In other cases we can recognise an inflectional property even though it is not independently contrastive: *alms* does not contrast with singular **alm*, but we can still analyse it as a plural form, and conversely *equipment* does not contrast with plural **equipments* but we can still analyse it as a singular form. In these cases we can invoke the concept of lexeme, so that *equipment*, for example, will be the singular form of the lexeme **equipment**. When we say that **equipment** has a singular form but no plural form we are talking about the same kind of entity as when we say that **tooth** has *tooth* as its singular form and *teeth* as its plural form. But it is of course contrasts like that between *tooth* and *teeth* that provide the raison d'être for the lexeme concept: if it were not for these we would have no lexeme–word distinction, **tooth** vs *tooth*, to generalise to cases like **equipment** vs *equipment*.

1.2 Constituent structure

Words are not the only units that we need in describing the structure of sentences. Although we can break a sentence down into a sequence of words, we will not go from sentence to word in a single step but will recognise units intermediate in size between sentence and word. For example, in

(1)   *The boss must have made a mistake*

it is intuitively obvious that although *a* is immediately adjacent in the sequence to both *made* and *mistake*, it is more closely related to the latter than to the former: this relationship between *a* and *mistake* can then be described by saying that they go together to form a **constituent** of the sentence. More generally, the syntactic analysis of a sentence will assign to it a **constituent structure** which identifies the full hierarchy of its constituents.

A standard way of representing constituent structure diagrammatically is illustrated in (2):

(2)

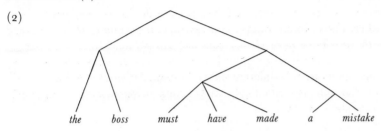

This diagram identifies eleven constituents: the seven words, represented by the bottom row of points, and four intermediate units, *the boss*, *must have made*, *a mistake*, and *must have made a mistake*. The point from which the lines lead down to *a* and *mistake* represents the constituent *a mistake*, and so on. By contrast *made a* is not a constituent: there is no point from which the lines lead down to just this pair of words.

If we read the diagram from the top downwards we see that the sentence is divided first into *the boss* and *must have made a mistake*: these are said to be the **immediate constituents** (or **ICs**) of the sentence. Each of them is then broken down into its own ICs, *the* and *boss* for the first, *must have made* and *a mistake* for the second – and so on until we reach the bottom.

'Constituent' is a relational concept: if *x* is a constituent, it must be a constituent of something. For example, in (2) *must have made* is a constituent of the sentence – and also of *must have made a mistake*. Similarly with 'immediate constituent': *must have made* is an IC of *must have made a mistake* (but only of this). It follows that the sentence itself is not a constituent: as the maximal unit in syntax it is not part of any other unit. We will then apply the term **construction** to the sentence and any constituent except the minimal ones, the words. Thus with 'constituent' we are as it were looking upwards: *x* is a constituent if it is part of some element higher in the hierarchy; and with 'construction' we are looking downwards: *x* is a construction if it is analysable into, i.e. constructed from, one or more elements lower in the hierarchy.[1]

---

[1] This allows for the special case where a construction has only one IC. For example the imperative sentence *Stop!* contains only one word, but we will still speak of it as a construction: it is constructed from that one word. It is for this reason that I say 'higher/lower in the hierarchy' rather than the more concrete 'larger/smaller'. (See 3.3 for further discussion of this issue.)

Finally we will use **form** as a general term covering both constituents and constructions. Thus in (2) there are eleven constituents, five constructions and twelve forms. Notice that this use of 'form' is consistent with that introduced in the last section, where we spoke of *teeth*, for example, as a form of the lexeme **tooth**: in *He cleaned his teeth* it is *teeth* not **tooth** that is a constituent of the sentence, so that *teeth* like *his teeth, cleaned, cleaned his teeth*, etc., will be a form.

A given sequence of words may be a constituent in one sentence but not in another. Thus *John and Bill* is a constituent of the sentence *He saw John and Bill at the races* but not of *He saw John and Bill did too*. Moreover, a single sentence may have two (or indeed more) constituent structure analyses, each corresponding to a different interpretation. *Liz attacked the man with the knife*, for example, is syntactically ambiguous, being analysable (approximately) as shown in (3) or (4);

(3) (4)

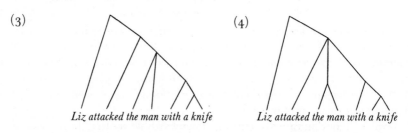

Liz attacked the man with a knife   *Liz attacked the man with a knife*

Analysis (3) corresponds to the interpretation "Liz attacked the man who had a knife" – here *the man with a knife* forms a constituent, and serves to pick out the person whom Liz attacked. Analysis (4), by contrast, represents the structure the sentence has under the interpretation "Liz used a knife in her attack on the man" – here *the man* and *with a knife* do not go together to form a constituent, but are both ICs of the larger constituent *attacked the man with a knife*, with *the man* identifying the person attacked and *with a knife* giving information about the means of attack, not about the man. Sometimes such ambiguities are resolved 'prosodically' – the different constituent structures are distinguished by the intonation and rhythm (similarly in writing they may be resolved by punctuation). An elementary example is *Liz saw John and Kim and Robin did too*, which can be analysed (again approximately) as either (5) or (6):

(5)

Liz saw John and Kim and Robin did too

(6)

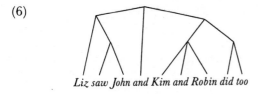

Liz saw John and Kim and Robin did too

(5) matches the interpretation "John and Kim were seen by Liz and they were also seen by Robin", whereas (6) corresponds to "John was seen by Liz and he was also seen by Kim and Robin". In any normal utterance of the sentence the prosodic features (or punctuation) would show clearly whether *Kim* was coordinated with *John*, as in (5), or with *Robin*, as in (6). But in general relatively little information about the constituent structure is derivable directly from the physical signal: constituent structure is an abstract property of sentences.

In discussing example (1) I said it was intuitively obvious that *a* goes with *mistake* to form a constituent, but clearly it will not do to proceed simply on the basis of intuition – we need to find less subjective evidence for our analysis. What kinds of evidence are relevant is a question we shall take up later – one cannot determine the constituent structure without considering other aspects of the syntax and it will therefore be better to proceed to the other main concepts, leaving till the next chapter the issue of how one chooses one analysis rather than another.

1.3 Syntactic classes and functions

The constituent structure analysis of a sentence identifies the forms and their hierarchical arrangement one within another. We must now consider how the various forms are to be further described.

In the first place, they will be assigned to syntactic **classes** and **subclasses** on the basis of various types of shared properties. Thus words will be assigned to such primary classes as noun, verb, adjective, etc., and to such subclasses as proper noun, common noun, transitive verb, etc. Forms occurring higher in the constituent hierarchy can be classified in an analogous way as noun phrases, verb phrases, clauses, interrogative clauses, and so on. If we return to our example sentence, *The boss must have made a mistake*, we can extend the earlier analysis by incorporating a sample of such classificatory information in the following way:

5

(7)

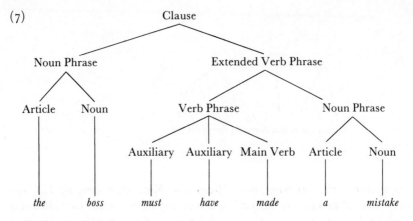

The relationship between this and diagram (2) above will be clear: classificatory labels have been attached to the points representing the twelve forms, and lines have been added linking the words with the word-class labels.

Secondly, we shall specify the **syntactic function** of each constituent. Thus *the boss* functions as subject, *a mistake* as object, and with the phrase *the boss* the word *boss* functions as head, *the* as determiner, and so on. Such functional information can be incorporated into our diagrammatic representation of the structure as shown in (8), where the classificatory labels of (7) have now been abbreviated.

(8)

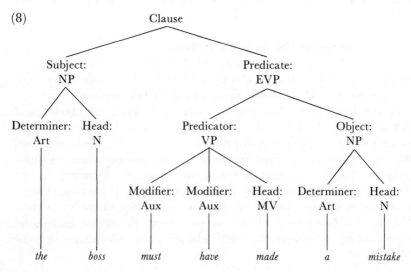

A considerable number of technical terms have been introduced here, and during the course of the book we shall need to explain them. At this stage, however, my aim is merely to make some general points about classes and functions, to give some initial idea of what kinds of concept they are.

Functions are inherently relational – and indeed are often referred to as 'grammatical relations'. Thus when we say that *the boss* is subject we mean that it stands in the subject relation to the clause: it is subject of the clause. Similarly *boss* is head of the phrase *the boss*. Syntactic functions are clearly of crucial importance for the meaning. The meaning of *The guard shot the intruder*, where *the guard* functions as subject, *the intruder* as object, is very different from that of *The intruder shot the guard*, where the functions are reversed. Or again, *the bottom saucepan*, where *bottom* is modifier, *saucepan* head, means something quite different from *the saucepan bottom*, where *saucepan* is modifier, *bottom* head. The meaning of a sentence depends in part on the meanings of the vocabulary items it contains, in part on their grammatical arrangement: much of the meaning attributable to the grammatical arrangement derives from the syntactic functions.

A syntactic class or subclass, we have said, is a set of forms sharing certain properties. These shared properties are of two main types: one concerns the internal structure of the forms, the other their functional potential.

(a) With **internal structure** (or simply structure), we are concerned primarily with the way a form is made up of forms lower in the constituent hierarchy. For example, the forms *in the garden, with considerable difficulty, behind the man I was talking to* all consist of a preposition (*in, with, behind*) functioning as head, followed by a noun phrase functioning as complement: they are alike in their (internal) structure, and this is the major factor determining their classification as preposition phrases. Conversely, *You are very careful* and *Be very careful* differ in their internal structure (they contain different inflectional forms of **be**, and only the first has a subject) and this difference determines their assignment to distinct classes, declarative clause and imperative clause respectively.[2] In this kind of classification we are considering forms as constructions, and the classificatory labels are thus commonly applied also to construction-types: we speak of *Be very careful* as an example of the imperative construction-type – or simply of the imperative construction. I also include under the heading of internal structure the analysis of a word into a lexeme plus its inflectional

---

[2] This account of the differences between the two classes is intended only as a rough approximation, but the refinements needed would not affect the point being made here; see 2.1 and 11.3 for fuller discussion.

properties, so that *took, wrote, saw*, etc., are alike in internal structure in that they consist of a lexeme plus the inflectional property past tense.

(b) With **functional potential** we are concerned with what functions a form can have in what kinds of construction higher in the constituent hierarchy. For example, *the boss, my uncle, some of it*, etc., are alike in being able to function as subject in clause structure, as in (9), object in extended verb phrase structure, as in (10), complement in preposition phrase structure, as in (11), and so on:

(9)   *The boss / my uncle / some of it arrived on time*
(10)   *[He] didn't understand the boss / my uncle / some of it*
(11)   *[She was dissatisfied] with the boss / my uncle / some of it*

This similarity of function is then a major factor justifying the classification of all three forms as noun phrases. Conversely, the reason why we assign *the* and *of*, say, to different word-classes is that they differ with respect to the functional positions they occupy in the structure of phrases: *the* functions as determiner in noun phrase structure (*the boss*), while *of* functions as head in preposition phrase structure (*of the wine*) – with noun phrases and preposition phrases likewise distinguished by their functional potential. A standard technique for investigating this kind of syntactic property involves substituting one form for another within a given sentence – a technique employed above to bring out the similarity between *the boss*, *my uncle*, and *some of it*. But it must be emphasised that it cannot be applied in any purely mechanical way. Two points should be borne in mind. First, the fact that we can substitute form A for form B in a given sentence will be relevant only if the syntactic function remains constant. Thus in *They left the meeting* we could replace *the meeting* by *rather late* to give *They left rather late*, but since *the meeting* functions here as object while *rather late* functions as 'adjunct', the substitution provides no evidence for a syntactic similarity between *the meeting* and *rather late*. The second point is that if substituting A for B results in a sentence judged to be unacceptable, this will provide evidence for a difference in functional potential only if the unacceptability is a matter of grammar. Suppose, for example, that we replace *my uncle* in (12) by *rather sadly* on the one hand, and by *the saucer* on the other:

(12)   i   *My uncle laughed with delight*
          ii   **Rather sadly laughed with delight*
          iii *The saucer laughed with delight*

Although (iii) might be judged unacceptable, it is not ungrammatical – it is just that the event it describes is one we regard as impossible on the basis of our knowledge of saucers. By contrast, (ii) clearly is ungrammatical, and hence, in accordance with the convention introduced in §1, is prefixed with an asterisk. Accordingly (12) provides no evidence for a difference in functional potential between *my uncle* and *the saucer*, but it does show *my uncle* and *rather sadly* to be different – and this kind of evidence is used in classifying *my uncle* as a noun phrase, *rather sadly* as an adverb phrase.

As we use functional potential as a major criterion for classification, there will of course be a significant degree of correlation between our syntactic functions (subject, object, modifier, etc.) and our syntactic classes (noun phrase, noun, adjective, adverb, etc.). The correlation is, however, by no means one-to-one. In the first place, a given class may be able to fill two or more different functional positions. This we have already seen to be the case for noun phrases, which can function as subject, object, complement of a preposition – and in a number of other positions too. Similarly, an adjective phrase like *very young* can function either as modifier in NP structure (as in *a very young child*) or as 'predicative complement' in clause structure (*The child was very young*). In the second place a given functional position may be able to be filled by members of different classes. For example, although the subject of a clause is usually an NP it can also be – under certain conditions – another clause, as in *That he was concealing something was becoming more and more obvious*, where *that he was concealing something* is a (subordinate) clause functioning as subject of the larger (superordinate) clause that forms the whole sentence. Similarly, what we have just introduced as the predicative complement position can be filled by an AdjP, as in *He was still very young*, or by an NP, as in *He was still a child*. Or again, the modifier position in NP structure can be filled by an AdjP (*[a man] eager for recognition*), a PP (*[a man] with a grudge*) or a 'relative clause' (*[a man] who knew her son*). (In discussing such cases I shall follow a convention whereby expressions like 'AdjP modifier', consisting of class label and function label, are to be interpreted as "modifier belonging to the class AdjP", not "modifier of/within the structure of an AdjP".)

The fact that we find a many-to-many rather than one-to-one correlation between functions and classes is of course a major reason for keeping the two kinds of category conceptually distinct. In certain specific cases the correlation is one-to-one: for example, the predicator is invariably filled by a verb phrase, and a verb phrase always functions as predicator; but for consistency we will maintain the distinction even when this is so – so that we will apply the term 'verb phrase' to a class of forms (such as *saw, has gone, may have been*) and 'predicator' to the function of a verb phrase in a larger construction (so that in *I saw the film*, say, *saw* is predicator and *the film* object).

1.4 Paradigmatic relations and kernel clauses

The linguistic relations between forms fall into two fundamentally distinct types: **syntagmatic** and **paradigmatic**. Less standard but more transparent terms are respectively 'and-relations' and 'or-relations'.

Thus on the one hand forms x, y, z, etc., stand in syntagmatic ('and') relation if x and y and z combine in the structure of some larger form. For example, in the clause *John knew Max* the forms *John, knew* and *Max* are related syntagmatically in that they occur together in the larger structure. On the other hand, we recognise a paradigmatic ('or') relation between forms x, y, z, etc., if one is substitutable for the other, if we have a choice between them. Thus the *knew* of *John knew Max* could be replaced by *had known, knows, warned, had warned*, etc. so that we recognise a paradigmatic relation at the predicator position between *knew, had known, knows, warned, had warned*, etc. Similarly the whole clause is in paradigmatic relation with *Did John know Max?, John didn't know Max*, and so on.

Syntactic functions, such as subject, predicator, object, are established to handle syntagmatic relations: the specific syntagmatic relations holding between the phrases in *John knew Max* are that *John* is subject, *knew* predicator and *Max* object. In this section, our focus of attention will be on paradigmatic relations. Let us therefore pursue the above example, where we have a paradigmatic relation between *knew, had known*, etc. Clearly the set of forms in paradigmatic relation with *knew* is enormously large: it would be an unprofitable undertaking to try to list them directly. We note, however, that the differences between them involve a number of distinct variables or dimensions of contrast:

(a) *knew* and *warned* are past forms in contrast to present tense *knows* and *warns*;

(b) *knew* and *warned* are non-perfect in contrast to perfect *had known, had warned*;

(c) *knew* and *warned* are positive in contrast with negative *didn't know, didn't warn*;

(d) *knew, knows, had known* and *didn't know* all contain as their final or only verb a form of **know**, whereas *warned, warns, had warned, didn't warn* contain a form of **warn**;

and so on.

Where a given variable has just a small number of possible values, we shall say that we have a grammatical **system**, with the values being mutually exclusive **terms** in the system. Thus past and present are terms in one system, (a), perfect and non-perfect are terms in a second system, (b), positive and negative in a third, (c) – but we will not have a system for variable (d) contrasting verb phrases with **know** and **warn** (or **admire**, **remember**, etc.) for the differences here depend simply on which dictionary item is selected. We will return to the relationship between grammar and dictionary in §8; in the meantime we will confine our discussion of systems to cases like those above where the terms are grammatical classes. Many but by no means all such systems have standard names: that contrasting past and present is called 'tense', perfect vs non-perfect is commonly referred to as a system of 'aspect', and so on.

The above example involved the VP – the multidimensionality of paradigmatic relations among clauses is illustrated in

(13) *Dillinger had sued Tom*
(14)   i *Had Dillinger sued Tom?*
       ii *Dillinger had not sued Tom*
      iii *Tom had been sued by Dillinger*
      iv *It was Dillinger who had sued Tom*
(15) *Was it not Tom who had been sued by Dillinger?*

Thus each of the examples in (14) contrasts with (13) in respect of a different variable: (i) is interrogative while (13) is declarative; (ii) is negative while (13) is positive;[3] (iii) is passive while (13) is active; (iv) is an *it*-cleft construction, while (13) is not – and (15) then contrasts with (13) on all four of these dimensions.

Generally one of the terms in a system can be regarded as syntactically **unmarked**, the other(s) as **marked**. The unmarked term is the one that is syntactically more basic, while the marked terms can be most conveniently described by reference to the way they differ from the unmarked term. In the most straightforward cases, being more basic is a matter of being simpler, of lacking some element(s) that characterise the marked term. (13), for example, is clearly simpler than any of (14ii–iv) in this very obvious sense. But there is a good deal more to it than that. Thus (13) and (14i) contain exactly the same elements: it's just the order that is different. There are nevertheless two reasons why we will regard the declarative (13) as unmarked, the interrogative (14i) as marked.

(a) In the first place, there are many cases where a declarative and its interrogative counterpart don't simply differ in order: compare declarative *Dillinger sued Tom* and interrogative *Did Dillinger sue Tom?* – and in these cases the declarative is simpler by virtue of lacking the auxiliary **do** that is required in the interrogative.

(b) The order of elements that we find in (14i) is very much more re-stricted than that of (13) with respect to the conditions under which it is found. Take, for example, the various kinds of subordinate clause in

---

[3] We treat positive vs negative as a system of the clause as well as of the VP because the negative element is not invariably in the VP – cf. *Nobody had sued Tom* where the clause is negative by virtue of its subject *nobody*.

(16)   i *[Those] who sued Tom [came to regret it]*
          ii *For Dillinger to sue Tom [would be a great mistake]*
         iii *Unless Dillinger had sued Tom [he would have been sacked]*

Here, as in numerous other contexts, only the order of (13) is possible. It is thus descriptively more economical to take this order as basic and that of (14i) as marked, exceptional, needing special statement: i.e. it is more economical to identify the conditions under which the order of (14i) is permitted or required, with that of (13) occurring everywhere else, instead of detailing each construction where we have the order of (13) and saying that others have that of (14i).

In some cases, indeed, the marked term may lack one or more elements found in the unmarked term:

(17)   i *She had written something*
          ii *[Something] she had written [was puzzling me]*
(18)   i *You are quiet*
          ii *Be quiet*

In (17ii) *she had written* is a subordinate clause (more specifically a relative clause), while (17i) is a main clause and we take (17i) as unmarked even though it contains an extra element, the object *something*. The reason is that although (17ii) lacks an object there is a sense in which one is 'understood' – this is why we could not replace **write** by such a verb as **die** which cannot take an object: the ungrammaticality of marked **[Something] she had died [was puzzling me]* thus follows from that of unmarked **She had died something*. In (18), (i) is declarative while (ii) is imperative; (ii) is structurally simpler in that it lacks a subject, but since there is nevertheless a subject 'understood' (namely *you*) we again take (i) as more basic. Notice, for example, that a predicate which can't take *you* as subject can't occur in construction (ii) – for example **seem** *that you're ill* can't take *you* as subject (it can only take *it*), so that the ungrammaticality of marked **Seem that you're ill* follows again from that of the unmarked **You seem that you're ill*. A further reason for taking the declarative as unmarked, the imperative as marked is analogous to that invoked in the discussion of (13) vs (14i) – there are significantly more restrictions on the imperative construction than on the declarative. For example, in the declarative we have a contrast of tense, with (18i) contrasting as present tense with *You were quiet* as past – but there is no such contrast for (18ii). Or again (18i) is 'non-modal' in contrast to *You must be quiet, You should be quiet, You may be quiet*, etc., which contain one of the 'modal auxiliaries' **must**, **should**, **may**, etc., but these verbs are excluded from the imperative construction.

A form which is maximally basic, one which does not belong to a marked term in any system, is called a **kernel** form. More particularly, for it is primarily in connection with clauses that we shall invoke the concept, we shall say that examples like (13), (17i), (18i) are **kernel clauses**, while (14), (15), (16), (17ii), (18ii) are non-kernel clauses. The set of possible clause structures is far too large and heterogeneous for us to be able to cope with them all at once: instead of treating them all as of equal status we will accord descriptive priority to the kernel clauses. We first describe the structure of kernel clauses and then deal with the non-kernel clauses derivatively by reference to the ways the various marked classes differ from the corresponding unmarked ones – how negatives differ from positives, interrogatives from declaratives, etc.

The differences will involve one or more of the following:

(a) The **addition** of some element(s) not present in the unmarked construction. Thus (14ii) differs from (13) by the addition of *not* – and in the pair *They like it* vs *They do not like it* the negative contains the additional elements ***do*** and *not*. Or again the subordinate [*The rumour*] *that Dillinger had sued Tom* [*was quite false*] differs from (13) by the addition of the 'subordinating conjunction' *that*.

(b) The **omission** of some understood element(s), such as the object in (17ii) or the subject in (18ii).

(c) The **rearrangement** of elements. The simplest kind of rearrangement is reordering, as (14i) differs from (13) with respect to the order of the subject and the first verb. A more complex kind involves the reassignment of grammatical functions, as in the difference between the passive (14iii) and active (13) (where there are also differences of type (a) – the addition of *by* and the auxiliary verb ***be***) – in (13) *Dillinger* is subject and *Tom* object, whereas in (14iii) *Tom* is subject and *Dillinger* is complement of the preposition *by*.

(d) The **selection** of some element(s) of a special kind instead of some ordinary element(s) with the same function in the unmarked construction. For example, in (19):

(19)   i *The film was interesting/good/quite passable/hopeless/...*
        ii *How was the film?*

(ii) is an interrogative clause (belonging to a different subclass of interrogative clause from that illustrated in (14i)) comparable in structure to the declaratives in (i): the difference is partly a matter of selection, with (ii) having the special interrogative word *how* as 'predicative complement' while (i) has the ordinary AdjPs *interesting, good*, etc., partly a matter of rearrangement (reordering), with (ii) having the predicative complement initial and the verb before the subject instead of the unmarked order of (i).

Differences of types (a)–(c) can conveniently be described by means of **transformations**, changes applied to the structure of an unmarked form to yield a marked form. Thus we will derive (14i) from (13) by a transformation called 'subject–operator' inversion: it moves *had* (a verb belonging to a class we shall call 'operators' – cf. 4.4) to the left of the subject. And we will derive (14iii) from (13) by the passivisation transformation – it changes the object into the subject, adds *by* and makes the original subject its complement, adds **be** and adjusts the verb inflections in ways we will specify (14.1). Such a use of transformations has a long tradition. They have long been invoked in language teaching, where the learner may be given drills in transforming declaratives into interrogatives, actives into passives, and so on. More recently, the idea has been developed, refined and formalised so that transformation is now a key concept in the theory known for that reason as transformational grammar. As explained in the preface, this book is not about transformational grammar, and my use of transformations will remain essentially pretheoretical and informal, differing in significant respects from the transformational grammarian's use of them. There are three points that should be made at this stage to clarify how the concept is to be understood:

(a) We take a transformation to be a syntactic process converting a more elementary construction into a less elementary one. We are concerned here solely with the description of the form of sentences, not with the mental processes involved in speaking or writing. In analysing (14ii) as transformationally derived from (13), for example, we are not suggesting that in uttering sentences like (14iii) speakers first formulate in their minds a sentence like (13) and then go through some mental operation of reformulating it: we are merely saying that (13) is structurally more basic or elementary and that the form of (14iii) can be conveniently accounted for in terms of its systematic difference from the simpler construction.

(b) I shall not invoke transformations to handle the selection of special elements like the *how* of (19ii). We cannot analyse the *how* into an 'interrogative component' and a 'residual component' that can be expressed on its own in a declarative, and hence there is nothing that we could regard as 'the declarative counterpart' of (19ii) – nothing, therefore, from which it can be illuminatingly derived by means of the substitution of *how* for the corresponding non-interrogative element.

(c) For the most part we will assume that the transformations apply to actual clauses (those of the transformational grammarian, by contrast, apply to abstract structures); to a limited extent, however, we will be willing to have them apply to postulated hypothetical clauses, indicated as such by the symbol '†'. Given, for example, that we are deriving interrogative clauses like *Did he try to finish it?* from declarative *He tried to finish it*, we will want, in the interests of simplicity and generalisation, to invoke the same transformation in the derivation of *Did he bother to finish it?* – but here there is no actual declarative counterpart because **bother** + *to* ... is restricted to clauses that are (as a first approximation) negative or interrogative, and hence the transformation will here apply to the hypothetical clause †*He bothered to finish it*. These matters will be taken up more fully in our discussion of non-kernel clauses in the later chapters of the book.

To conclude this section it will be helpful to identify more precisely the set of kernel clauses. We will understand them to have all of the following properties:

(a) A kernel clause forms a sentence on its own – i.e. it is not part of some larger syntactic construction. Thus it is neither **subordinate** to, nor **coordinate** with, some other clause. In (20):

(20) i *I know that he is ill*
      ii *Either he is ill or he has forgotten the appointment*

the subordinate clause *that he is ill* and the coordinate clauses *either he is ill* and *or he has forgotten the appointment* are all non-kernel by this criterion. Subordination and coordination are not always reflected in the internal structure of the clause concerned (compare, for example, *I know he is ill* where *he is ill* contains no overt marker of subordination), but we will still regard such clauses as non-kernel and simply allow that subordination and coordination may or may not lead to structural change. The most common kind of subordination is where the subordinate clause is a constituent of, i.e. is **embedded** within, the **superordinate** clause – as *that he is ill* is embedded as object within the superordinate *I know that he is ill*. The latter does satisfy the criterion of forming a sentence on its own and is (since it satisfies all the other criteria too) a kernel clause: a kernel clause can accordingly contain a non-kernel clause within it. Coordination and subordination of clauses is discussed in Ch. 12.

(b) A kernel clause is structurally complete, not reduced by ellipsis. In the exchange (21), for example:

(21) ⟨A⟩ *What are you doing?*
      ⟨B⟩ *Testing the chlorine-level*

B's reply does not have the form of a kernel clause, lacking as it does a subject and auxiliary verb – compare the non-elliptical and kernel *I am testing the chlorine level*. We will consider certain kinds of ellipsis associated with coordination and subordination, but limitations of space do not permit a more comprehensive treatment of the phenomenon.

(c) A kernel clause is **declarative**, not **imperative**, **interrogative** or **exclamative**, so that only the first of the following qualifies:

(22)
    i *You are careful*   Declarative
    ii *Be careful*   Imperative
    iii *Are you careful?*   Interrogative
    iv *How careful you are!*   Exclamative

This system is known as **clause type** and is discussed in Ch. 11.

(d) A kernel clause is **positive**, not **negative**; we thus include (i) but not (ii) in:

(23)
    i *They have seen it*   Positive
    ii *They have not seen it*   Negative

This is the system of **polarity**, discussed in Ch. 13.

(e) A kernel clause is unmarked with respect to all the **thematic** systems of the clause. Thus in each of the following pairs, (i) is a kernel clause but (ii) is not:

(24)
    i *My father wrote the letter*   Unmarked (Active)
    ii *The letter was written by my father*   Passive

(25)
    i *They invited John*   Unmarked
    ii *It was John that they invited*   Cleft construction

(26)
    i *Two policemen are at the door*   Unmarked
    ii *There are two policemen at the door*   *There* construction

(27)
    i *He has known her father for three years*   Unmarked
    ii *Her father he has known for three years*   Marked by thematic fronting

(28)
    i *That he should be so late is annoying*   Unmarked
    ii *It is annoying that he should be so late*   Marked by extraposition

In a restricted sense of the term 'meaning', (i) and (ii) can be said to have the same meaning; more precisely we will say that they have the same propositional meaning. The propositional meaning of a sentence defines the class of propositions it can be used to express, where propositions are the entities that can be said to be true or false. Notice then that it is not sentences themselves that are true or false: it doesn't make sense, for example, to ask whether (27i), a sentence of English, is true or false: the question can only arise for particular uses of it, where the context will determine who is referred to by *he* and *her father* and the limits of the time period involved in *has known for three years*, and thus what proposition is expressed. (27i) could accordingly be used in different contexts to express an indefinite number of distinct propositions, some true, some false. What is meant by saying that (27i) and (27ii) have the same propositional meaning is that if they were used in the same context, with *he* referring to the same person and so on, they would express the same proposition – and hence it would be logically inconsistent to assert one and deny the other. Propositional meaning is a central part of meaning, but it is not the whole of it, and in particular it would be a mistake to think that because (27i) and (27ii) have the same propositional meaning the choice between them is of no communicative significance. The grammar makes available a variety of different ways of expressing the same proposition so that at a particular point in a spoken discourse or written text we can select a form that is appropriate in the light of our assumptions about what information the addressee(s) will already possess, of what parts of our message we wish to emphasise or focus upon, of the contrasts we wish to draw, and so on. These are aspects of **thematic meaning**, and we accordingly say that (27i) and (27ii), while having the same propositional meaning, differ in their thematic meaning. The thematic systems of the clause are then those where corresponding members of the contrasting classes always or normally differ simply with respect to the thematic meaning. The set of kernel clauses excludes clauses belonging to a marked term in any of these systems.

For the most part traditional grammars tend to give relatively little attention to the thematic systems, and for this reason we do not have a well-established set of names for them. The main exception is (24), where (i) and (ii) contrast in the system of **voice**, with **active** the unmarked term, **passive** the marked: we will derive (ii) from (i) by a transformation of passivisation along the lines sketched above. In (25), (ii) is the **cleft** counterpart of (i): starting with (i) as basic, we select one element to focus attention on – *John* in this example – and make it complement of a clause of the form *it* + *be* + complement, which is followed by a subordinate clause containing the other elements from the thematically unmarked version. The effect is to divide the original into two parts: hence the term 'cleft'. In (26), we will derive (ii) by means of a transformation of *there* **insertion**: the subject of (i), *two policemen*, is moved to the right of the VP and the pronoun *there* is inserted into the position thus vacated. In (27) the difference is purely a matter of the linear order of the elements: we take (i) as representing the basic order and derive (ii) from it by a transformation called **thematic fronting** – it involves moving to front position in the clause some element, such as the object *her father* in this example, which does not belong there in the unmarked version. Finally in (28) the unmarked version (i) contains an embedded clause (*that he should be so late*) as subject: the marked version is derived by the **extraposition** transformation, which moves the embedded clause to the right and puts *it* in its place. Notice that of the two constructions in (28), (ii) is the more frequent: unmarked terms are typically more frequent than their marked counterparts but they are not invariably so. We take (i) rather than (ii) as unmarked on the grounds that it represents the more general and straightforward pattern – it has the same pattern as *His behaviour is annoying*, for example, with simply a subordinate clause subject instead of the NP subject of the latter, whereas the subordinate clause in (ii) is not in paradigmatic relation with an NP. We will take up these thematic transformations in the next chapter in the context of an investigation of the subject as a grammatical function (2.2), and will then look in more detail at the thematic systems of English in Ch. 14.

1.5 **Sentence and clause**

Syntax, we have said, is concerned with the way words combine to form sentences: the sentence is the largest stretch of language forming a syntactic construction. A larger stretch of connected speech or writing, such as a conversation, a debate, a speech, a letter, a newspaper article, a novel, we will call a **text**, using the term in a more general sense than it normally has outside academic linguistics, so that it covers spoken as well as written material. Texts typically consist of a sequence of sentences,[4] but although there are important connections between the sentences – a text does not consist of a random juxtaposition of sentences – the connections are not of the same kind as we find between the parts of a sentence, and their study thus falls within a different field, not syntax but 'discourse analysis' or (to use a more recent term) 'text-linguistics'. Within the sentence we have a much sharper distinction between permissible and impermissible combinations, which enables us to formulate rules distinguishing what is grammatical from what is not.

The difference between intra-sentence and inter-sentence connections is clearest when we are dealing with sentences that have the form of a clause, as in

(29)   *Your mother has borrowed the car. She should be back in about an hour.*

Here the first sentence is a clause with the structure 'subject + predicator + object', where these three functions are clearly distinguished from each other by the rules of syntax. The predicator differs from subject and object in respect of the class of forms that can occur there – VPs as opposed to NPs (and certain other classes); the subject differs from the object by virtue of its position relative to the predicator, the fact that the verb (often) agrees with it – if we change singular *your mother* to plural *your parents* we must also change *has* to *have* – and various other properties that we shall later be examining in detail. But we cannot set up supra-sentential constructions with functional positions differentiated in the same kind of way.

---

[4] In conversations and similar texts we will often find fragments of sentences rather than complete sentences, but this complication does not affect the present discussion.

Where a sentence consists of a sequence of two or more clauses, the connections between them will be less readily distinguishable from those holding between two sentences in a text. The approach adopted here will be to regard the central type of sentence as one with the form of a clause. We have already noted that a clause can contain a smaller clause as a constituent: recall the example *That he was concealing something was becoming more and more obvious,* with the (subordinate) clause *that he was concealing something* functioning as subject of the (main) clause that is coextensive with the whole sentence. We shall then allow a sentence to consist of a sequence of two (or more) clauses when the relationship between them is one that can occur between two clauses that are constituents of a single larger clause. Compare, for example:

(30)   i *He is staying with his aunt because the College food is wretched and the rooms aren't heated*
         ii *The College food is wretched and the rooms aren't heated*
        iii *The College food is wretched – I'm staying with my aunt*

The first sentence is a clause with the structure 'subject (*he*) + predicator (*is staying*) + complement (*with his aunt*) + adjunct (*because ... heated*)'. Within the adjunct position we have two smaller clauses joined by the 'coordinating conjunction' *and*: as *and* serves to relate two clauses in a syntactic construction here, we also allow that the two clauses of (ii) are joined in a syntactic construction and hence that (ii) is a single sentence. But the relation between the two clauses in (iii) is not found between clauses embedded within a larger clause and we accordingly treat (iii) as a sequence of two sentences. In applying this criterion we ignore the special case of quotation, as in *He said: 'The College food is wretched – I'm staying with my aunt'*; we set this construction apart because the quoted material is not structurally integrated, as far as its own internal form is concerned, with the clause in which it is embedded – as is evident from the fact that it could be in a different language. Even with this qualification, application of the criterion is not entirely straightforward and there may be some indeterminacy or room for disagreement as to whether or not in a given instance two clauses belong in the same sentence; nevertheless it yields clear results in a large class of cases and provides a principled basis for extending the domain of syntax beyond sentences that have the form of a clause.

As the sentence is, by definition, the maximal syntactic construction, we shall not allow for one sentence to occur inside another sentence (again leaving aside the special case of direct quotation, which is really a matter of one text occurring inside another). Thus although we regard *the College food is wretched* as a sentence in (30iii), it is not a sentence in (ii) or (i). The sentence is accordingly a different kind of concept from the clause. Whether a form is a clause or not depends on its internal structure: in the central cases a clause has a subject and a predicate, the latter position being filled by an extended verb phrase containing a predicator, alone or in construction with one or more objects, adjuncts, etc. But a clause or syntactically joined sequence of clauses will be a sentence only if it is not part of a larger syntactic construction. Where sentence and clause boundaries coincide, we will say that the sentence has the form of a clause or simply that the sentence is a clause, and that the clause forms a sentence: we will not say that the sentence 'consists of' a clause, in order to avoid any implication that the clause is a constituent of the sentence, for in an example like *the College food is wretched* in (30iii), the subject–predicate construction comes at the highest level in the constituent structure: there is no higher level construction with a single functional position filled by the clause as a whole. It is for this reason that I have used 'clause' as the label for the topmost point in diagrams (7) and (8) above.

I have spoken of the problem of identifying the sentence on the syntagmatic axis – of determining where one sentence in a text ends and the next begins. There is also the problem of identifying it on the paradigmatic axis – of determining whether two utterances are utterances of the same sentence or of different sentences. (Just as we generalise 'text' so that it covers speech as well as writing, so we generalise 'utterance' to cover writing as well as speech, so that the formulation just given applies equally to spoken and written sentences.) The main issue here involves the treatment of the **non-verbal** component of the utterance. The **verbal** component consists of the spoken or written manifestation of the words, while the non-verbal component consists of the rest. Thus in written English the verbal component consists of the letters, including the distinction between capital and non-capital letters insofar as this is determined by the individual word (as with the proper noun *Frank* vs the adjective *frank*), whereas the punctuation marks, other cases of the capital/non-capital contrast, the distinction in printed or typed material between different typefaces, italic vs roman, bold vs ordinary, and so on, constitute the non-verbal component. In spoken English, the verbal component consists, as a first approximation, of the consonants and vowels – the 'phonemes' to use a term covering both – and word-accent (as in the contrast between the noun '*import* and the verb *im'port*), whereas sentence stress (as in the contrast between *I saw Tom* and *I saw Tom*), intonation, tone of voice and so on constitute the non-verbal component.[5]

---

[5] We will also subsume under the non-verbal component variations in the pronunciation of words depending on sentence stress, tempo and the like – for example, we will regard /hæv/, /həv/, /əv/ and /v/ as variant pronunciations of the same word in a sentence like *I have seen it* (see 'Table of symbols and notational conventions' at the front of the book for explanation of the phonological symbols used here). It is for this reason that the verbal component is only approximately identifiable as the phonemes together with word-accent.

The verbal component is the more central, and significant differences in this component will be sufficient to distinguish one sentence from another. By 'significant' differences I mean those that reflect distinctions within the language as opposed to variation in, say, the sound of a given phoneme or the shape of a given letter as spoken or written by different people, or by the same person on different occasions. Thus there is no problem in recognising *It was a bin* and *It was a pin* as different sentences. With the non-verbal component matters are much more difficult, partly because of the problem of deciding which kinds of non-verbal signal would be relevant to sentence identity ('tone of voice' and overall loudness and speed would be generally accepted as irrelevant, whereas intonation is commonly but not invariably regarded as an aspect of the linguistic form of spoken sentences), partly because we are often dealing with continuous variation rather than with discrete units (with intonation, for example, we can talk grossly of rising or falling intonation, but it is unlikely that we can distinguish a fixed number of discrete types of fall or rise: the steepness and extent of the pitch movement is continuously variable over a certain range). It is accordingly hardly realistic to ask, for example, how many linguistically distinct ways there are of pronouncing a certain sequence of words, such as *Tom stayed in because he was ill.* Notice, moreover, that whereas in the verbal component speech and writing are in close correspondence, in the non-verbal component they are not – there is, for example, only a very rough and indirect correlation between punctuation and intonation, with the former providing for considerably less variation than the latter.

Given the limited scope and introductory nature of the present book, we need not worry about these problems: we shall not be dealing with those aspects of the meaning of utterances that depend simply on the non-verbal signal (and where syntactic constructions are differentiated non-verbally as well as verbally, we will be able to make do with a very limited set of intonational contrasts). We can accordingly work with the simplifying assumption that paradigmatic sentence identification depends solely on the verbal component, so that we shall continue to talk of sentence ambiguity – a single sentence with two or more meanings, as opposed to two or more different sentences each with its own meaning – even when utterances expressing the different meanings differ non-verbally, as with the sentence *Liz saw John and Kim and Robin did too* analysed in §2 above. This emphasis on the verbal component ties in with our failure to rely on punctuation in determining sentence boundaries on the syntagmatic axis: the criterion suggested above is neutral as between speech and writing.

1.6 Morphological processes

The two most basic units of syntax are the sentence and the word. The sentence is the largest unit of syntax: as we move upwards beyond the sentence we pass from syntax into discourse analysis; the word is the lowest unit of syntax: as we move downwards beyond the word we pass from syntax into morphology. And just as a sentence cannot normally contain any smaller sentence within it, so a word cannot normally contain any smaller word within it. Thus although we can analyse the word *blackbird*, for example, into *black + bird*, each of which occurs as a word in the sentence *The bird was black*, we shall not regard *black* and *bird* as words when they occur within the word *blackbird*: here they are merely **stems**.

The most elementary words, such as *boy, cat, good, in,* have the form of **simple stems**, 'simple' in the sense that they are not analysable into smaller morphological units. Other words are then formed from the stock of simple stems by various morphological processes. The two such processes traditionally recognised as the most important are compounding and affixation.

Compounding involves adding two stems together, as when we join *black* and *bird* to form *blackbird*, or *gold* and *smith* to form *goldsmith*, and so on. *Blackbird* and *goldsmith* are then said to be **compound stems**.

In **affixation**, an **affix** is added to a stem to yield a **complex stem**. More specifically, we can distinguish between **prefixes** like *pre-, sub-, un-,* which are added to the left of the stem, and **suffixes** like *-able, -ed, -ing, -iness,* which are added to the right. Thus the complex stems *substandard* and *unkind* are formed by prefixation, *payable* and *goodness* by suffixation.

It should be emphasised at this point that what was said earlier about the descriptive status of syntactic transformations applies equally to morphological processes. That is, it must not be thought that when we speak of compounding, affixation and so on, we are talking of mental operations performed by a speaker in using the words: we are simply concerned with the linguistic analysis of the morphological structure of words, relating the words to the more elementary units contained within them.

When two morphological units are put together – a stem and an affix, or two stems – either or both may undergo some modification of phonological form (and/or spelling). Thus if we suffix *-ion* to *decide* the result is *decision*; *abominate* and a considerable number of other verb stems drop the *-ate* when *-able* is suffixed, as in *abominable*, rather than *abominatable*; the vowel of *man* is reduced to /ə/ when it is compounded with *gentle, police* or whatever; and so on: the morphological rules of the grammar must clearly specify in detail such modifications.

Words may be formed by the application of more than one morphological process. In *unselfconsciousness*, for example, the first step is one of compounding, joining the simple stems *self* and *conscious* to form the compound stem *selfconscious*. To this is then added the prefix *un-*, yielding the complex stem *unselfconscious*; and finally *-ness* is suffixed, to give the final complex stem *unselfconsciousness*. We take the prefixation to apply before the suffixation in this example because it enables us to give a more general account of the **distribution** of the prefix *un-*, i.e. of whereabouts it can occur: *un-* can be added to a large set of adjective stems as in *kind, happy, wise* . . . – and *selfconscious*, but not (or at least not with the same sense as it has in *unkind, unhappy*, etc.) to noun stems: cf. **ungrace, *unwealth*, etc. The fact that we have a word *unselfconsciousness* but not a word **ungoodness* is thus attributable to the fact that *un-* can be prefixed to the adjective *selfconscious* but not *good*; we would not say that it can be prefixed to *selfconsciousness* but not *goodness*.

A third type of morphological process, particularly important in the grammar of English, is **conversion**. This is exemplified in the formation of the verb *bottle* (as in *I must bottle some plums*) from the noun *bottle*. We take the noun and verb to be distinct words (and hence distinct stems), with the noun *bottle* being primary: the verb is then formed by conversion of the stem from one class to another.

Just as we observed that compounding and affixation can combine, so either of them can combine with conversion. The verb *soundproof*, for example, (as in *I'm going to soundproof my study*), is derived by conversion from the adjective *soundproof* (as in *The room is soundproof*), which is in turn formed by compounding from the simple stems *sound* and *proof*. The plural noun *weeklies* ("magazines which are published each week") is based on the simple stem *week*: *-ly* is suffixed to this to yield the adjective stem *weekly*, which is then converted to the noun stem *weekly*, and finally the plural suffix is added. Or consider such an example as *fighter-bomber*, which involves all three types of process. *Fighter-bomber* itself is a noun stem formed by compounding from the two noun stems *fighter* and *bomber*. Each of these is in turn derived by suffixation of *-er* to a verb stem, *fight* and *bomb* (there being no question of any ordering between these two processes: they apply simultaneously). Of the two verb stems *fight* and *bomb*, the former is simple but the latter is derived by conversion of the noun stem *bomb* – *bomb* follows the pattern of *bottle* above, with the noun primary, as in *They found a bomb*, and the verb derived, as in *They planned to bomb the camp*.

Because conversion changes only the grammatical properties of the stem while leaving its pronunciation and spelling intact, it raises certain special problems of analysis. In the first place we have to distinguish conversion (one stem formed from another without any change in pronunciation or spelling) from the case where we simply have a single stem, a single word, used in two different grammatical constructions. For example, we have conversion of *bottle* because the *bottle* of *I must bottle some plums* is a different word from that of *I'll put it in a bottle*, but in *a happy man* and *The man was happy* we have two syntactic uses of the same word *happy*, so that there is here no conversion of one stem into another. The issue is not always as easy to decide as in the *bottle* and *happy* examples: we will look further in 3.2 into the problem of determining how much should be brought within the scope of the concept of morphological conversion. In the second place, in cases where we do have conversion, we are faced with the problem of deciding which is the original stem and which the derived. We will make the decision on the basis of meaning. Thus we take the noun *bottle* as primary and the verb as derived because it is the meaning of the noun that is basic: we would give the meaning of the verb as "put into a bottle", rather than take it as basic with the noun analysed as "container into which one puts what one bottles". Conversely, *catch* is primarily a verb, secondarily a noun: the meaning of the noun, as in *Chappell took a fine catch*, will be defined in terms of the verb, not the other way round. The same goes for *fight*, which is primarily a verb, with the noun stem in *They had a fight* derived by conversion – this is why we handled *fighter* differently from *bomber* in the *fighter-bomber* example above. But in between these clear extremes, there may be a small area of fuzziness. Which is primary in the case of *saw*, for example? Shall we say that the verb means "cut with a saw" (with the noun primary), or that the noun means "tool for sawing" (with the verb primary)?

To some extent this second problem – the problem of deciding the direction of derivation – arises also with pairs contrasting as stem vs stem + affix. From a historical point of view, a word of the form X + affix may exist in the language before a word of the form X: historical records show, for example, that the words *edit, scavenge, afflict* were introduced into the language later than the words *editor, scavenger, affliction* respectively. The process whereby a stem is formed by dropping an affix from a larger stem is known as 'back-formation'. Now as far as these particular examples are concerned it can be argued that the historical order is quite irrelevant to the morphological analysis of the words in the contemporary language – that, as far as the present day language is concerned, the morphological relation of *edit* to *editor* is precisely the same as that of *operate* to *operator*, *visit* to *visitor* and so on. We accordingly need to distinguish between **diachronic** processes, those involved in the historical development of the language, and **synchronic** processes, those that are descriptive of the structure of the language at a particular stage of its development. Then we will say that although *edit* is diachronically derived by back-formation from *editor*, it is synchronically a simple stem with *editor* derived from it by affixation. It is nevertheless arguable that there are other cases where back-formation needs to be recognised as a process in synchronic as well as in diachronic morphology. The most persuasive examples are verb stems like *stage-manage, house-keep, baby-sit*, etc. The meaning of *stage-manage* is derivative from that of *stage-manager* rather than the other way round and thus there is much to be said for allowing the synchronic analysis to match the diachronic analysis, so that the noun stem *stage-manager* will be formed by compounding of *stage* and *manager*, with the verb stem *stage-manage* then derived by back-formation from the compound.

There are various other types of morphological process besides the three major ones of compounding, affixation and conversion, and the relatively minor one of back-formation. Thus the past tense form *took* is formed by vowel change from the simple stem *take*. The noun *belief* is formed from the verb *believe* by changing the final consonant. The noun *import* is formed from the verb *import* by moving the accent from the second to first syllable. The past tense form *were* is formed from *be* by 'suppletion', the relatively rare process where one stem is replaced by another bearing no significant phonological resemblance at all to it. *Smog* is formed by 'blending' the stems *smoke* and *fog*. *NATO* and *TV* are 'acronyms', formed by putting together the initial parts of *North Atlantic Treaty Organisation* and *tele + vision*, and so on: we need not attempt an exhaustive listing, having covered the main processes and all that are relevant to the examples we shall be using.

1.7   Inflectional and lexical morphology

For each lexeme there is a single **lexical stem**: the forms of the lexeme are either identical with the lexical stem or are derived from it by inflectional processes. For example, the verb lexemes **wind** and **unwind** have *wind, unwind* as their lexical stems and the inflectional forms are either identical with these or derived from them by suffixation or vowel change: *winds, winding, wound, unwinds, unwinding, unwound*. We may speak of *winds, winding*, etc., as **inflectional stems**. With words that carry no inflectional properties, such as *clockwise, asleep, the, of*, the concept of inflectional stem is of course inapplicable, and such words will be said to have the form of lexical stems.

The distinction between lexical and inflectional stems yields a division of the field of morphology into two branches: **lexical morphology** and **inflectional morphology**. Lexical morphology deals with the processes whereby non-simple lexical stems are formed; inflectional morphology deals with the processes whereby the forms of a lexeme are derived from the lexical stem. Thus the prefixation of *un-* to *wind* to form *unwind* is a lexical process, whereas the suffixation of *-s* to *unwind* to give *unwinds* is an inflectional process. This follows directly from the fact that *unwind* and *unwinds* are forms of the same lexeme, while *wind* and *unwind* are not.

This is all straightforward enough, but how do we decide in the first place whether two words are forms of the same lexeme or of different lexemes? How can we distinguish between inflectional and lexical processes without begging this question? The crucial difference between the two types of morphological process lies in their significance for the syntactic classification of words. As a first and very close approximation we can put it as follows: the set of words with a given inflectional property make up a syntactic class, one having a distinctive functional potential; the set of words derived by a particular lexical process, however, will not be referred to by any rule of syntax. Let us see how this applies to a few examples.

Consider first the process forming what are traditionally called 'present participles' of verbs, such as *talking, laughing, nodding*, etc.: they are derived by adding *-ing* to the lexical stem. This clearly satisfies the criterion for inflection, for the set of these forms is a syntactic class: there are certain constructions where a verb must have this *-ing* form. Thus in *They kept talking* any verb we substitute for *talking* must also have the *-ing* inflection: *They kept laughing*, but not **They kept laughed*. Similarly in the 'progressive' construction: *They were talking / laughing / nodding*, but not **They were talk*. (We can of course also have the so-called 'past participle' after *be*, as in *They were seen*, but this is not an example of the same syntactic construction: it is passive, not progressive.)

Or, to take an example of noun inflection, consider the plural forms *dogs, cats, horses, men, children, mice*, etc. They are formed from the lexical stems by a variety of morphological processes, but the constant paradigmatic relation between *dogs* and *dog, men* and *man, mice* and *mouse*, enables us to group them all together: see below. And again the set of plural nouns is a distinct syntactic class: apart from being one term in the system of number contrasting plural and singular nouns, the class of plural nouns must be referred to in various rules of 'agreement': for example, the demonstratives **this** and **that** take the same number property as the noun with which they are in construction – *this dog / these dogs*, and so on.

Thus as we noted earlier, inflectional properties are morphosyntactic: they figure in both morphological and syntactic rules. The morphological rules specify the form a lexeme takes when it carries a certain inflection, while the syntactic rules are concerned with the conditions under which a lexeme may or must carry a certain inflection.

We may now contrast these inflectional examples with some lexical ones. The prefixation of *un-* as in *unwind* above, or *undo, unfasten, untie*, etc., does not satisfy the criterion for inflection: there are no rules of syntax saying that in such-and-such a construction a verb must or must not carry the *un-* prefix. In this example, indeed, adding *un-* does not affect the functional potential at all, for there is no difference between *wind* and *unwind* with respect to the constructions in which they can occur. *Un-* may accordingly be called a 'class-preserving' prefix. The *-en* of *enlarge, enable*, etc., is by contrast a 'class-changing' prefix, in that *enlarge* belongs to a different syntactic class (verb) than *large* (adjective). It is still lexical rather than inflectional, however, for the set of 'de-adjectival' verbs formed by prefixation of *en-* does not make up a syntactic class: there are no constructions where a verb of this type is required. Thus *He'll enlarge the gap* belongs to the same construction as *He'll close the gap*, and so on. The same applies with class-changing suffixes like the -*er* that is used to form 'deverbal' nouns such as *singer, talker, worker* and so on. Such complex forms do not differ from simple ones like *king* or *son* with respect to the constructions they enter into, so that the set of nouns in -*er* is not one that any rule of syntax need refer to. *Singer* is accordingly derived from *sing* by a lexical, not an inflectional, process: they are forms of different lexemes.

The property of defining a specific syntactic class is sometimes given as a necessary and sufficient condition for inflection. As so often, however, the distinction cannot be drawn in quite such absolute terms – hence the qualification ('as a first and very close approximation') with which I introduced the criterion. For example, words like *dog* and *dogs* can be uncontroversially regarded as forms of the same lexeme, but the syntactic class of plural nouns is not in fact quite coextensive with the set of nouns with the plural inflection. *Cattle* and *police*, for example, are syntactically plural, but their plurality is purely syntactic (it determines their functional potential and meaning) as opposed to morphosyntactic (it does not trigger any morphological process).

In spite of such occasional exceptions, we can still distinguish between inflectional and lexical morphology in terms of the significance of the processes for the syntactic classification of words. In addition, we should mention two properties that are typical, though certainly not definitional, of lexical processes and which tend to further differentiate the lexical and inflectional branches of morphology. Lexical processes are typically of restricted productivity and are characterised by a good deal of semantic unpredictability.

A morphological process is fully **productive** if it can apply to all members of a large and independently definable set of stems – for example the lexical stems of all 'transitive' verbs (verbs which take an object). Lexical processes vary considerably in their range of applicability, but it is doubtful whether any are fully productive. At one end of the scale we find, for example, the verb-forming prefix *en*- mentioned earlier: this combines with only a handful of adjective stems. The suffix -*age* is likewise of very limited distribution, and the stems to which it can be attached do not share any semantic, syntactic or phonological property distinguishing them from those which exclude it; they include *peer* but not *lord, marry* but not *divorce, parent* but not *father, yard* but not *metre, front* but not *back, break* but not *mend, band* but not *strip*, and so on. We are here clearly dealing with special facts about particular stems, not with general rules.

Towards the more productive end of the scale we find such a suffix as -*able*. To be more precise, we need to distinguish various types of stem to which it can be added. It occurs with a few noun stems, but is here as unproductive as -*age*: compare *knowledgeable, marriageable, objectionable, peaceable, pleasurable, treasonable*. Similarly it is found with a handful of stems which cannot stand alone as words, as in *amicable, durable, probable, unconscionable, vulnerable.* Where it does have a fairly high degree of productivity is with transitive verb stems as in *admirable, countable, payable,* and so on. Yet though the class is large there are numerous idiosyncratic restrictions: *-able* can be suffixed to *detest* but hardly to *hate* or *loathe* (compare *hateful* and *loathsome*), to *enjoy* but not *please,* to *laud* but hardly *praise, desire* but not *want,* and so on. Moreover there is a good deal of uncertainty as to whether the resultant form is acceptable or not – what is the status of *freeable, shortenable* and so on?

As a final example, consider the prefix *un-.* Where the sense is "reverse the act or process denoted by the stem", as in *unfasten, unpack, untangle, unwind, unwrap,* the range is very restricted, as it is where the sense is, roughly, "take from", as in *unearth, unhorse, unleash.* By contrast, the *un-* meaning "not" or "opposite of" that is added to 'gradable' adjectives (those denoting a property that can be possessed in varying degrees), as in *unfair, unkind, unreasonable, unsound, unwise,* has a very high productivity. Nevertheless it is still subject to various restrictions: in particular it is not used where there is some morphologically unrelated opposite available (*bad,* not **ungood; young,* not **unold*) or where some other less productive prefix is used (*disloyal* rather than **unloyal, improper* rather than **unproper*).

What emerges from such examples is that to a large extent, but probably not completely, the forms derived by the lexical processes have to be individually learnt by the language user and individually recorded by the linguist – in the dictionary or 'lexicon'. This of course is what makes the term 'lexical morphology' appropriate.

The classical treatment of inflection is a little different. Typically the members of a given lexeme class take the same inflectional properties, so that their forms can be put in correspondence. This is illustrated for a sample of English verbs in (31), where the columns are headed by lexemes, the rows by inflectional properties:

(31)	*take*	*write*	*sing*	*see*	*want*
Past tense	*took*	*wrote*	*sang*	*saw*	*wanted*
3rd pers sg present tense	*takes*	*writes*	*sings*	*sees*	*wants*
Present participle	*taking*	*writing*	*singing*	*seeing*	*wanting*

(Verb lexemes have, of course, more inflectional forms than shown here, but the three cited are sufficient for present illustrative purposes.) All the present participles are formed by the same morphological process – by adding *-ing* to the lexical stem. (The only restriction on the productivity of this rule is that a handful of verbs lack a present participle form: **beware, use** – as in *He used to like her* – and the 'modal auxiliaries' **can, may, must,** etc.) But the five past tense forms in (31) are all formed in different ways – by four types of vowel change and one type of suffixation. However, the systematic correspondences between the forms – *took* is to *takes* as *wrote* is to *writes* and so on – make it easy to recognise *took, wrote, sang*, etc. as having the same inflectional property in spite of the morphological differences between them. We can thus group a set of morphological processes together under the heading of rules for the formation of past tense forms – and similarly for other inflections; the present participle inflection simply illustrates the extreme case where there is just a single rule.

Of the processes involved in past tense formation all but one are of highly restricted productivity, so that the forms derived thereby will again have to be individually recorded; such forms – *took, wrote, sang, saw* and the like – are then said to be **irregular**. **Regular** forms, such as *wanted, pushed, robbed*, by contrast, do not have to be listed individually: as long as we have identified the verbs to which each of the irregular rules applies, we can simply say that for any other verb the past tense is formed in the following way:

(32)   (i) If the lexical stem ends in an 'alveolar stop', i.e. /t/ or /d/, add /ɪd/ (or /əd/ – there are variant pronunciations) as in *wanted, landed*

(ii) If the lexical stem otherwise ends in a voiceless consonant, add /t/, as in *pushed, laughed*

(iii) Otherwise add /d/, as in *killed, died, robbed*[6]

The regular rules are thus fully productive (or virtually so: we again find the odd verb, like **beware**, that lacks a past tense form); in particular, the rules are free to apply to any new lexical stem that is introduced into the language.

In lexical morphology we can in principle make a similar grouping of processes. For example, we can bring together the various processes used to form abstract nouns from adjectives, illustrated in pairs like *wise ~ wisdom, content ~ contentment, loyal ~ loyalty, able ~ ability, wet ~ wetness* – where the last, suffixation of *-ness*, would count as the regular rule, applying to all adjective stems not subject to the minor, highly restricted rules. However, there is no syntactic class consisting of abstract nouns derived from adjectives (which is of course why these processes are lexical, not inflectional), so that such pairings do not have the same syntactic importance as inflectional ones, and this grouping of lexical processes has not become anything like as standard as is the corresponding grouping in inflectional morphology.

Let us now consider briefly the meanings associated with morphological processes. In the most straightforward cases, a given process will introduce

---

[6] Again, see the 'Table of symbols and notational conventions' for the phonological symbols. The 'voiceless' consonants (other than /t/ covered by (32i)) which occur in stem-final position are /p, k, f, θ, s, ʃ, tʃ/.

can un- be used with phrasal verbs?
look up, think up, go out

a constant element of meaning. Thus in the pairs given earlier, *wind* ~ *unwind, fasten* ~ *unfasten, wrap* ~ *unwrap*, there is a constant semantic difference between the forms with and without *un-*: in such cases the meaning of the derived stem is predictable from its component parts. But often in lexical morphology the meanings are not fully predictable in this way. *Do* and *undo*, for example, do not exhibit the same difference as the above pairs: we can say *She must undo her blouse* but not *She must do her blouse* (rather *She must do up her blouse*). *I'll do the lawn* could mean that I'll cut it, whereas *I'll undo the lawn* suggests I am working on a tapestry or something of the kind. The *un-* of *undo* is clearly like that of *unwind*, but the *do* does not remain constant and one really has to learn the meaning of *undo* on its own. Or consider the meanings associated with the suffix *-able*. In the most straightforward cases, adding *-able* to a transitive verb stem *V* yields an adjective stem meaning "able to be V-ed" – *determinable* means "able to be determined", *answerable* can mean "able to be answered", and so on. But very often we find an additional component of meaning overlaid on this. To say that Smith is 'approachable' is to imply that it is easy to approach him. If a bill is 'payable', it isn't simply able to be paid: it has to be. If I say that your style is 'comparable' to Voltaire's, I'm saying more than that it can be compared – I'm suggesting that it is worthy of the comparison, which is high praise indeed. Any novel can be read, but a 'readable' novel is one that reads well, that can be read with pleasure. Where *-able* is added to an 'intransitive' verb stem *V* (one without an object), the basic meaning is "able to V": a 'workable' solution is one that will or is able to work. But again there will often be some extra or different meaning. If you are 'answerable' to the minister, it isn't that you are able to answer, but rather that you are obliged to.[7] 'Perishable' goods are goods that are liable to perish.

As a final example, note the semantic difference between such compound lexical stems as *blackbird* or *redskin* and the syntactic construction of adjective plus noun, as in *black bird* or *red skin*. The meanings of the latter are derived systematically from the meanings of the constituents, but the meanings of the compounds are not: 'blackbirds' are not necessarily black and birds that are black are not necessarily 'blackbirds', and a 'redskin' is a type of person, not a type of skin.

Such problems arise with inflections to only a very limited extent. In some cases it is not really possible to attribute any independent meaning

---

[7] Like a great many verbs, *answer* can be used both transitively and intransitively. In *They couldn't answer the question* it is transitive, with *the question* being object, whereas in *He has to answer to the minister* it is intransitive, for *to the minister* is not an object (cf. 5.5). The meaning of *answerable* that concerns us here is related to the intransitive use of *answer*, whereas its meaning of "able to be answered", mentioned above and illustrated in *The question wasn't easily answerable*, is related to its transitive use.

directly to an inflection. In examples like *He enjoys playing squash, He was talking, I avoided committing myself* the form of the second verb is determined by the nature of the syntactic construction and we can hardly identify a meaning contributed by the inflection itself. Where the inflection is not syntactically determined it will convey meaning – as with the past tense inflection in verbs or plural in nouns, and so on. And here the meaning will normally be constant, whatever lexeme the inflection is associated with: the past tense inflection has the same meaning in *took, wrote, sang, saw, wanted*, and so on.

Yet even with inflections we find occasional instances of semantic irregularity. The meaning of plural in *scissors* is not the same as in, say, *blades*. And while the meaning of *later* in *He arrived later than expected* is straightforwardly inferable from its analysis as the 'comparative' form of **late**, the meaning it has in examples like *He later realised his error*, namely "subsequently", is not. Nevertheless, such irregularity falls well within the bounds of tolerance for what we are calling systems, and we can accordingly expand on our original characterisation of inflection by noting that an inflectional property not only defines a syntactic class: the classes so defined will be terms in systems. Thus we have, as observed earlier, a system of the VP contrasting past tense and present tense, where the first verb in a past tense VP carries the past tense inflection, while that in a present tense VP carries one of the present tense inflections. And we have a system of number in the noun, with singular and plural nouns having singular and plural inflectional properties (save for the odd exception like *cattle* and *police* mentioned above).

Of the various morphological processes mentioned in the last section, suppletion standardly figures only in inflectional morphology – as there is no phonological resemblance between, say, *go* and *wen(t)* it is only by virtue of their place in the system of tense that we relate them. Conversely, processes such as acronym formation and blending are purely lexical, and, certainly as far as English is concerned, compounding is also restricted or virtually restricted to lexical morphology (the qualification relates to the reflexive forms *myself, yourself*, etc., which might be regarded as inflectional, though they are not normally so analysed – see 7.4). The example we gave of conversion – from noun *bottle* to verb *bottle* – was lexical, and the term tends to be restricted to that branch of morphology. Nevertheless, we find a very close analogue in inflectional morphology, as with **sheep**, whose plural form is identical with the singular form instead of being derived by suffixation or vowel change, or with such verbs as **hit**, **put**, **shut**, whose past tense forms are simply *hit, put* and *shut*. Affixation, of course, figures prominently in both branches of morphology, and it is worth noting that what from the point of view of pronunciation or spelling is a single affix can be involved in both inflectional and lexical processes. For example, the *-ing* of

[handwritten margin note: blend - smog]

31

They kept talking is inflectional, while that of *The building was destroyed* (where *building* belongs to the same syntactic class as a morphologically simple form like *house*) or *the singing of Joan Sutherland* (where *singing* could be replaced by, say, *voice*), is lexical. Similarly, in *He is taller than Ed* we have inflectional -*er* (an adjective must be in the comparative form in this construction), whereas in *singer, talker, walker* and the like, we have lexical -*er*.

The minimal units of morphology are simple stems and affixes; so far we have taken the distinction between these for granted, but to conclude this section we should look into it a little further. Words either have the form of simple stems or are derived from one or more simple stems by various morphological processes, so that simple stems are involved in the morphological structure of all words; affixes, by contrast, may or may not be involved, depending on the kind of word. In English, almost all simple stems, like stems in general, are **free**, that is, they can stand alone as words. Those that cannot are called **bound**: they include the *amic, dur, prob, conscion, vulner* of *amicable, durable* (or *duration*, etc.), *probable, unconscionable, vulnerable*, cited earlier; the *beknown* and (for most speakers) *kempt* of *unbeknown* and *unkempt*; *scissor* and *trouser* of *scissors* and *trousers* or of the compounds *scissor-movement, trouser-press*; and so on. *Unkempt* and *scissors* transparently have the same structure as *unkind* and *blades*, say, and it is on this basis that we assign *kempt* and *scissor* to the class of stems, as opposed to affixes: the distinction is based on their role in the structure of words, not on the ability vs inability to form a complete word. In a language like Latin, in fact, the majority of stems are bound: Latin has considerably more inflectional systems than English and much more complex rules of inflectional morphology. Whereas in English one form of each lexeme is normally identical with the lexical stem, in Latin all the inflectional forms are normally derived from the lexical stem by at least one morphological process, which is what makes the lexical stem bound: the characteristic property of simple stems in Latin is thus not that they can stand alone as words but that they can stand as lexical stems, i.e. the base from which the inflectional forms are derived.

Most bound stems in English are simple, but there are also a few that result from conversion. For example, the plural noun *remains* (as in *the remains of the meal*) is analysable into the suffix -*s* plus the noun stem *remain*, which is itself derived by conversion from the verb stem *remain*: the latter is free, but the noun stem is bound, as there is no singular noun *remain*. (Conversely, there is a free verb stem *scissor* derived by conversion from the bound noun stem.) In general, the distinction between stems and affixes can be drawn quite sharply, but historical change can involve a shift from one category to the other, resulting in some indeterminacy or overlap. A relatively recent example is that of *ism*, which is now recognised as a word on its own, and hence qualifies as a stem, though it is still regarded as a suffix in non-simple words like *heroism*. Similarly the prefix *anti-* is now sometimes heard functioning as a word (*He's very anti*, with the context making clear what he is opposed to). Such blurring of boundaries is quite typical of linguistic categories, and certainly does not undermine the validity of the distinction.

1.8 Components of a linguistic description

I observed at the beginning of this chapter that the term 'grammar' is used sometimes to cover the whole of a linguistic description, sometimes some specific component thereof – though not always the same component as here, where I include just syntax and morphology. In this section I will review briefly the contrast between grammar (as the term is employed here) and the other major components, phonology, graphology, the lexicon and semantics, and then take up the distinction that we draw within the grammatical component between syntax and morphology.

Phonology deals with the sound pattern of a language – with the distinctive vowel and consonant sounds (the phonemes), with the contrasts of word-accent, sentence stress, intonation and so on. It is an important property of natural languages – a property commonly called 'duality' – that they are structured in terms of two fundamentally different kinds of unit, which as a first approximation we can characterise as meaningful vs meaningless. For example, we can analyse the sentence *He fell off the bed* into a hierarchy of constituents (along the lines of §2) including *fell off the bed, off the bed, the bed, bed* each of which has a meaning, but if we continue the analysis dividing *bed* into *b, e* and *d* we move to a domain where the units are not individually meaningful but serve rather to distinguish one meaningful unit from another, as *b* distinguishes *bed* from *led, red*, etc., *e* distinguishes it from *bid, bud*, etc., and so on. These two levels of structure then provide the subject matter for grammar and phonology respectively: the way the units of grammar combine to form sentences is very largely independent of the way they are pronounced, whereas the way the units of phonology combine (such that, for example, we have a word *bed* in English but do not – and could not – have a word *dbe*) obviously is not.[8] In traditional grammar, phonology is usually regarded as a subcomponent of the grammar – which then leaves no single term to cover what I am here calling grammar, following a more modern usage. The terminology is of course of little significance: what matters is that we recognise the distinction between the two major levels of structure.

---

[8] It is not quite true that the units of grammar can all be assigned an independent meaning: it is doubtful, for example, whether this can be done for the *to* of *I want to go*, the *do* of *Did he go?*, the inflectional affix *-ing* of *He kept talking*, and so on – hence my qualification 'as a first approximation'. Note, however, that the distribution of these elements is likewise independent of the way they are pronounced and not describable in terms of phonological rules.

Graphology deals with the writing system of a language (if it has one!). A perhaps more familiar term, **orthography**, is concerned with the way words are spelt: it is thus that part of graphology which covers the verbal component of the signal (see §5 above). Phonology and graphology are outside the scope of this book. In the discussion of the grammar, forms will normally be cited in their standard orthographic representation (in italics); in the few cases where it is relevant to indicate the phonological representation directly, it will be enclosed between obliques, with the phoneme symbols having the values identified in the 'Table of symbols and notational conventions' at the front of the book.

The **lexicon**, or 'dictionary', deals with the **lexical items** of the language – the lexemes, words and so on that make up its vocabulary. The entry for each lexical item will give its meaning, its phonological and orthographic properties, determining respectively how it is pronounced and spelt, and its grammatical properties. Conventional dictionaries generally give only the most rudimentary account of the last of these, confining themselves, as far as the syntax is concerned, to information about the item's classification in terms of the parts of speech and certain major subclasses, such as transitive or intransitive verbs. A dictionary forming part of an integrated and theoretically-based linguistic description – and it is in this more specific sense that the term 'lexicon' is to be understood – would need to give a good deal more detail than this, as will become clear in the course of our later discussion of syntactic subclassification. Conversely, a lexicon, unlike the most usual kind of (monolingual) dictionary, will not deal with the etymology of lexical items, their historical origin or development from earlier forms: the integrated description of which it is a component is concerned with the state of the language at a certain limited period in time, not with its historical progression through time – it is, to use the standard technical terms introduced in §6 above, 'synchronic' as opposed to 'diachronic'.

The grammar will consist of rules saying how sentences are made up of smaller units and ultimately of the minimal units of this level of structure. As far as the syntax is concerned, the rules will be formulated in terms of classes of items, such as NP, noun, etc., or more specific classes such as singular common noun or whatever: they will not have occasion to mention individually such words as *daffodil* – or such lexemes as **daffodil**. There are no grammatical differences between the nouns **daffodil**, **tulip**, **car**, **chair**, **pen**, and the like: substituting one for another will never destroy the grammaticality of a sentence nor result in a change of construction; the differences between them, we will say, are purely lexical, to be handled simply in terms of the different meanings given to them in the dictionary.

In some cases, however, the syntactic rules do have to refer to particular words or lexemes. This arises: (i) when a construction determines the selection of one or more specific items, and (ii) when the terms in a system are specific items rather than classes. Examples of the first type are the extrapositioned construction, as in (28ii) above, which requires the insertion of *it*, and the passive construction, as in (24ii), whose description will mention the auxiliary verb ***be*** and the preposition *by*. Examples of the second type are the system of '3rd person singular definite personal pronouns', where we have a contrast between ***he***, ***she*** and ***it***, and the system of 'modal auxiliaries' operating at a certain place in the structure of modal VPs and where the terms are ***can***, ***may***, ***must***, ***will***, ***shall*** and two or three others. In general the terms in syntactic systems are classes, but under certain conditions we recognise systems with specific items as terms, as in these examples. I will not discuss these conditions in detail; for present purposes it will be enough to give the first and most elementary condition, namely that they be members of a small class, as is required by our general characterisation of a system. Thus ***he***, ***she*** and ***it*** belong to a three-member class defined by a set of grammatical properties unique to them (see 7.4 for details), and similarly the half dozen or so modal auxiliaries form a class of their own by virtue of their distinctive grammatical properties (see 4.2), whereas – as we have just observed – the grammatical properties of ***daffodil***, ***tulip***, ***car***, ***chair***, ***pen*** are shared with a large number of other nouns. Those items specifically mentioned in the syntax are commonly called 'grammatical items'. While grammar and dictionary are complementary, items differ in the way in which the burden of accounting for their distinctive use is shared between the grammar and the description of meaning in the dictionary. The grammar won't take you very far in determining how to use ***daffodil***, but with ***be***, say, the grammar will provide the bulk of the information; with grammatical items, then, it is the grammar that plays the major role in describing their distinctive use. We will look further into the relation between grammar and dictionary in the context of a discussion of the special status of 'words' later in this section; in the meantime we will continue with our survey of the scope of grammar by introducing the contrast between grammar and **semantics**.

Semantics deals with meaning. The meaning of a sentence depends in part on the meanings of the lexical items it contains, in part on the way they are put together grammatically: on this basis we can distinguish between **lexical semantics** and **grammatical semantics**. Lexical semantics is handled in the lexicon: the central part of the entry for a lexical item will be a description of its meaning. And traditionally grammatical semantics is likewise handled in the grammar: a traditional grammar will include information about the meanings of inflections, grammatical items, constructions, and so on. Modern linguistics, by contrast, generally argues for a distinction between questions of 'grammatical form', concerning how the units can be combined in grammatically well-formed sentences (like *He* *was reading a book*, in contrast to the ungrammatical **He have reading a book*, and so on) and questions of meaning, concerning the way the grammatical structure contributes to determining the interpretation of sentences (as the tense contrast, for example, in *He was reading a book* vs *He is reading a book* correlates with a difference in the location in time of the state of affairs in question). The relation between grammatical form and meaning is often quite complex – a good deal less straightforward than might at first appear. Many examples will emerge in the chapters which follow; here I will give just one illustration, involving the past tense inflection just mentioned. Consider, then, the sentences

(33)   i *The match started on 2 June*
         ii *You said the match started on 2 June*   *from: The match starts on 2 June (i.e. it is not yet 2 June)*

Both contain the past tense form *started*, but whereas in (i) (at least in its most salient and normal interpretation) the past tense inflection serves to locate the starting of the match in past time, (ii) would quite naturally be used at some time before 2 June (of the year in question). Thus we do not have any simple, one-to-one correlation between past tense and past time. It is accordingly essential to keep the two categories conceptually distinct – and to see that the *started* of (ii) has the same inflectional property as it has in (i), in spite of the difference in meaning, because there is identity of form, not just idiosyncratically for the lexeme **start** but systematically for all verb lexemes. More generally, it is important to distinguish between categories of meaning and categories based on the syntagmatic and paradigmatic relations between forms – between semantic categories and grammatical categories. It is in this sense that, in this book, grammatical analysis will be opposed to semantic analysis instead of subsuming (the non-lexical part of) it. Some of the traditional definitions of grammatical categories – whether functions, classes, constructions, inflections or whatever – are in part vitiated by a failure to give proper recognition to the nature of the relation between grammatical form and meaning: this is a point I shall take up and develop in the next chapter in the context of a comparison of the principles underlying grammatical analysis in what I am calling 'structural linguistics' on the one hand and traditional grammar on the other.

The term semantics is employed in a broader and a narrower sense: in the latter it contrasts with **pragmatics**, in the former it subsumes it. In the narrow sense semantics is concerned with the meaning of sentences (and parts of sentences) considered in abstraction from any particular context of use, while pragmatics deals with those aspects of the meanings of utterances that go beyond the meaning of the sentence uttered. One area where the contrast will be of relevance to us from time to time in later chapters is **implication**. Let us illustrate with the following example:

(34) i *The enemy opened fire and our platoon commander was killed instantly*
ii *Our platoon commander died*
iii *Our platoon commander was killed by the enemy's fire*

Here (ii) is a semantic implication, an **entailment**, of (i), while (iii) is only a pragmatic implication. (ii) follows from (i) directly by virtue of the meanings of the sentences: if the proposition expressed by uttering (i) in a given context is true, then that expressed by uttering (ii) in the same context is necessarily true too. The link between (i) and (iii) is less direct, and it is possible to imagine a context where the proposition expressed by (i) would be true while that expressed by (iii) would be false: it might be, for example, that there was a plot within the platoon to kill the commander and the enemy's opening fire was to be the signal for the deed to be done. Thus, when, in a more ordinary context, you infer (iii) from (i) you do so on the basis of an ASSUMPTION about the relation between the two events described in an utterance of (i): the specific nature of the relation is not encoded in (i), is not part of the sentence meaning. When we say that (i) pragmatically implies (iii), we mean that if I utter (i) I will normally be taken to have committed myself to (iii) unless the context specifically indicates otherwise. The qualification 'normally' and the possibility of contextual cancellation of the implication make pragmatic implication a much looser, fuzzier relation than entailment, but it is nevertheless of enormous communicative significance: in the ordinary use of language we do not spell out explicitly everything we wish to convey but leave a great deal for our audience to fill in on the basis of their non-linguistic knowledge and assumptions about our likely intentions.

Let us turn now, finally, to the division within grammar between morphology and syntax. It is based, as we have said, on the word, with morphology dealing with the form of words, syntax with their combination. What we shall be concerned with now is the motivation for dividing the grammar into separate subcomponents in this way.

What is it, then, that is special about words, that distinguishes them from units which are merely parts of words? The first point to make is that there is a significantly higher degree of cohesion between the parts of a word than between the words making up a larger syntactic unit. This strong internal cohesion of the word manifests itself in its virtual uninterruptability, i.e. its resistance to the insertion of further elements between the parts, and in the fixed order of the parts. Consider, for example, a word like *unrepentantly*. We could not insert anything at all between *un-* and *repent*, between *repent* and *-ant* or between *-ant* and *-ly* – and we could not change the relative order of the four morphological units. With *pigs* it is possible to insert *let* to give *piglets*, but such possibilities are enormously restricted and statable only ad hoc for specific items. Similarly one finds occasional examples of contrastive ordering, as in *outlook* vs *look-out*, but it is a mere coincidence that *out* and *look*

37

should be able to occur in either order, for there is no systematic relation between *outlook* and *look-out*. Contrast the situation found in syntax with such a phrase as *will finish*, as in *I will finish it*. There is massive potential for interruption (cf. *I will, I'm rather inclined to fear, never really finish it*), and the order can be systematically changed (cf. *I said I will finish it and finish it I will*).

From the point of view of motivating the division of the grammar into syntactic and morphological subcomponents, the significance of this difference between inter-word and intra-word cohesion lies in the consequences it has for the kind of description, the kind of rules that we need in the two areas. In the first place it is apparent that in syntax we must allow for reordering rules – *Finish it I will* is a thematic variant of *I will finish it* and will be derived from it by transformation. In such reordering rules the items moved will always be words or sequences of words, never just parts of words, and they will likewise never be moved to a position within a word. But there are no such rules in morphology – neither *outlook* nor *look-out* is derived from the other by such a rule.

Not all variations of order in syntax are comparable to *I will finish it* vs *Finish it I will*, where we can regard one order as basic, unmarked, the other as transformationally derived. There are certain types of expression – 'connective' adverbs like *however, nevertheless*, etc., 'parentheticals' like *I think, it is true, it seems*, etc. – which cannot be assigned a single basic position in the structure of sentences, so that neither *John, however, had misunderstood her intentions* nor *John had, however, misunderstood her intentions* is to be derived from the other (or from some third order). Thus, as a second point, we need to recognise in syntax classes of forms with no fixed basic position and to give rules specifying where they can appear; a minimum condition (more detailed conditions will be needed as well) is again that they must appear between words, never within a word.

Consider next some of the ways in which we will account for the interruptability of word sequences, as with, say, *a book*, where we could insert *new, good, rather interesting* and countless other forms between *a* and *book*. A third difference between syntax and morphology is that in syntax we will describe constructions by setting up functional positions, obligatory or optional, filled by specified classes (i.e. a description along the lines sketched in §3), thereby catering for a great many specific instances of the construction as particular members of the various classes combine in accordance with the general rule. For example – and simplifying a great deal – we might have a construction for the NP containing a 'determiner' (a functional position typically filled by words like *a, the, some, this, which, each*, etc.), optionally one or more 'modifiers' (filled by AdjPs like *new, good, rather interesting*) and a 'head' (filled by nouns). These rules will then yield or 'generate' a vast number of NPs: *a book, a good book, the book, the new book, this film, this rather interesting film*, and so on. It will of course be necessary to account for various restrictions on combinations – *a* can only occur with a singular noun in the head position, *many* only with a plural, and so on – but this doesn't affect the point that in syntax we are typically dealing with general rules involving classes of forms. But in morphology the restrictions are typically so great and idiosyncratic that it is normally not feasible to deal in general rules for combining classes: for example, with affixation we need to describe individually the distribution of particular affixes. We would not have a word construction A–B–C–D, with the four functions filled by morphological classes I, II, III, IV and treat *unrepentantly*, say, as simply resulting from the selection of particular members of these classes; rather we would look at the affixes in turn, noting that *repent* is one of a small number of verbs to which *-ant* can be suffixed to form an adjective, that the resultant *repentant* can then take the class-preserving suffix *un-* and that the adjective *unrepentant* can be changed into an adverb by suffixation of *-ly*.

Fourthly, we may note that 'coordination' is a relation that is found very generally in syntax but not – or virtually not – in morphology. Thus one source of the interruptability of such word sequences as *the books, has understood*, or *in Paris* is that we can insert coordinate forms: *the letters and books, has read and understood, in London or Paris*. By contrast we cannot analogously interrupt a word like *clearly*: we cannot say **She spoke clear-and-slowly*, with coordination of the morphological units (stems) *clear* and *slow* – we have to say *She spoke clearly and slowly*, with coordination of whole words. Or consider the contrast in the interpretation of, on the one hand, *old men and women* and, on the other, *unobjectionable and pleasant*. The first is a classic example of constituent structure ambiguity as discussed in §2: the constituent coordinated with *women* can be either (i) the word *men*, in which case *old* modifies *men and women* and the meaning is "old men and old women", or (ii) the phrase *old men*, in which case *old* modifies *men* alone and the age of the women is left unspecified. But *unobjectionable and pleasant* is not ambiguous: the unit coordinated with *pleasant* can only be the word *unobjectionable*, so that the meaning is "pleasant and unobjectionable" – it cannot be construed with *pleasant* coordinated with *objectionable*, for this is less than a whole word, so that the meaning cannot be "unobjectionable and unpleasant". It is true that we do find the occasional example of coordinated affixes, as in *pre- and post-war, pro- and anti-marketeers*, etc., but again we will need to state the possibilities in terms of combinations of specific affixes rather than in terms of general rules.

A further manifestation of the strong internal cohesion within the word, beyond the absence of systematic variations in order and the virtual non-interruptability, is that parts of a word cannot be omitted in ellipsis. A fifth difference to point out, therefore, is that ellipsis – the omission of elements recoverable from the context – is a syntactic phenomenon not a morphological one: it always involves whole words. Suppose, for example, you ask *Has he got two or three sisters?*: I might reply simply *Three*, with ellipsis of *He has got + sisters*. But if you ask *Do you think it is possible or impossible?*, I would not reply *Im-*, with ellipsis of *I think it is + possible*: the minimum reply selecting the second alternative would be *Impossible*. This difference between words and parts of words is more often discussed in terms of what can be retained than of what can be omitted – *Im-* is said to be excluded because it is not a full word rather than because there has been ellipsis of part of the word. In this case, of course, the two ways of looking at things are equivalent. But on the basis of the possibilities for retention it is commonly said to be a general characteristic of words that they can stand alone as an utterance. However, there are very many items we would certainly want to regard as whole words (by virtue of properties discussed above) that cannot naturally occur alone in this way – not just a handful of grammatical items like *the, our, every*, etc., but large classes. It is very difficult to accept, for example, that past and present tense forms of verbs can be so used: *took, came, sang, takes, comes, sings*, and so on.[9] A more useful criterion for distinguishing words from parts of words, certainly as far as English is concerned, is then that only whole words can be omitted in ellipsis. Two adjacent elements X and Y will thus not form part of a single word if one can be omitted in ellipsis while the other is retained. This shows forms like *has arrived* to be two-word sequences, not single words: cf. ⟨A⟩ *I wonder whether he has arrived* – ⟨B⟩ *Yes, he has*. Similarly we can distinguish between the 'infinitival' particle *to* (as in *to go*), which is a separate word, and the *-ing* of 'present participles' (as in *going*), which is not. Thus we have: ⟨A⟩ *Would you like to go with them?* – ⟨B⟩ *Yes, I'd like to* (with ellipsis of *go with them*) or ⟨A⟩ *What would you like to do?* – ⟨B⟩ *Go with them* (with ellipsis of *I'd like to*), but not ⟨A⟩ *Are you coming or going?* – ⟨B⟩ **Go* (with ellipsis of *I am + -ing*) or ⟨A⟩ *Was he reading his own copy?* – ⟨B⟩ **No, -ing Tom's* (with ellipsis of *He was read-*). This is not to suggest that we have here a necessary condition for word status. In an NP like *the book*, for example, neither *the* nor *book* could be omitted in this way. There is no single criterion to distinguish words from parts of words: one needs to consider a whole range of properties of the type introduced above. In the case of *the book*, for example, the divisibility into two words is very clearly established by the interruptability criterion, by what we said about the 'determiner +

---

[9] We must exclude cases where items are being 'cited' rather than used ordinarily, as in ⟨A⟩ *Did you say 'took' or 'borrowed'?* – ⟨B⟩ *'Took'*. For parts of words can also stand alone in citation, as in ⟨A⟩ *Does it take the prefix 'un-' or 'in-'?* – ⟨B⟩ *'Un-'*. I should also add that contraction, or 'cliticisation', as when *they are*, say, is reduced to *they're*, is not to be included under the concept of ellipsis as understood here; the phenomenon of cliticisation will be taken up later in this section.

optional modifier + head' construction and by the possibilities for coordination. The fact that *the* and *book* cannot be isolated as separate words by the ellipsis criterion does not invalidate the point that ellipsis is a syntactic not a morphological phenomenon; it merely shows that the rules of syntax governing ellipsis will need to specify what kinds of syntactic forms can be omitted in particular types of elliptical construction.

So far we have been looking at various kinds of construction or rule whose domain is limited to syntax. But we can also point to phenomena which are found only in morphology. Consider, for example, the rules of inflectional morphology for the formation of the past tenses of verbs – recall the discussion in §6. There are two aspects of these rules that distinguish them from the kind we have in syntax. Firstly we find a variety of different ways in which the one property 'past tense' is expressed or 'realised', and for irregular verbs (a considerable number) we must specify which process applies – that for **take** the form is *took*, for **write** it is *wrote*, and so on. Secondly the kind of process involved in most of the irregular verbs, vowel change, is itself distinctively morphological. Affixation is simply a matter of putting two items together in sequence and is not different in kind from putting together two words in a phrase – but vowel change is. It is primarily for this reason, indeed, that we treat 'past tense' as a PROPERTY accompanying a lexeme rather than as a constituent occupying a particular linear position in a construction. Similarly some of the minor processes in lexical morphology, such as blending, acronym formation, etc., are very distinctively morphological.

The syntax–morphology division assigns a special status to the word, and one final aspect of this special status is that we find in the word a significant (though certainly not complete) convergence of properties from different components of a language-description: grammar, lexicon, orthography and phonology. We have considered the grammatical properties first because the word (at least in the sense in which the term is employed here) is a grammatical unit and must accordingly be characterised primarily by reference to its grammatical properties. To conclude this section, let us now look at the way the word relates to the other components.

Firstly, there is a significant correlation between words and lexical items, the units described in the dictionary. 'Lexical item' is a technical term of modern linguistics, not part of the standard lay repertoire of terms for talking about language: the lay term is in fact 'word', so that a dictionary is conventionally defined, in part, as a book dealing with the words of a language. The reason for introducing 'lexical item' is of course that the correlation between the grammatical and lexical units is by no means complete. There is a stronger and a weaker sense in which the term 'lexical item' is employed. In the stronger sense, a lexical item is one whose meaning is not systematically derivable from the meanings of any smaller

41

items it may contain. Thus, to use an example from §7, *blackbird* is clearly a lexical item in this sense, while *black bird* equally clearly is not. In a weaker sense, a lexical item is one that is not formed by a general, productive rule, such as *cancellable*: recall our discussion of the limitations on the productivity of *-able* suffixation, again in §7. Conventional dictionaries very often list items of this second kind without giving a full entry, especially where the rule concerned is of relatively high but still restricted productivity. For example, there might be a full entry giving the meanings of **cancel**, followed simply by 'Hence *cancellable*', or the like: the properties of *cancellable* are assumed to be derivable by the dictionary-user from the entries for **cancel** and *-able* (for note that affixes of this kind are standardly listed individually in the dictionary). As we have seen, the output of the rules of lexical morphology are very often lexical items in the strong sense and if not then typically at least in the weaker sense, and lexical morphology is so called precisely because of this pervasive tie-up with the lexicon. The output of the rules of inflectional morphology are only very rarely lexical items in the strong sense, and for the most part – i.e. when the rules are regular – they are not lexical items in the weaker sense either: here it is accordingly the lexeme, not the various inflectional forms, the words, that correlates most closely with the lexical item, and again the term 'lexeme' is intended to be suggestive of this link. Irregular inflectional forms, however, will be lexical items in the weaker sense and as such are widely given partial dictionary entries like '*took*: see **take**'.

It should also be borne in mind that a lexical item (normally in the strong sense) may contain more than one lexeme or word: these are **idioms** such as **bury** *the hatchet* "renounce a quarrel", **spill** *the beans* "give away a secret", colloquial **kick** *the bucket* "die", **full** *of beans* "in high spirits", *down in the dumps* "depressed", **have** *a leg to stand on* "be able to support one's thesis with facts or sound reasons",[10] and countless others. The reason we say these contain more than one lexeme/word is that the grammatical arrangement is like that found elsewhere in what are clearly syntactic constructions, not morphological formations. Thus *He'll spill the beans* belongs to the same construction as *He'll prepare the beans*, with *the beans* an NP functioning in both cases as direct object; *He hasn't a leg to stand on* is like *He hasn't a bed to sleep in*, and so on. Indeed in the most obvious cases of idioms, such as those cited, the same elements can occur in the same syntactic construction with a non-idiomatic, or 'literal', meaning – *He buried the hatchet* has, as a less salient interpretation, "He covered up the light short-handled axe".

However, co-occurrence within an idiom deprives the component parts

---

[10] This last idiom normally occurs in the negative, as in *He hasn't a leg to stand on*; more precisely, it is restricted to what we shall call 'non-affirmative' contexts (see 13.2).

of some of the syntactic independence of words. Consider, for example, the matter of changes in order. While *He hasn't a bed to sleep in* is in paradigmatic variation with *He hasn't a bed in which to sleep* (with a difference, among other things, in the order of *sleep* and *in*), there is no corresponding variation with idiomatic *He hasn't a leg to stand on*. Or again, while *Tom kicked the bucket* is ambiguous between literal and idiomatic interpretations, *The bucket was kicked by Tom* (transformationally derived by passivisation) and *The bucket Tom kicked* (derived by thematic fronting) allow only the literal interpretation. Note, however, that there is some variation in the extent to which such syntactic processes are inapplicable to sentences containing idioms: passive *The hatchet was finally buried*, for example, has the same ambiguity as active *They finally buried the hatchet* (though the version with thematic fronting, *The hatchet they finally buried*, does not here have the idiomatic interpretation). The loss, in varying degrees, of syntactic independence is seen equally in the greatly reduced interruptability of word sequences belonging to an idiom. With **have** *a leg to stand on* we can insert material between **have** and the NP that is its object (cf. *He hasn't, however, a leg to stand on* – or the interrogative *Has he a leg to stand on?*) but the NP *a leg to stand on* is highly resistant to interruption. Similarly with *Tom kicked the bucket* we can freely insert modifiers between *the* and *bucket* in the literal interpretation, as in *Tom kicked the bright-red plastic bucket*, but in the idiomatic interpretation such modification is virtually excluded (though not quite: we could say *Tom kicked the proverbial bucket*). The parts of an idiom clearly have a lexical cohesion precisely by virtue of the fact that the meaning is associated with the whole, not derivable from the parts, and this lexical cohesion is accompanied, in varying degrees, by grammatical cohesion – the property we have seen to be characteristic of words.

There may then be some indeterminacy as to where we should draw the boundary between idioms and single words. How, for example, shall we analyse *wear and tear, spick and span, common or garden*? The fact that the parts are coordinated suggests that they are multi-word sequences, but on the other hand the degree of grammatical cohesion between the parts seems to be as great as for single words. Or again, is *in front* a two-word idiom or a single word, as used in, say, *She sat in front of the car*? We cannot reverse the order, neither part alone can be dropped in ellipsis and the sequence cannot be interrupted in any relevant way – for if we insert *the* to give *She sat in the front of the car* the meaning is changed in a non-systematic way, so that such an example no more establishes the interruptability of *in front* than *black, awesome bird* establishes that of *blackbird*. On the other hand, the degree of fusion between *in* and *front* is slightly less than that between *in* and *side* in *She sat inside the car*. *Inside* is a preposition taking an NP as complement: we shall not analyse it syntactically into a sequence of preposition (*in*) + noun (*side*) because nouns do not take NPs as complement and hence we could not take *the car* as complement of *side* on its own. But *in front* doesn't take NPs as complement: we need an *of* phrase (a type of complement that readily occurs with nouns, as in *the roof of the car*, etc.), so that *front* is thus somewhat more like an independent noun than *side*.[11] But it is a moot point whether this is sufficient to justify saying that, grammatically, *inside* is one word, *in front* two.

Before we leave the issue of the relation between words and lexical items, there is one further point that should be made. When they occur in sentences words obviously form constituents, but lexical items do not necessarily do so. This will already have become evident from what we have said about lexemes: in *He took the apples*, for example, **take** does not occur as a constituent in the sense discussed in §2 above – we can analyse *took* into **take** plus the inflectional property 'past tense', but these two elements are not linearly ordered, as constituents are. When we consider idioms, the point that lexical items are not always introduced into sentences as constituents becomes even clearer. In *Borg pulled the set out of the fire* "Borg saved the set when it seemed lost", the idiom involves the **pull** component of *pulled* and the PP *out of the fire – the set* is not part of the idiom (though there are considerable restrictions on what could be substituted for it). In *They pulled themselves together* "They rallied, recovered control of themselves", the idiom consists of **pull**, the 'reflexive' component of *themselves* (i.e. the property common to *themselves, himself, myself*, etc.) and *together*. In *She was pulling John's leg* "She was teasing John", it consists of **pull**, the possessive component of *John's* (what is common to *John's, Mary's, my*, etc.) and **leg** (with the choice between singular and plural inflectional forms dependent on the possessive phrase: cf. *She was pulling their legs*). And in *He'll spill the bloody beans*, the *bloody* is part of the NP *the bloody beans* but is not part of the idiom. The lexicon is thus not to be thought of as a set of units to be inserted at various points in a syntactic constituent structure: the entry for a lexical item will very often give only a PARTIAL specification of the syntactic constituents in which it can be instantiated.

Let us turn now, secondly, to the relation between grammar and orthography. Here, there is a very close correlation between the word as a syntactic constituent and what appears flanked by spaces in writing – so much so that this time we needn't introduce a wholly new term for the latter but can speak simply of an 'orthographic word'. Normally, then, a grammatical word is represented in writing by an orthographic word. We cannot assume, however, that it always will be, for the grammatical word must be established by grammatical criteria (which is why examples like *wear and tear* and *in front* are problems for the grammarian: if orthographic

---

[11] Note in passing that the *of* certainly is separable from *front* – cf. *I'll put it in front, or perhaps if you prefer on top, of the cabinet*; there can thus be no question of *in front of* being a single word.

criteria were paramount the issue would be clear-cut). There are just two points of complication in the relation between grammatical and orthographic words that merit brief mention here. One concerns compounds: many are written as two orthographic words (*birth control, income tax*, etc.), and very often there is fluctuation in writing between two or indeed all three of the possible ways of putting together the component stems of a compound – with a space, hyphen or neither, as in *starting point, starting-point, startingpoint*. The transition from space to hyphen to close juxtaposition reflects the pro- *lexicalisation* gressive institutionalisation of the compound. Compounds, however, are a problem for the grammar too, for again there is some indeterminacy over the precise boundary between compound nouns and phrasal sequences of modifier + head. The other minor point concerns the apostrophe: the orthography does not distinguish between, say, *fo'c'sle* (a variant spelling of *forecastle*), which grammatically is a single word, and *I've* (a contraction of *I have*), which grammatically is two words. Nevertheless, for the most part the grammatical word is distinguished clearly in the orthography, a fact that is indicative of the special status it has as a linguistic unit.

Thirdly, to a significant extent the word has distinctive phonological properties. Words typically carry a single accent – on the first syllable in *metaphor*, the second in *disinterested*, the third in *telegraphic*, and so on. This is standardly taken as one of the primary criteria for distinguishing between compound words and modifier + head phrasal constructions – compare our earlier examples, *blackbird* (a compound, with a single accent, on *black*) vs *black bird* (two words, each with its own accent), and note that *birth control* and *income tax*, which are orthographically separated, follow the accentuation pattern of *blackbird*, not *black bird*. Notice, however, that words belonging to the set of what we are calling grammatical items very often do not carry an accent, in which case they may not be clearly distinguished phonologically from affixes – compare *booklets, the books* and *new books*, where the second is like the first, not the third, in carrying one accent rather than two.

A further phonological property that is characteristic of words is that they normally contain at least one vowel; there are some affixes which, by contrast, lack a vowel and are thereby clearly unwordlike – notably the inflectional endings exemplified in plural nouns like *dogs, cats* and in verbs like *loved, kissed, runs, hits*. The clearest cases where a word lacks this property involve vowel elision, as when we say *I'll*, /aɪl/, rather than the uncontracted *I will* – and similarly in *I'd, I'm, he's, we've* and the like. We say here that /wɪl/ is 'cliticised', reduced to a **clitic**, namely /l/. A clitic is a word that merges phonologically with an adjacent word. We can then further distinguish between 'enclitics', like the above, which merge with the preceding word, and 'proclitics', which are attached to the following word, as when *Do we have to go?*, say, is pronounced /dwiː.../. Such cliticisation affects a relatively small number of verbs: certain inflectional forms of *be*, *have* and a number of auxiliaries such as *do* and *will*. The rules of inflectional morphology will have to specify not just the **strong** forms but also the **weak** variants. Thus one of the present-tense forms of *have* has /hæv/ as its strong variant, and /həv/, /əv/ and the clitic /v/ as progressively weaker variants. The four forms do not of course differ in their inflectional properties: the dimension of strength concerns variation in phonological prominence, not a difference in syntax.

The conditions under which we will say that a word lacks the phonological independence of a non-clitic word, that it merges with its neighbour, will depend on the phonology of the language in question. In English it is primarily a matter of the lack of a vowel, and grammatical items like *the* which normally lack word accent are not standardly analysed as clitics, whereas in Latin and Greek accentuation is the crucial factor. The English clitics mentioned above are all reduced variants of non-clitic words – but there is one very idiosyncratic and troublesome item which is best treated as a word that is inherently a clitic: the possessive *'s* of *the king's daughter* and the like. This is traditionally analysed as an inflectional suffix: *king's* is said to be the possessive or 'genitive' form of *king* and accordingly a single word. However, in terms of the criterion of interruptability, *king* and *'s* do not exhibit the strong degree of cohesion that characterises the parts of a single word, for there is considerable scope for inserting material between them. The possibilities are greater in 'informal' styles than in 'formal' ones (see §9 for this contrast): compare *the man's expression* vs *the man opposite me's expression* or *the man I was talking to's expression*, but even in formal style we can interrupt *the prime minister's main asset* to give *the prime minister, Mrs Thatcher's, main asset* or *the King's daughter* to give *the King of Spain's daughter*. And notice, further, that the unit preceding *'s* can be coordinated, as in *John and Mary's dislike for each other*. Examples like these argue very strongly for treating *'s* as a grammatical word on its own, not an inflectional suffix. Take *the King of Spain's daughter*, for example; here *Spain's* is not a syntactic constituent, for the constituent structure of the whole NP is surely essentially as shown in (35):

(35)

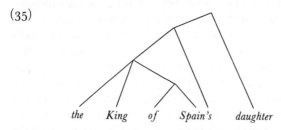

That is, the *'s* enters into construction not with *Spain* but with *the King of*

Spain, a phrase. Syntactically *'s* is basically analogous to the preposition *of*, except that it follows rather than precedes the NP that it combines with – compare *the daughter of the King of Spain*, where *of the King of Spain* is a preposition phrase (PP) having *of* as head and the NP *the King of Spain* as complement. We will thus take *the King of Spain's* to be a possessive phrase (PossP) with *'s* as head and the NP *the King of Spain* as complement. (If *'s* were inflectional we would expect *the King's of Spain daughter*, for in *the King of Spain* it is *King*, not *Spain*, that is head.) What makes it seem strange to say that *'s* is a word is that it is phonologically so unlike other words. In the examples given it is enclitic to the last word of the NP with which it enters into construction – but under certain grammatical–phonological conditions it has no separate phonological identity at all, as in *the boys' behaviour*, where the plural /z/ and the possessive /z/ fuse into one. That this example is so strikingly exceptional is, however, indicative of the generally close convergence in the word of grammatical and phonological properties.

One final point should be made concerning the syntax–morphology division. In view of the aims and scope of this book I have discussed the issue exclusively with reference to English, suggesting that in English the word is a basic unit with distinctive properties of its own such that there are appreciable differences in the kinds of rule we need for grammar above the word and grammar within the word. But this is an area where there is considerable variation across the range of languages: in some (such as Latin and Greek) the division of the grammar into separate subcomponents is much more highly motivated than in others (such as Turkish or Vietnamese). And because of its somewhat uncertain status as a universal, many modern treatments of English give rather less prominence to the syntax–morphology division than I have done here.

1.9   Descriptive grammar vs prescriptive grammar

To conclude this chapter we must introduce a distinction between two kinds of grammar, **descriptive** grammar and **prescriptive** (or 'normative') grammar. Descriptive grammar aims to present the grammar that underlies the actual usage of speakers of the language, while prescriptive grammar aims to tell its readers what grammatical rules they SHOULD follow: the difference is one of goals.

This book is, of course, an exercise in descriptive grammar. The reader should be aware, however, that there is a long and quite influential tradition of prescriptivism in school grammars and other manuals of grammatical usage (for which there is a large commercial market) – and that a good deal in the widely established prescriptive doctrine is open to objection from the point of view of descriptive linguistics. For this reason I shall have occasion from time to time to refer to various traditional prescriptive rules

47

that I would regard as descriptively unsound or in need of modification.

The main objection to the prescriptive tradition concerns the treatment of what we shall call variation in **style**. For most purposes it is sufficient to distinguish three styles, 'formal', 'informal' and 'neutral', illustrated, for example in

(36) i *He advised us by whom it had been designed*   Formal
      ii *Who had it been designed by?*   Informal
      iii *He knew who had designed it*   Neutral

Speakers of Standard English will normally have in their repertoire all three of these, but the first two will be restricted to certain contexts of use distinguished by the speaker or writer's attitude to the audience or to the occasion. In formal style we make use of grammatical and/or lexical features that convey the attitude that the occasion is one of some social formality – we come across as relatively deferential, stiff, cold, impersonal, distant; informal style contains features reflecting an attitude of social informality – here we come across as relatively relaxed, warm, friendly. The differences are thus analogous to those found, say, between formal and informal dress. And of course people vary a good deal with respect to the conditions under which they use formal and informal style, just as they vary with respect to the conditions in which they dress formally or informally. Now the prescriptive tradition very often treats constructions that belong to informal style as though they are not really grammatically 'correct'. For example, Fowler's *Modern English Usage*, one of the best-known prescriptive manuals, writes as follows of the construction illustrated in (ii): 'The interrogative *who* is often used in talk where grammar demands *whom*, as in *Who did you hear that from?*'. This is a very unsatisfactory way of putting it. (ii) is just as grammatical as (i), and more generally informal style is just as systematic, as 'rule-governed', as formal style. It is simply that the rules of grammar very often provide for variants – such as *from whom* and *who . . . from* – which are characteristic of different styles. People are often led by the prescriptive tradition to subscribe to such beliefs as the following: 'I say things like *Who did you hear that from?*, but I realise that I ought really to say *From whom did you hear that?*', but such beliefs are totally without foundation – there is not the slightest reason to think that that is what we ought to say. Neither construction is inherently any better than the other: they are equally grammatical, but differ in meaning, more particularly of course in non-propositional meaning.

It is worth observing that the contrast between (i) and (ii) is to be distinguished from that between

(37) i *I haven't seen anything*
      ii *I ain't seen nothing*

for here the difference is one of social dialect, not style: (i) belongs to the standard dialect, (ii) to a non-standard one, so that (37ii), unlike (36ii), is ungrammatical in Standard English. But in spite of this difference there is an important similarity between the pairs inasmuch as in neither case is there any sense in which one construction can be said to be inherently better, or more subject to grammatical rule, than the other. For while (37ii) is ungrammatical in Standard English, it is not ungrammatical tout court: it is completely grammatical, i.e. constructed in accordance with systematic rules of grammar, in its own dialect. The difference between (37i) and (ii) is a sociolinguistic matter, with speakers who use (i) belonging to socially more privileged groups than those who use (ii) – but on purely linguistic grounds there is no reason for saying that (i) is intrinsically better than (ii), just as there is none for saying that *From whom did you hear that?* is intrinsically better than *Who did you hear that from?* or that (37i) is intrinsically better, or worse, than French *Je n'ai rien vu.*[12]

FURTHER READING

A more advanced treatment of many of the topics dealt with in this chapter can be found in Matthews 1981. Lexemes are commonly represented in the literature in roman small capitals (see Matthews 1974: Ch. 2, 1981: Ch. 3) or in single quotation marks (see Lyons 1977: §1.5); my concept of lexeme is somewhat more restrictive, less closely related to that of lexical item. The term 'kernel' is most often found in combination with 'sentence' in early work on transformational grammar (e.g. Chomsky 1957); for 'kernel clause', see Matthews 1981: Ch. 12. On the contrast between verbal and non-verbal signals and its relevance to sentence identification, see Lyons 1977: §3.1, 1981a: 23–30, 130. On morphology, see Matthews 1974, and for descriptive accounts of lexical morphology – traditionally called 'word-formation' – in English, see Quirk et al. 1971: Appx 1, Marchand 1969, Adams 1973. On idioms, see Makkai 1972. On 'style' see Crystal & Davy 1969 and Quirk et al. 1971: §§27–29; on the descriptive/prescriptive contrast, see Palmer 1971: §1.3.

---

[12] Notice, in particular, that it is quite invalid to argue against (36ii) on the grounds that the two negatives cancel each other out by a rule of logic whereby two negatives make a positive (as *It is not the case that I haven't seen him* is logically equivalent to *I have seen him*). The rules of logic apply to the 'logical form' of sentences, and there is only one negative in the logical form of (36ii) (just as there is only one in that of *Je n'ai rien vu*, in spite of the fact that *ne* and *rien* can each occur in other sentences as the sole marker of negation): the two negatives in the grammatical form simply result from a rule of grammatical agreement. It is a matter of the most elementary empirical observation that (36ii) has the same propositional meaning as (i), and any argument based on the claim that it means " It is not the case that I have seen nothing" is no more valid than that claim.

2

The structural approach to linguistic analysis

2.1 General principles

The grammar of a language will be formulated as a set of rules – rules which specify the form of words (morphology) and the way words combine to make sentences (syntax). The various categories that figure in the rules – categories like verb, noun, noun phrase, clause, subject, object, and so on (there will inevitably be a considerable number of them) – are introduced so that we can express the rules in the most general way and thus make the grammar as simple as possible. This point may be illustrated with the following elementary example. Consider the data in (1):

(1)
    i *The nurse gave the patient the medicine*
    ii **Nurse the gave the patient the medicine*
    iii **The nurse gave patient the the medicine*
    iv **The nurse gave the patient medicine the*

Postulating a category of NP, covering expressions like *the nurse*, *the patient*, etc., allows us to exclude all of (ii–iv) by means of a single rule to the effect that within NP structure the determiner (*the* and similar items) must precede the head (the position filled by the noun). Notice that we could not express the rule simply in terms of permitted sequences of words in sentences, saying that the sequence 'noun followed by *the*' is excluded – for (1ii) does in fact contain the sequence *patient the*. We need a 'constituent structure' to define the domain within which the rule holds: *patient the* in (1ii) is not a counterexample to the rule because *patient* is the head of one NP while *the* is the determiner of another.

This is an obvious point, but it is worth emphasising for the general conclusion to be drawn from it. For it follows that concepts like 'NP', 'subject', 'past tense', 'verb', etc., can be understood only by looking at the role they play in the formulation of grammars. They are theoretical constructs which cannot be explicated or defined except by reference to their inter-relationships. The fundamental principle of what we are calling the structural approach to linguistic analysis is that the units and categories postulated for the grammar of a given language are determined by the syntagmatic and paradigmatic relations that obtain within the sentences of that language. (I use 'category' as a general term for all the more specific concepts dealt with in the last chapter: functions, classes, systems, terms in systems, and so on.)

This principle applies to all areas of linguistic analysis – phonology, morphology, syntax and the lexicon. Since our primary concern is with syntax, let me illustrate with a brief example from that field. Consider the following sentences:

(2)   i *Jill understood the problem and so did Ed*   *también*
         ii *Jill didn't understand the problem and neither did Ed*   *tampoco*

We will refer to *and so did Ed* and *and neither did Ed* as 'coordinate tags'. Our interest lies in the choice between *so* and *neither*. They are clearly not interchangeable, as we can see from the ungrammaticality of **Jill understood the problem and neither did Ed* or **Jill didn't understand the problem and so did Ed*. The choice depends on the structure of the clause to which the tag is attached, so that we distinguish positive and negative clauses, terms in a system of clause polarity, according as they require *so* in the following tag, like *Jill understood the problem*, or *neither*, like *Jill didn't understand the problem*. On this basis the first member of each of the following pairs will be classified as syntactically positive, the second as negative.

(3)   i *She must go with them*   ii *She mustn't go with them*   *must not go*
(4)   i *She can go with them*   ii *She can't go with them*   *cannot go*
(5)   i *She is unable to go with them*   ii *She isn't able to go with them*
(6)   i *She solved it in no time*   ii *She had no difficulty in solving it*
(7)   i *She almost touched it*   ii *She hardly touched it*

Thus the tags in (3) would be *and so must Ed* for positive (i), *and neither must Ed* for negative (ii); in (4) they would be respectively *and so can Ed, and neither can Ed*, in (5) *and so is Ed, and neither is Ed*, and so on. Notice that if we looked at the examples in isolation, instead of considering the syntactic relations they enter into, we would often have difficulty in arriving at the correct classification. Notice, for example, that the negatives in (3) and (4) are understood quite differently. (3ii) says that it is necessary for her not to go, but (4ii) doesn't say that it is possible for her not to go: it says that it is not possible for her to go. Semantically, "can" is part of what is negated in (4ii), while "must" is not part of what is negated in (3ii). When we turn to (5) we find that (i) and (ii) are just about equivalent in meaning, yet the first is positive, the second negative. (6i) and (6ii) are likewise very similar in meaning, and they both contain the word *no*, but again they differ in syntactic polarity. Finally in (7), notice that it is the positive (i) that entails that she didn't touch it, while the negative (ii) entails that she did!

As a second example of the way the analysis is determined by the syntactic relations between and within sentences, consider the constituent structure of (8) and (9):

(8)   *Ed found the key to the safe*
(9)   *Ed drove the minister to the station*

Superficially these look alike: in each we have the sequence 'noun + verb + article + noun + preposition + article + noun'. But the words are grouped together differently: in (8) *the key to the safe* forms a constituent whereas in (9) *the minister* and *to the station* do not go together but enter separately into construction with *drove*. Approximate structures are given in (10) and (11), where I simplify by omitting the functional labels, i.e. subject, object, etc.:

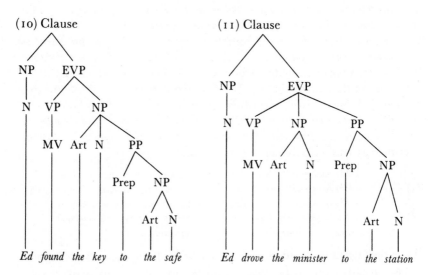

(10) Clause   (11) Clause

The evidence on which these analyses are based comes from various paradigmatic relations into which the sentences enter. Three such pieces of evidence are to be found in the way the sentences are related to their passive, cleft and *wh* interrogative counterparts.

(a) The passive counterparts. If we apply the passive transformation to (8) we get *The key to the safe was found by Ed*: this shows that *the key to the safe* behaves as the object of (8) and hence is a constituent – for we have seen (see 1.4) that the subject of a passive clause corresponds (generally, at least) to the object of its active counterpart. The passive of (9), by contrast, is *The minister was driven to the station by Ed* – not **The minister to the station was driven by Ed*. It follows that the object of (9) must be just *the minister*, which accordingly forms a constituent on its own, as shown in (11).

(b) Cleft counterparts. Here we are concerned with the systematic relation between thematically unmarked clauses like (12i) and cleft clauses like (12ii):

52

(12)   i *John saw Ed*   ii *It was Ed that John saw*

As we again noted in 1.4, the cleft construction picks out one element from the unmarked version and brings it into special focus. The highlighted element can be an NP, as in (12ii), a PP, as in *It was in London that Sue died*, a cleft counterpart of *Sue died in London*, and so on, but whatever the class it is always a single constituent. Now if we look at the cleft counterparts of (8) and (9) we again find that they are different. For (8) we have *It was the key to the safe that Ed found*, showing *the key to the safe* to be a constituent. But for (9) we cannot have **It was the minister to the station that Ed drove*: rather *It was the minister that Ed drove to the station* or *It was to the station that Ed drove the minister*, which respectively bring into focus the NP *the minister* and the PP *to the station*.

(c) *Wh* interrogative counterparts. The third piece of evidence comes from interrogative clauses introduced by one of the special interrogative elements *who, which, what*, etc. We can relate a declarative to various such interrogatives having an appropriate '*wh* phrase' in place of some constituent in the declarative. For example, (9) can be related to *Who did Ed drive to the station?*, with *who* in place of the object *the minister*. But for (8) the corresponding interrogative is not **What did Ed find to the safe?*, but simply *What did Ed find?*, with *what* selected in place of *the key to the safe*.

It would be easy to add further justification of the same general kind, but enough has been given to make the point. The rules that relate one type of construction to another make reference to constituent structure, to classes like NP, PP, etc., to functions like subject, object, etc., and thus the way such rules apply to a sentence provides an indispensable guide to its analysis.

Now it might be objected that the difference between (10) and (11) could be arrived at simply on the basis of the meanings of the sentences. In (8) *the key to the safe* refers to a particular object (with *to the safe* providing information as to which key is meant), whereas in (9) *the minister to the station* does not pick out a single object (and *to the station* does not serve to make clear which minister the speaker has in mind). Moreover, the ambiguity of *Liz attacked the man with a knife*, to which we assigned two constituent structures in 1.2, would be accounted for by giving it an analysis like (10) for the interpretation where *with a knife* is part of the description of the person attacked and an analysis like (11) for that where it indicates the means or instrument used for the attack.

It is true that in these examples there is a straightforward relation between the syntactic structure and the meaning – but things are not always so simple. The way grammatical units are grouped together syntactically and morphologically does not always match the way the corresponding meanings are grouped. We have already seen an example of this in (3ii) and (4ii). In both, the negative is expressed by an inflectional suffix on the verb, but they differ in what is negated from a semantic point of view: in (4) "she can go with them" is negated, whereas in (3) the negative applies to "she go with them", not "she must go with them". Or, as a second example, consider the sentence *John was believed by most of the staff to be a liar*. This is understood as meaning, essentially, "Most of the staff believed that John was a liar" – in particular, what most of the staff believed was not John, but the proposition that John was a liar. From a syntactic point of view, however, *John to be a liar* does not form a constituent even though "John was a liar" is a component of the meaning; rather the subject of *was believed* is simply *John*. Certain idioms provide other examples where the syntactic structure does not transparently show the way the components of meaning are grouped together, as we observed in 1.8. In *She was pulling John's leg*, for example, understood in its idiomatic sense of "She was teasing John", what corresponds to the semantic element "tease" is the syntactic non-constituent ***pull*** + *'s* + ***leg***; from a syntactic point of view *John's leg* is a constituent (more precisely, an NP functioning as object), but no part of the total sentence meaning corresponds to it.

The moral to be drawn from such examples is that the relationship between meaning and syntactic form is too complex, too indirect, for one to be able to determine the syntactic structure of a sentence from a mere consideration of its meaning. The structural approach, therefore, is to define categories by reference to their place within the grammar, to the rules in which they figure, to the relationships between them. As a brief and necessarily sketchy illustration of this approach let us examine two very familiar concepts from traditional grammar, first noun, then imperative clause. We may characterise them in structural terms as follows:

(a) Noun. The term 'noun' is applicable both to a class of lexemes and to a class of words: we will say both that ***man*** is a noun and that *man* and *men* are nouns; for reasons to be given later, I will regard the classification of words as the more basic, and will thus here consider the properties of noun words. One preliminary point that should be made is that not all nouns are identical with respect to their grammatical properties: we find rather that we have a core of what we may regard as **central** or **prototypical** nouns sharing a considerable number of distinctive properties, with other words classified as nouns by virtue of sharing a significant number of these properties and/or of being significantly more like a prototypical noun than like a prototypical adjective, verb or whatever. For example, *umbrage*, as in *He took umbrage*, occurs in a very restricted range of noun positions and thus differs quite appreciably from prototypical nouns like *boy, dog, song, fact*, but it is nevertheless quite clearly more like such words than it is like the adjectives *good, big, tall* or the verbs *go, goes, went, take, takes, took*, etc.

The most important distinctive properties of nouns have to do with their functional potential. They function primarily as 'head' in the structure of NPs (thus *farmer* is head of the NP *the farmer*), where NPs in turn function as subject in clause structure (*The farmer died*), object in clause structure (*He saw the farmer*), complement of a preposition (*He walked towards the farmer*), complement of the possessive clitic *'s* (*The farmer's death*), and so on. As head of an NP, the noun may stand alone (like *mother* and *lunch* in *Mother was preparing lunch*) or be accompanied by one or more 'dependents' of various kinds – 'articles' (like *the* in *the farmer*), adjectives (like *young* in *young children*), PPs (like *from Glasgow* in *people from Glasgow*), certain kinds of subordinate clause (like the 'restrictive relative clause' *that were far too large* in *clothes that were far too large*), and so on. Within NP structure, nouns can also function as a dependent of a following head noun: in *the saucepan bottom, a boy actor, student grants*, for example, the nouns *saucepan, boy* and *student* are modifiers, *bottom, actor* and *grant* heads.

Turning now to inflection, we note that prototypical nouns enter into contrasts of number, being singular with a contrasting plural counterpart or vice versa: *farmer ~ farmers, child ~ children, saucepan ~ saucepans*, etc. This is certainly not a necessary condition for nounhood since there are numerous words that are indisputably nouns by virtue of their functional potential which are non-contrastively singular (*equipment ~ *equipments, wetness ~ *wetnesses*, etc.) and a few which are non-contrastively plural (**scissor ~ scissors, *alm ~ alms*, etc.). It is nonetheless an important property of the prototype, and is almost a sufficient condition for nounhood, as the only inflectionally contrasting singular–plural pairs that are not nouns are the 'demonstratives' *this ~ these* and *that ~ those*.

Finally, there are a number of processes of lexical morphology which distinctively involve nouns. Some apply to noun stems, yielding stems of a different primary class (adjective in the case of *child → childlike*, *hope → hopeful*, verb in the case of *horse → unhorse, bottle* "container" → *bottle* "put in a bottle", and so on) or stems of a different subclass of noun (*man → manhood, London → Londoner*). Some, by contrast, apply to stems of other classes to yield noun stems (*happy → happiness, able → ability, hear → hearer, judge → judgement, victimise → victimisation*, etc.) The affixes appearing in these last examples often provide a clear signal that a word is a noun, but many nouns are of course morphologically simple, so that these properties are less important than those considered above. 'Noun' is a syntactic category: the essential properties of nouns have to do with their syntactic behaviour – their functional potential and their inflection.'

(b) Imperative clause. Imperative clauses (such as *Be careful*) contrast, in a system that we are calling 'clause type', with declaratives (*You are careful*), interrogatives (*Are you careful?*) and exclamatives (*How careful you are!*). Unlike the other terms in the system, imperatives cannot occur embedded inside a larger clause (except in the special case of quotation, which we suggested in 1.5 is to be regarded as the embedding of one text inside another).

As far as their internal structure is concerned, imperatives have the following properties. The first verb is inflectionally what we shall call a 'base' form – a form identical with the lexical stem; thus the *be* of imperative *Be careful* contrasts inflectionally with the *are* of declarative *You are careful*. A *you* as subject is optional, so that we can have either *You be careful* or just *Be careful*. Negatives are generally formed with *don't* or *do not*: *Don't be cheeky*, *Do not despair*; an expressed subject follows *don't*, as in *Don't you be so sure!*.

The structural approach contrasts with what is often called 'notional grammar', where syntactic categories are defined in terms of meaning. A standard notional definition of 'noun', for example, is that a noun is the name of a person, place or thing. Similarly, to say that an imperative clause is one that is used to issue a request or command is to give a notional definition of it: the criterion has to do with the meaning of the clause, not with its syntactic properties.

Notional definitions are characteristic of much traditional grammar – and of the grammar taught in schools in many places even now. Their appeal is clear. They avoid the apparent circularity of the structural approach, where a noun, say, is explained by reference to heads, noun phrases, subjects, objects, dependents, singular and plural inflections, and so on, all these other terms being just as much in need of explanation as 'noun' itself. The notional definition by contrast does not mention any technical terms of syntax beside the one being defined: it is expressed instead in terms of apparently everyday and intuitively obvious concepts like 'person', 'place', 'command', 'request'.

The trouble is that the notional definitions simply don't give the right results. Take first the one we have given for noun – the name of a person, place or thing. If we interpret 'thing' to mean "physical object", then clearly the definition does not provide a necessary condition for nounhood. There are innumerable examples of words that all grammarians would agree to be nouns but which do not denote persons, places or concrete objects: *fact, idea, joy, ability, indoctrination, rectitude, postponement*. And if we attempt to dispose of these counterexamples by claiming that such nouns denote 'things' in a more abstract sense of the term, then the definition becomes unworkable. For this more abstract notion of 'thing' is so vague that we have no independent way of determining whether or not a word does denote a thing – independent in the sense of not presupposing that we already know whether or not it is a noun. Or take the notional definition proposed for imperative clauses. 'Use as a command or request' is in fact neither a necessary nor a sufficient condition for a clause to be imperative. It is not a necessary condition because there are imperative clauses like *Sleep well, Get well soon,* and so on, which would normally be used to express wishes or hopes rather than requests or commands. And it is not a sufficient condition because requests or commands can be issued in other ways, e.g. by using a declarative like *Passengers are requested to remain in their seats* or an interrogative like *Would you please open the door.*

The reason why the notional definitions don't work has already been given: the relation between syntactic structure and meaning is in general too complex and indirect for one to be able to put syntactic and semantic categories in a one-to-one correspondence. And the notional approach is potentially harmful in that it can obscure the nature of the relationship between syntactic structure and meaning, and make the description of that relationship more difficult, by introducing conceptual confusion between syntactic and semantic categories. One of the things we want the grammar to do, for example, is to describe the correlations between the internal structure of sentences and their use in the performance of such acts as making statements, asking questions, making requests and so on. In order to do this, it is necessary to begin with a clear conceptual distinction between categories of syntactic form like declarative, interrogative, imperative, and categories of utterance use like statement, question, command: the notional definition, on the contrary, encourages a confusion between the two sets of concepts. Similarly, to take up an example from the last chapter, we need to describe the relation between the syntactic category of tense and the semantic category of time. A notional definition of past tense as a form used to express past time can lead to great confusion in cases like *I didn't realise the match started tomorrow* where *started* is inflectionally a past tense form although the time is future.

Moreover, it should be emphasised that the circularity we found in the structural approach in no way invalidates it. We can break out of the circle by checking our grammar against the data. The grammar makes predictions which can be tested by matching them with native speaker judgements about the acceptability of sentences, and so on. Suppose we said that *table* was a noun; then the grammar would predict, correctly, that sentences like *Their table intrigued me, I like that old table, He put it on the table that she had just bought, This table's value has increased enormously,* etc. are well-formed, whereas if we said that *obviously,* say, was a noun we would falsely predict that it occurred in sentences like **Their obviously intrigued me, *I like that old obviously,* and so on (the precise predictions would of course depend on whether we said it was a prototypical noun or a member of some less central subclass), and conversely we would fail to predict its occurrence in sentences like *He had obviously read it carefully, I was concerned at his obviously worsening condition.* The grammar is thus falsifiable. But we have no similar way of breaking out of the circle in the definition of noun as the name of a person, place or thing, where 'thing' is taken in an abstract sense: there are simply no testable predictions that follow from it. I can test to see whether a word can function as the head of a phrase in subject position, but how can I test whether a word denotes a thing?

2.2 Exemplification: the grammatical subject

In this section I shall develop the contrast between the structural and notional approaches to grammatical analysis with a further example, examined in somewhat greater detail than those introduced above. Our concern will be with the syntactic function 'subject'. This time we will begin by considering the notional approach, and then turn to a structural explication of the concept.

2.2.1 *The notional approach to a definition of grammatical subject*

The standard notional definition of subject equates it with the 'topic' of the sentence, i.e. what the sentence is about. The subject here contrasts with the predicate, which is equated with the 'comment', i.e. what is said about the topic. In a formulation from a recent book on English grammar, the subject 'names what we are thinking about in a sentence', while the predicate 'states what we are thinking about the subject' (Phythian 1980: 5). Consider, for example, sentence (13):

(13)   *Liz shot the intruder*

where *Liz* is subject, *shot the intruder* the predicate. Then according to the notional definition, *Liz* is subject because in uttering (13) I would be saying something about Liz (namely that she shot the intruder).

The definition is open to two objections. In the first place, the identification of the topic is very much more difficult and problematic than is that of the subject. How do we decide what the topic of a sentence is? The idea that a topic is a person about whom or a thing about which something is said is too vague, for in uttering (13) I surely say something about both Liz and the intruder: it would seem that we need some such qualification as 'primarily' – the topic is what the sentence is primarily about. But then there is no reason to believe that the distinction between what I am primarily talking about and what I am only secondarily talking about is directly reflected in the grammatical form of English sentences. Suppose, for example, that instead of (13) I say

(14)   *She shot him*

(with *she* referring to Liz, *him* to the intruder). Now if I said (14) in response to your question *What did Liz do?* (or *What did Liz do when she saw the intruder?*), it would be reasonable to suggest that I was saying something primarily about Liz; but if I said it in response to *What happened to the intruder?*, would it not be equally reasonable to suggest that I was saying something primarily about the intruder? If this is so, identification of the topic will depend on the larger context in which the sentence occurs – but we do not need to consider the larger context to determine the subject of (14), which can only be *she*. Further problems arise with certain kinds of subordinate clause. In *I stand to lose a lot of money if she shot him*, the embedded clause *if she shot him* has *she* as subject but it is very doubtful whether the concept of topic is applicable here: am I really 'saying something about Liz' in uttering this? The first objection to the definition of the subject as the topic, then, has to do with the problems of determining what the topic is in a given instance, with doubts as to whether it can be determined on the basis of the form of the sentence rather than being dependent on the larger context, and with doubts as to how generally the concept of topic is applicable to clauses, as opposed to sentences.

The second objection is that in spite of these problems we can find many perfectly ordinary sentences whose subject cannot be said to identify even a reasonably plausible candidate for topic status:

(15)   *Nobody likes John*
(16)   *It is time she had her hair cut*
(17)   *It turned out that she was related to him*
(18)   *There should be at least one student on the committee*
(19)   *Close tabs are being kept on all the radical students*
(20)   *In Queensland one can swim in the sea all the year round*
(21)   *The remaining issues they have left till the next meeting*

The subject of (15) is *nobody*, but it would be absurd to suggest that in uttering this sentence I would be saying something about 'nobody', namely that they like John: I could only be construed as saying something about John, namely that nobody likes him. The subject of (16) and (17) is *it*, but in these examples *it* is not being used to refer to anything: semantically it is quite different from the *it* of, say, *Be careful with that book – it's my father's*, where *it* refers to the book mentioned in the first clause and as such can plausibly be regarded as identifying a topic. Note that *it* in (16) and (17) is not in paradigmatic contrast with other NPs; it is what is sometimes called a 'dummy' subject – an element filling the subject position but without any identifiable meaning of its own. And since *it* doesn't refer to anything, it cannot refer to the topic. The same applies to (18), where *there* is another dummy subject: again it would be incoherent to suggest that (18) could be used to say something about 'there'. (18) illustrates one of the very few constructions where one encounters disagreement as to what the grammatical subject is; we will see below that there are strong reasons for taking *there* to be the subject, but we may note here that even if we followed those who regard *at least one student* as subject it would still be a counterexample to the notional definition, for the sentence would not be used to say something about 'at least one student': it would be used to say something about the committee (or the composition of the committee). (19) is likewise not about 'close tabs': *close tabs* is part of the idiom **keep** *close tabs on* and as such it has no independent meaning, no reference. The final two examples differ from (15)–(19) in that the subject – *one* in (20), *they* in (21) – is no longer the first element in the clause. And it is precisely the element that precedes the subject that can most plausibly be regarded as identifying the topic: (20) and (21) could be used to say something about Queensland and about the remaining issues, but surely not about 'one' and 'them'. Note that one device available in English for making explicit what the topic is, is an initial *as for*: both *As for Tom, he didn't like her* and *As for Tom, she didn't like him* would be construed as being (primarily) about Tom. And the points I have been making about the interpretation of (15)–(21) can be reinforced by observing the impossibility or implausibility of rephrasings along the lines of *As for nobody, they like John, As for one, one can swim all the year round in Queensland*, and so on.

Before turning to a structural account, it is worth considering one other notional definition, not of the subject as such, but one which nevertheless crucially involves the subject. I have drawn attention to the system of voice, with terms active and passive, illustrated in

(22)   i *Liz shot the intruder*   (= 13)   Active
         ii *The intruder was shot by Liz*   Passive

(The terms 'active' and 'passive' can be applied either to the whole clause or to the VP – *was shot* is passive, and so is *The intruder was shot by Liz*.) Now the standard notional definition of active and passive is in terms of the semantic role associated with the subject: in the active the subject is said to identify the 'actor', the performer of the action expressed in the clause, whereas in the passive, the subject identifies the 'patient', the 'undergoer' of the action. Let me again quote from the source used above: 'When the subject of a verb performs the action described in the verb, the verb is said to be *active* (or *in the active voice*) . . . When the subject of a verb receives or suffers the action of the verb, the verb is said to be *passive* (or *in the passive voice*)' (Phythian 1980:50). Thus in (22), (i) would be said to be active because Liz performed the action of shooting, while (ii) would be passive because the intruder underwent the action.[1] This notional definition is

---

[1] Note that Phythian, like many traditional grammarians, does not consistently distinguish between linguistic forms and the non-linguistic entities (people, physical objects, etc.) that they refer to, using 'subject' for both. I will use 'subject' only for the former, so that the subject of (22i) is *Liz*, while the performer of the action of shooting is not the subject *Liz*, but the person Liz – thus I will say of examples like this not that the subject 'is' the actor, but

again open to objection on two counts. In the first place, there are many active and passive clauses that do not express actions, and where the semantic roles of actor and patient are consequently inapplicable. Consider, for example,

(23)   i *The staff liked Tom*
         ii *Tom was liked by the staff*

Liking someone is not something we 'do': in the situation described here the staff are not performing any action and Tom is not undergoing any – but (23i) is nevertheless universally agreed to be an active clause, with *the staff* as subject, and (ii) a passive clause, with *Tom* as subject. Similarly for examples like *Everyone knew the answer* and *The answer was known by everyone*, which again describe states, not actions – and for countless others. A second point is that some clauses can report events in which there is more than one participant with an actor role:

(24)   *Max bought the car from Ed for $500*
(25)   *Jill married Max*

(24) reports the same event as *Ed sold the car to Max for $500*, an event in which both Max and Ed are actors inasmuch as they have control, make a decision – note that neither clause encodes information as to which participant took the initiative or first step in the transaction. Similarly in (25) Jill and Max are both actors, just as they are in *Max married Jill* or *Jill and Max married*: it would be absurd to suggest that in (25) Jill is actor, Max patient, that it reports Jill's doing something to Max. In such cases we cannot accept, therefore, that the subject refers to 'the actor', for such a formulation implies a single actor.

There is no one-to-one correlation between the grammatical subject in general – or, more particularly, the subject of active clauses – and any concept figuring in the semantic analyses of sentences: this is why it is impossible to give a notional definition that will enable us to find the subject of a clause. If we want to determine what the subject is we must look at the syntactic properties of the clause, not at its meaning – which brings us to the structural approach.

2.2.2 *A structural account of the grammatical subject*

If we want to understand what a subject is, we have to ask how the rules of syntax distinguish between the subject and other functions in the structure of the clause. There are in fact a considerable number of rules

that the subject 'is associated with' the role of actor or that that subject 'refers to' the actor. Note also that Phythian, again following the standard terminology of traditional grammar, uses 'verb' to cover both individual words (such as *was* and *shot*) and what I am calling verb phrases (such as *was shot*): see 3.2 for further comment.

that are sensitive to this distinction, so that the subject is an important category in English syntax, one that is particularly sharply delineated. We will not attempt an exhaustive review of such rules, but will consider the matter in sufficient detail to demonstrate how clearly distinct the subject is.

(a) Form-class. The prototypical subject is an NP. With respect to the class of forms occurring with a given function, the subject is most sharply distinct from the predicator, a function filled by VPs. Thus in the most elementary kind of kernel clause like *The farmer disappeared* the subject and predicator are clearly distinguished by the differences between the forms *the farmer* (NP) and *disappeared* (VP). The form class does not, however, distinguish the subject from the object, as the latter too is prototypically an NP.

Certain types of predicate allow an embedded clause as subject, as we have noted earlier, so that the subject is not necessarily an NP. One or two other classes of phrase can function as subject too – for example a PP in *From London to Manchester is about 180 miles* – but these occur only with a highly restricted range of predicates and thus differ rather sharply from the prototype.

(b) Verb agreement. Under certain conditions the VP agrees with the subject with respect to its person–number properties, as in

(26)   i *The moral objection is more important*
       ii *The moral objections are more important*

We have here an inflectional contrast between *is* and *are* such that the choice between them is determined by agreement with the subject: as we replace *the moral objection* by *the moral objections*, so we must replace *is* by *are*. Person and number are inherently NP properties: number is the system contrasting singular vs plural, while person contrasts 1st vs 2nd vs 3rd, where an NP is 1st person if its head is a form of *I* or *we*, 2nd person if its head is *you*, and otherwise 3rd person. Thus *the moral objection* is a 3rd person singular NP, and we then say that *is* is a 3rd person singular form of *be* because it occurs with a 3rd person singular subject. In *Tom likes Liz* all three phrases are 3rd person singular but we can easily see that *likes* agrees with *Tom* (the subject), not *Liz* (the object) by noting that if we replace *Tom* by an NP with other person–number properties we must also change *likes*, whereas a similar replacement of *Liz* has no effect on the verb: compare *My brothers like Liz* and *Tom likes my brothers*.

It must be emphasised that the VP does not always agree with the subject – there is, for example, no agreement in

(27)   *The moral objection had been more important*

for whatever subject we substitute for *the moral objection* the VP remains unchanged. Nevertheless the agreement criterion can even here be applied, but indirectly – we simply note that *had been* is in paradigmatic contrast with *is* and that the latter is 3rd person singular in agreement with *the moral objection*: we can say that *the moral objection* has subject property (b) in (27) as well as in (26i) in the sense that it is the element whose person–number properties will determine those of the VP if it has any. Similarly in (13) – *Liz shot the intruder* – one reason for saying that *Liz* is subject is that, although *shot* shows no agreement property, if we replace this past tense form by a present tense, then the 3rd person singular property of *Liz* will determine the selection of *shoots* rather than *shoot*.

(c) Pronominal case. A handful of pronoun lexemes – notably *I*, *we*, *he*, *she* and *they* – inflect for 'case', with 'nominative' forms (*I, we, he, she, they*) contrasting with 'accusative' forms (*me, us, him, her, them*): we will call such lexemes 'case-variable pronouns'. The choice between the two cases depends on the function of the NP of which the pronoun is head. We need not go into the rules in detail: it is sufficient for present purposes to note that in kernel and most types of non-kernel clauses a case-variable pronoun functioning as subject will take nominative case. Nominative forms are not wholly restricted to subject position, for they occur also in constructions like *It is I*, where the subject is *it*, not *I* (note that we have 3rd person singular *is* in agreement with *it*, not the 1st person singular *am* that would be required if *I* were subject) – but it is only in subject position that nominatives are obligatory, *It is me* being a stylistically less formal variant of *It is I*. Although only a very few lexemes have contrasting nominative and accusative forms, the case criterion for subject can – like the verb agreement property – be applied indirectly to examples like (13): *Liz* is in paradigmatic contrast with nominative forms of the case-variable pronouns, while *the intruder* is in contrast with accusative forms, so that we have a third property identifying *Liz* as subject: compare *She shot him*.

(d) Position in declarative clauses. The position of the subject in kernel clauses is before the predicator, and this is its normal position in all declarative clauses; the normal position of the object (and of other clause elements), by contrast, is after the predicator. Thus in our example (13) above, it is the position of *Liz* before the predicator *shot* and of *the intruder* after it that most clearly distinguishes them as subject and object respectively.

The order 'S + P + other elements' is not invariable. In (21) above, for example, the object (*the remaining issues*) is in initial position – and thus differs from a prototypical object; note, however, that the subject (*they*) occupies what is in other respects the normal subject position in that it occurs just before the predicator. In

(28)   *More important are the moral objections*

the initial position is occupied by what we shall call the 'predicative complement' (*more important*), while this time the subject (*the moral objections*) is in final position – it is not a prototypical subject. That *the moral objections* nevertheless is subject is evident from the combination of properties (a)–(c) above: it is an NP, while *more important* is an AdjP, it determines the person–number property of the verb *are* (compare *More important is the moral objection*) and to the extent that it is in paradigmatic contrast with a case-variable pronoun, the form required would be nominative *they* rather than accusative *them* (*More important are they* is somewhat unnatural, but hardly ungrammatical – compare the analogous construction *Humble was he, but also quite serene*; its status is quite different from that of the clearly ungrammatical **More important are them*).

(e) Position in interrogative clauses. One special case where the subject does not occur before the VP is the interrogative construction. We have noted that there is a systematic relation between the members of pairs like

(29)   i *The moral objections are more important* (= 26ii)   Declarative
             ii *Are the moral objections more important?*   Interrogative
(30)   i *Liz shot the intruder* (= 13)   Declarative
             ii *Did Liz shoot the intruder?*   Interrogative

The interrogative is formed from the declarative either by moving the first (or only) verb of the VP to the left of the subject, (29), or by adding an appropriate form of the auxiliary **do** to the left of the verb (and changing the form of the verb of the declarative to what we are calling the 'base' form – e.g. *shoot* in (30)); see 4.4 for discussion of the factors determining which of these two operations applies. This systematic relation between the two clause constructions provides one of the clearest criteria for determining the subject: we can identify *Liz* as subject of (30i) because when we compare this clause with its interrogative counterpart we note that it is *Liz* whose position relative to the VP has changed.

Before leaving this criterion we should note that subordinate clauses cannot in general occur as subject in interrogatives: we cannot perform the above operation on declaratives like (31i):

(31)   i *That John was late annoyed them*
             ii **Did that John was late annoy them?*   Did th that that ...

– this is the main reason for saying that a subordinate clause, like *that John was late* in (31i), does not make a prototypical subject. Notice that *that John was late* has properties (b), (c) and (d). As for (b), a subordinate clause counts as 3rd person singular and as subject determines accordingly any person-number property of the verb (compare *That John was late was annoying them*). As for (c), note that the clause is in paradigmatic contrast with a nominative form like *he* – and that *them* is an accusative form. And as for (d), the position of *that John was late* is the normal one for subjects.

(f) Conditions on omissibility. The final property we shall consider that distinguishes the subject from other elements of clause structure has to do with the conditions under which elements are omissible, optional. A kernel clause must contain a subject (and a predicator), but whether it contains an object depends on what the main verb is. Thus some verbs, such as **use**, require an object (*He used it*, but not **He used*); some, such as **eat**, occur either with or without an object (*He was eating some sandwiches* or *He was eating*); and some, such as ***disappear***, do not allow an object (*He disappeared*, but not **He disappeared the money*) – but we do not have an analogous classification of verbs with respect to their occurrence with a subject, for all verbs occur with a subject. In certain kinds of non-kernel clause, various elements may be missing that are present in comparable kernel clauses: for example, in *Ed lives in Paris, Peter in Berlin* the second clause lacks the predicator *lives* that is found in the non-elliptical counterpart *Peter lives in Berlin*. And again the conditions under which the subject can be omitted in non-kernel clauses are different from those applying to other elements. To give just one example: in imperative clauses, a 2nd person NP is optional if it is subject. We can accordingly have either *You be careful* or, omitting the subject, *Be careful* – but we cannot similarly drop the 2nd person object of, say, *Help yourself to some more wine* to yield **Help to some more wine*. Thus the relevant rule must evidently specify that it is the subject that is omissible in this construction – the rule is sensitive to the distinction between subjects and non-subjects.

As remarked above, this is by no means an exhaustive list of the properties that characterise a prototypical subject, but it is sufficient for our present purposes of illustrating structuralist principles and methodology. Let us now pursue our account of these subject properties by examining in turn some of the main transformations which relate marked and unmarked terms in the thematic systems of the clause – the transformation that converts actives into passives, and so on. The question we shall be concerned with is whether or not the transformation involves a reassignment of the subject function.

Passivisation

We are saying that (ii) is derived from (i) by the passivisation transformation in examples like (22), repeated below:

(22)   i *Liz shot the intruder*   (= 13)
         ii *The intruder was shot by Liz*

It is very easy to see that one effect of the transformation is to reassign the subject function, for while *Liz* is a prototypical subject in (i), *the intruder* is no less prototypical a subject in (ii). Consider the properties in turn.

(a) Form-class: both *Liz* and *the intruder* are NPs, so that in (i) this property is not distinctive; note, however, that in (ii) we have *by Liz*, a PP rather than an NP – the fact that *Liz* is related to the verb not directly but via the mediation of a preposition is a token of its having lost its subject function.

(b) Verb agreement: we have noted that although *shot* in (i) doesn't have any person–number properties, if we replace it with a VP that does, such as *has shot*, they will be determined by agreement with *Liz* (cf. *Liz has/ *have shot the intruders*); in (ii), by contrast, *was* agrees with *the intruder* (cf. *The intruders were shot by Liz*).

(c) Pronominal case: in (i) *Liz* is in paradigmatic contrast with a nominative form, *the intruder* with an accusative, whereas in (ii) the potential case-forms are reversed (cf. *She shot him* and *He was shot by her*).

(d) Position in declarative clauses: in (i) *Liz* occurs in the standard subject position, whereas in (ii) this position is occupied by *the intruder*.

(e) Position in interrogative clauses: the interrogative counterparts are *Did Liz shoot the intruder?* and *Was the intruder shot by Liz?* with *Liz* and *the intruder* respectively occupying the distinctive subject position after the first verb.

(f) Conditions on omissibility: note first that in (i) *Liz* is obligatory while *the intruder* (because of the properties of the verb **shoot**) is optional, whereas in (ii) it is *the intruder* that is obligatory while *by Liz* is optional (this *by* phrase being always omissible in passives, whatever the verb) – compare *Liz shot* and *The intruder was shot*. Notice also that in those non-kernel constructions that do allow the subject to be omitted, it is the element corresponding to *Liz* in the active (i) and to *the intruder* in the passive (ii) that is omitted – compare *Shooting the intruder was a regrettable mistake* and *Being shot by Liz was a regrettable mistake*.

Extraposition
This is the transformation that converts (i) into (ii) in

(32)   i *That John was late annoyed them* (= 31i)
          ii *It annoyed them that John was late*

Here too the subject function is reassigned: in (i) the subject is the subordinate clause *that John was late*, whereas in (ii) it is *it* (though neither conforms wholly to the prototype).
(a) Form-class: in (i) the subject is a clause, but in (ii) it is an NP: the transformation thus puts into subject position a form of a class that is more characteristic of that function.

(b) Verb agreement: we saw above that in (i) the property of determining any person–number property that the verb may have falls to *that John was late*; in (ii) this criterion cannot be used to select any one element as subject because both *it* and *that John was late* are 3rd person singular and neither is in paradigmatic contrast with forms having different person–number properties – the form *it* is required in the extrapositioned construction and is thus not paradigmatically variable. The agreement facts are consistent with the analysis of *it* as subject, but they do not provide positive evidence for selecting *it* rather than *that John was late*.

(c) Pronominal case: we noted above that *that John was late* is in paradigmatic contrast with nominative forms – but in (ii) it is not, for the only syntactically possible substitutions here involve other subordinate clauses (cf. *It annoyed them that she had left* but not **It annoyed them he*). We can thus say that *that John was late* loses this subject property in the transformation from (i) to (ii); we cannot, however, say that *it* takes on the property, for **it** is not a case-variable pronoun, and (as we have just noted) *it* is not paradigmatically variable and hence not replaceable by a nominative form any more than by an accusative. The evidence from this criterion is thus purely negative – *that John was late* lacks in (ii) the subject property that it has in (i).

(d) Position in declarative clauses: this supports our claim of a reassignment of functions, for in (i) the normal subject position is occupied by *that John was late* whereas in (ii) it is occupied by *it*.

(e) Position in interrogative clauses: (i) has no interrogative counterpart (cf. (31ii) above), but (ii) has, namely, *Did it annoy them that John was late?* with *it* occupying the distinctive subject position.

(f) Conditions on omissibility: by this criterion *that John was late* is subject of (i); in (ii) *it* is clearly obligatory, but we will also regard *that John was late* as non-omissible too, since if we leave it out we no longer have the extrapositioned construction (for note that in *It annoyed them* the *it* is in paradigmatic contrast with other subjects). It is not easy to test for non-kernel constructions with omissible subjects – there are, for example, no analogues here of the examples used above in our discussion of passivisation; nor, clearly, does an extrapositioned declarative like (32ii) contrast with an extrapositioned imperative. Constructions that can, however, be argued to be relevant are *That John was late seems to have annoyed them* and *It seems to have annoyed them that John was late*. **Seem** is not an auxiliary verb (for reasons we shall give in 4.4) and consequently *seems to have annoyed* is not a constituent: rather we will take *seems* as the predicator and what follows as its comple-ment. This complement will then be a non-kernel construction lacking a subject – and while in the first example the 'understood' subject is *that John*

67

was late, in the second it is *it*. Overall, then, there is strong evidence for saying that *it*, not *that John was late*, is subject of (ii). It is a rather special type of subject in that it is not paradigmatically variable – it is what we are calling a 'dummy' subject. The primary syntactic effect of the extraposition transformation is to deprive the embedded clause of subject status, but because the subject is obligatory in most classes of clause, this must be accompanied by the insertion of a dummy element to fill the vacated subject function.

There insertion

Our third thematic transformation converts (i) into the *there* construction (ii) in

(33) i *At least one student should be on the committee*
ii *There should be at least one student on the committee*

The transformation is rather similar in its effect to extraposition: *at least one student* loses its subject status and a dummy element, this time *there*, is inserted to take on the function of subject. Let us again consider the six properties in order to demonstrate that such a reassignment of subject function does take place.

(a) Form-class: *at least one student* is an NP – but what class does *there* belong to? We are distinguishing between the 'dummy' *there* of clauses like (ii) and the 'locative' ('place-indicating') *there* of *I put it there*, etc. – note that the two can combine, as in *There's a mistake there* (but with a phonological difference, dummy *there* being typically pronounced /ðə/, locative *there* /ðɛə/ – or /ðe/). Locative *there* is in paradigmatic contrast with *here* and other expressions indicating place (cf. *I put it here/on the table*); dummy *there* is not. Locative *there* is an adverb, and since dummy *there* derives historically from it, it is traditionally assumed to be an adverb too. Etymology, however, cannot be accepted as a sound basis for classification: we must consider its properties in contemporary English. Its appropriate classification is not in fact easy to determine. Morphologically it is a simple stem, so that there is no evidence from internal structure to guide us. And the technique of paradigmatic substitution, which normally provides major evidence for word classification, is barely applicable either, since dummy *there* (precisely because it is a dummy element) cannot be replaced by any other phrase in constructions like (33ii). However, it is arguable that under certain conditions we do have a paradigmatic contrast between *there* and *it*; compare *There/it was a siren blaring*; certainly *it* is the word to which it bears the closest syntactic resemblance, and they are best put in the same word-class, pronoun (see 7.4 for further comment). On this basis, then, the form class criterion is quite consistent with the analysis of *there* as subject of (ii), though it does not of course serve to select *there* in preference to *at least one student*.

(b) Verb agreement: at first glance this appears to invalidate our analysis, for contrasts like *There is at least one student on the committee* vs *There are at least two students on the committee* suggest that the criterion of determining any person–number property of the verb will, when applied to (ii), select not *there* but *at least one student* as subject. However, the matter is not so simple, as becomes evident if instead of varying the number we vary the person. Suppose, for example, someone said to me, *Who is there who could help her?*: I might reply, *Well there's always you*, not **There are always you*. Notice, moreover, that even if we consider only number variation in the 3rd person, we must distinguish between a plural attributable to the selection of a plural noun, like *students* above, and one attributable to the coordination of two singular NPs, like *a bottle of wine and a silver goblet*. That this is inherently plural is evident from the agreement in the kernel clause *A bottle of wine and a silver goblet were on the table* – but if we transform this into the *there* construction we get *There was a bottle of wine and a silver goblet on the table*, not **There were . . .* These considerations show that the normal rules of subject–verb agreement do not apply to the *there* construction: person–number inflection in the verb is shared between *there* (which is 3rd person singular, like *it*) and the NP following the VP. Certainly *there* is not a prototypical subject, but in the transformation from (i) to (ii) some aspects of verb person–number determination are transferred from *at least one student* to *there*.[2]

(c) Pronominal case: *there* is not in paradigmatic contrast with forms of case-variable pronouns but (under certain conditions, at least) the NP following the VP is – and we find accusative, not nominative, forms. An alternative response to the above *Who is there who could help her?*, for example, might be: *Well there's always me* – nominative *I* would be impossible here.[3] Thus in the transformation from (i) to (ii) *at least one student* loses its property of being in contrast with nominative forms, which supports our claim that it loses its subject status.

(d) Position in declarative clauses: *there* takes over from *at least one student* the property of coming before the VP.

---

[2] In some varieties of English we find *There's at least two students on the committee*, rather than *There are . . .*, so that *there* is here somewhat closer to a prototypical subject and (to the extent that the phenomenon is general, rather than being limited to clauses where the verb is contracted, i.e. *'s* rather than *is*, as may be the case for some speakers) the grammar is simplified by bringing the *there* construction under the normal rules of subject–verb agreement.

[3] *There am I* is of course grammatical, but it contains locative *there*, as is evident from: (a) the pronunciation (/ðɛə/, not /ðə(r)/); (b) the paradigmatic contrast with *here*, etc.; (c) the variant orderings *There I am, I am there*; and so on: it is thus not relevant to our present concerns.

(e) Position in interrogative clauses: the interrogative of (i) is *Should at least one student be on the committee?* while that of (ii) is *Should there be at least one student on the committee?*, with *there* taking over the subject position here.

(f) Conditions on omissibility: in (ii) itself neither *there* nor *at least one student* is omissible, but if we look at other constructions we find clear evidence for treating *there* as subject. Consider first ellipsis. If you ask, *Is he happy?*, I can reply: *Yes, he is* (with ellipsis of *happy*), *Yes, very happy* (with ellipsis of *he is*), *Yes* (with ellipsis of *he is happy*) – but not *Yes, is* (with ellipsis of *he* and *happy*) or *Yes, is happy* (with ellipsis of *he*). The rule is that if the VP (or just the first part of it) is retained, the clause must have a subject. Thus to *Is John on the committee?* a possible reply is *Yes, he is*, with the subject *he* obligatory once we put in the *is*. And to *Are there some students on the committee?* I might reply, *Yes, there are*: the *there* is obligatory, given the presence of *are*, but *some students* is omissible. It follows that with respect to the rules of ellipsis *there* is treated like a subject, *some students* like a non-subject. Or consider the 'relative clause' construction with *that* as in [*The paper*] *that impressed me the most* [*was by Dykes*] and [*The paper*] (*that*) *he was reading* [*was by Dykes*] – where the comparable kernel clauses are respectively *The paper impressed me most* and *He was reading the paper*. We note that in the second example, but not the first, the *that* is omissible. The rule is that *that* is omissible in this type of relative clause only when it is followed by the subject. And again *there* behaves like a subject: while *that* is not omissible in [*Everything*] *that was on the table* [*was Tom's*], it is omissible in [*Everything*] (*that*) *there was on the table* [*was Tom's*].

I have examined the *there* construction in some detail because traditional grammars tend to say that in an example like (33ii) the subject is *at least one student*. I hope to have shown that if we approach the analysis of such clauses by asking which element is most like a prototypical subject we can see very clearly that *there* must be subject. Negatively, *at least one student* loses virtually all its subject-like properties in the transformation from (i) to (ii) and, positively, *there* assumes a high proportion of the properties that characterise subjects.

Thematic fronting and subject postponement

All of the thematic transformations considered so far effect a reassignment of syntactic functions – in particular, of the subject function. They contrast with two others, whose effect is simply to reorder the elements in the clause without changing their functions; their effect is illustrated in

(34)   i *They have left the remaining issues till next week*
       ii *The remaining issues they have left till next week* (= 21)

(35)   i *The moral objections are more important* (= 26ii, 29i)
       ii *More important are the moral objections* (= 28)

In (34), (ii) derives from (i) by moving *the remaining issues* to initial position in the clause ('thematic fronting'); in (35), (ii) derives from (i) by moving *more important* to the front (again, 'thematic fronting') and moving *the moral objections* to final position ('subject postponement'). In introducing property (d) above, I gave some arguments for saying that *they* remains subject in (34ii) and *the moral objections* in (35ii): it is not necessary to repeat or expand on those arguments. One point that is worth drawing attention to, however, is that clauses like these with a marked order of elements differ from the other types of thematically marked clauses we have reviewed – the passive, extrapositioned, and *there* constructions – in that they are very much more restricted with respect to the range of clause constructions they can combine with (see our discussion of markedness in 1.4). For example, while we can form interrogative counterparts of (34i) and (35i) this is hardly possible with (34ii) (?*The remaining issues have they left till next week?*) and completely impossible with (35ii). Or again, thematic fronting and subject postponement occur very much less readily in subordinate clauses than in main clauses: we can have *if they have left the remaining issues till next week* or *if the moral objections are more important*, but hardly ?*if the remaining issues they have left till next week* and certainly not *if more important are the moral objections*. We do not find such restrictions with passives, etc., however: *if the intruder was shot by Liz* does not differ at all in acceptability from *if Liz shot the intruder*. One special case of this type of restriction is illustrated in

(36) i *He believed that the moral objections were more important*
ii *He believed the moral objections to be more important*
iii *He believed more important to be the moral objections*

With verbs like **believe, know, assume, suppose**, etc. we have a paradigmatic contrast between the constructions shown in (i) and (ii); just how the latter should be analysed raises problems that we need not go into here: what is relevant to our concerns is that it completely excludes the reordering effected by thematic fronting and/or subject postponement – compare also *He knew the remaining issues them to have left till next week*. But again, passive, extrapositioned and *there* constructions occur quite freely here: *He knew there to be a mistake in the plan, He believed the intruder to have been shot by Liz*, and so on. There are thus very clear differences between the 'side-effects', as it were, of reordering functions on the one hand, and reassigning functions on the other – and these differences lend further support to our putting passivisation, extraposition and *there* insertion into a single class of transformations, contrasting with thematic fronting and subject postponement.

To conclude this discussion of the concept 'subject' let us summarise the main theoretical and methodological points that emerge from it. Firstly, we argued that the standard notional definition does not work in the sense that we cannot find the subject of a clause by asking what the clause is 'about'. The subject is a syntactic category and it does not stand in a one-to-one relation with any semantic category figuring in the semantic analysis of clauses. To understand what subjects are, we have to investigate how the rules of syntax discriminate between this function and other functions in clause structure. The properties that we arrived at as characterising the subject critically involve reference to other categories of syntax: we cannot define the subject except by reference to its place within a network of related theoretical terms. Secondly, an important methodological point follows from this, namely that we cannot expect to be able to identify the subject of a clause by considering that clause in isolation: we must be prepared to see how it behaves under various types of manipulation – what happens when we turn it into the interrogative, when we subordinate it, when we replace such and such an NP by a case-variable pronoun, and so on? We need to perform such operations precisely in order to see how various elements are treated by the rules that are sensitive to the distinction between subjects and non-subjects. Finally, we have not provided a definition of the subject in the form of a set of 'necessary and sufficient conditions' for being subject (i.e. a set of properties such that an element will be subject if and only if it has each property in the set): rather we have given a set of properties which define the prototype, allowing for subjects to differ from the prototype in various ways. We shall see that there are numerous places in the grammar where it is necessary to recognize categories with a clear prototypical core but a somewhat fuzzily delimited periphery. Because we have so many properties distinguishing subjects from non-subjects there is in fact no significant difficulty in determining which element in a clause is subject – but we shall see that with categories having fewer distinctive properties some measure of indeterminacy may arise over the delimitation of non-prototypical instances.

2.3 Particular grammars and general grammatical theory

The basic principle of structural linguistics, we have said, is that the units, classes, functions, etc. that figure in the grammar of a language are determined by the relations between sentences and parts of sentences in that language. So far in this chapter we have been concerned with the consequences of this principle for the way in which we define our terms and justify our analyses. In this section I want to draw attention to a further consequence: that each language has its own individual structure. In describing a given language we must determine what distinctions it makes, instead of assuming in advance that they will be the same as in some other language (or some earlier stage of the same language).

A common criticism of traditional grammars of English is that they distort the description by foisting onto it analyses which are perfectly valid for Latin and Greek (and perhaps for Old English) but irrelevant to

Modern English. They vary a good deal in the extent to which they are guilty of doing this, but it is particularly common in the area of inflection.

One commonly-cited example concerns the system of case. This, along with number, is an inflectional system of the noun in Latin, so that a partial paradigm for the noun **puer** ("boy") is as follows:[4]

(37)

	Singular	Plural
Nominative	*puer*	*puerī*
Accusative	*puerum*	*puerōs*
Genitive	*puerī*	*puerōrum*
Dative	*puerō*	*puerīs*

(**Paradigm** is the traditional term for the set of inflectional forms of a lexeme; the modern term 'paradigmatic', which we have introduced for one of the two main kinds of linguistic relation, is derived from it, but with a generalisation of the meaning so that it covers other contrasts besides inflectional ones.)

Case indicates the syntagmatic relation between the noun and other elements in the sentence: in general, the case is determined by the syntactic function of the NP of which the noun is head and hence, indirectly, by its semantic role. The above four singular forms of **puer** are illustrated in (38) with (39) giving approximate English equivalents.

(38)

    i *Puer risit*
   ii *Puella puerum vīdit*
  iii *Puella librum puerī vīdit*
  iv *Puella puerō librum dedit*

(39)

    i *The boy laughed*[5]
   ii *The girl saw the boy*
  iii *The girl saw the boy's book*
  iv *The girl gave the boy the book*

It will be evident that English and Latin differ sharply with respect to the ways in which the syntactic functions and semantic roles are indicated. In Latin the functions are signalled primarily by inflection: as a first approximation, the subject will be in the nominative, the direct object in the accusative, the indirect object in the dative, and so on, as in these examples. The order of the elements is relatively free, so that in (38ii), for example, where *puella* is nominative, *puerum* accusative, we could switch the NPs to give *Puerum puella vīdit* without changing the syntactic functions or the propositional meaning: the difference would be purely thematic. In English, by contrast, order is typically crucial – if we switch the NPs in (39ii) we make *the boy* subject, *the girl* object, and thus drastically change the meaning. Also important in English for expressing the relations shown in Latin by case inflections are prepositions such as *of*, *to*, etc.: a thematic variant of (39iv), for example, is *The girl gave the book to the boy*, where the

---

[4] I simplify by omitting the vocative and ablative cases.

[5] Latin has no article corresponding to *the* and, depending on context, (38i) might equally well be translated as *A boy laughed*, and so on.

boy's role in the event is shown by the *to*. We have discussed the analysis of phrases like *the boy's* in 1.8. The *'s* differs from an affix in that it enters into construction with a phrase, not a stem, and need not even be attached to the head of the phrase: we accordingly analyse it as a separate word, a clitic, rather than an inflectional suffix, so that on this account *boy's* is not a genitive form of **boy**. For the rest, there is quite clearly no dative case inflection in Modern English, and the nominative/accusative contrast is confined – as we have also noted earlier – to a handful of pronouns (*I* vs *me*, *he* vs *him*, etc.). Yet it is not uncommon for traditional grammars to say that (39i–iv) contain respectively nominative, accusative, genitive and dative forms of **boy**, just as (38i–iv) do of **puer**. This is to confuse the syntactic concept of grammatical function (subject, direct object, etc.) with the inflectional concept of case; it distorts the description of English, forcing it into an alien mould appropriate for a quite different language. Languages vary a great deal in how much inflection they have. Some – like Vietnamese – have none at all, while Latin is at the other end of the scale, having a great deal. English has relatively little, and certainly much less than traditional grammars make it out to have. It will not do to analyse expressions in one language on the basis of their translation equivalents in another.

To insist that the analysis we present for a language must reflect the distinctions that hold within that particular language is not to deny that there are profound similarities between languages. I have cited an example of distinctions inappropriately transferred from one grammar to another, but it would be equally misguided to insist that every distinction is unique to a particular language. Terms like 'noun', 'verb', 'auxiliary', 'past tense', 'subject', 'head' and so on, are not coined ad hoc for the description of English, but belong to a set of **general** terms available for us in the grammar of any language where the conditions for their application are met.

We must therefore recognise two levels at which we should aim to define a grammatical concept like, for example, noun. At one level we are dealing with the definition of noun in a particular language – in the present instance, English. At this level we are concerned with the properties that in English distinguish nouns from other word-classes, with the criteria for determining whether some arbitrary word in English is a noun or not. This, then, is the level of **language-particular definitions** (which will, however, often involve reference to a prototype). The second level is that of **general definitions**, which determine the way general terms can be used in the grammars of particular languages. Suppose that in analysing a certain language we need, for reasons internal to that language, to distinguish five primary word-classes, A, B, C, D and E. Having made the distinctions and given language-particular definitions for the classes, we must consider what we are going to call them: What principled basis do we have, for example, for deciding which (if any) shall be called noun? What are the properties shared by the classes that we call nouns in different languages?

Earlier in this chapter, I was critical of notional definitions, interpreting them as language-particular definitions. The definition of a noun as the name of a person, place or thing does not provide workable criteria for determining whether any given word in English belongs to that class. At the level of general definitions, however, the appeal to meaning can be perfectly legitimate. Thus one property common to the classes we call noun in different languages is that they contain among their members – and particularly among those with morphologically-simple lexical stems – all or most of the words denoting persons and physical objects. (Note that the majority of nouns in English that do not denote persons or physical objects are derived by affixation and the like: *arrival, insanity, perseverance*, etc., as opposed to the simple *man, boy, girl, dog, cat, apple, tree*, etc.) The general definition does not enable us to determine that *arrival, insanity*, etc., belong to the class, but it does provide a basis for identifying classes across languages when their detailed language-particular definitions are inevitably different.

Similarly we have seen that the definition of an imperative clause as one that would be used to issue a command or request is not consistent with the analysis of *Sleep well, Get well soon* and the like as imperatives or of *Passengers are requested to remain seated, I order you to leave* as non-imperatives: it is not satisfactory as a language-particular definition. Nevertheless we can incorporate it into a general definition. If a language has a system of syntactically distinct clause constructions such that one is characteristically used in issuing commands or requests, while the others are characteristically associated with other types of 'speech act' (such as making statements, asking questions), then the construction associated with commands/requests will be called by the general term 'imperative'. On this account, *Get well soon* belongs to the same clause class as *Open the door, Pass the salt* and the like because it has the same distinctive properties (those outlined in § 1 above), and then this class will be called imperative, in spite of the fact that an utterance of *Get well soon* will not normally be construed as a command/request, because the great majority of members of the class do lend themselves to use as commands/requests.

We will not here offer a definition of the subject at the general level, because this would involve us in an investigation of certain significant differences between various types of languages that would take us too far from the primary concerns of this book – see the 'Further reading' recommendations at the end of the chapter for references to some of the extensive literature on the question. As a third example, however, we can take up the final notional definition quoted above, namely that for active and passive voice. Interpreted as a language-particular definition, it doesn't work because of the many examples like *The staff liked Tom* and *Tom was liked by the staff*, which are respectively active and passive even though the subject of the first does not refer to the actor nor that of the second to the patient. We can nevertheless make use of it in a general definition. Suppose in a given language we have a system of syntactically distinct clause classes (differing, among other ways, with respect to the form of the VP – inflectionally or in terms of auxiliaries), such that corresponding members of the two classes are normally thematic variants differing in the way the semantic roles are associated with the subject and other syntactic functions. Suppose, furthermore, that in clauses expressing an action (one involving a single actor and a single patient) the subject is associated with the actor role in one of the variants, with the patient role in the other. Then we shall say that the language has a system of voice, with terms active and passive, the active class containing among its members action clauses where the subject is associated with the actor role, the passive class those where it is associated with the patient role. *The staff liked Tom* and *Tom was liked by the staff* will then be respectively active and passive because: (i) they stand in the same syntactic relation as *Liz shot the intruder* and *The intruder was shot by Liz*; (ii) in examples like the latter pair, the subject of the first (*Liz*) refers to the actor, while that of the second (*the intruder*) refers to the patient.

These examples should not be taken to imply that the general definitions will be always or exclusively based on meaning: they too will often draw on the syntactic inter-relationships between the various grammatical categories. For example, a second property common to the classes we call noun in different languages derives from the contrast between the two elementary clause constructions illustrated in *The man died* and *The man killed the fox*. The first contains two phrases belonging to different classes, while the second contains three phrases, two of which belong to the same class; this latter class will then be the class of noun phrases, and noun will be the class of words functioning as the head of such phrases.

The distinction between language-particular and general definitions is an important one, and I shall be continually invoking it in the descriptive chapters that follow. It should be borne in mind, however, that grammarians have not had, and indeed still do not have, a completely authoritative and comprehensive reference manual of general terms at their disposal: the practice adopted in published grammars is accordingly not always as orderly, principled and consistent as one might wish.

Recognition of the distinction between the two levels of definitions and a renewed interest in investigating the deep-seated similarities between languages have made linguists more sympathetic to traditional grammar than they were thirty or forty years ago. The majority of general terms derive from traditional grammar, which provides at least the starting-point for their definition. But to make this point is in no sense to retreat from the basic principle of structural linguistics emphasised in this chapter.

2.4 Exemplification: English verb inflection

We turn now to a more detailed exemplification of the points made in the last section. I have chosen English verb inflection because in addition to providing a very sharp contrast between the traditional and structural approaches it occupies an important place within the grammar of English and will provide a useful point of entry into the description of English to be presented in Chs. 4–14.

The table given as (40) is extracted from the standard traditional paradigm for the verb **take**.[6]

(40)

		Indicative		Subjunctive		Imperative
		Past	Present	Past	Present	Present
Finite forms	1st Pers Sg	took	take	took	take	
	2nd Pers Sg	took	take	took	take	take
	3rd Pers Sg	took	takes	took	take	
	1st Pers Pl	took	take	took	take	
	2nd Pers Pl	took	take	took	take	take
	3rd Pers Pl	took	take	took	take	

Non-finite forms	Infinitive	Past Participle	Present Participle	Gerund
	take	taken	taking	taking

When two or more entries in an inflectional paradigm are orthographically and phonologically identical we say that there is **syncretism** between them. For example, there is syncretism between the singular and plural forms of the lexeme **sheep**: the *sheep* of *This sheep is ill* is a singular form, while that of *These sheep are ill* is a plural form – and that of *I saw the sheep* is ambiguously singular or plural. The analysis given in (40) postulates an enormous amount of syncretism: *take* appears fourteen times, *took* twelve and *taking* twice. I shall argue that most of this syncretism is unjustifiable – that a significant number of the inflectional properties included in it are simply carried over from Latin and have no validity in a grammar of contemporary English.

The relevant difference between English and Latin emerges very clearly

---

[6] For reasons given in 3.2, I omit periphrastic forms such as *have taken, will take, let's take*, etc., i.e. forms consisting of more than one word.

if we compare (40) with the partial Latin paradigm given in (41). I have again omitted the periphrastic forms – which is why there are only half as many passive forms in the table as active forms: the passives of the perfect series of forms (pluperfect, perfect and future perfect) consist of the past participle preceded by a form of the auxiliary **sum** ("be"). In English all passives are periphrastic, so that there is no equivalent in (40) of the Latin passives in (41): *capior* = *am taken*, and so on. Similarly the English equivalents of Latin pluperfects, futures and future perfects are periphrastic: *cēperam* = *had taken*, *capiam* = *will take*, *cēperō* = *will have taken*, and so on. The Latin perfect and imperfect will often both be translatable as an English past, thus *cēpī* and *capiēbam* as *took*, but elsewhere they will be better translated as *have taken* and *was taking* respectively (and similarly *capiō* may translate as *am taking* as well as *take*, *capiam* as *will be taking* as well as *will take*): the semantic distinctions drawn by the two languages differ somewhat in this area. What is of primary interest to us in the Latin paradigm, however, is that the indicative and subjunctive 'moods' and the six person –number combinations have distinct endings: the only instances of syncretism in (41) are between the future indicative and present subjunctive of the 1st person singular in both active and passive voices – and for most verbs these too would be distinct. Thus in Latin the mood, person and number properties are all clearly justified by the phonological contrasts between the forms. But this is not so for English.

Precisely because of the massive amount of syncretism in (40) it is likely to be extremely opaque to a reader not already familiar with it – or familiar with Latin: it is a serious indictment of the analysis that it is so much easier to understand for those who have studied the grammar of Latin or some similar language than for those who know only the language which it purports to describe. Let us therefore give some brief explanation of the grammatical terms that figure in (40) – most will be covered more fully in later chapters – before proposing certain modifications to the analysis: bear in mind, then, that the aim at this point is to explain the traditional analysis, not to endorse it, for we shall in fact discard a number of the traditional categories in arriving at a structural analysis of English verb inflection.

(a) **Indicative, subjunctive** and **imperative** are terms in the system of **mood**. General definitions may be given as follows. 'Indicative' (the unmarked term in the system) is used for a distinct inflectional verb form that is the one characteristically used in factual assertions (e.g. *He takes the bus to work*). 'Subjunctive' is used for the verb form associated with subordinate clauses involving non-factuality (e.g. *Liz insisted that he take the bus*, where *take* is in a subordinate clause and where I am not reporting a factual assertion of Liz's, but a speech act in which she was concerned to bring about a certain event), and 'imperative' is used for the verb form typically

(41) Partial paradigm for the Latin verb **capio** ("take")

			Singular			Plural		
			1st person	2nd person	3rd person	1st person	2nd person	3rd person
Active	Indicative	Imperfect	capiēbam	capiēbās	capiēbat	capiēbāmus	capiēbātis	capiēbant
		Present	capiō	capis	capit	capimus	capitis	capiunt
		Future	capiam	capiēs	capiet	capiēmus	capiētis	capient
		Pluperfect	cēperam	cēperās	cēperat	cēperāmus	cēperātis	cēperant
		Perfect	cēpī	cēpistī	cēpit	cēpimus	cēpistis	cēpērunt
		Future perfect	cēperō	cēperis	cēperit	cēperimus	cēperitis	cēperint
	Subjunctive	Imperfect	caperem	caperēs	caperet	caperēmus	caperētis	caperent
		Present	capiam	capiās	capiat	capiāmus	capiātis	capiant
		Pluperfect	cēpissem	cēpissēs	cēpisset	cēpissēmus	cēpissētis	cēpissent
		Perfect	cēperim	cēperīs	cēperit	cēperimus	cēperītis	cēperint
Passive	Indicative	Imperfect	capiēbar	capiēbāris	capiēbātur	capiēbāmur	capiēbāminī	capiēbantur
		Present	capior	caperis	capitur	capimur	capiminī	capiuntur
		Future	capiar	capiēris	capiētur	capiēmur	capiēminī	capientur
	Subjunctive	Imperfect	caperer	caperēris	caperētur	caperēmur	caperēminī	caperentur
		Present	capiar	capiāris	capiātur	capiāmur	capiāminī	capiantur

figuring in requests and commands (as in *Please take this letter to the post for me*). 'Mood' is then used for an inflectional system of the verb where the contrasts between the terms characteristically involve factuality vs non-factuality, assertions vs non-assertions, main clauses vs subordinate clauses. Remember that the above are to be interpreted as general definitions and will certainly not work as language-particular definitions: in *I wonder whether he takes the bus to work*, for example, *takes* is in a subordinate clause involving non-factuality but it is nevertheless indicative, not subjunctive (because the form is *takes*, not *take*). Note also that the definitions apply to the primary use of the terms – they are often extended so as to cover VPs and clauses as well as inflectional forms (verbs) – see the discussion of imperative in 11.3. Let us now consider some of the language-particular properties of the three moods as they are traditionally applied to English.

(b) Only indicative forms can occur as the first (or only) verb in what we are calling kernel clauses: *He took offence; I take French lessons; They take advantage of you*. Similarly interrogatives (normally), exclamatives, and subordinate clauses introduced by conjunctions like *because, since, before, after*, require indicatives as the first verb: *Who takes sugar?, What a long time he took!, [I'll help myself] before she takes them away*.

(c) The present subjunctive is almost wholly restricted to certain types of subordinate clause. It occurs after a relatively small class of verbs like **demand, insist, require**, or with similar adjectival expressions, as in *It is essential that he take her with him* (though some speakers may find this construction alien to their dialect). In main clauses, the present subjunctive is found only in archaic or formulaic sentences like *The devil take the hindmost; So be it*; and so on. The present subjunctive is most easily distinguished from the present indicative when the subject is 3rd person singular: the subjunctive lacks the *-s* ending. Thus in *I know that he takes the bus* the subordinate clause has an indicative verb, whereas in *I recommend that he take the bus* it has a subjunctive.

(d) The past subjunctive occurs mainly in a certain type of conditional construction, as in *If you took more care, you might do better*. It is also found after the verb **wish**, as in *I wish the paint took less time to dry*.

(e) Imperative forms occur in what we are calling imperative clauses: their properties were outlined in § 1 above.

So much for the moods: we turn now to the other categories in the traditional paradigm.

(f) Past and present are terms in the system of **tense**. The general definition of tense is that it applies to a system of the verb and/or VP, with terms differentiated inflectionally or by means of auxiliaries, where the primary semantic contrast has to do with <u>location in time,</u> especially location <u>relative to the time of speaking</u>. For example, in *He took the bus to work* I am talking about an event or situation located in the past, i.e. a period preceding the time of my utterance, whereas in *He takes the bus to work* the situation occupies a period of time that includes the moment of speaking (or at least this is so in the most salient interpretation of the sentence). Again we are dealing here with general definitions; the correlation between tense and time in English is not always as simple as this, as we have noted: we shall be examining it more carefully in 4.5.

(g) The term **finite** is related to its everyday use in the sense "limited, bounded". More specifically, as a grammatical term it is traditionally applied to verb forms that are limited with respect to person and number – e.g. *takes* is limited to occurrence with a 3rd person singular subject.

(h) The **infinitive** occurs after *to*, as in *There's no need to take it so seriously* (the *to* which functions in VP structure, as opposed to the preposition *to* of *He went to town* or *I object to her taking all the credit for it*); it also occurs after a small number of verbs, such as ***will***, ***can***, ***may***, ***do***, ***see***, ***make***: *You can take them all*; *He didn't take any*; *I saw him take it*.

(i) The **past participle** usually occurs either after the auxiliary ***have*** in the perfect construction, as in *He has taken umbrage*, or, prototypically after the auxiliary ***be***, in the passive construction, as in *She was taken to hospital*.

(j) The **present participle** occurs mainly after the auxiliary ***be*** in the progressive construction, as in *He was taking French lessons*; after a few other verbs such as ***keep***, as in *He kept taking offence*; and in modifying clauses, as in *[Everyone] taking the coach [should report here at 6 a.m.]*.

(k) The **gerund** occurs in subordinate clauses functioning as subject or object of a larger clause, as in *Taking exams was a waste of time* or *I don't anticipate taking much time over it*, or after a preposition, as in *He insisted on taking it to pieces*. It often occurs after a possessive phrase, as in *She resented his taking all the credit* (though we also have *She resented him taking all the credit*: see 5.6.3 for comparison of the possessive and non-possessive constructions). Gerunds are traditionally distinguished from participles as having noun-like functions in contrast to the adjective-like functions of participles: noun-like in that they (or more properly the clauses containing them) can typically be replaced by nouns (or noun phrases); compare the above with *The conference was a waste of time*; *I don't anticipate any difficulty*; *He insisted on a complete reappraisal*; *She resented his behaviour*.

(l) Finally, the systems of person and number, which were introduced in § 2 above: these differ from the others in that they are primarily systems of the

NP. Thus *the boy*, for example, is 3rd person singular (singular in contrast to plural *the boys*, 3rd person in contrast to 1st person *I* or 2nd person *you*). The systems then apply, derivatively, to the verb, in that we analyse *takes* as 3rd person singular because it occurs with 3rd person singular subjects.

Let us now look more critically at the syncretism in (40). A good deal of it involves the person–number properties. As we have just observed, these are carried over from the subject: the verb is said to agree with (i.e. make the same selection as) the subject with respect to person and number. But it is quite inappropriate to say that the rule of subject–verb agreement in English applies in the present subjunctive, past subjunctive, or (leaving aside the verb **be**) in the past indicative. A agrees with B if changing the properties of B requires a concomitant change in A. For example, in the noun phrase the demonstratives **this** and **that** agree with the head in number, for if in *this book* or *that book* we replace singular *book* by plural *books* we must also replace singular *this* and *that* by plural *these* and *those*. But if A remains constant while we change B, how can it be said to agree? In the present subjunctive, past subjunctive and past indicative of **take**, the verb does remain constant and there is accordingly no justification for attributing person–number properties to it. In the present indicative, there is variation in the verb-form – but not for person and number independently. The contrast (still leaving aside the verb **be**) is simply between 3rd person singular (*takes*) and everything else (*take*: I will call this the 'general' form).

If we remove the spurious agreement properties from (40) we arrive at the paradigm shown in (42):

(42)

		Indicative			Subjunctive	Imperative
Finite forms	Past	Present		Past	Present	Present
		3rd Pers Sg	General			
	took	takes	take	took	take	take

	Infinitive	Past Participle	Present Participle	Gerund
Non-finite forms	take	taken	taking	taking

This still contains more syncretism than can be justified. There is no verb in English where the present subjunctive, the (present) imperative and the infinitive are distinct, so that we have no grounds for making an inflectional difference here, a difference of morphological form. There are certainly grounds for recognising [*I insist*] *that he take it*, *Take care!* and [*He arranged*] *for the Smiths to take over next week* as distinct CLAUSE constructions,[7] but as far as

---

[7] See 11.3 for discussion of the first two and 12.3 for the third.

the VERB is concerned, the inflectional form is the same – I shall call it the **base** form. We will retain the distinction between the base form *take*, as in these constructions, and the general present indicative *take* of *The Smiths take over next week*, etc., because for the verb *be* we do have phonologically contrasting forms: compare [*He arranged*] *for the Smiths to be on the committee* with *The Smiths are on the committee*. The status of the distinction between the past indicative and the past subjunctive is, however, more problematical. For all verbs other than *be* they are identical, whereas with *be* in the 1st and 3rd person singular the past indicative is *was*, while the past subjunctive fluctuates between *was* and *were*: one finds both *I wish he was here* and *I wish he were here*, the latter belonging to more formal style. Given that the distinction is unstable and largely obsolescent even in the very small area where it is still found at all, I shall follow the practice of most modern grammars and conflate the two uses of *took* into a single inflectional form, called simply the past tense form; but there is certainly room for legitimate differences of opinion on this question.

Consider finally the remaining non-finite forms in (42). Again we find that there is no verb in English whose present participle and gerund are distinct, and I shall accordingly say that the paradigm contains only one form *taking*: we will call it the **-*ing* form**. *Taken* is of course a distinct form: to match the terminology proposed for *taking*, we will call it the **-*en* form**.

These changes leave us with just six different inflectional forms for *take*, instead of the thirty that we began with. The revised paradigm is shown in (43), where I have included the forms for three other verb lexemes as well – the analysis covers all but a handful of verbs.

(43)

			take	*want*	*find*	*put*
Tensed	Past tense		*took*	*wanted*	*found*	*put*
	Present — 3rd pers sg		*takes*	*wants*	*finds*	*puts*
	General		*take*	*want*	*find*	*put*
Non-tensed	Base form		*take*	*want*	*find*	*put*
	-*ing* form		*taking*	*wanting*	*finding*	*putting*
	-*en* form		*taken*	*wanted*	*found*	*put*

The correspondences with the traditional terminology are as follows:

(44)
i	Past tense	Past indicative or past subjunctive
ii	3rd pers sg present tense	3rd pers sg present indicative
iii	General present tense	Any of the other five present indicative forms
iv	Base form	Infinitive, imperative or present subjunctive
v	-*ing* form	Present participle or gerund
vi	-*en* form	Past participle

I have used 'tensed' vs 'non-tensed' in preference to 'finite' vs 'non-finite' for the distinction between the two major subsets of forms: as we have seen, the base form covers finite as well as non-finite members of the traditional paradigm and hence it would be potentially confusing to classify the revised inflectional forms as finite vs non-finite. The tensed forms are those which belong to one of the two terms in the inflectional system of tense and thus normally enter into a contrast of tense, as in the earlier *He took the bus to work* vs *He takes the bus to work* – the non-tensed forms, on the other hand, do not enter into inflectional contrasts of this kind. I shall also use the terms 'tensed' and 'non-tensed' for clauses according as the first (or only) verb is a tensed or non-tensed form; all kernel clauses, for example, will be tensed, in this sense.

The terms used for the non-tensed forms reflect their morphology rather than their characteristic meaning or use. The base form is identical with the lexical stem, which provides the input to the various morphological processes of suffixation and vowel change by which the other inflectional forms are derived. The *-ing* form is morphologically derived from the lexical stem by suffixation of *-ing*: this is the one area of inflectional morphology in English that is completely regular (though, as we have noted, a few verbs such as **beware**, **must**, etc. simply lack this form). A variety of morphological processes are involved in the derivation of *-en* forms, as is evident from (43) – suffixation of *-en* with **take**, of *-ed* (/ɪd/ or /əd/) with **want**, change from *i* to *ou* (/aɪ/ to /aʊ/) with **find**, and so on; suffixation of *-en*, however, is never used to derive any other inflectional form and thus provides a convenient mnemonic label for this form. The use of such morphology-based terms, though fairly common in modern grammars, cannot be regarded as wholly satisfactory; '*-ing* form' and '*-en* form' are particularly open to objection on the grounds that they are coined ad hoc for English rather than being general terms, so that the terminology does not recognise any correspondence between these forms and forms in other languages. My adoption of these three terms is thus based less on theoretical than on practical considerations – the desire to avoid confusion resulting from the use of a traditional term in a new sense. Since the base form covers the traditional present subjunctive, imperative and infinitive, no one of these ('infinitive' is the only real possibility) could safely be used. A similar argument can be given against using 'present participle' for the *-ing* form – and a further point is that the traditional distinction between 'present' and 'past' participle inappropriately suggests a contrast of tense, as though the relation of *taking* to *taken* were essentially the same as that of *takes* to *took*. And one final point is that the traditional term 'participle' is used to cover not only *-ing* and *-en* forms but also certain morphologically similar words that we shall want to analyse as adjectives rather than verbs (and likewise 'gerund' covers a certain type of noun as well as *-ing* forms of verbs) – see 3.2 for discussion of this issue.

The analysis presented in (43) has eliminated most, but not quite all, of the syncretism found in the traditional paradigm. In simplifying the paradigm we have applied the following two principles:

(a) We will not recognise syncretism unless it can be justified by reference to an overt and stable distinction in the paradigm of at least one lexeme. It is because this condition is not satisfied that we have conflated the traditional present subjunctive, imperative and infinitive forms, and so on.

(b) We will not generalise agreement inflections from one lexeme to another: we will not say, for example, that the two instances of *can* in *I can swim* and *He can swim* are inflectionally distinct, for **can** simply does not enter into agreement, i.e. co-variation, with the subject. Similarly we will not distinguish the *take* of *I take it* from that of *We take it* or the *took* of *I took it* from that of *We took it* by generalisation of the contrasts found with **be** between *I am* and *we are*, *I was* and *we were*.

We are then left with the following syncretisms in the English verb:

(a) All verbs other than **be** have syncretism between the base form and the general present tense form.[8]

(b) All regular verbs (such as **want** in (43)) and a number of irregular ones (such as **find**) have syncretism between the -*en* form and the past tense.

(c) A small number of verbs (**put**, **hit**, **cut**, etc.) have syncretism between the past tense and the base form.

It follows from the way the analysis was arrived at that there is a relatively simple test to decide which of two or more syncretised inflectional forms we have in a given instance – e.g. to decide whether the *wanted* of *That isn't what was wanted* is a past tense or an -*en* form. What we do is replace the lexeme by one which does not exhibit the syncretism in question and see which of its forms is required. Thus if we replace **want** by **take** in this example, the form we need is *taken*, not *took* (*That isn't what was taken/*took*), which shows that this instance of *wanted* is an -*en* form. It will not always be

---

[8] **Be** does not have a general present tense form, for in the present tense we have a three-way person–number contrast *is* (3rd person singular) vs *am* (1st person singular) vs *are* (2nd person or plural). The contrast of *am* vs *are* is purely a matter of person–number agreement properties and hence is not generalised to other verbs in accordance with principle (b), but the contrast between *am* and *are* on the one hand and *be* on the other is not purely a matter of agreement properties and hence justifies our inflectional distinction for other verbs between a non-3rd-person-singular (i.e. 'general') present tense form and a base form by virtue of principle (a). This is why the latter has been formulated as above rather than in more specific terms, such as 'We will not recognise syncretism between two forms unless there is at least one lexeme exhibiting an overt and stable distinction between them.'

possible to replace just the lexeme: changes may also have to be made to what follows. Consider, for example, the sentence *They take her for granted*. Is this *take* a base form or a general present tense form? The only verb which does not exhibit this syncretism is *be*, yet *be* cannot be substituted for **take** in our example, for **They are her for granted* and **They be her for granted* are both ungrammatical. We noted earlier in this chapter that verbs differ according as, in kernel clauses, they must, may or cannot take an object – our examples were **use**, **eat** and **disappear** respectively; an object is a particular type of what we shall call a 'complement', and, more generally, verbs differ according to what kinds and combinations of complements they take. The reason we cannot substitute **be** for **take** in *They take her for granted* is thus that **be** does not allow this pattern of complements. The inflectional properties of verbs, however, are not determined by their complements. In *They had taken her for granted* and *They had been friends*, for example, we have *-en* forms of **take** and **be** in spite of the difference in complements: the *-en* form is determined by the 'perfect auxiliary' **have** – and similarly in other examples it will always be some factor other than the complements that determines the verb inflection. It follows that we can use our test for resolving syncretism by allowing for changes in complements to accompany, where necessary, the substitution of one verb lexeme for another. In this way we can see that the *take* of *They take her for granted* is the general present tense form, not the base form, by comparing it with *They are/*be friends*: the form of **be** that we have in what is, in all relevant respects, the same construction is the present tense form *are*, not the base form *be*.[9] Interpreted in this way the test will enable us to resolve syncretisms of verbal inflections in all cases except those where the sentence is ambiguous. For example, substituting **mow** for **cut** in *I cut the lawn* gives either *I mowed the lawn* or *I mow the lawn*: the *cut* sentence is simply ambiguous between a past and a present interpretation.

As observed above, the inflectional system given in (43) applies to all but a rather small number of verbs. Some verbs lack one or more of the six forms. For example, the 'modal auxiliaries' **can**, **may**, **will**, **shall**, etc. do not have any non-tensed forms and in the present tense have no person–number contrast. There are also a few gaps that have to be specified for

---

[9] Two other 'tests' may be given for resolving this particular syncretism between the general present tense and the base form. They derive from the different contrasts into which the forms enter in paradigm (43). Firstly, we note that the general present contrasts with the 3rd person singular present in agreement properties. Thus if we replace the *they* of *They take her for granted* by *he* we must change *take* to *takes*: this shows that *take* is the general present tense form. Note that replacing *they* by *he* in *They may take her for granted* doesn't have any effect on the *take*: this *take* is accordingly the base form. Secondly, the general present tense form contrasts in tense with the past: we may contrast *They take her for granted* with *They took her for granted*. But the base form does not enter into inflectional tense contrasts, so that the *take* of *They may take her for granted* is not replaceable by *took*.

individual verbs, rather than for a whole subclass: **use** (as in *I used to live there*) has only a past tense and – for those who say *He didn't use to be like that* and the like – a base form (the two forms are always followed by *to*, a fact which has brought about a phonological syncretism between them), and so on: see 4.1 for further discussion. Conversely some verbs have forms not shown in (43). We have already noted that **be** has more person–number variation. More interestingly, verbs belonging to the class of 'operators' (the modal auxiliaries plus **do**, **be** and **have**: see 4.4) have a contrast in the tensed part of the paradigm between positive and negative forms: *will* vs *won't, shall* vs *shan't, had* vs *hadn't*, and so on.

The contrast between *will* and *won't*, etc., is not traditionally regarded as a matter of inflection – partly, perhaps, because there are no negative verb inflections in Latin, but primarily, no doubt, because *won't* is simply taken to be a contraction of *will + not*, just as *I've*, say, is a contraction of *I + have*. There are, however, three differences between *won't* and *I've*. In the first place, the phonological form of *won't* is not predictable by general rule as a reduction of *will + not*: it has, rather, to be specified as an individual item. Historically it derives from *will + not*, but the fusion between the parts is greater than with *I've* and in the analysis we are proposing this is reflected in the recognition of *won't* as a single word while *I've* remains, grammatically, two. This phonological unpredictability is not found with all our negative verb forms, but the next two points do hold for them all. The second difference between *won't* and *I've* is that with the former we find syntactic contexts allowing *won't* but not *will not* whereas *I've* is always syntactically replaceable by *I have*. Thus interrogatives like *Won't it hurt?* do not have as variants forms like **Will not it hurt?*: the variant is, rather, *Will it not hurt?*. The sequence verb + *not* + subject is not wholly excluded but it is quite rare and is restricted to 'weightier' subjects than personal pronouns (cf. the attested example *Is not this system in any case 'fairer'?*): the normal rule for forming interrogatives from declaratives leaves the *not* in post-subject position. Instead of deriving *Won't it hurt?* from **Will not it hurt?* by obligatory contraction, we will regard it as the interrogative of *It won't hurt*: it is then covered by the general rule whereby interrogatives are normally formed by moving the tensed verb to the left of the subject (as in *It will hurt* → *Will it hurt?*, *It will not hurt* → *Will it not hurt?*). The point is, then, that *won't* behaves here syntactically like a single word, a tensed verb, whereas there are no syntactic rules that treat *I've* as a single word. The third difference is the converse of the second: we find syntactic contexts where *I have* is not reducible to *I've* but where *won't* can still occur as an alternative to *will not*. The construction concerned is that where there is ellipsis of material following the *have* or *not*: *Ed hasn't seen it but I have/*I've* (with ellipsis of *seen it*) vs *Ed will be going but I will not/won't* (with ellipsis of *be going*). The significant point here is not just that *won't* behaves differently from *I've*: it's that *won't* is permitted even though the version with *will not* will here have contrastive stress on the *not*, just as *have* is stressed in the first example. The contraction found in *I've* is the extreme case of 'weakening' of /hæv/, with /həv/ and /əv/ as intermediate cases (see 1.8), and such weakening doesn't occur when the word concerned is stressed: the fact that *not* would be stressed in the above example thus argues against deriving *won't* by weakening of *not*.

I remarked in 1.8 that the distinction between one word and two cannot always be drawn sharply and we are here dealing with cases that are close to the boundary. Nevertheless the differences that we have just pointed out between *I've* and *won't* do provide very reasonable grounds for assigning them to different sides of the boundary, with *I've* two words, *won't* one. Note that while it would be absurd to ask what word-class (part of speech) *I've* belongs to, the corresponding question for *won't* is not at all absurd: no problems arise from analysing it as a verb. We will accordingly treat *won't* and *will not* as differing in the 'verbal' component of the signal as one word vs two, while *I've* and *I have* differ 'non-verbally' – so that, in accordance with the position set out in 1.5, we will regard *It won't hurt* and *It will not hurt* as different sentences, while *I have seen it* and *I've seen it* are merely different manifestations of the same sentence. And once it is recognised that *won't* is grammatically a single word, it will be clear that the contrast between *will* and *won't* satisfies our criteria for an inflectional contrast. Our paradigm for the lexeme **will** will accordingly be:

(45)

	Positive	Negative
Past tense	*would*	*wouldn't*
Present tense	*will*	*won't*

This concludes our discussion of English verb inflection. The primary aim has been to show how an examination of the relations between forms and between syntactic constructions leads to an analysis which is significantly different from the traditional one; different and a good deal simpler. Traditional grammar incorporates into the verbal paradigm a number of distinctions that are quite clearly justified in a grammar of Latin but equally clearly out of place in a grammar of Modern English – and omits one distinction that can be argued to be valid for the class of operator verbs in English.

FURTHER READING
On the contrast between notional and structural – or 'formal' – approaches, and between language-particular and general definitions, see Lyons 1968: Chs. 4, 7. The term 'structural linguistics' (or 'structuralism') is unfortunately used in a variety of senses: see Lyons 1981b: §7.2 for discussion; I intend it in the broad sense mentioned by Lyons (p. 220) – 'the sense in which particular

emphasis is given to the internal combinational and contrastive relations within a language-system, [a sense] that makes the term "structuralism" appropriate to several different twentieth-century schools of linguistics [including transformational-generative grammar]'. On the category 'subject' as a general term, see Li 1976, Foley & Van Valin 1977, Comrie 1981: § 3.3, Matthews 1981: Ch. 5. On the concept of 'prototype', see Comrie 1981: 34–5; closely related is the idea of 'serial relationship' – see Quirk 1965. For the terms '*-ing* form' and '*-en* form', see Palmer 1974: 14, Quirk et al. 1971: § 3.9 use '*-ing* participle' and '*-ed* participle' (and they do not distinguish inflectionally between the base and general present tense forms). In spite of my criticisms of traditional grammar, it must be emphasised that such scholarly traditional grammars as the following provide invaluable source material and descriptive insight into the grammar of English: Curme 1931, 1935, Jespersen 1909–49, Kruisinga 1925, Poutsma 1926–29, Scheurweghs 1959, Sweet 1891–98, Visser 1963–73, Zandvoort 1972.

3
The parts of speech

3.1 The traditional classification

Traditional grammars of English standardly recognise eight parts of speech, listed here with typical examples:

(1)
Noun	*boy, woman, cat, apple, truth*
Pronoun	*I, he, everyone, nothing, who*
Verb	*be, become, come, die, believe*
Adjective	*big, happy, careful, old, wooden*
Adverb	*quickly, very, here, afterwards, nevertheless*
Preposition	*at, in, on, by, for*
Conjunction	*and, but, because, although, while*
Interjection	*ouch, oh, alas, grrr, psst*

The part-of-speech classification plays a central role in the organisation of traditional grammars: a major section of the work will typically consist of a set of chapters each of which is devoted to a particular part of speech. This aspect of traditional grammar has come in for a large amount of criticism from structural linguists – and many modern grammars, while using the categories noun, verb, adjective, etc., refer to them as 'word-classes' or 'form-classes', rather than 'parts of speech', partly in order to dissociate themselves from the traditional doctrine.

Traditional grammars generally provide short definitions for each part of speech, and it will be helpful to preface our discussion with a representative set of such definitions; the following are taken from Curme 1935, the work of a respected US scholar.

(a) 'A noun, or substantive, is a word used as the name of a living being or lifeless thing: *Mary, John, horse, cow, dog; hat, house, tree, London, Chicago; virtue*' (p. 1).

(b) 'A pronoun is a word used instead of a noun' (p. 7).

(c) 'The verb is that part of speech that predicates, assists in predications, asks a question, or expresses a command: The wind *blows*, He *is* blind, *Did* he *do* it? *Hurry!*' (p. 63). (By 'predication' Curme evidently means 'assertion', the term that appears in the shorter version of his grammar (1947:

90

22): 'The verb is that part of speech by which we make an assertion or ask a question: The wind *blows*, *Is* the wind *blowing*?'.)

(d) 'An adjective is a word that modifies a noun or pronoun, i.e. a word that is used with a noun or pronoun to describe or point out the living being or lifeless thing designated by the noun or pronoun: a *little* boy, *that* boy, *this* boy, a *little* house' (p. 42).

(e) 'An adverb is a word that modifies a verb, an adjective or another adverb' (p. 71).

(f) 'A preposition is a word that indicates a relation between the noun or pronoun it governs and another word, which may be a verb, an adjective or another noun or pronoun: I live *in* this house' (p. 87).

(g) 'A conjunction is a word that joins together sentences or parts of a sentence: Sweep the floor *and* dust that furniture, He waited *until* I came' (p. 92).

(h) 'An interjection is an outcry to express pain, surprise, anger, pleasure, or some other emotion, as *Ouch!*, *Oh!*, *Alas!*, *Why!*' (p. 105).

Substantially the same definitions are to be found in countless grammars and handbooks written in the last hundred to two hundred years and more. The only place where there is significant variation is in the definition for the verb: a common alternative account is that a verb denotes 'action or being' or 'action or a state of being'.

The first point to be made about these definitions, one that will be evident from what has been said in the last chapter, is that they are quite inadequate as language-particular definitions: they do not provide clear criteria that would enable one to assign words to the 'correct' class (i.e. the one to which they are in practice assigned by traditional grammarians). We have argued this for the definition of a noun as 'the name of a person, place or thing', a variant of the one given by Curme, and it is easy to show that the point holds equally for the other definitions. Consider the pronoun, for example. We can accept that in *The boss said he was ill*, interpreted with *he* referring to the boss, the pronoun *he* is used instead of a noun (except that given our concept of constituent structure we would relate it not to the noun *boss* but to the NP *the boss*); we might even be persuaded to accept that in *I am ill* the pronoun *I* is used instead of a noun (phrase), though this case differs in important ways from the first; but in examples like *Nobody came, Everything was destroyed, What is the new boss like?, It was John who broke the window* it is not remotely plausible to say that the pronouns *nobody, everything, what* and *it* are used instead of nouns. Curme's definition of the verb is particularly unhelpful, since assertions, questions and the like involve whole sentences, not just their verbs: what reason is there to say that in *Are you ill?* it is the verb *are* that asks a question? Notice, on the other hand, that in saying *If he knows her we're in trouble* I do not assert that he knows her, though *knows* is nevertheless a verb. The definition of a verb as a word denoting an action or state of being fares no better. There is nothing in the definition that will enable us to include the *destroyed* of *They destroyed the residue unnecessarily* while excluding the *destruction* (a noun) of *Their destruction of the residue was unnecessary*. And how is 'state of being' to be interpreted in such a way as to include verbs like *know* or *love* while excluding adjectives like *knowledgeable* or *fond*? Again, if an adjective is a word that 'describes' what is designated by a noun or pronoun, why is it that in *They are fools* the word *fools* is a noun, not an adjective (like the *foolish* of *They are foolish*)? And so on: the point is too obvious to need further demonstration. It is important to see that these objections cannot be overcome by any small-scale modification or clarification of the definitions. The complexity of the phenomena to be handled will defeat any attempt to provide a simple set of definitions of the above kind that will work at the language-particular level.

The distinction between language-particular and general definitions drawn in 2.3 is not made in traditional grammar, which can be argued to have an inadequate understanding of the relation between particular grammars and 'universal grammar'. The definitions do not make reference to specific properties of English and are certainly conceived of as being applicable to other languages as well. On the other hand there can be no doubt that they are normally presented as providing the criteria by which the individual words and lexemes of English are assigned to their respective part-of-speech category. In terms of the framework developed here, therefore, we can say that the failure of the definitions stems from the implicit but false assumption that a single set of definitions will work at the general and language-particular levels.

The criticisms made by structural linguists have concentrated on the weaknesses of the definitions at the language-particular level, partly because it is here that they are most striking, but also because until relatively recently structural linguists were more concerned with emphasising the diversity of languages than in investigating universal grammar. The severity of the criticism – discussions in modern textbooks of the traditional part-of-speech analysis are quite often overwhelmingly negative in spite of the fact that there is undoubtedly a great deal of value in it – is related to the dominant place that the definitions held in the teaching of English grammar in schools for many generations. And certainly within that context an unsophisticated use of the definitions can well promote confusion or even intellectual dishonesty. For they are in the main couched in terms of the meaning of the words to be classified rather than of their grammatical properties: as such they fail to mention the kind of property that in fact provides the basis and raison d'être for the classification. To take up just one of the above examples: the reason why we distinguish *fools* as a noun from *foolish* as an adjective in *They are fools/foolish* is that *fools* is a plural form contrasting with singular *fool* (cf. *He is a fool*), that *fools* can take words like *the, some, many, these,* etc. as dependent, that we can say *They are very foolish* but not **They are very fools* and conversely *They are utter fools* but not *They are utter foolish*, that *foolish* but not *fools* occurs in constructions like *her foolish brothers* (cf. **her fools brothers*), and so on. Any satisfactory account of the parts of speech must make clear that the classification depends on the grammatical function and form of words in sentences. And it must also give recognition to the distinction we have drawn between prototypical or central members of a category and more or less marginal members, with the possibility of some indeterminacy over just where the boundaries are to be drawn.

A second point to be made about the definitions is that they are not all of the same kind – though the categories they are meant to define are intended to be of the same kind, namely contrasting classes of words or lexemes. It will be noticed that the noun and verb are defined independently of the others, while the pronoun, adjective, adverb and preposition definitions refer to nouns and/or verbs. Thus, for example, the noun is defined in terms of a word's inherent semantic properties whereas the adjective is defined in terms of the semantic relation between a word and the noun or pronoun with which it is in construction. The trouble with this (which might otherwise be thought to have the advantage of imposing a logical ordering on the parts of speech in such a way as to avoid circularity in the definitions) is that the definitions are not mutually exclusive. Consider one of Curme's own examples: *a boy actor.* Here *boy* satisfies the definition for noun by virtue of denoting a person and also the definition for adjective by virtue of modifying *actor.* Is it then to be classified as a noun or an adjective? Curme's answer is that it is a noun used as an adjective. And this type of locution, 'an X used as a Y', with X and Y standing for different parts of speech, is extremely common in traditional grammar; it is, however, quite unclear and in need of explication. Is it being claimed that an X used as a Y actually is a Y or that it is merely functionally like a Y? If it actually is a Y, then in what sense is it also an X? If it is not a Y but just functionally like one, how can this be reconciled with a definition of Y in terms of function – if Y is defined as a word having a certain function, how can a word occur with that function and yet fail to be a Y?

Let us see what Curme says about a few examples. Of *John's book* he says quite explicitly that *John's* is not an adjective: it has the 'force' of an adjective but is 'formally' the genitive of a noun. It has the 'force' of an adjective in that it 'points out' which object is being designated by *book* – but precisely by virtue of having this 'force' it satisfies the definition of adjective. He contrasts *John's book* with *We are the same age*, saying that *the same age* not only has the force of an adjective but actually is one – it is 'formally' an adjective; this is a very strange sense of 'formally' because in terms of its internal structure *the same age* is clearly quite unlike a standard adjective: it has the structure of what we are calling a noun phrase. Curme does not in fact employ the locution 'a noun used as an adjective' for the *John's* of *John's book*, and the contrast between his treatment of this example and of the *boy actor* type suggests that for him, *boy*, unlike *John's*, is an adjective. But he then goes on to contrast a 'true adjective' with a 'noun used as an adjective': in discussing the subclass of adjectives traditionally called 'proper' adjectives, he says 'proper adjectives are of two kinds – true adjectives [like *English* in *the English navy* or *Shakespearian* in *a Shakespearian scholar*] and proper nouns used as adjectives [like *Mississippi* in *the great Mississippi flood*]'. What does it mean to say that *Mississippi* is an adjective, but not a true adjective? Thus among the words satisfying the definition for adjective some, like *Shakespearian*, are true adjectives, others, like *Mississippi* and presumably *boy*, are not true adjectives but nouns used as adjectives, and others, like *John's*, are not adjectives at all but nouns having the force of an adjective.

I draw attention to these bewildering analyses not in order to belittle Curme's work – his *Grammar* is unquestionably an impressive and valuable scholarly contribution – but to illustrate the kind of problem that is created by the traditional definitions, in particular by their failure to give proper recognition to the distinction we have drawn between syntactic classes and syntactic functions. In general, traditional grammar makes this distinction quite clearly in analysing clauses, but not in analysing noun phrases – indeed it does not have a comparable category of noun phrase. Thus where we would say of an example like *Young Tom was reading a book on astronomy* that the subject is the NP *young Tom* and the object is the NP *a book on astronomy*, traditional grammars typically say that the subject and object are the nouns *Tom* and *book* respectively: *young, a* and *on astronomy* are analysed as subordinate elements of the sentence. They do speak of modification, with *young* modifying *Tom*, etc., but this is not handled by means of a construction where *young* has the function 'modifier', *Tom* the function 'head': rather *young* is said to modify the SUBJECT *Tom*. In introducing the distinction between class and function in 1.3, I pointed out that one obvious reason for keeping them conceptually and terminologically separate is that there is not a one-to-one relation between them: in *Tom saw Ed*, for example, *Tom* and *Ed* belong to the same class but have different functions, while in *Tom worried me* and *That he was late worried me*, on the other hand, *Tom* and *that he was late* have the same function but belong to different classes. And the same holds for NP structure: in *a boy actor*, say, *boy* and *actor* belong to the same class (noun) but have different functions (modifier and head respectively), while in *a boy actor* and *a great actor*, by contrast, *boy* and *great* have the same function (modifier) but belong to different classes (noun and adjective). The inconsistencies in Curme's analysis stem largely from the attempt to make a single pair of categories, adjective and noun, do the work of two pairs, the functions modifier and head, and the classes of adjective and noun: the adjective is defined as though it were a function but is intended as a class, Curme's 'true adjectives' being the words which belong to this intended class. The relation between classes and functions in the NP is, admittedly, not completely the same as in the clause. In the clause both subject and object functions are prototypically filled by NPs, whereas in the NP the modifier and head functions are prototypically filled by adjectives and nouns respectively: a word that could function as modifier but not head could not be a noun. This strong association between modifier and adjective facilitates the confusion between the two concepts – but it does not make it any the less important to draw the distinction: the range of forms that can function as modifier in NP structure is far too heterogeneous for us to use the ability to appear in this function as the defining criterion for a syntactic class. Take again, for example, the contrast between *a boy actor* and *a great actor*: although *boy* and *great* both have modifier function there are considerable differences between them, and it is for this reason that we assign them to different classes. Thus we can say *a rather great actor* but not **a rather boy actor* (*rather* modifies adjectives but not nouns); we have *a great new actor* (with a sequence of two adjective modifiers), but not **a boy new actor* (we need *a new boy actor*, with the adjective preceding the noun); we can relate *a great actor* to *The actor is great* but not *a boy actor* to **The actor is boy* (rather we have a contrast of number in *The actor is a boy* vs *The actors are boys*, with *boy* and *boys* being singular and plural forms of the noun lexeme **boy**). And so on: see 9.3.2 for further discussion.

Before leaving this issue of the interpretation of the traditional locution, 'an X used as a Y', I should point out that it is also employed in cases quite different from those discussed above. For example, Curme gives *the ups and downs of life* as an illustration of the way adverbs can be 'used as nouns'. What we have here, however, is lexical–morphological conversion in the sense of 1.7. In *He went up and down*, say, *up* and *down* are adverbs, but in *the ups and downs of life* the words *ups* and *downs* are not adverbs at all: there is nothing at all adverb-like about them. They are quite straightforwardly nouns: they carry the plural inflection, they combine with *the* and similar words, they could take an adjective as modifier (*the turbulent ups and downs of life*), they occur as heads of phrases functioning as subject or object in clause structure, complement of a preposition, and so on. Thus *ups* and *downs* are clearly forms of the noun lexemes **up** and **down**, whose lexical stems are derived by conversion from the adverb stems *up* and *down*. This is quite different from the case of *boy actor*, where instead of lexical conversion we simply have a word of one class (a noun) occurring with a function which is prototypically associated with another class (adjective). Thus a further reason for avoiding the 'X used as Y' locution is that it fails to distinguish between these two types of case, an important distinction even if it is not always so easy to decide between them as in these examples.

The criticisms I have been making so far have been of a theoretical kind, concerned with the general nature of the definitions and explications that traditional grammar provides for the parts of speech; in addition there are criticisms of a more purely descriptive kind: it is argued that the traditional parts of speech, with the membership that they standardly have, do not provide the best system of classification for the words and lexemes of English. I will here draw attention briefly to four areas where the analysis is open to question – some of these points will be taken up in more detail in the descriptive chapters that follow.

(a) In the first place there are strong grounds for saying that the pronoun should not be a distinct primary class on the same taxonomic level as noun, verb, adjective, etc., but should be regarded as a subclass of an enlarged primary class 'noun'. The functional potential of phrases headed by a pronoun like *it* or *something* is almost the same as that of phrases headed by common nouns like *dog* or proper nouns like *Fido* and differences in the internal structure of these phrases are not such as to justify a distinction of primary class. This point will be developed in 7.1, and I shall henceforth assume that the noun class includes pronouns as well as common nouns and proper nouns – and the NP class will accordingly cover phrases headed by any of these three subclasses of noun. This is a fairly minor change to the traditional scheme: the other deficiencies are very much more difficult to rectify.

(b) The most common descriptive criticism of the traditional parts of speech concerns the adverb class, whose members are a good deal more heterogeneous than is the case with the other primary classes. The definition is very broad, and its standard interpretation is arguably even broader: it is far from obvious, for example, that in *Even John liked it* the adverb *even* can properly be said to be modifying a verb, adjective or adverb. The result of having a broad definition liberally interpreted is that the adverb has something of the character of a residual or miscellaneous class, a class to which items are assigned that lack the more specific positive properties associated with the other primary classes. Consider, for example, such words as *however, very, quickly, downstairs, even, not*: it is questionable whether we have given any significant or useful information about how these words are used when we have said simply that they are adverbs. In general, the members of a single class enter into relations of paradigmatic contrast with each other. In the simplest cases of such contrast we can substitute one item for another in a given functional position in specific sentences. For example, in *John touched the glass* we could substitute *broke* for *touched*, *cup* for *glass*, and so on, without loss of grammaticality or change of construction-type. As noted in 1.3, we cannot expect that all members of a class will always contrast in this way, so that we allow for paradigmatic contrast of a more abstract kind, defined by reference to functional positions in a construction rather than a specific sentence. For example, we cannot substitute *disappeared* for *touched* in the above sentence, but we can still speak of paradigmatic contrast in that both occur as head of a VP functioning in turn as head (predicator) in clause structure. The heterogeneity of the adverb class is thus not convincingly demonstrated by giving example sentences where one adverb cannot be substituted for another (by observing, for example, that *very* cannot replace *downstairs* in *He ran downstairs*): the point is, rather, that there is a lack of paradigmatic contrast in the more abstract sense. And note, again, that although we could substitute *quickly* or *however* for *downstairs* in *He ran downstairs*, this does not show the words to be paradigmatically contrastive in the relevant sense, for they could all three occur here (non-coordinately), as in *He ran quickly downstairs, however.*

It is one thing to argue that the adverb is a more heterogeneous class than the others, quite another to decide on an alternative analysis involving a set of smaller primary classes instead. Various proposals have been made, but none has established itself as anything remotely like a standard analysis, and I shall therefore not pursue this matter in much detail in later chapters. There is no reason to assume, however, that all parts of the word/lexeme taxonomy can be made equally rigorous: we have to accept that some aspects of sentence structure are subject to stricter, more specific rules of grammar than others – we shall take up this point briefly in the contrast we shall draw between 'nuclear' and 'peripheral' elements of clause structure.

(c) A more specific charge of heterogeneity is often levelled against the traditional class of adjectives – namely that words like *the, a, this, each, some, few*, etc. differ so clearly from such prototypical adjectives as *big, happy, old* that they should be extracted from the adjective class and assigned to a distinct primary class of their own. This proposal has a good deal to commend it, though we will not find a sharp boundary between the two new classes (see 8.2). Some traditional grammars do indeed treat *the* and *a(n)* separately from adjectives, calling them 'articles' (definite and indefinite respectively) – and for convenience I followed this analysis in Ch. 1; once a distinction of this kind is drawn, however, there is no reason to restrict the smaller class to just *the* and *a(n)*, for *this, each, some* and *few* are clearly more like these than they are like *big, happy, old*. Probably the most usual term for this new class is 'determiner', but as I shall be using this as the name of a function I will use the related term 'determinative' as the class label.

(d) The final point of this kind that I shall mention concerns the preposition – more particularly the way in which it is distinguished from the conjunction and the adverb. A traditional analysis of (2) would say that *before* was a preposition in (i), a conjunction in (ii) and an adverb in (iii):

(2) i *He had met her before Easter*
  ii *He had met her before he left school*
  iii *He had met her before*

Many would argue that these distinctions are not soundly based and that some reorganisation of the taxonomy is needed in this area. Again, however, there is no consensus among contemporary grammarians as to just what form the reorganisation should take, and I shall accordingly confine myself in Ch. 10 to explaining the traditional analysis and showing why it is open to objection, without arguing for any specific alternative analysis.

To conclude this section, let us now ask what evaluation can be made, in summary, of the traditional doctrine of the parts of speech, as it applies to the grammar of English. On the debit side, there is no doubt that the standard definitions are unsatisfactory in that they do not provide criteria that justify the standard assignment of words to the various parts of speech, do not in several major cases give any indication of the kind of grammatical property that in fact distinguishes one class from another, and are not based on a sound grasp of the distinction and relation between syntactic classes and functions. And leaving aside the definitions, the analysis itself is certainly in need of some modification. On the credit side, there is much in the analysis that is clearly sound. It is inconceivable, for example, that one might write a viable grammar of English that failed to distinguish classes of nouns, verbs and adjectives with very much the same coverage as in traditional grammar (for differences in the treatment of pronouns or determinatives, etc. concern a rather small number of items in relation to the total set of nouns, verbs and adjectives); similarly it is clear that such words as *in, on, by, at, for, of, to* belong together in a very small grammatical class even if there is room for argument as to whether they should be distinguished from *because, if, while* and the like; and so on. Moreover, the modifications to the taxonomy that have been proposed have not achieved majority acceptance among modern grammarians, so that from a pedagogical point of view the traditional scheme arguably provides the best starting point for discussion: other schemes can then be considered in terms of their departure from the tradition. And finally, as will become clear in later chapters, the grammatical differences between the parts of speech are of major importance, so that it is inevitable that they should play a central role in the organisation and presentation of the grammar.

3.2   Nature of the units classified

In this section we will be concerned with the question of what kind or kinds of unit are assigned to the various parts of speech. We have already noted that the classification applies both to words and to lexemes: we say, for example, that the word *took* is a verb and that the lexeme **take** is a verb. From the point of view adopted here, where a lexeme is an abstraction from a set of inflectional forms, we will take the classification of words to be primary, with the classification of lexemes derivative from it: we do not say that *took* is a verb because it is a form of the verb lexeme **take** but because of its own immediate properties. The two main kinds of property that determine syntactic classification in general are functional potential and internal structure (see 1.3), and these apply in the first instance to words: it is words rather than lexemes which occur as constituents of sentences. And note that it is only to words that the classification applies in its entirety: there are no preposition, conjunction or interjection lexemes.

Nothing that we have said about inflection requires that all the forms of a lexeme should belong to the same part of speech – and traditional practice, initially in the grammar of Greek and Latin, subsequently and derivatively in the grammar of English and other languages, has been to recognise certain exceptions to the normal case where all the words in a paradigm are of the same class. Again we will confine our attention to English, where it is in fact very questionable whether the traditional practice is sound.

The main problem area concerns the traditional non-finite forms of verb lexemes, the participles, the gerund and the infinitive. A participle is said to be a 'verbal adjective', while the gerund and – for some grammars at least[1] – the infinitive are 'verbal nouns'. According to the traditional doctrine, a gerund like *writing* in *She likes writing letters* is a noun because it is object of the verb *likes*. Just as we noted in the last section that in *Young Tom was reading a book on astronomy* the object of *was reading* is traditionally said to be *book*, rather than *a book on astronomy* as we would have it, so in the present example the traditional analysis generally treats *writing* alone, rather than *writing letters* as the object. This failure to recognise a constituent structure, to consider fully the role of the gerund within the intermediate unit rather than immediately within the sentence, leads the traditional grammarian to classify together as nouns words which are syntactically very different, such as the *writing* of (3) and that of (4):

---

[1] Cf. the entry for 'infinitive' in the *Shorter Oxford English Dictionary*, which says that it is usually classed as a mood, though it is 'strictly a substantive [i.e. a noun] with certain verbal functions'.

99

(3)   *Actually writing the letters took only a couple of hours*
(4)   *The actual writing of the letters took only a couple of hours*

Instead of saying that both are nouns because they are subject of *took*, we
will say that the *writing* of (3) is a verb because it is head of the extended
verb phrase *actually writing the letters*, while the *writing* of (4) is a noun
because it is head of the noun phrase *the actual writing of the letters*. We say
that *actually writing the letters* is an extended verb phrase because of its clear
structural resemblance to a prototypical EVP like [*She*] *actually wrote the
letters*, and similarly that *the actual writing of the letters* is a noun phrase
because it is like a prototypical NP such as *the actual size of the letters*. Note
that in (3) *writing* is modified by the adverb *actually* whereas in (4) it is
modified by the adjective *actual*; that in (3) *writing* takes an object, the NP
the letters, whereas in (4) what we will call the complement of *writing* is a PP,
of the letters; that in (4) but not (3) *writing* enters into construction with the
determiner *the*; and so on. The word *writing* in (3) is an inflectional form –
what we are calling the *-ing* form – of the lexeme **write**, and both word and
lexeme are verbs. By the criterion of 1.7, the relation between *writing* of (4)
and the stem *write* is lexical rather than inflectional, and thus although this
writing is a noun it is not a form of **write**. Instead of speaking of the *writing* of
(4) as a 'verbal noun', I will call it a 'deverbal noun', i.e. a noun derived by
a lexical-morphological process from a verb stem. Analogously with participles, as in

(5)   *Anyone disturbing these papers will be severely dealt with*
(6)   *I've just had a very disturbing experience*

Instead of saying that *disturbing* is a verbal adjective in each of these, we
will say that it is a verb in (5), an adjective in (6) – and again in (5),
disturbing is an inflectional form of the lexeme **disturb** but in (6) it is not:
disturbing in (6) is lexically derived and hence a deverbal adjective. The
argument for this analysis will be presented in Ch. 9, where we will also
take up again the question of gerunds. It would be foolish to suggest that
there are no problems, for this is a very complex area of English grammar;
nevertheless, a strong case can be made for saying that recognition of a
fully-fledged constituent structure and of the fact that there need be no
one-to-one correlation between functions and classes permits a significant
clarification of the status of so-called gerunds and participles. And in
particular we can proceed with a straightforward relation between the
part-of-speech classification of words and lexemes here: all the inflectional
forms of a verb lexeme belong to the class of verb words.

   A second problem area concerns possessives. We have noted some
equivocation in the traditional treatment of forms like *John's* in *John's book*:
it is regarded as an inflectional form of the noun **John** but is also said, in

Curme's formulation, to have the force of an adjective. And when *John's* occurs without a following noun head, as in *My hand is larger than John's* Curme analyses it as a 'substantive possessive adjective'! This particular issue can be disposed of very quickly in the light of the analysis of *'s* as a clitic rather than an inflectional suffix: *John's* is not syntactically a single word, not a form of **John**, so that the issue of whether a lexeme and a member of its paradigm belong to the same part of speech does not arise. Less easily resolved is the problem raised by the possessive forms *my, your, his, her, its, our* and *their* – which some traditional grammars treat as adjectives, others as pronouns. There are in fact two problems here: are these to be analysed as inflectional forms of **I**, **you**, etc. (or are they inflectionally related at least to *mine, yours*, etc.) and what syntactic class do they belong to? Neither of these questions allows a dogmatic answer. I shall take up the issue in 7.4; here we may note simply that only if the answer to the first question (in either version) is 'yes' and that to the second is 'adjective' (or 'determinative') would we have here a discrepancy between word and lexeme classification – and the fact that it would apparently be the only instance of such a discrepancy in the grammar could reasonably be advanced as one argument against that particular combination of answers.

As well as covering words and lexemes, the part-of-speech classification is standardly applied to stems – except to bound stems like the *poss* of *possible*, and the like. In *those blackbirds*, for example, the lexical stems *bird, blackbird* are said to be nouns, *black* an adjective. Such classification of stems is directly derivative from the classification of words: *black* is an adjective because that is the part of speech it belongs to when it occurs as a word (with the relevant meaning – for in *There's only one black on the committee*, say, *black* is a noun). There is little danger of confusion in the use of the same terms for stems and words, since in one case we are dealing with morphology and in the other with syntax.

In addition, the part-of-speech labels are also commonly applied in syntax to units larger than a word, in both traditional and modern grammars. I am not concerned at this point with their use in expressions like 'noun phrase': a form like *a book on astronomy* is not a noun but a phrase with a noun as head – I will take up this matter in the next section. The issue here is the application of the part-of-speech labels on their own to word sequences. Two cases of this kind may be distinguished.

(a) The first involves the so-called **periphrastic** forms, such as *will take, have taken, are taking, were taken, will have been taken*, and the like. These are traditionally analysed as forms of the lexeme **take** (*will take* is a future form, *have taken* a perfect form, and so on), and by virtue of being members of the paradigm of **take** they enter into the part-of-speech classification: each is said to be a verb. Since they consist of more than one word, the separate words are also classified: thus, for example, *have taken* as a whole is a verb but the words of which it consists, *have* and *taken*, are also verbs. We will not follow this practice here: rather, we will say that *have taken* is a 'verb phrase' and will restrict the term 'verb' to the component words *have* and *taken*. We take the parts of speech to be syntactic classes, and it is clear that the rules of syntax distinguish between forms like *have taken* on the one hand, *have* and *taken* on the other: it is for this reason that we assign them to different classes. For example, in forming the interrogative of *They have taken it* we move the verb *have*, not the verb phrase *have taken*, to the front: *Have they taken it?*; in elliptical constructions like *Ed has taken it to heart and I have too* we retain the verb *have* not the verb phrase *have taken*, and so on. We accordingly distinguish between a form like *have taken*, say, on the one hand and *took* on the other: the latter has no syntactic constituent structure, but the former has – and again our departure from the traditional analysis is associated with our adoption of a fully-fledged constituent structure mode of description. Thus while the form *took* will be derived by a rule of inflectional morphology from the lexical stem of ***take***, the form *have taken* will not: it is a rule of syntax that says that perfects are formed by means of the auxiliary verb ***have*** followed by an *-en* form. For this reason we will not regard *have taken* as a form of the lexeme ***take***: it is a form of ***have*** in construction with a form of ***take*** (just as *this man* is not a form of ***man***, but a form of ***this*** in construction with a form of ***man***). Notice that we do not need to say that *have taken* is a form of ***take*** in order to account for the fact that it is ***take*** that determines what pattern of complements the phrase will allow (e.g. that we can say *have taken the bus, have taken it for granted* in contrast to **have disappeared the bus*, **have used it for granted*, and so on): this is catered for by saying that the 'head' of the VP construction here is a form of ***take***.

All the forms of a lexeme will therefore be single words[2] – which means that we shall have no use for the concept of a 'periphrastic form', for this term is standardly employed precisely for a form in the paradigm of a lexeme that consists of more than one word. Instead of contrasting *have taken* and *took* as periphrastic vs non-periphrastic we can use an alternative pair of traditional terms which do not carry any implication that they belong to the same lexeme, and say that in English the perfect is 'analytic' while the past tense is 'synthetic': a perfect VP is marked as such by the presence of a particular word, while the marker of the past tense is a morphological process.

---

[2] It was in anticipation of this principle that we adopted the convention of representing verb lexemes as '***take***', '***go***', '***be***', etc., i.e. the base form in bold face, rather than following the traditional practice. Our convention differs from the latter in two respects: it uses bold face to distinguish lexemes from forms, and the form which is selected to represent the lexeme (the 'citation form') is the base form, not the infinitive with *to*. *To take* is not a single word (for reasons given in 1.8), and hence not a form of ***take***, and thus not a suitable candidate for a citation form.

Somewhat less straightforward than these examples is the system of **comparison**, which applies to certain subclasses of AdjP and AdvP: the complication stems from the fact that while the perfect is invariably analytic, the **comparative** and **superlative** can be either synthetic or analytic:

(7)

		Absolute	Comparative	Superlative
AdjP	*noisy*	$\left\{ \begin{array}{l} \textit{noisier} \\ \textit{more noisy} \end{array} \right.$	*noisier* *more noisy*	*noisiest* *most noisy*
AdvP	*often*	$\left\{ \begin{array}{l} \textit{oftener} \\ \textit{more often} \end{array} \right.$	*oftener* *more often*	*oftenest* *most often*

That *more* is a separate word while *-er* is not will be clear from the criteria of 1.8: compare, for example, *It was getting more and more noisy* with *It was getting noisier and noisier* (not *It was getting noisier and -er*) or *It was getting less noisy, not more* with *It was getting less noisy, not noisier* (not *It was getting less noisy, not -er*), and so on. We must in fact distinguish syntactically between two types of comparative, which for convenience I will call types 'A' and 'A/S'. Unlike the more usual type A/S, type A is invariably analytic: an example is *Ed is more noisy than naughty*, where the comparison is not between different degrees of noisiness, as in type A/S, but between different degrees of appropriateness of the terms 'noisy' and 'naughty' as applied to Ed. The type A comparative is a quite straightforward syntactic construction, but the type A/S fits in less well with the distinction we have drawn between syntax and morphology, for while some adjectives or adverbs allow either analytic or synthetic forms (*It was more noisy/noisier than ever*) with many only the analytic form is grammatical (*He's more intelligent/ *intelligenter than Tom*) and conversely for some others only the synthetic form is found (*It's getting worse/ *more bad*): the rule for the formation of A/S comparatives thus bears some resemblance to the kind of rule that is characteristic of inflectional morphology. These complications will have to be handled in the lexicon. Where synthetic comparatives and superlatives exist, the lexical item will be recorded as a lexeme: **noisy**, **bad**, etc. and the entry for **bad** will also record that it is syntactically exceptional in that it cannot enter into the analytic comparative construction in type A/S comparatives. Where there is no inflectional paradigm, the lexical item will be recorded directly as a word: *intelligent* – and the fact that its failure to enter into inflectional contrasts is predictable from the phonological properties of the stem (it contains more than two syllables) would be handled by a lexical generalisation valid for the lexicon as a whole. We thus have no need to postulate a lexeme '**intelligent**' as an abstraction from *intelligent, more intelligent* and *most intelligent*, and no need to apply the term adjective to forms like *more intelligent*: it is an AdjP, consisting of the adverb *more* as modifier and the adjective *intelligent* as head.

(b) The second case, after the traditional periphrastic forms, where the part-of-speech labels will often be found applied to units larger than single words involves certain types of idiom. Expressions like **give** *up*, **put** *up with* are commonly spoken of as verbs, *in front of* or *on behalf of* as prepositions, *so that* or *in order that* as conjunctions, and so on. Given the approach to the relation between lexical items and syntactic structure sketched in 1.8, we shall have little if any occasion to follow this practice. Lexical items do not always occur in sentences as syntactic constituents, but it is to syntactic constituents that, in the first instance, the part-of-speech classification applies. In *He had put up with it for long enough* the words *put up with* do not form a constituent (as we shall argue in 5.5), so that the question of what syntactic class the sequence as a whole belongs to does not arise – and the abstraction of **put** *up with* from EVPs like *had put up with it, was putting up with his father* and so on, is a lexical abstraction, not a grammatical one like the abstraction of **tolerate** from the verbs *tolerated, tolerate, tolerates*, etc.: the resemblance between **put** *up with* and **tolerate** is essentially a lexical-semantic one rather than a syntactic one and hence does not justify their assignment to the same syntactic class. We saw earlier that the generally high degree of correlation between lexical items and words is responsible for the common use of the same term, 'word', for both, but precisely because the correlation is imperfect we need to distinguish two concepts – and we are reserving the term 'word' for the grammatical one; similarly here with the term 'verb'. The other types of example – *in front of, so that*, etc. – would need to be considered on their particular merits (see 10.5 for some discussion), but certainly as far as the major parts of speech are concerned, i.e. the noun, verb, adjective and adverb, I know of no convincing reason for including within their membership any expressions consisting of more than one word/lexeme.

Up to this point the nature of the units classified in a parts-of-speech analysis has been discussed relative to their syntagmatic delimitation; the issue needs also to be considered with respect to the paradigmatic axis. The question here is how we handle the phenomenon exemplified in

(8)   i *He put it in the wrong bottle*
        ii *I must bottle these plums*
(9)   i *What kind of thing are you looking for?*
        ii *What are you looking for?*

'*Bottle*' is standardly analysed as a noun in (8i) but a verb in (8ii), and similarly '*what*' is taken to be an adjective (or determinative, or the like) in (9i) but a pronoun in (9ii). The question then is: does '*bottle*' represent the same word in (8i) as it does in (ii), and similarly for '*what*'? If the answer here and in all analogous cases is 'no', then we can say quite simply that we are classifying words and the parts of speech will be mutually exclusive in the sense that no one word belongs to more than one of them – but we will need to bear in mind that words will not be fully identifiable by their pronunciation or spelling. If on the other hand the answer, here or in some analogous cases, is 'yes', then the classification will apply in the first instance to uses of words rather than to words as such: it will only be with respect to the uses of words that the parts of speech will be mutually exclusive.

Discussions of the problem of identifying words on the paradigmatic axis have tended to focus on the relevance of semantic differences rather than grammatical differences. In lexical semantics a distinction is standardly drawn between **homonymy** and **polysemy**, where homonymy is the relation between two or more different lexical items which are pronounced and spelt the same (or, in the case of lexemes, whose forms are pronounced and spelt the same), while polysemy is the property that holds of a single lexical item that has two or more different senses. Thus there is homonymy between the ***bat*** of *The bats flew down from the belfry* and that of *He struck the ball with the bottom edge of his bat*, whereas *My foot hurts* and *He sat at the foot of the bed* illustrate the polysemy of ***foot***: "nocturnal mouse-like winged quadruped" and "club or instrument for striking the ball in cricket, baseball, etc." are senses of different lexical items, while "terminal part of leg beyond ankle" and "lower end of table, bed, etc." are senses of a single lexical item. The decision as to whether two senses should be associated with distinct homonymous lexical items or with a single polysemous one is made on the basis of semantic and etymological criteria. Thus on the one hand the two senses of ***foot*** that we have illustrated are clearly connected, while those for the homonymous items ***bat*** are not, and on the other hand whereas there is a single etymological source for ***foot***, ***bat*** in the first sense ("nocturnal animal") derives from Middle English *bakke*, which is of Scandinavian origin, but in the second sense ("club") derives from Middle English *batte*, from Late Old English *batt*. Conventional dictionaries have distinct entries for homonyms but cover the different meanings of a polysemous item under a single entry – so that there will be two entries headed '***bat***' (or rather, usually, one headed '***bat***[1]' and another '***bat***[2]' or the like), whereas a single entry for the noun ***foot*** will list both the above senses (and various others too, of course). ***Bat***[2] is in fact also polysemous, for as well as denoting the club it can be applied to the person who uses it, as in *He's a very good bat* "He bats very well", and so on. The etymological criterion and the more intuitive semantic criterion generally yield the same results, which supports the recognition of the distinction as a significant one. In consequence we find a very high measure of agreement among dictionaries as to whether different senses are to be handled under a single entry or separate ones – disagreements arise when the criteria do not, or do not clearly, match, with some dictionaries giving more weight to etymology, others to meaning (for example, some have a single entry covering the *fast* of *He's a fast bowler* and *After the damp weather all the drawers became fast*, others have two: there is a single etymological derivation but the senses are not very close or clearly connected). Where, by contrast, we have words or word uses that differ primarily in grammar rather than in meaning, as in our examples (8) and (9), dictionaries vary quite markedly in their practice. Some, especially the smaller ones, have a single entry for '*bottle*', for '*what*', and so on, while others (such as *Webster's*) have distinct entries whenever there is a difference in the part of speech. Others again do not treat such cases in a uniform way: the *Concise Oxford Dictionary* (7th edn), for example, has separate entries for the noun *hammer* and the verb *hammer*, but a single entry covering '*saw*' as a noun and verb; for '*calm*' it has two entries, one covering the noun (*I admired his calm*), the other the adjective and verb (*The sea is calm*; *You must calm down*), while for '*empty*' one entry covers the adjective and the noun (*The bottle is empty*; *Leave the empties for the milkman*), another the verb (*I'll empty it*). Insofar as a single-entry solution assimilates this phenomenon to polysemy, while a multiple-entry solution assimilates it to homonymy, the former would seem to be preferable in the light of the standard criteria for distinguishing polysemy and homonymy. There is surely something unsatisfactory about handling in the same way the contrast between, on the one hand, the adjective *utter* of *an utter fool* and the verb *utter* of *I didn't utter a word* and, on the other, the adjective *humble* of *He is very humble* and the verb *humble* of *We must humble them* – only the former pair can be properly subsumed under the concept of lexical homonymy.

Be that as it may, our concern here is with the identification not of lexical items but of words, which are grammatical units: the above discussion has been intended to show that there is no standard practice in dictionaries to guide us. From a grammatical point of view, there are good reasons for saying that (8) contains two different words '*bottle*'. We are analysing words, where appropriate, into a lexeme plus one or more inflectional properties: we accordingly need to distinguish two lexemes '*bottle*', one an abstraction from *bottle* and *bottles*, the other from *bottle*, *bottled*, etc. – we will identify them respectively as '*bottle*$_N$' and '*bottle*$_V$'. The word '*bottle*' in (8i) is thus analysable into the lexeme *bottle*$_N$ plus the inflectional property 'singular', while that in (8ii) is analysable into the lexeme *bottle*$_V$ plus the inflectional property 'base form'. Because they contain different grammatical 'components', we will say that they are different words: as the word is a grammatical unit we will treat the grammatical difference, not the phonological and orthographic sameness, as decisive. Similarly '*writing*' and '*disturbing*' represent different words in (3)–(4), '*writing*$_V$' and '*writing*$_N$', and in (5)–(6), '*disturbing*$_V$' and '*disturbing*$_{Adj}$'. For the same reason, we will distinguish the '*bottle*' of (8ii) from that of *I always bottle plums at this time of year*, since the latter is analysable as **bottle**$_V$ plus the inflectional property 'general present'. We could then identify the three words as '*bottle*$_N$', '*bottle*$_{V:Base}$', '*bottle*$_{V:GP}$': the phonological and orthographic sameness of the first and second will then be handled in terms of the morphological process of conversion, while that of the second and third is a matter of syncretism. Conversion is more important than syncretism from the point of view of the present chapter, for it is conversion, not syncretism, that yields pairs of phonologically and orthographically identical words belonging to different parts of speech – and conversion from one part of speech to another is, as we noted earlier, one of the major morphological processes in English, so that we find a vast number of such pairs.

Analysis into lexemes plus inflectional properties is not applicable, however, to the two occurrences of '*what*' in (9) – and in the absence of other sound reasons for distinguishing them I will assume that (9i) and (9ii) contain the same word *what*. (Where it is relevant to specify that we are talking of a particular use, we may write '*what*^{detve}' or '*what*^{pro}': the convention will be that while subscripts distinguish words or lexemes, descriptive superscripts distinguish uses/senses: we might then, on another dimension, differentiate notationally between '*what*^{interrog}', as in (9), and '*what*^{relative}', as in *What money she had was in the bank* or *What remained was mine* – see 12.4.5 for the interrogative/relative contrast; we have of course used numeral superscripts to distinguish lexical homonyms, such as **bat**^{1} vs **bat**^{2}, following standard dictionary practice, but as no one could postulate lexical homonymy in *what* there will be no danger of confusion arising from this convention.) The fact that '*what*' belongs to a different part of speech in the two examples in (9) will not, then, be regarded as sufficient reason for denying that it is the same word. Although we are not allowing phonological and orthographic identity to be the decisive criterion for word identity, we shall not want to override it without good reason. We shall not say, for example, that '*open*' represents a different word in *He won't open the door* (where it is transitive) than in *The door won't open* (where it is intransitive) – or that there are different words both spelt '*hope*' in *I hope it rains* and *I hope for the best* (where the complement is a subordinate clause in the first case, a PP in the second): otherwise we would have a quite pointless proliferation of different words – and a usage quite at variance with our pretheoretical or common-sense idea of what constitutes a single word. The '*what*' example falls somewhere between two cases that we have been at pains to contrast: the case of conversion, illustrated in (8), and the case where a word belonging to a single class occurs with two different functions (one of which may be prototypically associated with another class), illustrated in

(10)   i *He's only a boy*
         ii *They're looking for another boy actor*

If we were to adopt the same kind of analysis for *what* as for *boy*, we would say that it was a pronoun functioning as determiner in (9i) and head in (9ii), but this would obscure significant differences between the *what* and *boy* pairs. As we have seen, *boy* in (10ii) differs quite clearly from a prototypical adjective like *great*, whereas *what* in (9i) does not similarly show clear differences from a prototypical determinative like *the* – and whereas any (non-pronominal) noun can occur in modifier function, not all pronouns would (in the analysis we are considering) be able to function as determiner: the ones which could would have to be specifically indicated in the lexicon. It accordingly seems better not to force *what* into either of the types illustrated respectively by *bottle* and *boy*; if this is correct, we will need to allow for all three of the cases shown in (11).

(11)   Word   Part of speech   Function
                                          (class)

      i *bottle* (8i) vs *bottle* (8ii) different   different   different
      ii *what* (9i) vs *what* (9ii)   same   different   different
      iii *boy* (10i) vs *boy* (10ii)   same   same   different

There will be fewer instances of case (ii) than of the others: it will arise most clearly when relatively small classes are involved, such as determinative and pronoun in this example, rather than with large classes like common nouns and main verbs – for these are characterised by a whole cluster of positive properties, so that instances involving them are likely to be more sharply distinguished and hence to fall into one of the outer cases (i) or (iii). But as so often, we cannot expect that the boundaries between (i) and (ii) or (ii) and (iii) will be clear-cut.

3.3 Associated phrase classes

We have said that we are interpreting 'noun', 'verb', 'adjective', etc., as applying in the first instance to classes of words; derivatively they apply to classes of stems and, in part, to classes of lexemes. In addition, the distinctions are crucial for the classification of units higher in the constituent hierarchy than words, in that we have 'noun phrase', 'verb phrase', 'adjective phrase', and so on, as classes of phrase whose head position is filled respectively by a noun, verb, adjective, and so on: it is a measure of the importance of the part-of-speech distinctions that they pervade the classification of the full range of units in the constituent structure of sentences. In this section I want to look at the relation between the phrase and word classifications, first making some general points, and then contrasting the concept of phrase adopted here with that found in traditional grammar.

Let us begin with a simple example:

(12)   *The third candidate was getting very impatient*

Here *the third candidate* is a noun phrase with the noun *candidate* as head; *was getting* is a verb phrase with the verb *getting* as head; and *very impatient* is an adjective phrase with the adjective *impatient* as head. Within the structure of phrases we distinguish between the **head** element and **dependent** elements: 'modifier', 'complement', 'determiner', etc. are particular types of dependent. The distinction between head and dependent is based on the following factors:

(a) The head element is obligatory, except in the special case of ellipsis; dependents are often (and prototypically) omissible. Consider first the obligatoriness of the head. In (12) *impatient* is obligatory in the most elementary sense that its omission leads to ungrammaticality. *Candidate* could be omitted in ellipsis: *The second candidate was holding forth at great length while the third was getting very impatient*. Here the interpretation and grammatical structure of *the third* derives from its relation to the non-elliptical *the second candidate*: the phrase *the third* will accordingly be described not directly but indirectly, by reference to the fuller phrase *the third candidate*. In such cases we accordingly allow a phrase to consist wholly of dependents, so that *the third* here will be a noun phrase even though it lacks an overt noun head. In this example the missing item, *candidate*, is straightforwardly recoverable from the surrounding linguistic context; whether, and if so how far, we should extend the concept of ellipsis beyond this prototypical case is a difficult question which we will leave for consideration with respect to a number of specific problems in later chapters. Finally, the head of the verb phrase *was getting* is obligatory in a more abstract sense. We can of course omit the word *getting* in the particular example cited as (12), ending up with (13), which is neither ungrammatical nor elliptical:

(13)   *The third candidate was very impatient*

But what we have done here is not simply drop the *getting*: we have changed the function of *was*, so that it is no longer a dependent but is itself the head. As far as the structure of the VP is concerned, then, we haven't omitted the head – we have changed it, and at the same time dropped the dependent: the VP *was getting* in (12) has the structure 'dependent + head', while the VP *was* in (13) consists of the head alone. Thus the grammaticality of (13) does not establish that the head of the VP in (12) is an optional element: it merely demonstrates that in testing for omissibility we must consider not just the grammaticality of the resulting word sequence but also its structure, the relation between its structure and that of the original.

So much for the obligatoriness of the heads in (12); consider now the dependents. *Very* and *third* are straightforwardly omissible and illustrate the simplest type of dependent. In the VP we cannot drop *was* in the same way – but we can omit it if we change the inflection on **get**: *The third candidate got very impatient.* We can say then that the auxiliary verb is optional, and hence has dependent function, in the sense that we can have (non-elliptical) VPs without it – but it has a more important structural role in the VP than *very*, say, in the AdjP, in that its presence or absence before the verb head affects the inflectional form of the latter, and this difference will be relevant to deciding between the various kinds of dependent that we shall need to distinguish. *The*, finally, is not omissible in (12), but we can find many NPs where it is omissible and for this reason we will regard it as a dependent element – compare, for example, *The dogs were howling* and *Dogs were howling*, and so on. Obligatoriness vs optionality does not provide a simple or absolute criterion for distinguishing between heads and dependents, but it certainly takes us a long way towards an analysis in terms of these functions.

(b) Within the structure of the phrase itself, the head often imposes restrictions on what kinds of forms can occur as dependent. For example, within the AdjP, the adjective head *eager* takes a *for* phrase dependent, while *intent* takes an *on* phrase: *He was eager for/*on vengeance* vs *He was intent on/*for vengeance*. Where the head is a form of a lexeme, such restrictions will normally be statable for the lexeme in general rather than for specific forms; for example, we will say that **proud** takes an *of* phrase, **keen** an *on* phrase: *He is proud of his daughter, He is keen on football.* Similarly in the NP: **belief** takes an *in* phrase, **knowledge** an *of* phrase, as in *her belief in herself, her knowledge of the law.* Or, to take an example where the restriction involves not the choice of preposition but the possibility of having a clause dependent of a certain class, nouns like **fact**, **idea**, **belief**, **knowledge** can take what we shall call a 'content clause' as dependent, whereas the great majority of nouns cannot: cf. *He was obsessed with the idea/*book that he was going to die.*

(c) When the phrase combines with one or more other phrases in a larger form, there are commonly restrictions of one sort or another affecting the head but not the dependents. Consider, for example, a clause like *He had gone quite mad*, where (leaving aside the subject *he*) the VP *had gone*, with a form of **go** as head, combines with the AdjP *quite mad*, whose head is a form of **mad**. Restrictions holding over this pair of phrases affect the heads but not the dependents *had* and *quite*. In the first place, there is only a limited set of verbs that can combine with an AdjP in this way: we could not replace **go** here by **murder**, **invent**, **use**, etc. Secondly, and more specifically, where **go** does combine with an AdjP we find severe restrictions on the head adjective: **mad**, **black**, **sour** and the like are permitted, but hardly *indecent*, *careless, intelligent.* But no similar restrictions hold in *He had gone quite mad* over **go** and the dependent *quite* or over **mad** and **have**.

(d) We have noted that there is often not a one-to-one correlation between functions and classes; in the light of the distinction we have now drawn we can say more specifically that it is only dependent functions that can be 'realised' by members of different classes. For example, in *a man eager for recognition, a man with black hair, a man I hadn't met before* the noun head *man* is modified by an AdjP in the first, a PP in the second and a clause in the third. Or, to take a different subtype of dependent, determiner rather than modifier, the determiner in *this car* is what we are calling a determinative, while that in *my father's car* is a PossP. Similarly in the structure of the AdjP: an adjective like **proud**, for example, can take as complement either a PP, as in *proud of her achievements*, or a clause, as in *proud that she had achieved so much.* The head, by contrast, will be realised by members of a single class: the head of an NP will be a noun, the head of a VP a verb and so on; if this were not so, we could not of course incorporate the part-of-speech labels into our phrase-class labels in the way that we have been doing.

So far we have been working with a simple distinction between a phrase and the word which is its head, between noun phrase and noun, and so on. It seems clear, however, that we cannot get by with just these two hier-archical 'levels'. Consider, for example, the sentence

(14)   *A Ministry of Defence official had denied the claim categorically*

It is arguable whether the constituent structure of *a Ministry of Defence official* is as shown in (15) or in (16):

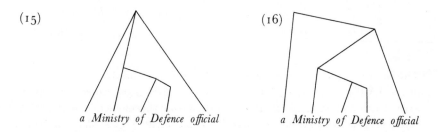

(15)   a Ministry of Defence official   (16)   a Ministry of Defence official

but what is not in doubt is that *Ministry of Defence* forms a constituent, and that *a Ministry of Defence* does not, for *a* is determiner to *official* or *Ministry of Defence official* not to *Ministry of Defence.* Now *Ministry of Defence*, which functions as dependent (more particularly, modifier) of *official* is clearly not a word, not a noun. But nor does it belong to the same syntactic class as the whole expression *a Ministry of Defence official*, which, in accordance with standard usage, we are calling a noun phrase. It differs from an NP in both functional potential and internal structure: it cannot occur as subject, complement, etc. and cannot take a determiner (we have *an official from the Ministry of Defence*, but we cannot say **a the Ministry of Defence official*). *Ministry of Defence* is thus intermediate between noun and noun phrase. There is no generally recognised term for it, and I shall not need to introduce one here, for it is a much less important category than noun and noun phrase. Nor shall I argue for the choice of one of (15) and (16) rather than the other – I shall simply adopt (15) for convenience of presentation, for (15) allows us to continue with our assumption that an NP has a noun as head (in (16), by contrast, the head of the NP is *Ministry of Defence official*, which belongs to our unnamed category: in (16) the noun *official* is the 'ultimate' but not the 'immediate' head of the NP).

The same kind of issue arises with phrases headed, immediately or ultimately, by a verb. A partial structure for *The official had denied the claim*, assuming the analysis presented in Ch. 1, is as follows:

(17)

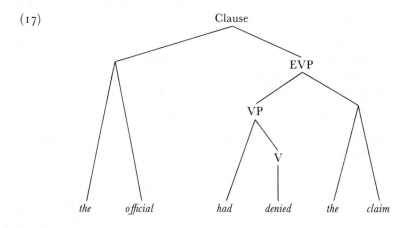

The (main) verb *denied* is head of the VP *had denied*, and this in turn is head of the EVP (extended verb phrase) *had denied the claim*, by criteria given above: although *the claim* cannot be omitted from this particular sentence, it is the verb, as we have noted, that determines whether the clause must or may contain an object (compare *The official had spoken*, where there is no dependent within the EVP), and the dependent *the claim* can be replaced by one of a different class, a subordinate clause rather than an NP (as in *The official had denied that there had been any casualties*). It is also arguable that within the clause construction the predicate *had denied the claim* is head, and the subject *the official* dependent. Although the subject is an obligatory element in kernel clauses, so that the presence or absence of a subject is not determined by the verb, there are two related factors indicating that the predicate is head. First, the predicate position is filled by members of a single class, the EVP, while the subject is not invariably an NP but can be a subordinate clause or, occasionally, a PP (see 2.2.2). Second, which form-class we can have as subject does depend on the choice of predicate, usually on the verb: while any verb can take an NP as subject, only certain verbs (e.g. ***please*** but not ***enjoy***) can take a subordinate clause (*That he had been so thoughtful pleased/ *enjoyed them*) – and more specifically the verb determines what subtype of subordinate clause is allowed (e.g. ***puzzle*** can take an interrogative subordinate clause subject, as in *Why he was so thin puzzled us all*, whereas ***prove*** allows only a declarative: *That/ *why he was so thin proved the point*). For these reasons, I will regard subject and predicate as special cases of the more general functions dependent and head respectively. In (17), then, *had denied the claim* is head of the whole clause, *had denied* is head of *had denied the claim* and *denied* is head of *had denied*: it is in this sense that we can speak of *denied* as ultimate head of the whole clause. From this point of view, the term 'clause' is simply the name for a particular class of phrase, one at the next higher level than the EVP in the hierarchy of phrases with a verb as ultimate head – a 'further extended verb phase', as it were.

As I have said, the term 'extended verb phrase' is itself not one that will be found in the literature: in part this is due to the practice inherited from traditional grammar of calling a form like *had denied* a verb (which saves 'verb phrase' for *had denied the claim*), and in part it is due to the fact that many grammarians will assign a somewhat different IC structure. Thus in addition to (18i) – which is the same as (17) above save for the class labels – one will also find (ii) and (iii), not to mention other possibilities:

(18) i

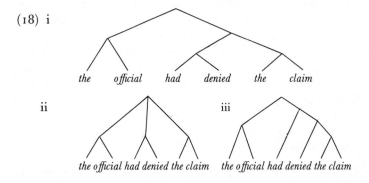

(ii) simply omits that level in the hierarchy which I have called the EVP, so that the clause is described immediately in terms of the functions subject, predicator, object, etc. In (iii) *had* is treated as entering into construction not with *denied* alone but with *denied the claim*: since *had denied* is not here a constituent, the term 'VP' is freed for application to *had denied the claim*, thus again, at the next level down from the clause. The present book is not the place to discuss the relative merits of (18i–iii), but the reader should be aware that this is an area where differences in analysis will be found; as we noted in the last chapter, some grammatical categories are more highly justified than others (no other functional category in English, for example, being characterised by such a cluster of distinctive properties as the subject), and this is naturally reflected in the quite sharply varying degrees of consensus about them to be found among structural linguists. In an introductory book, it is of course better to give priority to the more strongly motivated aspects of grammatical analysis. (And although I have adopted (18i), which incorporates a constituent with the traditional function of predicate, I will not make much use of the EVP category and will handle its internal structure within the discussion of clause structure in the manner of those who adopt (18ii).)

Because dependents are often omissible, we have constructions consisting of a head alone, and in such cases a single form will be a constituent at two places in the constituent hierarchy, a member of two different classes. For example, in *Dogs were howling* we say that *dogs* is both an NP (functioning as subject of the clause) and a noun (functioning as head of the NP). Why do we do this, instead of saying that the noun functions directly as subject of the clause? There are a number of points to be made in answer to this question.

(a) The most important and most general point is that it would in fact gratuitously complicate the description of NP structure if we insisted that it always contain at least two elements. We shall distinguish several different kinds of dependent, some of which are seen in combination in an example like *the enormous debts that he had incurred*: here *the* is a 'determiner', *enormous* a 'pre-head modifier' and *that he had incurred* a 'post-head modifier' (see 6.4 for the distinction between determiners and modifiers). Each of these dependents is separately optional in NP structure: we can have *enormous debts that he had incurred, the enormous debts, the debts that he had incurred, the debts*, and so on. There is then no reason to say that NP structure requires the presence of some dependent: as each kind of dependent is optional, special ad hoc provision would need to be made to block the case where the head is unaccompanied by a dependent of any kind.

(b) A closely related point, but one that is of less general application than the first, is that in the particular example we are considering – *Dogs were howling* – the word *dogs* has the potentiality for expansion by means of the kinds of dependent we find in NP structure: we could have *the dogs, some ferocious dogs, dogs that had been overfed*, and so on. We can simplify the description by handling the properties of *dogs* under two headings, noun phrase and noun; as a noun phrase it is in paradigmatic contrast with *the dogs, some ferocious dogs*, etc., and as a noun it is in contrast with *foxes, wolves, dog, fox*, etc. I distinguish point (a) from point (b), in that (a) is an argument for accepting that an NP may consist of a head alone, while (b) is an argument for accepting *dogs* as a particular instance of this construction. Examples like *dogs*, where such expansion is possible, illustrate the clearest case of a construction consisting of a head alone, but once a certain construction of this kind has been established on the basis of an argument like (a) we shall not require that each individual head should allow for expansion by means of dependents. For example, the 'relative pronoun' *which*, as in [*He's coming on Good Friday,*] *which falls on 4 April this year* cannot take any dependents, but we will still say that it is an NP consisting of a head alone.

(c) A third point is that if we did not allow *dogs* to be an NP as well as a noun, we would have to say for each of the functional positions subject, object, complement of a preposition, and so on, that it could be filled either by an NP or by a noun: it is simpler to say that they can be filled by an NP and then cater for the contrast between *dogs* on the one hand, *the dogs, some ferocious dogs*, etc. on the other, at just one place in our description, namely the section dealing with NP structure. This then is one reason why we will take the relative pronoun *which* as an NP, for as well as occurring as subject, as in the above example, it can occur as object ([*He ordered the other book,*] *which he himself had edited*), complement of a preposition ([*They gave him another car,*] *for which they paid $1000*), and so on. Notice, by contrast, that the ability of a subordinate clause to function as subject, object, or complement of a preposition (*Whether Tom was the culprit* [*is unclear*], [*I don't know*] *whether Tom was the culprit*, [*There was some doubt as to*] *whether Tom was the culprit*) does not establish that such clauses are also NPs. The subordinate clause case differs from the *dogs* case in two respects. First, *whether Tom was the culprit* clearly does not have the internal structure of an NP: it does not have a noun as head accompanied by various dependents – it is precisely by virtue of its internal structure that we classify it as a clause. Second, we could not in fact handle the choice between forms like *whether Tom was the culprit* and, say, *the reason*, at a single place in the grammar, the NP section, for whether the subject or object of a clause can be a subordinate clause depends on properties of the higher clause: **be** *unclear* allows a subordinate clause as subject while **be** *green* does not, **know** allows one as object, while **eat** does not, and so on. This is quite different from the choice between *dogs* and *the dogs* or *some ferocious dogs*, which doesn't depend in an analogous way on the properties of the clause in which the NP occurs.

These are, then, the main factors – though certainly not the only ones – which will lead us to allow a word to constitute a phrase (or, more generally, to allow a single form to occur as a unit at two or more levels in the constituent hierarchy). But it does not follow that every word in a sentence will be analysed as the head of a phrase of the corresponding class. In *Dogs were howling* and *The dogs were howling* the noun *dogs* is head of a noun phrase, but we shall not analyse the determinative *the* in the second as the head of a determinative phrase. Nor shall we say of *He had already left, however* that *however* is the head of an adverb phrase. Analyses such as these will be found in the literature, but they have little to commend them: we must beware of analysing the language in a way that makes it out to have a more uniform, neat and regular organisation than in fact it has. We will thus regard *the* as entering into NP structure and *however* into clause structure directly as words. The decision as to whether we have a word functioning as head of a phrase without dependents (as in the *dogs* example) or one functioning itself as dependent in a different kind of phrase (as with *the*) will thus be made on the merits of the particular case, taking account of factors like (a)–(c) above, rather than by imposing a general prohibition on one or other of these two types of analysis.

The senses in which I am employing the terms 'phrase' and 'clause' are significantly different from those they have in traditional grammar, and to conclude this section we will look briefly into these differences and their relevance to the part-of-speech classification. First, the 'phrase'. As the term is most standardly used in traditional grammar, a phrase has the following properties:

(a) It is a group of two or more words – traditionally a phrase cannot consist of just one word, which is one reason why I have been concerned to show why one-word phrases are theoretically justifiable within the framework adopted here.

(b) It does not contain a 'finite' verb – so that *who came to dinner* in *The man who came to dinner stole the silver*, for example, will not be a phrase (it is, rather, a clause).

(c) It is functionally equivalent to a single word, and will thus be classified according to the part of speech of the kind of word to which it is equivalent. Consider such examples as

(19)   *She bought it from a man with a French accent*
(20)   *She spoke with a French accent*

In (19) *with a French accent* functions as modifier to a noun (*man*), a function characteristically performed by an adjective: it would thus here be traditionally analysed as an adjective phrase (or 'adjectival phrase'). In (20), on the other hand, it is modifying a verb (*spoke*) and is accordingly traditionally analysed as an adverb phrase (or 'adverbial phrase'). Notice, however, that *a French accent* is not normally treated as a noun phrase in traditional grammar: as observed above, the noun *accent* itself would be taken as the object of *with*, with *a* and *French* being simply subordinate to the noun. Thus the idea of functional equivalence in this condition (c) is not to be understood as including cases where a group of words can be regarded as an expansion of one of the words in the group.

In the approach we are adopting in this book, by contrast, the term 'phrase', and its relation to 'word', is to be understood by reference to the constituent structure assigned to sentences. Words occur as the ultimate syntactic constituents of sentences, whereas phrases occupy positions at higher levels in the hierarchy. There is a good deal of variation among structural linguists with respect to the more specific understanding of the term 'phrase': here I shall restrict its application to those higher level units that have a structure involving a head element, alone or in combination with one or more dependents. Not all constructions have this kind of structure: most obviously, coordinate constructions (such as *black and white, Jill or her husband*) do not. Phrases are then classified primarily according to the type of head they have, in the manner outlined above – and the reason why I restrict the term 'phrase' to head or head + dependent(s) constructions is that it is only in such cases that this type of classification is directly applicable. Notice, for example, that in *He was very tired and in a terrible temper* the 'predicative complement' position is filled by a coordination of an AdjP and a PP, but the coordinate expression as a whole, *very tired and in a terrible temper*, cannot be assigned to either of these phrase classes.

It will be apparent, then, that none of the traditional conditions (a)–(c) applies to the conception of the phrase adopted here. Condition (a) we have already discussed at some length. As for (b), I am taking the view (though it is certainly one that many would dispute) that the subject + predicate construction, although differing in important ways from the most proto-typical dependent + head construction, can nevertheless be subsumed under that very general construction-type, and hence that a clause is a kind of phrase – one with a verb as 'ultimate' head. And as for (c), although we will certainly regard *with a French accent* as a phrase in (19) and (20), it will be classified in both as a preposition phrase: the differences are adequately handled by saying that the phrase is functioning in (19) as modifier in NP structure and in (20) as modifier in clause (or EVP) structure – there is no reason to posit, in addition, a difference in the class of the phrase itself.[3]

Let us now turn, finally, to the clause. There are two points to be made here. The first concerns the delimitation of the category of clause. As I have

---

[3] Many traditional grammars do in fact call it a prepositional phrase as well as an adjectival or adverbial one – but then of course the sense in which a phrase is prepositional is quite different from that in which it is adjectival or adverbial. We have seen that the parts of speech can be regarded as mutually exclusive, as applied to word occurrences, and we will take the corresponding phrase-classes to be mutually exclusive in the same way.

implied, traditional grammar usually makes it a defining property of a clause that it contain a finite verb: only finite verbs were regarded as fully or strictly verbal, the non-finite forms being verbal nouns or verbal adjectives. From the point of view adopted here, where we have rejected the concept of a verbal noun or verbal adjective, there is no motivation for restricting the application of the term 'clause' in the traditional way. It is true the prototypical clause contains a tensed verb (see 12.3 for the relation between 'tensed' and 'finite'), but we can find essentially the same syntagmatic relations between the constituents of a form containing a non-tensed verb. Compare, for example:

(21)   i *He resented that there were so many professors on the committee*
         ii *He resented there being so many professors on the committee*
(22)   i *All he wants is that you should enjoy yourself*
         ii *All he wants is for you to enjoy yourself*

Given that we are regarding the clause as a kind of phrase a certain number of hierarchical steps above the verb, its ultimate head – three steps according to the constituent structure analysis in (18i) – we shall treat *there being so many professors on the committee* as a clause in (21ii), having the same structure (save for the initial *that*) as *that there were so many professors on the committee* in (21i), and analogously in (22). More difficult to decide is how necessary it is for a clause to have a subject. We have noted that the subject is an obligatory element in kernel (and other prototypical) clauses: where no subject is present, can we nevertheless still have a clause or will the phrase be simply an EVP? As we have argued that we should not rule out the possibility of a construction consisting of a head alone, there would seem to be no reason in principle why we should not allow for a subjectless clause. The strongest candidates for such an analysis are constructions where a subject could in fact be added, as in imperatives like *Be careful* (cf. *You be careful!*) or subordinate constructions like *To do that* [*would be unwise*] (cf. *For us to do that* [*would be unwise*]). Where there is no possibility of such expansion, as in [*She tried*] *to get elected to the committee* (cf. *[She tried] for him to get elected to the committee*), the case for saying that the EVP is head of a subjectless clause (rather than that it enters directly, qua EVP, into construction with **try** or whatever) is much weaker. However, as we are here assigning little importance to the EVP category, subsuming the description of EVP structure under our account of clause structure, we will make the simplifying assumption that all these subjectless constructions are clauses – but with the understanding that this analysis might well need to be revised in the light of a fuller investigation of the conditions under which a construction may consist of a head unaccompanied by any dependents.

The second point has to do with the classification of subordinate clauses. Traditionally these are, like phrases, regarded as functionally equivalent to single words, and classified accordingly as noun clauses, adjective (or 'adjectival') clauses and adverb (or 'adverbial') clauses. The three classes are illustrated in (23)–(25) respectively:

(23)   *That he finished first was no surprise*
(24)   *This is the piece that he finished first*
(25)   *He ran so fast that he finished first*

The subordinate clause *that he finished first* functions in (23) as subject of the larger clause, in (24) as modifier in NP structure and in (25) as modifier in AdvP structure. This case, however, differs from the traditional classification of phrases discussed above. There we suggested that we don't need to assign *with a French accent* to different classes in (19) and (20), for we have said all there is to say about the differences when we have given its function, whereas here we certainly have not fully accounted for the difference between *that he finished first* in (23) and (24) when we have said that it is subject in (23), modifier in NP structure in (24). In (23), *that he finished first* corresponds to the kernel clause *He finished first*: the subordination is reflected simply in the addition of the subordinating conjunction *that*. In (24), by contrast, it is comparable to some such kernel clause as *He finished the piece first*: the subordination involves here not just the addition of the conjunction *that* but the loss of the object (this being recoverable from the NP, *the piece that he had finished first*, in which it is embedded).[4] Notice in this connection that whereas in (23) we could replace *that he finished first* by *that he disappeared*, in (24) we could not: while **finish** can occur either with or without an object, **disappear** cannot take an object, so that there is no kernel clause **He disappeared the piece* from which we could derive the kind of subordinate clause we need in (24). It follows, then, that the difference between the subordinate clauses in (23) and (24) is not simply a matter of their function within the larger construction containing them, but also involves their internal properties, so that this time we shall want to recognise a difference in class as well as in function.

Nevertheless, the appropriate classification of subordinate clauses is not, I believe, one based on functional similarities to nouns, adjectives and adverbs. There are several reasons for not taking over the traditional classification into noun clauses, adjective clauses and adverb clauses. In the first place, the adverb clause class is again too heterogeneous to be useful, covering such examples as [*He set out*] *although it was snowing*, [*We live*] *where the road crosses the river*, [*He has more money*] *than she has*, etc., as well as the *that he finished first* of (25) and the like: since we want the classification

---

[4] Traditionally *that* would be analysed as the object of *finished* in (24), and it would accordingly be regarded as a pronoun rather than a conjunction. The contrast between this analysis and the one I have adopted will be discussed in 12.4.2: it is not relevant to the point being made here.

to complement, not merely duplicate, the functional analysis, a class covering such a diverse range of clauses gets us nowhere: we need more specific classes, such as 'comparative clause' for *than she has*, and so on. Secondly, there are many places where the functional analysis does cater fully for the difference, so that there is then no more need for a class distinction than in the case of our *with a French accent* example. For example *if he is sentenced to prison* is functioning as modifier in *I shall resign if he is sentenced to prison* and complement in *The only circumstances under which I shall resign will be if he is sentenced to prison* – but there are no other differences, and hence we gain nothing by saying that it is an adverb clause in the first but a noun clause in the second. Similarly, while I argued that there are internal differences between the subordinate clauses of (23) and (24), we do not find similar differences between those in (23) and (25), so that it would be simply duplicating the functional distinction to assign *that he finished first* to distinct classes in (23) and (25). Thirdly, functional analogy with the parts of speech provides a somewhat uncertain criterion for classification in a number of cases. To which class, noun clause or adjective clause, should we assign the subordinate clause of examples like *The suggestion that he might be lying was very worrying* – is its role like that of a noun (in 'apposition' to *suggestion*) or an adjective (modifying or 'limiting' *suggestion*)? Curme handles this type under the heading of adjective clauses (1947: 162), but says at another point (1947: 158) that they are noun clauses (which is, in fact, how most traditional grammars classify them). Or again which class should *who had done his first degree at Edinburgh* belong to in *John, who had done his first degree at Edinburgh, was now enrolled for a Ph.D at Leeds*? It is standardly taken to be an adjective clause, but could we not say that its role is at least as similar to that of a noun (or NP) as to that of an adjective? Compare *John, a graduate of Edinburgh, was now enrolled for a Ph.D at Leeds*. And it is even less clear that the subordinate clause of *I am getting grey and wrinkled, which is not particularly cheering* (another of Curme's examples) is adjective-like. Lastly, as we are regarding a clause as a kind of phrase, it will be more consistent with the principles underlying our classification of phrases if we avoid using the terms 'noun clause', 'adjective clause' or 'adverb clause' for phrases which do not have nouns, adjective and adverbs as their (immediate or ultimate) head. I shall accordingly classify *that he finished first* as a 'content clause' in (23) and (25) and as a 'relative clause' in (24); we will take up the issue of the classification of subordinate clauses more fully in 12.3.

3.4 Open and closed classes

Word and lexeme classes fall into two groups, commonly called **open** classes and **closed** classes. Of the traditional parts of speech, the noun, verb, adjective and adverb are open classes, while the pronoun, preposition, conjunction and interjection are closed. The open classes have very large numbers of members, while the closed ones are highly restricted in membership; a large grammar could be expected to list all members of the closed classes (they will, in effect, be grammatical items in the sense of 1.8), whereas for the open ones we would be referred to the dictionary.

Open classes are so called because they readily accommodate the addition of new members as the vocabulary of the language adapts itself to the changing needs of its speakers. The two main avenues for the introduction of new members are: (i) borrowing from other languages (as with the noun **sputnik**, for example); (ii) the use of lexical-morphological processes of the type discussed in Ch. 1 – for each of the open classes we find a number of such processes, some of a relatively high degree of productivity, such as the formation of deverbal adjectives in *-able*, de-adjectival verbs in *-ise*, de-adjectival adverbs in *-ly*, and so on. A third avenue for adding to the membership of a class, very rarely used in comparison with the other two, is the creation of a new simple stem from the phonological resources of the language (as with *nylon*, coined in the 1930s).

Closed classes, by contrast, are highly resistant to the addition of new members (though the term 'closed' should not be taken to imply that such expansion is strictly impossible). A topical illustration of the difficulty of adding to the closed classes is to be found in the failure to satisfy the widely perceived need for a singular personal pronoun to replace the **he** of examples like *If any student wishes to take part in the seminar, he should consult his tutor*: many people understandably find it offensive for **he** to be used for a non-specific member of a set containing both males and females. We can of course say *he or she* or reformulate using plural NPs, but it would be much handier to have a singular pronoun neutral as to sex and distinct from both **he** and **she**. The existing personal pronouns all have simple stems, so that there is no morphological process appropriate for filling the gap and attempts to create a new simple stem (such as *thon*) have not been successful.[5]

---

[5] An alternative to filling the gap by introducing a new stem, whether simple or complex, is to extend the use of an existing pronoun. And of course there is already a pronoun that is commonly used with the sense "he or she", as well as with its more central sense, namely **they**. This use of **they** is particularly frequent where the 'antecedent' is an 'indefinite pronoun' like *anyone, someone, everyone*, etc. (as in *If anyone feels aggrieved, they should say so*), but is certainly not restricted to such cases; it has a long tradition, so that, unlike the use of compounds in *-person* (*spokesperson, chairperson*, etc.), the title *Ms*, and so on, it is not specifically related to the feminist movement – and doubtless occurs in the speech of many who have no sympathy with that movement. However, there is also a long tradition, fostered by the teaching of prescriptive grammar, of condemning this use of **they** as 'incorrect' on the grounds that it violates the rule that a pronoun agree in number with its antecedent. It is for this reason that we can properly speak of a 'gap' here – not in the language as a whole, but in that variety that is fully accepted as standard.

The open–closed distinction applies to secondary classes (subclasses) as well as the primary ones: transitive verbs and auxiliary verbs, for example, are respectively open and closed subclasses of verb. (We can accordingly speak of the pronoun as a closed class independently of whether it is regarded as a primary class, as in traditional grammar, or as a subclass of the noun, as suggested here.) As we shall see, items belonging to closed classes or subclasses typically present more difficulty for the analyst than open class items: disagreements among grammarians over the part-of-speech classification generally involve the treatment of closed class items.

Of the four open primary classes, the adverb differs from the others in having only a small number of members with morphologically simple lexical stems – a high proportion of adverbs are formed from adjectives by -*ly* suffixation. Thus the great majority of simple stems are verbs, nouns or adjectives, and for this reason these may be regarded as the three major parts of speech. And of these three, the verb and noun classes are of special status in that all kernel clauses contain at least one verb and one noun; moreover, phrases headed (immediately or ultimately) by verbs or nouns are of much greater structural complexity than those headed by the other parts of speech. As we noted earlier, the traditional scheme of definitions for the parts of speech treats the verb and noun as more basic than the others in that they are defined independently of the rest, while the definitions of adjectives and adverbs make reference to verbs and nouns. Finally, of the verb and the noun, it is the former that functions as ultimate head of the clause, with the most central kind of sentence having the form of a clause: we can accordingly think of the verb as having the highest ranking in importance in the organisation of the grammar – a view reflected in the etymology of the term 'verb' which derives from the Latin for "word".[6]

This ranking of the parts of speech, together with the distinction I have drawn between kernel and non-kernel clauses, provides the basis for the organisation of the descriptive chapters of the book, which now follow. I begin with verbs and verb phrases, and then move up the hierarchy to the clause, though I confine my attention at this stage to kernel clauses. Chapters 6 and 7 are devoted to nouns (including pronouns) and the phrases they head, and the following, much shorter, chapter deals with adjectives and their associated phrases. Chapter 9 then attempts to clarify the distinction between the three major parts of speech. Chapter 10 covers the remaining parts of speech – except that I shall not say anything more about interjections, which are integrated into sentence structure in only the most tenuous way. The final four chapters then take up the clause again, examining the main classes of non-kernel construction.

---

[6] Note that this etymology explains the sense of the term 'verbal' introduced in 1.5: the verbal component of an utterance covers all the words in it, not just the verbs.

FURTHER READING

Discussion of the traditional parts of speech can be found in Lyons 1968:§7.6, Gleason 1965:Ch. 6, Palmer 1971:§2.3, Matthews 1967 – and of word-classes in English in Crystal 1967 (which also deals in some detail with the contrast between open and closed classes). For an alternative view of the relation between word and lexeme classes, see Lyons 1981b:§4.3. On periphrastic forms, see Matthews 1981:55–9, 274–8. On the relation between phrase- and word-class, see Lyons 1968:327–32 and the current approach known as 'X-bar' syntax as presented in, for example, Jackendoff 1977. On non-finite constructions, see Koster & May 1982 (infinitives), Schachter 1976, Horn 1975 (gerunds), Matthews 1981:Ch. 8. On the distinction between homonymy and polysemy, see Lyons 1977:§13.4, 1981a:43–7. The term 'content clause' is taken from Jespersen 1909–49, Pt III:23, but is generalised to cover interrogatives, etc., as well as declaratives; the standard term in transformational grammar is 'complement clause'.

4
Verbs and verb phrases

4.1 Verbs

The most central members of the word-class verb have the following two properties:

(a) Inflection. They are tensed: they have one or other of the inflectional properties 'past tense' and 'present tense'. Thus in *He lived in Sydney* and *He lives in Sydney* the words *lived* and *lives* are prototypical verbs. In the present tense the verb – again prototypically – agrees with the subject as 3rd person singular vs general (i.e. not 3rd person singular): *He lives in Sydney* vs *I/you/we/they live in Sydney*.

(b) Functional potential. They function as the ultimate head of the clause (with the EVP and VP as intervening categories), as explained in the last chapter.

It is tensed verbs that are most sharply distinct from words belonging to other parts of speech: this is why non-tensed verbs may be regarded as less central members of the class. As we have seen, the non-tensed forms (more specifically the non-finite forms of the traditional paradigm) are traditionally spoken of as verbal nouns or verbal adjectives, and although we are rejecting that kind of description there is no doubt that they have closer affinities with nouns and adjectives than do tensed verbs. We thus take tensed forms as the prototype and include other words within the class on the basis of their functional resemblance to the prototype. The status of a non-tensed word as a verb is then clearest when it is functioning as ultimate head of a tensed clause as in *He was writing the letter*. Although *writing* is not itself tensed, it is functioning as head of a VP that is – the tense inflection is located in the *was*; there is a direct paradigmatic contrast between *was writing* and *wrote*, so that the inclusion of the heads *writing* and *wrote* within the same primary word-class presents no problems. In non-tensed constructions like [*The one*] *writing the letter* [*was her brother*] we shall take *writing* to be a verb rather than an adjective on the grounds that it takes the same kind of dependents (at the next higher level in the constituent structure hierarchy than the VP) as a prototypical verb – that *writing* resembles *wrote*

124

in selecting a 'complement' like *the letter* (i.e. an object), and so on: we will take up this issue in some detail in Ch. 9.

   The above discussion is concerned with the classification of words: as we have said, we take the part-of-speech classification as applying in the first instance to words, and then derivatively to lexemes. Turning now to the latter, we can characterise the central members of the lexeme-class verb in terms of their inflectional paradigms and the functional potential of their forms.

(a) Inflection. They have tensed forms; more specifically the great majority of verbs have the six inflectional forms discussed in 2.4 and repeated here summarily with examples from **take**.

(1)

	Tensed		Non-tensed		
Past	Present		Base form	*-ing* form	*-en* form
	3rd pers sg	General			
took	*takes*	*take*	*take*	*taking*	*taken*

Morphologically, the base form is the lexical stem, and the general present tense is identical with it – recall our earlier discussion.

   The *-ing* form is wholly regular, being derived from the lexical stem by suffixation of *-ing* (which has /ɪŋ/, /ɪn/ and /ɪŋg/ as socially or regionally distinguishable variant pronunciations). In regular verbs, the past tense and *-en* form are syncretised, being derived from the lexical stem by the rule given in 1.7; for details of the rules for irregular verbs, the reader should consult the works mentioned in the 'Further reading' recommendations at the end of this chapter. The 3rd person singular present is formed in the following way:

(2)   i If the lexical stem ends in a 'sibilant', i.e. /s, z, ʃ, ʒ, tʃ or dʒ/, add /ɪz/ or /əz/ (again there are variant pronunciations), as in *kisses, watches*

   ii If the lexical stem otherwise ends in a 'voiceless consonant', add /s/, as in *hops, walks*

   iii Otherwise add /z/, as in *lobs, runs, sees*

The only irregularities here involve the lexemes **be** (*is*), **have** (*has*), **do** (*does*, /dʌz/) and **say** (*says*, /sɛz/), the last two irregularities not being apparent from the spelling.

   A few verbs have forms other than those given in (1). The 'operators' (see 2.4 and below) have negative forms in the tensed part of the paradigm: *hadn't, hasn't, isn't, shouldn't, won't,* etc.; the regular negatives are formed from the corresponding positives by simple suffixation of /nt/, while the irregular ones involve some change to the stem to which it is attached, as in *don't, can't, won't, shan't, mustn't* (though again the stem-modification in the last example, the loss of final /t/, is not reflected in the spelling). In addition, the verb **be** has extra person–number forms: *was* and *were* instead of a single past tense form, *am* and *are* instead of the normal general present tense form.

There are also some verbs which lack certain of the forms shown in (1). The most important are the modal auxiliaries **can**, **may**, **must**, etc., which have no non-tensed forms and have no contrast in the present tense between 3rd person singular and general forms. The lack of non-tensed forms is a matter of **defectiveness**: the forms are simply missing from the paradigms and as a result the verbs cannot occur in constructions where these forms are required. Thus we cannot say **I'd like to can ski*, for this construction requires a base form (cf. *I'd like to be able to ski*). Nor can we say **I don't anticipate musting pay any more*, for here we need an *-ing* form (cf. *I don't anticipate having to pay any more*). The lack of contrasting 3rd person singular and general present tense forms is, by contrast, a matter of **neutralisation**: the modals have instead a single present tense form which cannot be equated with either of those in (1), but which occurs both in constructions normally requiring a 3rd person singular (*He takes it, He can take it*) and in those normally requiring a general present (*They take it, They can take it*). We will refer to *can, may, must* simply as the (positive) present tense form: there are no person–number properties involved. In addition, one or two modals, such as **must**, are defective in lacking a past tense form (*I had to leave before he finished* but not **I musted leave before he finished*). There are a few defective verbs besides the modals, though we will mention only one more. **Beware** has only a base form: the defectiveness is clearly related to the fact that the lexical stem is formed by compounding of the verb stem *be* and the bound stem *ware*. We include **beware** with the verb class, as a very peripheral member of course, mainly because the one form it does have can occur in some of the major constructions where we find the base forms of prototypical members of the class – e.g. in imperative clauses like *Beware of the dog* or after the infinitival *to*, as in *I warned him to beware of the dog*.

Defectiveness is a property of lexemes: we shall not invoke this concept where not all forms of a lexeme occur in a certain use of it. For example, the *-en* form of **have** does not occur in the 'perfect auxiliary' use (in *had gone*, for example, *had* can only be the past tense form), but we shall not speak of defectiveness here since there is no reason to regard the perfect auxiliary as a different lexeme from the **have** that is used as a main verb and which does have an *-en* form *had* (as in *He has had enough*).

(b) Functional potential. For the great majority of verb lexemes their forms can function as the ultimate head of a clause – and the immediate head of a VP. The only exceptions here are the modal auxiliaries, whose forms function only as dependents in VP structure: see §2 below.

Before turning to the VP, let us briefly consider the lexical morphology of verbs. In general the processes used in the formation of verb stems are fewer and typically less productive than those used in the formation of nouns. We will confine our attention here to affixation, conversion and compounding/back-formation.

(a) Class-changing affixation. There are a few suffixes used to form verb stems from stems of other classes. Much the most productive is *-ise (-ize)*, which forms denominal verbs like *hospitalise* or de-adjectival verbs like *popularise*. Others are *-ify* (*beautify, simplify*) and *-en* (*sadden, widen*). There are also a few prefixes, but of very low productivity: *be-* (*becalm*), *de-* (*debug*), *en-/em-* (*enlarge, endanger, empower*), *un-* (*unhorse*).

(b) Class-preserving affixation. Affixes used to form verb stems from more elementary verb stems are prefixes: they include *co-* (*co-exist*), *counter-* (*counteract*), *de-* (*desegregate*), *dis-* (*dislike*), *fore-* (*foretell*), *mal-* (*maltreat*), *mis-* (*misbehave*), *out-* (*outlive*), *over-* (*overcharge*), *re-* (*re-enter*), *sub-* (*sublet*), *under-* (*undercharge*). Notice, however, that although there is here no change in primary class, some of these prefixes may change the secondary class, by affecting the type of 'complements' the verb may take: for example, **live** could not be substituted for **outlive** in *He outlived his rivals*, nor **act** for **counteract** in *This counteracted the effect of the tax reductions*.

(c) Conversion. The most frequent process forming denominal verbs is conversion, as in the *bottle* example that we have mentioned several times. There are many such verbs, showing a variety of semantic relations to the underlying noun: *brake, corner, cripple, elbow, father, grease, peel, plaster, ship,* etc. Less productive is the conversion of adjectives into verbs, as in *calm, empty, humble, soundproof*.

(d) Compounding/back-formation. Compounding especially is vastly less frequent in verbs than in nouns and indeed it is highly questionable whether the relatively few stems that look like compounds are in fact to be so analysed: we suggested in 1.6 that forms like *stage-manage* are more properly regarded as deriving by back-formation from the noun compound *stage-manager* than by the compounding of *stage* and *manage*. The resultant 'pseudo-compounds' are of two main kinds. In one, exemplified in *house-keep* and *lip-read*, the semantic role of the nominal element is analogous to that of a syntactic object (cf. *They kept house for us*); in the other, exemplified in *chain-smoke* or *day-dream* the analogous syntactic construction consists of verb + PP (cf. *He dreams during the day*).

4.2 Structure of the verb phrase

The verb phrase consists of a head element, obligatory except in cases of ellipsis, and optionally one or more dependents. In [*He*] *may have seen* [*her*], for example, we take *may* and *have* as dependents. The dependent positions may be filled by:

(a) **Auxiliary verbs,** like the *may* and *have* of this example. Auxiliary verbs are precisely those verbs which do function as dependent in VP structure, and are contrasted with **main verbs**, which function as head. Most verbs belong exclusively to one or other of these subclasses, but a few, most clearly forms of *be*, *have* and *do*, belong to both: in *He is sleeping* we have an auxiliary use of *is* (and hence, derivatively, of *be*), in *He is sad* a main verb use. The precise delimitation of the auxiliary class raises a number of problems which I shall take up briefly in §4 below: in the meantime we will confine our attention to the most central cases.

(b) *To*, as in *To resign* [*now would be a mistake*]. Although it has certain affinities with an inflectional affix, *to* quite clearly satisfies the criteria for separate word status (see 1.8), and is accordingly regarded here as entering into the syntactic structure of the VP, not the morphological structure of the verb. It is, however, very different in its syntactic properties from other words, and little is achieved by assigning it to any general word-class; I shall speak of it as the 'infinitival particle' *to*, in order to distinguish it from the preposition *to* of *He went to Paris*, etc.

(c) *Not*, as in [*He*] *had not seen* [*her*]. This bears some resemblance to words like *never, often, usually*, etc. but differs from them in that it cannot be freely moved away from the verb it follows: compare *He had never seen so many errors* with *Never had he seen so many errors* or *She would often stay up all night* with *Often she would stay up all night* – **Not had he seen her*, by contrast, is clearly ungrammatical. Furthermore, under conditions we shall be detailing below, *not* requires the presence of a form of *do* in the VP: *She does not like it* rather than **She not likes it* (but cf. *She never/usually likes it*). For these reasons we shall regard *not* as belonging within the structure of the VP itself, with *never, usually* and the like entering into the structure of the clause (or EVP), but this is not an aspect of our constituent structure analysis that is particularly strongly justified.

Our main interest in this section will be in VPs containing auxiliaries as dependents. The main verb may be preceded by up to four auxiliaries. If we provisionally leave aside auxiliary *do*, which cannot (except in imperative constructions) combine with any of the others, we can distinguish the four auxiliary positions shown in (3):

(3)

		Auxiliaries		Main Verb
Modal	**Perfect**	**Progressive**	**Passive**	
can	*have*	*be*	*be*	*take*
may				etc.
must				
shall				
will				
.				
.				
.				

The modal auxiliaries are distinguished from other verbs, whether main verbs or other auxiliaries, by three main grammatical properties, the first two of which have been mentioned above:

(a) They have only tensed forms and do not occur in any syntactic environment where a non-tensed form is required – recall the examples **I'd like to can ski* or **I don't anticipate musting pay any more*. Notice that since the position following a modal is itself one where a non-tensed form, a base form, is required (cf. *He may be ill*), we cannot have non-coordinated sequences of modals within a single VP: **Soon he will can swim*, **I may shall regret it*. It is for this reason that we have a single modal position in (3): the modals are in paradigmatic contrast with each other.[1]

(b) They do not enter into person–number agreement with the subject: they have a single present tense form occurring with any kind of subject.

(c) Only modals can occur as the first verb in the main clause of an 'unreal' conditional construction. The contrast between **real** and **unreal** conditional constructions is exemplified in

(4)   i *If Ed comes tomorrow, we can play bridge*
       ii *If Ed came tomorrow, we could play bridge*

Semantically the difference is a matter of the way the speaker presents the chances of fulfilment of the condition expressed in the subordinate clause: the unreal condition (ii) presents Ed's coming as less likely, a more remote possibility, than the real condition (i) does. Syntactically – and this of course is what defines the distinction – the unreal construction is subject to certain restrictions on the form of both subordinate and main clauses: the subordinate clause must be in the past tense, while the VP of the main clause, as we have said, must begin with a modal auxiliary – also in the past tense if the lexeme in question has a tense contrast. Thus in (i) we could

---

[1] Some dialects do in fact allow certain combinations of modals such as *might could*, but such combinations have to be specified individually, they cannot be derived by any general syntactic rule.

replace *we can play bridge* by the non-modal *we are playing bridge* (or even by an imperative like *give him my regards*), but no analogous changes are possible in (ii).

Each of the auxiliary positions in (3) is optional, so that ignoring differences in the choice of modal it allows for 2^4, i.e. sixteen, different possibilities. They are illustrated in (5), where **may** is used as a representative of the modal class:

(5)	Modal aux	Perfect aux	Progressive aux	Passive aux	Main Verb
i					*takes*
ii				*is*	*taken*
iii			*is*		*taking*
iv			*is*	*being*	*taken*
v		*has*			*taken*
vi		*has*		*been*	*taken*
vii		*has*	*been*		*taking*
viii		*has*	*been*	*being*	*taken*
ix	*may*				*take*
x	*may*			*be*	*taken*
xi	*may*		*be*		*taking*
xii	*may*		*be*	*being*	*taken*
xiii	*may*	*have*			*taken*
xiv	*may*	*have*		*been*	*taken*
xv	*may*	*have*	*been*		*taking*
xvi	*may*	*have*	*been*	*being*	*taken*

Notice that the relative order of the auxiliaries is rigidly fixed – for example, if the perfect and progressive auxiliaries combine, the former must precede the latter: *has been taking*, not **is having taken*. Examples like (viii) and (xvi), which contain perfect, progressive and passive auxiliaries, sound somewhat awkward and strange. This is especially so when they are considered in isolation: acceptability is increased by adding appropriate time expressions, as in *He has been being interrogated without a break since 8 o'clock last night* or *She may still have been being tortured when the police entered the building*. Actual examples can be attested, but they are certainly rare; the boundary between what is grammatical and what is not cannot always be sharply drawn on the basis of speakers' judgements about the grammatical acceptability of sentences and these constructions fall in the fuzzy area. The grammar will of course be simpler if we take them to be grammatical, for we would need to make special provision to exclude them.

One very important principle governing the structure of the VP is that each auxiliary determines the inflectional form of the FOLLOWING verb. The rules are given in (6):

(6)

Auxiliary	Inflectional form of following verb
modal	base form
perfect	-*en* form
progressive	-*ing* form
passive	-*en* form

In (5), for example, modal **may** is followed by one of the base forms *take*, *have* or *be*, perfect **have** is followed by *been* or *taken*; progressive **be** by *being* or *taking*; and passive **be** by *taken*. It is this generalisation that enables us to identify the *been* of (vi), say, as the passive auxiliary in contrast to the progressive *been* of (vii) – or to identify the first **be** of (iv) as the progressive auxiliary, the second as the passive and hence to put the progressive auxiliary before the passive in (3).

4.3 Systems of the VP

The rules given in (6) determine the inflectional form of each verb in the VP other than the first. In VPs functioning as head of kernel (and many classes of non-kernel) clauses, the first verb carries one of the tense inflections, as in all the examples of (5), where the initial verbs – *takes* in (i), *is* in (ii–iv), *has* in (v–viii) and *may* in (ix–xvi) – are present tense forms. Each of these has a past tense counterpart, *took, was, had, might* respectively, and if we allow for this inflectional contrast of tense we double

(7)

System	Terms	Corresponding structural property of VP
Tense	i Past	Initial verb carries past tense inflection
	ii Present	Initial verb carries present tense inflection
Analytic Mood	i Modal	Contains modal aux.; next verb is base form
	ii Non-modal	[Unmarked: no modal aux.]
Perfect Aspect	i Perfect	Contains aux. **have**; next verb is -*en* form
	ii Non-perfect	[Unmarked: no perfect aux.]
Progressive Aspect	i Progressive	Contains aux. **be**; next verb is -*ing* form
	ii Non-progressive	[Unmarked: no progressive aux.]
Voice	i Passive	Contains aux. **be**; next verb is -*en* form
	ii Active	[Unmarked: no passive aux.]

the number of possibilities from sixteen to thirty-two, 2^5. Note that there is only one tense selection per VP, determined by the inflection of the first verb: all non-initial verbs are non-tensed, as we see from (6), and we can accordingly handle the tense contrast at the VP level, along with those relating to the selection of auxiliary verbs. We thus now have five dimensions of contrast for the VP and each of these dimensions yields what we are calling a system. The names of the systems and their terms are given in (7).

The correlation between the structure and the classification is illustrated in the following examples:

(8)

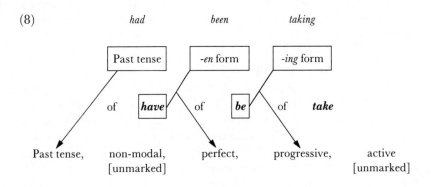

(9)

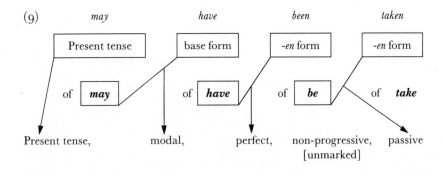

The system of voice applies in the first instance to the clause, with *John took the money* an active clause, *The money was taken by John* its passive counterpart; general definitions of the categories 'voice', 'active' and 'passive' as they apply to clauses were given in 2.3 and their application to VPs is straightforwardly derivative from those definitions. Precisely because voice is primarily a clause system, we will not consider it further in this chapter. We will look into the semantics of the tense, analytic mood, and perfect and progressive aspect systems in §§5–8 below and in the light of that discussion will offer general definitions for these categories; their English-specific definitions are given in (7), in that a perfect VP is one containing auxiliary **have** plus a following *-en* form, and so on.

The most striking difference between this analysis and that found in traditional grammars is that it has a tense system with two terms, past vs present, instead of the traditional system of three terms, past vs present vs future (e.g. *took* vs *takes* vs *will take*). This is because **will** is here analysed as a modal auxiliary, not a tense auxiliary. It has the three distinctive properties of modals given above: it cannot occur in constructions requiring a non-tensed inflectional form (*I hope that I will do better next time*, but not **I hope to will do better next time*, and so on); it does not have contrasting person–number forms, selected by agreement with the subject (compare *They will swim* and *He will swim* – not **He wills swim*); its past tense form *would* can occur as the first verb in the main clause of an unreal condition (*If Ed came tomorrow, we would play bridge*). As we have noted, the modals enter into relations of paradigmatic contrast with each other, but not syntagmatic combination: the contrast is illustrated in *can take* vs *will take*, while the combinations **can will take* and **will can take* are quite ungrammatical. On the other hand **will** does combine with either of the tense inflections, rather than being in paradigmatic contrast with them. The contrast between past tense *could take* and present tense *can take* is paralleled by that between *would take* and *will take*, as can be seen from examples like

(10)   i *Last time no one could/would help me*
        ii *This time no one can/will help me*
(11)   i *I thought it could/would be done*
        ii *I think it can/will be done*

Thus just as *could* and *can* are past and present forms of **can**, so *would* and *will* are analysed as respectively past and present forms of **will** – this is why we say that **will** combines rather than contrasts with the tense inflections. It is true that a form like *will take* will often translate as a future tense form in some other language (e.g. Latin *capiet*, etc.) – but as argued in Ch. 2, it is not a valid procedure to analyse forms in one language on the basis of their translation equivalents in another. If we examine the paradigmatic and syntagmatic relations between forms in English, it is clear that **will** belongs with the modal auxiliaries, not with the tense elements. I believe that such an analysis can also be more illuminating from a semantic point of view: I will take up this point later in the chapter in the context of our discussion of the semantics of tense and mood, but within the methodological framework developed in Ch. 2 it is the grammatical argument just presented that is the crucial factor in the decision to depart from the traditional analysis of tense.

In addition to the VP systems tabulated in (7), there are a number of others that we can deal with fairly summarily.

(a) Person–number. As we have noted, there is a small amount of person–number variation in the VP. It is reflected in the inflectional properties of the verb carrying the tense inflection, and the contrasts depend on the lexeme concerned. The details are given in (12):

(12)	Tense	1st verb	Contrasts
	Past	*be*	1st or 3rd pers sg (*was*) vs plural or 2nd person (*were*)
		others	nil
	Present	*be*	1st pers sg (*am*) vs 3rd person sg (*is*) vs plural or 2nd person (*are*)
		modal aux.	nil
		others	3rd pers sg (e.g. *takes*) vs general (*take*)

The person–number property, where there is one, is normally determined by agreement with the subject; certain cases of 'discord' are discussed in 6.5.2.

(b) Kind of VP. Just as we can apply the terms 'past tense' and 'present tense' to VPs as well as to verbs, so we speak of VPs as tensed or non-tensed, according as the initial verb is or is not one of the tensed inflectional forms. Thus in *Having considered all the arguments, he decided against it*, the VP *having considered* is non-tensed: it begins with an *-ing* form. By further extension, we will also speak of tensed and non-tensed clauses, depending on the kind of VP they have as head. And just as we have said that tensed verbs are more central than non-tensed ones with respect to the word-class verb, so tensed clauses are more central than non-tensed ones with respect to the phrase-class clause – as we have noted, the status of forms like *having considered all the arguments* as clauses is somewhat problematic. All three non-tensed verb forms can occur in initial position in the VP, and a base form may or may not be preceded by the infinitival particle *to*; this then yields the following possibilities:

(13)

			Corresponding structural property of VP	
System	Terms		Form of initial verb	Particle *to* present?
Kind of VP	i Non-tensed	base < +*to*	base form	yes
		base < −*to*	base form	no
		-*ing*	-*ing* form	[no]
		-*en*	-*en* form	[no]
	ii Tensed		tensed form	[no]

The four kinds of non-tensed VP are exemplified in (14):

(14)   i   [*She hoped*] *to be photographed*
        ii [*He wouldn't let her*] *be photographed*
        iii [*She resented*] *being photographed*
        iv [*He had her*] *photographed*

The base kind without *to* occurs in imperative clauses (cf. our earlier *Be careful*) but for the rest non-tensed VPs are virtually confined to subordinate clauses. The choice between them depends in part on the particular subclass of subordinate clause involved, in part on properties of the superordinate clause; in (14), for example, the subordinate clauses are all functioning as 'complement' within the superordinate clause, and the choice depends on the verbs **hope**, **let**, **resent** and **have**.

Non-tensed VPs do not allow the full range of auxiliaries shown in (3). The restrictions are as follows: none of the four kinds allows a modal, as already noted; the *-en* kind allows no auxiliaries at all; the base kind without *to* hardly allows perfect **have** (cf. **He wouldn't let her have finished*).

'Kind of VP' is an informal label, not an accepted general term. The primary distinction within the traditional analysis, as we have seen (2.4), is between finite and non-finite verbs, and the standard term for that contrast is 'finiteness'. I shall retain 'finiteness' for a system of the clause, but not for the VP: see 5.6 and 12.3 for the relation between the contrasts finite vs non-finite clause, and tensed vs non-tensed VP.

(c) Polarity. Cutting across the distinctions we have drawn so far is that between **positive** and **negative** VPs – what is sometimes called the system of **polarity**. Positive is the unmarked term in the system. Negative VPs are marked by the word *not* functioning as dependent in the structure of the phrase, as in *is not working*, or by a negative form of the verb, as in *isn't working*: these may be distinguished as respectively analytic and inflectional negatives, 'analytic' being a term quite widely used for a construction that is realised by the presence of some word as opposed to one that is realised morphologically (see 3.2).

(15) | System | Terms | Corresponding structural property of VP |
        |--------|-------|---|
        | | i Negative ⟨ analytic | *Not* as dependent |
        | Polarity | inflectional | First verb carries negative inflection |
        | | ii Positive | [Unmarked: lacks the above] |

Except in imperatives (e.g. *Don't panic*), inflectional negatives are restricted to tensed VPs: there is no inflectional counterpart to [*I regret*] *not having seen* [*it*]. With analytic negatives, the usual position for the *not* is after the first verb in tensed VPs (*has not finished*) and at the beginning of the phrase in non-tensed ones (*not having seen, not to be working*), though these are not the only possibilities.

Polarity is also a system of the clause, but a negative clause is not always marked as such in the VP (cf. *No one came*, where it is marked in the NP subject): we will look further into these matters in Ch. 13. One distinction that it will be convenient to make here, however, is that between emphatic and unemphatic polarity in tensed VPs. With emphatic polarity, the stress is placed on the tensed verb, the semantic effect being to emphasise that the proposition being expressed is positive as opposed to negative or negative as opposed to positive. The emphatic form may be used to deny something that has been previously asserted, as when you say *He can't swim* and I reply: *That's not true – he can swim*. But the contrast may be with a proposition that is merely implicit: *I don't know whether he'll go, but if he is there I'll tell him*. Corresponding clauses with emphatic and unemphatic polarity will be thematic variants in the sense of 1.4, and the thematically marked variants, the emphatic ones, will be non-kernel. In the examples given, the distinction has been realised in the non-verbal component, the stress, but it also has relevance for the verbal component, and it is for this reason that we shall need to take it up again in our discussion of operators, to which we now turn.

4.4 Operators, auxiliaries and catenatives

There are four constructions which require that the VP contain what we will call an **operator**; the central operators are the modal auxiliaries, **be** and – in certain but not all of their uses – **have** and **do**. All four of the constructions may be regarded as marked, contrasting with more elementary, unmarked, constructions. Let us take them in turn.

(a) Tensed negative VP. In a tensed VP that is negative (whether analytic or inflectional), the tensed verb must be an operator:

(16)		Unmarked: positive	Marked: negative
	i	*You must tell her*	*You mustn't tell her*
	ii	*She has arrived*	*She has not arrived*
	iii	*They are here*	*They aren't here*
	iv	*He drinks*	**He drinks not*

We see that **must**, **have** and **be** are operators, while **drink** is not. Notice that examples like *He prefers not to tell them* or *They want not me but you* are not in conflict with this rule for the *not* does not here belong in a tensed VP: in the first it is the non-tensed *to tell* that is negated, not tensed *prefers* (as is evident from the fact that a coordinate tag – see 2.1 – would be *and so does she,* not *and neither does she*), and in the second *not* goes with *me*, not with the verb.

(b) Tensed verb preceding subject. The order of elements in kernel clauses has the subject preceding the VP but, as we have noted, there are various classes of non-kernel clause where the subject follows the tensed verb, which is then required to be an operator:

(17)   Unmarked order: Marked order:
               subject + tensed verb   tensed verb + subject
      i *He will tell her*   *Will he tell her?*
      ii *I had never seen such chaos*   *Never had I seen such chaos*
      iii *Jill was there*   [*Max was there*] *and so was Jill*
      iv *She wants something*   **What wants she?*

Will, **have** and **be** are here seen to occur in the marked construction, while **want** is excluded. The marked order occurs: in interrogative clauses (see 11.4 for details), including interrogative tags (*He can't swim, can he?* vs **He saw nothing, saw he?*); in thematically marked clauses where a negative phrase – or a phrase of certain other kinds – has been moved to initial position (*At no time had she spoken to him* vs **At no time spoke she to him*); in coordinate tags introduced by *so, neither, nor* (compare (iii) above with **He likes her and so like I*). These constructions are to be distinguished from that where the subject is thematically moved to post-VP position, as in *On top of the cupboard were stacked no less than a dozen suitcases, Over the hill appeared a camel*, and the like, where there is no requirement that the tensed verb be an operator (see 14.4.2 for discussion of the difference between the two marked orders).

(c) Tensed VP with emphatic polarity. The tensed verb of a VP with emphatic polarity must again be an operator. If the VP is negative, the tensed verb is already required to be an operator by condition (a) above, so here I will give examples of emphatic positives:

(18)   Unmarked: unemphatic polarity   Marked: emphatic polarity
      i *She can swim*   *She <u>can</u> swim*
      ii *She has gone*   *She <u>has</u> gone*
      iii *I am ill*   *I <u>am</u> ill*
      iv *I know her*   **I <u>know</u> her*

I <u>know</u> her is not ungrammatical as such, but is nevertheless not the emphatic polarity counterpart of *I know her*: rather the stress is here used to emphasise the lexical content of **know** as opposed to the polarity. For example, I might say *I <u>know</u> her but I'd hardly call her a friend*, where the contrast is between knowing her and being a friend of hers, not between knowing her and not knowing her. Thus (18) again illustrates how the syntax differentiates between operators such as **be**, **have** or modal **can** and non-operators such as **know**.

(d) Post-verbal ellipsis. Where there is ellipsis of post-verbal material recoverable from the context, the last non-ellipted verb must be an operator:

(19)

	Unmarked: non-elliptical	Marked: post-verbal ellipsis
i	*He may go*	[*I'm not sure he'll go*] but he may
ii	*Ed could have seen her*	[*I certainly saw her*] and Ed could have too
iii	*I have been a member since May*	[*He didn't realise I was a member*] but I have been since May
iv	*Ed enjoyed the concert too*	*[*We enjoyed the concert*] and Ed enjoyed too

The last is ungrammatical because **enjoy** is not an operator. Post-verbal ellipsis is to be interpreted as ellipsis of material following a verb immediately, as in (19), or with an intervening subject or negative particle. Thus in *Ed will go, but will Max?* the second clause corresponds to *but will Max go?*, with ellipsis of what follows the tensed verb + subject, and in *Ed will go but Max will not* there is ellipsis of what follows the tensed verb + *not* in the corresponding full clause *but Max will not go*. This fourth construction differs from the other three that require the presence of an operator in that here the operator does not have to be tensed: in (19ii), for example, *have* is a base form, and in (iii) *been* is an *-en* form.

The ungrammatical examples in (16)–(19) can all be corrected by using the verb **do**:

	Unmarked	Marked
(20)	*He drinks*	*He does not drink*
(21)	*He wants something*	*What does he want?*
(22)	*I know her*	*I do know her*
(23)	*Ed enjoyed the concert*	[*We enjoyed the concert*] and Ed did too

There are a number of syntactically distinguishable uses of **do**; for our purposes it will be sufficient to distinguish just three. In the first place it may be used as a transitive main verb: *He did a wonderful job, I haven't done it yet, What are you doing?*, where *a wonderful job*, *it* and *what* are objects. Secondly, it can be used as what we may call a 'substitute', as in *Jill took more time over it than she had ever done before*, where *done* may be thought of, intuitively, as substituting for *taken over it*. This use of **do** is analogous to that of **she** in the same example, which is traditionally regarded as serving to avoid the repetition of *Jill*: we will look more carefully at this phenomenon in our discussion of pronouns (7.2). In its substitute use, **do** is a main verb: it functions as head in VP structure and can, as the example shows, take auxiliaries as dependents. Thirdly, **do** can be used as a 'dummy' operator, as in *He does not drink*. It is a dummy in the sense that it has no identifiable meaning of its own but is inserted to satisfy the syntactic requirement that the tensed negative VP contain an operator; again we can find an analogous use of a pronoun – recall the discussion of *It is time she had her hair cut* in 2.2, where we spoke of *it* as a dummy subject. Dummy operator **do** can function as dependent to transitive main verb **do**, as in *He didn't do it* – transitive **do** is not itself an operator, as is evident from the ungrammaticality of *He did not it, *Did he a good job?, etc. In some varieties of English, the dummy operator can likewise combine with substitute **do**, as when you ask *Did he finish it?* and I reply *No, he didn't do*, with *do* substituting for *finish it*. (I could of course also reply *No, he didn't*, with ellipsis of *finish it* rather than its replacement by a substitute – and for many speakers only the version with ellipsis would be acceptable here.)

Returning now to (20)–(23), it is clear that in the first three the marked constructions contain **do** in its dummy operator use: our rules for deriving constructions (a)–(c) from their unmarked counterparts will say that if the unmarked form does not contain an operator then **do** must be introduced as a dummy operator.[2] Some grammars treat construction (d) in the same way and accordingly analyse the **do** of (23), as well as (20)–(22), as the dummy operator. An alternative and, I believe, preferable analysis is to say that *and Ed did too* in (23) is not in fact an example of construction (d) inasmuch as it involves not ellipsis but the use of **do** as a substitute. We have already noted one difference between construction (d) and (a)–(c), namely that in (a)–(c) but not (d) the operator has to be tensed; a second difference, it is now suggested, is that whereas the rules for (a)–(c) provide for the insertion of a dummy operator, the rule for (d) does not: if the unmarked form does not contain an operator, then reduction by ellipsis is simply not possible, and we have to use substitution instead. Ellipsis and substitution are clearly related: both serve to avoid repetition and permit the use of a form that is in general shorter than would be necessary if the interpretation were not derivable from other forms in the sentence or text. And precisely because

---

[2] Auxiliary **do** also occurs in negative and emphatic polarity imperatives – *Don't take any notice*, <u>*Do*</u> *take care*. Here, however, the **do** appears even when the unemphatic positive counterpart contains the operator **be** (compare *Be cautious* and *Don't be cautious*): it does not appear, therefore, that the insertion of **do** in imperatives can be accounted for by means of the same rules as apply to other clause classes.

they are so similar, it is not always a straightforward matter to distinguish between them – hence the different views on the analysis of *Ed did too* in (23) (and see also 7.3 for problems in distinguishing in NP structure between ellipsis and substitution involving the use of a pronoun). As we are drawing the distinction here, speaker B's reply to A's question will involve ellipsis in (24), substitution in (25):

(24)	⟨A⟩ *Do I pay the bill?*	⟨B⟩ *Yes, you do*
(25)	⟨A⟩ *Who pays the bill?*	⟨B⟩ *You do*

In (24), *you do* is elliptical for *you do pay the bill*, where the operator **do** is required because we have an emphatic positive; in (25) *do* substitutes for *pay the bill*. Note that we could not insert *pay the bill* after *do* in (25) as we could in (24) – and conversely, in (25) we could drop the *do* to yield the elliptical answer *You*, whereas in (24) *do* cannot be dropped because the important feature of the answer is not that the subject is *you* but that the polarity is positive, i.e. that the operator is *do*, not *don't*. The issue is complicated, however, by the fact there are a number of restrictions on the use of **do** as a substitute. It cannot occur in the passive construction: **Kim was seen by the caretaker and I was done too* (only the elliptical *and I was too* is possible here). And it does not readily occur in the progressive: many find unacceptable such examples as ⟨A⟩ *Will they be taking part?* – ⟨B⟩ *Yes, they will be doing*; and similarly there are varieties of English where it is excluded in the base form, as in ⟨A⟩ *Will you see him?* – ⟨B⟩ *Well, I hope to do*. These restrictions reduce the force of what would otherwise be a very strong argument for saying that (23) and (25) contain substitute **do**, namely that if they were not so analysed we would need to introduce into the grammar an ad hoc restriction preventing substitute **do** from appearing in a tensed form.

Let us now consider the relation between the operator and auxiliary classes. 'Auxiliary' is a general term, i.e. one that has a general definition in the sense of 2.3, a definition that provides a basis for its employment in the grammar of particular languages. The traditional concept of an auxiliary verb is that of a verb having the same kind of meaning as a verbal inflection – and hence being involved in contrasts of tense, aspect, mood, voice and the like. For example, the perfect auxiliary of *I have seen it* expresses a rather similar meaning to the past tense inflection of *I saw it* and while the passive construction is marked inflectionally in Latin non-perfects, in Latin perfects – and in English – it is marked by an auxiliary. 'Operator', by contrast, is an English-specific term, one without a general definition. We are defining it language-specifically by reference to constructions (a)–(d), but since the restrictions on what verbs can appear in these constructions have no close analogue in other languages, they do not provide the basis for the general definition of any syntactic category. It would in fact be perfectly consistent with the principles outlined in Ch. 2 if we dispensed with the term 'operator' altogether, applying the term 'auxiliary' to the class that we have been calling 'operator': we would have a class defined at the language-particular level by reference to constructions (a)–(d) and since the members of this class have, for the most part, the properties given in the general definition of 'auxiliary' we would be entitled to apply that general term to the class. And some writers do indeed do that. I have nevertheless avoided that usage here for two, largely practical, reasons.

In the first place, it would be very much in conflict with the standard use of the term 'auxiliary' to say that *be* was an auxiliary in examples like *Kim is ill*, where *is* is not functioning as dependent to any other verb. I am following the standard use in restricting 'auxiliary' to cases where the verb is a dependent, but this means that I need another term for the verbs occurring in constructions (a)–(d), for *be* does so irrespective of whether it is functioning as dependent or as head. It is particularly handy to have two terms to deal with uses of the verb *have*. We need to distinguish three uses of *have*, which I shall refer to as 'perfect', 'dynamic' and 'non-dynamic'. The perfect use is found in *I have seen it, She had gone*, etc., where *have* is the marker of perfect aspect: in this use, *have* is both an auxiliary and an operator. Dynamic *have* is found in *She always has a swim before breakfast, I'm having lunch with Pat, We had difficulty understanding it* – 'dynamic' in the sense that it involves an action or process, as opposed to a state. In this use *have* is neither an auxiliary nor an operator – witness the deviance of **Has she a swim before breakfast?*, **I haven't lunch with Pat*, etc. Finally non-dynamic *have* is found in *They have a car, Ed has to leave*: this *have* is interchangeable, subject to considerations of style, with the idiom *have got* (which contains perfect *have*), as in *They've got a car, Ed has got to leave*. Non-dynamic *have* is clearly not a dependent, but it can be an operator, as is evident from examples like *Have they a car?, Ed has to leave and I have too.*[3] The important point is, then, that the operator uses of *have* are not coextensive with the auxiliary uses, so that we need two categories not one.[4]

The second point is that the status of the class of auxiliary verbs, in the sense of verbs functioning as dependent of a main verb, is a matter of some controversy. The issue here is whether we are justified in drawing a

---

[3] I say 'can be' rather than 'is' an operator because we also find *Do they have a car?, Ed has to leave and I do too*; US English has only this latter construction, where *have* is not an operator, while the construction without *do* is more characteristic of British English, for example, though many speakers use both types quite freely.

[4] It doesn't follow, however, that we need two CLASSES. Given that we do not require a one-to-one relation between functions and classes, we could define the class auxiliary verb in terms of constructions (a)–(d) and allow that some auxiliary verbs can function both as head and as dependent within VP structure: this is why I characterised my reasons for not using 'auxiliary' for the operator class as 'largely practical' – it would conflict with standard usage but would not be theoretically unsound.

distinction between auxiliaries and what are commonly known as **catenatives**. Catenatives are main verbs like **keep**, **promise**, **seem**, **want** and numerous others that take non-tensed clauses as complement, as in *They kept laughing*, *I promise to tell her*, *She seemed to lose her balance*, etc. In the analysis we have adopted here, we will assign quite different structures to the two sentences in, say, (26):

(26)   i   *They were laughing*
         ii *They kept laughing*

If we simplify by omitting the EVP level, the structures will be essentially as follows:

(27)

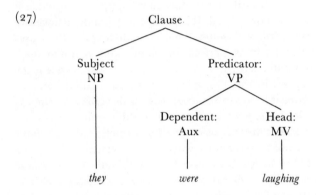

(28)

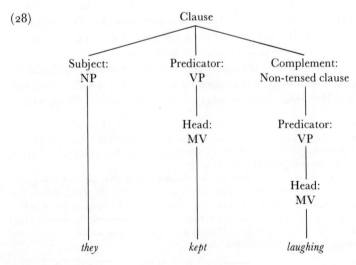

Note that the ultimate head of the sentence in (27) is *laughing*, with *were* a dependent, whereas in (28) the ultimate head is *kept*, with *laughing* dependent on it (even though head of its own clause). An alternative analysis denies that there is any such difference in the direction of dependency and hence assimilates auxiliaries to catenatives, so that (26i) would likewise have a structure where *laughing* was a non-tensed clause dependent on the ultimate head *were*. On this view all verbs would be 'main verbs': there would be no auxiliary vs main verb distinction, no VP construction like that described in §2 above. The present book is not the place to examine this controversy, and I will continue to follow the more conservative line that recognises a class of auxiliaries functioning as dependent in VP structure. But the controversy does provide a reason for not applying the term 'auxiliary' to what I am calling the operator class. The dispute is over the validity of a structural analysis like (27) contrasting with something like (28): there is no dispute (how could there be?) over the distinction between two subclasses of verb, one containing verbs like **be** which occur in constructions (a)–(d), one containing verbs like **keep** which do not; and since the debate is generally presented in terms of 'auxiliaries' vs 'main verbs', it would only confuse the issue to employ the term 'auxiliary' for the uncontroversial operator class.

We have observed that not all operators are auxiliaries: whether all auxiliaries are operators is another question that we will not attempt to resolve. Certainly the central auxiliaries are, i.e. those given in (3), but if we make it a necessary condition for auxiliaries that they have the operator properties this will exclude from the auxiliary class a number of verbs which might otherwise appear to be strong candidates for inclusion, such as the **get** of passives like *He got arrested by the police* (see 14.1), the **let** of imperatives like *Let's go* (see 11.3), and so on.

4.5 Tense

In the remainder of this chapter we will return to four of the VP systems introduced in §3 above, tense, progressive aspect, perfect aspect and (analytic) mood, considering them this time primarily with respect to the meanings of the contrasting terms. We will begin with tense – but since there are close connections between the semantics of tense and the semantics of aspect and mood we will in this section confine our attention, except where otherwise stated, to VPs that are unmarked in aspect and mood.

We will examine the semantic contrast between the tenses under three headings: location in time, factuality and backshifting.

(a) Location in time. The primary use of the past tense is illustrated in (29):

(29)   i *Kim lived in Berlin*
         ii *I saw Jill yesterday*

Let us use 'situation' as a completely general technical term covering actions, events, processes, relations, states of affairs or whatever a clause expresses. Situations may be either 'dynamic', in which case they may be said to 'take place', or 'static', in which case they 'obtain'. (In its everyday, non-technical sense a situation will normally be a state, but it is useful to generalise it so as to have a term that is neutral with respect to the dynamic/static contrast.) We can then talk about the 'time of the situation' as the time – a point or period of time – at which the situation takes place or is presented as obtaining. The primary use of the past tense is then to indicate that the time of the situation is in the past. The past time may be identified more specifically by a temporal expression like *yesterday* in (29ii), or by the context. In (29i), for example, Kim may have lived in Berlin all her life, with her lifetime then specifying the time period, or else she may simply have lived there at the time being spoken about in the discourse in which the sentence occurs. But whether identified elsewhere in the clause, in the surrounding text or else simply by the context, there will be some 'definite' past time that is being referred to.

It follows from what we have just been saying that the past tense inflection does not create any entailment that the situation obtaining at the past time in question no longer obtains at the present time. This is clear in an example like

(30)   *Kim was able to speak French, so we got around quite easily*

This evidently does not entail that Kim is not now able to speak French – nor that she is: it tells us something about what situation obtained at a particular period in the past (such as the time when the speaker and Kim went to France for a holiday) but nothing at all about what situation obtains at the time of utterance.

One special case of this primary use of the past tense is, indeed, where there is a pragmatic implication that the past situation does still obtain, as in

(31)   [*Are you free for a couple of moments? –*] *there was something I wanted to ask you.*

You would understand from this that there is something I want to ask you, but I don't explicitly say so. Presenting the situation as obtaining in the past distances it from the here and now of the utterance itself, and this is a conventional means of achieving politeness: (31) is more polite – more deferential, less brusque – than it would be with *there is something I want to ask you.*

It should be emphasised that past time is an inherently relational concept. The past tense inflection indicates that the time of the situation is past relative to some other time – usually the time of uttering the sentence. Let us, for convenience, use the abbreviation 'TS' for the time of the situation,

'TU' for the time of utterance, and 'TR' for the time to which TS is related – so that the past tense indicates that TS precedes TR. Usually, as we have said, TR = TU, but they are not invariably the same, and this is why we need to keep them conceptually distinct. The above examples, where TR is the same as TU, may thus be contrasted with

(32)   *If Kim doesn't see him, she'll tell you he wasn't there*

where we are concerned with the past tense form *wasn't*. Here TS, the time of his (allegedly) not being there, is presented as past not relative to TU, the time at which (32) itself is uttered, but relative to the time when Kim tells you he wasn't there. Normally, but not always (as we shall see below), it is only in subordinate clauses that TR can differ from TU.

Let us now consider, by contrast, the use of the present tense, as in

(33)   i *Kim lives in Berlin*
         ii *Kim gives her first lecture in Berlin*

With the present tense, TS will normally be present or future: the natural interpretation for (33) is that TS is present in the first and future in the second. Whether the situation is interpreted as present or future may be determined by temporal expressions (such as *now* vs *soon, next week*, and so on), by the content of a superordinate clause (compare the different temporal interpretations of the subordinate *when* clause in *When she gets home, she always has a swim* and *When she gets home I'm going to tell her about it*), by the nature of the situation (this is the factor which makes the examples in (33) conducive to different temporal interpretations), or simply by the context (*He goes with me*, for example, would be interpreted as present in a context where I've been saying that I regularly go to London on Tuesdays, but as future in a context where I'm talking about a visit of mine to London scheduled for next week).

Clearly, then, the present tense does not have the meaning "TS is present". Nevertheless, there are two factors which justify our selection of the general term 'present' – as opposed to 'non-past' – for this tense. In the first place, the future interpretation is less frequent and subject to fairly strong pragmatic constraints. Except in certain kinds of subordinate clause (such as conditional ones like *if she arrives tomorrow*), it is restricted to cases where the future situation can be regarded as assured in the present – by virtue of being already organised, as with *We leave for Paris next week* (dynamic) or *We are in Paris next week* (static), or being determinable from the laws of the natural sciences, as in *The sun rises at 5.15 tomorrow*. *He has a heart attack next week* or *He is ill next week*, by contrast, are not normal (though they are not of course ungrammatical – which is why I described the constraints as pragmatic – and it is possible to contextualise them in such a way as to make them acceptable, as when I use them in talking about a TV programme to be shown next week but whose content I already know). In the second place there is an analogous use of the past tense – compare:

(34) i *The match starts tomorrow*
      ii *[Ah, yes, but] at that time the match started next week*

In (ii) the past tense clearly does not locate the start of the match in past time – we are concerned with a state of affairs in the past where an event was scheduled or organised for some subsequent time. Certainly this use of the past tense is vastly less frequent than the future use of the present tense, but that doesn't entitle us to disregard it altogether (and note that it occurs perhaps more readily with the past progressive: *At that time the match was starting next week*). The point of the analogy between (34i) and (ii) is that it supports the view that (i) does not involve simple futurity but some element of present scheduling as well as the futurity of the situation.

When we have a future interpretation of TS with the present tense there will be reference to some definite time – just as we noted above that with past tense there is usually reference to some definite time in the past. In *I leave for London next Tuesday* the time is identified by the temporal expression *next Tuesday*, in *He goes with me*, interpreted as future, the time will be clear from the context. When the interpretation of TS is present, however, things are not so straightforward. With past time, TS precedes TR and with future time, TS follows TR; if present time were understood as TS equals TR, then it too would be definite, for TR is definite (this is obvious in the usual case where $TR = TU$, TU being the time of the utterance, but TR will always be some definite time even when not identified with TU). However, a present tense clause where the interpretation is not future will not necessarily or even usually involve a present conceived of as virtually coextensive with TR: it will, rather, be a time which includes TR – cf. (33i), for example. But just how far beyond TR the 'present' extends will generally be indeterminate, and this is why I am saying we need not have reference to a definite time. Indeed there are cases where time would seem to be simply irrelevant: when I say

(35) *The square root of four is two*

I am surely not referring to present or any other time, and it doesn't make sense to ask what the time-period is of the situation of the square root of four being two (philosophers would say that the proposition expressed in an utterance of (35) is 'timeless', outside of time altogether).

There are, moreover, three cases where the present tense can be used even though TS is in fact past relative to TU. They are illustrated in

(36)   i *I'd only just got on the bus when this guy comes up to me and asks for a light*
        ii *PM resigns*
        iii *Bill tells me you are moving to Sydney*

The first is traditionally referred to as the 'historic present'; it is a device employed in certain narrative styles of speech or writing (and found in a great many languages) where we use the same verb forms as are used for running commentaries in order to lend added life to the narrative. Instead of saying that TS, the time of the guy coming up and asking for a light, is identified directly as past relative to TU, we can think of it as present relative to a TR that is in the past: in using the historic present I transport myself, as it were, into the past and narrate the events as they unfold from that vantage point instead of from that of the context in which the utterance is actually taking place.

The second example is characteristic of news headlines. Whereas (i) contrasts stylistically with the past tense (... *this guy came up to me and asked for a light*), (ii) contrasts stylistically with the present perfect (*PM has resigned*). One factor favouring it therefore is that it is shorter than the latter – though that is more relevant to newspaper headlines than radio bulletin headlines. In addition there is presumably, as with the historic present, the element of extra vividness: the event reported is presented as so recent that the report is virtually a running commentary.

Consider now the third case, (36iii). I would typically use this in a context where Bill's telling me about your move to Sydney was in fact in past time: why then do I say *tells* rather than *told*? The answer seems to be that the focus of attention is not on Bill's act of communication itself but rather on its content: I am not primarily concerned with the occurrence in the past of a particular event wherein Bill told me you were moving to Sydney but rather with the proposition that you are moving to Sydney and the fact that Bill subscribes to that proposition (that I implicitly claim this to be a fact is evident from the pragmatic unacceptability of continuing (36ii) with *but he now admits he was lying* or the like). There is thus clearly a present time component in such examples – but what is present is not the situation actually expressed, Bill's telling me, but one which is implied, his commitment to the truth of what he told me. Examples like this are found only with a small set of verbs of communication such as **tell**, **say**, **hear**.

(b) Factuality. One secondary use of the past tense was illustrated in (4) above in connection with the syntactic properties of the modals; it is repeated in (37) together with the contrasting present tense:

(37)   i *If Ed came tomorrow, we could play bridge*
        ii *If Ed comes tomorrow, we can play bridge*

Clearly the *came* in (i) does not serve to indicate that the time of Ed's coming is past. The semantic difference between (i) and (ii) is not a temporal one: as we have said, (ii) presents Ed's coming as less likely, as a more remote possibility than (i) does. In what we are calling the 'unreal' conditional construction exemplified in (i), it may be pragmatically clear that the hypothetical situation does not obtain, is counterfactual: *If you were me, wouldn't you do exactly the same?*. But counterfactuality is not part of the meaning of the past tense itself: (37) does not altogether rule out the possibility of Ed's coming tomorrow. For this reason this use of the past tense is better described as indicating 'factual remoteness': counterfactuality is just a special case, subsumed under that more general notion. Notice, however, that where the condition is known to be counterfactual, the 'real' conditional construction is out of place: *I realise he's not here, but if he is, what will he be able to do about it?* is semantically anomalous.

It has been proposed that the concept of remoteness is sufficiently general to cover both the primary use of the past tense and the one we are concerned with here. According to this view, the inflection itself would simply indicate remoteness, and it would depend on other features of the sentence or context whether this is interpreted more specifically as remoteness in time or remoteness in factuality. The problem that faces us here is of a type which commonly arises in semantic analysis. As we try to bring more and more uses of a category or item within the scope of our semantic analysis of it, the meaning proposed will become more and more general, with less and less content – and the burden of accounting for the more specific features of the interpretation of sentences containing it will fall elsewhere, on other linguistic elements in the sentence or on pragmatics. The alternative to giving a single very general meaning, which may be fairly empty, is to allow for polysemy, recognising a range of related senses (some of which may be more central than others): different writers may take quite widely varying positions on this issue. As far as the particular case of it that we have raised here is concerned, my own view would be that we do need to recognise distinct senses of the past tense, for it is not clear why remoteness as such should select past time as opposed to future time when interpreted temporally (we do not say *He was here yesterday, is here now and was here tomorrow*). Nevertheless the proposal is certainly useful in showing a relation between the past time and factual remoteness uses.

We may distinguish three subcases of the factual remoteness use of the past tense. First, it appears in the unreal conditional construction, as in (37i) – with *if, unless, suppose, supposing*, etc. Second, it is found in clauses functioning as complement to the verb **wish** or in construction with *it is time*: *I wish I had the latest edition, It's time you were in bed*. Here there is no contrast of tense: we cannot say **I wish I have the latest edition* or **It's time you are in bed*. The semantics of **wish** and *it is time* involve an element of counterfactuality: for example, *I wish I had the latest edition* implies that I believe I haven't, and a rule of grammar requires a subordinate clause verb that matches this interpretation. (Notice, however, that the rule does not apply to **pretend**, which is semantically analogous to **wish** in that *He pretends he knows how to cure them* implies that he believes he doesn't.) Third, it occurs with modal auxiliaries: *You might be right* (for many speakers at least) presents the possibility of your being right as somewhat more remote than *You may be right*; *He'd be about seventy* (with *'d* a contraction of *would*) is more tentative than the present tense counterpart *He'll be about seventy* (said in response to, say, *How old do you reckon he is?*); and so on – further examples of this third subcase will be given in the discussion of the modals.

Traditional grammar analyses the *came* of (37i) as a past subjunctive form, inflectionally distinct from the past indicative *came* of *Ed came yesterday*. I observed in 2.4 that there is room for debate as to whether or not we should recognise distinct inflectional forms here: it depends on whether we generalise to all verbs the obsolescent contrast found in *if Ed were here tomorrow* vs *Ed was here yesterday*. We are not doing so here, but there are several points relevant to the concerns of this chapter that should be borne in mind if one did draw an inflectional distinction between two forms, syncretised for all verbs other than **be**. The first is that we would not want to follow traditional grammar in calling *came* in (37i) a 'past' subjunctive. There is no justification for saying that *came* and *comes* in (37) contrast in both mood and tense. The traditional past subjunctive *came* is opposed to the 'present subjunctive' *come* that appears in constructions like *It is essential that Ed come tomorrow* – this *come* and the *came* of (37i) are surely not different tenses of the same mood. The relationship between them is not in any way comparable to that between 'indicative' *comes* and *came* in *The point comes/ came across clearly*: if the two forms of **come** in (37) differ in mood it will be only the indicative *comes* that enters into an inflectional contrast of tense. The second point is that it is also questionable whether 'subjunctive' is the most appropriate general term to apply to the proposed mood inflection. If the *come* of *It is essential that Ed come tomorrow* were a distinct inflection (instead of just one syntactic use of the base form) then 'subjunctive' would be the appropriate term for it, but the *came* of (37i) would be better called 'irrealis'. Both subjunctive and irrealis are general terms used for moods characteristically associated with non-factuality; the difference is that the subjunctive is primarily used in subordinate clauses and tends to involve a wider range of types of non-factuality (compare again the *It is essential* example) than irrealis, which primarily expresses counterfactuality or factual remoteness. Although the *came* in (37i) is in a subordinate clause, the unreal conditional construction has the same inflection in the main clause (carried by the modal auxiliary) – and the *might, would*, etc. of *You might be right, He'd be about seventy* occur freely in main clauses. The third point is that even those who use *were* rather than *was* in *if he were here, I wish I* *were at home* and the like, normally use *was* after *it is time*: *It is time I was/*were in bed*. Thus even if we did recognise a system of inflectional mood contrasting indicative and irrealis, we would still have to allow for a factual remoteness use of the past indicative.

So much for the implications of making an inflectional distinction between the *came* of *if Ed came tomorrow* and *Ed came yesterday*. Given that we are not doing so here but are rather recognising different uses of a single inflectional form, it remains only to explain why we treat the difference between *came* and *come(s)* as one of tense. We will say that a language has a system of tense if it has contrasting classes of verb or verb phrase, differentiated inflectionally or by auxiliaries, such that the primary semantic contrast between them has to do with the relation between the time of situation and the time of the utterance. And clearly the primary use of the inflectional system *came* vs *come(s)* is to make contrasts of the kind discussed in (a) above rather than those considered here in (b). That the use of the past tense to locate in past time, as in (29), is primary while its use to indicate factual remoteness, as in (37i), is secondary is evident not simply from the fact that the former is vastly more frequent than the latter but also from the fact that only the former is found in kernel clauses for virtually all verbs. Again we see the importance of distinguishing between general and language-particular definitions. At the general level we will define past tense as a syntactically distinct category of the verb or VP whose primary use is to locate the situation in past time. At the level of definitions specific to English, the past tense is defined by reference to the inflectional paradigm given in (1): to determine whether a verb is a past tense form we ask whether it occupies the position of *took, wrote, saw*, etc. in its paradigm, not whether it is being used to indicate past time.

(c) Backshifting. A further secondary use of the past tense is illustrated in (38):

(38)   *Kim said that the match started tomorrow*

The past tense inflection accompanying **start** clearly does not have the primary sense: it does not indicate that TS is past, where the situation is the starting of the match. The clause containing *started* is a non-kernel one by virtue of being embedded in a larger clause; the kernel clause to which it corresponds is

(39)   *The match starts tomorrow*

The structure of the subordinate clause in (38) can then best be understood by reference to the way it differs from its main clause counterpart. When (39) is embedded inside a clause whose own VP is in the past tense as with *said* in (38), the present tense *starts* is changed to past tense *started*. This process is commonly known as 'backshifting': the present tense verb is shifted back to the corresponding past tense.

The particular case of backshifting in (38) is an instance of what is traditionally called 'indirect reported speech': in uttering (38) I report Kim's act of speech but I do so indirectly in the sense that I give the content of what was said, not the actual words – *Kim rushed in and yelled: 'Out of bed, the lot of you!'* is, by contrast, an example of 'direct reported speech', i.e. quotation. The phenomenon of backshifting is, however, a good deal more general than indirect reported speech: in *Kim didn't know that the match started tomorrow*, for example, there is no report of any act of speech (**know** is not a verb of communication, and in any case it is negated) but we have the same use of the past tense *started* as in (38). Moreover, precisely because the reported speech in (38) is indirect, we do not know what sentence Kim actually used: it might have been (39), but it might equally have been *It begins on Saturday*, *The date on which the match is scheduled to start is 23 September*, and so on: given an appropriate context (38) could be used to give a true report of Kim's utterance of any of these. For these reasons, backshifting is best described by reference to the relation between a subordinate clause and its main clause counterpart, rather than that between indirect reported speech and the actual speech utterance being reported.[5]

Traditional grammars speak of a 'rule' for the 'sequence of tenses': (38) conforms to the rule in that it has a past tense *started* 'following', 'in sequence with', the superordinate clause past tense *said*; the rule is recognised to have exceptions, however, and instead of (38) we can say, without backshifting, *Kim said that the match starts tomorrow*. This way of putting it is not entirely satisfactory, but it is correct in implying that the backshifted construction is more normal, semantically more neutral, than the non-backshifted one. For there are conditions under which it would be inappropriate not to apply backshifting, but none under which backshifting of a present tense is excluded. Suppose, for example, that the main clause to be embedded is not (39) but (40), so that the subordinate counterparts with and without backshifting are as in (41i) and (ii) respectively:

(40)   *The match starts on 2 June*
(41)   i *Kim said that the match started on 2 June*[6]
             ii *Kim said that the match starts on 2 June*

---

[5] Backshifting can, however, occur in main clauses in what is called 'free indirect style': *The match started the next day so he would have to hurry* (with *he thought, he said to himself* or the like understood). This is a stylistic device found mainly in narrative writing. Although there is no formal embedding here, we will regard the backshifting as sufficient evidence for treating such clauses as non-kernel. There is also some affinity between backshifting and the use of the past tense found in examples like (34ii).

[6] This sentence is ambiguous in that it may involve the embedding without backshifting of *The match started on 2 June* – I am concerned with it only in the interpretation where it involves the embedding, with backshifting, of (40).

If Kim's utterance of (40) or of a pragmatic equivalent is being reported before 2 June, then either (i) or (ii) would be in order, but if it is being reported after 2 June clearly only (i) would be acceptable. Or consider a case where the present tense clause to be embedded has not a future time interpretation like (40), but a present time interpretation like

(42)   *The water is too cold for bathing*

Then in a context where there has been a significant change in the temperature of the water between the time of Kim's utterance and the time of mine, I would have to backshift: *Kim said that the water was too cold for bathing*. It would be inappropriate to say *Kim said that the water is too cold for bathing* precisely because that would imply that what Kim said was equivalent to what I would be saying if I uttered (42) now. These are of course pragmatic matters: (41ii) and *Kim said that the water is too cold for bathing* are perfectly grammatical – it would simply be inappropriate to use these sentences in the contexts described. Another pragmatic factor that is relevant is the speaker's attitude to the proposition expressed in the subordinate clause. If I believe that an assertion of (40) would be false, then I am more likely to prefer (41i) over (ii): backshifting distances the speaker somewhat from the content of the embedded clause.

It is difficult to say whether there are any conditions under which backshifting is grammatically obligatory. A sentence like *I knew you like her* sounds thoroughly unacceptable, but can we formulate a rule of grammar to exclude it? Certainly we cannot say that backshifting is obligatory with **know** but optional with **say**, for we shall not want to exclude *Did you know that Jill's in hospital again?* and the like. In the absence of clear evidence that conditions for obligatory backshifting have been partially grammaticalised, I shall simply say that there is a rule of grammar which PERMITS backshifting when a clause is embedded within a larger clause whose tense is past; (41ii) is not an exception to the rule, but a case where a grammatically optional process has not been applied.

In the examples we have been considering, the past tense in the superordinate clause has its primary use of indicating past time. The TS for the backshifted subordinate clause is then related not to TU but to the past time referred to in the superordinate clause, whereas in the non-backshifted construction $TR = TU$. The backshifting rule is equally applicable, however, when the superordinate past tense indicates factual remoteness: *If he knew that the match started tomorrow, he would surely be here by now*, and in this example $TR = TU$ in spite of the backshifting. Nevertheless the backshifting here still has the distancing effect that it has in the former case: in neither case is the backshifted clause presented from the vantage point of the actual here and now of the utterance itself.

4.6 **Progressive aspect**

As the name suggests, the progressive presents the situation as being 'in progress'. This implies that the situation is conceived of as taking place, not simply obtaining – i.e. it is conceived of as having a more or less dynamic character, as opposed to being wholly static. It also implies that the situation is viewed as having at least the potential for continuation and hence is being viewed not in its (potential) temporal totality but at some 'subinterval' of time, a point or period within that total interval of time. The non-progressive by contrast does not present the situation as in progress: the situation may be either static or dynamic, and in the latter case the action, process or whatever will be viewed in its temporal totality, and hence presented as an event.

Consider, for example, the contrast between

(43) i *It was raining*
     ii *It rained*

The verb **rain** denotes a dynamic situation. In (i) this situation is in progress at the time being referred to (cf. *I opened the curtains and saw that it was raining*), and the time being referred to will be a subinterval of the total interval of time during which it rained; (ii) on the other hand presents the situation as a whole, as an event.

The implication that the situation continued or will continue beyond the time at which it is presented as being in progress is a pragmatic one, not an entailment, and hence the progressive is not inconsistent with other indications that in fact the situation was halted at the time in question: *Ed was watching television* will imply, other things being equal, that the situation continued after the subinterval being talked about, but in *Ed was watching television when the blackout occurred* other things are not equal and there would here normally be no such implication. It is for this reason that I spoke above of the situation as having the 'potential' for continuation rather than as simply continuing.

Let us now consider certain more specific contrasts of meaning to be found in progressive/non-progressive pairs; to a large extent but probably not completely, they can be regarded as special cases of the above general contrast, predictable from the interaction of the aspectual contrast with other features of the sentence.

(a) Take first a pair like

(44) i *Kim was opening the parcel*
     ii *Kim opened the parcel*

This pair differs from (43) in that (43i) entails that it rained, while (44i) does not entail that Kim opened the parcel. Certain types of expression, such as **open** *the parcel* in contrast with **rain**, can be used for situations involving some inherent completion point. You cannot go on 'opening a parcel' once it is open, and similarly the fire cannot go on 'destroying all the paintings', say, once they have been destroyed. We may thus contrast, for example, **drink** *the bottle of whisky* with **drink** on its own: the former but not the latter has an inherent completion point, a difference reflected in the fact that we can say *It took him only ten minutes to drink the bottle of whisky* or *He drank the bottle of whisky in ten minutes* but not (with the same interpretation of *it* and *in ten minutes*) *It took him only ten minutes to drink* or *He drank in ten minutes*. Where the situation has an inherent completion point, then, the progressive indicates incompleteness at the time in question, while the non-progressive indicates completeness.[7]

(b) Consider next the contrast in

(45) i *Kim is living in Berlin*
      ii *Kim lives in Berlin*

Here (i) implies a situation of limited duration, something relatively temporary, whereas (ii) suggests a longer, indefinite duration. This is related to the fact that living somewhere is basically static rather than dynamic (note that it would not normally be conceived of as something one does). The most natural aspect for **live** *in Berlin* to appear in is accordingly the non-progressive. The progressive, as we have said, presents the situation as in progress, a process – and this is incompatible with its being an unchanging state of unlimited duration; since the element of change required by a process is not inherent in the meaning of **live** *in Berlin* we infer that it comes from the impermanence of the situation – it is progressing towards its end. Notice, however, that limited duration could also be indicated by a suitable temporal expression such as *at the moment*, and though such an expression may well favour the use of the progressive it does not require it: *at the moment* could be added to either sentence in (45). Thus if I know that you are in temporary accommodation I might say *Where are you living?, Where are you living at the moment?* or *Where do you live at the moment?* – but hardly just *Where do you live?*. The difference noted in (45) will also apply in the past tense.

(c) Our next pair is (46), where the present tense is more significant:

---

[7] This account needs to be refined or qualified to handle expressions like **read** *'Emma'*: the situation here would seem to be one with an inherent completion point (reached when the whole book has been read), yet we can say *I read 'Emma' for half an hour last night before going to sleep*, which doesn't imply that I read the whole book (rather, the contrary). Note by contrast that *Kim opened the parcel for half an hour* cannot be interpreted as "Kim spent half an hour opening the parcel".

(46)   i *Kim is reading 'The Australian'*
         ii *Kim reads 'The Australian'*

In the absence of indications to the contrary, one is likely to interpret (i) as involving a single occasion of reading 'The Australian', (ii) repeated or habitual reading of it. This, however, is a matter of the relative salience of particular interpretations, not a difference in the meanings of the sentences themselves. It is possible to contextualise (i) with regular reading: *We've decided to change our newspaper allegiances for the vacation – I'm reading 'The Age' and Kim is reading 'The Australian'*, and (ii) could be used for a single occasion of reading in a stage direction. Thus it would be a serious mistake to conclude that the semantic difference between progressive and non-progressive is to be equated with that between "single-occasion" and "habitual" (or "repeated regularly or characteristically"): this latter distinction is not grammatically encoded in the structure of the VP in English. The difference in salience of the single-occasion and habitual interpretations of (i) and (ii) results from the combination of aspect, tense and the meaning of **read** *'The Australian'*. **Read** *'The Australian'* is inherently dynamic but like all or most such expressions it can appear in clauses involving situations conceived of as obtaining rather than taking place – states of affairs characterised by the habitual or regular occurrence of an event: if we consider the past tense *Kim read 'The Australian'* it is easy to see both single-occasion and habitual interpretations, neither being obviously more salient than the other. A present tense normally indicates present time or future time. Reading 'The Australian' is not the sort of thing one readily thinks of as being organised for the future so that we will most naturally seek a present time interpretation of (ii). The non-progressive, we have said, is used for events considered in their temporal totality or for states – but for the former it is used in the present tense with a present time interpretation only when the duration of the event does not extend significantly beyond TR, as in running commentaries (*Hughes plays defensively forward*), demonstrations (*I take two eggs ...*), and so on. A single act of reading 'The Australian' is of much longer duration than this – so we will normally be left with the state interpretation, involving habitual reading. In (i), on the other hand, the progressive focuses on a subinterval of time, so that there is no bar to the single occasion interpretation, and this is more salient for the progressive than the habitual interpretation because two extra conceptual steps, as it were, are required for the latter. First we have to move from something basically dynamic to a state characterised by habitual or regular occurrences of an event, and then we have to move from a state of this kind of indefinite duration to a process involving the progression towards the end of such a state of affairs, as in (45i).

(d) Next we note the interaction between aspect and a certain type of temporal expression, as in

(47)   i *Ed was having lunch when I arrived*
         ii *Ed had lunch when I arrived*

In (i) *when I arrived* gives the time at which the situation of Ed's having lunch is presented as being in progress, whereas in (ii) it is interpreted as the time that situation began. The first is unproblematic: the progressive focuses on a subinterval of time, and this is simply the time when I arrived. In the second the non-progressive, in conjunction with the semantics of **have** *lunch*, indicates that the situation is a total event, and since having lunch takes time while arriving is instantaneous, the two events cannot be simultaneous. Notice that *Ed stood when I arrived* is interpreted in the same way: although standing up takes less time than having lunch it is still not instantaneous – only in a case like *Ed arrived when I arrived* are the two events simultaneous (though *as* would be probably preferred to *when* for simultaneity). *Ed was in bed when I arrived* is interpreted differently because Ed's being in bed is a static situation. *Ed was very pleased with himself when I arrived* allows either type of interpretation – though the reading where my arrival gives the time when his being pleased with himself began will carry the further pragmatic implication that my arrival caused him to be very pleased with himself.

(e) (48) illustrates a special conventionalised use of the progressive:

(48)   i *They are always playing chess*
         ii *They always play chess*

The progressive here carries an emotive component of meaning not present in (ii): it suggests that I find their behaviour somewhat tiresome. The adverb *always* (or some near-equivalent such as *continually*) is crucial for this use – and *always* is in fact interpreted rather differently in the two examples. In (ii) the *always* needs elaboration from the context or further temporal expressions – cf. *They always play chess on Friday evenings*: it means "on all occasions of some contextually determined kind". In (i) it is interpreted without any such limitation, so that it implies, when taken literally, that at any time you care to mention they will be engaged in playing chess; this will obviously be recognised as 'hyperbole' or overstatement – and the element of disapproval is presumably derived precisely from this hyperbole.

(f) Both progressive and non-progressive can be used for future situations:

(49)   i *John is leaving tomorrow*
         ii *John leaves tomorrow*

The difference in meaning is difficult to pin down precisely. We have noted that there are pragmatic constraints on the use of a present tense with a future time interpretation – and these constraints seem somewhat stricter for the progressive. Thus *The sun rises at 5.15 tomorrow* is quite normal, whereas *The sun is rising at 5.15 tomorrow* is not: the progressive is not used where we simply have a projection into the future of events following a regular pattern in nature. The progressive also typically suggests more initiative, intention on the part of the person referred to by the NP subject: compare *I can't come to the party because I'm doing / I do my marking tonight*, where the progressive presents it as a matter of personal intentions, the non-progressive as a matter of some more general schedule. It is doubtful whether the difference between the two aspects under the future interpretation can be regarded as a special case of the general semantic difference with which we began this section.

In the above discussion we have been concentrating on examples with contrasting aspects; we should also mention that certain verbs are highly resistant to aspectual variation, occurring predominantly or wholly in the non-progressive. Among the clearest are those denoting a variety of static relations, such as **belong**, **consist**, **contain** (as in *It contains calcium*, as opposed to *He contained himself*, etc.), **entail**, **possess**, and so on. With some, the semantic and pragmatic conditions for the progressive would seem simply not to arise: **entail**, for instance, as in *'John forced Peter to resign' entails that Peter resigned* denotes a relationship that is (at least for practical purposes) permanent and static, so that it is difficult to see how it could be represented as a process. But for the most part the inherent meaning of the verb provides only a partial explanation. Take **belong**, for example: certainly this denotes a relationship and would therefore be expected to favour the non-progressive, but we have noted that situations that are inherently states can be represented as processes when they are conceived of as progressing towards a relatively imminent change, as in *Kim is living in Berlin at the moment*: why then can we not say *The car is belonging to me at the moment though I'm selling it to John tomorrow*? There is a great deal more that could be said on this difficult issue; for further discussion the reader is referred to the works mentioned under 'Further reading'.

Progressive and non-progressive contrast in a grammatical system to which we are applying the general term 'aspect'. It will be clear that the meaning difference is quite unlike that which figures in the general definition of tense given above. 'Aspect' is employed for grammatical systems where the primary semantic contrast between the terms has to do with what has been called the 'internal temporal constituency' of the situation – whether it is viewed as static (unchanging through time) or dynamic, as complete or incomplete, as habitual/iterative or not, as durative (stretching out over time) or non-durative, as in its initial stage, its terminal stage or neither – and so on: there is a considerable variety of aspectual systems in the world's languages. In English we have a number of catenative verbs that have aspectual type meanings – verbs like **begin**, **start**, **cease**, **finish**, **stop**, **continue**, **keep** (compare *He keeps losing his temper* and *He's always losing his temper*), *going* (in the idiom **be** *going* as in *It's going to fall*, **use** (as in *I used to go to work by bicycle*), and so on; as these are main verbs, not auxiliaries, however, we can talk of them as 'aspectual verbs' but will not set up grammatical systems of aspect with the marked terms containing these verbs (as some traditional grammars treat *It started to rain* as having 'ingressive' aspect, and so on). We are also applying the term aspect to the system contrasting *has taken* and *takes* – though, as we shall see, the meaning involved is not one that places the system very clearly within the domain of the general term 'aspect', as opposed to 'tense'.

4.7 Perfect aspect

Perhaps the most obvious semantic difference between perfect and non-perfect in a contrasting pair like

(50)   i *Kim has been ill*
        ii *Kim is ill*

is that the situation of Kim's being ill is located in (i) in past time and in (ii) in present time. But that is also the difference that we find between *Kim was ill* and *Kim is ill*. We will accordingly begin our discussion of the perfect by examining the contrast between it and the past tense (in its primary use): we will at this stage be concerned solely with cases where they are, as it were, in competition – with the contrast between, say, *has seen* and *saw* (or *has been seeing* and *was seeing*, *has been seen* and *was seen*), where perfect **have** carries a present tense inflection. Cases where **have** carries the past tense inflection (*had seen*) or is non-tensed (*to have seen, having seen, may have seen*) will be taken up later. In the interests of readability I shall, in this initial discussion, speak simply of the 'perfect' and the 'past tense' to refer to VPs that are respectively present, non-modal and perfect (*has seen*) and past, non-modal and non-perfect (*saw*): it must be borne in mind that what is at this stage said about the 'perfect' applies only where **have** is in the present tense.

The essential difference between the perfect and the past tense is this: the perfect locates the situation within a period of time beginning in the past and extending forward to include the present (TU, or more generally, TR), whereas the past tense is used where the time of the situation is identified as wholly in the past, as a past that excludes the present. With the perfect we have an 'inclusive past', with the past tense an 'exclusive past'.

This distinction between an inclusive past and an exclusive past immediately accounts for certain restrictions on the temporal expressions that can combine with the two forms:

(a) Expressions such as *at present, as yet, since last week, lately* combine with the perfect but not the past tense: *At present I have written/*wrote three chapters.* The inclusion of the present time is very clear in *at present, as yet, so far,* which can equally well combine with a present non-perfect: *So far she has three novels to her credit.* Similarly *since last week* means, essentially, "from last week until the present (TR)". The occurrence of *lately* in this class is not so clearly motivated by the semantics: note that *recently* does combine with the past tense.

(b) Expressions such as *three days ago, at that time, last week, yesterday,* and so on, combine with the past tense but not with the perfect: *I saw/*have seen her last week.* These expressions all identify periods that are quite distinct from, exclusive of, the present.[8]

(c) A third class of temporal expressions, including *this morning, today, always, never, recently,* can occur with either form:

(51)   i *He has overslept this morning*
         ii *He overslept this morning*

This morning can be used with the perfect only if it is still morning at the time of utterance, i.e. the period identified by *this morning* must include TU. But its use with the past tense is not restricted to the afternoon and evening: either (i) or (ii) could be uttered appropriately in the morning. In (ii) the time of his oversleeping is conceived of as over, as separate from the present – although the morning as a whole need not be over, that part of it within which his oversleeping is located (for instance the part associated with waking and getting up) is. Thus, if he is still asleep, I would normally use (i), whereas if he got up at 6 a.m. instead of his usual 5.30 and it is now mid-morning, (ii) is the form I would use.

It will be apparent that the choice between a perfect and a past tense, between an inclusive and an exclusive past, is generally not determined by the actual temporal location of the situation, but depends on the speaker's subjective conception of it. Suppose, for example, that I broke my leg on a climbing expedition last weekend: I could now say either *I have broken my leg* or *I broke my leg.* It is not the time of the event that differs, but my perspective. With *broke* I am talking about a past thought of as over: if I am now back at home with my leg in plaster I might say *The expedition was marred by the fact that I broke my leg* – not *have broken.* But if, on the other hand, I am talking not about the expedition as such but about my present incapacity, I

---

[8] It is in fact a slight overstatement to say that they never occur with the perfect: occasional examples like *There have been more deaths in Northern Ireland yesterday* (from a radio news bulletin) are found, but I will regard them as sufficiently rare and questionable to be ignored under a reasonable idealisation of the data: if these occurrences turn out to be of more significance, this will reflect a weakening of the semantic contrast between the perfect and the past tense.

would say *I have broken my leg*. Let us therefore consider some of the main factors influencing the choice between the perfect and the past tense.

(a) In the first place, the choice may be determined, as we have seen, by the selection of a temporal expression allowing only one or the other of the two forms: this overrides any of the factors mentioned below.

(b) To indicate that a state of affairs prevailed continuously throughout a period beginning in the past and extending up to the present, a perfect is required: *He has lived in Canberra all his life*. There is a clear contrast here with the past tense *He lived in Canberra all his life*. With the former, *all his life* must indicate a period inclusive of the present, from which it follows that he is still alive; with the latter, it indicates a period exclusive of the present, so he must be dead. English differs from such languages as French and German in using a perfect rather than a present non-perfect for a state prevailing from past time into the present time. It is easy to see that such a difference is quite reasonable. Disregarding the cases of future time interpretation, the time of a situation expressed in a clause with a present non-perfect is present, but with static situations, as we have seen, the time period can extend beyond the immediate present, as in *He lives in Canberra*, where I am not talking exclusively of the present instant. Now in English, specification of the time in the past at which the present situation began requires the perfect: *He has lived/*lives in Canberra since 1975*. But in French and German the temporal expression corresponding to *since 1975* would just be added to the present non-perfect. Thus English here uses a past inclusive of the present, while French and German use a present inclusive of the past.[9]

(c) The perfect is often used for recent events – it is the very recency which provides the connection with the present: *Max has just bought a new car*. This is the source of the large number of perfects heard in radio news bulletins: *The American actor Charles Henry has died at his home in California at the age of 92* (but recall our discussion of examples like (36ii)). Recency is neither a necessary nor a sufficient condition for the use of the perfect, but it may create the context in which the meaning of the perfect is an appropriate one to express.

(d) The perfect is commonly used for past events considered as causes of their present effects or results – or, more generally, considered for their 'current relevance': *I have broken my leg, so I can't go with them*. The effects or relevance will often be left implicit and thus be heavily dependent on the

---

[9] It is also relevant to add that although French and German have a VP construction analogous to the English perfect in that it consists of the auxiliary "have" + a 'past participle inflection' on the next verb it does not have the "inclusive past" meaning of the English (as is evident from the fact that it occurs freely with expressions meaning "yesterday", etc.) and hence is less appropriate for the type of situation we are considering here.

particular context; *Liz has gone to London*, for example, might be used to account for her absence, but there could be any number of other reasons for its relevance. The concept of current relevance is rather vague and it is perhaps general enough to cover all uses of the perfect – but there is certainly no question of the past tense being used only for states or events lacking current relevance. For example, in *I broke my leg yesterday so I can't go with them* the relevance is just as clear as in the above example, but the specification of a period of time excluding the present makes the past tense necessary.

(e) The perfect is often used for past events where the actual time of occurrence is unimportant: what matters is their taking place within the experience of the participants. Compare here a pair of examples like *Have you read 'Middlemarch'?* and *Did you read 'Middlemarch'?*. The latter suggests that I am asking about some particular occasion: you were intending or were intended to read it, say, and I am asking whether the intention was realised. The perfect, on the other hand, could be used when I have no particular time in mind. There is one use of the verb **be**, meaning approximately "go" or "visit", which occurs only in the perfect and it quite characteristically has this 'experiential' interpretation – compare *I haven't been to Moscow before*.

The various uses of the perfect illustrated in (b)–(e) are not intended as distinct senses (meanings) of the form. 'Use' is a pretheoretical term – methodologically prior, that is, to a proper semantic analysis. In the case of the past tense inflection, the three uses that we distinguished in §5 do, I believe, correspond to different senses, in that they do not appear to be predictable from the interaction between a single general sense and other semantic/pragmatic factors in the sentence or context. But the above uses of the perfect can all be subsumed under the account given of it at the beginning of this section, and merely illustrate some of the ways a past situation may be connected with the present so as to motivate our representing it as located in an inclusive rather than an exclusive past. And although there is a constant distinction of meaning between the perfect and the past tense, the significance of choosing one rather than the other may vary considerably depending on the context. With the pair *He has lived in Canberra all his life* and *He lived in Canberra all his life*, the choice involves, as we have seen, a matter of life or death; but at the other extreme we find pairs like [*Good-bye,*] *it has been a pleasure to meet you* and [*Good-bye,*] *it was a pleasure to meet you*, where it will often make little difference to what is communicated whether we choose an inclusive or an exclusive past. And it should also be borne in mind that there is some variation in usage across dialects, with some using the past tense where the account given above would predict the perfect (e.g. *Did you read it yet?* instead of *Have you read it yet?*).

As emphasised above, what we have been saying about the perfect applies just where the auxiliary **have** carries a present tense inflection. We have said that the perfect indicates a past inclusive of the present, and it is the present tense that is the source of this "present" element (for the present tense cannot sustain a future time interpretation when it combines with perfect **have**). Because the present is included in this way, the perfect does not trigger back-shifting – cf. **Kim has said that the match started tomorrow*. It is also worth observing that in the idiom **have** *got*, which contains auxiliary **have** + an -*en* form, the meaning (when the **have** is present tense) is concerned solely with the present: in *I've got a headache*, or *I've got to mow the lawn* I'm not talking at all about any past situation. This of course is what makes it an idiom, but it is of interest that it is the present time component from the meaning of the perfect, not the past time component, that is retained in the idiom.

Let us now turn to cases where perfect **have** either carries the past tense inflection or is untensed. Consider first the past perfect, as in [*I arrived at six,*] *but she had left a few minutes before*. The time of her leaving is past relative to the time of my arriving, which is in turn past relative to the time of utterance: TS for *had left* is thus past in past, i.e. past relative to a past. The more distant past derives from the perfect, the less distant one from the past tense inflection. We have noted that some temporal expressions indicate a past inclusive, others a past exclusive of TR, occurring with the present perfect and past non-perfect respectively. The past perfect, however, occurs with both types. *A few minutes before*, in the example above, indicates a past exclusive of TR (compare *a few minutes ago* which combines with the past non-perfect), but we could also have *since three*, which is inclusive of TR: [*I arrived at six,*] *but she had been there since three*. Thus the perfect here no longer indicates a specifically inclusive past: we simply have a past time that is relative to (but is indifferently inclusive or exclusive of) another past time. Analogously when the past tense of a past perfect is used to express factual remoteness:

(52) i *If you had been here yesterday, you'd have seen some fun*
ii *If you had been here since this morning, you'd have seen some fun*

The 'real' condition counterpart of (i) is *If you were here yesterday, you will have seen some fun*, where the *if* clause has the past non-perfect *were* (with its primary use), while that of (ii) is *If you have been here since this morning, you will have seen some fun*, where we have the present perfect *have been*: as we move from the real to the unreal, the contrast between exclusive *were* and inclusive *have been* is lost, both becoming *had been*. And the same holds when we apply backshifting to a past non-perfect and a present perfect: both become past perfects, witness *She told me that Ed had been here yesterday/since this morning*.[10]

---

[10] When the clause for embedding has a single past, however, the construction without backshifting will often be used: *She told me that Ed was here yesterday*. If the clause for embedding already has a past perfect, then there is no possibility of backshifting – it can

Finally we find the same loss of contrast within the VP in non-tensed constructions: *Ed is known to have been here yesterday/since this morning.* In these non-tensed constructions, TR – the time relative to which the situation is past – is determined by the superordinate clause: in the example given TR = TU (because of the present time interpretation of *is known*), in *They believed him to have died of cancer*, it is past (the time of the believing) and in *I hope to have finished by six* it is future (because **hope** projects into the future).

What emerges from the discussion of the last two paragraphs is that it is only when auxiliary **have** carries the present tense inflection that the perfect indicates an inclusive past. Elsewhere it simply indicates a past: if that past is interpreted as specifically inclusive or exclusive (and there is no reason to assume that it always will be), this interpretation will derive from other features of the sentence or context – the distinction is not encoded in the VP itself. It is not difficult to see why this should be so. The non-perfect is unmarked relative to the perfect (it lacks **have** + following -*en* inflection) and present tense is unmarked relative to the past tense (the general present tense form is identical to the base form, while the past tense form involves the application of some morphological process): the present non-perfect, as in [*They*] *take*, is thus unmarked relative to both [*They*] *have taken* and [*They*] *took*, and the latter pair, present perfect and past non-perfect, can be seen to be in grammatical contrast, not in the sense that they are different terms in a single system but in the sense that they represent contrasting ways of departing from the maximally unmarked present non-perfect. Corresponding to this contrast in the grammar we have the semantic contrast between inclusive and exclusive past. But elsewhere the perfect is not in grammatical contrast with the past tense: either they combine (the past perfect) or the past is not grammatically possible (**have** being in a non-tensed construction); since there is then no grammatical contrast, the semantic contrast is neutralised, and the perfect simply indicates an undifferentiated past.

To conclude this section, let us consider the implications of the general term 'perfect aspect'. 'Perfect' is to be understood in the sense "complete": in its strictest use, perfect will thus be applied to a formal category of the verb or VP whose primary meaning is to denote the state characterised by the completion of some earlier situation. Completeness is closely related to pastness: if something is now complete the process or whatever of reaching that point will have taken place in the past; thus perfect aspect is closely related to past tense. The difference is that with perfect aspect the emphasis is on the present state while with the past tense it is on the past situation. The English auxiliary **have** + -*en* form construction does not by any means

only remain a past perfect: *She told me that Max had already been here three hours when she arrived.* The reader is invited to consider whether it is possible to have an unreal counterpart of a real condition containing a past perfect in the *if* clause.

fall at the centre of the semantic area covered by the concept of perfect aspect, even if we consider only the case where *have* carries the present tense inflection – i.e. where the form contrasts with the inflectional past in the sense explained above (and it is reasonable to regard this as the primary use, the one on the basis of which an appropriate general term will be selected). It is often used for a situation obtaining from a time in the past up to and including the present, as in *He has lived in Canberra all his life* (discussed above), *She has been ill since last week, We've known them for years,* etc., where there is no implication that the situation is now complete, finished – quite the contrary. And there are many other places where, even though the situation does not still obtain or is not still taking place, it would be quite unnatural to paraphrase with 'complete': *Have you seen Kim?, I've met them three times,* and so on. Nevertheless, the past situation is presented as crucially connected with the present: this is what we have been emphasising in talking of a past inclusive of the present; while the past tense is used when there is simply reference to a situation in the past, the *have* + *-en* form construction is not. It is for this reason that we are regarding the system contrasting *takes* with *has taken* as one of aspect. Clearly, however, the system of perfect aspect is very much closer to a tense system than is that of progressive aspect – and this is reflected in the fact that when *have* does not carry the present tense inflection we have a neutralisation of the aspect-type and tense-type meanings.

4.8   Analytic mood

The general term 'mood' is applied to grammatical systems of the verb or VP whose terms are differentiated semantically primarily in the contrast between factual assertion and various kinds of non-factuality and/or non-assertion. The traditional inflectional system indicative vs imperative vs subjunctive clearly falls under this definition, with indicative, the unmarked term, the one used in factual assertions. We are taking the view that there is no inflectional system of mood in Modern English, but the contrast between *He is downstairs, He may be downstairs, He must be downstairs,* and so on, also falls within this semantic area and we will accordingly regard the VPs *is, may be* and *must be* as differing in mood; since the terms in the VP system are differentiated not inflectionally but by means of auxiliaries, we will talk of an analytic mood system. The initial distinction is between non-modal and modal VPs, with the latter being then subdivided into more specific mood categories according to which modal auxiliary they contain.

The distinctive grammatical properties of the modal auxiliaries were given in §2: they are always tensed, they don't enter into person–number agreement with the subject and they can occur as the tensed verb in the main clause of an unreal condition. The central members of the class of modal auxiliary verbs – or 'modals', as they are often called – are **may**, **must**, **can**, **will** and **shall**. Also to be included are **need** and **dare**, as in *He need/dare not show his face*. In *He needs/dares to show his face*, by contrast, **need** and **dare** are main verbs (catenatives) not auxiliaries – compare *Does he need/dare to show his face?*. Given the concept of lexeme adopted in this book, we will recognise distinct lexemes **need**$_{Mod}$ and **need**$_{MV}$, **dare**$_{Mod}$ and **dare**$_{MV}$, since we have abstractions from distinct sets of inflectional forms – as evident from the above contrast between *need* and *needs*, *dare* and *dares* in construction with *he* as subject. **Need**$_{Mod}$ and **dare**$_{Mod}$ occur only in 'non-affirmative' contexts – roughly in negative or interrogative clauses (see 13.2 for a fuller account of what is meant by 'non-affirmative'). **Ought** is on the periphery of the class: it is questionable whether it can occur as the tensed verb in the main clause of an unreal condition – and in certain non-standard varieties it has a base form combining with the dummy operator **do** (*You didn't ought to have done that*); it also differs from the central modals in being followed by infinitival *to* instead of directly by a base form. In addition **have** and **be** in certain uses have some affinities with the modals. **Have** occurs only in the past tense in the idiom where it combines with *better*: *I had better leave* (where the past tense is clearly not used in its primary sense); it doesn't here show agreement, but given that the tense is past this is of no significance, and as it doesn't satisfy the unreal condition criterion the case for including it is fairly weak. (Note that the **have** of *I have to leave*, though semantically very close to **must**, has none of the modal properties and is very clearly a catenative, not a modal.) In the use exemplified in *You are not to tell him*, **be** occurs only in tensed forms – but it lacks the other two modal properties, and is thus again better classified as a catenative.

The semantics of the modal auxiliaries is a highly complex matter, and the subject of a large literature. Some writers claim to bring all the uses of any one modal within the scope of a single broad definition of its meaning, while others allow for polysemy but with widely varying views on how many different senses are to be distinguished in any given case. There are no generally accepted criteria for determining rigorously how many senses should be distinguished for a lexical item or grammatical category, so that disagreements of the kind just mentioned are commonplace in semantic analysis. The problem is nevertheless particularly acute in the analysis of the modals and in the short space available here there is no need to take any very explicit stand on the question – though I shall assume that at least some polysemy needs to be recognised. The aim here will thus simply be to introduce some of the main concepts and issues in this area of grammatical semantics.

The first concept we need is that of **modality**: this is a rather broad term for the kind of meaning characteristically expressed by the modals – its sense will become clearer as we distinguish various types of modality.

Note, then, that we are using 'mood' as a category of grammar and 'modality' as a category of meaning: the distinction is analogous to that between 'tense' and 'time' (and it would be useful if we had a similar pair of terms for talking about aspect). It will already be clear that it is not only modal auxiliaries that express semantic modality: the meanings of catenative **need** and **dare** are the same as those of the corresponding modals, catenative **have** and **be** (*He has/is to leave tomorrow*) overlap with **must**; the adverbs *perhaps* and *surely* are semantically similar to certain uses of **may** and **must** respectively; the adjectives **able** and *possible* commonly figure in paraphrases offered for sentences containing **can** – and so on: modality is expressed by a considerable range of syntactically quite diverse items. Whether the modal auxiliaries have any senses falling outside the domain of modality is less clear. **Dare** is semantically somewhat different from the others, and its meaning is at best very peripheral to modality – and **will** and **shall** have uses that fall in the boundary area between modality and time, a point we will take up below.

The two most central notions in modal logic, that branch of logic that deals with modality, are possibility and necessity, and we will begin our investigation of modality by distinguishing two kinds of possibility and necessity, known as **epistemic** and **deontic**. Examples are given in (53):

(53)

		Epistemic	Deontic
Possibility	i	*You may be under a misapprehension*	ii *You may take as many as you like*
Necessity	iii	*You must be out of your mind*	iv *You must work harder*

The distinction can also be illustrated by means of the ambiguous sentences in (54), which can be interpreted in either of the ways shown in (55) and (56) respectively:

(54)　　i *You may have a bottle*
　　　　ii *You must be very tolerant*

(55)　　i "Perhaps you have a bottle"　　　　　　　　　　　Epistemic
　　　　ii "You are permitted to have/take a bottle"　　　　Deontic

(56)　　i "I am forced to conclude that you are very tolerant"　Epistemic
　　　　ii "You are required to be very tolerant"　　　　　　Deontic

Since we are not concerned here with determining precisely how many senses the modals have, we will examine the contrast between epistemic and deontic modality with the aim not of providing rigorous criteria to decide whether any given instance of a modal expresses one or the other (or neither) kind of modality, but of highlighting the differences between the prototypical examples: scholars vary considerably in how far beyond the prototype they allow the categories to extend. I will discuss four main differences between prototypical epistemic and deontic modality – and in presenting them below, I will for convenience use the informal term 'residue' for what is left of the meaning expressed in an utterance of the clause when the modality is abstracted away.

(a) In epistemic modality the residue has the status of a proposition, something that is either true or false: in (55i), for example, the modality applies to the proposition that you have a bottle, in (56i) to the proposition that you are very tolerant. And the issue is whether or not the proposition is true. More precisely, epistemic modality is concerned with its truth status in the light of what the speaker knows – the term 'epistemic' is related to the Greek word for "knowledge". With epistemic possibility I imply, minimally, that I do not know that the proposition is false: if I say *It may be Kim's* I cannot, without contradiction, add *but I know/realise it's not* – though I could add anything from *but I think that's very unlikely* to *and I'm pretty sure it is*. (Indeed it is possible to use *may* when the proposition is known to be true, as in *You may be older than me but that doesn't give you the right to push me around*, though *may* is here quite clearly not expressing prototypical epistemic possibility.) With epistemic necessity I imply that, on the basis of the knowledge I have, I cannot accept that there is any possibility of the proposition not being true – note again that it would be contradictory to say *It must be Kim's though I concede it's just possible that it isn't*. Because *It must be Kim's but it isn't* is contradictory we can say that *It must be Kim's* (interpreted epistemically) entails *It is Kim's*. Nevertheless, there is a clear sense in which I commit myself more strongly in saying *It is Kim's* than in saying *It must be Kim's*: with the former I imply that this is something I simply know, while with the latter I imply that I conclude that the proposition is true through the (usually tacit) rejection of other possibilities. Notice that the implicit reasoning involved with epistemic **must** may in practice vary widely in soundness. In *Tom is Bill's father and Bill is John's father so Tom must be John's grandfather* it is impeccable – and here it would make little pragmatic difference if non-modal *is* were substituted for *must be*. In *Tom must have overslept*, on the other hand, said when he has failed to turn up for a 6 a.m. rendezvous, it is probably very shaky, since there might well be other possible reasons for his non-appearance.

In the account just given, epistemic modality is oriented towards the speaker – it is 'subjective'. **May** and **must** can, however, be used 'objectively'. To cite an actual example from a political incident in Australia a few years ago, the Prime Minister was reported as saying: *Senator Withers may have misled Parliament*, where it was clearly not a matter of what the Prime Minister himself personally knew or thought – rather he was acknowledging that the possibility existed that the Senator had misled Parliament, and it would be one of the tasks of an official inquiry to establish whether in fact he had done so. But such cases are among those where we find disagreement as to what kind of modality is expressed, and it is for this reason that subjectivity is included in our characterisation of the prototype.

While in epistemic modality the residue has the character of a proposition, in deontic modality it has, by contrast, the character of an action. What is at issue is not whether something is true but whether something is going to be done. Again I will take the prototypical case to involve the speaker, to be subjective. Thus with deontic necessity, as in *You must come in now*, I require that the action be performed, I'm telling you to come in now – the etymology of 'deontic', also from Greek, involves the notion of "binding": I bind you, as it were, to come in. With deontic possibility I give permission for the action to be performed: *You may/can come in now*. Deontic **must** does not countenance the possibility of the action not being performed: *You must come in immediately though you can stay out a while longer if you prefer* is inconsistent. Deontic **may/can** are of course weaker and merely facilitate the performance of the action – though in certain contexts permission may be interpreted as binding: someone in a subordinate role will generally take *You may go now* as a dismissal. As we move away from the prototype, we find **must**, **may**, **can** used where the source of the obligation or permission is not the speaker, and where it is not a matter of performing some action but of satisfying some condition (cf. *Applicants must have postgraduate qualifications in psychology*): again I leave open the question of how broadly deontic modality is to be interpreted.

(b) It follows from what has just been said that with prototypical deontic modality the time involved in the residue is future: I require or permit something to be done after the obligation is imposed or the permission granted. With epistemic modality, by contrast, the time of the residue is generally present (*Tom must be John's grandfather*) or past (*Tom must have overslept*); the past time is expressed by the perfect construction, and since **have** occurs in the base form after a modal, the past can be either inclusive or exclusive. **Must** is rarely used in a similar way with future time (*The rain must surely ease soon*). **May**, on the other hand, does occur freely with future time, as in *It may rain tomorrow* – and epistemic modality is invariably interpreted broadly enough to include this. Nevertheless we can think of present and past as more central to it than future, partly because of the frequency pattern with **must**, partly because with the future the residue is less readily thought of in terms of a proposition: in *It may rain tomorrow* the issue is not so much the truth of some proposition but the occurrence of some event.

(c) Epistemic and deontic modality interact somewhat differently with negation. We must first note that negation can apply either to the residue or to the modality. Thus the natural interpretation of *She may not have known him* is "It may be the case that she did not know him": the negation is within the residue (here the proposition) that is modalised – and is accordingly commonly said to be 'internal'. In *She can't have known him*, by contrast, what is negated is the possibility of it being the case that she knew him: the negation applies to the modality and is hence 'external' (i.e. not within the residue). Let us now assemble examples of internal and external negation for epistemic and deontic possibility and necessity:

(57)		Negation	Possibility	Necessity
	Epistemic	Internal	i *It may not have been Tom*	ii *It mustn't have been Tom*
		External	iii *It can't have been Tom*	iv *It needn't have been Tom*
	Deontic	Internal	v *You may nŏt go*	vi *You mustn't go*
		External	vii *You mây not go*	viii *You needn't go*

(v) and (vii) are alike in the verbal component but are distinguished prosodically: in (v) there will be a phonological break between *may* and *not* (which will be stressed) to show that the negative relates to *go* – I have used '⌒' to link *not* to *go* in (v) and to *may* in (vii) as an ad hoc way of indicating the intended interpretation, "You are permitted not to go, i.e. permitted to stay" (v) and "You are not permitted to go" (vii). **Can** could be substituted for **may** in either, again with the special prosodic marking in (v), with the inflectional negative *can't* allowed in (vii) (for most speakers there is no inflectional form *mayn't*). Notice, by contrast, that with epistemic possibility **may** and **can** are not interchangeable.

Possibility and necessity are logically related in such a way that:

(α) If X is not possible, then not-X is necessary, and vice versa;
(β) If X is not necessary, then not-X is possible, and vice versa.

Thus from (α), (iii) is logically equivalent to (ii), and (vii) to (vi), and from (β) (i) is logically equivalent to (iv), and (v) to (viii). We nevertheless find a difference between the epistemic and deontic sets. (i) illustrates a more usual pattern than (iv), as does (iii) than (ii), which many speakers find at best marginally acceptable: with epistemic modality there is a tendency to prefer a formulation in terms of possibility when negation is involved. With deontic modality, however, the tendency is reversed – certainly (viii) is vastly more frequent than (v) (with *may* or *can*). For these and related reasons it has been plausibly argued that epistemic modality takes possibility as more basic than necessity, while with deontic modality necessity is more basic than possibility (and the reader may have noticed that the etymology of 'deontic' relates more directly to obligation than to permission).

(d) There are also differences relating to tense. The modals of necessity, **must** and **need**, lack past tense forms, so it is only with possibility that the issue arises, **may** and **can** having the past tense forms *might* and *could*. Our account of prototypical epistemic and deontic modality in (a) related them to the speaker, and hence by implication to the present time of the utterance – the speaker expresses a current epistemic judgement or places an obligation, gives permission, at the time of speaking. In these central cases, therefore, we do not find past tense modals with the past tense having its primary, temporal meaning. *Might* indeed is very rarely used at all to indicate past time; *could* certainly is so used, with examples having clear affinities with the types of modality we have been discussing, especially the deontic: cf. *We could stay out as long as we wanted at that time* ("We were permitted to . . ."). Both *might* and *could* occur with backshifting, but more interesting for present purposes is the case where the past tense indicates factual remoteness: only modal auxiliaries have past tense forms that occur in this use in main clauses, including constructions where there is no explicit or implicit unreal condition: we will consider only these. With epistemic **may** we have then a contrast between *may* and *might*, with the latter indicating (for many speakers) a more remote possibility than the former, as in the pair *You may/might be right*. As *can* is not used epistemically in kernel clauses, we could not substitute it for *may* in *You may be right* and hence have no analogous *can/could* contrast here; *You could be right* is possible, however, and similar though probably not quite identical in meaning to *You might be right*. With deontic **may** and **can** the past tense is not used to indicate a more remote possibility: deontic possibility is permission, which is not scalar like epistemic possibility, and hence it is not clear how factual remoteness could combine with it (outside of the conditional construction). *Might* can, however, be used deontically – but with a stronger, not a weaker, force than **may**: *You might take your dirty feet off the sofa*. Here I am not giving permission, but asking or telling you (with some element of rebuke at the same time): this must be recognised as a special use of *might*, not predictable from the meanings of **may** and the past tense.

So much for epistemic and deontic possibility and necessity. Of the modals we have been considering, **may**, **can**, **must** and **need**, it is clear that **can** at least has certain uses that do not fall under the concepts of epistemic and deontic modality, however broadly they are interpreted. Among the most obvious is that where **can** indicates ability of some kind, as in *Sue can speak ten languages*. The modality here is sometimes described as 'dynamic', though this is nothing like so standard a category as the other two. I will not go into it here, except to note that the most central cases involve some property or disposition of the referent of the subject NP – in the example given we are talking about an ability of Sue's. (Note then that if we take **dare** to express modality, it will be of the dynamic kind.)

Let us now turn to **will**. It has a quite wide range of uses, only some of which can be mentioned here. Some fall within the domain of what we have just introduced as dynamic modality – notably when it is a matter of volition or willingness on the part of the subject referent: *They won't give me any reason, Will he lend us the car?*. This element of 'disposition' is clearest perhaps in non-affirmative contexts, as in these negative and interrogative examples, and in such cases the past tense form *would* appears in the primary, past time, use: [*I complained bitterly*] *but they wouldn't give me any reason*. **Will** is also used in a way which has obvious affinities with more central cases of deontic modality: this use is found in military orders (*Company will parade at 0800 hours*) but also more generally in contexts where the speaker has the authority to lay down what is going to be done (*You will all stand when the headmaster enters*). Thirdly, it is used, with a present or past time residue, to express what is very clearly some type of epistemic modality:

(58) i   *That'll be Sue*
      ii *They will have received your letter yesterday*

– where the first might be said, for example, on hearing the telephone ring or someone knock at the door. We noted in discussing epistemic **must** that an example like *It must be Kim's* excludes the possibility of it not being Kim's but nevertheless involves a somewhat weaker commitment than *It is Kim's*. The same holds for epistemic **will**: it would be inconsistent to add *but it might be her brother* or *though it is possible that it hasn't yet reached them* to the above, but they are epistemically weaker than *That is Sue* and *They received your letter yesterday* – they are not construed as simple factual statements. It is commonly said that **will** is weaker than **must**; there may well be something in this, but I do not think it satisfactory to distinguish **must** and **will** as occupying slightly different positions on a single scale of 'strength', with **may** at the lower end. Intuitively **will** has a less clear-cut meaning than **must** and **may** – epistemic *will be* is less sharply distinguishable from *is*, semantically, than is *must be* or *may be*. This is reflected in the fact that a VP with *will* combines just as freely as its non-modal counterpart with the full range of AdvPs expressing epistemic modality – (*just*) *possibly, perhaps, probably, most likely, surely,* (*quite*) *certainly*, and so on: cf. *They will just possibly/quite certainly have received your letter yesterday*. **Must** and **may** on the other hand are not neutral with respect to the selection of an AdvP from this range: examples like *They must just possibly have received your letter yesterday* and *They may most likely have received your letter yesterday* are, to say the least, much less natural than *They must surely have …* and *They may possibly have …* A second point is that with epistemic **will** internal and external negation cannot be contrasted anything like so sharply as with **may** and **must**. It is quite clear that *It may not be Sue* and *It mustn't be Sue* (in the absence of very special prosodic marking) have internal negation, and they can be compared with *It can't be Sue, It needn't be Sue*, where the negation is external. But what of *It* *won't be Sue?* We may argue that the negation here is internal, but it is not obviously so and there is no contrasting modal giving an external negation counterpart. (A third reflection of the relative 'neutrality' of epistemic *will* can perhaps be seen in the considerable difference of opinion found in the literature as to what its meaning is, and the absence of any widely accepted label, analogous to 'necessity' for *must* and 'possibility' for *may*.)

Consider now the use of *will* when there is reference to future time, as in

(59)   *He will be seventy tomorrow*

We have already noted that a present tense non-modal VP can be used when the time of the situation is future, so that (59) contrasts with *He is seventy tomorrow*. Thus *is* contrasts with *will be* in both present and future time:

(60)   Present time   Future time

     − *will*   i *He is seventy now*   ii *He is seventy tomorrow*
     + *will*   iii *He will be seventy now*   iv *He will be seventy tomorrow*

Clearly then the semantic difference between *is* and *will be* is not a matter of "present time" vs "future time". This is not to suggest, however, that time is irrelevant, for the relation between *is* and *will be* is not simply the same with future time as with present time. One difference is that with present time *will* is often replaceable by *would* without any implications of conditionality. Thus in answer to *How old do you reckon he is?* I could say any of *He is seventy, He'll be seventy, He'd be seventy*, with *would be* involving a weaker commitment to the factuality of his being seventy than *will be*, just as the latter is weaker than *is*: the relation of *would* to *will* matches that of epistemic *might* to *may*. For the future, however, *He would be seventy tomorrow* is used only with explicit or implicit conditions (e.g. ... *if he had lived*) – we will take up the use of *will* in conditions below. A second difference is that with present time *will* seems always to have the element of subjectivity that we mentioned in discussing epistemic *may* and *must*, but with future time it does not; with respect to both time and subjectivity, the *will* of (60iii) falls within the domain of prototypical epistemic modality, while that of (iv) does not. A third difference, the most obvious, is that with present time the form without *will* is very much more frequent than the one with *will*, whereas with future time the reverse is the case: as we have noted, the use of a present tense non-modal for future time is subject to quite strong pragmatic conditions (see §5 above), so that while (60ii) and (iv), say, are equally normal and acceptable, *She'll soon forget she ever knew me* and *She soon forgets she ever knew me*, are not. There is thus some significant correlation between *is* and present time, *will be* and future time, even though it is nowhere near a one-to-one correlation. This correlation can be seen as reflecting an inherent connection between modality and time: by the very nature of things we cannot in general talk about the future with the same assurance as about the present or past, and it is accordingly only under quite special conditions that it is appropriate to make a modally unqualified assertion about the future. Her forgetting in the future that she ever knew me is not the sort of thing for which I can have, at the time of speaking, anything like the same kind of evidence as I can for her doing so in the past: hence the difference in acceptability between *She forgot she ever knew me* and *She soon forgets she ever knew me*. This suggests that the meaning of **will** has at least some latent element of modality about it even when used with future time, even though it is certainly less evident than when it is used with present or past time. A further reason for thinking that this is so emerges when we consider certain kinds of subordinate clause, including those belonging to the class of temporal expressions:

(61)   *When you feel better, [get in touch with me]*

The time is future, but we do not here use *will*: *When you will feel better, get in touch with me* is quite un-English (the sort of mistake that might be made by a non-native speaker whose own language has a future tense). Why should this be so? The answer is surely related to the fact that in uttering (61) I do not 'assert' that you feel better at some future time (compare it with a main clause like *You feel better tomorrow*, which would be pragmatically odd): what is at issue is simply the time, not the factuality, of your feeling better and hence modal qualification would be out of place, and *will* is no more acceptable here than *may* or *must*.

Finally, **will** occurs frequently in conditional constructions:

(62)   i *If she was there, he will have told her*
        ii *If there's any left, it will be in the top drawer*
        iii *If you do that again, you will be fired*

Here the time of the situation (for subordinate and main clauses alike in these particular examples) is respectively past, present and future.[11] In all three cases a non-modal VP could be used: ... *he told her*; ... *it is in the top drawer*; ... *you're fired* (or else one with another modal such as *may* or, for (i) and (ii) though hardly (iii), *must*). The semantic difference between the non-modal versions and those in (62) again involves modality, the non-modal versions reflecting marginally greater assurance. The examples in (62) are all 'real' conditions: the unreal counterparts have *would* in place of *will*:

[11] With past time, when *if* is construed as "whenever", we find *would* + non-perfect rather than *will* + perfect: *If you turned the volume up, it would distort horribly, [so I decided to get a new one]*.

(63)   i *If she had been there, he would have told her*
           ii *If there were any left, it would be in the top drawer*
          iii *If you did that again, you would be fired*

This time we cannot replace the modal VP by a non-modal one: compare *If there were any left it were in the top drawer*, etc. – there is a grammatical requirement (referred to in our list of distinctive properties for the modals) that the main clause contain a modal. In conditional constructions, whether real or unreal, the content of the main clause alone is not asserted: even in the modally unqualified *If there's any left it's in the top drawer* I am not saying that it actually IS in the top drawer; the unreal condition removes the content of the main clause one step further from actuality than the real condition, and the grammar requires that this non-actuality be reflected in a double marking of modality, once in the selection of a modal VP, once in the selection of a past tense inflection with the factual remoteness sense. (This rule does not apply in earlier stages of English – witness Macbeth's *If it were done when 'tis done, then 'twere well it were done quickly* – and one still occasionally finds, in archaic style, sentences which violate it.)

In §3 I argued that **will** belongs syntactically with verbs like **may**, **must** and **can**, and this section has shown that it belongs with them semantically too. It distorts the syntax to set **will** aside as a marker of future tense as opposed to mood, but it is also unsound from a semantic point of view to set it aside from them as expressing future time as opposed to modality. In several of its uses the meaning very clearly involves modality of one kind or another – and even where, with future time, the modality component is least apparent, there is evidence that it is not entirely lacking. The various uses are moreover, closely related (to take just one example, the connection between futurity and conditionality is suggested by the fact that 'if x then y' can also be put as 'y follows from x': we use 'follow' for both temporal and logical relations): it would certainly be impossible to draw any reasonably clear boundary between an allegedly purely temporal use and the others.

The traditional grammarian's future tense has *shall* as an auxiliary as well as *will*: *shall* occurs with 1st person subjects, *will* with 2nd and 3rd person, as in *I shall go, You will go*, and so on. There is a good deal of dialect variation concerning the relationship between *will* and *shall*, but there are surely few speakers who consistently follow the prescriptive rule requiring *shall* with 1st person subjects for future time where no volitional component is involved – the rule that proscribes examples like *I will be surprised if she wins*. Nevertheless many speakers have *shall* as an alternative to *will* (semantically equivalent but differing in style) only with 1st person subjects. In addition *shall* has a number of uses involving deontic modality or something very close to it. The most frequent is in interrogatives with a 1st person subject: *Shall I open the window?* (though again some dialects use *will*). This differs from the prototypical deontic modality in that the speaker does not say what is to be done but invites the addressee to do so (compare *May I open the window?*, where the addressee is asked to give permission). Note that the natural positive answer to *Shall I open the window?* would be *Yes, (please) do*, not *Yes, you shall*, for in Modern English *shall* is not used with the relevant kind of deontic modality in declarative clauses (but cf. the biblical *Thou shalt not kill*). Secondly, *shall* is used in constitutions, regulations, etc., in legal or semi-legal writings: *The committee shall consist of the Head of Department and three members of the academic staff elected annually*. The writer here has the authority to determine the situation. Finally it is used in examples like *You shall have your money tomorrow*: this is deontic in that I, as speaker, impose upon myself the obligation to ensure that you have your money tomorrow.

The past tense of **shall** is *should*, and this occurs as the counterpart of *shall* in the backshifting and unreal condition constructions: *I realised I should soon have nothing left*; *If I continued to spend at this rate I should soon have nothing left*. (In *I should like to thank you for your hospitality*, the conditional element is at best implicit: *should like* is semi-formulaic here.) In addition *should* has several uses that are not explicable in terms of the combination of **shall** plus past tense – and some analysts accordingly recognise a distinct lexeme **should** for these cases: certainly it requires separate lexical description.

One of these uses expresses a type of epistemic modality and another a type of deontic modality: they can both be illustrated in *He should be very tactful*, which exhibits the same kind of ambiguity as (54). A context like '... *if Sue's description is anything to go by*' invites the epistemic interpretation, which can be roughly glossed as "It is to be expected that he is very tactful". Conversely, a context like '... *because she is unusually sensitive*' encourages the deontic interpretation, "The right thing for him to do is to behave very tactfully". In either case the 'strength' of the modality falls somewhere between that expressed by *may* on the one hand, *must* or *will* on the other. Epistemic *should* does not exclude the possibility of the modalised proposition being false (cf. *The meat should be ready by now, though it may need a few more minutes*), and deontic *should* does not exclude the possibility of non-compliance (cf. *You should give it back to her but I don't suppose you will*) – yet we are clearly not concerned in these examples with mere possibility or permission. However, the relation between the epistemic and deontic senses tends to be somewhat different from what we have seen in the case of, say, **must**. The epistemic sense involving a judgement, generally the speaker's, as to what can be expected to be the case occurs as freely with future time situations as with present and past, while the deontic sense involving a judgement, again generally the speaker's, as to what is 'right' occurs with present or past time as well as future. Moreover, epistemic 'expectability' is often based on the assumption that things 'go right': in

Tom should be in Paris by now the expectation or reasonable assumption that he is in Paris by now is likely to be based on the calculation that he will be if everything has gone according to schedule. From this point of view, then, the senses are not so distinct as with **must**. But on the other hand, when the deontic sense combines with a present or past time situation, the latter is often known or assumed to be counterfactual. *Sue should be in bed now* can be used deontically when it is known that she's not: the interpretation is then roughly "It is wrong that she is not in bed", but this of course is not possible with epistemic *should*, "It is reasonable to expect that she is in bed now": the contrast is here very sharp, but has no analogue for **may** or **must**. In both epistemic and deontic uses, *should* could be replaced by *ought* without perceptible change of meaning. There are other uses unique to *should*, but we need not pursue them here: my aim has been to introduce the main concepts and issues in the semantics of modality, not to catalogue all the uses of the various modal auxiliaries.

FURTHER READING

Two book-length studies of the English verb and verb phrase are Palmer 1974 and Leech 1971; shorter overall treatments differing somewhat from 'mainstream' analyses are Langacker 1978 and Halliday 1984: Ch. 6. On the much-debated issue of the validity of a distinction between main verbs and auxiliary verbs, see Matthews 1981:155–6, 164; for a detailed listing of potential criteria for defining auxiliary verbs in general or modal auxiliaries in particular, see Huddleston 1980. I have given the function of auxiliaries as dependent, without further specification; Matthews identifies it as that of 'determiner' (a concept generalised from NP structure). The term 'operator' is taken from Quirk et al. 1971: §§2.2, 2.17–23. On **do** as a substitute, see Halliday & Hasan 1976: §3.3. On tense, see Lyons 1977: §§15.4, 17.3 (p. 820 for the concept of 'remoteness', deriving from Joos 1964). Dudman 1983 questions the long-accepted account of the semantics of tense in conditional constructions and proposes a more unified, wholly temporal, account of the meaning of tense. On the various ways of expressing future time in English, see Wekker 1976; on the more specific issue of future time in conditionals, Comrie 1982. The construction where a non-modal present tense is used for future time is commonly called the 'futurate'; see Prince 1982 for recent discussion. On aspect, see Comrie 1976 (where the concept of 'internal temporal constituency' is developed) and Lyons 1977: §15.6; a recent collection of papers on tense and aspect is Tedeschi & Zaenen 1981. On the perfect construction, see McCoard 1978; Dinsmore 1981; the term 'phase' is sometimes used in place of 'aspect' for the perfect system, as in Joos 1964, Palmer 1974. On modality, see Lyons 1977: Ch. 17, Palmer 1979; in the classification of different kinds of modality an initial distinction is commonly drawn between epistemic modality on the one hand and 'root' modality on the other – see Sweetser 1982 for recent discussion of the relationship between the two. There is a significant amount of regional variation within Standard English concerning the verb and verb phrase: see Trudgill & Hannah 1982, esp. §4.11.

5
The structure of kernel clauses

5.1 Complements and adjuncts

Some of the initial concepts that we need in talking about the structure of kernel clauses may be introduced with reference to an example like

(1)   *Unfortunately, my uncle was using an electric drill at that very moment*

We are taking the verb *using* as ultimate head of the clause, and immediate head of the VP *was using* (see 3.3); intuitively we can see that *my uncle* and *an electric drill* are more closely related to the VP and hence more tightly integrated into the structure of the clause than are *unfortunately* and *at that very moment*. We can think of *my uncle, was using* and *an electric drill* as combining to form, as it were, the structural 'nucleus' of the clause, with *unfortunately* and *at that very moment* being 'extra-nuclear' elements – or **adjuncts** as we shall call them. Adjuncts are always omissible, so that (1), for example, can be reduced to

(2)   *My uncle was using an electric drill*

Let us now temporarily confine our attention to kernel clauses like (2), containing only nuclear elements, no adjuncts. At the first level of structure, such clauses consist of a subject followed by a predicate. The predicate we are analysing as the head, with the subject a dependent of it. The predicate position is always filled by an extended verb phrase; the subject is usually an NP, but it can also be an embedded clause or, occasionally, a PP (see 2.2). At the next level down, the EVP has a VP as head, for which we are employing the more specific term 'predicator'. The predicator may constitute the whole of the EVP, as in *My uncle was resting* or it may be accompanied by one or more **complements**, like *an electric drill* in (2). The structure of (2) is thus as appears on page 178. As noted in 3.3, we are giving relatively little prominence to the Predicate/EVP constituent, and will understand 'clause structure' to cover both the levels of structure shown in (3).

There are a number of different types of complement, and we shall be looking at these in the following sections; first, however we must attempt to

(3)

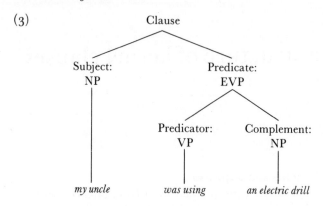

clarify the distinction that we have drawn between complements and adjuncts. In what sense are complements more 'nuclear' than adjuncts?

(a) In the first place, the occurrence of a complement of a given kind depends on the presence of a verb of an appropriate subclass, whereas there are no such restrictions on the occurrence of adjuncts. Suppose, for example, that in (1) we replaced **use** by **arrive**: this would require that we drop the complement *an electric drill* (cf. **My uncle was arriving an electric drill*), but *unfortunately* and *at that very moment* would be unaffected. *An electric drill* is a complement of a kind that we shall call 'object', and only certain verbs, 'transitive verbs', take objects: **use** is transitive, **arrive** intransitive, and so on. But we do not have a subclassification of verbs according as they can or cannot occur with an 'attitudinal' adjunct like *unfortunately* or a 'time' adjunct like *at that very moment*. The syntactic information given about particular verbs in the lexicon will include a specification of what types of complement they can or must take, but will not mention adjuncts.

(b) We have noted that adjuncts are syntactically omissible: dropping an adjunct will not result in ungrammaticality. Omitting the adjuncts from (1), for example, results in (2), which is equally grammatical. Complements, by contrast, may be obligatory: dropping *an electric drill* from (1) or (2) does lead to ungrammaticality (**Unfortunately, my uncle was using at that very moment*). This relates to the traditional explanation of the concept. In clauses like *Ed died, I awoke, It rained*, the predicate is composed simply of the verb – but not all verbs can occur in clauses of this pattern: we cannot say **Ed became, *My uncle used*, and so on. Verbs like **become** and **use** are then said to be 'verbs of incomplete predication' – they cannot constitute the whole of the predicate. To complete the predicate, we need one or more elements in addition to the predicator, and these are the complements. Thus in *Ed became ill* and *My uncle used the drill*, for example, *ill* and *the drill* are complements in that they complement the verb in such a way as to form a composite unit which can serve as a predicate. We will regard a dependent as obligatory not only in the elementary case where its omission leads to ungrammaticality, but also where its omission results in a radical change in the meaning of the verb. It is in this second sense that *mad* is obligatory in *He drives the minister mad*: dropping it gives *He drives the minister*, which is grammatical but quite different in meaning from the original, involving a clearly different sense of **drive**. If a dependent of the predicator is obligatory, we shall accordingly regard it as a complement. We shall not, however, take obligatoriness to be a necessary condition for complements. In *She was reading a novel*, for example, we analyse *a novel* as a complement even though *She was reading* is perfectly grammatical (and doesn't involve a change in the meaning of **read**). *A novel* is here a complement by criterion (a), and in addition there are good reasons, as we shall see, for regarding *She was reading a novel* and *She was using a drill* as having the same structure. The optional/obligatory distinction thus doesn't provide a simple test, and we are giving greater weight to the subclassification criterion; if a dependent element is obligatory, it is a complement, if it is optional it can be either a complement or an adjunct, depending on other factors.[1]

It follows from these two points (rather than constituting a separate distinctive difference) that complements are much more subject to grammatical rules than are adjuncts. The selection of a given verb as ultimate head of the clause determines, completely or within quite narrow limits, what kind or kinds of complements will occur, whereas the occurrence of adjuncts is in general not grammatically determined[2] – and while there will be a maximum of three or so complements in any one clause, there is no grammatical limit to the number of adjuncts that may appear: complex combinations of adjuncts will be excluded by semantic and stylistic factors rather than grammatical ones.

(c) A third difference concerns the class of phrase realising the two functions. Complements are prototypically NPs or AdjPs, while adjuncts are prototypically AdvPs or PPs – and note that nouns and adjectives (along with verbs) are the major word-classes, in the sense discussed in 3.4. These correlations between function and class are by no means perfect, however,

---

[1] It will be recalled that we invoked the contrast between obligatory and optional elements in discussing the distinction between heads and dependents (3.3), with heads obligatory, dependents prototypically optional; complements are dependents by our other criteria, but with respect to obligatoriness they are more like heads than are prototypical dependents, and this grouping of head and complements together in contrast to adjuncts is reflected in our concept of nuclear elements.

[2] Certain kinds of temporal adjunct depend on tense–aspect features of the VP (as we saw, for example, in 4.7). Although there is a grammatical rule involved in such cases, the restrictions do not involve lexical subclasses of verbs and hence do not bring the temporal expressions concerned into the nucleus.

and at the level of language-particular definition we will not allow this factor to override (a). Let us nevertheless look a little further at the correlation. In (1) the complement *an electric drill* is an NP, while the adjuncts *unfortunately* and *at that time* are respectively an AdvP and a PP: (1) thus illustrates the usual pattern. Certain types of NP can, however, appear as adjuncts, mainly temporal NPs like *this morning, last Tuesday*, etc., so that we may contrast, for example,

(4) i *He died the following morning*   S–P–A
     ii *He wasted the following morning*   S–P–C

In (i) *the following morning* is a time adjunct, like *at that very moment* in (1), while in (ii) it is object, like *an electric drill*. (i) and (ii) are distinguishable by criteria (a) and (b) above, but note also the great difference in the substitution possibilities for *the following morning* in the two examples. Apart from the fact that in (ii) we could substitute a non-temporal NP (such as *his opportunity*), a more clearly grammatical point is that in (ii) but not (i) we could have a pronoun – cf. *He wasted/ *died it* or, to use a non-kernel example, [*the following morning,*] *which he wasted/ *died,* . . ., and so on. We shall also allow for PP and AdvP complements. In *He congratulated Liz on her promotion*, for example, the PP *on her promotion* is clearly a complement by our first criterion (the lexical entry for **congratulate** must specify that it can take an NP + *on* phrase), and similarly in *He treated us badly* the AdvP *badly* is a complement, being obligatory inasmuch as *He treated us* involves a different sense of **treat**. Nevertheless, these do not belong to the most central kind of complement – note that what is standardly analysed as an object, for example, cannot be either a PP or an AdvP. (We should add that embedded clauses can function as either complement or adjunct, though there are differences in the functional potential of various subclasses of subordinate clause.)

The boundary between complements and adjunct is not a sharp one, and differences will be found among grammars as to just where it is drawn (with different weightings being given to the above three points). In the rest of this chapter we will pay much more attention to complements than to adjuncts, precisely because they are more nuclear, more subject to grammatical rule – and of the various kinds of complement, we will concentrate on the most central, those that are most clearly distinct from adjuncts.

Although the term 'complement' is usually applied, in the analysis of clause structure, only to certain dependents within the predicate, there are good reasons to generalise it so that it covers the subject as well: on this view the subject would be a special case of complement, just as the object is. In kernel clauses the subject is an obligatory element; the prototypical subject is an NP; and verbs are subclassified according to what kind of subject they take (e.g. according to whether, like **emerge**, say, but not **arrive**, they allow an embedded clause as subject) – these properties bring the subject within the concept of complement as characterised above.

The more specific properties of subjects have already been given in 2.2 and need not be repeated here. Our concern henceforth in this chapter will accordingly be with those complements that fall within the predicate; we begin with the contrast between two of the main kinds.

5.2 Objects and predicative complements

In this section we shall be examining the two most standardly recognised kinds of complement, objects and predicative complements. Initially we will confine our attention to clauses with a single complement, in order to focus on the contrast between these two kinds; the analysis will then be extended to cover a wider range of constructions.

Our concern, then, is with the contrast illustrated in

		S	P	O		S	P	PC
(5)	i	Ed	engaged	a lawyer	ii	Ed	was	a lawyer
(6)	i	Ed	shot	Kim's lover	ii	Ed	became	Kim's lover
(7)	i	Ed	appointed	a real idiot	ii	Ed	seemed	a real idiot
(8)	i	Ed	got	the best seat	ii	Ed	got	angry

We will examine the distinction first from a semantic point of view, with the aim of characterising object and predicative complement as general terms, and then turn to a consideration of the ways in which they are syntactically distinguished in English.

The semantic distinction is intuitively quite sharp in examples like (5)–(7), where we have the same NPs used in the two functions. In (6i), for instance, *Kim's lover* serves to pick out some person who is assigned a certain role in the event expressed in the clause, the role of 'patient' or 'affected participant', but in (ii) it denotes a property that Ed came to have, the property of being lover to Kim. In (7i) *a real idiot* describes an individual distinct from Ed, whereas in (ii) it denotes a property ascribed (with the qualification implied by **seem**) to Ed – and analogously for (5).

The relationship between semantic and syntactic structure is more straightforward in S–P–O clauses than in S–P–PC clauses, as is suggested by such pairs as

		S	P	O		S	P	PC
(9)	i	Ed	loves	Kim	ii	Ed	is	fond of Kim
(10)	i	Ed	admired	the Beatles	ii	Ed	was	a fan of the Beatles

where (ii) is in both cases semantically very similar to (i) but is syntactically more complex. Let us therefore start with the S–P–O construction and introduce some of the semantic concepts we shall need.

If I use (9i) to make a statement I express a certain **proposition**. As we observed in 1.4, it is propositions, not sentences, that are true or false, and a sentence like (9i) can be used to express an indefinite number of propositions, distinguished according to who is identified in the context in which it is used by the NPs *Ed* and *Kim*, and according to the time at which the situation of Ed's loving Kim is said to obtain, a time identified as including the moment at which the sentence is used. Some of these propositions, we may assume, will be true, others false: the sentence can be used to express both true and false propositions but is not itself, considered simply as a sentence of the language, assessable as either true or false. In the most elementary cases a proposition is analysable into a **semantic predicate**[3] accompanied by one or more **arguments** representing particular persons, other kinds of living creature or inanimate entities of various kinds. In (an utterance of) (9i) the arguments are expressed by the NPs *Ed* and *Kim* while the semantic predicate is expressed by the verb ***love*** (I simplify by ignoring the tense inflection: we may consider the proposition in abstraction from the time specification). ***Love*** has a quite different semantic function than *Ed* and *Kim*. The latter are used to **refer** to particular individuals, to pick out the persons about whom something is said. ***Love***, by contrast, is used to **predicate** something of the individuals referred to by the NPs, to say something about them – to ascribe a relation to them. Thus a semantic predicate ascribes a property or a role in a relation, action, event, etc., to what is represented by its argument or arguments.

Semantic predicates may be classified according to the number of arguments they take. Thus "love" (the semantic predicate expressed by ***love***) takes two; "sleep" (as in *Ed was sleeping*) takes one; "give" (as in *Ed gave me the key*) takes three. From a simple 'two-place' semantic predicate like "love", however, can be derived a complex 'one-place' semantic predicate incorporating the other argument. For example, we have said that in a normal utterance of (9i) ***love*** is used to predicate something of the pair Ed and Kim, to ascribe a relation to them, but we might also say that ***love Kim*** is used to predicate something of the individual Ed, to ascribe a property to him. This is where the semantic and syntactic concepts of predicate come together: in syntax the term 'predicate' is employed for the function of the constituent which enters into construction with the subject – one which typically expresses a one-place semantic predicate that is either simple or derived from a simple one by the incorporation of all arguments other than that expressed by the subject. (It will be clear that we are concerned here with an explanation of the general term 'predicate': nothing that is said here

[3] Usually called, simply, a 'predicate'; since there is not, however, a one-to-one correlation between semantic predicates and syntactic predicates, I shall restrict the unqualified term 'predicate' to syntax, using 'semantic predicate' when talking about the analysis of propositions.

invalidates our criticism in 2.2 of the notional definition of the subject, construed language-specifically, as identifying the topic of a sentence, that about which something is said, or predicated.) We are employing 'predicator', by contrast, for the function of the VP, whose main verb will typically express a simple semantic predicate, whether one-place, two-place, or whatever. And finally 'object' is the function of an element within the predicate which typically expresses an argument of a simple semantic predicate and is related to the main verb without the mediation of a preposition. The last part of this definition distinguishes the *Kim* of (9i), which is an object, from that of *Ed relies on Kim*, which is not: see §5 below for this latter construction.

Consider now (9ii). From a semantic point of view, **fond** is similar to **love** – they express the two-place semantic predicates "fond" and "love", which represent similar relations. From a syntactic point of view, however, they are very different, for **fond** is an adjective while **love** is a verb. This part of speech difference has two consequences. First, because **fond** is an adjective it cannot carry a tense inflection: as we have observed, it is the chief distinguishing property of verbs that only they inflect for tense. In (9ii) the tense inflection is carried by the verb **be**, and it is plausible to suggest that the only role of **be** here is precisely to carry the tense inflection – that it does not itself express a semantic predicate. **Be** (as used here) is traditionally said to be a **copula**, a term reflecting the idea that it serves to 'fasten or link' the rest of the predicate to the subject. The second consequence of **fond** being an adjective is that in (9ii) *Kim* is introduced by a preposition: unlike verbs, adjectives do not (with one or two exceptions) take objects. Because of these two syntactic differences between the adjective **fond** and the verb **love**, (9ii) has two extra layers in its constituent structure:

(11)

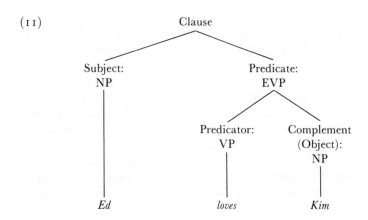

(12)

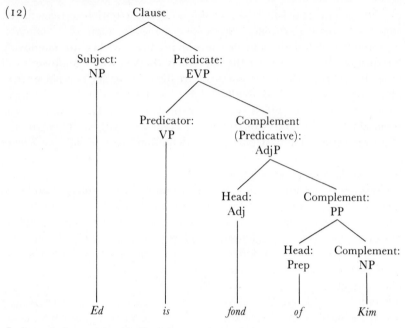

In kernel clauses the predicate must always contain a tensed VP: this is the obligatory element common to all, and is accordingly analysed as the head. In structures like (12), however, the expression of the semantic predicate falls not within the VP but within its complement. This then is why the general term 'predicative complement' is applied: it is associated with the semantic function of predicating – not that of identifying an argument of a semantic predicate expressed elsewhere.

The contrast in (10) is the same. In (i), **admire** expresses the semantic predicate, *the Beatles* one of its arguments – *the Beatles* would be used to refer to the group of singers so named. In (ii) the semantic predicate is expressed by **fan**: as this is a noun, it cannot carry the tense inflection and cannot take an object complement, so that the structure is analogous to (12) (except that the noun *fan*, unlike the adjective *fond*, takes the determiner *a*). While the noun **fan** expresses a two-place simple semantic predicate, the NP *a fan of the Beatles* expresses a one-place complex semantic predicate, incorporating one of the arguments of the simple "fan". Note then that the NP *a fan of the Beatles* is here used to predicate, not to refer: it expresses a property ascribed to Ed (as does the AdjP *fond of Kim* in (9ii)) rather than picking out some individual about whom something is said (contrast *I bought it from a fan of the Beatles* where the same NP would be used referentially).

We have suggested that the **be** of (9ii) and (10ii) is semantically empty – that it does not express a semantic predicate but serves rather to carry the tense inflection and to link the phrase that does express the semantic predicate to the subject. But other verbs that take predicative complements are clearly not semantically empty in this way. In *Ed became fond of Kim*, whose syntactic structure is the same as (12) save for the replacement of *is* by *became*, both **fond** and **become** express semantic predicates ("become" involving a change of state). Verbs occurring in the S–P–PC construction we shall call **copulative** verbs, a term based on 'copula' in the sense explained above, but it must be emphasised that it is only **be** itself (much the most frequent of them) that can be regarded as semantically empty, a syntactic element that merely links the PC to the subject. Thus although from a syntactic point of view *Ed became fond of Kim* is a single clause, semantically there are two predicates – the fact that a semantic predicate need not be expressed by a verb means that we can have more than one semantic predication in a simple clause (i.e. a clause that does not have another clause embedded within it). This is a further reason why the relation between semantic and syntactic structure is in general less straightforward in the S–P–PC construction than in the S–P–O construction.

So much for the semantics, and for an explanation of object and predicative complement as general terms; let us now turn to the syntax, to the ways in which the two kinds of complements are distinguished in the grammar of English. Although the semantic distinction illustrated above is so basic, the syntax does not differentiate between them as sharply as one might expect (or as it does in languages with more case inflection). The three main syntactic factors that discriminate between them are form-class, number and passivisation.

(a) Form-class. The first difference is that whereas NPs can function as either O or PC, AdjPs can function as PC but not O. Note, for example, that in (5)–(7) the NPs *a lawyer*, *Kim's lover* and *a real idiot* are in paradigmatic relation with AdjPs in (ii) but not (i) – cf. *Ed became fond of Kim*, but **Ed shot fond of Kim*, and so on. AdjPs don't occur as subject either (in kernel clauses), and their exclusion from both object and subject positions is related to the fact that they cannot be used referentially.

Although the PC position can be filled by either an AdjP or an NP, there are grounds for regarding the AdjP as somewhat more central inasmuch as there are greater restrictions on the occurrence of NPs than of AdjPs in this function. Thus a number of copulative verbs allow only AdjPs as PC: we can say *She fell sick/pregnant* but not **She fell an invalid*, etc.; *She got ready/ tired/angry* but not **She got a lunatic* (except where *a lunatic* is O and **get** has the meaning of (8i), not (ii)); *The substance tasted salty* but not **The substance tasted salt*, and so on. With **go** NPs are not excluded altogether but are much more limited in range than AdjPs – compare *He went pale/mad* and *He went a strange colour/*a madman*. The only copulative verb that shows the reverse pattern is **make**, as in *He made a good husband/an excellent Iago*: this verb does not take AdjPs as PC (unless we include **make** *merry* and **make** *good*, whose syntactic structure is somewhat obscured by the idiomatic nature of the constructions).

A further more specific point concerning the class of the complement expression is that with nouns denoting various institutional roles, such as **queen**, **president**, **prime minister**, **treasurer**, etc., the definite article *the* can be omitted in PC but not O position – compare *She became president/Queen of England* and **He shot president/Queen of England*. Given what was said in 3.3 about the need for a unit intermediate between noun and NP, it is arguable whether *president* and *Queen of England* are properly analysed as NPs here; be that as it may, they are not of the type that can be used with the syntactic function of object (or subject) – or the semantic function of referring. English (unlike French, for example) does not allow for the analogous dropping of the indefinite article – we say *He became a teacher*, not **He became teacher*.[4]

A further point of detail is that the PC position can be filled by a PossP, as in *These shoes are my father's*. Forms like *my father's* can also occur as object, but in this case they have the status of elliptical NPs: *I couldn't find my shoes so I borrowed my father's* ("my father's shoes") – note that *my father's* is semantically non-referential in the first example, referential in the second; see 7.3–4 for further discussion.

(b) Number. The second difference is illustrated in the following pair:

(13)   i *Ed engaged a lawyer/some lawyers*
        ii *Ed was a lawyer/*some lawyers*

As a first approximation we can say that where an NP functions as O, its number – singular or plural – is selected independently of that of S, but where it functions as PC its number agrees with that of S. Hence the deviance of **Ed was some lawyers* and **Ed and his sister are both a lawyer*. This, however, is very much a first approximation: the matter is not at all straightforward and it is in fact unclear how much can be brought within the scope of a syntactic rule of agreement, for the semantic properties of the NP play a significant role in number selection. Most of the qualifications to our initial statement concern the PC, but let us first clarify one point about the number of the O.

In *She hurt herself* and *They hurt themselves* the complements – the 'reflexive pronouns' *herself* and *themselves* – agree in number with the subject, but we will nevertheless regard them as O, not PC. The agreement here is of a quite different kind: the relevant rule is not that the complement agrees with the

---

[4] *He turned traitor* is an exception – but the **turn** + NP-PC construction is of very low productivity. Although **He became teacher* is ungrammatical under the construal "He became a teacher", it is arguable that there are contexts where it would be acceptable with the interpretation "He became the teacher".

subject but that a pronoun agrees with its 'antecedent'. It just happens that in these examples the pronoun is complement, the antecedent subject, but this is of no significance for the formulation of the rule. Thus on the one hand, there are innumerable cases where pronoun and antecedent do not have these functions (such as *He told Liz she was hurting him*, in the interpretation where *she* has *Liz* as antecedent and hence refers to Liz – or, to use an example involving a 'reflexive' pronoun, *He told Liz some home-truths about herself*). And on the other hand the *herself* of *She hurt herself* is in paradigmatic contrast with plural NPs: *She hurt them* (where *she* is not antecedent to *them*). It is true that such paradigmatic contrasts do not apply for all reflexive pronouns. A handful of verbs, such as **perjure**, permit only a reflexive pronoun as complement (*Ed perjured himself/ *them*) – but the agreement can still be handled by the rule applying to pronouns and antecedents, so that there is no reason to regard the reflexive here as PC rather than O.

Consider now some of the qualifications that must be made to the rule of number agreement between S and PC. It is very easy to find examples of plural S with singular PC. One type of example is illustrated in *Ed and Kim are an amiable pair/a nuisance/a good choice*, where something is predicated of Ed and Kim conceived of as a single unit rather than being predicated of them individually. "An amiable pair" obviously could not be predicated of an individual person (*Ed is an amiable pair* being semantically anomalous – in the same way as *Ed and Kim are an amiable trio*); "nuisance" and "good choice" can be predicated of individuals – and here we can find *Ed and Kim are both nuisances/good choices*. But we can still have singular *a nuisance* and *a good choice* even with *both* (which excludes the 'single unit' interpretation), so that the lack of agreement is not fully explicable on semantic grounds. A further type is illustrated in *They are a strange colour/the same age/pure cotton* where the semantic predicates are clearly of a different kind from that in *She is a lawyer/They are lawyers*. Clauses with singular S and plural PC are much rarer. In *He is not friends with her* we must treat *friends with* as an idiom – and in the slang *He is nuts/bonkers* and the like it is arguable that *nuts* and *bonkers* are denominal adjectives rather than NPs. The only type of any generality is exemplified in

(14)   *One thing we don't want now is more taxes*

Semantically **be** here has an 'identifying' function – (14) identifies the one thing we don't want. We shall have more to say about this identifying use of **be** later (see, especially, 14.5): we shall see that there are other respects in which the complement behaves in a syntactically idiosyncratic way – so much so that the complement of identifying **be** can certainly not be regarded as a prototypical PC.

(c) Passivisation. O can normally be made subject by passivising the clause, whereas PC never can:

(15)   i *Ed shot Kim's lover → Kim's lover was shot by Ed*
         ii *Ed became Kim's lover → *Kim's lover was become by Ed*

Subject and object, as we have said, typically express arguments of the semantic predicate, and the grammatical system of voice allows for different ways of associating the argument roles with syntactic functions – in (15), for example, the actor is associated with subject function in the active, the patient in the passive (see 2.3); the PC, which generally expresses a semantic predicate, does not qualify for conversion to subject in this way. Passivisation does not provide an absolute criterion for distinguishing O from PC, however, because not all S–P–O clauses have passive counterparts – hence the need for 'normally' in the formulation given above. The restrictions on passivisation are discussed in 14.1: here it is enough to illustrate with a pair like *The coat doesn't fit her* / *She isn't fitted by the coat*.

   In addition to the three factors we have been considering, mention should also be made of case: a case-variable pronoun functioning as O will be in the accusative form (*Ed shot him* / *he*) whereas one functioning as PC may be nominative or accusative (*This is he* / *him*). In Latin, case provides probably the clearest criterion for distinguishing PC from O and for this reason it figures prominently in traditional grammars of English too: the traditional rule is that an NP in PC function agrees with S in case as well as number. It will be clear from what has already been said that this rule cannot be accepted as valid for English. In the first place, the great majority of NPs carry no case property. Thus in *Ed was a lawyer* neither NP has case and it is quite inappropriate therefore to talk of case agreement; clauses where both S and PC select for case, as in *I am he*, constitute a very small proportion. In the second place, the intention of the rule is to allow as grammatical clauses like *It was I* but not *It was me*, whereas in fact both of these are grammatical in Standard English: they differ in style, not as standard versus non-standard. Notice, moreover, that there are many types of example where only an accusative PC sounds at all natural: *The only one who didn't get to see it was me*; *Which is me?* (said, for example, on seeing a kindergarten group photograph); *How could that little monster have been* / *become me?*. A speaker inhibited by knowledge of the prescriptive rule from using *me* here would hardly just substitute *I*: a more radical change would normally be made – *I was the only one who didn't get to see it* might be preferred to the first, and so on, with the case-variable pronoun no longer in PC position.

   One further point about case should be made. We observed in discussing the syntactic properties of the subject (2.2.2) that although only a handful of pronouns select for case, case provides an important diagnostic for the subject because an NP without case occurring with this function will very often be in paradigmatic contrast with a nominative pronoun – in *Liz shot the intruder* we can substitute nominative *she* for caseless *Liz*. With NPs functioning as PC, however, the scope for this kind of substitution is extremely limited. In *Ed seemed a decent guy*, for example, we cannot replace the second NP with a form of **he**: **Ed seemed he/him*. Likewise in *Ed would make an excellent Iago*: we cannot say **Ed would make he* and *Ed would make him* involves a different sense of **make** with *him* O, not PC. Or again *Kim's lover* is not replaceable by *he* or *him* in *Ed became Kim's lover*. Even with **be** the substitution is possible only in the syntactically special construction where **be** has the 'identifying' sense – thus not in examples like *Ed's a lawyer, Ed's the sort of guy who'd do anything to help a friend*, and so on. Thus case-variable pronouns do not in fact occur in prototypical PC function. And this in turn is related to the semantics: the prototypical PC is used to predicate, not to refer, whereas personal pronouns can be used to refer but not to predicate. It follows from what we have been saying that, in English, case is of very limited relevance to the syntactic characterisation of the PC – hence its omission from the list of major properties given above distinguishing PC and O.

It will be clear from a comparison of the above discussion with that in 2.2.2 that the object is much more sharply distinguished from S than it is from PC. With some verbs it is indeed far from clear whether the complement is O or PC. Among these are certain verbs taking 'measure' NPs as complement – **cost**, **weigh**, **measure**, etc.: *The tie cost $20, He weighs twelve stone, The flex measured five metres*. These complements lack the positive properties of both O and PC: they cannot become subject through passivisation (**$20 was cost by the tie*), they do not agree with the subject and they are not in paradigmatic contrast with AdjPs. Not surprisingly, some grammars take them as O, other as PC.[5]

We have been concerned up to this point with the contrast between PC and O; let us now take up briefly the relation firstly between PC and head, and secondly between PC and adjunct. We are taking the head to be the element realised by the VP – but it is evident that in examples like *Di was ill/a teacher*, where we have as main verb **be** in its non-identifying sense, the AdjP *ill* and NP *a teacher* have some of the characteristics of a head: it is they rather than **be** that limit the range of permitted subjects. *Ill* and **teacher**, for example, unlike **clear** and **puzzle**, do not allow a subordinate clause as subject: *Why she resigned was clear/*ill/a puzzle/*a teacher*. This again is related to the semantics, for a semantic predicate will impose limitations on the type of arguments it can take and we have suggested that **be** does not express a semantic predicate in clauses like these. Notice, however, that **be** is not the only verb that takes a PC, and the others typically restrict the range of permitted PCs

---

[5] *He weighed the baby, He measured the flex* and (with a different lexeme **cost**$_{\text{Reg}}$, regular in its inflectional morphology) *They costed the project* are, by contrast, straightforward S–P–O constructions.

(and often subjects too) – cf. *Ed went mad,* **Di went a teacher,* **Why she resigned went unclear.* As we have said, there are here two semantic predications, but only one clause – and from a syntactic point of view we will regard the VP as having the head function on the basis that this is the element that is obligatory in all kernel clauses (along with the subject), that is not in paradigmatic contrast with phrases of other classes, and that most generally determines the range of other elements permitted in the nucleus of the clause. Nevertheless, *was ill, was a teacher* fall at the far limits of what can reasonably be analysed as a 'head + dependent' construction (and some would take the view that they fall beyond these limits).

AdjPs and (to a more limited extent) NPs can function both as PC and as A. The functional contrast is clear in pairs like

(16) i *He was furious at this deception*
      ii *Furious at this deception, he vowed never to see them again*
(17) i *Ed seemed a man of considerable talent*
      ii *A man of considerable talent, Ed had little difficulty in overcoming these obstacles.*

Furious at this deception in (16i) and *a man of considerable talent* in (17i) are straightforwardly PCs of the most central kind, but in (ii) we will regard them as extranuclear elements, as adjuncts. In (i) they are obligatory, in (ii) optional; in (i) they depend on the presence of a syntactically appropriate verb, whereas in (ii) there are no such constraints – in (ii) they are attached only loosely to the rest of the clause (a point reflected in the prosodic pattern) and evidently fall outside the nucleus. Much less easy to analyse, however, are examples like

(18) *She ran naked across the pitch*
(19) *She died a millionaire*

Naked and *a millionaire* here fall at the borderline between PC and A. They differ from a prototypical PC in being omissible, but they are certainly more closely integrated into the structure of the clause than are the initial elements in (16ii) and (17ii). It is not entirely clear whether they require the presence of a verb of a particular subclass; the restrictions on the occurrence of an NP, like *a millionaire*, seem somewhat greater than for an AdjP, like *naked* – and (19) is probably more resistant than (18) to a prosodic pattern marking off the item in question as parenthetical. We will not pursue the issue further here, leaving undetermined the analysis of examples like (18) and (19).

Clauses containing an object are called **transitive** clauses – and those without an object **intransitive**. The term 'transitive' derives from Latin *trans* "across" + *ire* "go" – it reflects the idea that in an elementary example like *Ed killed Bill* the action 'goes across' from Ed to Bill. In active clauses expressing an action, the object is typically associated with the semantic role of 'patient', but just as there is no one-to-one correlation between subject and actor role, the object does not always correspond to the patient, in the sense of the entity that 'undergoes' some action, or to which something is done. It may be associated with a variety of semantic roles, as is evident from examples like

(20)   i *She painted a picture*
          ii *I heard an explosion*
         iii *It jumped the fence*
          iv *He gave a shout*

In (i) the picture comes into existence as a result of the action – its role is quite different from that of the fingernails in *She painted her fingernails*, where we can invoke the idea of something being done to the nails. In (ii) I clearly didn't do anything to the explosion: if anything, the explosion did something to me, namely cause me to have a certain sensation – the semantic role associated with the object here is that of stimulus for some sensory perception. (This notion of sensory stimulus might be generalised to cover the stimulus for various emotional states or attitudes, as in *I like chamber music*, which again doesn't involve doing anything to the chamber music.) In (iii) the fence is likewise unaffected by the action; the object here specifies what has been called the 'range' of the action, identifying the spatial limits, as it were. (iv) has a good deal in common with (i) inasmuch as the (fleeting) existence of the shout results from the action; I have included it for separate mention because it illustrates a quite common pattern where a combination of verb + NP object expresses a meaning that can also be expressed by a verb alone – *give a shout* or just ***shout***, ***take*** *a rest* or just ***rest***, ***make*** *a reply* or just ***reply***, and so on. Similarly we may relate ***take*** *place* to ***occur*** – ***take*** + its object *place* forms a single lexical item, an idiom. Like the subject, then, the object is a semantically 'neutral' element in the sense that there is no unique semantic role associated with it: the interpretation of the role is crucially dependent on the particular verb. Attempts have been made to devise a small set of semantic roles that can be assigned to the arguments of a semantic predicate – roles like actor, patient, experiencer, instrument, range, and so on – but it is extremely difficult to establish a set of roles that are both exhaustive and clearly defined, and whatever the value of these concepts for semantics, it seems clear that they are of very little relevance, at the language-particular level, to the formulation of the rules of English syntax.

The terms 'transitive' and 'intransitive' are also applied to verbs: ***take*** is a transitive verb, ***disappear*** an intransitive one, and so on. A great many verbs, however, occur in both transitive and intransitive clauses – certainly a majority of those that can take an object can also occur without (a property that may be regarded as something of a peculiarity of English, for languages generally make a sharper division within the lexicon between transitive and intransitive verbs). In such cases, then, we will talk about transitive and intransitive 'uses' of the verbs – illustrated respectively for **write**, say, in

(21)   i *Ed was writing a letter*
         ii *Ed was writing*

Where a verb enters into both transitive and intransitive clause constructions, the semantic relation between the two will normally be of one or other of two broad types (I ignore cases of lexical homonymy). In one the semantic role associated with the subject remains constant whereas in the other the subject of the intransitive clause corresponds semantically to the object rather than to the subject of the transitive clause: let us consider them in turn.

(a) The first type is illustrated by the two **write** clauses in (21). The subject *Ed* is associated with the same role in each, the difference being simply that the transitive specifies an additional argument while the intransitive does not. Note then that (21ii) differs semantically from an intransitive like *Ed was dying* in that it implies that Ed was writing SOMETHING, even though the something is not expressed.

The nature or identity of the unexpressed something is recovered from the context in which the sentence is used or from the lexical-semantic properties of the verb. It may be very specific or quite general. For example, *I can't see* could convey that I can't see the particular thing that I am trying to see (perhaps the stage in a theatre where I find myself in a bad seat) or alternatively that I am blind. Some verbs denote activities where there is some standard or typical kind of object-argument: with **eat** it is food, or more specifically meals; with **read** it is books, newspapers and the like; with **wash** it is clothes; with **study** scholarly reading matter; and so on – and these verbs are very often used intransitively with some unspecified object-argument of the characteristic kind understood: *She's eating/reading/washing/studying*. If Ed were studying his income tax form or a baby were eating plasticine, it would be very unnatural to say *Ed is studying* or *The baby is eating*.

A few verbs denote activities that one characteristically and regularly performs on oneself, e.g. **shave**, **dress**, **wash**, and these are commonly used intransitively with a reflexive object understood. Thus *Ed is shaving* will normally be interpreted as "Ed is shaving himself". Or rather, to be more precise, **shave** is characteristically applied to the activity of removing one's FACIAL hair: we would not normally say *Di is shaving* when she is removing the hair from her legs.

It will be noticed that **wash** figures in both the lists given above – for the sentence *She is washing* is interpretable as either "She is washing the clothes" or "She is washing herself" (though *She's doing the washing* is probably a more frequent way of expressing the former meaning). This is not to say, however, that intransitive **wash** is always interpreted in one or other of these two ways.

In the context of cleaning a car, for example, I might say *Ed washed and I polished*, where it is "the car" that is understood as the object-argument of both verbs.

Some writers have treated examples like (21ii) – in contrast to *Ed was dying* – as non-kernel clauses, syntactically derived by a transformational process deleting some lexically unspecified object. Few would now subscribe to such an analysis, however, for it is clear that one cannot avoid dealing with the matter in the lexical entries for the verbs concerned. In the first place, there are certainly some verbs such as ***exert***, ***further***, ***necessitate***, etc., where the object cannot be left unexpressed. Moreover, where the object is omissible, one finds considerable differences among verbs with respect to the conditions under which the intransitive construction can be used. For example, we may contrast ***read*** or ***wash*** above with ***annihilate***: the first two occur as readily without an object as with one, whereas the third might be used intransitively in clauses expressing a general property of the subject-referent (*This weapon doesn't merely kill, it annihilates*), but hardly in the narration of a particular event (*?Yesterday he went out and annihilated*). And in the second place, the particular interpretation must often be lexically specified; this will be evident from the discussion above, but is particularly obvious with verbs like ***drink***, ***propose***, ***expect***. While intransitive ***drink*** can be used in a way analogous to intransitive ***eat***, it commonly has a more specific sense, "drink liquor", and similarly ***propose*** can be used intransitively in the sense "propose marriage", while intransitive ***expect*** (probably only with progressive aspect, ***be*** *expecting*) is often used with the sense "expect a baby", i.e. "be pregnant".

Somewhat different from the above, but still falling within the general category where the semantic role associated with the subject remains constant in the transitive and intransitive constructions, are verbs like ***die***, ***laugh***, ***sleep***, etc. These are usually used intransitively – but they can also take what are known as 'cognate' objects, as in *He died an agonising death, She slept a fitful sleep*, where ***death*** and ***sleep***$_N$ are cognate with, lexically related to, ***die*** and ***sleep***$_V$. Having a cognate noun here enables us to add an adjectival modifier – without such a modifier, the object would be pointless and the sentence hardly acceptable (cf. *He died a death*).

(b) The second type, where the subject of the intransitive corresponds semantically to the object of the transitive, is illustrated in

(22) i *I broke the glass*
      ii *The glass broke*
(23) i *You don't iron this shirt*
      ii *This shirt doesn't iron*

In (22) it is in both cases the glass that becomes broken, and similarly in (23) the semantic role associated with *this shirt* is the same in both clauses, namely 'patient'/'undergoer'. We can distinguish two subtypes, illustrated by **break**, representing a quite large class of verbs (**move**, **open**, **close**, **roll**, etc.) and **iron**, representing a much smaller class (including **wash**, **frighten**, **sell** and the like). With the **iron** subtype, the transitive use is clearly primary, with the intransitive use occurring when it is a matter of characterising the subject-referent with respect to its readiness or suitability to undergo the process denoted by the verb; for this reason the intransitive use normally requires a negative or a manner adverb or the like (*It irons well, It'll sell easily*, etc.): one would not say simply *The shirt ironed*.

A number of verbs occur in intransitives of type (a) and type (b). **Iron** indeed is one of them, for besides (23ii) we have also *You should be ironing*, where the subject is associated with the same role as in the transitive. Similarly we may compare *She's reading*, type (a) and *The paper reads well*, type (b). Which type any given intransitive belongs to will normally be obvious from pragmatic considerations: the two arguments of "read", for example, represent quite different kinds of things, typically people for one and reading matter for the other, and the interpretation of *They read well*, say, as (a) or (b) will depend on whether *they* refers to people or texts.

5.3 The complex-transitive construction

In the last section we were concerned with clauses containing a single complement within the predicate, either O or PC. These two elements can, however, combine, as in

(24)   *Ed made Liz angry*
(25)   *Ed considered Liz a great asset*

Here *Liz* is O, *angry*/*a great asset* PC. The PC is here related to the object rather than to the subject, as in the copulative clauses *Liz was angry*/*a great asset*: we can distinguish them as **objective**, 'PC°', and **subjective**, 'PC^s', so that (24) and (25) will have the structure S–P–O–PC° while the copulative structure is S–P–PC^s. (24) and (25) are transitive by virtue of containing an O: the more specific clause construction where O combines with PC° we will call **complex-transitive**.

The three main syntactic properties of PC outlined in §2 apply to PC° as well as to PC^s, mutatis mutandis – and this of course is what justifies assigning the same general function to both.

(a) Form-class. Virtually all complex-transitive verbs allow an AdjP as PC° (compare (25) with *He considered Liz very able*), and some exclude an NP (compare *He drove her mad*/ *a lunatic, He drank himself senseless*/ *an alcoholic*). A few, such as **appoint** or **elect**, do not permit an AdjP, but they do take NPs like *secretary of the committee*, with the definitive article omitted, which we have noted do not function as object: *They elected her secretary of the committee*, but not **I dislike secretary of the committee*.

(b) Number. An NP in PC° function typically agrees in number with O: *He considered Liz a genius/*geniuses*. Again, the agreement rule holds only for the core of most straightforward complements, and examples like *He considered Ed and Kim an amiable pair/a nuisance/a good choice* parallel the instances of non-agreement given for the copulative construction. Note similarly with **call**: with a noun like **idiot** we have agreement, as in *He called her an idiot/*idiots*, but with **name**$_N$ we do not, witness *He called her rude names*.

(c) Passivisation. PC° cannot be made subject by passivising the clause, so that (25) can be transformed to *Liz was considered a great asset (by him)*, but not to **A great asset was considered Liz (by him)*.

In (24) and (25) the PC is non-omissible in the sense explained above: *He made Liz* and *He considered Liz*, though not ungrammatical, involve different meanings of **make** and **consider**. Whether or not we allow copulative clauses with omissible PC – see the discussion of (18) and (19) – it seems clear that the AdjP, though omissible, is a complement (and hence PC) in

(26)   *Ed painted the shed green*

for its occurrence certainly depends on the selection of a verb of an appropriate subclass.

Semantically, the complex-transitive construction involves two predications: in (24), for example, "angry" is predicated of Liz, and "made Liz angry" is predicated of Ed. Correlating with the distinction between omissible and obligatory PC, however, we have a contrast according as there is or is not a direct semantic relation between the verb and the object. In (26) there is: *the shed* expresses an argument of the predicate "paint" (as is obvious from the fact that the sentence entails *Ed painted the shed*). In (24) and (25) there is not: the second arguments of "make" and "consider" are not "Liz" but "Liz be angry" and "Liz be a great asset". Thus (24) says that Ed brought about the situation of Liz's being angry, not that he made Liz, and (25) says that in Ed's opinion Liz was a great asset, not that he considered her. (Note, however, that **make** can also occur in the same subtype as **paint**: compare (24) with *I've made the dress too large*.)

5.4   **The ditransitive construction**

Complex-transitive clauses like (25) with an NP functioning

as PC° are to be distinguished from **ditransitive clauses** like (27), which contain two objects, **indirect** (O^i) and **direct** (O^d):

(25)	*Ed considered Liz a great asset*	S–P–O–PC°
(27)	*Ed gave Liz the key*	S–P–O^i–O^d

It is clear that both syntactically and semantically the function of *the key* is quite different from that of *a great asset*. *The key* lacks the positive properties characteristic of a prototypical PC: it is not in paradigmatic contrast with an AdjP (or an NP like *secretary of the committee*), and its number is not determined by agreement with any other element in the clause. And for some speakers, though not all, it has the positive O property of being able to be made subject by passivisation: *The key was given Liz* (*by Ed*).[6] Semantically, *the key* expresses an argument of the semantic predicate: "give" is a 'three-place' semantic predicate, with the three arguments expressed by the three NPs *Ed, Liz* and *the key* – unlike *a great asset* in (25), *the key* does not express a semantic predicate taking "Liz" as its sole argument. A few verbs enter into both complex-transitive and ditransitive constructions, and with these we can devise ambiguous examples which bring out the semantic contrast quite clearly:

(28)	i	*He called her a nurse*
	ii	*I'll make you a colonel*

The complex-transitive meanings are "He applied the term 'nurse' to her" and "I'll bring it about that you become a colonel", whereas the ditransitive meanings are "He summoned a nurse for her" and "I'll make a colonel for you" (as in a context of making toy-soldiers, perhaps).

From a semantic point of view (27) differs only in thematic meaning from

(29)	*Ed gave the key to Liz*

Many grammars posit a transformational relation between the two, with (27) deriving from (29) by a rule which deletes the preposition and moves the NP *Liz* to the left of *the key*. The preposition deleted is normally either *to*, as here, or *for*, as in

(30)	i	*Ed found a seat for Liz*
	ii	*Ed found Liz a seat*

There is no analogous variant of a complex-intransitive like (25): **Ed considered a great asset to/for Liz*. We will be looking further at the relation between pairs like (27)/(29) and (30i/ii) in 14.2, but it is worth observing at this point that not all ditransitive clauses have such variants: with **allow**, for example, we have *He allowed me another try* but not **He allowed another try to me.*

---

[6] All speakers have *The key was given to Liz by Ed* but this is the passive not of (27) but of (29) below.

Thus although the existence of such a relationship is relevant to the differentiation of the ditransitive and complex-transitive constructions, it does not provide a simple test for distinguishing them.

If ditransitive clauses are transformationally derived from constructions containing a PP complement, they will not be kernel clauses and hence will fall outside the scope of this chapter. We will see, however, that it is questionable whether the relationship is sufficiently systematic to warrant a transformational derivation, and for this reason it is appropriate to include some discussion of them here – especially as they are highly relevant to our present concerns of examining the various kinds of complement that we need to recognise in analysing clause structure. For I am here taking the view that whether or not (27) and (29) are transformationally related, it is only (27) that contains an indirect object. Traditional grammars generally apply the term 'indirect object' to both the NP complement *Liz* in (27) and the PP complement in (29) – and some modern grammars follow this usage. Such an analysis reflects the identity of the associated semantic role, ('recipient', let us call it), but is not, I believe, justifiable from a syntactic point of view. Note first that *Liz* is associated with this same semantic role of recipient in the passive

(31)   *Liz was given the key by Ed*[7]

where it is nevertheless clearly subject, not indirect object. Thus what we are saying is that (27) differs not just from (31) but also from (29) with respect to the way the semantic roles are paired with the syntactic functions.

The indirect object is a particular kind of object and in excluding the *to Liz* of (29) we are in the first place simply applying a criterion for objects in general that they may take the form of an NP but not of a PP – in *Ed ran to Liz, Ed worked for Liz, Ed relied on Liz*, for example, the PPs *to Liz, for Liz* and *on Liz* are not objects. But apart from this difference in form-class between the NP complement *Liz* of (27) and the PP complement *to Liz* of (29) – or between the NP *Liz* in (30ii) and the PP *for Liz* in (i) – there are two reasons for distinguishing syntactically between the two kinds of complement, two respects in which the rules of syntax differentiate between them.

(a) Resistance to fronting. The indirect object, but not the PP complement, is resistant to fronting by various movement processes, as illustrated in the following examples.

---

[7] This contrasts thematically with another passive variant of (27), namely *The key was given Liz by Ed*, cited above. In principle ditransitives have two passive counterparts according to whether it is O^i or O^d that is made subject; the type where O^i is made subject, as in (31), is more usual and in certain cases the only one available – see 14.1.

(32)   i   *Ed gave Liz the key* (= 27)
           ii   **Who(m) did Ed give the key?*
           iii *To whom did Ed give the key?*

(33)   i   *He lent them books*
           ii   **[He kept a record of those] who(m) he lent books*
           iii *[He kept a record of those] to whom he lent books*

(34)   i   *He ordered Liz a gin and tonic*
           ii   **Liz he ordered a gin and tonic*
           iii *For Liz he ordered a gin and tonic*

In (32) we have the fronting of the '*wh* phrase' in an interrogative clause, in (33) that of the *wh* phrase in a 'relative' clause and in (34) what we have called thematic fronting – see 11.4, 12.4.1 and 14.4.1 for discussion of these non-kernel constructions. The starred sentences and others like them do not all sound thoroughly deviant, but (for most speakers at least) we can nevertheless distinguish clearly between the result of fronting an indirect object, which is at best marginally acceptable, and that of fronting a PP complement, which is completely acceptable – just like that of fronting a direct object (*What did Ed give Liz?*) or the NP within a PP complement (*Who did Ed give the key to?*) and so on.

It is worth adding that this resistance of O^i to fronting distinguishes further the ditransitive construction from the complex-transitive – compare

(35)   i   *He considered them bores*
         ii *[He avoided those] who(m) he considered bores*

Bores is here PC^o, so that there is only one object, and this can readily be fronted. It follows that the restriction must be stated as applying to indirect objects – rather than, for example, to the first of two NP complements.

(b) Passivisation. Unlike the indirect object, the PP complement can never be made subject by passivisation. Thus (29) cannot be passivised to **To Liz was given the key by Ed,*[8] as (27) can be passivised to (31). As emphasised above, the indirect object is a kind of object, and thus like the object in general it can prototypically be made subject by passivisation. The failure of *to Liz* in (29) to permit such reassignment to subject function makes it like all other PP complements – compare **To Liz was run by Ed*, **For Liz was worked by Ed*, **On Liz was relied by Ed*, and so on.

This point is probably more obvious than (a) – but it is in fact somewhat less general, for by no means all ditransitive clauses permit such passivisation: cf. *This error lost us the match/*We were lost the match by this error*; *They saved*

---

[8] *To Liz was given the key* is not ungrammatical, but it does not have *to Liz* as subject, being a mere thematic reordering of *The key was given to Liz*. This can be confirmed by consideration of the syntactic properties of subjects given in 2.2.2 – note the deviance of **Was to Liz given the key?*, the agreement of the verb with the following NP in *To Liz were given the keys*, and so on.

me some rice-pudding/*I was saved some rice-pudding, and so on. The matter is complicated by differences of dialect, with US English, for example, being more restrictive than British English in not allowing passivisation of clauses like (30ii), where the corresponding PP has *for* rather than *to*. But whatever the actual restrictions, we have already noted that the ability to be made subject by passivisation is not a necessary condition for object status in general, and hence it need not worry us that it is not a necessary condition for indirect object in particular.

In kernel clauses containing just one object, it is not at all clear that a syntactic distinction between O^i and O^d can be maintained. Normally the second object of a ditransitive clause is non-omissible – note, for example, that if we leave out *some money* from *He sent Liz some money* we have to reinterpret the role associated with *Liz* from recipient to patient. With a few verbs, however, we can omit the second object without changing the semantic role associated with the object that remains:

(36)   i *He told me the news*
         ii *He told me*
(37)   i *He envied her her success*
         ii *He envied her*

But from a syntactic point of view it is doubtful whether we are justified in analysing the *me* of (36ii) and *her* of (37ii) as O^i. In the first place, the restrictions on the fronting of O^i do not apply here: cf. *Who(m) did he tell?*, [*She was the one*] *whom he envied most*, and so on. And in the second place it would be somewhat arbitrary to analyse (36ii) and (37ii) on the basis of a comparison with (36i) and (37i) as opposed to, say, *He told me about it* and *He envied her for her success*, which are not ditransitive clauses. In the absence of convincing evidence to the contrary, therefore, I shall distinguish between O^i and O^d in the analysis of kernel clauses only in ditransitives, speaking simply of O in the case of 'monotransitives'.[9]

We have seen that there is no one semantic role consistently associated with the object in S–P–O constructions. The indirect object exhibits a narrower range of semantic variation, but variation there still is. The most typical role is that of 'recipient', as in *He gave Liz some flowers*, *He handed Kim the hammer*, where Liz received the flowers, Kim the hammer. *He ordered Jill a drink* does not entail that she received one – Jill is the 'intended' recipient. Commonly O^i indicates the addressee of some act of communication – the recipient of the communication, as in *He told her the news*. In *He gave Sue an*

---

[9] One single-object construction where it may be appropriate to have O^i is exemplified in *He made her a good husband*: cf. **[Liz,] whom he would make a good husband* [, . . .]. *A good husband* is here PC – but instead of being PC^o, like the PC of a complex-transitive such as *He made her a good wife*, it is PC^s, as in *He made a good husband*. The S-P-O^i–PC^s construction, if this is what it is, appears, however, to be unique to **make**.

examination we might say that Sue is a recipient, in that she receives an examination, but the semantic role could equally be viewed as that of patient, one to whom something is done, just as in *He examined Sue*. With some verbs the situation expressed by the clause is the opposite of one where the O^i referent receives something – opposite in either of two ways. In *I'll save you the bother* the meaning is that I'll bring it about that you do not have the bother – whereas in *They charged Kim £5* Kim didn't receive the money but on the contrary parted with it. We thus have a family of rather closely related meanings for O^i, but certainly not any single role that it can be said to express: the particular interpretation is again determined by the verb (or verb $+O^d$). The terms 'direct' and 'indirect' reflect the traditional idea that in an example like *He gave Liz some flowers* the flowers are more directly, immediately involved or affected than Liz inasmuch as they 'undergo' the transfer. The terms are thus based on the associated semantic roles: from a syntactic point of view both O^i and O^d are complements of the verb and given the language-particular definition of O^i adopted here they are both in a direct syntactic relation to the verb (phrase) – they are both ICs of the EVP.

5.5   PP and AdvP complements

All the complements considered in the last three sections have been NPs or AdjPs: here I shall extend the analysis to cover certain kinds of complement with the form of PPs or AdvPs.

5.5.1   *'Prepositional verbs'*

I begin with a construction whose analysis is in fact somewhat problematic:

(38)   *Ed relied on the minister*

The question is whether the *on* belongs with the preceding verb or with the following NP – is the constituent structure of the EVP to be represented as in (39i) or (ii)?

(39)   i

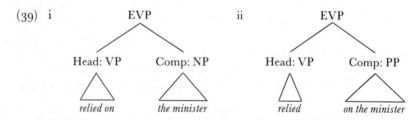

According to (i) the complement will be an object, whereas in (ii) it is not. Let us consider some of the factors that might be adduced in choosing between them.

200

(a) One respect in which (i) is intuitively appealing is that it reflects the close relation between **rely** and *on*, such that the verb determines the choice of preposition – it could not be replaced by *onto, in, to* or whatever. There are numerous combinations of this kind: **apply** *for*, **approve** *of*, **attend** *to*, **belong** *to*, **care** *for*, **come** *across* ("find"), **conform** *to*, **consist** *of*, **hint** *at*, **look** *for*, **object** *to*, **refer** *to*, **resort** *to* – and many more. This selectional dependence of the preposition on the verb does not, however, constitute a sound argument for analysis (i). For our description must be able to provide a mechanism for handling such a selectional relation between items that do not form constituents. One very clear example is found with catenative verbs, as in

(40) i *I kept him waiting*
      ii *I expected him to wait*

Keep selects a following *-ing* form, **expect** a base form with *to* – but there can surely be no question of treating **keep** + *ing* or **expect** + *to* as single syntactic constituents. And with prepositions we find examples like (41) where the preposition follows the first complement:

(41) i *He congratulated Kim on her promotion*
      ii *He accused me of bias*

We shall not want to say that *Kim* and *her promotion* are two complements of a verb **congratulate** *on*: rather we will say that **congratulate** takes two complements, one an NP, the other a PP with *on* as head. Thus the lexical entry for verbs must be able not simply to say what general kind of complements they take but also to give quite specific details about the complements (see 1.8). And of course once we can do this for **keep**, **expect**, **congratulate**, **accuse**, etc., we can also do it for **rely**: the selectional relation between **rely** and *on* can thus be handled in the lexical entry for **rely** and does not require that they be analysed as forming a syntactic constituent.

(b) A second point that might at first be thought to support analysis (i) is that we find passive clauses like *The minister could be relied on* – comparison with *The minister could be trusted*, and so on, suggests a paradigmatic contrast between VPs *could be relied on* and *could be trusted*. However, the existence of such passives would count as firm evidence for (39i) only if it could be shown that the subject of a passive clause always corresponds to an object of an active. This is the correspondence we find in the most elementary active/passive pairs like *Ed shot Max* and *Max was shot by Ed* where *Max* is object in the active, subject in the passive, but it certainly does not hold for all passives:

(42) i *That bed had been slept in by Queen Victoria*
      ii *Queen Victoria had slept in that bed*

In (42ii) the *in* is not uniquely determined by the verb, but is in paradigmatic contrast with other prepositions such as *on, underneath, beside*, etc. – and *in that bed* can provide the answer to a *where* question: *Where did she sleep?*. There can be no doubt that *in that bed* forms a constituent in (42ii), and this argues that passivisation can apply in such a way as to pick out the complement in a PP, not just the object in a clause: passives like *The minister could be relied on* are accordingly consistent with either (39i) or (ii) as analyses of the active construction.

We must conclude that neither (a) nor (b) provides any real evidence in favour of (39i); let us turn therefore to the arguments supporting analysis (39ii).

(c) One important point to note is that the preposition together with the following NP may be moved as a unit (just like expressions whose status as a PP is not in question) in transformations deriving certain non-kernel constructions, such as relative clauses: compare

(43)   i *Ed relied on the minister*
         ii [*the minister*] *on whom Ed relied*

(44)   i *She cut it with the knife*
         ii [*the knife*] *with which she cut it*

In (44i) *with* belongs uncontroversially with *the knife*, not with *cut*, and the examples show that *on the minister* is treated for purposes of relative clause formation just like the PP *with the knife*, a fact which is consistent with (39ii) but not with (i). There is of course an alternative form of the relative clause, [*the minister*] *who*(*m*) *Ed relied on*, but this is not relevant to the issue since it is consistent with both analyses (for whether *the minister* is complement of a so-called verb **rely** *on* or simply of the preposition *on* it will still be a constituent). Notice that this second kind of relative clause construction does not distinguish (43i) from (44i) since (44ii) likewise has the variant [*the knife*] *which she cut it with*.

(d) Further evidence for structure (39ii) is that adjuncts can be inserted between the verb and the preposition, but not between the preposition and the NP:

(45)   i *Ed relied steadfastly on the minister*
         ii **Ed relied on steadfastly the minister*

Analysis (39ii) allows for *steadfastly* to be inserted as an IC of the EVP, as is normal for adjuncts – and again we may compare *She cut it carefully with the knife* vs **She cut it with carefully the knife*.

(e) One other factor supporting (39ii) is the coordination in an example like

(46)   *Ed relied on the minister and on his solicitor*

which points to *on* + NP forming a constituent – compare again the coordination of undisputed PPs in *He had seen her in Paris and in London*.

These last three points combine to provide very strong evidence for the second analysis, and this is the one we shall adopt. One complicating factor is that the verb–preposition pairs may vary with respect to the tightness of the lexical bond between them. With ***come*** *across* ("find"), for example, the preposition does not move to initial position in relative clauses (cf. *[*the letters*] *across which he came*), is not repeated in coordination (cf. **He came across* *some old coins and across some stamps*), and does not readily allow the insertion of an adjunct before it (cf. ?*He came later across some interesting letters*). However, it is very doubtful whether we could make a viable distinction between separable and inseparable combinations that would justify adopting an analysis like (39ii) for the former and one like (i) for the latter. What we can do is adopt (39ii) for all and allow that various syntactic processes may be inhibited from applying if their effect would be to separate items over which a close lexical tie holds. This phenomenon has to be recognised elsewhere in the grammar in any case – for example, in the passivisation of clauses containing idioms, which applies quite normally for some (*The cat was let out of the bag, The beans have been spilled, The hatchet was finally buried*), but is inhibited with others (**The bucket was kicked*; ?**The line must be toed*): see 1.8.

A distinction corresponding to that we have drawn between O and PC is applicable to the complement of the preposition – compare (38) above with

(47)   *She counts as a full member of the society*

In (38) *the minister* is, as it were, an 'oblique' object, while in (47) *a full member of the society* is an oblique predicative complement, where by 'oblique' we mean that the syntactic relation between the element and the verb is not a direct one, but is rather mediated by the preposition. In (47), the oblique PC is subjective; it can also be objective, as in *They regarded him as stupid, They took him for dead*. The prepositions that occur with an oblique PC are fewer than those that occur with an oblique object: the clearest are *as* and *for*, as in the examples given; we should perhaps also include *into* (*It turned/degenerated into a slanging-match*), though this does not allow AdjP complements.

There is no term in standard use for the kind of complement illustrated by *on the minister* in (38). I shall call it a 'neutral PP complement', with 'neutral' suggesting that there is no constant semantic role associated with it: the interpretation depends on the verb + preposition and will have to be specified in the lexical entry for the verb. Verbs taking this kind of complement are commonly called 'prepositional verbs'. As we have noted, they may be either intransitive (***rely*** [*on*]; ***consist*** [*of*]; etc.) or transitive (***congratulate*** [. . . *on*]; ***cure*** [. . . *of*]). Among the transitive ones are to be included many that also belong to the ditransitive class (***give*** [. . . *to*]; ***find*** [. . . *for*]) – compare (27)/(29), (30i/ii).

5.5.2   *The verb–particle construction*

Structure (39ii), which we have adopted for [*Ed*] *relied on the minister* will not serve for the superficially similar EVP of (48):

(48)   *Ed backed up the minister*

(with the sense "Ed supported the minister"). *Up* here is traditionally analysed as an adverb; for present purposes I will adopt the term 'particle', which is commonly used in discussions of this construction and which may tentatively be regarded as denoting a subclass of adverb. (38) and (48) may be differentiated structurally as shown in (49):

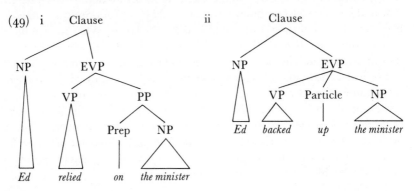

The main syntactic differences between the two constructions are as follows:[10]

(a) Corresponding to (38), as we have seen, is the relative clause [*the minister*] *on whom Ed relied* – the fact that *on* moves with the 'relative pronoun' *whom* to initial position was our first argument for saying that *on* is head of a PP. But there is no relative clause of this form for (48): *[*the minister*] *up whom Ed backed*. More generally, there is no transformation which moves the particle *up* together with the following NP: compare interrogative *Up which minister did Ed back?*, cleft *It was up the minister that Ed backed*, and so on.[11]

(b) Adjuncts can be inserted after the verb in (38) (as we have noted), but not in (48): *Ed relied steadfastly on the minister* vs *Ed backed steadfastly up the minister*. This does not provide any positive support for the analysis given in (49ii) but is nevertheless quite consistent with it, for there are other complements that do not permit adjuncts to intervene between them and the verb – for example NPs (objects), except when they are relatively long (cf. *Ed read carefully the book* vs *Ed read carefully all the papers she had lent him*).

(c) In (48) we can reverse the order of the particle and the NP: *Ed backed the minister up* (contrast *Ed relied the minister on*). Where the NP is an unstressed

---

[10] There is in addition a prosodic difference: the particle in (48) will normally be more prominent than the preposition in (38).

[11] (48) must be distinguished from *Ed backed up the hill*, where **back** means "reverse (e.g. a car)": here *up* is a preposition with *the hill* as its complement, and it is possible to say [*the hill*] *up which he was backing*, and the like.

'personal pronoun' it must precede the particle: *Ed backed her up* but not *Ed backed up her*, except with stress on *her*.

Points (a) and (c) provide compelling evidence against treating *up the minister* in (48) as a constituent (PP), while point (c) gives some support to the analysis of *up* as a separate element in the EVP, rather than as forming a syntactic unit with **back**: we will say that **back** takes two complements in the EVP, one (the object) an NP, the other a particle, such that the complements can occur in either order. (There are grounds for taking verb–NP–particle as the kernel order, with a thematic transformation shifting the object to the right to give it extra prominence.)

Back and *up* make up an idiom, and it is a lexical characteristic of English that it contains a great many idioms of this kind – cf. **bring** *up* ("raise [children]"), **fill** *in* ("complete [a form]"), **give** *up* ("stop trying", "surrender"), **make** *up* ("become reconciled", "fabricate [an alibi, etc.]"), **put** *off* ("alienate", "postpone"), **turn** *up* ("arrive"), and so on. But the occurrence of particles as complements is not restricted to idioms: compare *They brought the clothes in*, and the like. Where it is part of an idiom, we will regard it as a 'neutral complement'; in *They brought the clothes in*, the particle *in* is what we shall be calling a 'goal', and is in paradigmatic contrast with other forms of goal complement, as in *They brought the clothes into the kitchen* (and the fact that the latter clearly exhibits the kernel order of elements is a reason for regarding *They brought the clothes in* as more basic than *They brought in the clothes*).

Particles may occur as the only complement within the predicate (*They fell out*) or combine with either an object (*Ed backed up the minister*) or a neutral PP complement (*She came up with a brilliant idea, She looked down on the servants*); in the latter combination, the particle must come first: **She came with a brilliant idea up*. Note again the discrepancy between the lexical and syntactic grouping: **come** *up with* is not a syntactic constituent, for the *with* forms a unit with the following NP (cf. [*the idea*] *with which she eventually came up*).

5.5.3 *Place, goal and time complements*
Let us consider next the complements in such examples as

(50)   *The cat is in the lounge*
(51)   *John went into the kitchen*
(52)   *The meeting is at 5 o'clock*

The PPs here clearly satisfy our criteria for complements: those in (50) and (52) are obligatory, while that in (51) depends on a verb of the *go* subclass. They differ from the neutral PP complements in that the preposition is not determined by the verb – the prepositions could be replaced by others in the same semantic set. Thus (51) may be compared with *The cat is near/outside/ over/beyond the lounge*. Moreover the PPs are in paradigmatic contrast with expressions belonging to other classes: particles (*The cat is in, John went out*); certain other words traditionally classified as adverbs (*The cat is here/there*); a limited set of NPs (*The meeting is this evening*). Note in particular that they can be questioned with adverbial *where/when* (*Where is the cat?, Where did John go?, When is the meeting?*), whereas neutral PP and particle complements cannot – **Where did she rely?* is ungrammatical (in contrast to *Who did she rely on?/On whom did she rely?*) and *John eventually turned up* does not answer *Where did John eventually turn?*.

(51)–(53) contain **place** (or **locative**), **goal** and **time** complements respectively. Place is to be understood as static, goal as dynamic, involving movement to or towards. There is a very high degree of overlap between the expressions that can function as place complement and those that can function as goal: *in the car* and *under the ladder*, for example, are place complements in *He remained in the car, He was under the ladder* but goal complements in *He got in the car, He went under the ladder*. But the overlap is not complete: *into the kitchen*, for example, could only be goal, while *at church* could only be place.

These three kinds of complement have some affinity with predicatives. In the first place, the distinction between subjective and objective, which we drew for predicatives, can be applied also to place, goal and time complements. Thus the relation between the complement and the subject in (50)–(52) matches that between the second complement and the object in (53)–(55):

(53)   *She keeps her books in the lounge*
(54)   *They pushed John into the kitchen*
(55)   *They have kept the meeting at 5 o'clock*

Secondly, there are PPs containing non-literal uses of primarily place and goal prepositions which are semantically close to AdjPs – compare

(56)   i   *He was on top of the cupboard*   Place
         ii *He was on top of the world*
         iii *He was elated*   PC
(57)   i   *He got into a taxi*   Goal
         ii *He got into a bad temper*
         iii *He got bad-tempered*   PC

What kind of complements do we have in (56ii) and (57ii)? The non-literal place expression has the same distribution as an AdjP in that it can occur with verbs that take predicative but not place complements: *She seemed elated/on top of the world/*on top of the cupboard*; similarly with **look**, **feel** and also **appear** in the sense "seem" as opposed to "make an appearance, arrive". It is therefore best to analyse *on top of the world* (in its non-literal sense of course) as a PC and thus to allow a predicative to consist of an idiomatic PP as well as an AdjP or NP. The non-literal goal expression, on the other hand, behaves distributionally more like a literal goal than a PC. Thus it cannot occur with such verbs as **become** (intransitive) or **make** (transitive), which allow PCs but not goals: *He became bad-tempered/ *into a taxi/ *into a bad temper; He made her bad-tempered/ *into a taxi/ *into a bad temper.* And note that if we replace **make** here by **put** or **throw**, which take goals but not PCs, the non-literal goal is acceptable: *He puts her *bad-tempered/into a taxi/into a bad temper.*[12]

This by no means exhausts the range of complements that can consist of a PP. For example in

(58)   *I washed the stain out of the shirt*
(59)   *The meeting lasted for five hours*

the PPs are integral parts of the nucleus and may be analysed respectively as complements of source (involving movement away from) and duration. We will not pursue the analysis further in this direction: it is sufficient for our purposes to have introduced the most central and frequent structures.

5.6   Subordinate clause complements

We turn now to complements having the form of a clause, as in *She believed that they were genuine*, where *that they were genuine* is complement of *believed* – note that its occurrence is dependent on the selection of a verb of a particular subclass: compare **She slept/used that they were genuine*. The subordinate clause *that they were genuine* is, more specifically, what we are calling a 'content clause' (3.3), and our task in this section is to survey the kernel clause constructions containing complements of this very general kind.

We will look first, and quite briefly, at those where the subordinate clause is finite. 'Finite' covers all tensed clauses, together with a subset of clauses containing a base kind VP without *to* – those which, like (60ii), share with tensed clauses the property that the subject is required to be in nominative form when it is a case-variable pronoun:

(60)				
	i	*[I believe] that Ed/he/ *him took the car*	Finite	Tensed
	ii	*[I insist] that Ed/he/ *him take the car*	Finite	Non-tensed
	iii	*[I saw] Ed/ *he/him take the car*	Non-finite	Non-tensed

As we have noted, traditional grammars analyse the *take* of (ii) as a finite verb form (more specifically, subjunctive) and that of (iii) as non-finite (infinitive): we have not accepted any inflectional distinction in the verbs of (ii) and (iii) (see 2.4), but from the point of view of clause structure, there is much to be said for grouping (ii) with (i) rather than with (iii), and we are accordingly taking over the traditional terms 'finite' and 'non-finite' for classes of

---

[12] It is not quite true to say that **put** cannot take a PC (cf. *She put the rods straight*), but the construction is of very low productivity, with *straight* and *right* more or less the only possibilities for PC.

clause as opposed to verb form. In addition to their similarity with respect to pronominal case, (i) and (ii) have it in common that they are introduced by the subordinating conjunction *that*. *That* can very often be omitted (as here), but when present it provides a clear constituent structure signal: *that Ed/he took the car* and *that Ed/he take the car* are quite clearly constituents, whereas the status of *Ed/him take the car* as a constituent in (iii) is very questionable, as we shall see.

5.6.1 *Finite clauses*

Finite subordinate clauses are classifiable in terms of the system of 'clause type':

(61) i [*She assumed*] *that he was right*   Declarative
      ii [*She asked*] *who I was*   Interrogative
      iii [*She remembered*] *what a struggle it had been*   Exclamative
      iv [*She demanded*] *that he be told*   Jussive

These distinctions will be explained later, after we have examined the clause type system as it applies to main clauses (Ch. 11), and most of our examples here will use the unmarked term, declarative. But it is relevant to our present concerns to point out that verbs must be subclassified not merely according to whether they can take a content clause as complement but, more specifically, according to which of the four types they take. Thus **assume** and **believe** take declaratives, **inquire** takes interrogatives, **ask** interrogatives or jussives, **remember** declaratives, interrogatives, or exclamatives, **decree** jussives, and so on.

Where a clause complement is in paradigmatic contrast with an NP it is traditionally given the same more specific functional analysis as the NP. Thus the subordinate clauses in (61) are analysed as objects since they are replaceable by NP objects: *She assumed his innocence, She asked a probing question, She remembered her schooldays, She demanded a recount.* In (62), by contrast, the content clause would be predicative complement:

(62)   *Her main worry is that he drinks too much*

Be is here used in its identifying sense, and the complement is accordingly not a prototypical PC – a finite clause does not express a semantic predicate, so that the complement here is not semantically predicative. Very few of the copulative verbs other than **be** take finite clause complements: we could not, for example, replace **be** in (62) by **become, appear, seem, sound** – though **remain** is allowed.

Finite clause complements are not always in contrast with NPs, however: verbs like **hope** and **insist**, for example, take clause but not NP complements, as in *She hoped (that) she would recover quickly* vs **She hoped a quick recovery* or *She insisted (that) he was innocent* vs **She insisted his innocence.* Instead of NP objects, these verbs take neutral PP complements: *She hoped for a quick recovery, She insisted on his innocence.* Finite clauses – more specifically, declarative and jussive ones: see 10.4 for the others – cannot occur as complement to a preposition (**of/for/at that she would recover quickly*), and hence the distinction that elsewhere we find between verb + NP (*She expected a quick recovery*) and verb + PP (*She hoped for a quick recovery*) is lost with clause complements (*She expected/hoped that she would recover quickly*). But there is no reason to give a different functional analysis according as the clause is replaceable by an NP or a PP: if *that she would recover quickly* is object of *expected*, then it is also object of *hoped.* One respect in which finite clause complements are like NPs, objects, is that in general the superordinate clause can be passivised – compare

(63)   i *Everyone accepted this explanation*
        ii *This explanation was accepted by everyone*
(64)   i *Everyone accepted that it was a genuine case of mistaken identity*
        ii *That it was a genuine case of mistaken identity was accepted by everyone*

Usually, however, passivisation is accompanied by extraposition: *It was accepted by everyone that it was a genuine case of mistaken identity.* Notice that such passives (particularly with the *by* phrase omitted) are typically possible whether the clause is replaceable by an NP or by a PP: *It was expected/hoped that she would recover quickly.*

In the examples given so far the content clause has been the only complement, but it may also combine with various others, such as an NP object or neutral PP complement:

(65)   *The boss told/persuaded them that it was genuine*
(66)   *The boss suggested to Bill that he might resign*

The latter has passive counterparts of the kind exemplified above (*It was suggested to Bill by the boss that he might resign*), but for the former it is only the NP that can be moved into subject function by passivisation: *They were told/persuaded by the boss that it was genuine* but not **It was told/persuaded them by the boss that it was genuine.*

5.6.2   *Non-finite clauses, 1*

We turn now to complementation by non-finite constructions, as in

(67)   i *He tried to sell it*
        ii *She advised me to buy it*

This is one of the most difficult areas of English grammar and despite a great deal of intensive study over the last twenty years there remains much disagreement over quite basic aspects of the analysis. In the limited space available here, we can do no more than give a short survey of the range of complements involved and consider very briefly some of the problems that arise in their description. We will divide the discussion into two parts: in the present subsection we confine our attention to constructions where the VP of the non-finite clause immediately follows the superordinate clause VP, as *to sell* immediately follows *tried* in (65i), and then in §6.3 we take up those where there is an intervening NP, like the *me* of (ii).

All four kinds of non-tensed VP distinguished in 4.3 are to be found:

(68) i   [*Ed hoped*] *to repair it*   ɪ base kind, + *to*
      ii   [*Ed helped*] *repair it*   ɪɪ base kind, − *to*
      iii [*Ed remembered*] *repairing it*   ɪɪɪ -*ing* kind
      iv   [*It got*] *repaired*   ɪᴠ -*en* kind

The base form verbs in non-finite content clauses are all infinitives in the traditional verbal paradigm, and we may accordingly use the standard term 'infinitival' for such clauses; the -*ing* forms, however, are in some cases traditional gerunds and in others present participles, so that we will do better to continue with '-*ing* clause' instead of generalising either 'gerundive' or 'participial', as in many modern grammars.

The verbs **hope**, **help**, and so on which take complements like those in (68) belong to the class of catenative verbs (see 4.4, where we alluded to the problem of distinguishing auxiliaries and catenatives). The choice among the four non-finite constructions depends primarily on the catenative to which they are complement. Some catenatives allow only one kind, as **hope** allows only ɪ, **enjoy** only ɪɪɪ. Others allow two or three possibilities, but without any uniform semantic distinctions correlating with the syntactic ones. This will be evident from the different semantic relations between the pairs *He remembered to repair/repairing it, They need to eat/eating* (the -*ing* clause here is passive, though its VP does not have the normal structure of a passive: *They need eating* is equivalent to *They need to be eaten*), *I'll try to eat less/eating less, He likes to do the crossword-puzzle/doing the crossword-puzzle* (that ɪ and ɪɪɪ are not equivalent with **like** can be seen by replacing *being* by *to be* in such an example as *He likes being married to a politician*), *I intend to finish it/finishing it* (one of the few cases where there is no apparent semantic difference at all). This is not to say that the choice is totally arbitrary: catenatives with similar or related meanings (such as **wish** and **desire** or **remember** and **forget**) will typically take the same kind or kinds of complement. Moreover there is a tendency for the -*ing* kind to be associated with factuality, the base kind with non-factuality: compare, for example, *he enjoyed reading it, He hoped to read it*, where the former but not the latter implies that he actually did read it. This is no more than a tendency, however, and there are numerous cases where it does not apply – we could not, for example, predict that **anticipate** would take an -*ing* clause complement, and so on. Thus there is no getting away from the fact that the lexical entries for verbs must specify which kinds of complement they take and, where more than one is involved, the semantic differences (if any).

Of the four constructions in (68), only I and III occur with significant numbers of catenative verbs: for most dialects only *get* takes IV, and leaving aside a few idioms like *make do*, *let slip*, etc., only *help* and *dare*$_{MV}$ take II. IV also differs from the others in that the *-en* class clause is invariably passive; we will take up the relation between *It got repaired* and *It was repaired* in 14.1 – we will not consider it further in this chapter.

The non-finite complements in (68) do not contain subjects and I observed earlier (3.3) that it is arguable whether they should be analysed as subjectless clauses or simply as EVPs. In either case, however, it is intuitively clear that the semantic interpretation of the whole sentence involves finding what is in some sense an 'understood subject' for the non-tensed EVP. In (69), for example,

(69)   *Liz expected to impress the panel*

what Liz expected was that she, Liz, would impress the panel – not that Tom, for example, would do so or that someone simply not specified would. Here, then, the understood subject of the subordinate clause/EVP is recovered from the actual subject of the superordinate one. This illustrates the normal case, but before raising the question of what is meant by an 'understood' subject we should note that with a small number of catenatives, such as *advocate* (with construction III), *help* (I or II), *say* (I), it is not recoverable from any element in the sentence. Consider, for example, *help* as in *Further study may help to resolve this problem* (I) or *Ed helped wash up* (II). The semantic predicate "help" basically takes three arguments, the first representing the one(s)/thing(s) that provide the help, the second the one(s) who receive the help, and the third the matter with respect to which the help is given: in the examples cited the second argument is not expressed but has to be pragmatically inferred from the context – and it is then from this inferred second argument that the understood subject of the non-finite construction is recovered. For example, it might be clear from the context for *Ed helped wash up* that it was Liz that Ed gave help to, and in this case it will be Liz who washed up (with Ed's help). Or take *say*, as in *She said not to listen to old wives' tales* (a construction restricted to informal styles): here the understood subject represents the addressee(s) and/or speaker, the meaning being approximately "She said that you/we should not listen to old wives' tales".

These, however, are quite exceptional cases: with the great majority of catenatives, the understood subject of the non-finite construction is recovered from the actual subject of the catenative. But what do we mean by an 'understood subject'? We are taking 'subject' to be a syntactic concept, so that when we talk about the subject of a clause (a clause, that is, that has an actual subject, not an understood one) we are referring to some linguistic form: the subject of *Liz shot the intruder* is the NP *Liz*, not the semantic argument representing the person Liz. Is 'understood subject' to be taken in the same way? A positive answer would imply that the subjectless construction is to be syntactically derived from a more basic construction, a clause, containing an actual subject – *to impress the panel* in (69) would derive from *Liz to impress the panel* by the deletion of *Liz*, and so on. This kind of analysis may seem plausible enough at first, but there are cases, such as (70), where it yields semantically unsatisfactory results:

(70)   *Both candidates expected to impress the panel*

For the expectation of the two candidates was not that both candidates would impress the panel – rather, if the candidates were Ed and Liz, then Ed expected that he, Ed, would impress the panel and Liz expected that she, Liz, would do so. We shall accordingly not want to derive *to impress the panel* from *both candidates to impress the panel*: the 'understood subject' must be more abstract, not a form repeated elsewhere in the sentence.

Perhaps we should therefore interpret 'understood subject' as a semantic argument rather than a syntactic form (in which case 'understood subject-argument' would be a better term). Thus in (69) the understood subject-argument for the predicate expressed by *impress the panel* would be "Liz", whereas in (70) it would be what is known as a 'variable' covering the set of two candidates – using "x" for the variable, we would then have something along the lines of "x expected x to impress the panel, for either x in the set". This interpretation in terms of an understood subject-argument cannot be generalised to all cases, however, as can be seen by considering an example like

(71)   *There seem to be too many people with vested interests on these committees*

The non-finite complement is relatable to the main clause *There are too many people with vested interests on these committees*, which has *there* as subject – but *there* is a dummy subject: it does not express a semantic argument. Thus we cannot say that *to be too many people with vested interests on these committees* expresses a semantic predicate predicated of some understood subject-argument: rather we have a syntactic predicate understood as related to a syntactic subject *there*.

In some cases, then, we apparently need a semantic interpretation of 'understood subject', a semantic argument not expressed in the non-finite complement but inferable from elsewhere (or from the context), while in other cases we need a syntactic interpretation, a linguistic form not present in the non-finite complement itself, but retrievable from elsewhere in the sentence. It turns out, however, that the catenatives (such as **expect**) where the first interpretation is needed are different from those (such as **seem**) where the second interpretation is needed. And this is related to a further difference between the two classes of catenatives. It may be explained by reference to a contrasting pair like

(72)   *Ed expects to amuse Kim*
(73)   *Ed seems to amuse Kim*

The difference we are concerned with is that in (72) but not (73) there is a direct semantic relation between the catenative and its subject *Ed* – "Ed" is an argument of "expect" but not of "seem". Thus (72) attributes to Ed a certain psychological state – it expresses a relation between Ed and the situation of his amusing Kim. By contrast, (73) has just about the same meaning as *Seemingly, Ed amuses Kim*. If I say simply *Ed amuses Kim* I commit myself unequivocally to the truth of the proposition that Ed amuses Kim, whereas if my evidence is weaker I can qualify my claim by adding the adverb *seemingly* or the verb **seem**. Thus in terms of the propositional meaning, **seem** in (73) relates to *Ed + to amuse Kim* as a whole rather than to the two parts separately.

The difference between (72) and (73) can perhaps be most clearly brought out by comparing them with the following:

(74)   *Kim expects to be amused by Ed*
(75)   *Kim seems to be amused by Ed*

(72) and (74) have clearly different propositional meanings, for one attributes a psychological state to Ed, the other to Kim: it is accordingly easy to imagine a context where one could truthfully assert one and deny the other. (73) and (75), by contrast, have the same propositional meaning: it would always be inconsistent to assert one and deny the other. This follows from what was said in the last paragraph, for we can give the meanings very informally as

(72')   "Ed expects p" $\Big\}$ where "p" = "Ed amuses Kim"
(73')   "Seemingly p"

(74')   "Kim expects q" $\Big\}$ where "q" = "Kim is amused by Ed"
(75')   "Seemingly q"

"p" is equivalent to "q", and from this it follows that (73') is equivalent to (75'), but not that (72') is equivalent to (74'). In (73), we have said, **seem** relates semantically to *Ed + to amuse Kim* as a whole: the passive counterpart of the latter is *Kim + to be amused by Ed*, which is what we have in (75), and this is why (73) and (75) differ only in thematic meaning.

Similar relationships are found when we consider thematic systems other than voice that involve a difference in the selection of the subject (see 2.2.2). Take, for example, the pair of thematic variants:

(76)   i *Too many people with vested interests are on these committees*
            ii *There are too many people with vested interests on these committees*

where we take (i) as unmarked, and (ii) as derived by *there* insertion. If we replace *are* by infinitival *to be* and insert **seem**, we get

(77)   i *Too many people with vested interests seem to be on these committees*

           ii *There seem to be too many people with vested interests on these committees* (=
71)

which are likewise thematic variants. But with **expect** only version (i) is
grammatical:

(78)   i *Too many people with vested interests expect to be on these committees*

           ii **There expect to be too many people with vested interests on these committees*

The subject of **expect** expresses a semantic argument and hence cannot be
filled by a dummy element like *there*.

This then is why examples like (71), which we used to show that what we
have been calling the 'understood subject' cannot always be interpreted as a
missing subject-argument, occur only with catenatives of the **seem** class in
contrast to the **expect** class. Conversely, the case against a syntactic interpretation of 'understood subject' can be made only with examples containing
expect class catenatives, not **seem** class ones. For if we replace **expect** by **seem**
in (70) we get

(79)   *Both candidates seemed to impress the panel*

and this time there is no semantic problem in relating the non-finite construction to one with *both candidates* as subject, for the meaning is "Seemingly,
both candidates impressed the panel".

We will not pursue the distinction between the **expect** and **seem** constructions beyond this very informal account, which is non-committal on the
question of whether and, if so, how the distinction should be handled in
syntactic terms (except that the analysis of examples like (78ii) as ungrammatical implies that the distinction is not purely semantic). Numerous
different analyses will be found in the literature, varying according to the
particular formal framework adopted. Of the catenative classes the **seem**
class is a good deal smaller than the **expect** class; representative examples are
given in (80)–(81):

(80)   **Expect** class: **abhor, detest, hate, like, love, prefer, resent, want;**
                         forget, remember; attempt, endeavour, strive, try;
                         manage, neglect, risk; consider

(81)   **Seem** class: **begin, continue, keep, cease, finish, stop; appear; happen;**
                        fail; tend; need, have^{Oblig} (as in *You have to fill in both forms*)

The contrast applies with non-finite constructions I and III; there are no **seem**
class verbs taking construction II. The assignment of verbs to the two classes
depends of course on whether they follow the pattern of **expect** or **seem** with
respect to the relation between pairs like (72):(74)/(73):(75) and
(77i:ii)/(78i:ii) – the reader is invited to check the above classification by
constructing and testing relevant examples. Thus, to illustrate with *-ing*

class non-finites, the non-equivalence of *The hecklers enjoyed barracking the minister* and *The minister enjoyed being barracked by the hecklers* shows that *enjoy* belongs to the **expect** class, and conversely the equivalence of *The hecklers kept barracking the minister* and *The minister kept being barracked by the hecklers* puts **keep** in the **seem** class. One point should be borne in mind when the tests are being applied. We are saying that with **seem** class catenatives, pairs like (73):(75) and (78i:ii) will be alike in propositional meaning, so that each will entail the other – but they differ in thematic meaning, and it follows from this that they will not be freely interchangeable; indeed one or the other will often sound quite unnatural. Consider, for example, the verb **begin**. The propositional equivalence of pairs like *His colleagues began to resent his overbearing attitude* and *His overbearing attitude began to be resented by his colleagues*, analogous to (73):(75), is unproblematic. But in the pair *Ed began to unwrap the parcel* and *The parcel began to be unwrapped by Ed*, the second sounds very odd, hardly a sentence one could imagine oneself actually using. Nevertheless in a context where the first was true, we would not say that the second was false, only that it was unnatural. The relationship is quite different from that found with **expect** class verbs: compare *Ed preferred to open the parcel* and *The parcel preferred to be opened by Ed*, where we would say that the truth conditions were different, since the first attributes a psychological state to Ed, the second to the parcel (and since we do not believe parcels to have minds, the second will be judged anomalous except in the context of fairy-tales and the like).

5.6.3 Non-finite clauses, II

In this subsection we examine constructions where the non-tensed VP is preceded by an NP, as in

(82)
    i *Ed intended Liz to repair it*   I base kind, + *to*
    ii *Ed let Liz repair it*   II base kind, − *to*
    iii *Ed remembered Liz repairing it*   III -*ing* kind
    iv *Ed had it repaired by Liz*   IV -*en* kind

All four kinds of VP are found, and again the choice among them depends on the catenative. Complements with -*en* kind VPs are invariably passive, and hence construction IV will again be taken up in 14.1.

I shall frequently refer informally to the NP preceding the non-tensed VP – *Liz* in (i–iii), *it* in (iv) – as the 'intervening NP'. This term has the advantage of being neutral with respect to the difficult question of where the NP figures in the constituent structure. There is some evidence that the constituent structure is different in the -*ing* construction than in the others, and it will accordingly be convenient to treat it separately after the others.

With constructions I, II and IV, I shall take the intervening NP to be an object of the catenative, so that the structure will be as shown in (83) rather than (84):

(83)

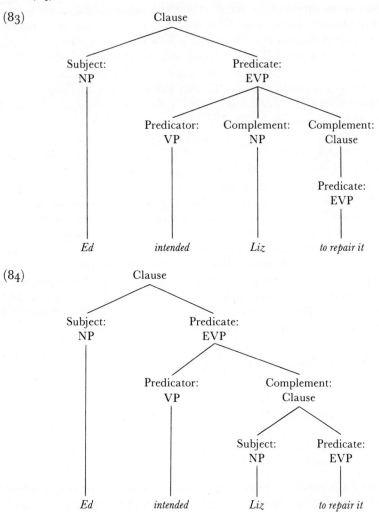

(84)

Structure (84) matches the meaning more closely than (83) – at least for this example, and analogously for (82ii) and (iv). For Ed's intention was that Liz should repair it – what was intended was an event, not a person, so that "Liz" is not a semantic argument of "intend". From a syntactic point of view, however, there are grounds for preferring the analysis shown in (83). Firstly, it is to be noted that a sequence like *Liz to repair it* does not occur elsewhere as a constituent: we cannot say, for example, **Liz to repair it was intended*, **Liz to repair it would be useful*, **The intention was Liz to repair it*, **What he intended was*

Liz to repair it. In this respect the construction is analogous to a complex transitive clause where object + PC° can jointly express a single semantic argument, as in *Ed considered Liz a genius.* Notice that (82i) differs from the construction with *for*:

(85)   *Ed arranged for Liz to repair it*

for such a sequence as *for Liz to repair it* does occur as a clear constituent in a number of constructions: *The arrangement was for Liz to repair it, What he'd like best would be for Liz to repair it, It would be useful for Liz to repair it* (interpreted as deriving by extraposition from *For Liz to repair it would be useful*). We will therefore take *for Liz to repair it* in (85) as a single complement of **arrange** (an infinitival clause), but *Liz to repair it* in (82i) as a sequence of two complements, an NP and a subjectless clause (with the same doubt as in (68) as to whether the non-finite element is a clause or just an EVP).

A second point is that the intervening NP in (82i) can become subject by passivisation: *Liz was intended (by Ed) to repair it.* Again, (82i) contrasts with (85), which cannot be passivised in this way: **Liz was arranged (by Ed) for to repair it.* The passivisation transformation cannot extract an NP from a subordinate clause to make it subject of the superordinate clause: this is evident not only from the **arrange** example but also from others involving a finite subordinate clause: *Ed thought Liz was ill* ↛ **Liz was thought (by Ed) was ill*, and so on. What we do have as the passive of (85) is *It was arranged (by Ed) for Liz to repair it*, where the extraposition process has applied obligatorily to **For Liz to repair it was arranged (by Ed)*: this is further evidence for taking *for Liz to repair it* as a constituent. Passivisation is not always possible with clauses like (82i): we can have *Liz was intended to repair it* but not, for example, **Liz was liked to repair it.* However, we have already noted exceptions to the passivisation rule in clauses with a single NP complement (*The suit fits me* ↛ **I am fitted by the suit*), so we shall not take this inapplicability of passivisation as a reason for assigning to *Ed liked Liz to repair it* a different structure than to (82i), given that there are apparently no other grounds for distinguishing them.

Having argued for (83) as the analysis for clauses like (82i), let us now draw a distinction between two subclasses of catenative entering into this construction, analogous to that drawn between **expect** and **seem** classes for the construction without an intervening NP. Our model verbs this time will be **persuade** and **intend**:

(86)   *Ed had persuaded Liz to photograph the child*
(87)   *Ed had intended Liz to photograph the child*

Whereas in (72) and (73) the issue was whether there was a direct semantic relation between the catenative and its subject, here it is whether there is a direct semantic relation between the catenative and its object, the intervening NP. In (87) there is not: this point was made above when we were observing that structure (84) provides a closer match with the meaning than does (83). But in (86) catenative and object are directly related semantically: to 'persuade' Liz to do something is to act directly on her – it involves reasoning with her, applying pressure to her or whatever; the object *Liz* in (86) thus does express a semantic argument of "persuade".

There are several consequences of this semantic distinction between (86) and (87): we will mention just two, analogues of those discussed for the **expect/seem** contrast. First, note the different relationships between (86) and (88) on the one hand, (87) and (89) on the other:

(88)   *Ed had persuaded the child to be photographed by Liz*
(89)   *Ed had intended the child to be photographed by Liz*

The two **intend** sentences have the same propositional meaning, whereas the two with **persuade** do not: in (86) Ed had exerted persuasion on Liz, in (88) on the child. With **intend** the semantic relation is between the verb and the sequence NP + non-finite complement as a whole, so that any purely thematic manipulation of this sequence will not affect the overall propositional meaning. But **persuade** relates directly to the object, and hence changing the object will not leave the propositional meaning intact. It is worth observing that the result of applying the passivisation process to the sequence following **persuade** (and other verbs in the same class) will often be anomalous. Thus *Ed persuaded the letter to be signed by Liz* (in contrast to *Ed persuaded Liz to sign the letter*) is anomalous because "the letter" is not an appropriate object-argument for "persuade". But even where the object-argument remains an appropriate one, the passive non-finite may sound unnatural, as in *Ed had persuaded Max to be invited by Liz* (in contrast to *Ed had persuaded Liz to invite Max*). The reason is that the meaning of **persuade** is such that the understood subject-argument of the infinitival complement is assigned an **agentive** role, one involving some measure of control, decision, responsibility. In passive clauses, however, the subject-argument is normally construed non-agentively: the main clause *Max was invited by Liz*, for example, will not normally be interpreted with Max having an agentive role, for being invited is something that happens to you, not something you do. (88) itself is not completely felicitous – one would tend to say instead something like *Ed had persuaded the child to let Liz photograph him/her*. This in no way detracts from the point being made. On the contrary, it reinforces the distinction between **persuade** and **intend**, such that in the **persuade** construction the intervening NP is interpreted as having two semantic roles, one being 'patient' with respect to the act of persuading, the other being some kind of agentive role with respect to the situation expressed in the infinitival complement, whereas in the **intend** construction the intervening NP has a single semantic role, determined by the content of the infinitival complement.

The second consequential difference between **persuade** and **intend** concerns the *there* construction. With **intend** we find equivalences between pairs like

(90)   *He had intended a reporter to be at the meeting*
(91)   *He had intended there to be a reporter at the meeting*

Again, we have applied a thematic transformation to the sequence following the catenative, and since **intend** relates semantically to the sequence as a whole the thematic change is allowed. But we could substitute **persuade** for **intend** only in (90), not in (91) – the NP object expresses a semantic argument of "persuade" and can thus never be filled by a dummy element like *there*.

Other catenatives taking an intervening NP + infinitival complement (constructions I and II) may be grouped with **persuade** or **intend** on the basis of their behaviour with respect to the constructions illustrated in (86)–(91); representative members are as follows:

(92)   **Persuade** class: *advise, ask, assist, challenge, dare*$_{MV}$, *entreat, invite, oblige, remind, request, teach, tell, urge*
(93)   **Intend** class: *desire, hate, like, love, want, wish; allege, believe, claim, know, prove, remember, report, suspect, think; hear, see, watch*

For example, the equivalence of pairs like *Ed believed Liz to have wronged Max* and *Ed believed Max to have been wronged by Liz*, and the possibility of having *there* as object, as in *Ed believed there to have been a mistake,*[13] shows clearly that **believe** belongs with **intend**, not **persuade**.

The classification, however, is not always obvious or straightforward, as may be seen from a consideration of such verbs as **allow** and **make**. Given a sentence like *Ed allowed his son to watch the match* it is tempting to put **allow** with **persuade**, interpreting it as "give permission" with the object-argument having the role of recipient of the permission – and one would certainly be very unlikely to say *Ed allowed the match to be watched by his son*. But there are many examples where **allow** cannot be interpreted as "give permission": *He allowed the situation to get out of hand, They didn't allow the weather to ruin the outing.* Note that the latter is equivalent to *They didn't allow the outing to be ruined by the weather,* and that *there* can occur as object, as in *He hadn't allowed there to be any misunderstanding about his intentions.* On the strength of the latter data we must accept that **allow** belongs in the **intend** class with the approximate meaning "not prevent". Does it also have a distinct meaning, "give permission",

---

[13] Note that this has no counterpart without *there*: **Ed believed a mistake to have been*; as we shall see in 14.7 the *there* transformation is often obligatory.

where it belongs with **persuade**? I do not think that this is the proper solution, partly because of the difficulty of distinguishing between the two proposed meanings in particular instances,[14] partly because, even where verbal permission or consent seems to be involved, the referent of the intervening NP does not have to be interpreted as the recipient of the permission. For example, in *He wouldn't allow the chauffeur to drive his daughter*, to whom is the permission refused – the chauffeur, the daughter or someone else? Surely the sentence simply doesn't encode that information, and we must conclude that **allow** belongs only in the **intend** class.

Make is more difficult. Semantically it has affinities with both **force** and **cause** – but **force** belongs with **persuade**, **cause** with **intend** (cf. *This caused/ *forced there to be a malfunction*). **Make** is like **force** in that such pairs as *Ed made Liz photograph Kim* and *Ed made Kim be photographed by Liz* seem to differ in propositional meaning and in that it does not take *there* as intervening NP: **He made there be an accident, *He made there be something wrong with it*. However, with **force** the semantic role associated with the intervening NP with respect to the infinitival complement is always agentive – so that **force** could be inserted in '*Ed ____ Liz to lie down*', but not naturally in '*This ____ Liz to lose her balance*': losing one's balance is not normally conceived of as being under one's control. **Make**, by contrast, could be inserted equally naturally in both – like **cause** it does not associate a necessarily agentive role with the intervening NP. And although it doesn't take *there*, it does allow dummy *it*: *He made it appear that she was lying* – here *it* cannot express a semantic argument of "make", and **make** resembles **cause** and hence **intend**. The properties of **make** cannot be fully accounted for by assigning it to the **persuade** class, nor by allowing it to belong to both classes (for this would not predict its failure to take *there* or the contrast between *This caused the meeting to be delayed* and **This made the meeting be delayed*, and so on): some measure of ad hoc description of its distribution seems unavoidable.

Let us now turn to the construction with intervening NP + *-ing* class complement, as in (82iii). Again we can contrast one variant where the intervening NP has a direct semantic relation to the catenative with another where it does not:

(94)   *Ed caught your father opening the mail*
(95)   *Ed resented your father opening the mail*

Thus while the second is equivalent to *Ed resented the mail being opened by your father*, the first is not equivalent to the anomalous *Ed caught the mail being opened by your father*, and similarly we can have *Ed resented there being a reporter at the meeting* but not **Ed caught there being a reporter at the meeting*. The reason for

---

[14] Neither of the glosses given captures the full semantic properties of **allow**, for *Ed allowed her to do it* entails that she did it, whereas *Ed didn't prevent her doing it* and *Ed gave her permission to do it* do not.

giving the *-ing* construction separate consideration is that although a constituent structure like (83) is needed for (94), it may well be that for (95) a structure like (84) is appropriate.

With complements of the infinitival class we contrasted constructions with and without *for* – e.g. (82i) vs (85) – and found evidence for treating *for Liz to repair it* as a single constituent, but *Liz to repair it* as a sequence of two constituents. With complements of the *-ing* class we must compare the intervening NP construction with that involving an intervening PossP:

(96)   *Ed resented your father's opening the mail*

Here, *your father's opening the mail* undoubtedly forms a single constituent: there is no question of *your father's* on its own being a complement of **resent**. But the *-ing* constructions with PossP and with NP do not differ in the same way as the infinitival ones with and without *for*. In the first place, the PossP can always be replaced by the corresponding NP, as *your father's* can be replaced by *your father*, giving (95) instead of (96): the difference is stylistic, with the PossP variant being more formal. The converse, however, does not hold: some catenatives allow an NP but not a PossP, as in *I heard the boss/*the boss's interrogating Liz.* (Verbs belonging to the **catch** class do not take a PossP, as we would expect, but we are concerned here only with the **resent** class – I include **hear** in the latter class on the strength of the equivalence between the above and *I heard Liz being interrogated by the boss.*) Moreover, where an NP is replaceable by a PossP it can never become subject through passivisation: **Your father was resented opening the mail by Ed.* A second point is that a sequence like *your father opening the mail* (unlike *Liz to repair it*) can occur elsewhere as a constituent: *He objected to your father opening the mail, What Ed resented most was your father opening the mail.* Although the evidence is by no means conclusive, it does suggest that *your father opening the mail* is also a constituent in (95), though not of course in (94). In this case, there would be some correlation between the semantic and syntactic differences – except that some verbs, such as **hear** in the above examples, might go semantically with **resent** but syntactically with **catch**. It is often assumed that the infinitival and *-ing* constructions are wholly parallel, but there is reason to doubt whether this is so. Be that as it may, it has to be recognised that the constituent structure in these constructions with intervening NP is by no means clearly determinable.

It will be noticed that some catenatives, such as **want**, occur either with or without an intervening NP, while others, such as **persuade**, occur only with, and others again, such as **seem**, only without. The overlap is greatest between what we have been calling the **expect** class and the **intend** class (with **expect** and **intend** themselves belonging to both).

That there should be overlap here is not surprising. Compare, for example,

(97)   *Ed expected/intended to finish the job quickly*
(98)   *Ed expected/intended Liz to finish the job quickly*

In (98) the subject-arguments for the predicates "expect"/"intend" and "finish" are different and have to be expressed separately, whereas in (97) they are the same and need be expressed only once. It would be a mistake to think, however, that we could merge the *expect* and *intend* classes, resulting in a three-way classification with the *seem* class containing those verbs that exclude an intervening NP, the *persuade* class those that require one and the *expect/intend* class those that occur with or without one: things are nothing like as simple as this. Thus some *seem* class verbs, such as *keep* and *start*, also occur with an intervening NP; some *expect* class verbs, such as *manage* and *try*, do not allow one; some *intend* class verbs, such as *believe* and *see*, require one; and finally some *persuade* class verbs such as *dare*$_{MV}$ and *help* also occur without one. The presence or absence of an intervening NP is accordingly not predictable from the semantic distinctions on which we based our four classes, but involves a partially independent dimension of classification. As we have noted, the contrast between the four kinds of non-finite construction provides a further dimension. And in the construction with intervening NP, the possibility of passivising the clause headed by the catenative also correlates imperfectly with other properties of the catenative. All this inevitably makes for a quite complex description, with a good deal of detailed classification of individual verb lexemes: the reader is invited to follow up the references at the end of the chapter to see some of the numerous different ways in which this area of verb complementation has been handled in the recent literature.

There is one final point to be made concerning the non-finite complements surveyed in this section. Where they are in paradigmatic contrast with NP objects traditional grammar tends to analyse them as objects too. Thus in both *He wanted a glimpse of it* and *He wanted to see it* the verb *wanted* would be analysed as having an object. Although there is some justification for extending the concept object to cover finite clauses (see above), its extension to non-finites is not helpful: they are better regarded as a distinct kind of complement. Notice, in the first place, that only a very small minority of catenatives can occur in passives like *It is hoped to return to this matter at a later date* (extraposition is obligatory here: we cannot have **To return to this matter at a later date is hoped*). Secondly, there is no point in distinguishing those non-finites which are replaceable by NP objects from those which aren't (cf. *He attempted/endeavoured to solve the problem* vs *He attempted/*endeavoured the problem*). Traditional grammars attach great importance to the contrast between transitive and intransitive constructions – this is reflected in the standard dictionary practice of classifying all verbs as transitive, intransitive or both. It will be clear from what has been said in this chapter, however, that this represents only a very gross classification: a syntactically adequate lexicon would have to give much more specific information about the range of complements allowed by individual verbs. Within the framework proposed here, the object will be only one of a variety of complements, and the transitive/intransitive contrast will have a good deal less importance.

5.7 Adjuncts

We will deal with adjuncts quite briefly. Numerous kinds are commonly distinguished, though in some cases the distinctions are more semantic than strictly syntactic. I give here examples of some of the major ones without making any attempt at exhaustiveness.

			Kind of adjunct
(99)	i	[*He drives*] *very carefully*	Manner
	ii	[*I opened it*] *with the master-key*	Instrument
	iii	[*Liz came*] *with John*	Comitative
	iv	[*She died*] *in 1942*	Time
	v	[*They rested*] *for a few minutes*	Duration
	vi	[*She*] *often* [*faints*]	Frequency
	vii	[*He was reading*] *in the bath*	Place/Locative
	viii	[*He worked late*] *to impress the boss*	Purpose
	ix	[*They stayed in*] *because it was raining*	Reason
	x	[*I enjoyed it*] *very much*	Degree
	xi	*From a philosophical point of view,* [*it is quite unsound*]	Viewpoint
	xii	*Perhaps* [*he likes her*]	Modal
	xiii	[*She resigned,*] *however*	Connective

The terms used for (i–x) are all traditional ones and are semantically transparent, except for 'comitative', which is used for adjuncts indicating accompaniment. Of the three newer terms, the first, 'viewpoint', is also semantically transparent; modal adjuncts – *perhaps, possibly, probably, certainly*, etc. – express the same kinds of meaning as the modal auxiliaries; and connective adjuncts like *however, therefore, nevertheless* serve to connect or relate the clause to what has gone before and thus contribute to making the text 'cohesive'.

Adjuncts are most often realised by AdvPs, as in (i), PPs, as in (ii), or subordinate clauses, finite (ix) or non-finite (viii). Notice, then, that we distinguish the function of *to impress the boss* in (viii) from that in, say, *He wanted desperately to impress the boss*, where it is a complement such as we discussed in the last section. Infinitival clauses of purpose differ from the complements of catenatives in that they may be introduced by *in order: He worked late in order to impress the boss* but not **He wanted desperately in order to* *impress the boss* (the two may combine, as in *He tried hard to win the contract in order to impress the boss*). As noted above – cf. examples (4i), (16ii), (17ii) – adjuncts may also, but to a much more limited extent, be realised by NPs and AdjPs.

I began by saying that adjuncts are less closely integrated into the structure of the clause than are complements. However, there are not just two degrees of integration, one associated with complements, the other with adjuncts, for we can see some rather clear differences on this dimension within the set of examples in (99). Thus some of these adjuncts but not others share with the most central kinds of complement (including subjects) the property of being able to be brought into contrastive focus in such constructions as the thematically marked cleft construction (100) or the 'disjunctive interrogative' (101):

(100)   Thematically unmarked   Cleft

     i *She saw John*   iv *It was John she saw*
     ii *She died in 1942*   v *It was in 1942 that she died*
     iii *She resigned, however*   vi **It was however that she resigned*

(101)   i *Did she see John or Bill?*
     ii *Did she die in 1942 or 1943?*
     iii **Did she resign however or therefore?*

Notice, moreover, that there are significant differences regarding their linear position. It is reasonable to say, for example, that (99ii) represents an unmarked order, while *With the master-key I opened it* is thematically marked (just as *John she saw* is marked relative to *She saw John*). But it would be quite arbitrary to select just one position for *however*, say, and treat the other possibilities as derived by some movement transformation.

There are thus good grounds for making a major division between what we will call **modifiers**, those adjuncts which share the above properties with complements, and **peripheral** dependents, those which do not – though, as with the adjunct–complement distinction, there are severe problems in drawing a sharp boundary between them. In general, modifiers, but not peripheral dependents, impose additional 'truth conditions' on the sentence – i.e. the conditions under which it could be used to express a true proposition. Clearly, for example, the conditions under which *She died in 1942* would be true are more restrictive than those under which *She died* would be true, but we could not have a situation where *She died* was true while *She died, however* was false. The correlation, however, is by no means perfect: modal adjuncts, for example, are syntactically peripheral but affect the truth conditions.

As far as the constituent structure is concerned, there is a case for saying that modifiers belong, like complements (other than the subject), within the predicate, whereas peripheral dependents enter into construction with the rest of the clause as a whole. According to this proposal, the ICs of (99i), say, would be *he* and *drives very carefully* (so that what I have informally called the 'nucleus' would not in fact be a constituent), whereas those of (xii) would be *perhaps* and *he likes her*. The precise position of adjuncts and the precise number of steps in the constituent hierarchy is, however, a difficult question on which there is relatively little consensus among modern grammarians; it is not necessary for us to adopt any very explicit stand on the issue here.

5.8   **Vocatives**

One final functional concept I will, for convenience, introduce here is that of a **vocative** element, such as the *Kim* of

(102)   *Kim, your father's here*

The most central use of the vocative is to attract the attention of the one(s) addressed, to make clear who it is that is being addressed. But it can also serve a purely 'emotive' purpose, as when A says to B in a context where no one else is present and where B is already attending: *I think, Kim/dear/Sir, that the issue is worth pursuing* – here it would be a mark of friendliness, of warmth, or of respect and formality, and so on. In some languages, such as Latin, the vocative function is associated with a special nominal case inflection, contrasting with nominative, accusative, etc., and the primary use of the term 'vocative' is for this inflectional category (see 2.3 – the vocative case of **puer** is syncretised with the nominative, but in such a noun as **dominus** "master" we have a phonologically distinct form *domine*); extension of the term to the function of the NP is, however, well-established and we can apply it to the *Kim* of (102) without implying any inflectional contrast between this *Kim* and that of *Kim has left*. The vocative function is filled by NPs; in some cases, as with proper names, the NP is one that can also be used referentially in the central nominal functions of subject and object, but in others it is not – *my dear, son, Sir, old man*, etc. (except that *Sir* is used referentially in the speech of some children in a schoolroom type context: *Sir said . . .*).

I spoke above of introducing vocatives at this point 'for convenience' because it is very doubtful whether they are properly regarded as entering into the structure of a kernel clause (or any other kind of clause). They can stand alone non-elliptically, as when I simply call *Kim!*: they are thus hardly dependent elements within the clause. Their distribution is rather similar to that of interjections and the like; they can precede a clause, as in (102), follow it, as in *Your father's here, Kim*, or interrupt it, as in *Your trouble, Kim, is that you've never had to work for your living*. We shall not have occasion to mention them again except for the purpose of distinguishing subject and vocative in imperative clauses (11.3).

FURTHER READING

On the distinction between complements and adjuncts, see Matthews 1981:Ch.6; for the concept of nucleus, see Lyons 1968:§8.1.1. Not all grammars treat objects and predicative complements as different subcases of a more general function complement – the term 'complement' is commonly contrasted with 'object', thus corresponding to my 'predicative complement', with 'subject complement' then corresponding to my PC^s and 'object complement' to PC^o. The distinction predicative vs non-predicative complements is sometimes expressed as 'intensive' vs 'extensive' complements – this terminology derives from Halliday 1967–68 (which includes a detailed survey of different kinds of complement), and is taken over, for example, in Quirk et al. 1971; the term 'predicative complement' derives from Jespersen (e.g. 1924:88). The permitted array of complements (in the sense which includes the subject) that a verb takes is commonly referred to as the 'valency' of the verb – and the complements as its valents; see Lyons 1977:§12.4, Allerton 1982. On the indirect object construction see Matthews 1981 (refer index), Green 1974, Allerton 1978, Ziv & Sheintuch 1979. In 'relational grammar' (see Perlmutter 1980), the *Liz* of *Ed gave Liz the key* is referred to as the 'direct object' – the clause is derived from *Ed gave the key to Liz* by a transformation which is regarded as depriving *the key* of its object status. The term 'complex-transitive' is from Quirk et al. 1971; on the copulative construction and the idea of a 'complex-intransitive', see Matthews 1980. On the **rely** *on* kind of construction, see DeArmond 1977, and on the verb-particle construction, Dixon 1982. On the catenative construction, see Palmer 1974:Ch. 7, Matthews 1981:Ch. 8; the constituent structure of examples like (82) has been the subject of a good deal of controversy in transformational grammar – see, for example, Postal 1974, Lightfoot 1976; verbs of the **seem** and **intend** classes are commonly called 'raising verbs' in the transformational literature. As examples of the problems associated with particular catenative verbs, the verbs of perception, see Kirsner & Thompson 1976, Akmajian 1977, Declerck 1981. For a detailed description of adjuncts, see Quirk et al. 1971:Ch. 8 (where the term 'adjunct' is, however, used in a narrower sense than here). On vocatives, see Quirk et al. 1971:§§7.39–40.

6
Nouns and noun phrases

6.1 Nouns

The most central members of the word-class noun have the following three properties:

(a) Functional potential, I. They function as head in the structure of NPs. NPs in turn realise a variety of functions, notably (but not exhaustively) subject, object or predicative complement in clause structure, complement in PP or PossP structure.[1]

(b) Functional potential, II. As heads of NPs, they take a different range of dependents from the other parts of speech. Most distinctively, they take determiners like *the, which, a, every, my, three* (*the book, my cousin, three days*) and adjectives as pre-head modifiers (*young boys, valuable paintings*).

(c) Inflection. They enter into inflectional contrasts of number, singular vs plural (*dog* vs *dogs*, *cousin* vs *cousins*).

The first property can be said to be the most general, inasmuch as all nouns function as head in NP structure – there is no close analogue of auxiliary verbs, which we have analysed as functioning only as dependent in VP structure. Properties (b) and (c) characterise only central nouns, with marginal members differing from them in varying degrees here. Notice in particular that there are quite a few words belonging uncontroversially to the noun class which do not have plural counterparts (*equipment, furniture, wetness*), and some without singular counterparts (*alms, dregs, remains*): it is for this reason, and also because there are fewer inflectional contrasts, that we have given somewhat less weight to inflection in the characterisation of nouns than we did for verbs.

Property (a) by itself does not, however, provide a simple test for nouns. Of the four NP functions mentioned, only one is uniquely realised by NPs, the complement in PossP structure – but only a restricted range of NPs can function here: compare *her sister's success* with **her perseverance's success*, and so

---

[1] Recall that we are analysing *the King of Spain's* (as in *the King of Spain's daughter*) as a PossP, with the possessive clitic as head and the NP *the King of Spain* as complement: see 1.8.

on. The subject, object, predicative complement and complement of preposition positions can all be filled by non-NPs, so that what distinguishes an NP from a clause, an AdjP or a PP, say, is not in general its actual function in some given instance, but rather its range of potential functions and its internal structure, including its potential for expansion and systematic variation. Thus in an example like *The project was worrying me* we take *project* as a noun not simply because *the project* is subject (for the subject could also be a clause, as in *That everything was so quiet was worrying me*): rather we note the potential for *the project* to occur in positions like *He approved the project, He spoke of the project, The project's success amazed him*; we note that *project* has *the* as dependent, that we could add such other dependents as adjectives (*the new project*), 'restrictive relative clauses' (*the project that had just been approved*), etc.; that singular *project* contrasts with plural *projects*.

The properties given above are formulated so as to apply to words: central members of the lexeme class can again be defined derivatively in terms of the functional potential of their forms and their inflectional paradigm. Within the latter, the singular form is the lexical stem, and the plural is formed from it by a variety of morphological processes. Regular nouns form the plural by adding one of the following suffixes: (i) /ɪz/ or /əz/, as in *churches, garages, roses*; (ii) /s/, as in *hats, mints, ropes*; (iii) /z/, as in *kings, queens, relatives* – the choice among (i)–(iii) is determined phonologically by the rule given for 3rd person singular present tense forms – see (2) of Ch. 4. Some irregular nouns (e.g. **sheep**) exhibit syncretism between singular and plural; others are formed by processes of relatively low productivity: *man → men, child → children, crisis → crises*. Again we will not attempt a detailed account, though it is worth mentioning that a number of nouns have coexisting regular and irregular plurals: *hoof → hoofs/hooves, formula → formulas/formulae*, and so on.

Many nouns have morphologically simple lexical stems, but there are also numerous lexical-morphological processes that yield non-simple noun stems. We will here attempt no more than a brief illustration of some of the main types.

(a) Class-changing suffixation. A number of suffixes, some of high productivity, form deverbal and de-adjectival nouns. Thus *-er, -ee, -ation, -ment, -ing*, etc. are added to verbs to form nouns like *player, employee, organisation, punishment, singing*, while *-(i)ty* and, most productively, *-ness* form de-adjectival nouns like *diversity, loyalty, happiness*.

(b) Class-preserving suffixation. Other suffixes yield nouns from nouns, often with a difference in subclass: *man → manhood, friend → friendship, slave → slavery, kitchen → kitchenette, actor → actress*.

(c) Class-preserving prefixation. Prefixes yielding nouns from nouns include *counter-* (*counterexample*), *ex-* (*ex-wife*), *mini-* (*minibus*), *super-* (*superman*); the prefixation generally makes no syntactically relevant difference to the stem.

(d) Conversion. Just as conversion can yield verbs from nouns ($man_N \rightarrow man_V$), so it can work in the opposite direction: we find many deverbal nouns like *attempt, catch, cover, fall, need, run, swim, turn.* Conversion of adjectives to nouns, as in *comic, intellectual, weekly,* is less productive; we also find a handful of conversions from other stem classes: *There are too many ifs and buts about it.*

(e) Compounding. The majority of compounds are nouns, and there are also far more different types of compound noun than compounds of other classes. They may be classified according to the nature of the component parts and the relationship between them. In *rainfall* we have noun stem + deverbal noun stem in a semantic relation analogous to that expressed in a clause as subject–predicator (*rain falls*); in *haircut* the same kind of stems but in a relation analogous to predicator-object (*they cut hair*); in *tugboat* verb stem + noun stem related like predicator–subject (*the boat tugs*); and so on.

(f) Minor processes. The minor lexical processes of blending and acronym formation (see 1.6) also yield predominantly nouns. The majority of acronyms – whether pronounced as sequences of letters, like *IRA* (*Irish Republican Army*) or as ordinary words, like *CREEP* (*Committee for the Re-election of the President*) – serve as proper names and as such are rather peripheral to the language: a standard dictionary will include only a small proportion, those with the widest currency.

6.2 Subclasses of noun

There are numerous syntactically distinguishable subclasses of noun, a number of which will be introduced in the following sections; at this point it will be sufficient to distinguish just three major subclasses, as shown in (1):

(1) Nouns
- Common nouns — **boy**, **dog**, **car**, **book**
- Proper nouns — **John**, **Smith**, **London**, **Easter**
- Pronouns — **we**, **who**, *everybody*, *none*

The **common** subclass is the unmarked one: nothing special need be said about it. **Proper nouns** characteristically function as the head of NPs serving as **proper names**. It is necessary to distinguish between proper

NOUNS and proper NAMES because, although a proper name will consist simply of a proper noun in the most elementary cases like *John* or *Paris*, it may also be structurally more complex than such examples. *The University of Cambridge* and *Cambridge University Press* are both proper names, but they are not proper nouns; although they contain the proper noun *Cambridge* their heads are the common nouns *University* and *Press*, while *Central Station* is a proper name containing no proper noun at all.

In the most straightforward cases – that is, where the proper name is a full NP, not just part of one – proper names are most often used to refer to the person, place, institution, etc. that bears the name: *John was arrested, I'm going to Melbourne*. Of course ordinary NPs can also be used referentially, so that these examples may be compared with *The man who stole the silver was arrested, I'm going to the station*. An obvious difference here is that *the man who stole the silver* provides a description of the 'referent' (i.e. that which is referred to), whereas *John* does not. However, proper names may be derived from descriptions (which is why they need not have proper nouns as heads): *the University of Cambridge* names a university in Cambridge. What makes a proper name different from a (mere) description is the conventional association between the name and its bearer: in the central cases proper names are institutionalised – for example, by some kind of registration. Notice in this connection that the referent of *the University of Queensland* is not the only university in Queensland; it was when it was founded (so that the description provided an appropriate basis for the name), but the fact that there are now two other universities in the state does not make *the University of Queensland* any the less appropriate as a means of referring to it – precisely because it is the institutionalised name.

We will not go into the grammar of proper names except to note that they are inherently 'definite'. With other NPs we normally have a contrast of definiteness realised by the choice of determiner: for example, definite *the boy, the boys* contrast with indefinite *a boy, boys* and so on: see §6 below. Proper names can only be definite; they will either have the 'definite article' *the* as an integral part of the name (*The Hague, the Himalayas*) or, more often, they will have no determiner at all (*John, Paris*). Note that with ordinary NPs, by contrast, lack of determiner indicates indefiniteness (*books, coffee* as opposed to definite *the books, the coffee*).

Let us return now to proper nouns. The most central type are those, like **John** and **Paris** above, which can stand alone as proper names: this is what distinguishes them from common nouns. (We will also include, as less central members, nouns like **Hague** and **Himalayas** which occur only in proper names with *the*.) Notice, however, that central proper nouns are not restricted to functioning as the head of a proper name NP. Thus in examples like *We weren't talking about the same Jones, We could do with another Churchill, There were two Paulines in my class*, the NPs *the same Jones, another*

Churchill and *two Paulines* are themselves clearly not proper names. This is why they select for definiteness like ordinary NPs, with indefinite *two Paulines* contrasting with definite *the two Paulines*, and so on. It is commonly said that in such constructions *Jones*, *Churchill* and *Pauline* are common nouns, or that they are 'used as' common nouns. Thus some grammars posit a conversion process deriving a common noun *Jones* from the proper noun *Jones*, analogous to that deriving $catch_N$ from $catch_V$. But the two cases are not comparable. In the first place, we do not have two distinct lexemes '*Jones*' as we have two lexemes '*catch*', i.e. abstractions from two contrasting sets of inflectional forms (see 3.2): we are restricting the concept of conversion to cases involving a change of lexeme. In the second place, the phenomenon is quite general: any central proper noun behaves like *Jones*, so that the phenomenon should be handled in the syntax rather than in lexical morphology. We will, moreover, avoid talking of 'a proper noun used as a common noun' because of our general objection to that type of locution (see 3.1). Nor do we want to distinguish 'common' and 'proper' as mere uses of nouns, rather than lexical subclasses, for clearly our lexical entries must distinguish nouns like *boy* from those like *Jones*. The distinction we are drawing between nouns and NPs, between proper nouns and proper names, enables us to avoid these problems. Instead of handling the difference between *Jones arrived* and *We weren't talking about the same Jones* by saying that the first *Jones* is (or is used as) a proper noun, the second a common noun, we will say that of the two NPs *Jones* and *the same Jones* only the first is a proper name, although both NPs have a proper noun as head. We will of course need semantic rules to give the interpretation of NPs like *the same Jones*, and so on – in this case "the same person bearing the name *Jones*".

Proper names are generally not listed in ordinary dictionaries, because they do not have any meaning definable for the language as such. That is, we can specify the reference of *Jones*, say, on some particular occasion of its use (as when I say *Jones thinks there'll be no problem*, using *Jones* to refer to my bank manager), but we cannot give a general meaning to it, as we can to a common noun like *dog*, for example. This is no reason why proper nouns should not be included in our lexicon, however – and note that like common nouns they may undergo processes of lexical morphology (cf. *Jonesian*, *un-Joneslike*, etc.). They nevertheless do raise a problem in that there is no determinate list of proper nouns: one reason for this is that many are carried over from language to language (cf. names like *Nkomo* or *Nkrumah*, which do not even follow the normal rules that determine what is a phonologically permitted word). Proper nouns thus constitute an 'open' class in the most literal sense.

The remaining subclass in (1) is that of pronouns – a closed class. As observed in 3.1, the analysis adopted here differs from that of traditional grammar in treating pronouns as a subclass of nouns, rather than as a distinct primary class. They are like other nouns in having property (a) above – they function as head of phrases filling the position of subject, object, etc. – and insofar as they take any dependents at all within the phrase, they are like those found in NPs rather than phrases of other classes. They differ from other nouns, however, in that they do not combine with determiners (or at least not with the central determiners). There is a good deal to be said about the various different subclasses of pronoun and it will be convenient therefore to treat them in a chapter on their own: at that point we will elaborate on what has just been said about the relation between pronouns and nouns.

6.3 Dependents in NP structure

As a first approximation, we may say that all (non-elliptical) NPs contain a head element, realised by a noun, and optionally one or more dependents. There is a wide range of types of dependents and no definable limit on how many we can have in a single NP: the potential complexity of NP structure matches that of the clause.

Some dependents precede the head, others follow: we will refer to them as **pre-head** and **post-head** respectively. Among the pre-head dependents we distinguish between **determiners** and **modifiers**, as in

(2)	*the	intelligent	women*	Determiner Modifier Head

Post-head dependents are of three main kinds, complements, modifiers and peripheral dependents,[2] exemplified in

(3)	*the	destruction	of Carthage*	Determiner Head Complement
(4)	*a	girl	with red hair*	Determiner Head Modifier
(5)	*Max,	who knew Greek*	Head Peripheral-dependent

These structures do not cater for such items as *only* and *even* in clauses like *Only the people in the first few rows could hear him, They included even her grandparents in the invitation.* As will become apparent, *only* and *even* here function quite differently from what we are calling determiners and modifiers, and thus on the assumption that *only the people in the first few rows* and *even her grandparents* are constituents (an assumption that by no means all grammars accept), we will need some other pre-head dependent function and – since the ICs of such constituents would surely be *only* + *the people in the first few rows* and *even* + *her grandparents* – we will need to recognise different levels of phrase with a noun as ultimate head in order to distinguish *even her grandparents* from *her grandparents*. We will not pursue this issue here,

---

[2] There is also one determiner, *enough*, which optionally follows the head: compare *enough money* and *money enough*.

however, but will confine our attention to phrases without these 'focusing' elements – it is to such phrases that we will apply the term noun phrase.

Of the various dependent functions in NP structure introduced above, we will deal first with determiners; we will then examine the NP systems of number, boundedness, definiteness, etc. to which determiners are crucially relevant, and then take up the other functions in turn.

6.4 **Determiners**

The determiner function is realised by closed-class words like *the, a, some, any*, etc., or by expressions of more complex structure such as *how much, a few, my uncle's*, and so on. An NP may contain up to three determiners: *ideas* has none, *her ideas* one, *her many ideas* or *all her ideas* two, *all her many ideas* three. Where there is more than one, the order is fixed (cf. **many her ideas*), so that we need to distinguish three determiner positions, which will be simply labelled I, II and III. Particular items are then associated with one or other of these positions on the basis of their potential for combining with other determiners – thus *all* is assigned to position I, *her* to II, *many* to III, and so on. Some examples of these structures are given in (6):

(6)

	Determiners			Modifier	Head
	I	II	III		
i	all	her	many	good	ideas
ii		her	many	good	ideas
iii	all	her		good	ideas
iv				good	ideas
v			many	good	ideas
vi	all			good	ideas
vii	what	a		marvellous	suggestion
viii		the	one	constructive	proposal
ix		a few			remarks
x	both	my father's			parents

(7) gives the forms, or illustrates the types of forms, that can occur in the three determiner positions:

(7) I *all, both; half, one-third, three-quarters* . . .; *double, twice, three times* . . .; *such, what*[exclamative];

II i *the; this, these, that, those;* PossP;
ii *we, us; you;*
iii *which, what*[relative]*, what*[interrogative]*; a, another, some, any, no, either, neither; each, enough, much, more, most, less; a few*[positive]*, a little*[positive];

III *every; many, several, few*[negative]*, little*[negative]*; one, two, three* . . .; *(a) dozen*

However, only a relatively small number of combinations from the three positions are permitted. Position II is the most basic: this is where we find the definite article *the* and the demonstratives **this** and **that**, arguably the most central of the determiners. Forms are assigned to position I and III (sometimes called 'pre-determiners' and 'post-determiners') on the basis of their ability to precede or follow a position II determiner. Items like *some, any, each*, etc., which cannot combine syntagmatically with any other determiner, are assigned to position II, where they are in paradigmatic contrast with *the*, etc. The combinational restrictions can then be stated in terms of position I and III items. Examples of these restrictions are as follows:

(a) *All* and *both* can occur only with II (i), (ii) or alone: *all the wine, both these points, both my father's parents, all you women, all men, *all much cheese.*

(b) *Such* and exclamative *what* occur only with *a* or alone: *what/ such a nuisance, what/ such fine singing.* (Exclamative *what* is distinguished from the interrogative *what* of *What time is it?* and the relative *what* of *What money he had was in the bank*: in these latter uses, *what* belongs to II – cf. **What a department is he in?.*)

(c) *Many* can occur only after II (i) or alone: *the many mistakes, those many crimes, her many attractive qualities, many people.* (Note that *much*, in spite of its close semantic relationship to *many*, occurs only alone and hence is assigned to position II.)

(d) *One, two*, etc., occur after II (i), (ii), *which, any, no*, or alone: *the four sons, those three crooks, John's one mistake, you two girls, which/ any one article, no one man, five cats.*

The reader is invited to work out the restrictions holding over the other I and III position items.

It will be clear from (6) and (7) that a determiner need not be a single word. We need then to distinguish between the structure where we have a sequence of two determiners and that where we have a single determiner containing a sequence of words. Let us consider one or two cases of the latter kind, contrasting them where relevant with the double-determiner construction.

(a) In *a few mistakes* we analyse *a few* as a single determiner to the head *mistakes*. The justification for grouping *a few* together is that *a* is dependent here on *few*, not on *mistakes*, as is evident from the deviance of **a mistakes*. Notice also that there is a difference in meaning between *a few* and *few* which is not predictable from the presence or absence of *a*: *a few* means "a small number (of)", whereas *few* on its own means roughly "not many" – I have distinguished them in (7) as 'positive' and 'negative' respectively.[3] That there is a real semantic difference here can be seen by considering a family

---

[3] Semantically the *few* of *her/ these few mistakes* also seems to go with the one we have labelled negative, though there are certainly differences as far as the syntax of negation is concerned: see Ch. 13.

with, say, two dogs, three cats, a parrot, a couple of rabbits and a tortoise: one might say that they had 'a few pets', but hardly that they had 'few pets' – *few* is more dependent on a comparison with what is normal or expected than is *a few*. We can make a similar distinction between *a little help* ("a small amount") and *little help* ("not much"). Contrasting with *a few mistakes*, containing a single determiner, are NPs like *her few mistakes*, *these few mistakes* containing a sequence of two, *her/these* from position II followed by *few* from position III. *Her* and *these* are not dependent on *few* here – note for the second in particular that we have plural *these*, not the singular *this* that would be expected if it were in direct paradigmatic contrast with *a*.

(b) *Many, much, few*[negative], *little*[negative], take 'degree' expressions as modifiers: *as, how, so, this, that, too, very*. Note then that we distinguish *that many mistakes*, with *that many* a single determiner, from *those many mistakes*, where *those* and *many* are separate determiners. When ***that*** is a dependent of the head noun it agrees with it in number (*that mistake* ~ *those mistakes*), but when it is a dependent of *many, much*, etc. it is invariably singular (*that much confusion* ~ *that many mistakes*). Degree expressions may themselves be the heads of phrases containing their own modifiers, as in *far too few friends, all that much difficulty, twice as many letters* – here the determiner to *friends* is the phrase *far too few*, which has *few* as head and *far too* as modifier. The above degree expressions, it may be added, also modify adjectives and adverbs – thus not only *how/so/that many books*, but *how/so/that pleasant, how/so/that quickly*, and so on. One difference between the determinatives and the adjectives/adverbs is that the former do not take the comparative modifiers *more* and *less*: *more/less careful*, **more/less many mistakes*, **more/less much confusion*; the gaps are filled by *more* and *less* functioning as determiners by themselves: *more/less mistakes, more/less confusion*.[4] I am assuming that in examples like *some/five/many more mistakes* there is a single determiner with *more* as its head, but the distinction between a single complex determiner and a sequence of two single ones is very difficult to draw here; if the assumption is false, we will need to allow *more* to follow position III determiners.

(c) In examples like *many a soldier*, the *a* cannot be omitted, so that *many a* is best treated as a single constituent with *many* as modifier.

(d) A less obvious example involves the 'cardinal numerals' *two, three, four*, etc., (but not *one*), which can occur as heads of phrases containing their own determiner:

---

[4] *Less* + plural noun – *less mistakes*, etc. – is condemned by prescriptive grammarians, and though it is commonly used there are many who follow the prescriptive rule, especially in careful speech and writing. In that case the gap left by the ungrammaticality of **less many mistakes* is filled by the logically equivalent *fewer mistakes* ("less many" is equivalent to "more few") – *few* does have an inflectional comparative. For further discussion of these matters, see 12.5.

(8)	*another two candidates*
(9)	*an enjoyable three days*
(10)	*the first four miles*

There is a good case for treating *another two, an enjoyable three* and *the first four* as constituents, single determiners of the heads *candidates, days, miles*. In (8) and (9) the numerals could not be omitted, although *another* and *an enjoyable* could be, which argues that *two* and *three* are the heads of phrases with *another* and *an + enjoyable* as their dependents. In (10) the numeral can be omitted – but in otherwise similar examples like *the second four motions* it cannot be. Treating *first* and *second* as dependents of *four* rather than *miles/ motions* here enables us to account neatly for the distinction between pairs like *the first three prizes* and *the three first prizes* or *the second three attempts* and *the three second attempts*. In *the second three attempts*, for example, *second* modifies *three*, so that the meaning is "the second set of three attempts"; in *the three second attempts*, on the other hand, *second* modifies *attempts*, so that each of the three is a second attempt – which suggests that they are by different people or are attempts at different things. (8) is to be distinguished structurally from *these three candidates* where *these* and *three* do not form a single constituent but function separately as position II and III determiners to *candidates* – note that the plural form *these* agrees with *candidates*, whereas in (8) *two* has as its dependent *another* which does not function as determiner to a plural head (**another books*). One problem that arises here, however, is that of finding evidence to decide whether examples like *the two books, the premier's four sons, any three records, which two countries* belong to the single determiner construction of (8)–(10) or the double one of *these three candidates*.

(e) *Almost* and *nearly* can modify a variety of forms occurring in positions I, II and III: *almost one-third his salary, nearly enough money, almost twenty mistakes*. Similarly, *not* can modify *all*, fractions, *much, many, every, enough* and perhaps one or two more: *Not all women [will agree with you]*.[5]

It will be clear from the foregoing that we are dealing here with a very complex area of the grammar: there is much that has to be said in terms of particular words or very small ad hoc classes; this is a major reason for there being a certain amount of indeterminacy over the constituent structure. To conclude this section, we will take up one further problem in constituent structure: what is the analysis of NPs like *a lot of eggs, a number of mistakes, plenty of friends*? More particularly, which is head: *lot* or *eggs*, *number*

---

[5] *Almost, nearly* and *not* also occur in such NPs as *Almost the whole country [was covered with snow]*, *Not the least important point she made [was that . . .]*. Semantically *almost* goes with *whole*, *not* with *least important*, but this is not the grouping made in the syntax. We should probably add *almost/nearly* and *not*, as used here, to the position I determiners given in (7).

or *mistakes, plenty* or *friends*? If we take *lot* as head, the structure will be as in
(11); if we take *eggs* as head, it will be along the lines of (12):

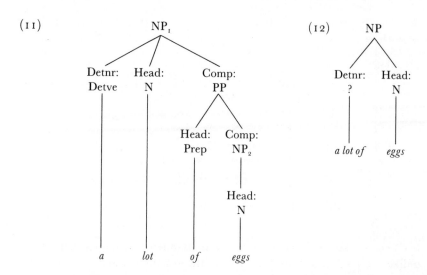

(11) is the kind of structure that is evidently needed for such NPs as *a history
of ethics, an interest in painting, a diet of vegetables, a taxonomy of birds*, where the
heads are clearly *history, interest, diet* and *taxonomy*. (It is also needed for *the
number of mistakes*, where *number* is uncontroversially head.) (12) relates *a lot
of eggs* more directly to NPs like *several eggs* or *a dozen eggs* – though whereas
the nature of the determiner is unproblematic in these latter examples
(*several* is a determinative, *a dozen* an NP) it is unclear how *a lot of* should be
further described in terms of its classification and internal structure.

The clearest syntactic difference between *a lot of eggs* and, say, *a diet of
vegetables* is that in the former, the number of the whole NP depends on the
second noun (*eggs*), whereas in the latter it depends on the first noun (*diet*).
Thus *a lot of eggs* is a plural NP, whereas *a lot of milk* is singular – compare *A
lot of eggs were needed* with *A lot of milk was needed*; with *diet*, on the other hand,
it makes no difference when we replace plural *vegetables* with singular *milk*,
as is evident from the form of the verb in *A diet of vegetables/milk was
recommended*. The attraction of an analysis like (12) is, then, that it brings *a
lot of eggs* into line with the standard case where the number of an NP
depends on the head noun.

This argument becomes less persuasive when we note that the noun
following *of* can have its own determiners: *a lot of the eggs, a lot of this milk*.
Here *eggs* and *milk* again make the number of the whole NP respectively
plural and singular, but an analysis along the lines of (12) is somewhat less
plausible than an extension of (11):

237

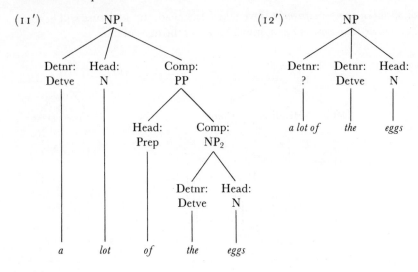

(11′) shows the sequence beginning with *of* to be a constituent, and this – unlike (12′) – accounts for the fact that the *of* sequence may in these cases be moved as a unit by various thematic transformations: *Of the eggs that came from her father's farm, a lot were so small they could only be used for cooking.* Further support for analysis (11′) derives from its ability to account for the ambiguity we find in examples like

(13)   *A lot of the soldiers, only two of whom had had previous experience of such conditions, were thoroughly exhausted*

In one interpretation, only two of the full set of soldiers had had previous experience; in the other, it is only two from the subset who are said to have been thoroughly exhausted. Structure (11′) has one NP embedded inside another, so that we can say that in the first interpretation *whom* relates to NP₂, *the soldiers*, whereas in the second it relates to NP₁, *a lot of the soldiers*. Structures like (12′) provide no natural way of handling the first interpretation, for they do not show *the soldiers* to be a constituent.

Whether *a lot of eggs* should be assigned the same kind of structure as *a lot of the eggs* is a question on which different views, explicit or implicit, will be found in the literature. (Note that the argument from thematic movement does not apply to *a lot of eggs* – compare *Of the eggs, a lot were broken* and **Of eggs, a lot were broken.*) I shall not attempt to resolve the issue here by detailed argument. Given that we have found reasons for preferring (11′) to (12′), I shall simply assume for the sake of simplicity that (11) is also to be preferred to (12). It remains only to note that accepting (11) and/or (11′) makes it necessary to allow that the syntactic number of an NP may not be determined by its head noun. We will say that the expression *a lot* is

238

'number-transparent': it allows the number of the NP in the complement to pass through and determine the number of the NP headed by *lot*. Other expressions having this property are *lots, plenty, the rest, the remainder* and (for some but not all speakers) *a number*: *The rest of the eggs were/ *was wasted, The rest of the milk was wasted*; *A number of problems arise/*arises*.

Determiners precede modifiers,[6] and differ from them in that they are typically involved in one or more of the following systems: number, countability and boundedness, definiteness, clause type and polarity. The last two are systems of the clause and will be discussed in Chs. 11 and 13 respectively. Here it is sufficient to note that two of the marked terms in the system of clause type, interrogative and exclamative, may be marked as such by the presence of an interrogative or exclamative determiner in NP structure (*Which piece do you want?*, *What a shambles it was!*), and similarly the marked term in the polarity system, negative, may be marked as such by a negative determiner (*Neither solution was entirely convincing*). The other systems mentioned apply to the NP, and we will take these up in turn, including in the discussion an account of the role of the determiners, before moving on to the other functions in NP structure.

6.5 Number

The system of number, contrasting singular and plural, is applicable both to nouns and to NPs. With nouns, number is primarily an inflectional category: *boy* and *boys*, for example, are the singular and plural forms of the lexeme **boy**. In this example we have a lexeme, **boy**, that is inherently unspecified or neutral as to number; in any particular occurrence of the lexeme, number will be selected independently and will be formally expressed inflectionally. However, neither of these two features – selection of number independently of the lexeme and inflectional expression of number – holds in all cases: we will look at the less normal cases in subsection 3 below.

With NPs, number is generally determined by the noun functioning as head: the plurality of the NP *the boys* derives from that of the noun *boys*. But again it is not always so. One case where it is not has already been introduced: the plurality of *a lot of the eggs* derives from that of the complement. A second case is illustrated in *We bagged three elephant that day*, where the NP *three elephant* is plural although its head, the noun *elephant*, is singular: this construction will be analysed below.

Co-occurrence restrictions involving the category of number hold both within the NP and between an NP and other elements in the clause. The internal restrictions hold primarily over the head and the determiner: these are the concern of subsection 1. The external restrictions hold over the

---

[6] Except where the modifier begins with *how, so, too*, as in *so great a success, too large a deficit*.

subject and the tensed verb, and over the subject and the subjective predicative complement (or object and objective PC); the latter were discussed in 5.2, while the former will be dealt with in subsection 2.

6.5.1 Determiner–head co-occurrence restrictions of number

Some determiners, such as, *the, my, which*, etc., can occur with either a singular or a plural head: *the boy* or *the boys*. Others are restricted to occurrence with a singular or with a plural; in the following lists, the roman numerals refer to the three determiner positions we have distinguished.

(14)   Determiners requiring a singular head
       II *this, that, a, another, either, neither, each, much, less* (see footnote 4), *a little*;
       III *every, little, one*;
(15)   Determiners requiring a plural head
       I *both*;
       II *these, those, we, us, a few*;
       III *many, several, few, fewer, two, three* (etc.), *(a) dozen*

This and *these* are respectively singular and plural inflectional forms of the lexeme **this**, and analogously for *that* and *those*. As far as these forms are concerned, then, the co-occurrence restrictions are a matter of agreement: the 'demonstrative' determiners agree with the head in number. For the rest, the restrictions are not of the agreement type: *many, several, two, dozen*, etc. require a plural head but there is no reason to say that they are themselves plural forms. On the contrary, to the extent that these words occur as the head of a phrasal determiner in the form of an NP, they can be shown to belong to the singular category: cf. *a great many eggs, a dozen eggs, another two eggs* (contrast *dozens of eggs, They left in twos*, where we have plural forms of **dozen** and **two**). It is for this reason that the lists in (14) and (15) are labelled as shown, not as 'singular determiners' and 'plural determiners'.

Exceptions to the internal co-occurrence restrictions occur in the type of construction illustrated above: *We bagged three elephant that day*. Here the whole NP is plural, but the head position is filled by the singular form *elephant* rather than the plural *elephants*. This phenomenon, which has been called 'collectivising', is to be distinguished from that found in *We came across three sheep*, where there is no violation of the normal determiner–head co-occurrence restrictions, for *sheep* is here a plural form. It is simply a fact of inflectional morphology that with **sheep** there is syncretism between the singular and plural forms, whereas collectivising is a syntactic phenomenon, involving the selection of a singular form in lieu of a plural.

Collectivising characteristically occurs with nouns denoting animals hunted for food or sport, and with some of them is restricted to contexts involving hunting – if we were talking about a circus performance rather than big-game hunting, for example, we would say *three elephants*. It is where this contextual restriction obtains that syntactic collectivising is most sharply distinct from morphological syncretism – but there is a certain grey area in between, involving nouns such as **deer**, **carp**, **trout**, etc., where the regular plurals are used so rarely that for some speakers they may be non-existent, with the result that what for others is collectivising is for them syncretism. Collectivising is also found with various nouns denoting plants – **cabbage**, **cauliflower**, **lettuce**, **beetroot**, tree-names, etc.: *She bought a couple of lettuce*. The explanation suggested by the term collectivising is that the particular members of the plural set are not thought of as having significance as individuals: attention is directed rather to the set as a whole, whether it be game or food or wood or whatever.

Other exceptions to the co-occurrence restrictions occur in certain measure NPs. The exceptions are optional in cases like *three foot/feet tall*, obligatory in *two dozen/*dozens eggs* (which contrasts with the *of* construction, *dozens/*dozen of eggs*).

NP-internal co-occurrence restrictions involving number are not confined to the determiner–head relation: they apply also in NPs containing some of the number-transparent expressions mentioned in §3 above. For example, *a number* requires a plural complement (*a number of mistakes/*confusion*), and conversely *a (great/good) deal* requires a singular (*a great deal of confusion/*mistakes*).

6.5.2   Subject–verb agreement

The co-occurrence restrictions between subject and tensed verb illustrated in *My brother lives/*live in Washington* vs *My brothers live/*lives in Washington* involve agreement: if the subject is 3rd person singular, so is the verb, and if the subject is not 3rd person singular, nor is the verb. To a significant extent we find inflectional co-variation: in the examples given, we change the inflectional form of **live** as we change that of **brother**. But clearly it isn't purely a matter of inflection. The agreement involves number in combination with person, and person is not an inflectional category in nouns. Moreover, number is not purely inflectional – *I* and *we*, for example, are not different inflectional forms of a single lexeme, as we shall argue in 7.4.

We have examined in detail which verb-forms enter into agreement with the subject (see 4.3). What remains to consider here are various types of exception to the basic agreement rule.

(a) Collectives. The first exception involves singular **collective** nouns like *committee, government, team, herd*, etc. – nouns denoting a set or collection of separate members. Here both forms of the verb occur:

(16)   *The committee has/have rejected the idea*

(though in US English there is a tendency to keep to the 3rd person singular). The general present tense form, here *have*, lacks the singular property found in the subject, and hence breaches the agreement rule. The semantic effect of the breach is to focus on the individual members of the set rather than on the set as a unit. Thus if the predicate is one that necessarily applies to the set as a whole, not to each of the members separately, then agreement is required: *The committee consists/*consist of three professors and two students.*

Breach of agreement – or 'discord', as we may call it – with collectives thus has the opposite effect from that of collectivising. **Elephant** is not a collective noun (*an elephant* can only denote a single animal), but the syntactic construction of collectivising in a plural NP shifts attention away from the members of the plurality. **Committee** is a collective noun, so that in the singular it still denotes a set, but the syntactic construction of discord shifts the attention more towards the individual members. The lexical factor (collective or non-collective noun) outweighs the syntactic, so that *the committee have* is more unified than *three elephant*, though less so than *the committee has*. Discord with collectives is also related to the phenomenon of number-transparency discussed in §4. Thus in an example like

(17)   *The board of governors have decided not to make any further appointments*

we have a choice between saying: (i) that *have* is in discord with the 3rd person singular subject headed by collective *board*; and (ii) that *board* is number-transparent, with *governors* determining the number of *the board of governors* as plural. It is better, I believe, to adopt the first analysis here, since *have* in (17) can be replaced by *has* with the same difference of meaning as in (16); we would then restrict number-transparency to cases where there is no choice, as in *The rest/A lot of the eggs have/*has been broken.* Here the subject is plural and the verb is required to follow the agreement rule. In (17), by contrast, the subject is singular and the discord is contrastive. The distinction is theoretically clear, but, as so often, the assignment of particular expressions between the two cases may not be, and may vary from speaker to speaker (cf. *A bunch of crooks have/?has gained control of the station*).

(b) Quantities. The opposite type of discord – a 3rd person singular verb with a 3rd person plural NP as subject – occurs under certain conditions when the plural NP is interpreted as denoting a single quantity or amount rather than a plurality of individuals:

(18)   i   *Three mistakes in one line is not good enough*
         ii *Five inches is too long*
         iii *Two pounds of sugar is all you need*

There is perhaps some uncertainty as to whether *are* would be an acceptable alternative to *is* here – uncertainty and variation from case to case, for *are* seems a good deal better in (iii) than in (ii), for example.

(c) Proper names. Where a plural NP is used as the name of a single entity (as *The Three Musketeers* is the name of a novel), the verb form will be 3rd person singular:

(19)   *'The Three Musketeers' is/*are her favourite novel*

Here the semantic predicate "be her favourite novel" is predicated of something singular – a novel – and it is this semantic fact that determines the form of the verb.

A proper name may be a collective, and in such cases point (c) will feed into point (a). For example, *The United States* is a plural NP naming a single nation, so that it will take a 3rd person singular verb, just like the singular proper name *Australia*, etc., in examples like *The United States/Australia currently has an inflation rate of about 10%*. The names of countries, however, can be used as collectives (e.g. when applied to sporting teams representing the country), and as such allow the general form of the present tense: *The United States/Australia have a lead of two matches to one.*

It will be clear from this discussion that the choice between the 3rd person singular and the general present tense is not determined in a purely mechanical way. The main determining factor is of course the syntactic number of the subject, but the grammar allows for a breach of agreement under certain conditions, so that the choice of a verb-form can express various kinds of meaning.

6.5.3 *Lexically inherent number in nouns*

We began the discussion of number by noting that in nouns it is primarily a matter of inflection, so that *boy* and *boys*, for example, are the singular and plural forms of the lexeme **boy** that is itself neutral with respect to the category of number. With a minority of nouns, however, there is no inflectional contrast and the number property, singular in some, plural in others, is an inherent property of the noun lexeme itself. Examples are given in (20) and (21):

(20)   Nouns which are inherently singular
         i *equipment, homework, knowledge, music, perseverance, wetness*
         ii *linguistics, mathematics, news; measles, mumps*
(21)   Nouns which are inherently plural
         i *arms* ("weapons"), *clothes, dregs, earnings, greens* ("green vegetables"), *remains, surroundings, thanks. . .; binoculars, pyjamas, scissors, trousers . . .*
         ii *cattle, people* ("persons"), *police* ("policemen/women")

I have divided the examples in (20) into two sets: those in (i) are straight-forward enough, whereas those in (ii) look like plurals though they are in fact singulars.[7] Note that we say, for example, *This news is bad*, not **These news are bad*. It would not be appropriate to regard this as another case where there is a breach of agreement, as in *Three mistakes is too many*, and the like. The difference is that in the discord cases, the verb is in contrast with one that agrees and/or is restricted to certain kinds of construction (compare *Three mistakes is too many* with **Three mistakes was made*): linguistics, news, and so on, by contrast, behave throughout their distribution as syntactically singular. As far as present-day English is concerned, there-fore, there is no reason for saying that they are syntactic plurals. The best way of accounting for their morphological form is probably to treat the *-s* ending as a lexical rather than an inflectional suffix, to handle the form under lexical not inflectional morphology – but they do point to a certain degree of fuzziness in the lexical/inflectional boundary. We will say, then, that the stem of the inherently singular noun lexeme **linguistics** is formed by suffixation of *-s* to the adjective stem *linguistic*, and analogously for the others, with *measle-* and *mump-* being bound stems.

The nouns in (21i) are all inflectionally plural: they are formed from the lexical stems by the regular rule for plural inflection. The lexical stems themselves are in some cases derived from other stems by standard pro-cesses of lexical morphology – e.g. *remain* is formed by conversion of the verb stem. When compounds are formed from them, it is sometimes the inflected stem that is used, sometimes the uninflected one – compare *the arms-race, a clothes-basket* with *a scissor-movement, a trouser-press*.

The nouns in (21ii), by contrast, are non-inflected plurals. *Cattle*, for example, is clearly a syntactically plural form (cf. *These cattle are unhealthy* vs **This cattle is unhealthy*), but it is not inflected for plural – it is not derived from any more elementary stem by a morphological rule. The plurality is thus purely syntactic, not morphosyntactic, i.e. not inflectional. Similarly for *police* and *people* – in the relevant sense, for we must distinguish the *people* of, say, *People were rushing in all directions*, which is lexically plural, from that of *They are a people of great courage*, which is the singular form of a regular collective noun with *peoples* as its plural counterpart (cf. *the English-speaking peoples*). Other examples are to be found among the pro-nouns: *we* and *they*, for instance, are syntactic plurals not derived by any inflectional process – *we* is not inflectionally related to *I*, as mentioned above and argued in 7.4. It follows, then, that the set of plural-inflected nouns is not quite coextensive with the set of syntactically plural nouns, but is rather included within it.

---

[7] Except that the last two, and similar disease names, apparently belong in (21i) for some speakers.

6.6   **Countability and boundedness**

Noun lexemes that lack singular or plural forms naturally cannot enter into construction with determiners that require such forms in head position: inherently plural **surroundings** cannot combine with *every*, nor inherently singular **phonetics**, with *many*, and so on. There are, however, co-occurrence restrictions between determiners and nouns that are not explicable in terms of a simple contrast between singular and plural – witness the ungrammaticality of expressions like *two clothes, *another equipment*, and so on. To account for such restrictions, we need to classify nouns in terms of their degree of **countability**. At one extreme we have uncountable nouns like **equipment**, which are incompatible with any of the following determiners:

(22)　　　i the cardinal numerals *one, two, three*, etc.;
　　　　　ii other numerically quantifying expressions such as *both, a dozen*, etc.;
　　　　　iii the 'fuzzy' quantifiers *many, several, few*;
　　　　　iv *a, another, each, every, either, neither*, which take singular heads.

At the other extreme we have fully countable nouns like **dog**, which can combine with any of these (given the appropriate number inflection, of course).

Just how many intermediate classes we need is not easy to determine, for judgements concerning the acceptability of relevant determiner–head combinations are not always clear or constant from speaker to speaker. Here we will content ourselves with four such intermediate classes, giving in all six 'countability classes'.

(23)	Degree	Examples	Determiners permitted from list (22)
Uncountable	I	*equipment, outskirts*	None
	II	{ (α) *knowledge, phonetics* { (β) *clothes, dregs*	*a* *many, few*
	III	*cattle*	*many, few*, and relatively large round numbers
	IV	*police, people* ("persons")	All except those requiring a singular head
Fully countable	v	**cake, dog**	All

Examples: **a good equipment*, *a good knowledge of Latin*; **the few outskirts*, *the few dregs*; *many clothes*, **a hundred clothes*, **two clothes*; *many cattle*, *a hundred cattle*, **two cattle*. I treat the difference between *knowledge* and *dregs* as qualitative rather than quantitative: they are both slightly more countable than the uncountable nouns but we can hardly say that one of them is more countable than the other. The reader may find it helpful to classify such nouns as *alms, earnings, information, news, remains, scissors,* and so on. Note that proper nouns like **John** are fully countable – we can talk for example of 'the three Johns' in a tutorial group, and so on.

Countability has to do with a noun's potential for combining with various types of determiner, but we must also consider the interpretation of actual instances of nouns. Notice, for example, that the noun **cake** is interpreted somewhat differently in *I'd like another cake* and *You shouldn't have eaten so much cake.* The difference may be described in terms of the concept of **boundedness**. In *another cake,* **cake** has a bounded or **individuated** interpretation: it is conceived of or perceived as a unit, a discrete entity; in *so much cake* it has an unbounded or **mass** interpretation: we are simply concerned with the substance as such rather than some bounded unit consisting of that substance. **Cake** is a 'concrete' noun (one denoting material substance or a material object), but the same distinction is to be found in 'abstract' nouns – compare *He then pointed out another difficulty* and *He hadn't expected to have so much difficulty in persuading her.* In the first example, the difficulty is presented as more particularised, more delimited – more bounded – than in the second.

The interpretation as mass or individuated depends in part upon the number (singular or plural), in part upon the determiner and in part upon the noun itself. Plurals normally have an individuated interpretation: *The box was full of little cakes; He listed several major difficulties.* With inherently plural nouns of low countability, however, we have a mass interpretation, as in *the remains of the meal,* which is not thought of as a set of discrete units. (In an example like *She has too many clothes,* the mass/individuated distinction becomes somewhat blurred.)

With singulars, certain determiners yield a mass interpretation, others an individuated one:

(24)   Determiner   Interpretation

                  enough, much, more, most, little
                  unaccented *some* or *any*   } Mass
                  what[exclamative] (when not followed by *a*)

                  one, a, another, each, every, either, neither   Individuated

Other determiners are consistent with either interpretation: with *the cake,* for example, one might have in mind some cake-substance or some cake-unit. Similarly, accented *some* occurs in an NP with an individuated interpretation in *She was talking to some guy from the tax-office* and with a mass interpretation in *She has some knowledge of it, but not much,* whereas unaccented *some,* as noted, yields a mass interpretation: *Do you want some cake?* (Unaccented *some* is commonly reduced to /sm/, while accented *some* retains the full vowel, as in /sʌm/.)

Finally, if there is no determiner at all in the singular, an individuated interpretation is normally possible only if the head noun is proper as opposed to common – compare *I like John* (the individual) and *I like cake* (mass: the substance).

Boundedness is clearly related to countability. Thus an uncountable noun cannot bear an individuated interpretation. For example, with *equipment, information* and the like, if we wish to talk about one or more individual units we have to use expressions like *a piece of equipment, an item of information*. Each of these consists of a mass NP embedded inside an individuated NP – just as in *a piece of cake*, where the NP *cake* has the mass interpretation (substance), not the individuated one (unit). The embedded NP has a mass interpretation in accordance with the rules given above: it consists of a singular common noun without a determiner. It should be noted that this property of *equipment* and *information* is a contingent fact about English; it is not in any sense a necessary consequence of any aspect of extralinguistic reality – there is no reason why the meaning 'lexicalised' (i.e. expressed in a lexical item) should not have been "piece of information" or "information in abstraction from the mass/unit distinction". Note in this connection that the French word *renseignement* is glossed as "(piece of) information", and is not syntactically uncountable.

An uncountable noun, we have said, cannot sustain an individuated interpretation; the converse, however, does not hold. As the examples with **cake** and **difficulty** show, particular instances of countable nouns can receive mass interpretations. It is precisely for this reason that I have treated countability and boundedness as distinct concepts. Such a treatment differs from that commonly found in grammars of English, where a single contrast of mass noun versus count noun is recognised.

The latter approach inevitably requires that we allow for a great deal of overlap between the two classes. Some grammars handle this in terms of conversion, a process of lexical morphology. There might then be one conversion process deriving count nouns from mass nouns (e.g. **coffee**$_{count}$, as in *He ordered four coffees*, might derive from **coffee**$_{mass}$, as in *He drinks too much coffee*) and another operating in the opposite direction (with the **carpet**$_{mass}$ of *We need another two square feet of carpet*, say, deriving from the **carpet**$_{count}$ of *We need another carpet*). The phenomenon is, however, quite different from that which we are handling here by means of conversion: there is no reason to posit two different lexemes '**coffee**' – no reason to handle the overlap as a matter of MORPHOLOGY. Rather, we will have a single lexeme '**coffee**', classified in the lexicon as fully countable, with particular instances taking a mass or individuated interpretation depending on the syntactic structure of the NP containing it and/or the context.

What is more difficult to decide is how far we need to posit lexical POLYSEMY: to what extent are the more specific differences between mass and individuated interpretations to be accounted for in the lexical entries for the nouns themselves rather than by general rules applying to NPs? Certainly the semantic contrast between mass and individuated uses varies somewhat across lexical items (or sets of lexical items). Consider, for example, the following contrasts involving **knowledge** and **lamb**:

(25)   i *She had more knowledge of the subject than Tom*
         ii *She had a very good knowledge of the subject*
(26)   i *I'd rather have lamb than pork*
         ii *I'd rather have a lamb than a goat*

There is little effective difference between the mass and individuated interpretations of **knowledge** in (25i) and (ii) respectively; individuation merely delimits her knowledge of the subject in question from other knowledge that she has, thereby permitting its characterisation as good. In (26), by contrast, the most salient interpretation of the mass use of **lamb** is as meat and of the individuated use is as an animal. Notice, however, that these are not the only specific interpretations that occur. Thus in *I'd rather have lamb than mink*, we think of the skin rather than the meat, and if in a restaurant I say *We ordered three lambs and two porks*, the individuated unit would be a serving of meat for one person, not an animal. Just how we determine the specific interpretation attaching to a particular mass or individuated use of a given noun is a problem for semantic theory rather than for grammar in the narrow sense: I will not pursue it further here.

Related to the variation in the specific differences of interpretation associated with mass and individuated uses is variation in the ease or frequency with which particular nouns take a mass interpretation. Compare, for example, **coffee** and **book**. The former readily occurs in a mass use, indicating the substance (solid or liquid) – individuated uses typically apply to servings of the liquid (*Would you like another coffee?*) or varieties of the substance (*This is a better coffee than that one*). **Book** on the other hand is normally used with an individuated interpretation – mass uses (*These wretched creatures have been living on a diet of book*) sound somewhat contrived. It is nevertheless arguable that the rules of grammar provide for a mass use of any fully countable noun, even if the resources thus made available are not always normally exploited; even an expression like *three pounds of John* would then be quite grammatical, though pragmatically somewhat macabre. This is the view adopted here, where the grammatical category of countability, with the classes shown in (23), makes no distinction between **coffee** and **book**.

6.7   Definiteness, specificness and genericness

Two of the most important determiners are the **definite article** *the* and the **indefinite article** *a(n)*. We will begin with *the*, focusing in the first instance on its use in singular NPs, where there is a potential contrast with *a(n)*, and leaving aside at this stage its 'generic' use, as in *The whale is an endangered species*, where one is making a generalisation about the class of whales, rather than talking of any individual member of that class. We will be concerned with its occurrence in NPs used to **refer**, to pick out some person, animal, inanimate object or whatever that the speaker wishes to say something about. Examples of this use of *the* are given in (27):

(27) i *The man who succeeded Gough Whitlam as leader of the Australian Labor Party was a very different sort of person*
      ii *Go and put it in the fridge*
      iii *The boss has just returned from lunch*
      iv *A man and a woman got on the bus; the man was carrying a heavy suitcase*
      v *I took a taxi to work this morning; the driver turned out to be a part-time university student*
      vi *The father of one of my students rang me up last night*
      vii *It turned out that John had been to the same school as Max*

The head noun, together with any complements or modifiers, provides a description of the **referent**, what is referred to, and the selection of *the* indicates that this description is presented as one which is sufficient to define the referent, to distinguish it from everything else.

In the most straightforward cases, the description defines by virtue of there being a unique person, object or whatever satisfying it. Thus there is only one man who succeeded Whitlam as ALP leader (namely Bill Hayden), and this justifies the *the* in (i). Similarly the descriptions in *the first man to run the mile in under four minutes, the Prime Minister of Britain from 1963 to 1970, the fact that Liz is married*, and so on, are all unique – in the last, for example, 'that Liz is married' constitutes a fact, and it is a different fact from all others.

Far more often, however, the description is not unique in this way – there are a great many objects satisfying the description *fridge*, for example, but we can still present it as defining. Here the speaker relies on the context to supplement the description: what we have is not absolute uniqueness but uniqueness relative to the context of discourse. The tacit assumption is that there is only one thing that both satisfies the description and is associated in some standard way with some feature or features of the context in which the utterance takes place. The relevant relationship may be visible presence in the context: I might say *Pass me the newspaper* when there is a unique object that is both a newspaper and visible to the addressee. But the relationship does not have to be of this kind. In (ii) the fridge might well not be visible but would probably be associated with the place in which the utterance takes place – in or near a house containing a single refrigerator. (iii) is likely to be uttered by (and/or to) an employee of the person described as *boss*: there is just one person who is both a boss and in the boss-relationship to the speaker (and/or addressee). Similarly *the prime minister* will typically be understood as the prime minister of the country in which the utterance takes place and/or of which the participants are residents.

Frequently the relationship which supplements the description to yield uniqueness is with something that has been mentioned previously in the discourse. This is illustrated in (iv) and (v). In (iv) the relationship is the elementary one of identity. The referent of *the man* will be understood as the man introduced in the first clause by the indefinite *a man*. The indefinite is used first because at that stage the description *man* would not be defining: it is not inherently unique and there is nothing in the context to provide the necessary implicit supplementary information. But once I have said *A man and a woman got on the bus* I have created a context in which there is a person who can henceforth be defined by that description. (v) does not exhibit the repetition of the descriptive term (*man*) or the elementary identity relation that we have seen in (iv), but is otherwise similar – for it is the mention of a taxi in the first clause that makes the description *driver* defining. I draw on your knowledge of the standard association between taxis and drivers in order to pick out the one person satisfying the description *driver* and associated with the taxi just mentioned.

Writers on definiteness often say that a definite description provides 'identifying' information about the referent. I have here preferred the term 'defining', partly because of its transparent relationship with 'definite', partly because I want to make a systematic distinction between defining and identifying. Thus in a sentence like *The only member of the group who didn't enjoy it was Jill*, I shall say that the referent of the NP in subject position is defined by the description therein (*only member of the group who didn't enjoy it*) and identified by the predicate (*was Jill*). Identifying predication has already been introduced in connection with our discussion of verb complementation; we will have more to say about it in Ch. 14.

Defining information distinguishes the intended referent from everything else. In successful communication, then, a definite description forestalls a *which* question. If I say '*the* . . .' and you respond with '*which* . . .?', this signals a hitch in the communication: you are in effect challenging my implicit claim to have provided defining information. And of course such hitches do occur in ordinary conversation. For example, I might say *I'm going to see the Deputy Vice-Chancellor this afternoon* even though there are in fact two deputy vice-chancellors at my university, one responsible for academic matters, the other for fabric and finance – if you knew this, you might then reply: *Which one?*. But this simply means that I had not been strictly entitled to present my description as defining – it does not alter the fact that I had so presented it, and thus does not invalidate the above account of the meaning of *the*.

Definite NPs can be appropriately used in situations where the addressee has widely varying amounts of information about the referent. Suppose you and I are employees in the same firm, and I address (iii) to you: *the boss* would then pick out someone about whom you presumably already have a good deal of information – you will probably know his or her name, know what he or she looks like, and so on. Yet in (vi) you might have no prior knowledge of the person referred to as *the father of one of my students* – and even if by chance you did, you wouldn't be aware of it because I don't say which student he is the father of. We can nevertheless still say that *father of one of my students* provides defining information. The example bears some similarity to (v): there I assume you accept that there is a taxi which I caught (even though you know nothing else about it) and the driver is then defined by his or her unique relationship with that taxi; similarly in (vi) I assume that you accept that I have a certain student in mind (even though you don't know who it is), and the father is then defined by his unique relationship with that student: it would be out of place for you to ask *Which father of one of your students?*, because that would imply that a student can have more than one father, which goes against our knowledge of the world. The difference between the examples is that in (v) the indefinite NP is introduced before the definite, whereas in (vi) the indefinite is a constituent within the definite. In (vii) one term in the implicit defining relation is not directly expressed, but we understand "Max went to a certain [indefinite] school", and then *same school as Max* is satisfied uniquely by the school related by identity to that one. You would be entitled to ask *Which school was that?*, but not *Which same school as Max?*, for there is only one.

It follows, then, that there can be considerable variation in the amount of new information imparted by the use of a definite NP. In uttering (iii) to you in the context suggested above, I would not be informing you of the fact that there exists a unique person in the boss-relationship to us; rather I would be drawing on your knowledge of that fact in order to convey to you who I was talking about. But if in reply to your asking *Why is John looking so miserable?*, I say *The girl he was going out with tonight has just phoned to say she doesn't want to see him again*, I do not assume you already knew John was scheduled to go out with a certain girl – the existence of a unique girl satisfying the description can be part of the new information imparted. It is important to bear in mind, therefore, that prior knowledge or familiarity with the referent on the part of the addressee is not a necessary condition for the appropriate use of *the*; what matters is that the description together with any necessary contextual supplementation should provide (or be regarded as providing) defining information about the referent.

The indefinite article indicates that the description is not presented as defining. Generally, this will be because the description is not unique and the context fails to provide the further implicit information that would supplement it to the point of uniqueness. As we saw, this accounts for the use of *a man* in the first clause of (iv).

If a description is necessarily unique, the indefinite will be excluded: this is built into the grammatical rules governing the distribution of *a(n)*, as we see from **a fact that Liz is married*, **a youngest member of this committee*. If the description is not unique but there is an obvious relationship with the context that would make it defining, use of an indefinite will be not ungrammatical but pragmatically baffling and/or inappropriate. For example, if a mother said to a child at the dining-table: *Take these plates into a kitchen*, her failure to present *kitchen* as defining in the context would suggest that she did not specifically have in mind the kitchen associated with the house they were in, and yet it would be difficult to understand how she could be indifferent as to which kitchen the plates were taken to.

Nevertheless, non-uniqueness is not part of the propositional meaning expressed by *a(n)*. Suppose you ask *Do you know anything about the tense system of Tiwi?*, and I reply *Well, actually, a Ph.D. student in our department is currently writing a thesis on it*. It is clearly not a condition for the truth of my answer that there should be more than one Ph.D. student in our department. If there is in fact only one such student, I could use *the*, but I don't have to. Use of *the* would convey that there was only one, and I might simply not wish to impart that information, judging it not germane to the issue. It is for this reason that we can say that *a(n)* is 'semantically unmarked' relative to *the*: it does not indicate that the description is non-defining – it merely fails to present it as defining.

What has been said about the meaning of *the* can be generalised to cover its use in plural NPs, as in

(28) i *The headmasters of Britain's public schools had come together for their annual conference*
   ii *The parents of one of my students came to see me*
   iii *I didn't buy the car because the tyres were worn*

As before, *the* indicates that the description is presented as defining. But we no longer have uniqueness, either absolute or relative to the context. Rather, the reference is to all the persons, objects or whatever that satisfy the description (together with any implicit supplementation from the context). Thus the NP in subject function in (28i) refers to the set of all those who are headmasters of Britain's public schools, that in (ii) to the full set of those who are parents of the student in question; (iii) is one where the description *tyres* is implicitly supplemented by an associative relationship with the car just mentioned, but the reference is still to the set of all tyres belonging to that car. The uniqueness component in the earlier examples is attributable to the singular noun rather than being part of the meaning expressed by *the* itself. Whether the NP is singular or plural, *the* indicates that the description (together with any contextual supplementation) provides defining information and that the reference is to the set of all persons or whatever satisfying it: uniqueness is the special case, marked by the number property of the noun, where that set has a single member. Putting *all* before *the* emphasises, reinforces the meaning of totality, rather than introducing it. If there are three bottles on the table, two empty and one full, it would be just as false to say *The bottles on the table are empty* as to say *All the bottles on the table are empty*.

The class of definite NPs can be extended beyond those containing *the*. Other determiners that mark an NP as definite are the demonstratives ***this*** and ***that***, *we/us* and *you* (*we Queenslanders*), the position 1 determiner *both* (as in *both parents*), and PossPs like *my, the old man's, one girl's*, etc. As with *the*, the NP is presented as providing defining information – but this time part of that defining information is expressed by the determiner itself. If I pick up a glass, for example, and say *This glass is dirty*, then some such meaning component as "proximate to the speaker" contributes to the definition of the referent. Similarly in *One girl's spectacles were broken* the information contained in the PossP is crucial to the definition – it is equivalent to "the spectacles of one girl".[8]

Alternatively, an NP may be marked as definite by the head alone, when this position is filled by a proper noun, personal pronoun (***I***, ***we***, etc.) or demonstrative pronoun (***this/that***). Thus in *Liz is due to arrive soon* I present the referent as defined by the name. Names, like descriptions, are commonly not unique, so that we again rely on the context to provide further specification. There are obviously many people named *Liz*, but it can often be assumed that only one will be salient in the particular context. If such an assumption can't be made, I can forestall a *which* question (*Which Liz are you talking about?*) by giving a fuller name (*Liz Jenkins*) or adding descriptive information, which will necessitate the introduction of a determiner (*the Liz who was with John*). Note also that one can add stressed

---

[8] The inclusion among the definites of NPs with possessive determiners is not entirely straightforward. We may contrast *my friend*, say, with an indefinite like *a friend of mine* (or *one of my friends*), but the relation between *my x* and *an x of mine* is not quite the same as that between *the x* and *an x* – doubtless because with the possessives there is a sharp difference in the syntactic complexity of the two phrases. Thus where there is a small set, not just one entity, satisfying the description *x of mine*, one will often nevertheless use *my x* rather than *an x of mine*. For example I would say *He trod on my foot*, not *He trod on a foot of mine* even when there's nothing in the context to indicate which foot it was, and a father of two sons would normally prefer *I'm going to visit my son this week-end*, not *I'm going to visit a son of mine* . . . In a sense the *which* questions would be out of place here because it doesn't matter which – the significance of his treading on my foot is unlikely to be affected by which foot it was and if the addressee knew of the two sons the father could easily say *my son Bill* or the like: *a foot/son of mine* would draw attention to the fact that the description was not defining in a way that would normally be quite gratuitous.

the, /ðiː/, to a name, as in *But surely it can't have been the Attlee*, to refer to one regarded as having, as it were, the first claim to be known by the name on account of his or her fame. Normally when one makes reference by means of a proper name alone one assumes that the addressee has some measure of familiarity with the referent – I would hardly say *I had coffee with Liz Jenkins this morning* if I believed you had no idea who she was (such an assumption holds more generally with proper names than with *the* phrases – recall the discussion above). One can then avoid appearing to make such an assumption by using an indefinite NP: *A Mrs Smith phoned while you were out*; *He introduced me to a girl called Liz Jenkins*. In *a Mrs Smith* I fail to present the title plus name as defining, suggesting I think you may not know who she is.

It will be noticed that I have defined and discussed definiteness in semantic terms; just what its syntactic status is, is at present rather uncertain. It has not yet been convincingly demonstrated, I believe, that there are clear distributional differences between definite and indefinite NPs.

Not to be confused with the distinction between definite and indefinite NPs is that between **specific** and **non-specific**. This latter contrast is illustrated in the following pair:

(29)   i *Ed bought a house in Honour Avenue*
         ii *Ed would like to buy a house in Honour Avenue*

In (i) there must have been some specific, some particular house that he bought. The speaker may or may not know which it was, but that is beside the point: if Ed bought a house there, there must have been a specific house that he bought, No 5, No 8, or whatever. But (ii) is different: Ed need not have any given house in mind, so that it may be simply a matter of what SORT of house he'd like to buy. (ii) is in fact widely analysed as ambiguous, with *a house in Honour Avenue* specific in one interpretation (the case where he does have a particular house in mind), non-specific in the other (the interpretation involving the sort of house).

If we replace indefinite *a* by definite *the* in (29ii), a non-specific reading is hardly possible. Since *house in Honour Avenue* is not inherently unique (let us assume), the descriptive information will need contextual supplementation to make it defining, and this will typically come from prior mention – but then if the house has been mentioned before, there will be a specific house involved, not just a type of house. Nevertheless, if we choose the content of the description suitably, we can still have a definite non-specific in this kind of construction: *John is still looking for the right house to buy*.

We have seen then that both indefinite *a* and definite *the* can occur in both specific and non-specific NPs, and the same goes for most determiners. Whether an NP is interpreted as specific or not depends in general on properties of the sentence containing it rather than being predictable from the form of the NP itself. The crucial difference in (29), for example, is between *bought* (where the buying is actual) and *would like to buy* (where it is merely potential). Nevertheless, there are two determiners, *any* and *either*, which are inherently non-specific. In *Do you know any/either of the women Ed danced with last night?*, for example, the question is not whether you know some particular woman. Conflict will then result if the sentence requires a specific interpretation – hence the anomaly of examples like **As soon as she phoned this morning to say she was coming to tea, I dashed out and bought any/either cake*. Thus *any* and *either* characteristically occur in 'non-affirmative' contexts – we will take up this issue in 13.2.

Also cutting across the definite–indefinite contrast is that between **generic** and **non-generic**:

(30)   i *The/a leopard has a dark-spotted yellowish-fawn coat*
        ii *The/a leopard was growling menacingly in its cage*

The first can be used to make a general statement about animals belonging to the species leopard: in this case we will say that the NP *the/a leopard* has a generic interpretation. The same NP in (ii), however, can have only a non-generic interpretation: the sentence could only be used to make a statement about some one individual leopard.

Genericness is clearly related to specificness. Specific NPs cannot be generic, and as is evident from the above examples, the interpretation as generic or not again depends on the form and meaning of the sentence, not just of the NP itself; we will not go into the question of how far a generic interpretation can be regarded as simply a special case of non-specificness.

It is difficult to detect any significant difference between *the* and *a* in (30i): whether or not the description is presented as defining seems not to matter. And the same effect can be obtained with a plural indefinite – *Leopards have dark-spotted yellowish-fawn coats.* (Plural definites are not used in this way, except with nationality terms, as in *The Italians have a marvellous sense of humour.*) In other cases, however, we find that *the* is permitted while *a* is excluded; *a* could not be substituted for *the* in the example mentioned at the beginning of this section, *The whale is an endangered species.* The difference between this and (30i) has to do with the kind of semantic predicate involved. Having a dark-spotted yellowish-fawn coat is something that applies to individual members of the class leopard, whereas being an endangered species applies to the class whale as a whole. The class leopard doesn't have a single coat belonging to it, and individual whales do not constitute species. Only *the* can be used when the semantic predicate applies to the class as a single unit.

255

6.8 **Pre-head modifiers**

The syntactic and semantic role of modifiers is typically somewhat different from that which is characteristic of determiners. Consider an example like the NP subject of

(31)   *The two large black dogs were sleeping peacefully*

Notice first that when this is used to make an assertion, it is the whole NP *the two large black dogs* that serves to refer, to pick out the entities, Fido and Rex say, who are said to have been sleeping peacefully. We will thus not speak of the lexeme ***dog*** as having reference: rather we will speak of its **denotation**, which is the class of all entities x of which it can be truly asserted that 'x is a dog'. Thus ***dog*** denotes the class of canine animals, and the referents of the NP *the two large black dogs* will be members of that class. Now the modifiers *black* and *large* specify further properties of the class from which the referents are drawn: members of the class are not just canine animals, but are also black and large (large relative to the average size of dogs, we assume: whether something is large depends not on its absolute size but its size relative to some understood norm). But *two* does not specify still further properties of members of the class. Rather it gives the number of members of the class that are being picked out. And likewise *the* does not identify any property of the dogs. It indicates, as we have seen, that the speaker is presenting the expression *two large black dogs* as a sufficient description to define the referents. As usual, these semantic observations are relevant to the general definitions of modifiers and determiners: they do not give criteria for analysing particular examples.

The most straightforward pre-head modifiers are adjectives – like *large* and *black* in the above example. We have already noted, however, that there are good grounds for not taking all modifiers to be adjectives – recall the contrast drawn in 3.1 between *a great actor* and *a boy actor*, where *actor* is modified by the adjective *great* in the first and by the noun *boy* in the second. There are similar arguments for recognising verb modifiers. Thus any of the three major parts of speech can occur in this function – though verbs do not appear here in their central, i.e. tensed, forms:

(32)	Class of modifier	Determiner	Modifier	Head
	Adjective	*that*	*glorious*	*sunset*
	Noun	*a*	*Yorkshire*	*dialect*
	Verb $\Big\langle$ *-ing* form	*the*	*simmering*	*stew*
	-en form	*the*	*captured*	*terrorist*

We will take up this issue again, in Ch. 9, after we have completed our initial review of the three major parts of speech and their associated phrases.

Strictly speaking, the modifiers should not be analysed (immediately) as words but as phrases, for although they are most frequently single words,

there is in general the potential for them to have their own dependents –
compare *that absolutely glorious sunset, a North Yorkshire dialect, the gently
simmering stew, the recently captured terrorist.* A partial structure for the first of
these will thus be as follows:

(33)

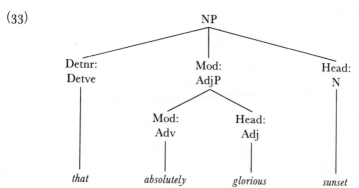

Adjectives functioning as pre-head modifier are said to be used **attributively**; those functioning as predicative complement, by contrast, as in
They are black, They seemed large, are said to be used **predicatively**. And, in
general, attributive adjectives have much the same potential for expansion
as predicative adjectives. Thus corresponding to the predicative construction *The proposal was very much more attractive* we have the attributive *a very
much more attractive proposal.* However, where a predicative adjective has a
dependent following rather than preceding it, either the corresponding
attributive AdjP will be discontinuous, (34), or there will be no corresponding attributive construction, (35):[9]

(34)	i	*The deficit was much larger than had been expected*	Predicative
	ii	*a much larger deficit than had been expected*	Attributive
(35)	i	*The minister was quite confident about the outcome*	Predicative
	ii	**a quite confident minister about the outcome*	Attributive

In (34ii) the embedded clause follows the head of the NP, but we continue
to analyse it as a dependent of the adjective *larger* rather than of the noun
deficit. This is the kind of construction that invites description in transformational terms: we would posit a hypothetical basic structure †*a much
larger than had been expected deficit,* which is then transformed into (34ii) by a
rule which shifts the post-head dependent of the AdjP to the right of the
head noun.

With attributive nouns and verbs the possibilities for expansion are
severely limited. With nouns we find pre-head modifiers as in the earlier *a*

---

[9] Exceptions are restricted to cases where the dependent is very short and some of them
approach the status of compounds: *a larger than expected deficit, an easy-to-clean frying pan.*

Nouns and noun phrases

North Yorkshire dialect or *a State Government inquiry* but no determiners (we cannot have **a the State Government inquiry* in the sense "an inquiry by the State Government"), and post-head dependents, as in *a Ministry of Defence official*, discussed in 3.3, are of very low productivity; as we suggested in that earlier discussion, it may well be that forms like *North Yorkshire*, *State Government* and *Ministry of Defence* as used here should not be assigned to the NP category but to a distinct phrase category intermediate in the constituent hierarchy between noun and NP. With verbs, the scope for expansion is even less: it is virtually limited to the addition of adverb pre-head modifiers – and again there are problems in deciding what phrase category forms like *gently simmering* and *recently captured* should be assigned to.

In addition to adjectival, nominal and verbal modifiers, we should recognise one other fairly productive pattern – that where the modifier is realised by a PossP, as in *a men's toilet, an old people's home*. PossPs, as we have seen, can also function as determiner, so that we must distinguish between the constructions in (36):

(36)	i	*an*	*old people's*	*home*	ii	*the old fellow's*	*home*
		Detnr	Mod	Head		Detnr	Head

In (i) *an* is determiner to *home*, whereas in (ii) *the* is determiner to *fellow*. The semantic difference between the examples is very clear: (i) is interpreted as "a home for old people", with *old people's* specifying what kind or class of home it is, while (ii) is interpreted as "the home belonging to the old fellow", with *the old fellow's* specifying whose home it is. An example like *the old people's home* can be analysed in either way, with a clear semantic distinction: the meaning it has with structure (i) is "the home for old people", while that corresponding to structure (ii) is "the home belonging to the old people". The semantic difference will not always be so sharp, however. For example, *a cat's tail* structured like (i) would mean "a tail of the kind that cats have" and structured like (ii) "the tail of a cat", and in practice it might not matter how we took it. Where a PossP has modifier function, the complement of the possessive clitic – *old people* in (i) – cannot contain any determiner of its own: we cannot have, for example, **an the old people's home*; *old people* (unlike *the old fellow*, which is complement of *'s* in (ii)) might again then not be an NP but a member of the suggested 'intermediate' phrase category.

This does not exhaust the range of possible kinds of modifier, but other constructions – as in *his couldn't care less attitude*, for example – are of such low productivity that we need not consider them further here.

Instead we turn briefly to NPs containing two or more pre-head modifiers, as in

(37)	i	*a*	*very long*	*metal*	*rod*	ii	*a*	*big*	*black*	*Holden*	*sedan*
		Detnr	Mod	Mod	Head		Detnr	Mod	Mod	Mod	Head

The relative order of modifiers is marginally less rigidly fixed than that of determiners, for there is some scope for alternative orderings: both *pornographic Swedish films* and *Swedish pornographic films* are grammatical, for example. The second is probably a less normal order than the first, but it could perfectly well be used if one was drawing a contrast between pornographic films from Sweden and those from France. To a large extent, however, the order is fixed: we could not have **a metal very long rod*, and so on. There is not space to go into details, but one generalisation we can make is that modifiers denoting 'gradable' or 'scalar' properties precede those denoting 'non-gradable' or 'categorial' properties. Thus length is gradable – we can ask how long a rod is or say that one rod is longer than another, and so on, but we could not ask 'how metal' the rod is: rather we simply assign the rod to the metal category as opposed to the wooden or plastic categories, say. Notice that this principle is also relevant to the example where we had contrasting orders. *Swedish* will normally be interpreted as non-gradable – the films will be Swedish or British or French, etc., and we will not have a scale of Swedishness. But *pornographic* can be interpreted either gradably or categorially; in the former case it will precede *Swedish*, in the latter it will follow. Hence the possibility of *extremely pornographic Swedish films* but not **Swedish extremely pornographic films*: in *Swedish pornographic films* we are concerned with Swedish films of a certain category, contrasting, say, with musicals or Westerns. As gradable properties are characteristically expressed by adjectives rather than nouns, adjectival modifiers will generally precede nominal modifiers, as in (37). There is obviously much more to the ordering constraints than this, but for a more detailed discussion the reader is referred to the literature mentioned in the 'Further reading' recommendations.

As we move to the rightmost modifier positions we are faced with the problem of distinguishing between modifier–head phrasal constructions and a compound noun – e.g. *gold watch* vs *goldsmith*. The easiest criterion to use is that of accent: in *gold watch* the accent will fall (in the absence of contrastive emphasis) on *watch*, whereas in *goldsmith* it falls on the *gold*. This gives intuitively correct results in the majority of cases but it also has the effect of including within the compounds some expressions which involve a productive and semantically transparent pattern (such as *history teacher*) and excluding a few which clearly have a meaning not systematically derivable from the meanings of the parts (such as *common sense* and *ice-cream*, at least for those who pronounce this *ice-'cream*) – we have to accept that the distinction between the phrasal and compound noun constructions is somewhat fuzzy.

The construction with a sequence of modifiers is of course to be distinguished from that where we have a single modifier realised by a phrase containing its own modifier, as in (33) and other examples discussed above.

The contrast between *that absolutely glorious sunset* and *the large black dogs* is easy to see because *absolutely*, an adverb, can modify an adjective (*glorious*) but not a noun (*sunset*) and conversely *large*, an adjective, can modify a noun (*dogs*) but not an adjective (*black*). Where there is a noun modifier, however, the constructions are not differentiated by the part of speech sequences in this elementary way – compare

(38)	i	*an*	*attractive*	*gold*	*watch*	ii	*a*	*solid gold*	*watch*
		Detnr	Mod	Mod	Head		Detnr	Mod	Head

In (i) the adjective *attractive* modifies the noun *watch*, while in (ii) the adjective *solid* modifies the noun *gold*, with *solid gold* as a whole modifying *watch* – here *solid gold* contrasts with *gold-plated* and the like. From a purely syntactic point of view both expressions are potentially ambiguous between the two constructions: which syntactic analysis is appropriate in a given instance will in general be pragmatically clear (our knowledge about gold and watches, for example, will favour the analyses shown): it need not be prosodically signalled.

6.9 Complements

The relationship between the head and the post-head dependents we are calling complements parallels that between the predicator and its complements in clause structure. The parallel is particularly clear in NPs whose head is a deverbal noun; compare

(39)	i	*She relied on her father*
	ii	*her reliance on her father*
(40)	i	*They believe in God*
	ii	*their belief in God*
(41)	i	*Ed assumed that it was genuine*
	ii	*Ed's assumption that it was genuine*

One major difference, however, is that whereas in clause structure a complement can be – and indeed most often is – an NP, in NP structure it cannot: the complement corresponding to the NP object of a clause will be a PP, generally – though not invariably – having *of* as the preposition:

(42)	i	*He criticised the book*
	ii	*his criticism of the book*
(43)	i	*She married her cousin*
	ii	*her marriage to her cousin*

It is not only deverbal nouns that take complements. We shall see that adjectives enter into construction with complements and parallels like those above are then found between AdjPs and NPs with de-adjectival nouns as head: compare *He was eager to win* and *his eagerness to win* where *to win* is a complement of the adjective *eager* in the first, and of the noun *eagerness* in the second. In addition complements occur with a number of nouns whose lexical stems are not morphologically derived from other parts of speech – nouns like **author**, **king**, **fact**, **idea**:

(44)			
	i *the*	*author*	*of both books*
	ii *the*	*idea*	*that she might be pregnant*
	Detnr	Head	Complement

Complements are generally realised by PPs or subordinate clauses, finite or non-finite. Some deverbal nouns also take what we have been calling 'particles' as complement, as in *His looking up of the information*, where the particle *up* and the PP *of the information* are separate complements. The number of complements in any one NP is strictly limited. This last example has two, as does *his criticism of the book for its repetitiousness*, while *his purchase of the land from the Government for $10,000* has three, but NPs with more than one complement are generally rather infrequent. Typically the number of complements permitted with deverbal nouns will match those found in clauses with the corresponding verb as head of the predicator (but cf. §13 below).

6.10   **Post-head modifiers**

Post-head modifiers are mainly realised by PPs, subordinate clauses (again finite or non-finite), AdjPs, or NPs:

(45)	Class of modifier		Detnr	Head	Modifier
	PP	i	*a*	*girl*	*with red hair*
	Clause ⟨ Finite	ii	*the*	*man*	*who stole the silver*
	Non-finite	iii	*the*	*man*	*working in the garden*
	AdjP	iv	*a*	*poem*	*full of alliteration*
	NP	v	*the*	*opera*	*'Carmen'*

We will be looking a little further into the relationship between pre- and post-head adjectival modifiers in §12 below; at this stage we will note only two points:

(a) Only the post-head position is available when the head is realised by an 'indefinite pronoun' – *someone, everybody, anything*, etc.: *I said something ridiculous*.

(b) Other than in the construction just identified, a post-head AdjP will normally contain its own post-head dependent, as in (45iv) – compare **a poem long* (exceptions like *matters political* tend to be stylistically marked: archaic, literary, jocular or the like).

The last example in (45) differs from the others in that the dependent NP could stand alone instead of the larger NP: *He began work on the opera 'Carmen'* and *He began work on 'Carmen'* are equally grammatical, and though they are not of course semantically identical (since only the first explicitly encodes the information that 'Carmen' is an opera) they involve reference to the same thing – the opera was 'Carmen'. For this reason *'Carmen'* is traditionally said to be in **apposition** to *(the) opera*. Apposition is used for a variety of constructions where one form (an NP in the central cases) is 'placed alongside' another, to which it is in some sense equivalent. Such equivalence puts apposition at the margin of the dependency, subordination relation – and in some cases, perhaps, beyond it. In the present type there is, nevertheless, a significant functional likeness between *'Carmen'* and, say, *who stole the silver* in (ii): just as the latter gives information defining which man is being referred to, so *'Carmen'* gives information defining which opera is being referred to, and it is on this basis that they are analysed alike.[10]

Let us consider now the distinction between modifiers and complements. From a semantic point of view, complements generally correspond to arguments of a semantic predicate expressed in the head noun, while modifiers generally give properties of what is denoted by the head. Consider, for example, the pair

(46) i	*a*	*king*	*of England*	ii	*a*	*king*	*of considerable intelligence*
	Detnr	Head	Complement		Detnr	Head	Modifier

The head noun **king** in (i) may be analysed as expressing a two-place semantic predicate, rather like the verb **reign**, as in *William reigned over England*, where the arguments are "William" and "England". Where the phrase headed by **king** is predicative complement, as in *William was King of England* the first argument will be expressed by the subject, *William* – compare our earlier discussion of *Ed was a fan of the Beatles*, example (10ii) of Ch. 5. Otherwise the first argument will be expressed by the whole NP headed by **king**, as in *They saw the king of England*, where the NP *the king of England* might be used to refer to William. In either case the second argument of "king" is expressed by *England*, part of the PP we are analysing as a complement. The semantic relations in (ii) are clearly quite different. Instead of having two arguments (corresponding to William and England)

---

[10] Traditional grammars also analyse the subordinate content clauses in (44ii) and (41ii) above as being in apposition to *(the) idea* and *(Ed's) assumption* respectively. We again have a kind of equivalence relation in that the idea was that she might be pregnant and Ed's assumption was that it was genuine. But here the clause is not so uniformly substitutable for the whole NP, so that the relation is less marginally one of dependency – cf. *He rejected the idea that she might be pregnant, Ed's assumption that it was genuine was quite unfounded*, where *the idea* and *Ed's assumption* could not be omitted.

with a "king" relation between them, we have a single argument (corresponding, we again assume, to William) with the two properties of being king and of being of considerable intelligence.

Syntactically the distinction is a good deal more difficult to draw than that between complements and modifiers (or adjuncts) in clause structure – and indeed it is much less generally drawn in grammars of English. In our discussion of the distinction for dependents of a verb in 5.1 we drew attention to three properties of complements: (a) the occurrence of a complement of a given kind depends on the presence of a verb of an appropriate subclass; (b) complements are obligatory with certain verbs; (c) prototypical complements are realised by NPs or AdjPs. When we move from clause to NP structure, we find significantly less differentiation.

Take point (c) first. Leaving aside predicative complements, NP dependents within the predicate of the clause are normally objects, but NP dependents of a noun are appositional and not at all analogous to objects in clause structure. Thus the distinction between transitive and intransitive – to which traditional grammar assigns such fundamental importance, as we have seen – is not applicable to nouns: there are no transitive nouns. Thus those grammars which for clause structure emphasise the contrast between adjuncts and objects (as opposed to complements) will not see a parallel contrast in NP structure.

Nor does point (b) provide us with any basis for a distinction, for in NP structure, complements are to all intents and purposes as freely omissible as modifiers. It is probably an overstatement to say that complements are always omissible, but examples like *a denizen of the forest*, where the PP dependent is arguably obligatory, are so few that we will not want to base a major functional contrast upon them.

This brings us to point (a). A difference with respect to the subclassification of head nouns is clearest with subordinate clause dependents, since those functioning as complement are readily distinguishable from those functioning as modifier:

(47)　　　i [*the fact*] *that John had overeaten*　　　　　　　　Complement
　　　　　ii [*the fact*] *that John had overlooked*　　　　　　　Modifier

The subordinate clauses here are respectively 'content' and 'relative' clauses – see 3.3 above for this contrast. And what we find is that any noun (save a few pronouns) can take a relative clause as dependent, whereas only a small subclass of nouns can take a content clause: they are mainly nouns with stems derived in lexical morphology from verbs or adjectives that take clause complements (e.g. *belief, knowledge, eagerness*, etc.) plus one or two with morphologically simple stems (*fact, idea*). Thus nouns like *boy, apple, king*, and so on, could replace *fact* in construction (47ii) but they could not do so in (i). We thus have a quite sharp distinction between two

263

kinds of clause dependent – though, as we have observed, traditional grammar treats (47i) and the like as involving apposition rather than complementation.

With PP dependents the distinction is more problematic, because we do not have clear internal differences that would give distinct subclasses of PP correlating with a functional distinction between complement and modifier. Nevertheless we can see a difference in

(48) i [*her reliance*] *on her father*   Complement
      ii [*the book*] *on the table*   Modifier

where the *on* in (ii) has its ordinary locative meaning, while that in (i) has no obvious meaning of its own but is, rather, determined by the head noun **reliance** – and then, plainly, the kind of PP we have in (i) is dependent on the selection of an appropriate noun as head. In (46) there are a number of ways in which we can differentiate between the *of* phrases. In the modifier (ii), but not the complement (i), *of* is more or less equivalent to *with* and is in paradigmatic contrast with *without*; this kind of *of* phrase can occur as dependent to any noun, or at least any common noun – compare *a man of/without honour, a poem of/without distinction, an event of/without importance*, and so on. Conversely with an NP like (46i), but not (ii), the dependent (or part of it) can be moved to the front of the clause containing the NP as predicative complement in a construction like *What country was he (the) king of?* (compare **How much intelligence was he a king of?*, and the like), and again this will be possible only for the limited subclass of nouns taking an *of* phrase complement. It would be idle to suggest that such criteria can yield a sharp distinction between complements and modifiers: there is bound to remain a considerable area of indeterminacy – but this does not mean that we should simply abandon the distinction proposed for (46).

One further difference between complements and modifiers involves their linear order: complements precede modifiers, as in *a king of England of considerable intelligence*, not **a king of considerable intelligence of England*.

There is no grammatical limit to the number of post-head modifiers occurring in a single NP, but considerations of style and comprehensibility will normally keep them to one or two. Where we have more than one, the relative order tends to depend on the related properties of length and class, with shorter modifiers preceding longer ones, PPs preceding clauses: *a guy from France who I was talking to last night.*

6.11 Peripheral dependents

Peripheral dependents are distinguished prosodically from modifiers and complements: they occur with a separate intonation contour; in writing they are typically marked off by commas (or some stronger punctuation, dashes or parentheses):

(49)   i *my father, who had just returned from Paris*
         ii *her suggestion – that we should pay half the costs*
        iii *her uncle, an infantry colonel*

The subordinate clause in (i) is a 'non-restrictive relative clause'; the content clause *that we should pay half the costs* in (ii) and the NP *an infantry colonel* in (iii) are again traditionally analysed as being in apposition to the preceding noun, but with the apposition being 'loose' or 'non-restrictive' in contrast to the 'close' or 'restrictive' apposition of (45v), (44ii) and (41ii).

   We will look more closely at the contrast between restrictive and non-restrictive constructions in 12.4.3, contenting ourselves here with a provisional account based on a prototypical pair such as

(50)   i *The necklace which Elvis had given her was in the safe*   Restrictive
         ii *The necklace, which Elvis had given her, was in the safe*   Non-restrictive

In (i) the subordinate clause is intonationally linked to the head noun, whereas in (ii) it is intonationally separate, rather like an interpolation or parenthesis. In (i) we could replace *which* by *that* or simply omit it, but in (ii) we could not. Semantically the relative clause in (i) forms part of the description that serves to pick out the referent: it would be appropriate in a context of discourse where there was more than one necklace, with the property of having been given to her by Elvis thus distinguishing the necklace being referred to from other necklaces – the description *necklace which Elvis had given her* is presented as more 'restrictive' than that of *necklace* alone. In (ii) by contrast *necklace* is presented as sufficient by itself to pick out the referent: the referent is defined independently of the information about it contained in the relative clause. The same clearly applies to (49i): the referent is uniquely defined by the property of being my father. That he had just returned from Paris is given as supplementary information rather than as information necessary to clarify, as it were, which father I am referring to: as I have only one, that question cannot arise.

   The appositive elements in (49ii) and (iii) are semantically non-restrictive in the same sense. The former has a straightforward restrictive analogue, *her suggestion that we should pay half the costs*. The difference can be brought out by observing that only in the non-restrictive construction could we insert *other* before *suggestion*. There is necessarily only one suggestion of hers that we should pay half the costs (she might have said it more than once, but it would still be the same suggestion); thus where the content clause is used restrictively, to define which suggestion is being referred to, *other* will be out of place. But in (49ii), where it is used non-restrictively, *other* is possible because we clearly can have two different suggestions of hers, as opposed to suggestions-that-we-should-pay-half-the-costs. (iii) does not have a direct restrictive analogue: an NP like *an infantry colonel* (indefinite and with an individuated interpretation) cannot occur in restrictive apposition. The earlier example (45v), however, illustrates restrictive apposition of a definite NP and can be contrasted with the non-restrictive *the opera, 'Carmen'*.

Non-restrictive dependents are peripheral in that they can be omitted with relatively little loss – never loss of grammaticality, and loss only of supplementary information as opposed to information integral to the main message. They should probably be regarded as occupying a different position in constituent structure from modifiers and complements: we might distinguish *the opera, 'Carmen'* from *the opera 'Carmen'* for example along the following lines:

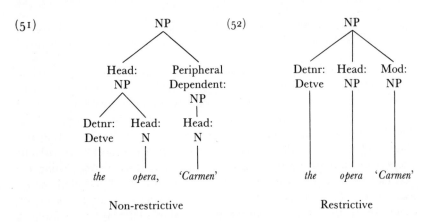

(51)   Non-restrictive   (52)   Restrictive

Where the dependent is non-restrictive, the remainder (*the opera*) forms a constituent, as in (51); but in the restrictive construction, shown in (52), it does not – if there is any further structure here it would involve grouping *opera* and *'Carmen'* together as a constituent in construction with *the*. It must be admitted, however, that it is difficult to find strong syntactic evidence for determining such details of NP constituent structure and, as in the rather analogous case of the clause, a good deal of variation will be found among grammars in this regard.

6.12   **The relationship between pre- and post-head modification**
There are a number of cases where the same or similar meaning can be expressed by different kinds of dependent – for example, *a green-eyed monster* is almost synonymous with *a monster with green eyes*, where the first has a pre-head modifier realised by an adjective, the second a post-head modifier realised by a PP. (They are 'almost' rather than 'completely' synonymous because *green-eyed* does not encode information about the number of eyes, whether singular or plural.) We do not have space to

review all such relationships, but will comment briefly on two – one (in this section) involving pre-head AdjP modifiers and post-head relative clauses, the other (in the next section) PossP determiners and *of* phrase complements.

We begin, then, with the constructions exemplified in

(53)   i *an incredibly offensive attitude*
         ii *an attitude that was incredibly offensive*

In (i) we have an AdjP as pre-head modifier, in (ii) a post-head modifier realised by a relative clause containing the same AdjP as predicative complement to the verb *be*. On the basis of the apparent equivalence between the two constructions, it might be suggested that the first should be derived from the second – by a transformation that deletes initial *that* (or a relative pronoun) plus *be* and moves the AdjP to pre-head position. However, the semantic and syntactic relationship between them is by no means as straightforward as might appear from the elementary example in (53). The following differences should be pointed out.

(a) In the relative clause construction we have a contrast between restrictive and non-restrictive (as discussed above) which is not systematically made in pre-head modifiers. It is true that in the AdjP + Head construction we have a distinction according as the main stress falls on the head (unmarked) or the modifier (marked), as in *her younger sister* vs *her younger sister*, but this is not to be equated with the distinction we have made within the post-head dependents. Placement of the stress on the modifier will direct attention to it and in this case it will normally be interpreted as semantically restrictive – but placement of the stress on the head certainly does not imply that the modifier is semantically non-restrictive. For example, I might say *It's just behind that blue car* in a context where the *blue* helps to pick out the intended referent even though the stress falls on the head. Thus where the stress is on the head, it will depend on the context and on non-linguistic knowledge whether the modifier is construed restrictively or not: it is not encoded in the form of the NP.

(b) The relative clause makes a distinction of tense, so that we have a contrast between, say, *the tomato that was ripe* and *the tomato that is ripe* but in *the ripe tomato* the temporal contrast is not encoded and the time of the ripeness has to be inferred pragmatically.

(c) There is a tendency for attributive adjectives to correspond to properties that are relatively permanent or at least characteristic of the referent, whereas the relative clause construction can be used for permanent or temporary properties. Thus *the navigable rivers* would typically be understood as referring to the rivers that are characteristically navigable, whereas *the rivers that were/are navigable* could be used of those that were/are navigable on some specific occasion.

(d) Not all adjectives can be used in both constructions (or at least not with the same sense). Some of the restrictions are related to point (c), in that certain adjectives denoting inherently temporary properties cannot be used attributively: *an afraid man, *an asleep child, *the ready meal. Among those that occur only in the attributive construction are *mere, utter, principal, major,* and so on.

In general, then, the differences between the two constructions are too great for us to regard one as systematically derived from the other.

6.13 **The relationship between PossP and *of* phrase dependents**
In this final section we will consider the relationship between NPs like

(54)   i *the prime minister's son*
       ii *the son of the prime minister*

The possessive clitic and the preposition *of* serve to relate two NPs, one (*the prime minister*) forming a constituent of the other (*the prime minister's son/the son of the prime minister*): we will speak of them as, respectively, the 'subordinate' and 'superordinate' terms in the relationship. Similarly in the inflectional possessive construction, the personal pronoun in abstraction from the inflection will be the subordinate term – compare *your appointment as dean* and *the appointment of you as dean*.

Traditionally grammars apply the name 'genitive' to this relationship and commonly refer to the constructions in (54) as '*s* genitive' and '*of* genitive' respectively. We will not adopt that terminology here, however, partly because the primary use of the general term 'genitive' is for a case inflection (see 2.3) and partly because the use of a single term for the two constructions risks obscuring the important syntactic difference between them, namely that the PossP in (i) is a determiner while the *of* phrase in (ii) is a complement. As a determiner the PossP is in paradigmatic contrast with other determiners (more precisely, others from position II – see (7) above), such as *the, this, a,* etc.; as a complement the *of* phrase can combine syntagmatically with a determiner. In general, the construction with *of* allows a choice of determiner – we could replace *the* in (ii) by *each, any, another,* etc.; with some heads, however, only *the* (or perhaps one of the demonstratives *this, that*) is permitted – cf. *the/*a height of the building, the/?this/*some singing of Joan Sutherland*. The PossP determiner marks the superordinate NP as definite, even if the subordinate one is indefinite: *a reviewer's responsibility,* for example, means "the" (not "a") "responsibility of a reviewer".

(54i) and (ii) have the same propositional meaning. The two constructions are not, however, in anything like a one-to-one relationship: there are many cases where only one is acceptable. Thus we can have *your nose* but not **the nose of you* and conversely *the writing of letters* but not **the letters' writing*. Some of the factors that contribute to determining whether one or other of the constructions is possible are as follows:

(a) Complexity of the subordinate term. Consider such a series of NPs as

(55)
     i *you*
     ii *Peter*
     iii *the prime minister*
     iv *the former prime minister, Sir William McMahon*
     v *the only other person to whom the manuscript had been shown*

With a personal pronoun like (i) as subordinate term, only the PossP determiner construction is in general available: compare *your car* and the unacceptable *the car of you*; examples like *the appointment of you as dean* are handled under factor (c) below. With an NP like (v) containing a finite subordinate clause within it, only the *of* construction is normally possible: *the opinion of the only other person to whom the manuscript had been shown* but not *the only other person to whom the manuscript had been shown's opinion*. With a short NP like (ii) there is normally a strong preference for the PossP: *Peter's hat* is much more natural than *the hat of Peter*. Other things being equal, an NP like (iii) fits just as naturally into one as into the other, as we see from (54), while increasing the complexity to the level illustrated in (iv) generally makes the *of* construction more natural. The complexity of the remainder of the superordinate NP may also be relevant: (55iv), for example, would more readily enter into the PossP construction if followed by *attitude towards this issue* than by something shorter, like *voice*. For the most part at least, we are dealing here with preferences and tendencies, not with syntactic rules (which is why I have not used the asterisk in this paragraph). *The hat of Peter* sounds so unnatural that it is tempting to say that it is ungrammatical – but it is questionable whether we could devise rules of syntax to exclude such examples while admitting the perfectly acceptable *the thoughts of Mao, the voice of Ferdinand*, and the like. Similarly, while the PossP example with (55v) is unacceptable, we might, in informal speech, get away with examples where the finite clause is shorter: *the woman he was talking to's evident repugnance*. The strongest case for a syntactic rule is to exclude examples like *the car of you*, but again this would depend on point (c) below.

(b) Humanness and animacy of the subordinate term. If the subordinate term refers to one or more humans, the PossP construction is almost always possible and often preferred; if it refers to something inanimate the same applies to the *of* construction. Compare *the man's left eye*, more natural than *the left eye of the man*, and *the eye of the needle*, more natural than *the needle's eye*. Similarly, *the doctor's removal from the board* is much better than *the error's removal from the draft*. Notice – and this might be considered a distinct factor – that the latter becomes significantly worse if we replace singular *error* with plural *errors*: in speech at least we would be just about bound to say *the removal of the errors*.

(c) Nature of the relationship between the subordinate and superordinate terms. Traditional grammars commonly distinguish a number of different types of 'genitive' according to the semantic relationship involved. Thus *Ed's stamp collection* would typically be classified as a 'genitive of possession'; *Ed's telegram* ("the telegram Ed sent") as a 'genitive of origin'; *the city of Rome* as an 'appositive genitive' (*the city* and *Rome* are semantically equivalent in the same sense as *the opera* and *Carmen* in our earlier example of apposition); *a few of the candidates* as a 'partitive genitive'; *the minister's arrival* as a 'subjective genitive'; *the city's destruction* as an 'objective genitive'; *an old people's home* and *a king of considerable intelligence* as 'descriptive genitives' (the PossP and *of* phrase here are, in our analysis, modifiers rather than determiner or complement); and so on. There is not space here to consider all of these types or to examine the linguistic status (whether syntactic, semantic or pragmatic) of the classification. We may note, however, that the appositive and partitive *of* phrases do not have PossP counterparts (**Rome's city*, **the candidates' few*) – and that the distinction between the subjective and objective constructions is also relevant to the choice between PossP and *of* phrase. The subjective and objective constructions occur where the head of the superordinate NP has a lexical-morphological relationship to a verb or adjective, as with **arrival** ~ **arrive**, **destruction** ~ **destroy,** *eagerness* ~ *eager*, etc. The subordinate NP is said to be subjective if it stands in the same semantic relation to the head as the subject of a corresponding active clause does to the verb or predicative adjective – compare *the minister's arrival* with *The minister arrived*, *Bill's eagerness to win* with *Bill was eager to win*. Similarly the subordinate NP is objective if its relation to the head matches that of object to verb – compare *the city's destruction* with *They destroyed the city*. Where the two occur together, the subjective NP will be within a PossP, the objective NP within an *of* phrase: thus corresponding to *Ed removed the manuscript* we have *Ed's removal of the manuscript*, not **the manuscript's removal of Ed* or **the removal of the manuscript of Ed*.[11] This suggests the PossP is the unmarked construction for the subjective type, the *of* phrase for the objective type, an association supported by various other restrictions. We have seen, for example, that personal

---

[11] We can often have two complements if they are not both *of* phrases: *the removal of the manuscript by Ed*. Note that this construction with *by* is limited to actions: we can have, for example, *Ed's knowledge of Greek* but not **the knowledge of Greek by Ed*, since **knowledge** does not denote an action.

pronouns are generally restricted to the PossP construction but in the objective type they occur also in the *of* construction – cf. *the appointment of you as dean* above. Notice that *my photograph* can be interpreted subjectively ("the photograph I took") or objectively ("the photograph taken of me"), whereas *the photograph of me* admits only the latter interpretation.[12] Conversely, *the shooting of the hunters* is a commonly cited example allowing either interpretation (cf. *The hunters shot* vs *They shot the hunters*), whereas *the hunters' shooting* hardly admits the objective interpretation. *The writing of the letters* can only be objective for pragmatic reasons (letters don't write), and this time, as we have seen, the PossP construction is excluded: **the letters' writing*. Finally, note the difference between *the king's fear* and *the fear of the king*: the former can only be subjective, while the latter very strongly favours the objective interpretation. Thus some nouns (such as ***fear***, ***writing***) require an objective subordinate term to be within an *of* phrase; and more generally there is a tendency for an association between subjective and PossP and between objective and *of* phrase – but this tendency interacts with factors (a) and (b) above.

This necessarily sketchy discussion should give some indication of the highly complex relation between the two constructions. They do not lend themselves readily to an analysis where one is derived transformationally from the other – certainly not in terms of the very informal concept of transformation that we are working with here.

FURTHER READING

For general accounts of NP structure, see Quirk et al. 1971: Chs. 4 & 13, Strang 1968: Chs. 7 & 8, Halliday 1984: Ch. 6; for discussions within a generative approach, more particularly X-bar syntax, see Jackendoff 1977: Chs. 4 & 5, Selkirk 1977. On number and countability, see Allan 1976 (source of the term 'collectivising'), 1980, 1981, Quirk 1978, Mufwene 1981, Mühlhaüsler 1983; on the constituent structure of NPs like *a number of people*, within a more abstract framework than that adopted here, see Akmajian & Lehrer 1976. On reference, including definiteness, specificness and genericness, see Lyons 1977: §7.2; on definiteness in particular, see Hawkins (J.) 1978 – and for the definiteness of NPs like *a friend's wife* Woisetschlaeger 1983; on generics, see Burton-Roberts 1976, Smith N. 1977. On the distinction between complements and modifiers, see Matthews 1981: Ch. 7; on apposition, see Burton-Roberts 1975, Matthews 1981: Ch. 10. On the relation between pre-head adjective modifiers and post-head relative clauses, see Bolinger 1967b, and on the relation between PossP and *of* phrase dependents Hawkins (R.) 1981.

---

[12] *My photograph* (but again not *the photograph of me*) can also be construed possessively, "the photograph I have, the one that is mine". 'Possession' is to be understood in a rather broad sense – for example, the photograph might simply have been temporarily assigned to me in some situation where a group of people each have to describe, talk about, enlarge or whatever some photograph: thus the specific interpretation depends very heavily on the context.

7
Pronouns

7.1   Types and distinctive properties of pronouns

Traditional grammar has a number of different subclasses of pronoun: we will be looking at them in turn later in the chapter, but it will be helpful to begin by identifying at least their central members:

(1)   Personal pronouns: *I, me; we, us; you; he, him; she, her; it; they, them*

(2)   Reflexive pronouns: *myself, ourselves, yourself, yourselves, himself, herself, itself, themselves*

(3)   Possessive pronouns: *my, mine; our, ours; your, yours; his; her, hers; its; their, theirs*

(4)   Demonstrative pronouns: *this, these; that, those*

(5)   Interrogative and relative pronouns: *who, whom, whose, what, which,* together with compounds in *-ever – whoever,* etc.

(6)   Indefinite pronouns: *anybody, anyone, anything; somebody, someone, something; everybody, everyone, everything; nobody, no one, nothing; none*

Pronouns, we have said, are better analysed as a subclass of nouns than as a separate part of speech. We analyse them as nouns because the phrases they head are like those headed by common or proper nouns in terms of their functional potential and, though to a lesser degree, their internal structure. Functionally, pronoun-headed phrases are like other NPs in that they occur as subject, object, complement of a preposition, and so on: *Everybody left; John criticises everybody; The change will be of benefit to everybody.* There are, it is true, some differences in functional potential. A handful of pronouns have contrasting case-forms (*I* vs *me,* etc.), such that nominative forms like *I* and *he* don't occur as object or complement of a preposition, and accusative forms like *me* and *him* do not occur as subject, at least in kernel clauses. And reflexive pronouns like *myself* similarly do not have the full range of NP functions. But these differences are quite minor in comparison with the likenesses, and in any case involve only a subset of the pronouns. As for the internal structure of pronoun-headed phrases, pronouns are more restricted than other nouns with respect to the dependents they take (and some, such as the reflexives, do not allow any at all) – but such dependents as we do find are of the same kind as occur with common or proper nouns. Most significantly perhaps, a considerable number of the

272

pronouns take restrictive relative clause modifiers: *everything that he could find, that which he gave her, those who know his work, we who survived the ordeal* – such clauses are not found as dependents to verbs or adjectives. Some pronouns take AdjP modifiers, which is also noun-like, but with a few exceptions like *poor old you* they are limited to post-head position: *someone fond of children, something terrible. Fond of children* would follow a common noun, but *terrible* would not: the compounding of *some* and *thing* makes it impossible for it to occupy its normal pre-head position. Other dependents found with certain pronouns are PPs: *someone with talent, who among you* [*is willing to help?*] – in this too they are like other nouns, though less distinctively so since PPs function as dependent to a wide range of words. The pronouns constitute a closed class and as such it is only to be expected that there should be various restrictions and peculiarities concerning their distribution (mainly applying to individual pronouns or subsets of them, rather than to the class as a whole), but there is no reason to allow these to outweigh in our classification the more general properties that they share with ordinary nouns.

We have noted that pronouns permit a considerably narrower range of dependents than other nouns. It is on this basis that, at the language-particular level, we will define pronouns as a syntactically distinct subclass of nouns. In particular, they do not combine with position II and III determiners: **the he, *a who, *this/these everybody*, and so on.[1] Most pronouns, indeed, cannot occur with determiners at all, but the demonstratives **this** and **that** allow such position I determiners as *all* and *both*, as in *All this will be yours one day* – and *all* is for many speakers also able to combine with at least one personal pronoun, *you*, as in *all you over there* (though probably only when there is a post-head dependent like *over there*).

With some pronouns, the failure to take a determiner results from the fact that the pronoun is a compound of a noun stem and a determinative stem: *everybody, someone, nothing*, etc. Syntactically these differ from the two-word sequences *every body*, etc., in that only in the latter may the two parts be separated by other dependents of the head: compare *Every other body* [*was buried*] and *Everybody else* [*agreed*]; there are also, of course, semantic differences, with the meaning of the compounds not fully predictable from that of the individual stems. With other pronouns we do not have any morphological combination of determinative plus noun, but certain marked

---

[1] Examples like *He's a nobody* do not invalidate our criterion for pronouns, for this *nobody* is a common noun: it differs from the pronoun of *Nobody saw him*, etc., not just in taking a determiner but also in its inflectional number contrast (cf. *They are both nobodies*) – and in its meaning ("person of no significance"). Similarly for *somebody* and *nothing/something* (*They whispered sweet nothings to each other, I've brought a little something for the baby*) – and for *he* and *she*, as in *Is it a he or a she?*, where the common nouns **he** and **she** inflect for number (*hes, shes*), not case.

NP categories that with other nouns are indicated by a determiner of the relevant kind are here indicated directly by the pronoun itself. Thus interrogative *who* may be compared to *what person*, while the personal pronouns **I**, **you**, **he**, etc., have the property of definiteness elsewhere expressed by the definite article, so that **he** (in its most frequent use) may be analysed semantically as "the male one", and so on. Proper nouns like **Mary** are also inherently definite when used as proper names (*Mary is here*), but as we observed in 6.2, they also have other uses where they can combine with determiners (*We could do with another Mary*), so that in spite of certain resemblances they are syntactically distinguishable from pronouns by this criterion.

7.2 **Pronouns, anaphora and deixis**

The traditional definition of a pronoun is that it is 'a word used instead of a noun'. We argued in 3.1 that this is quite unsatisfactory as a language-particular definition of pronouns for English – and it is clear that a very significant proportion of the words in (1)–(6) cannot reasonably be held to satisfy it. Nevertheless there can be no doubt that something along the lines of the traditional criterion should figure prominently in a general definition of pronouns. Let us therefore see whether we can make the traditional idea more precise.

It will be helpful to begin with the most elementary type of example, as in

(7)   *The Empress hasn't arrived yet but she should be here any minute*

The most natural interpretation of the second clause is "but the Empress should be here any minute", so that it is not unreasonable to think of the pronoun *she* as being used instead of repeating *the Empress*. Note, however, that given our conception of constituent structure and our distinction between nouns and noun phrases, we would want to say, if we are to use this kind of formulation at all, that the pronoun *she* is here used instead of an NP, not a noun.

We will say that (in the interpretation we are concerned with) *the Empress*, as it occurs in the first clause, is the **antecedent** of *she* in the second. Traditional grammars tend to say that a pronoun 'refers' to its antecedent, but that is clearly a quite different sense of **refer** from that which we have adopted: the relation between *she* and its antecedent (the NP *the Empress*) is not to be confused with that between *she* and its referent (the Empress – a person, not a linguistic form). Instead we will draw on another traditional term and say that *she* is **anaphoric** to *the Empress*; **anaphora** is then the name for the relation between *she* and *the Empress*, and extending the terminology one step further we will say that *she*, as used here, is an **anaphor**. One important component of a general definition of pronouns can now be formulated as follows: the pronoun class will include among its most central members words which are characteristically used as anaphors to NP antecedents. I say 'characteristically used' because in general those pronouns which can be used anaphorically at all are not invariably so used. Suppose, for example, we are watching a circus act in which some woman is walking a tightrope – I might then say, without there having been any previous mention of the woman,

(8)   *She looks remarkably old for a tightrope-walker*

In this case *she* is not being used anaphorically: the context is such that the referent can be picked out simply from the sense of *she* without the need of further information deriving from an antecedent NP. In (7), by contrast, the interpretation of *she* as referring to the Empress is dependent upon the LINGUISTIC context – if the first clause had been *the Queen hasn't arrived yet* then the *she* would have been interpreted differently.

   Anaphora is an important relation with a considerable variety of manifestations: there are numerous different kinds besides the elementary one exemplified in (7). We cannot give a systematic account of it here – instead we will take (7) as our starting-point and show how a number of specific properties of it are not criterial for anaphora in general: this will enable us to give some indication of its scope at the same time as we attempt to clarify what is essential to it.

(a) The first inessential property of (7) is that the anaphor is a pronoun and the antecedent an NP: the same relation can hold between forms of other classes. Consider, for example,

(9)   *Sue sang the aria more movingly than she had ever done before*

Here the interpretation of *done* as "sung the aria" is determined by its anaphoric relation to its antecedent in the superordinate clause, just as that of *she* is determined by its anaphoric relation to *Sue*. (9) illustrates what in 4.4 we called the 'substitute' use of **do**: with the terminology now introduced we can speak instead of anaphoric **do**. Similarly *there* and *then* are used as anaphors in examples like *I'm not going to London this year because I went there last year* (with *there* interpreted as "to London") and *He's coming on Tuesday but I doubt whether I shall still be in Brisbane then* (with *then* interpreted as "on Tuesday"). Note that **do** is a verb, *there* and *then* adverbs, so that the anaphor class in part cuts across the main part-of-speech classification. And this is in fact another reason for dissatisfaction with the traditional analysis of pronouns as a primary word-class. Why should nominal anaphors be treated so differently from verbal and adverbial ones? If the anaphoric status of **do** and *there* does not prevent their classification as verb and adverb respectively, why should that of **she** prevent its classification as a noun?

A less obvious example of an anaphor that is not a pronoun is *one*, as used in

(10)   *You'd better get a tin of paint because this one is nearly empty.*

Unlike the items in (1)–(6), *one* can combine with determiners, as we see from this example. Given that the potential for use as an anaphor is not part of the language-particular definition of pronouns in English but that incompatibility with determiners is, it would be inconsistent to classify *one* as a pronoun. There are, moreover, two other respects in which it differs from pronouns like *it*. In the first place it inflects for number, with singular *one* contrasting with plural *ones*: this is not in general a property of pronouns, for *it* and *they*, say, are not forms of the same lexeme (see §4 below). And in the second place the antecedent of this *one* is always less than a whole NP: in (10), for example, the antecedent of *one* is simply *tin of paint* not the whole NP *a tin of paint*.

One last word-sized anaphor we should mention is *so*, as in

(11)   *I don't know whether Jill will be here, but I very much hope so*

where the interpretation of *so* as "that Jill will be here" is clearly determined by its anaphoric relation to the clause functioning as complement to *know*. It is very doubtful whether *so*, as used in such examples, can be properly assigned to any of our part-of-speech classes. In particular, we shall hardly want to include it among the pronouns, for this would imply that it functions as head of an NP, whereas its distribution is significantly different from an NP: it cannot function as subject or as complement to a preposition, for example, and in (11) it is in paradigmatic contrast with clauses, not NPs. Like the infinitival *to* of *I want to go*, etc., *so* differs from the clear members of all our primary word-classes to such an extent that it seems pointless to include it in the classification: it requires ad hoc description.

In referring to 'word-sized' anaphors in the last paragraph I implied that there are other kinds. In an utterance of an example like

(12)   *Three men and a woman got on the bus at the traffic lights, but the woman got off again at the next stop*

we will understand *the woman* to refer to the woman mentioned in the first clause. The relation between *the woman* and *a woman* is thus the same in relevant respects as that between *she* and *the Empress* in (7) and can accordingly be subsumed under our concept of anaphora, with the whole NP *the woman* being the anaphor. The referential interpretation of *the woman* depends on its anaphoric relation to its antecedent *a woman* just as that of *she* in (7) depends on its anaphoric relation to *the Empress*.

Finally, **ellipsis** too may be anaphoric, as in

(13)   *Ed advised me to sell my shares but I don't want to*

where *I don't want to* is structurally incomplete, hence elliptical. Again the interpretation "I don't want to sell my shares" is determined anaphorically, with *sell my shares* in the first clause being the antecedent. Whether we should treat the elliptical construction *don't want to* as the anaphor or talk instead of a 'null' or 'zero' anaphor (as many writers do) is a question we will not pursue at this stage.

(b) A second property of (7) and of the other examples we have given that is clearly not criterial for anaphora in general is that antecedent and anaphor are in the same sentence. All the examples given could be replaced by ones where the same anaphoric relation holds across a sentence boundary. Instead of (7), we might have

(14)   ⟨A⟩ *Has the Empress arrived yet?*
             ⟨B⟩ *No, but she should be here any minute now*

and so on. This is not to say that all kinds of anaphoric relations are free to cross sentence boundaries: a minority are more limited. The antecedent for a reflexive pronoun like *himself*, for example, must normally be within the same clause (at least in most dialects), so that in (14), for example, B could not reply to A's question with **I haven't seen herself.* Similarly in the restrictive relative clause construction of *the necklace which Elvis had given her* and the like, the antecedent for the pronoun *which* must obviously be within the NP containing the relative clause.

(c) We have noted that *she*, whose anaphoric use is illustrated in (7), can also be used non-anaphorically, as in (8). The same holds for most kinds of potential anaphor – but not for all. There is some correlation between this property and the last, inasmuch as items which cannot derive their interpretation from an antecedent in a preceding sentence cannot derive their interpretation non-anaphorically. But it is not a perfect correlation: it may be that the antecedent can be in a preceding sentence, but that nevertheless an antecedent is always required. This applies to the *so* of (11), for example. In (14) B could reply to A's question with *I hope so*, with the antecedent to *so* being in the preceding sentence, but the interpretation of *so* must be derivable from some actually expressed proposition.

(d) A further property of (7) that does not hold for all cases of anaphora is that the antecedent precedes the anaphor. Etymologically, both 'antecedent' and 'anaphora' do imply that the antecedent comes first, but we will follow the practice of the many writers who generalise the terms to cover cases where the order is reversed, as in

(15)   *As soon as he realised what had happened, John phoned his solicitor*

with *he* interpreted as referring to John by virtue of its anaphoric relation to its antecedent *John*. The order antecedent + anaphor is vastly more frequent than the reverse, which is subject to rather restrictive conditions, so that the two orders may be distinguished as 'unmarked' and 'marked ' respectively. With some kinds of anaphor, only the unmarked order is possible. For example *so*, as used in (11), requires a preceding antecedent – we cannot say *If you hope so, I'll tell Liz* with *so* deriving its interpretation from the following *I'll tell Liz*. Furthermore, with anaphors that do allow the marked order, it is normally possible only under a much narrower range of structural conditions than the unmarked order. As a rough first approximation, we can say that the anaphor may precede its antecedent only if it is in a clause subordinate to the one containing the antecedent. Thus in (15) the clause containing *he* is subordinate to that containing *John*, but in *He phoned his solicitor as soon as John realised what had happened* it is not and thus *he* cannot be interpreted as anaphoric to *John*. With the unmarked order, antecedent + anaphor, by contrast, *he* can be anaphoric to *John* in either (16i) or (ii):

(16)   i *As soon as John realised what had happened, he phoned his solicitor*
          ii *John phoned his solicitor as soon as he realised what had happened*

Notice, moreover, that even where we do have the marked order, as in (15), it will very often be that the referent of the pronoun has been mentioned earlier in the discourse.

(e) In (a normal utterance of) (7) both the antecedent *the Empress* and the anaphor *she* will be used as referring expressions, and they will of course have the same referent (the Empress): they will be, as we shall say, **co-referential**. But again co-reference between antecedent and anaphor is not an essential property of anaphora in general. Clearly the issue of co-reference can arise only when both terms in the anaphoric relation are used referringly, and in many cases of anaphora one or both terms are not so used. In *Liz ran faster than she had ever done before*, for example, neither the antecedent *ran* nor the anaphor *done* (or, perhaps we should identify them as **run** and **do** respectively) refers: we would say, rather, that they express the same predicate. Similarly in (10), neither the antecedent *tin of paint* nor the anaphor *one* is a referring expression. (The whole NP *this one* that contains the anaphor is, but it so happens in this example that the NP containing the antecedent, i.e. *a tin of paint*, is not, because it is non-specific in the sense of 6.7; in *Pass me that tin of paint, this one is empty* both *that tin of paint* and *this one* would refer, but not of course to the same thing.) A third example where the conditions for co-reference are not satisfied is to be found in one interpretation of

(17)   *Nobody would admit that they/he had heard anything unusual*

This could be used with *they/he* having an antecedent in a preceding sentence (in which case there would be co-reference), but the more salient interpretation is that where the antecedent is *nobody*, and in this case neither antecedent nor anaphor refers. The anaphor *they/he* here serves as a 'variable' such as we spoke of in our discussion of example (70) in 5.6: the meaning can be given informally as "There is no person x such that x would admit that x had heard anything unusual".

Although antecedent and anaphor can be co-referential only if both refer, the issue of identical reference also arises when the antecedent contains a referring expression within it. In (9), for example, the antecedent **sing** *the aria* is not itself a referring expression (it expresses a semantic predicate), but it contains within it the NP *the aria*, which is. And when we interpret the anaphor **do** as "sing the aria" it is of course the same aria. **Do** is not a referring expression and unlike its antecedent does not contain one, but in such cases we must surely be allowed to speak of 'implicit' reference. Similarly in (11): *so* does not refer but there is implicit reference to the same Jill as is referred to within the antecedent *Jill will be here*. A full study of anaphora must accordingly investigate the conditions under which there is identity of reference – and this of course cannot be undertaken except in the context of a study of reference in general.

(f) In (7) it would be possible – though somewhat clumsy and unnatural – to replace the anaphor by a repetition of its antecedent, giving *The Empress hasn't arrived yet but the Empress should be here any minute*: it was this property of the example that we related to the traditional formulation wherein a pronoun is 'used instead of' a noun (or NP, as we would put it). It will be evident that this too is not an essential property of anaphora. One quite general case where it fails to apply is illustrated in

(18)   ⟨A⟩ *Has your father arrived?*
         ⟨B⟩ *Yes, he's downstairs*

The antecedent for *he* is *your father* but because of the change of speaker the pronoun is equivalent to *my father* – and this phenomenon can arise with all kinds of anaphora that involve explicit or implicit reference and cross boundaries. A second, less obvious case is found in

(19)   *If the boss finds out, she will be furious*

(in the interpretation where *she* is anaphoric to *the boss*). Although *she* will here be co-referential with *the boss* it encodes information about the sex of the referent which the antecedent does not: replacing it by a copy of the antecedent would thus involve some loss of meaning. Similarly in (12) the anaphor is definite while the antecedent is indefinite; if we substituted *a woman* for *the woman* the meaning would be changed – the implication of co-reference would be lost. A third case is to be found in (17), where replacement of *they* or *he* by *nobody* would result in a very clear change of meaning. The same will hold for all constructions where the pronoun is used as a 'variable' in this way – compare *Both candidates expected that they would impress the panel* where *they* is not replaceable by *both candidates* (at least not in the interpretation "x expected that x would impress the panel, for each of the two candidates"). Various other cases could be added, but enough has been said to demonstrate that we cannot accept any general analysis of anaphora in which a clause containing an anaphor is necessarily non-kernel, deriving from a more basic clause by the transformational substitution of the anaphor for a copy of the antecedent – e.g. in which the second clause in (7) is transformationally derived from [*The Empress hasn't arrived yet*] *but the Empress should be here any minute*. Whether this form of analysis can be justified for any kinds of anaphora is a question we cannot go into here: it is sufficient for present purposes to see that it is not valid for all kinds – and in particular not for personal pronouns.

All the examples of anaphora that we have given are clear and central instances of the phenomenon. What they have in common is the presence of two expressions such that the interpretation of one, the anaphor, derives from that of the other, the antecedent. Anaphors belong to that class of expressions whose interpretation is 'context-dependent' rather than being fully determined by their lexical and grammatical properties. In any normal utterance of *but she should be here any minute* the pronoun *she* will be interpreted as referring to some female (or to some ship, or the like) – but which female (or ship, etc.) it is will depend on the context of the particular utterance. And with anaphors, this contextual determination of the interpretation derives from an antecedent expression. Notice that determining whether *she* refers on some particular occasion to the Empress Catherine, to Queen Elizabeth or whoever it might be is not a matter of resolving any ambiguity in **she**. The phenomenon we are concerned with is thus quite different from that exemplified in, say, *Just as the bowler was about to begin his run, Chappell left the crease and prodded the pitch with his bat*, where the context would lead us to interpret **bat** as "club for hitting the ball" rather than "person who bats" – or "nocturnal flying animal". **Bat** is certainly not an anaphor. The difference is that **bat** is ambiguous: a dictionary will list these as different meanings of **bat** – more precisely the first two as different senses of the polysemous **bat**^{2} and the third as a sense of **bat**^{1} (see 3.2) – but it will not of course give "the Empress Catherine", "Queen Elizabeth" and so on as different meanings of **she**. Anaphorically-determined interpretation is thus not a matter of resolving ambiguity (attributable to homonymy or polysemy) but of filling in various aspects of the interpretation of an expression that are simply not given in the lexical and grammatical description of the language itself. In (7) it is a matter of determining the reference of *she*, in (9) of determining the set over which the variable expressed by *they/he* 'ranges', and so on.

The account just given, although it might reasonably be held to cover the central cases, is still too restrictive for anaphora in general. One fairly minor extension is needed to allow for an anaphor to have 'multiple antecedents', as in

(20)   *Ed discussed with Jill the proposal that had just been put to them*

This allows an interpretation of *them* as referring to Ed and Jill, hence as anaphoric to *Ed* and *Jill* jointly.

A trickier case is exemplified in

(21)   *I haven't got a car myself but Tom has, and I think I'll be able to persuade him to let us borrow it*

The natural interpretation of *it* here is that it refers to Tom's car. It cannot be said to derive this interpretation from the NP *a car* in the first clause, for the latter NP does not refer to Tom's car (or indeed to any car). The interpretation of *it* is dependent on the prior interpretation of the elliptical *Tom has*: we take this to mean "Tom has a car" and *it* is then interpreted as referring to that car. In contrast with such NPs as *the picture hanging over the fireplace in Uncle Harry's dining-room*, pronouns like *she* and *it* have such general meanings that they can be used to pick out successfully an intended referent only when the latter is of a high degree of salience in the context of discourse: I will hardly be able to get my addressee to interpret *I quite like it* as "I quite like the picture hanging over the fireplace in Uncle Harry's dining-room" unless the picture is actually present or has been explicitly or implicitly referred to in the closely preceding text. (21) is then like (7) in that the salience of the pronoun's referent results from its having been introduced into the context of discourse in the immediately preceding text: for this reason most analysts would take *it* in (21) as anaphoric. The difference is that in (21) the referent is introduced into the context of discourse without being overtly referred to, so that there is nothing that can be identified, strictly, as its antecedent – it is this that puts it outside the central or prototypical cases of anaphora.

Another non-prototypical case is found in

(22)   ⟨A⟩ *How's the baby?*
            ⟨B⟩ *Oh, she's been crying a good deal recently*
            ⟨A⟩ *Well, they often do, you know*

with the interpretation of *they* as "babies" made possible by the fact that it is an easy and frequent step to move from talking about the particular to talking about the general. But it is questionable how far it is proper to talk of *the baby* as the 'antecedent' of *they* – especially in view of the fact that the particular baby could have been referred to by name or, if present in the context, by the pronoun *she*. Such examples are by no means uncommon; they show that there is no sharp boundary between anaphoric and non-anaphoric uses of the personal pronouns.

Although not all anaphors are pronouns and not all pronouns have anaphoric uses, anaphora is, we have suggested, relevant to a general definition of pronouns – among the central members of the pronoun class will be found those words which characteristically stand in an anaphoric relation to an NP antecedent. But there is another important component of the general definition: the pronoun class will also include among its central members words which are used **deictically**.

We say that an expression is used deictically when its interpretation is determined in relation to certain features of the utterance-act: the identity of those participating as speaker and addressee together with the time and place at which it occurs. Take, for example, an utterance of

(23)   *I want to know why you are here*

Clearly the referents of *I* and *you* are respectively whoever is uttering the sentence and whoever is being addressed: if Tom Smith utters (23), *I* refers to Tom Smith, if Sue Jones utters it, *I* refers to Sue Jones, and so on. Similarly the referential interpretation of *here* is determined by where the utterance takes place, and the time of the wanting and of your being here is determined by the time of the utterance. We accordingly say that *I*, *you*, *here* and the tense are deictic elements.

Among the most obvious deictic elements are the personal pronouns **I**, **we**, **you** and their reflexive and possessive counterparts; the demonstratives **this** and **that**; the locatives *here* and *there*; the inflectional category of tense and a variety of temporal expressions such as *now, then, today, tomorrow, yesterday, last week, next month*, including PPs like *on Tuesday*, adverbs like *soon* and phrases ending in *ago*. Thus in *He's arriving on Tuesday* the reference of *Tuesday* is determined in relation to the day on which the utterance takes place – the first Tuesday after that day (but the last Tuesday before that day in *He arrived on Tuesday*): note the contrast between deictic *on Tuesday* and non-deictic *on the Tuesday*, as in *I'm giving my paper on the Tuesday*, where the reference is to the Tuesday of the period being talked about (the period of some conference, say) rather than to some Tuesday identifiable by its relation to today. Definite NPs with *the*, such as *the door*, can also be used deictically: in *Please open the door* the reference will normally be to the door that is present in the situation of utterance (see the discussion of definiteness in 6.7).

Just as with anaphora we saw that very often a single form can be used now anaphorically, now non-anaphorically, so with deixis we find that some forms have both deictic and non-deictic uses. For example, *soon* is used deictically in *They'll be here soon* but non-deictically in *He soon discovered his error*: *soon* means roughly "within a short time period after T", with T being the time of utterance in the deictic use but some other, contextually-determined time in the non-deictic use. Similarly it will be clear from our discussion of tense in 4.5 that the past tense is sometimes interpreted deictically, sometimes non-deictically: in *Kim said that the match started tomorrow*, for example, the past tense accompanying **say** is deictic in that it locates the time of Kim's saying relative to the time of my utterance, while the past tense accompanying **start** is non-deictic for it does not relate the time of starting to that of my utterance. Or again, while *the door* is interpreted deictically in the above *Please open the door*, it is interpreted non-deictically in *When Tom finally reached her house, he found that the door was locked*. And finally it will now be clear that while the *she* of (7) is anaphoric, not deictic, the non-anaphoric *she* of (8) is, more specifically, deictic, for it is interpreted as referring to a female present and salient in the situation of utterance.[2]

Anaphora and deixis are related not only in that a single form can, like **she**, be used now anaphorically, now deictically – we also find uses that are simultaneously anaphoric and deictic:

(24)   *Max came to Australia when he was five, and has lived here ever since*
(25)   *Sue's coming in today – we're having lunch together*

In (24) *here* is deictic in that it refers to the place where the utterance occurs but at the same time it is anaphoric to *Australia*, which determines the reference more explicitly. In (25) *we* will be interpreted as referring to a group consisting of the speaker and Sue: the inclusion of the speaker is determined by the deictic component in the meaning of **we**, while that of Sue is determined anaphorically.

I began this section by quoting the traditional definition of a pronoun as a word used instead of a noun. The idea of one form being used instead of another is a somewhat nebulous one and can be discarded in favour of the clearer concepts of anaphora and deixis: the core of the pronoun class will consist of those nouns which are generally used anaphorically and/or deictically. Some pronouns – the interrogative and negative pronouns and the negative indefinites (*nobody, nothing*, etc.) – are restricted to non-kernel

---

[2] It should not be assumed, however, that in its non-anaphoric use a pronoun like **he** or **she** can refer only to someone present in the situation. I could perfectly well come home from work and say something like *Did he get away on time this morning?* referring to someone neither previously mentioned in the discourse nor present in the situation: it might be my father, say, who had been visiting, so that he and his departure would be sufficiently salient in the day's events for me to be able to refer to him simply by means of *he*. It is questionable whether the concept of deixis should be extended to embrace such uses.

clauses of one kind or another, but the rest are not: it will be clear from what has been said here that we shall not want to regard the inclusion of a pronoun within a clause as itself an indication of non-kernel status.

7.3 Pronouns and ellipsis

We have seen that it is not only pronouns that may be interpreted anaphorically: in particular, elliptical constructions may be. Let us therefore compare examples like

(26) i *Max took the large dish. He filled it with fruit salad*
      ii *Max took the large dish, Ed the small*

In (i), *he* and *it* will normally be interpreted anaphorically as referring to Max and the large dish respectively, while in (ii) *Ed the small* will be interpreted anaphorically as "Ed took the small dish". The difference is that *He filled it with fruit salad* is structurally complete (it is in fact a kernel clause), while *Ed the small* is not – it is precisely for that reason that we say it is elliptical. More specifically, there is ellipsis of the predicator of the clause and of the head of the NP object.

The analysis of elliptical constructions is derivative from that of corresponding non-elliptical ones. Thus in (26ii) *Ed* is subject and *the small* object in clause structure, and *the* is determiner, *small* modifier in NP structure. We would have no more reason for analysing *small* as head of the NP than for analysing *the small* as head (i.e. predicator) of the clause.

There are many different kinds of elliptical construction, depending on what elements are omitted, on the conditions under which the ellipsis is permitted, on whether the interpretation is determined anaphorically, non-anaphorically or in either way. Our interest here, however, lies not in ellipsis for its own sake but in the problem of distinguishing an NP with ellipsis of the head from one with a pronoun as head. *The small* in (26ii) is a very clear example of ellipsis. We do not want to take *small* as a pronoun here: that would imply a lexical treatment, with the lexical entry for **small** assigning it to the pronoun as well as the adjective class, an unsatisfactory analysis given the generality of the phenomenon – virtually any adjective could occur in the position of *small* in this kind of construction. Conversely, *he* and *it* in (26i) are very clear examples of NPs that ARE pronominal, not elliptical. In between these extremes, however, are others where the analysis is not so obvious. Consider first

(27)   *Ed had hardly any friends, whereas Max had many*

Many here would traditionally be analysed as a pronoun, but we might alternatively say that the final NP is elliptical, with no head and *many* a determinative functioning as determiner, just as it does in the non-elliptical *many friends*.

One significant but not insurmountable problem for an analysis which denies pronominal status to *many* is that it occurs in the **partitive** construction, as in *many of the boys*. The partitive construction has the form '*X of Y*', where *Y* indicates the set of individuated entities or the mass of substance (cf. *much of the paintwork*) from which *X* is selected. How shall we analyse NPs like *many of the boys*? The most obvious solution is to take *many* as head, *of the boys* as complement, and then to say that by virtue of its function *many* is here a noun (more particularly, a pronoun). However, the word before partitive *of* is certainly not necessarily a noun, for again we find what are clearly adjectives in this position: *the more important of these objections, the best of her novels*. The fact that we could have just about any 'gradable' adjective here and that such adjectives enter into the comparative and superlative constructions (whether synthetic, as with *best*, or analytic, as with *more important*) rules out a lexical treatment involving dual class membership. Yet we will not want to say that the adjective is functioning as head of an NP, for a phrase with an adjective as head is an adjective phrase: this follows from our general understanding of the concept 'head'. The remaining possibility is to say that *the more important of these objections* is elliptical, with the head element missing. This is probably the best solution, but it involves some stretching of the concept of ellipsis. In the standard case of ellipsis we can reinstate the missing element(s) without loss of acceptability – as we could insert *friends* after *many* in (27). In the present case, however, it is questionable whether this can be done: the only serious candidate for insertion is **one** (in either singular or plural form, for note that *the more important of these objections* can be interpreted as referring to a single objection or to a set of objections), but a phrase like *the more important ones of these objections* seems quite unnatural. With *many*, insertion of *ones* is less acceptable still: there can be little doubt that *many ones of the boys* should be treated as ungrammatical.

Before leaving the partitive construction, we should note that there may be ellipsis of the *of* PP. In *He made two objections, the more important being that it was dangerous*, the NP *the more important* is implicitly partitive, being equivalent to *the more important of them*. Similarly we may contrast (27) with (28):

(28)   *He found nearly a hundred stamps but many were torn*

In (28) *many* is understood partitively ("many of them"), but in (27) it is not ("many friends", not "many of them").

The cases where we have difficulty in drawing the distinction between elliptical head and pronominal head involve a group of items having the potential to function as determiner. To conclude this section we will distinguish four groups of these items: in the first three our problem does not arise or is easily resolved, while the fourth contains the difficult cases like *many*.

(a) Firstly, there are those which occur only with a following head noun (or pre-head modifier): the 'attributive' possessives *my, your*, etc.; *no, the* and *a*. These cannot occur in examples like (27), and consequently the question of distinguishing between ellipted and pronominal head does not arise: cf. **Ed had hardly any friends and Max had no; *John's shirt was brown and my was green.* (We could of course have *none* instead of *no* here, *mine* instead of *my*, but since *none* and *mine* do not function as determiner there is clearly no question of ellipsis in *Max had none*, or *mine was green*.)

(b) A second group consists of possessives based on ordinary nouns, like *the doctor's*. These can occur without a following head, but as they are not word-sized units there is no question of them being pronouns in such cases. In *My car had broken down but fortunately I was able to borrow the doctor's*, it is clear that *the doctor's* is an elliptical NP, equivalent to *the doctor's car*. In *I'll have to take him to the doctor's* there is no anaphora, but it is probably still reasonable to posit ellipsis, with *the doctor's* thus determiner in a headless NP (we understand roughly, "the doctor's surgery or place of work"), though the ellipsis is so conventionalised that it would be artificial to insert a head noun. In *Those are the doctor's* ("Those belong to the doctor"), there is little justification for positing ellipsis, but there is likewise little reason for saying that the complement of *be* is an NP rather than simply a PossP.

(c) *This/these, that/those* and *what* occur without a following head in cases where we shall not want to posit ellipsis: *Look at this!, That is why he resigned, What is it?*. *This* and *that* are here used as referring expressions which are interpreted deictically or anaphorically as full NPs, not as elliptical versions of *this/that X*, with the value of X being given by the context. Similarly *What is it?* is not understood as "What X is it?". We must thus surely allow that **this**, **that** and *what* can be used either as pronouns, as in the examples just given, or as determinatives, as in *This knife is blunt, I've forgotten those wretched letters, What course are you taking?*. This is what we assumed for *what* in 3.2, where we suggested that as there are no inflectional differences involved it is better to posit a single word *what* with different part of speech uses than to have distinct words *what*$_{Pro}$ and *what*$_{Detve}$. And for the same reason we will have just one **this** and one **that**, each assigned in its lexical entry to both pronoun and determinative classes. Notice that the two uses of *what* are further distinguished by the fact that in the pronominal use we have a paradigmatic contrast with *who* (*What is it?* vs *Who is it?*), so that *what* here indicates "non-human" (or at least it usually does – see 11.4 for fuller discussion), whereas in the determinative use there is no equivalent contrast, with *what* functioning as determiner to nouns denoting humans as well as non-humans (e.g. *What car?, What parent?*).

(d) The last group consists of the problem cases: *many, few, much, enough, some, any, several, which,* etc. These are certainly not as clearly pronominal as the items in group (c) above, but the case for dual classification as determinative and pronoun is greater than the case for classification as pronouns as well as adjectives with words like *important*, as in *the more important of the objections* vs *It is very important*, because we need to specify the items found in the various constructions instead of giving a general rule.[3] There are in fact differences among them: for example, although all can occur without a following head noun in the partitive construction (whether it is explicitly or implicitly partitive) and all except *which* occur in anaphoric non-partitives like (27), *many, few, some* differ from *several, any* in that they can be used non-anaphorically in non-partitives, with the interpretation "many people", etc.:

(29)   *Many/ *several would disagree with this judgement*

To this extent *many* is more noun-like than *several*. It is not clear that we can avoid some element of arbitrariness or indeterminacy with respect to the boundary between ellipsis and classification as pronoun. In either case we will take the construction determinative as determiner + noun as head to be in some sense more basic: if we choose the ellipsis analysis we are saying that the noun head is missing, whereas if we choose the pronoun analysis we are saying in effect that the semantic contents of determiner and head are fused within the pronoun, and it is not surprising that it should be difficult to choose between such alternatives.

7.4 Personal, reflexive and possessive pronouns

In this section and the next we will look at the various subclasses of pronoun listed summarily at the beginning of the chapter. We begin with the personal, reflexive and possessive classes, which are closely related inasmuch as the forms can be put in correspondence as shown in (30):

(30)

		Personal		Reflexive	Possessive	
		Nominative	Accusative		Attributive	Absolute
1st person	sg	*I*	*me*	*myself*	*my*	*mine*
	pl	*we*	*us*	*ourselves*	*our*	*ours*
2nd person	sg	*you*		*yourself*	*your*	*yours*
	pl			*yourselves*		
3rd person	sg	*he*	*him*	*himself*	*his*	
		she	*her*	*herself*	*her*	*hers*
		it		*itself*	*its*	
	pl	*they*	*them*	*themselves*	*their*	*theirs*

[3] The 'cardinal numerals' *one, two, three*, etc. will be treated like *important*, for here the phenomenon is completely general: all occur both with and without a following head noun (*four men* vs *Four were killed*).

Let us examine in turn the various categories that figure in this classification.

(a) Person. This is a deictic category: the referential interpretation of the two marked terms in the system, 1st person and 2nd person, is determined wholly or partially in relation to the speaker/writer and the addressee(s) of the utterance act. Normally, the 1st person forms refer to the speaker/writer, while the 2nd person refers to the addressee or a group including at least one addressee but no speaker/writer. Note then that the speaker/writer takes precedence over the addressee: if both are involved in the reference, a 1st person form is used; this is one factor that makes the terms '1st', '2nd' (and analogously '3rd') appropriate. I prefaced the above account with 'normally' because two qualifications are needed. In certain restricted contexts such as a doctor speaking to a patient, 1st person *we* can be used to refer to the addressee, thereby expressing some element of 'empathy', of personal involvement. And in the 'generic' use of *you*, as in *You need extraordinarily high qualifications to get admitted to Dunbar College*, it is doubtful whether we should say that there is reference to a group containing the addressee(s): *you* is here a stylistically less formal variant of non-deictic *one* – and could be used with a male addressee even if Dunbar College admitted only females. 3rd person is the semantically unmarked term in the system in that reference to the speaker/writer or addressee is not excluded (though it is rare) – cf. *The writer has to admit that he has not explored all these possibilities*, where *he* could be anaphoric to *the writer* and hence refer to the one performing the utterance-act.

As we have seen, person is involved in subject–verb agreement, and for this reason needs to be recognised as a category of NPs not just of pronouns. But the NP classification is determined by that of the noun head, with all nouns not listed in (30) being 3rd person.

(b) Number. We noted in 6.5 that for nouns in general, number is predominantly an inflectional category. But in the personal pronouns it is not. Thus whereas *book* and *books*, say, are the singular and plural forms of a single lexeme **book**, *I* and *we* (and similarly *me* and *us*, etc.) are forms of different lexemes. There are two reasons for handling pronominal number as non-inflectional. Firstly, the semantic contrast of *we* to *I* is not the same as that of *books* to *book*. *Books* is used for a set containing two or more books, but the meaning of *we* is not "two or more speakers/writers": rather it is applied to a group of two or more individuals at least one of whom is speaker/writer of the utterance containing the form. *We* can be used for a group speaking or writing jointly, but this is quite rare, being found only in chanting (e.g. *We want the Queen*, chanted by a crowd outside Buckingham Palace), petitions (*We the undersigned . . .*), joint letters to the press and the like: usually it is used for a group consisting of a single speaker/writer plus one or more others – me and you, me and him/her, me and them, and so on. (And perhaps we should still allow for the 'royal' – or papal – *we* referring to a single speaker/writer.) The second point is that in the 3rd person we have differentiation in the singular between *he, she* and *it* (and *him, her, it*, etc.) but only *they* in the plural: *they* can apply to a group the individual members of which would be referred to by means of different singular pronouns, so that plural *they* clearly does not have a singular counterpart.

(c) Gender. **He**, **she** and *it* are commonly classified as respectively 'masculine', 'feminine' and 'neuter', the three terms in a system of **gender**. Gender is, however, a category of very minor significance in English in comparison with, for example, familiar European languages. As a general linguistic category, it figures primarily in the description of languages where there is agreement between some element X and a noun N in respect of the lexical subclass of N (as opposed to agreement in respect of number or case, which are not normally inherent properties of noun lexemes). The agreement may be of two kinds. In the first, X stands in some specific grammatical relation to N, typically dependent to head in NP structure or predicative complement to the subject NP of which N is head. Thus in German we may contrast *eine kleine Nachtmusik* and *ein kleines Nachthemd*, where *eine* and *ein, kleine* and *kleines* are respectively feminine and neuter forms of **ein** "a" and **klein** "small, little", selected in agreement with the lexically inherent properties of **Nachtmusik** (feminine) "serenade" and **Nachthemd** (neuter) "nightshirt". In the second kind of agreement, X is a pronoun and N is head of the NP to which X is anaphoric – for example in German the feminine personal pronoun **sie** and the neuter **es** would be used with the above NPs as their respective antecedents. It is clear that English does not have any gender agreement of the first kind: determinatives, adjectives and so on do not inflect for gender. Nor is it appropriate to say that the choice between **he**, **she** and *it*, when they are used anaphorically, is determined by gender agreement with the antecedent. We cannot divide English nouns into three classes, masculine, feminine and neuter, such that **he**, **she** or *it* is required as the corresponding anaphoric pronoun. Rather, the choice between the pronouns is determined semantically, primarily by the properties of the referent and secondarily, to a very limited extent, by the speaker's attitude to the referent. Typically, **he** is used of males, **she** of females and *it* elsewhere, but we need to add several qualifications to this initial account.

In the first place, *it* can be used for male or female animals and human infants. This is the area where it is the speaker's attitude, rather than the properties of the referent, that determines the choice between *it* on the one hand, **he** or **she** on the other. One is unlikely, for example, to use *it* for one's own baby or pet cat. **He/she** suggest that the speaker regards the referent as having, as it were, a personality, while *it*, which doesn't encode information about sex, distances the speaker more from the referent.

Secondly, **she** is commonly used of ships and – mainly by male speakers – of various other kinds of inanimates (e.g. *She's about to fall*, said by someone felling a tree). This can reasonably be regarded as a non-literal use of **she**, a kind of personification.

Thirdly, **he** is used by many speakers as a 'variable' ranging over a set containing both males and females (normally human), as in the example given in 3.4: *If any student wishes to take part in the seminar, he should consult his tutor*. The semantic distinction male vs female is here neutralised, and the fact that **he** is used makes it the semantically unmarked member of the pair **he/she**.[4] As we noted earlier, **they** has long been used as an alternative to **he** in this sense.

It will be clear, then, that in a typical example like (19) above – *If the boss finds out, she will be furious* with *she* interpreted as anaphoric to *the boss* – we should not say that *she* agrees in gender with *boss*. The NP *the boss* can be used to refer to a man or to a woman because **boss** does not encode any information about sex: it just happens that in the particular context of our example the speaker is using it to refer to a woman, and it is that non-syntactic fact that determines the selection of *she* rather than *he*. The most we can say is that the pronoun and antecedent must not encode incompatible properties: *The king had taken her own life* is anomalous because *king* and *her* encode the mutually incompatible properties male and female. But it is arguable that the anomaly should be regarded as a matter of semantic inconsistency (attributing incompatible properties to a single entity) rather than as a violation of a syntactic rule. There will then be no grammatical rule of gender agreement in English, and no grammatical category of gender applying to ordinary nouns.

(d) Case. The distinction between lexemes and inflectional forms is considerably more difficult to apply to the closed class of pronouns than to the open classes of ordinary nouns, verbs or adjectives, where we have systematic correspondence over large sets of forms. The clearest example of an inflectional category in pronouns is case, with nominative *I* and accusative *me* being forms of a single lexeme. The syntactic rules specify when the pronoun may or must appear in one or other case, and the morphology specifies the form – though we cannot give any worthwhile rules for deriving the forms: we must simply list them. We will not attempt here a detailed description of the uses of the cases: it is sufficient to give a simplified account whereby the nominative is used when the pronoun is subject of a tensed clause (or, more generally, of a finite clause – see 5.6),

[4] One change that has taken place in the last few years is that some speakers have consciously reversed the semantic marking in the cause of feminism, and use **she** rather than **he**.

and under certain, mainly stylistic conditions, when it is functioning as subjective predicative complement (see 5.2); elsewhere the pronoun takes the accusative form.

(e) The reflexive pronouns. These are traditionally presented separately from the personal pronouns, but the highly regular and systematic relation between the two sets makes it very reasonable to treat reflexive as an inflectional property, with *myself* the reflexive form of *I*, and so on.[5] Two uses of the reflexive pronouns may be distinguished:

In the first, they function as complement in clause or PP structure: *You underestimate yourself; I didn't do myself justice; John voted for himself.* Here the reflexive is normally in contrast with a non-reflexive form, or indeed a non-pronominal NP (cf. *I didn't do him justice; John voted for Fraser*), although a few verbs require that a complement be reflexive – I can 'perjure' myself but I cannot perjure you or my boss, I can 'pride' myself on my spaghetti, but not my wife on hers, and so on. Notice, however, that even where the reflexive pronoun is in paradigmatic contrast with a non-reflexive NP there is reason to doubt whether it is used in a straightforwardly referential way. This may be seen from a comparison of

(31) i *Tom despised the boss; Ed did, too*
      ii *Tom despised himself; Ed did, too*

In both, the interpretation of the second clause is determined anaphorically, with the first clause, or part of it, as antecedent. In (i) with *the boss* used referentially, the interpretation is "Ed despised the boss too", with implicit reference to the same boss. But in (ii) the most salient and for many the only possible interpretation is "Ed despised himself too" (as opposed to "Ed despised Tom too"); if *himself* were straightforwardly referential, one would expect implicit reference in the anaphor to its referent. Instead the reflexive can be regarded as serving as what we have been calling a variable: in (ii) the first clause says that "x despised x" holds for x = Tom, while the second says that it holds also for x = Ed.

The second use of the reflexive pronouns is called 'emphatic', as in

(32) i *Tom himself had written the letter*
      ii *Tom had written the letter himself*

In (i) *himself* is in apposition to its antecedent *Tom*, its semantic effect being that of emphasising that it was Tom, not someone else, who had done it. The meaning of (ii) is essentially the same – in particular it does not involve a third argument of the verb **write**. We will regard (i) as the more

---

[5] One complicating factor, however, is that there are contrasting singular and plural forms *yourself* and *yourselves* corresponding to *you*: if reflexive is taken as an inflectional property we shall need distinct lexemes **you**$_{sg}$ and **you**$_{pl}$.

basic construction, allowing then for the optional movement of the apposed reflexive to a later position in the clause.

The two uses may be contrasted in an ambiguous sentence like *Tom had offered them himself*. In the non-emphatic use, where it is equivalent to *Tom had offered himself to them*, the reflexive is direct object and expresses one of the arguments of **offer** (with *Tom* and the indirect object *them* expressing the others). In the emphatic use, where it is equivalent to *Tom himself had offered them*, only two arguments of **offer** are expressed – by the subject *Tom* and the direct object *them*.

The non-emphatic reflexive construction contrasts with the **reciprocal** construction: compare

(33)   i *Tom and Max hurt themselves*
        ii *Tom and Max hurt each other*

In (i) each of Tom and Max hurt himself – "x hurt x, for x = Tom and for x = Max". In (ii), by contrast, each of them hurt the other – we need distinct variables x and y: "x hurt y, for each x–y pair in the set consisting of Tom and Max". It is not easy to decide how *each other* should be analysed syntactically. The strongest evidence for saying that it forms a single constituent, more specifically an NP, is that it can occur as complement to the possessive clitic: *They were criticising each other's proposals*. But it is not a prototypical NP: if it were, examples like *It was only each other that they hurt* or *The only ones they hurt were each other* should be acceptable, but judgements about such examples tend to be variable or uncertain. Assuming that it is an NP, it evidently is not a 'determiner + head' construction like *each book*; the construction is to a significant extent sui generis, and attempts to handle *each other* in terms of more general categories are not likely to be very illuminating; the traditional analysis has *each other* (and similarly *one another*) as a 'reciprocal pronoun'.

Whether we take reflexive to be an inflectional property or not, we need to ask what determines the choice between a reflexive and a non-reflexive pronoun – between *themselves* and *them*, *myself* and *me*, and so on. This is in fact a difficult question, and we can here do no more than take some initial steps towards answering it. We will consider only the non-emphatic uses of the reflexives, for it is only here that there can be contrast between the two sets of pronouns, as in

(34)   i *Tom hurt himself*
        ii *Tom hurt him*
(35)   i *Max said that Tom had hurt himself*
        ii *Max said that Tom had hurt him*

In (34) *himself* is anaphoric to *Tom*, whereas *him* cannot be: assuming that *him* is interpreted anaphorically rather than deictically, its antecedent must be in the preceding text. In (35) we find, similarly, that *himself* can only be anaphoric to *Tom* whereas *him* can be anaphoric to *Max* but not to *Tom*. We might then hypothesise that a reflexive is selected when the antecedent is subject of the clause containing the pronoun. This certainly covers the great majority of examples, but there are some that it doesn't account for, such as

(36)   *Liz had told Tom certain things about himself that he had not expected to hear*

Himself will again be interpreted as anaphoric to *Tom*, but *Tom* is object, not subject, of the **tell** clause. Examples like (36) are commonly cited in support of a modified version of the rule, saying that a reflexive is used when pronoun and antecedent are in the same clause.

This modified version, however, is likewise not without its problems. In the first place, there is reason to doubt whether 'being in the same clause' is quite the right structural relation; we will not pursue that issue here, contenting ourselves with it, for present purposes, as a reasonable approximation. In the second place, it is not clear that the relation in question is in fact to be regarded as holding between pronoun and antecedent. Where the reflexive is 1st or 2nd person, as in

(37)   *I hurt myself*
(38)   *Don't hurt yourself*

should we not say, in the light of our discussion in §2 above, that the pronouns are interpreted deictically rather than anaphorically? (And note in passing that these differ further from (34) and (35) in that the reflexives are not here grammatically replaceable by their non-reflexive counterparts: **I hurt me, *Don't hurt you.*) (38) has no subject expressed; there is of course an understood subject-argument representing the addressee, but to call this the 'antecedent' of *yourself* is certainly to stretch the concept of antecedent to a considerable distance from the prototype. We have suggested that a reflexive pronoun is interpreted as a variable paired in the semantic analysis with another instance of the same variable: "x hurt x" (considered in abstraction from time) will figure in the semantic analysis of all of (34i), (37) and (38). It may be, then, that instead of formulating the rule in terms of the structural relation between the pronoun and its syntactic antecedent (a form) we should approach it in terms of the relation between the pronoun and the semantic argument consisting of the other instance of the variable: it must be an argument of the semantic predicate expressed in the clause containing the reflexive pronoun. I will not develop this point further either: it is sufficient for my purposes to have drawn attention to the problem raised by invoking the concept of antecedent in such cases. The concept needs to be more fully explicated than it has been here before we can properly judge whether it should figure in the formulation of the rule for reflexives – and the reader should beware of assuming that everything discussed in the literature in terms of a relation between anaphor and antecedent should in fact be subsumed under a single relation.

(f) The possessive pronouns. These present problems for analysis because of the uncertain status of the possessive construction in English. Distributionally, *his* is entirely parallel to a possessive based on an ordinary noun, like *the king's*: how parallel should the analyses of their internal structure be? There are two possible analyses of *the king's*, as suggested in the discussion in 1.8. In one it would be an NP with the head position filled by the possessive inflectional form of the noun **king**. This extends without difficulty to *his*: it too would be an NP with the possessive form of **he** as head. On such an account *his* would have the properties proposed above as definitional for the class of pronouns. In the second analysis of *the king's* the *'s* is a syntactic constituent, functioning as head of a PossP and taking an NP as complement: this was the analysis we adopted because it accounts better for examples like *the King of Spain's*, where the *'s* is attached to the end of the NP, not to its head. But this analysis cannot be extended directly to *his* since the possessive component and **he** are fused instead of being sequentially separate syntactic constituents. If we were to generalise the analysis to cover *his*, we would have to express it in more abstract terms than it has been our practice to adopt in this book: we would need to recognise an element 'Possessive', which sometimes appears as the clitic *'s*, as in *the man's*, sometimes as 'zero', as in *the boys'*, and sometimes is fused with its complement, as in *his*. On this account, *his* itself would not be a pronoun (since it wouldn't be the head of an NP), though it would of course contain one. The abstractness of this analysis will make it unacceptable to many, who will prefer the first analysis or else to handle pronoun-based possessives quite differently from ordinary noun-based ones.

One property peculiar to the personal pronoun-based possessives is that in general we have two distinct series: *my* vs *mine*, and so on. In (30), I have labelled them respectively 'attributive' and 'absolute'. *My, your*, etc., occur in pre-head position, as do adjectives in their attributive use. *Mine, yours*, etc., occur as predicative complement, as in *The book is mine*, in a way which parallels the predicative use of adjectives (compare *the blue tie* and *The tie is blue* with *my book* and *The book is mine*), and for this reason they are sometimes called 'predicative possessives': I have avoided this term because it reflects just one of several uses of these forms. They also occur as complement of *of* in NPs like *a friend of mine*, and as anaphors in examples like

(39)   *John's reaction was negative and so was mine*

The attributive possessives function as determiner in NP structure, where they are in paradigmatic contrast with determinatives like *the, this, that, each*, etc. We have noted that the latter are traditionally analysed as adjectives and, on the basis of this functional similarity, *my, your*, etc. are often classified as possessive adjectives rather than pronouns: in this analysis *my* is related to *I* syntactically (by its classification as 1st person singular) but not inflectionally. The analysis of *mine* as a pronoun then derives from its use in examples like (39), where it is equivalent to *my reaction*.

His occurs in both the attributive and the absolute series. *Its* (which is phonologically segmentable into *it* + *s*, but orthographically fused in that it lacks the apostrophe of *John's*) is more or less restricted to the attributive series: examples like *The food wasn't its*; *a hair of its*; *Their fur was black but its was grey* are of doubtful acceptability.

It is a distinctive property of the personal pronouns that they can function as subject in 'interrogative tags' like the *wasn't it?* of *The car was a write-off, wasn't it?* (see 11.6). Only two words not listed in (30) can appear in this position, and they might accordingly be best included as marginal members of the class of personal pronouns: *one* and *there* as in *One could scarcely do better, could one?* and *There's an error in it, isn't there?*.

Semantically *one* is normally very close to one use of *you* (the use where *you* is not, or only minimally, deictic): compare *One/You could feel the tension developing*, where the difference is one of style. *One* is also used by some speakers in referring to themselves, apparently as a means of avoiding *I* (a characteristic of some members of the British Royal Family that is much exploited by parodists). The inclusion of *one* among the personal pronouns is valid only for some varieties of English: in others it belongs quite clearly with the indefinite pronouns like *someone*. In varieties where it is a personal pronoun, it not only occurs in interrogative tags, but is also like the central members in having reflexive and possessive counterparts *oneself* and *one's*. In varieties where it is an indefinite pronoun, it is paired – as antecedent to anaphor – with *he*, etc. Compare

(40) i *One shouldn't pamper oneself* Personal pronoun
  ii *One shouldn't pamper himself/ him- or herself* Indefinite pronoun

Both constructions are found in US English, but only the first in British English.

What we have called 'dummy' *there* is not traditionally analysed as a pronoun at all; its classification is non-obvious because of its clearly unique properties and because it is generally not in paradigmatic contrast with any other form: nothing can substitute for it in *There are two mistakes on the first page, There remain many difficulties*, and so on. However, as noted in 2.2.2, we do seem to have a contrast between *there* and *it* in *It/there was a siren blaring away*, etc., and this, together with the fact that it functions as subject in tags, suggests that we should group it with the personal pronouns.

7.5 Other subclasses of pronoun

(a) Demonstrative pronouns. The demonstratives are **this** and **that**, which, as we have noted, can be used either as determinatives or as pronouns; they are the only members of either class that inflect for number. The term 'demonstrative' is suggestive of the pointing gesture or suchlike which often (though of course not necessarily) accompanies their use – compare *This is mine and this is yours*, with the two instances of *this* in a single utterance having different referents, identified by pointing, touching or the like. We will confine our attention here to their use as pronouns.

The most basic use of **this** and **that** is as deictics, the semantic contrast between them involving the relative proximity of their referents to the speaker – **this** is commonly labelled 'proximal', **that** 'non-proximal' (or 'distal'). We find the same deictic contrast in *here* vs *there* and (with relative proximity to the time of utterance) *now* vs *then*. As deictic pronouns, the demonstratives normally refer to non-humans: in *Take that downstairs* the *that* will refer to a thing, not a person – if, as is perhaps just possible, it were used of a person, it would be grossly offensive and contemptuous precisely by virtue of treating the person as a mere thing. They can, however, have human reference when functioning as subject to a predicate expressing some kind of identification as in *This is my fiancée, Sue Jones* or *That may be Peter* – in contrast to the non-human *that* of *That is in the wrong place*. The restriction to identification predicates explains why *That looks like Peter* allows the interpretation "It looks as though that person is Peter", but not "That person resembles Peter".

This and **that** can also be used as anaphors:

(41)   *She eventually bought him a tie, but this/that turned out to be a bad mistake*

where the interpretation "her buying him a tie" derives from the first clause. Usually anaphoric **this** and **that** refer to events, actions, situations, propositions and the like rather than physical objects – compare *She eventually bought him a tie, but it turned out to be the wrong colour*, where *that* would not naturally replace *it*. They can, however, be used of physical referents when contrastive: *She offered him another tie, but that was no better than the first*. Anaphoric *this* differs from *that* in being able to precede its antecedent, as in *Remember this: in a few weeks you will be taking over from me*. Where the antecedent precedes, as in (41), the semantic difference between **this** and **that** is elusive: it can perhaps be regarded as derivative from the basic deictic distinction, with **this** suggesting more immediate personal involvement on the part of the speaker. We should also note that **that** is the unmarked member of the pair, in that it occurs in certain syntactic environments where **this** is excluded, as in *His behaviour was like that of a child*. We could not replace *that* by *this* here, and the corresponding non-pronominal NP would be *the behaviour*, not *that behaviour*.

This contrast in markedness brings us, finally, to a use of pronominal **that** which is neither deictic nor anaphoric: *Those who play with fire may get their fingers burnt, That which impressed us most was the concern he showed for his opponents*. The plural *those* has a human interpretation, singular *that* a non-human one; *that* is always followed here by a relative clause, while *those* allows a slightly wider range of modifiers (cf. *Those in the know will tell you . . .*). This use of *that* is found only in formal style, and even there is subject to heavy restrictions.

(b) Interrogative and relative pronouns. Pronominal *who, whom, whose, what* and *which* (and their compounds in *-ever*) can be used either interrogatively (*Who said that?*) or relatively ([*The one*] *who said that* [*is John*]). *Who* and *whom* are different case forms of **who** – nominative and accusative respectively. The choice between them, however, is determined in a slightly different way than that between the nominative and accusative forms of personal pronouns. For both kinds of pronoun, subject function normally selects nominative, but for the rest the parallelism is lost because *whom* is restricted to comparatively formal style. It consequently does not occur as an informal variant of the nominative in predicative complement function: compare *It was he/him* with *Who/*whom is he?*. In (clause-initial) object function, *who* occurs as an informal variant of *whom*: *Who did you see?*, for example, is much more usual than *Whom did you see?*. Where **who** is complement to a preposition, we have three possibilities: *To whom did you give it?*, *Who did you give it to?*, *Whom did you give it to?*. The first is formal, the second informal, while the third is the least usual, involving a mixture of the formal choice of *whom* rather than *who* and the informal property of having the preposition left 'stranded' at the end of the clause.

For the rest, the distinctions between the various pronouns are somewhat different in interrogative clauses than in relatives, and we will accordingly look at the two series separately in the context of a consideration of the two clause-classes concerned, in 11.4 and 12.4 respectively;[6] we will see, in fact, that *when* and *where* also have pronominal uses in addition to their more frequent uses as adverbs.

(c) Indefinite pronouns. The most straightforward of the indefinite pronouns are those derived by compounding of *every, some, any* or *no* with *thing*,

---

[6] Indeed even with *who/whom* there is a difference in that the use of *who* as object or complement of a preposition is significantly more frequent in interrogative than in relative clauses – in the latter the formal *whom* can be avoided by not using **who** at all: compare *The guy whom she married/ The guy who she married/ The guy that she married/ The guy she married* [*was a teacher*] (see 12.4).

one or *body*; *everything, someone, anybody*, etc. Note that with *no* + *one* the compounding is generally not reflected in the orthography; syntactically and phonologically we regard *no one* as a single word in *No one came* but as a sequence of two words in *No one of the texts would suffice alone* – compare *anyone* and *any one of the texts*. (As a separate word, *one* contrasts here with *two*, etc.: *any two of the texts*; as part of a compound, of course, it does not.) Also included in the indefinite pronouns is *none*, as in *Ed had little money and I had none*. As we have seen, *none* is the pronominal equivalent of the determinative *no*; it is not usefully analysed as *no* + *one*, for while *one* forces an individuated interpretation, *none* does not, as can be seen from the examples just given, where it has a mass interpretation.

For the rest, the indefinite subclass will contain *many, much, several, few, all, both*, etc., if these are in fact to be analysed as pronouns at all: see §3 above. Because of the doubtful status of these, the set of indefinite pronouns is the least clearly defined of the pronoun subclasses, and considerable differences will be found from grammar to grammar with respect to its membership, its name and further subdivisions within it.

FURTHER READING

On the grammar of pronouns and the various subclasses, see Quirk et al. 1971:§§4.106–28. Anaphora has attracted a great deal of attention in the last twenty years: see, for example, Hankamer & Sag 1976 (followed up in Sag 1979), Halliday & Hasan 1976, Lyons 1977:§15.3, Wasow 1979, Evans 1980, Carden 1982, Reinhart 1983. Some scholars, e.g. Quirk et al. 1971, Halliday & Hasan 1976, restrict the term 'anaphora' to what I am calling unmarked-order anaphora (with the antecedent preceding the anaphor), using 'cataphora' for marked-order anaphora (where the antecedent follows). Where 'anaphora' covers both, the two orders are distinguished in the transformational literature as 'forwards anaphora' vs 'backwards anaphora', while Lyons uses respectively 'backward-looking' and 'forward-looking' (or 'anticipatory'); the conflict arises from the fact that the transformational terminology reflects the early (but discredited) analysis where an anaphor is transformationally substituted for a copy of the antecedent: this leads one to focus on the antecedent and move 'forwards' in the case where the anaphor follows or 'backwards' when it precedes; Lyons' terminology focuses on the anaphor and looks backwards to a preceding antecedent or forwards to a following one – although this is surely a better way of looking at it the conflict with the earlier terms is potentially a source of confusion and I have accordingly preferred to speak of unmarked order vs marked order, where there is no possibility of misinterpretation. Some writers extend the term anaphora to cases where there is no antecedent and the pronoun or whatever is interpreted deictically – Hankamer & Sag, for example, call this 'pragmatically controlled anaphora', as opposed to 'syntactically controlled anaphora' for cases where there is an antecedent; Halliday & Hasan, by contrast, distinguish these cases as respectively exophora vs endophora (with the latter equivalent to anaphora in the sense in which I have used it). On deixis, see Lyons 1977: Ch. 15, 1981a:228–35. On gender as a general category, see Lyons 1968:§7.3. On reciprocals, see Dougherty 1974.

8
Adjectives and adjective phrases

8.1 Adjectives

The most central members of the word-class adjective have the following four properties:

(a) Functional potential, I. They occur as head in phrases functioning as predicative complement in clause structure: this is what we have called the predicative use of adjectives. Thus the prototypical adjectives *careless, intelligent* and *tiresome* are used predicatively in *He was careless, She seemed very intelligent, They found it rather tiresome.*

(b) Functional potential, II. They occur as head in phrases functioning as pre-head modifier in NP structure: this is the attributive use. It is illustrated in *a careless mistake, a very intelligent woman, that rather tiresome politician.*

(c) Functional potential, III. They occur as head in phrases functioning as post-head modifier in NP structure: this we will call the **postpositive** use. Thus the above adjectives are used postpositively in *people careless in their attitude to money, someone very intelligent, something rather tiresome.* The postpositive use is much less frequent than the first two, and subject to quite restrictive conditions (see 6.10), but it is nevertheless a significant property of central adjectives that they can be used in this way.

(d) Modification and inflection. Prototypical adjectives are 'gradable' (see 6.7) and as such take modifiers indicating degree, notably *very, rather, quite, so, too, how,* etc.: *very careless, rather intelligent, how tiresome.* More particularly, gradable adjectives either enter into inflectional contrasts of comparison, as in

(1) | Absolute | Comparative | Superlative |
|----------|-------------|-------------|
| *big* | *bigger* | *biggest* |
| *pretty* | *prettier* | *prettiest* |
| *good* | *better* | *best* |

or occur in the analytic comparative and superlative constructions marked by *more* and *most*: *careless, more careless, most careless.*

No one of these properties is unique to adjectives, but only adjectives possess all four. For example, nouns generally have properties (a) and (b), and to a more limited extent (c) too, but they lack (d) – cf. the noun *bastard* in *He is a bastard, his bastard son, his son the bastard, *a very bastard child*. This is not to suggest, however, that it is only property (d) that distinguishes adjectives from nouns – we must of course also take account of the other properties of nouns discussed in 6.1: their ability to take determiners as dependents, to head phrases functioning as subject, object, etc. Thus, to continue with the same example, *bastard* shows clear noun properties in *He is a bastard* (determiner *a*), *That bastard needs watching* (determiner *that*, and subject function), in its inflectional contrast with *bastards*, and so on. We will take up the distinction between nouns and adjectives in the next chapter, but it will be clear from what has been said already that the central members of the two classes are very sharply distinct in terms of the kinds of dependent they take and the range of functions realised by the phrases they head. We should add that property (d) does not distinguish adjectives from adverbs: note in particular that a number of adverbs enter into inflectional contrasts of comparison (*badly ~ worse ~ worst; soon ~ sooner ~ soonest*, etc.).

As in earlier chapters, the above properties have been formulated so as to apply to words, but it is a trivial matter to reformulate them so as to apply to lexemes. There are, however, very many adjective words which carry no inflectional property and where the concept of lexeme is consequently inapplicable – the examples used above, *careless, intelligent* and *tiresome*, are of this type. As argued in 3.2, we will invoke the concept of lexeme only where we have inflectional, as opposed to analytic, contrasts of comparison.

Whether an adjective stem can undergo the inflectional processes that yield comparative and superlative forms is to a large extent predictable from the morphological and phonological properties of the stem. Lexical stems like *bored* or *worried* that are derived by conversion from the *-en* forms of verbs (see 9.3) do not permit these processes to apply: **He felt boreder than he had ever felt before* (cf. *He felt more bored* ...). For the rest, if the stem is monosyllabic, inflection is normally possible: *big ~ bigger, sad ~ sadder, tall ~ taller*, and so on. Disyllabic stems that take inflectional suffixes are normally either: (i) morphologically simple, ending in syllabic /l/ (*gentle, simple*), /ər/ or /(j)ʊər/[1] (*clever, obscure*), /əʊ/ (*hollow, narrow*) and certain other unaccented syllables (*common, quiet*) – *polite* is a rare example where the second syllable is accented; (ii) morphologically complex, ending in one of the suffixes *-ly* (*deadly, friendly*) or *-y* (*funny, noisy*) or beginning with the prefix *-un* (*unkind*). Stems of more than two syllables do not inflect, except for a few (such as *unfriendly*) formed by adding a negative prefix to a disyllabic stem that inflects.

[1] In many varieties of English, including for example English Received Pronunciation, the final /r/ is dropped unless followed without an intonational break by a vowel (in some styles by a vowel within the same word).

The morphological rules forming comparatives and superlatives are relatively simple: for regular adjectives, the suffixes /ər/ (see footnote 1) and /ɪst/ respectively are added. There are one or two concomitant phonological modifications: stem-final syllabic /l/ loses its syllabicity (so that the marked forms of *feeble* are disyllabic, like the absolute form) and final /ŋ/ becomes /ŋg/ (*young*, /jʌŋ/ in most varieties, is paired with *younger*, /jʌŋgə/, and so on). There are only a handful of irregular adjectives. *Better* and *best* are the comparative and superlative forms of the adjective *good*, and also of *well*, which can be used as an adjective or an adverb; adjectival *well* means "in good health" and the meaning of *better* is then not fully predictable from its analysis as the corresponding comparative, for *I am now better* can be, and usually is, interpreted as "I am now recovered, i.e. well again" (cf. the semantic irregularity of the adverb *later* mentioned in 1.7). *Worse* and *worst* likewise serve as the marked forms of the adjective *bad*, the adverb *badly* and of *ill*, which has both adjectival and adverbial uses. *Far*, which again belongs to both adjective and adverb classes, has the irregular forms *farther/further* and *farthest/furthest*. *Elder* and *eldest* might be analysed as irregular forms of *old*, coexisting with the regular forms in a specialised use – or else we might treat them as forms of a defective lexeme lacking an absolute form. In either case they require ad hoc lexical description: they are used only attributively with a kinship term like *brother* or *daughter* or (for *elder*) the noun *statesman* as head – and they cannot take modifiers of their own (cf. *a much older/*elder brother*). One comparative form that very clearly has no absolute or superlative counterpart is *other* – note that this behaves syntactically like an ordinary comparative in that it enters into construction with *than* (*anyone other/taller than Ed*). In *upper* (cf. *the upper level*) the suffix is added to a stem which does not belong to the adjective class: *upper* is not the comparative form of an adjective *up*, but an adjective derived from an adverb/ preposition. Its opposite, *lower*, is the comparative form of *low*, and forms like *upper* (cf. also *inner* and *outer*) thus provide further illustration of the lack of a sharp division between inflectional and lexical morphology.

Let us turn now to the central cases of lexical morphology. Although there are many adjectives with simple lexical stems, a high proportion have stems derived by affixation, conversion or compounding. As in the verb and noun chapters, we will give only a brief outline of the processes involved; not all the examples cited will be prototypical adjectives – for example, a number will lack property (d) (see §2 below).

(a) Class-changing suffixation. There are a considerable number of suffixes forming denominal adjectives: *-ful* (*careful*); *-less* (*careless*); *-ly* (*friendly*); *-like* (*childlike*); *-ish* (*childish*); *-esque* (*Picassoesque*); *-al, -ial, -ical, -ic* (*musical, editorial, philosophical, heroic*); *-ous* (*grievous*); *-ian, -ese* (*Christian, Japanese*); and so on. The suffix *-ed* also forms denominal adjectives, as in *walled* (*a* *walled garden,* "a garden with a wall around"), but more often it is added to adjective + noun sequences, as in *long-haired, flat-chested, simple-minded, giant-sized,* etc.: the process is relatively productive. Such forms make it impossible to maintain a rigid division between morphology and syntax: we have here a morphological element added to a syntactic construction (but note that the noun is always in the singular form, the form that coincides with the lexical stem: thus *a blue-eyed baby,* not **a blue-eyesed baby*).

(b) Class-preserving suffixation. Two of the suffixes mentioned in (a), *-ish* and *-ly,* can also derive adjectives from simpler adjectives. With *-ish* the class-preserving use is relatively productive, applying especially to adjectives of colour, shape and the like: *greenish, squarish, longish,* etc.; class-preserving *-ly* is found in a few stems such as *kindly, lowly, poorly* where the resultant meaning is of rather low predictability.

(c) Prefixation. Prefixation is predominantly class-preserving. Most of the exclusively class-preserving prefixes are negative or else involve degree. Among the negative prefixes, *un-* (*unkind*) and *non-* (*non-scientific*) are of high productivity, while *a-²* (*amoral*), *dis-* (*dishonest*) and *in-* (*intolerant*) are much more restricted; *im-* (*impossible*) and *il-/-ir,* phonologically /ɪ/ (*illegal, irrelevant*), are variants of *-in,* occurring with stems beginning with /p/ and /l/ or /r/. Among the degree prefixes, *super-* (*superhuman*), *hyper-* (*hypersensitive*), *ultra-* (*ultraconservative*), *over-* (*overconfident*) grade upwards, whereas the only one of any productivity grading downwards is *sub-* (*subhuman*). A few prefixes involving temporal or spatial relations, *pre-, post-, inter-, trans-,* attach to adjective stems (especially denominal ones) or else to nouns, so that they can be either class-preserving (*pre-classical, post-classical, intercontinental, transcontinental*) or class-changing (*pre-war, post-war, inter-university, trans-Mississippi*).

(d) Conversion. Given that we are not postulating conversion in cases like *the Queensland government,* where we take the modifier *Queensland* to be a noun, not an adjective, adjectives derived by conversion are virtually restricted to *-ing* and *-en* forms of verbs: *amusing, interesting, bored, distressed,* and so on. We will take up this matter in Ch. 9.

(e) Compounding. The most productive kinds of adjective compound have an *-ing* or *-en* form of a verb as the second component: [*a*] *record-breaking* [*swim*], [*a*] *much-debated* [*question*]. The first component may be a noun (*hair-raising, hand-made*), including the *self* that appears in reflexive pronouns (*self-fulfilling* [*prophecies*], *self-addressed* [*envelopes*]); an adjective (*good-looking, true-born*); or an adverb (*well-meaning, well-meant*). With *-ing* form compounds, the noun may have a semantic role corresponding to an

---

² The prefix *a-* also forms adverbs or prepositions like *aboard* in *He went aboard (the ship);* cf. Ch. 10.

object in clause structure (cf. *a swim that broke the/some record/records*) or the complement of a preposition (*a law-abiding citizen* may be compared with *a citizen who abides by the law*). In *-en* form compounds, the verb component is almost always understood passively: *a much-debated question* is equivalent to *a question that is/was much debated* (we have to say 'almost always' because of examples like *newly-arrived*); again, see Ch. 9 for further elaboration. In addition there are a considerable number of compounds formed from noun + adjective: *tax-free, carsick*, etc.; a particularly productive subtype has a colour adjective as second component: *sky-blue, blood-red*. Finally, there are adjectives compounded from a pair of adjectives, or from a bound stem in *-o* plus an adjective, where neither stem is subordinate to the other: *bitter-sweet, Sino-Tibetan, socio-historical*.

8.2   **Some non-central subclasses of adjectives**

The four properties given at the beginning of the last section – ability to be used predicatively, attributively, postpositively and to take modification pertaining to degree – characterise the prototypical adjective, but they are not necessary conditions for membership of the adjective class. In this section we will mention briefly some subclasses of adjective that lack one or more of the properties.

(a) In the first place, we must recognise a quite large subclass of non-gradable adjectives like *anthropological, philatelic, phonetic, set-theoretic* ("pertaining to set theory"), which do not take modifiers of degree. Thus we might have *a philatelic gem/magazine/rarity* but not **a very philatelic gem/ magazine/rarity*. It should be emphasised, however, that gradability is primarily a semantic matter: the possibility of adding a degree modifier depends on the meaning of the adjective, not on some semantically-arbitrary syntactic property. From a semantic point of view, a gradable adjective denotes a scalar property as opposed to a categorial one – where a scalar property is one that can be possessed in varying degrees; and precisely because the property denoted can be possessed in varying degrees the adjective can take degree modifiers. Many adjectives, however, are polysemous, denoting a categorial property in one sense and a scalar one in another. For example, a nationality adjective like *British* denotes a categorial property in its central sense, as in *a British passport, the British Parliament*, but also has an extended sense denoting a scalar property ("like typical or stereotypical British people or things"), as in *He's very British*; the primacy of the categorial sense is reflected in the fact that the adjective will not normally be interpreted in the scalar sense unless there is some grading modifier present. To a significant extent, therefore, the gradable/non-gradable contrast applies to uses of adjectives, rather than simply to the adjectives themselves.

(b) As we have noted, a few adjectives cannot be used attributely: *afraid, asleep, awake, loath, tantamount* ..., and for many speakers *well* "in good health", *unwell, content*, and a few others. Compare *They were afraid* (predicative), *anyone afraid of heights* (postpositive), **some afraid sheep* (attributive). We will see below (§4) that AdjPs containing complements do not normally occur attributively: the inclusion of *loath* and *tantamount* in the present subclass is then related to the fact that with them a complement is normally obligatory. In one or two cases the inability to appear in predicative position applies to some but not all senses of an adjective: thus *glad* and *sorry* are not used attributively in the sense "pleased" and "regretful", but they can be in other senses, as in *glad tidings, a sorry sight*.

(c) Conversely, there are a few adjectives (all non-gradable) that are used ONLY attributively: *main, principal, mere, utter*, etc.

(d) Finally, a small number of adjectives (again non-gradable) are used neither attributively nor predicatively: *designate, elect*, etc., as in *the bishop designate*; these are very peripheral members of the adjective class – but they are clearly not candidates for inclusion in any of the other primary word-classes.

8.3 Determinatives

The term 'determiner' is commonly used both as a functional label (like 'modifier', 'subject', etc.) and as a class label (like 'adjective', 'NP', etc.). It is evident, however, that we do not have here a one-to-one relation between function and class, and I am accordingly restricting the term to one of the above senses, the functional. The determiner function has been discussed in our analysis of NP structure, but at that point we paid little attention to questions of class. The easiest case to deal with is illustrated in, say, *the bishop's proposal*, where the determiner is realised by a PossP, *the bishop's*. Some of the other forms given in list (7) in 6.4 rather clearly have the internal structure of NPs: *one-third, three-quarters, three times, a few* (cf. *a good few*), *a little, a dozen*, etc. This then leaves us with the closed class items *the, all, a, some, every, many* – the items to which 'determiner' as a class label is commonly applied, and which I am instead referring to as 'determinatives' (see 3.1). Traditional grammar has the term 'article', but it is generally restricted to *the* (the 'definite article') and *a* (the 'indefinite article'): I have preferred to use the relatively unfamiliar term 'determinative' rather than stretch 'article' so far beyond its traditional application.

The determinatives are traditionally analysed as a subclass of adjectives ('limiting adjectives' as opposed to 'descriptive adjectives' like **big, good, beautiful**), whereas modern grammars more often treat them as a distinct primary class. Clearly they have little in common with proto-typical adjectives. In general their only adjective-like property is that of occurring as pre-head dependent in NP structure – though even here we have made a functional distinction between determinatives (determiners) and adjectives (modifiers). Nevertheless we have just noted that *main, principal, mere,* etc., are restricted to pre-head dependent position – and some of the determinatives have additional adjective-like properties: one or two are gradable (cf. *very much money*), and *many* at least can, under rather restricted conditions, be used predicatively, as in *How many were you?*. As noted in 3.4, the classification of closed class items is typically much more problematic than that of open class items, and the informal framework developed in this book is certainly not sophisticated enough to allow us to choose in a well-motivated way between an analysis where determinatives are a subclass of adjective, and one where they constitute a separate class.

8.4 Dependents in AdjP structure: complements

The range of dependents found in AdjPs is somewhat less varied and complex than in NPs or EVPs. We can again distinguish, however, between complements and modifiers along the same lines as with dependents of nouns and verbs. Let us begin with a brief consideration of complements.

A clear example is found in example (9ii) in 5.2, *Ed is fond of Kim,* where the PP *of Kim* is complement of the adjective *fond.* As we suggested in the earlier discussion, **fond** expresses a two-place semantic predicate (like the verb **love**): one of the arguments is expressed by the subject *Ed,* the other by the NP *Kim* within the PP complement. Apart from the semantic property of including the expression of an argument, *of Kim* has the two syntactic properties that we have seen to be characteristic of complements:

(a) It depends for its occurrence on the presence in head function of an adjective of the appropriate subclass: we could replace **fond** by *afraid,* say, but not by **keen, sorry, tall,** etc. Where the complement is a PP, the choice of preposition is determined by the adjective: **fond** *of,* **keen** *on,* **sorry** *for,* **similar** *to,* etc.

(b) It is obligatory: we cannot have **Ed is fond.* However, very few adjectives take obligatory complements – compare *afraid* (*of the dark*), *keen* (*on the idea*), *sorry* (*for the inconvenience*), etc., where the parenthesised PP complements are not syntactically obligatory.

Complements of adjectives are generally realised either by PPs, as in the above examples, or by subordinate clauses, as in

(2)   *Ed was angry that he had gone*
(3)   *I am unsure whether she can do it*

where *angry* has a declarative content clause as its complement, *unsure* an interrogative. Examples like (2) and (3) are to be distinguished from *It was odd that he had gone* and *It is questionable whether she can do it*: these are non-kernel constructions derived by extraposition from *That he had gone was odd* and *Whether she can do it is questionable*, so that the adjective and content clause do not here go together to form a phrase.

In addition to finite clauses like those in (2) and (3), we also find non-finite clauses functioning as complement to an adjective – more specifically infinitival clauses with *to*:[3]

(4)   *Ed was keen for me to see the manuscript*

Some details of the structure of a form like *for me to see the manuscript* are problematic: I am assuming that *for* is a 'subordinating conjunction' (see 10.4) and that *me* is subject – it differs from a prototypical subject, of course, in that the case-variable pronoun takes the accusative form in infinitival clauses. More often, the infinitival complement has no subject expressed, as in

(5)   *Ed was keen to see the manuscript*
(6)   *Ed was likely to see the manuscript*
(7)   *The dye was ready to use*
(8)   *The dye was easy to use*

There are several different kinds of infinitival complement; the four illustrated here may be distinguished along the following lines:

(a) In (5) and (6) the understood subject (or subject-argument) of the infinitival clause is recovered from the subject of the superordinate clause – i.e. *Ed*. Thus the semantic relation between *Ed* and **see** *the manuscript* is the same as in the tensed clause *Ed saw the manuscript*, in which *Ed* is the actual subject of **see** *the manuscript*. In (7) and (8), by contrast, the infinitival clauses lack not only a subject but also an object – and it is the understood object (or object-argument) that is recovered from the subject of the superordinate clause (cf. *We used the dye*). To be subsumed under the same construction are those where it is the complement of a preposition that is missing from the infinitival clause, as in *The knife was ready/easy to cut with*. The understood subject-argument in (7) and (8), on the other hand, is recovered pragmatically – "The dye was ready for us/me/him/her/one . . . to use", depending on the context.

(b) (5) and (6) differ from each other in just the same way as the catenative constructions *Ed expects to amuse Kim* and *Ed seems to amuse Kim* discussed at some length in 5.6.2. Thus **keen** expresses a two-place semantic predicate: "x was keen for x to see the manuscript, for x = Ed" (note that *Both scholars*

---

[3] Normally, *-ing* class clauses require a preposition, rather than entering directly into construction with the adjective: *He's not very keen on marking assignments*. An exception is *worth*, as in *The idea is worth pursuing further*.

were keen to see the manuscript is not equivalent to *Both scholars were keen for both scholars to see the manuscript*). Conversely, **likely** expresses a one-place semantic predicate: "That Ed would see the manuscript was likely"; this is why *The manuscript was likely to be seen by Ed* has the same propositional meaning as (6) (while the pragmatically anomalous *The manuscript was keen to be seen by Ed* is not propositionally equivalent to (5)), why we can say *There were likely to be too many people with vested interests on the committee* (but not **There were keen to be . . .*), and so on. As with the catenative examples, I leave open the question of whether, and if so how, this initially semantic distinction should be reflected in our syntactic analysis. *Eager, reluctant,* **glad, sorry,** etc. belong with **keen**, while *certain, sure* and one or two others belong with **likely**. With the **likely** class, the infinitival clause cannot contain an overt subject (**Ed was likely for me to see the manuscript*), whereas with the **keen** class it generally can, as in (4).

(c) It may well be that (7) and (8) differ from each other in the same way. **Ready** certainly expresses a two-place semantic predicate (cf. *Ed was ready for the conference*), and indeed it can also enter into the construction of (5), as in *Ed was ready to go*: ambiguities can then arise between the two constructions, as in *The lamb was ready to eat*, where "the lamb" can be taken as either the understood subject-argument of "eat" ("The lamb was ready to eat its food or whatever") or its understood object-argument ("The lamb was ready for them/us/ . . . to eat it"). The semantic analysis of (8) is more problematic. The case for treating **easy** as expressing a one-place semantic predicate rests primarily on the relation between (8) and *To use the dye was easy* (or, equivalently but more naturally, *It was easy to use the dye*). On the other hand, the **easy** of (8) can be used attributively, as in *an easy dye to use*, which suggests an interpretation of (8) as predicating a property "easy to use" of "the dye", i.e. one where "the dye" is an argument of "easy". We will therefore leave open the nature of the semantic distinction between (7) and (8); syntactically they differ precisely in that it is only the AdjP in (8) that has an attributive use – cf. **a ready dye to use*.

We have been looking at complements with the form of PPs or clauses: NPs, by contrast, cannot normally function as complement of an adjective. In this respect, adjectives resemble nouns: verbs take a greater range of complements, with NPs being among the most central. There are just two or three adjectives that do take NP complements, such as *like* and *worth*, as in *He is very like his father* and *The land was worth a fortune*, but they lie on the periphery of the adjective class and are not sharply distinguishable from prepositions (see Ch. 10).

Most AdjPs contain no complement at all or just one, but a small number of adjectives allow two: *critical of Max for his indecisiveness, responsible to the directors for implementing the proposal*.[4]

---

[4] In the first example, *for* has to be replaced by *of* if the other complement is omitted: *critical of his indecisiveness*.

In general, AdjPs containing complements cannot be used attributively – even in the discontinuous construction mentioned in 6.8. Thus we can have, for example, *She is keen on hockey* (predicative) or *a woman keen on hockey* (postpositive) but neither **a keen on hockey woman* nor **a keen woman on hockey*; similarly with finite clause complements: *He was angry that he had gone* but not **an angry that he had gone man* nor **an angry man that he had gone*. The exception involves infinitival complements of the kind found in (8) as noted above: *an easy car to drive, a difficult person to get on with*.

8.5 Dependents in AdjP structure: modifiers

Modifiers normally occur only with gradable adjectives and are concerned primarily with the expression of degree. In pre-head position we find a large number of de-adjectival adverbs in *-ly* (*absolutely, completely, enormously, incredibly, profoundly, utterly,* etc.) and a small number of other adverbs whose stems are for the most part morphologically simple (*how, quite, so, too, very* and the non-simple *rather, somewhat*): *absolutely useless, quite good, rather thin*. Most of these can take their own modifiers (*as profoundly wrong, ever so pretty, just how intelligent*), so that we should have the pre-head modifier function realised by phrases rather than, immediately, by words.

Among the morphologically simple items, special mention should be made of those which belong to both adverb and determinative classes: *the, this, that, much, no, any, all*. These are adverbs by virtue of their potential to modify adjectives and other adverbs, determinatives by virtue of their potential to function as determiner in NP structure. Thus the adverbial use is illustrated in *He was much the wiser for it, It wasn't all that satisfactory, It was no different from last time, Was it any good?*, and so on, while the determinative use is found in *He hadn't much patience, He lost all that money, It was no mean feat, Do you want any milk?*. For the most part nouns and adjectives differ with respect to the pre-head dependents they take, but these examples show that there is some overlap – so that the presence of *the, this*, etc. cannot be taken as sufficient to indicate a nominal construction. Except for the demonstratives, however, these adverbs can modify only a quite restricted range of adjectives/adverbs – *the*, for example, occurs only with comparatives and with *same*: *I'm all the more grateful to you, My feelings are the same as before*.

Post-head modifiers are exemplified in

(9)   *Ed was so tall that he could see over the wall*
(10)   *It was more useful than I had expected*
(11)   *It was as long as six feet*
(12)   *Ed was too sleepy to concentrate*
(13)   *Ed was rather young to send on such a mission*
(14)   *It was warm to be wearing an overcoat*

In some cases the post-head modifier is closely linked to a pre-head modifier: in (9), for example, if we dropped the *so* the *that* clause would have to go too, and similarly in (10) the *than* clause could not remain if *more* were dropped. There is thus something to be said for analysing the subordinate clauses here as dependents of *so* and *more* (rather than of the adjectives), with the AdjPs each containing a single discontinuous modifier. I have preferred to take the clauses as separate modifiers of the adjective for two reasons. Firstly, the analytic comparative in (10) may be matched with the inflectional comparative of *It was longer than I had expected*. If we replace *longer* by *long* we must again drop the *than* clause, yet the latter does not form a syntactic constituent with the comparative inflection: within the framework we have adopted, the ICs of *longer than I had expected* could not be *long + -er than I had expected*, because *-er* is part of the word *longer*. Secondly, it would be very difficult to distinguish the discontinuous construction from that where there is a post-head dependent of the adjective. In (12), for example, the infinitival clause seems to be closely linked to the *too*: the meaning is that the degree of sleepiness was excessive relative to the goal of concentrating, and if we drop the *too* while retaining the infinitival clause the result sounds quite unnatural. Yet if we change the lexical content to, say, *He was too old to be doing that kind of work*, it is certainly possible to drop just the *too*. Similarly in (11) we could not drop the first *as*, but in examples like *She was as slim as a reed* we could.

Examples (12)–(14) illustrate three distinct kinds of infinitival clause modifier. In (12) the understood subject-argument of the infinitival clause is recovered from the subject of the main clause (it is a matter of Ed's concentrating), whereas in (13) and (14) it is recovered pragmatically – and these latter may contain an overt subject after *for*: *rather young for them to send on such a mission*, and so on. The difference between (13) and (14) is that the infinitival clause in (13) is structurally incomplete in that it lacks an object (or the complement of a preposition, as in *The wall was too high to climb over*), with the understood argument being recoverable from the subject of the main clause (in (13) it is a matter of sending Ed on the mission).

Infinitival clauses, as we saw in the last section, also function as complement in AdjP structure: let us therefore pause briefly to clarify the distinction between the two constructions as exemplified in, say,

(15)			
	i	*He was anxious to be a minister*	Complement
	ii	*He was young to be a minister*	Modifier[5]

(a) Semantically, the complement corresponds to an argument of the adjectival semantic predicate: (i) may be compared to *He wanted to be a*

---

[5] As with verb and noun heads, we can probably not make a completely sharp distinction between complements and modifiers; it is possible, for example, that the constructions of (7) and (8) above should also be differentiated as involving a complement and modifier respectively.

minister. The modifier, on the other hand, is concerned with the specification of degree. Gradable adjectives generally involve some kind of comparison – explicit, as in *Ed is smaller than Max*, or implicit, as in *Ed is small*. That there is implicit comparison in the latter becomes evident when we imagine what sizes the clause would attribute to Ed if he were a six-month-old baby, a ten-year old boy, an adult human or, say, a circus elephant: the standard with which he is being compared and judged small would be quite different. The semantic effect of the modifier in (ii) is thus to specify the standard – "young in comparison with the standard age for ministers".

(b) The complement, as noted earlier, depends for its occurrence on the selection of an adjective head allowing an infinitival complement: we could replace *anxious* in (i) by *afraid, eager, reluctant*, etc., but not by *considerate, responsible, similar* and the like. The modifier, however, can occur with all gradable adjectives, though it will often sound more natural if there is also a pre-head modifier, as in our **sleepy** example, (12).

(c) The two can combine, with the complement preceding the modifier: *He was too anxious to win to appreciate such niceties* (some pre-head modifier is just about obligatory in such cases).

(d) There is, potentially, a prosodic distinction between (i) and (ii): a natural pronunciation of the latter would have two intonation contours, the first having the stress on *young*, the second on *min(ister)*, but (i) would not be spoken in this way.

It is not always easy to distinguish clearly between modifiers in AdjP structure and adjuncts in clause structure. Consider the examples

(16)   *He was too indiscreet*
(17)   *He was obviously indiscreet*

The first is straightforward: *too*, in the sense "excessively", cannot function as an adjunct – we could not replace *excessively* by *too* in this sense in *She had loved him excessively* and the like (the corresponding degree adjunct is *too much*); in (16) the *too* is thus clearly a modifier of *indiscreet*. *Obviously*, on the other hand, can be an adjunct – what we have called a modal adjunct, as in *She obviously loved him* – and it clearly has this function in *Obviously he was indiscreet* or *He obviously was indiscreet*. If we take a copulative verb other than **be**, such as **become** or **seem**, we find a clear semantic contrast between *He obviously became indiscreet* ("It is obvious that he became indiscreet") and *He became obviously indiscreet* ("He came to exhibit obvious indiscretion"): in the first it is the becoming indiscreet that was obvious, and here *obviously* is an adjunct, in the second there is a change from one state to another, with *obviously* characterising the indiscretion of the second state – and here it is natural to analyse *obviously* as a modifier of *discreet*. With **be**, the analysis is more difficult. One might argue that we can again distinguish between an interpretation where *obviously* relates to the being indiscreet ("It is obvious that he was indiscreet") and one where it relates just to the indiscretion "He was blatantly indiscreet"). *He obviously was indiscreet* allows only the former interpretation, but (17) allows either – and it is then tempting to say that (17) is structurally ambiguous. Notice, however, that *obviously* can enter into construction with an adjective used attributively, as in *his obviously indiscreet ex-secretary* – and this allows either of the above interpretations. It seems that attributive AdjPs permit a wider range of modifiers, with some of them corresponding to adjuncts in clause structure in the matching predicative construction – compare *her at that time still industrious husband* with *Her husband was at that time still industrious*.

FURTHER READING
On adjectives in general, see Quirk et al. 1971: Ch. 5, Bowers 1975. On the adjective + infinitive construction, see Bolinger 1961, Silva & Thompson 1977, Nanni 1980.

9
Verbs, nouns and adjectives: the boundaries between them

In Chs. 4, 6 and 8 we have set out the grammatical properties which characterise the three major parts of speech – and it is clear that in a sentence like *Both men became very angry*, for example, we can distinguish very sharply between the verb *became*, the noun *men* and the adjective *angry*. Non-central members, however, are often significantly less easily distinguishable: the frequent appearance in grammars of expressions like 'verbal noun', 'noun used as an adjective', and so on, attests to this. In the present chapter I will consider in turn each of the pairs verb/noun, verb/adjective and noun/adjective, partly in order to develop and sharpen the earlier account of the distinctive properties of the classes, partly in order to draw attention to certain problems that arise in drawing boundaries between them or between the associated phrase classes.

We noted in 2.4 that what we are calling *-ing* forms of verbs are traditionally analysed as either gerunds (as in *Taking [exams was a waste of time]*) or present participles (as in *[Everyone] taking [the coach should report here at 6 a.m.]*). We argued against making any inflectional distinction between them on the grounds that no verb in the language exhibits any morphological contrast here. The traditional concepts are worth taking up again at this point, however, because they also cover words that we do not regard as *-ing* forms of verbs. Thus *killing* in *the killing of kangaroos* is a gerund that we will take to be a noun rather than a verb, while the *amusing* of *an amusing incident* is a present participle that we will take to be an adjective rather than a verb. Traditional grammarians were not a little exercised by the question of where to draw the boundary between gerunds and present participles; from our point of view, however, the interest lies not in that issue but in the problems they raise for the boundary between verbs and nouns (in the case of gerunds) and between verbs and adjectives (in the case of present- and also past-participles).

9.1 Verbs vs nouns: gerunds

Gerunds are illustrated in the following examples:

(1)   *[She disapproved of his] being [so extravagant]*

(2)	[*She resented*] *being demoted*
(3)	[*She regretted*] *having told* [*him the truth*]
(4)	[*She likes*] *writing* [*letters*]
(5)	*Hunting* [*wild animals can be a dangerous pastime*]
(6)	[*The*] *hunting* [*of wild animals for sport should be banned*]
(7)	[*The*] *singing* [*of Joan Sutherland was a delight to listen to*]
(8)	[*These*] *killings* [*must stop*]
(9)	*Fox-hunting* [*arouses great passion*]

Not all traditional grammars would include the last one or two items of this list, but at least some do, and it will suit our purposes here to take gerund in its broadest sense. Note that 'gerund', like 'verb', is traditionally applied not only to single words but also to phrases containing one or more auxiliaries, such as *being demoted* in (2) or *having told* in (3).

Gerunds are defined by two properties, the first making them verb-like, the second noun-like:

(a) A gerund contains (at least) a verb stem and the suffix *-ing*.

(b) A gerund has one of the functions that are characteristic of nouns – or rather, as we would put it in terms of the framework introduced in Chs. 1–3, a gerund heads a phrase with one of the functions that are characteristic of NPs, subject in (5)–(9), complement within EVP structure in (2)–(4), complement of a preposition in (1).

Strictly speaking we should add a third property to exclude words denoting concrete objects, as in

(10)   [*The*] *building* [*collapsed*]

for concrete nouns like this fall outside even the broadest extension of the term 'gerund'.

The combination of verb-like and noun-like properties given in (a) and (b) underlies the traditional characterisation of gerunds as 'verbal nouns'. Note, however, that this latter term, 'verbal noun', implies that greater weight is attached to (b) than to (a): a verbal noun is primarily a kind of noun, not a kind of verb.

We shall certainly not want to follow that line here and indeed, as implied above, we shall not treat all gerunds alike, regarding the verb-like characteristics as outweighing the noun-like ones in some cases, vice versa in others. We thus draw a sharp distinction between (1)–(5), on the one hand, where the gerunds – or rather the *-ing* words (i.e. *being*, rather than *being demoted* in (2), and so on) are verbs, and (6)–(9) on the other, where they are nouns (like the non-gerund *-ing* word in (10)).

Central members of the verb class, we have said, are tensed, with non-tensed forms being admitted into the class on the basis of their systematic resemblance to tensed forms. *Fox-hunting* in (9) can then be very quickly dismissed as a candidate for verbhood by the lack of corresponding tensed forms: we do not say **He fox-hunts/fox-hunted;*[1] it bears no significant syntactic resemblance to a verb at all and is quite clearly a compound noun. Central members of the noun class enter into inflectional contrasts of number, and we can immediately see that *killings* in (8), contrasting with *killing*, belongs by this inflectional criterion in the noun class (like *building* in (10), which contrasts with *buildings*).

The main justification for distinguishing (1)–(5) from (6)–(9), however, is based not on inflectional contrasts but on syntagmatic relations. In (1) *being* is like a central verb such as *was* in that it enters into construction with an AdjP functioning as predicative complement – the relation is like that in [*He*] *was so extravagant* (and unlike that between the AdjP modifier and the pronoun head in an NP like *anyone so extravagant*). In (2) and (3) *being* and *having* are related to *demoted* and *told* as the tensed auxiliaries *was* and *had* are in the central VPs *was demoted* and *had told*; again we do not find comparable relations within the NP. And in (3)–(5) the gerunds have NP objects. Note the contrast between the verb *hunting* in (5), which takes the NP *wild animals* as complement (cf. *They hunt wild animals*, with *hunt* clearly a verb), and the noun *hunting* in (6), which takes the PP *of wild animals* (cf. *the pursuit of wild animals*, with *pursuit* clearly a noun): nouns do not take dependents of the object kind. Similarly, verbs take adverbs as modifiers while the corresponding modifiers of nouns are adjectives, so that in *He was accused of driving dangerously* vs *He was accused of dangerous driving*, the first *driving*, modified by the adverb *dangerously* is a verb (cf. *He drove dangerously*), while the second, modified by the adjective *dangerous*, is a noun (cf. *a dangerous fellow*). Again, the complement in (7) is of the kind found in NPs (cf. *the arrival/autobiography of Joan Sutherland*) rather than in clauses (in the corresponding central-verb construction it would appear as an NP subject: *Joan Sutherland sang*).

Where the gerund has no dependents present we will of course decide the classification on the basis of its potential for expansion – and if both types of dependent can be added it will be analysed as ambiguous. In *I like singing*, for example, *singing* can be either a verb or a noun. In the verb construction we could expand with a following NP complement like *Schubert's Lieder* (with *singing Schubert's Lieder* comparable to [*I*] *sing Schubert's Lieder*), in the noun construction with a preceding AdjP modifier like *choral* (with *choral singing* comparable to *choral music*). Where *singing* is a verb, *I like singing* will be interpreted with "I" as the understood subject-argument of "sing",

---

[1] Strictly speaking, the lack of tensed counterparts is not sufficient to exclude a word from the verb class, for *beware* is a verb in spite of the deviance of *He bewares/bewared of the dog* (see 4.1). But in the absence of special factors such as obtain in the case of *beware* (note that, like a tensed form, it can function as predicator in a main clause) we will take the absence of tensed forms as a clear indication that a word is not a verb.

but where it is a noun we are concerned with singing by people (or singers) in general, and a further difference is that while the verbal interpretation involves the activity of singing, the actual performing, the nominal interpretation is more likely to involve the product, as it were, of the activity – i.e. the sound. The semantic distinction will not always be as sharp as in this example, but there will in principle be no difficulty in deciding whether some given instance of a (one-word) gerund is a verb, a noun or ambiguous.

One further difference we should note between nouns and verbs in *-ing* is that the morphological process deriving nouns in *-ing* is, although very productive, nevertheless still significantly less so than that deriving *-ing* forms of verbs, and this is one reason why we regard the one as lexical, the other as inflectional. Virtually all verbs other than the modal auxiliaries (which can be established as a special subclass on independent grounds) have inflectional *-ing* forms. Many abstract nouns, however, are formed from verbs by other processes: *arrive ~ arrival, grow ~ growth, pay ~ payment, resign ~ resignation*, etc. In some cases both kinds of formation are found: *the growth/growing of tomatoes, the payment/paying of the bill*; in others only one seems acceptable: *the arrival/*arriving of Joan Sutherland, the resignation/*resigning of the prime minister*, but as is quite typical of lexical morphology it is not possible to define precise limits to the *-ing* noun construction.

Although a word-class distinction between the *-ing* words in (1)–(5) and those in (6)–(9) is well motivated, the analysis of the first set raises significant problems. For verbs and verb-headed phrases, we have postulated four hierarchical levels of form-classes: verb, verb phrase, extended verb phrase and clause – with a clause having an EVP as head, an EVP having a VP as head, and a VP having a verb as head. Our arguments for treating the *-ing* words in (1)–(5) as verbs were based on syntagmatic relations at the VP and EVP levels. But what of clause level relations? A prototypical clause has an EVP as head (predicate) and an NP as dependent (subject). In earlier chapters we have assumed, for the sake of simplicity, that *-ing* class EVPs either constitute subjectless clauses on their own or enter into construction with a subject to form a clause. This assumption is perfectly consistent with the fact that the resultant constructions can function within the structure of a larger clause as subject or of a larger EVP as object, etc., for finite constructions, whose status as clauses is not in dispute, can likewise appear in these functions – compare

(11)   i *Missing the bus didn't matter*
      ii *That we had missed the bus didn't matter*
(12)   i *We regretted missing the bus*
      ii *We regretted that we had missed the bus*

Nevertheless, there are a number of respects in which the *-ing* constructions differ from *that* clauses: in some respects they have properties characteristic of NPs rather than clauses.

(a) They can follow the tensed verb in interrogative clauses and the like (see 4.4):

(13)   *Is* $\begin{Bmatrix} \text{i} & \textit{her atheism} \\ \text{ii} & \textit{her being an atheist} \\ \text{iii} & \textit{*that she is an atheist} \end{Bmatrix}$ *really relevant?*

As we see from (13), NPs can occur in this position, but finite clauses cannot – and *-ing* constructions follow the distributional pattern of NPs.

(b) They resist being shifted out of subject position by extraposition:

(14)   i   *That she is an atheist is highly relevant*
         ii   *It is highly relevant that she is an atheist*
(15)   i   *Her being an atheist is highly relevant*
         ii   **It is highly relevant her being an atheist*
(16)   i   *Her atheism is highly relevant*
         ii   **It is highly relevant her atheism*

The examples numbered (ii) are to be read without an intonational break after *relevant* – see 14.3. In general, NPs cannot be extraposed (again see 14.3 for some exceptions), so that here too the distribution of the *-ing* construction resembles that of an NP. But the resemblance is not absolute: for many speakers at least, extraposition of an *-ing* construction is possible if it and the superordinate clause EVP over which it is moved are relatively short, especially where the *-ing* construction has no subject: *It's been nice meeting you, It's pointless getting worked up about it*. Native speaker judgements are not uniform on this issue – and some indeed will regard (15ii) as acceptable. But there is no doubt that *-ing* constructions allow extraposition very much less readily than finite clauses.

(c) They can function as complement of a preposition:

(17)   *There is a good chance of* $\begin{Bmatrix} \text{(i)} & \textit{a complete recovery} \\ \text{(ii)} & \textit{her recovering completely} \\ \text{(iii)} & \textit{*that she will recover completely} \end{Bmatrix}$

Notice, however, that finite clauses are not wholly excluded from this function: interrogative and exclamative clauses are found here, as in *There is the question of whether she will ever recover completely*.

(d) Adjectives normally take neither NPs nor *-ing* constructions as complement – the only one taking an *-ing* construction is *worth* (*The film is worth seeing*), which is also one of the handful that take NPs (*That is worth a fortune*); many adjectives, however, take finite clause complements – see 8.4.

(e) What we are treating as the subject of the *-ing* construction may be a PossP:

(18)   *He objected to my being given the best seat*

My cannot function as subject of a tensed clause – its most characteristic function is of course that of determiner in NP structure. Again, however, we should note that very often a PossP and the corresponding NP are both possible, with the latter characteristic of less formal style (see 5.6.3): *He resented my/me opening the mail*. And the pronoun *there*, which has no possessive counterpart and cannot function as determiner in NP structure, can certainly enter into construction with an *-ing* class VP: *He objected to there being so many professors on the committee.*

What emerges from the above is that the *-ing* construction is something of a hybrid: it has both clause-like and NP-like properties and clearly differs quite significantly both from a prototypical clause and from a prototypical NP – it lies towards the boundary between them. But this does not undermine the distinction we have drawn between (1)–(5) and (6)–(9). Let us introduce the term 'nominalisation' for a grammatical process resulting in forms bearing a resemblance to nouns or NPs – a greater resemblance than the forms from which they are derived. Then we can distinguish different kinds and degrees of nominalisation. (6)–(9), like (10), involve lexical nominalisation processes that yield nouns: the words in *-ing* are sufficiently like prototypical nouns for their inclusion in that word-class to be well justified. Subordination of a clause by means of *that* can also be regarded as nominalisation: *that we had missed the bus* is more like an NP in its functional potential than is the kernel clause *We had missed the bus*. But clearly the nominalisation here does not create a noun, i.e. a WORD of a certain class. It is evident from points (a)–(d) above that the *-ing* constructions in (1)–(5) involve a higher degree of nominalisation than we find in *that* clauses (particularly in the variant with initial PossP, *my opening the mail*, rather than initial NP, *me opening the mail*), but the points made earlier in this section show that here too the nominalisation does not create a noun. The status of *his being so extravagant* in (1) as a clause is certainly problematic, but the case for treating *being* here as a verb, not a noun, remains compelling.

It is worth adding that the degree of nominalisation involved in infinitival constructions is appreciably less than in *-ing* constructions: they differ from *-ing* constructions with respect to all of (a)–(e). Traditional grammar often applies the term 'verbal noun' to infinitives as well as to gerunds, but it will again be evident that the process deriving an infinitival construction like [*It would be wiser*] *to give him both copies* does not create a noun: within the framework adopted here, there can be no question of *to give* (or just *give*) being a noun.

9.2 **Verbs vs adjectives: participles**

Whereas gerunds are traditionally described as 'verbal nouns', participles are said to be 'verbal adjectives'. The term 'participle' is etymologically related to 'participate' and the idea behind it is that participles 'share' the properties of verbs and adjectives. Two kinds of participle are distinguished: 'present participles' like *taking* and 'past participles' like *taken*; we will consider them in turn.

9.2.1   Present participles

We will proceed as before with a set of examples illustrating the range of constructions containing present participles, again adding the proviso that some scholars use the term more restrictively than others, excluding the examples towards the end of the list.

(19)   [*He was*] *telling* [*the truth*]
(20)   [*No one saw him*] *leaving* [*the building*]
(21)   *Being* [*only three-foot tall, he had to stand on a chair*]
(22)   [*Anyone*] *owning* [*more than $200,000 will have to pay wealth tax*]
(23)   [*The bill*] *being debated* [*at the time was hardly controversial*]
(24)   [*He pointed towards the*] *setting* [*sun*]
(25)   [*He was concerned about the rapidly*] *falling* [*share prices*]
(26)   [*She was resting after her*] *record-breaking* [*swim*]
(27)   [*He was a*] *charming* [*fellow*]
(28)   [*It seemed very*] *interesting*

Again the term 'present participle' is not restricted to single words but covers phrases containing an auxiliary, like *being debated* in (23) – more specifically we should say that a present participle may contain the passive auxiliary *being*, for *having left* (in its non-gerundive use) would traditionally be analysed as a 'perfect participle' rather than a 'present perfect participle'.

Like a gerund, a present participle contains (at least) a verb stem and the suffix *-ing*. But whereas a gerund or, as we have preferred to put it, the phrase headed by a gerund, has nominal properties, a present participle, or again the phrase headed by one, allegedly has adjectival properties. I say 'allegedly' because it is difficult to see any significant functional resemblance to an adjective or AdjP in the first two or three examples on the list: it is in (22)–(28) that such a resemblance is evident, for here we have phrases functioning as post- or pre-head modifier in NP structure or as predicative complement in clause structure.

Gerunds we were able to divide quite sharply into verbs and nouns, but the analysis of present participles is not quite so straightforward. The *-ing* words in (19)–(23) are clearly verbs, while those in (26)–(28) are equally clearly adjectives: it is examples like (24) and (25) that are problematic.

The verb status of (19)–(22) is evident from the fact that they have the same dependents – more specifically, complements – as the corresponding tensed verbs: cf. *He told the truth, He left the building, He was only three-foot tall, They own more than $200,000.* Adjectives do not take this kind of complement. The *being* in (23) is a form of the passive auxiliary; it has the same syntagmatic relation to *debated* as the tensed *was* of *It was debated.*

Charming and *interesting* in (27) and (28) are central members of the adjective class. They occur attributively, predicatively, postpositively and are gradable – cf. *a very charming fellow, He was very charming, someone very charming.* Some grading items can modify either verbs or adjectives, so that with *quite* or *rather*, for example, we can have both *I quite / rather liked it* and *It was quite / rather enjoyable*; others, however, are restricted – and in particular *very* modifies adjectives: *Did you like it much/*very?* vs *It was *much/very enjoyable.*[2] The fact that *charming* and *interesting* take *very* as modifier is thus strong evidence for analysing them as adjectives. We accordingly need to recognise a process of lexical morphology which converts *-ing* forms of verbs into central adjectives. Notice, moreover, that with *interesting* the stem so formed can undergo the further lexical-morphological process of prefixation by *un-*, a process which we have seen to apply very productively to adjective stems. The compound *record-breaking* in (26) is not a form of a lexeme with tensed forms (cf. **It record-broke*) and hence is disqualified from the verb class. It is not gradable and can hardly be used predicatively (cf. *?*The swim was record-breaking*), but given that it is not a candidate for any other class the fact that it is used attributively is sufficient to qualify it as an adjective, albeit a non-central one. We may add that certain otherwise similar compounds do have the full properties of central adjectives: cf. *It was very spine-chilling.*

Consider now *setting* and *falling* in (24) and (25). They are evidently not central adjectives: they are not gradable and cannot function as predicative complement. We can of course have *The sun was setting* or *The share prices were falling* but the **be** here is the progressive auxiliary and *setting, falling* are main verbs, heads within the predicator, not predicative complements. This is evident from the meaning but is confirmed by their inability to occur after other verbs taking predicative complements, notably **seem**, **appear**, **become**: **The sun seemed setting, *The share prices seemed falling.* Note also the contrast between *falling* and the central adjective *interesting* functioning as objective predicative complement: *He made/considered them interesting/*falling.* Should we then analyse *setting* and *falling* as verbs? They are unlike normal verbs in that they cannot have any following dependents:

---

[2] *Much* can modify comparative adjectives (e.g. *much taller*) and one or two others (*much different*; [*It wasn't*] *much good*). In active clauses *much* (when not itself modified by *very*) tends to be restricted to negative or interrogative constructions (or to 'non-affirmative' constructions in the sense of 13.2): compare *I didn't like it much* and *?*I like it much.*

*the setting slowly sun, *the falling to a new low share prices.* However, it is a general characteristic of NP structure that pre-head modifiers cannot normally contain dependents following their own heads (see 6.8). As for pre-head dependents, they are also unverblike in disallowing *not* (*the not falling share prices*), but the dependents that are found – generally manner adverbs like *slowly, gently, rapidly,* etc. – are ones which characteristically modify verbs rather than adjectives, so that there is some evidence here favouring a verb analysis. Moreover, the construction is highly productive, being found with words formed from the stems of verbs that occur freely without complements: *The baby was sleeping ~ the sleeping baby; The guests were departing ~ the departing guests; The minister was relying on her staff ~ *The relying minister; The troops were annihilating the enemy ~ *The annihilating troops.* (Note that the adjectives *charming* and *interesting* are, by contrast, derived from transitive verb stems.) This provides some evidence in favour of a syntactic rule governing the distribution of *-ing* forms of verbs rather than a morphological rule converting verbal *-ing* forms into adjectives. We might also add that the meaning of *setting* and *falling* is more characteristic of verbs than adjectives, and again they contrast with *charming* and *interesting.* 'Falling share prices' are share prices that are in the process of falling at the time in question – *falling* denotes a more or less temporary process; but a 'charming woman' is one with a certain kind of personality and need not be exercising her charms at the time in question – the adjective *charming* denotes a relatively permanent state or quality.

In summary, forms like *setting* and *falling* in (24) and (25) lie towards the boundary between the verb and adjective classes. They lack several of the properties of central members of the two classes, but are on the whole somewhat closer to verbs than to adjectives: we will analyse them as such, rather than as deverbal adjectives. The *-ing* words in (19)–(23), on the other hand, are quite clearly verbs, as we have seen, while those in (26)–(28) are adjectives.

9.2.2 Past participles

The forms to which the term 'past participle' is traditionally applied likewise do not make up a unified syntactic class: some are clearly verbs, others clearly adjectives, and some are more problematic – but these last are not entirely parallel to *setting* and *falling* above in their properties. A representative range of examples is given in (29)–(40):

(29)   [*He had*] taken [*my umbrella*]
(30)   [*He was*] given [*some money by his grandmother*]
(31)   [*He saw them*] killed
(32)   *Struck* [*on the cheek by a bouncer from Lillee, he fell to his knees in agony*]
(33)   [*The officer*] considered [*responsible for the accident refused to resign*]
(34)   [*The concert began with a rarely*] heard [*work by Purcell*]

(35)   [*He came across a*] broken [*vase*]
(36)   [*The vase was already*] broken
(37)   [*They were searching for the recently*] escaped [*prisoner*]
(38)   [*He's the director of a*] Sydney-based [*car hire firm*]
(39)   [*He's a*] worried [*man*]
(40)   [*He was very*] surprised [*at the result*]

Morphologically, past participles are less homogeneous than present participles in that they exhibit a variety of morphological processes applied to verb stems: suffixation of *-en* (*taken*), *-ed* (*killed*), vowel change of one kind or another (*strike* ~ *struck*; *ring* ~ *rung*), and so on – these processes are united syntactically by the fact that they yield forms capable of entering into construction with the perfect auxiliary **have**.

Before turning to an analysis in terms of verbs and adjectives, we should make a distinction between 'passive past participles' like the *given* of (30) and 'perfect past participles' like *taken* in (29). This reflects the fact that in the structure of the VP there are two auxiliaries that require the following verb to be in the *-en* form, the passive auxiliary **be** and the perfect auxiliary **have** (see 4.2). Constructions where neither auxiliary is actually present, as in (31)–(40), can then be related to the two elementary constructions of (29)–(30) and classified as passive or perfect accordingly. For example (31) can be related to the passive *They were killed* while (37) can be related to the perfect *The prisoner had escaped*, and so on; all the remaining examples above are passive past participles.

The past participles in (29)–(33) are undoubtedly verbs. This is clearest in the perfect construction of (29), since here the participle takes exactly the same range of complements as does a tensed verb. Such is not the case in the passive construction, since in the most straightforward kind of passivisation the object complement of the active becomes the subject of the passive. Thus the passive *killed* in (31), for example, cannot take an object although the central, i.e. tensed, forms of **kill** can; conversely the passive participle optionally takes a *by* phrase complement of a kind which the tensed verbs do not. Apart from this, however, the participles in (30)–(33) are like the corresponding tensed verbs with respect to their actual or potential complementation. Notice in particular that *given* in (30) does have an object, since in the active **give** allows two objects and only one of them is assigned a new function by passivisation – compare *His grandmother gave him some money*. And in (33) *considered* has a predicative complement, which – like an object – does not occur as a dependent of an adjective. Thus, save for the one readily identifiable difference attributable to the effect of passivisation, passive past participles like those in (30)–(33) are like central verbs and unlike adjectives in their complementation.

The past participles in (37)–(40) are, by contrast, clearly adjectives; they are very similar to the adjectival present participles in (26)–(28)

respectively. *Worried* and *surprised* are gradable – in particular, modifiable by *very*; moreover, they differ partly in their complementation from the corresponding verbs – witness the *at* phrase complement of *surprised*, the *about* phrase in *He was very worried about it* or the finite subordinate clause in *He was worried/surprised that she was late*.[3] Furthermore, *worried* and *surprised* occur in all three adjectival positions – attributive in (39), predicative in (40), postpositive in *someone very worried*. We must accordingly recognise a process of lexical morphology which converts certain verbal *-en* forms into central members of the adjective class.

Sydney-based in (38) is a compound adjective: as there are no corresponding tensed forms (**They Sydney-based the company*) it cannot be a verb. The first part of such morphological compounds corresponds to what in equivalent syntactic constructions is an NP related to the verb by a variety of prepositions – compare *Sydney-based* ~ *based in Sydney*, *syntax-related* ~ *related to syntax*, *hand-painted* ~ *painted by hand*, and so on.

Let us turn now to the less obvious cases in (34)–(37). The perfect past participle *escaped* in (37) has some affinities with the present participle *falling* in (25): it cannot be used predicatively, it is non-gradable and it has a modifier, *recently*, which characteristically enters into construction with verbs. An important difference, however, is that only a handful of forms behave like *escaped*: *a retired officer*, *the vanished Indians* – but not **the disappeared Indians*, and so on. A lexical solution, involving morphological conversion from verb to adjective, would thus seem to be more appropriate than a syntactic rule for the distribution of verbal *-en* forms.

Broken in (35) and (36) is not a central adjective in that it is not gradable, not modifiable by *very*. But, unlike the present participles *setting* and *falling* above, it can be used both attributively and predicatively, as the examples show.

At this point we must draw a distinction between two kinds of passive construction contrasted in (41):

(41)   i *The vase was broken by Tim*
       ii *The vase was already broken*   (= 36)

Example (i) is an **actional** passive, (ii) a **statal** passive. In the actional passive *be* is an auxiliary, the past participle is head of the VP and – provided there is a *by* phrase complement of the appropriate kind – the clause can be straightforwardly related to an active counterpart: it is for such cases that we have posited a passive transformation deriving (41i) from *Tim broke the vase*. In the statal passive, the *be* is a main verb, head of the VP predicator, while the past participle functions as (head of) a predicative complement, and there is no equivalent transformational derivation: (41ii)

---

[3] The difference in complementation is only partial, for the adjectives also allow a *by* phrase like the verbs: *He was very surprised by the result* (see 14.1).

is not derivable from [*Someone*] *already broke the vase*. If we remove the complement from (ii) and the modifier from (i) we are left with *The vase was broken*, which can belong to either construction, with clearly different interpretations in the two cases. As an actional passive it says that a certain event took place, namely the breaking of the vase. As a statal passive it attributes a certain property to the vase, that of being in the state resulting from the event wherein it was broken in the actional sense. The same ambiguity is found in *They were married* (*to each other*), "The marriage ceremony took place" (actional) or "They were husband and wife" (statal); in *The gate was closed*, "The closing of the gate took place" (actional) or "The gate was in a closed state, i.e. the opposite of open" (statal); and so on. One good reason for saying that in the statal passive the participle is complement rather than main verb is that it can occur with other copulative verbs than **be**: *The vase appeared/looked/seemed broken*, and so on (compare the non-participial predicative complements in *The vase appeared/looked/seemed very valuable*).

The past participle of the actional passive is, we have argued, a verb; that of the statal passive is better analysed as an adjective. This means that in addition to the morphological process converting *-en* forms into central adjectives like *worried, surprised*, we have one converting *-en* forms into more marginal adjectives like *broken*. The evidence for analysing *broken* as an adjective is as follows:

(a) As we began by noting, it can be used both attributively and predicatively. The contrast between actional and statal passives was introduced here to show that *broken* is indeed used predicatively in the way in which adjectives are, i.e. that it functions as head of the predicative complement.

(b) This kind of past participle can generally take the prefix *un-* meaning, essentially, "not", which elsewhere is added to what are clearly adjectives (*faithful ~ unfaithful, kind ~ unkind*, etc.) but not to verbs. Taking the statal participle as an adjective and the actional one as a verb then accounts for the fact that *The vase was unbroken, They were unmarried* are unambiguously based on the statal constructions.[4]

(c) The statal construction is somewhat less productive than the actional passive and hence more characteristic of lexical morphology. Examples like *They were killed, He was blamed for the accident, The error was noticed* are unambiguously actional – notice that **be** could not here be replaced by **seem**. The gaps are typically semantically motivated: noticing something

---

[4] A few verbs can take *un-* as prefix, but with a quite different sense, as in **untie, unwind**, etc. (see 4.1). And examples like *His shoe-laces were untied* will then exhibit the same ambiguity as *The vase was broken*, with *untied* a verb in the actional sense ("They untied his shoe-laces") and an adjective in the statal sense (as in *His trousers were at half-mast and his shoe-laces* (*were*) *untied*).

does not really affect it (as breaking something manifestly does), so that we do not need an adjective denoting the state resulting from being noticed – and the same holds for blaming someone. Killing obviously does affect the person or whatever that is killed, but the resulting state is not in general different from that resulting from the more general process of dying, which is denoted by *dead*.

This last point leads us to the final example in our set of past participles, (34). For *heard* does not occur in the statal passive construction, as is evident from the deviance of *It seemed heard, etc., and the unique interpretation of *They were heard* (which expresses a happening, not a resultant state) – and again there is little need for a word denoting the state resulting from being heard. (34) thus differs significantly from (35): *heard* cannot be used as predicative complement and the meaning corresponds to that of the actional (verbal) passive rather than the statal (adjectival) passive. (34), unlike (35), provides the analogue among past participles to the *setting* and *falling* examples among our present participles, and it too seems best analysed as a (marginal) verb. Other examples with verbal past participles used attributively include *the hastily read document, a carelessly driven car, the unjustly blamed petty officer, an atrociously sung aria, a frequently used recipe*, and so on.

Past participles thus illustrate well the tendency for the parts of speech to be very clearly different at their centres but much less easily distinguishable at their margins. We can range them on a scale from most verbal to most adjectival with at least three intermediate positions, as shown in (42):

(42)

Verbal   Adjectival

←——————————————————————————————————→

A	B	C	D	E
[He had]	[He was]	[a rarely] heard	[a] broken [vase]	[a] worried [man]
taken [it]	killed [(by Tim)]	[work by Purcell]	[it seemed] broken	[He seemed] worried

B is slightly less verbal than A with respect to its complementation, while C is much less verbal still by virtue of the severe restrictions on permitted dependents. D is less adjectival than E because it is ungradable, while C is less adjectival than D because it cannot occur as predicative complement. I have put the boundary between C and D, but other divisions will be found in the literature, while some writers – on principle or out of expediency – are inexplicit about the status of C and D.

boundary between nouns and adjectives as gerunds and participles straddle

9.3 Nouns vs adjectives

There is no morphologically special type of word straddling the those between verbs and nouns and between verbs and adjectives: our discussion of the noun–adjective boundary will thus differ slightly in form from the earlier sections. It will again be helpful to use the informal term 'nominalisation' for a grammatical process resulting in forms bearing some resemblance to nouns or NPs: this time we shall be concerned with the nominalisation of adjectives or of larger forms headed by adjectives: we will distinguish two types of nominalisation and then turn to the 'adjectivalisation' of nouns or of larger forms headed by nouns.

9.3.1 Nominalisation of adjectives

One type of nominalisation involves processes of lexical morphology. Where an affix is added, as with *happy* → *happiness*, adjective and noun are clearly distinct and we need not trouble ourselves further about such cases. Very often, however, the process is one of conversion, as with **white**$_{Adj}$ (as in *His hair is very white* or *This nappy is whiter than that one*) → **white**$_N$ (as in *There's too much white in the picture* or *Which of these whites would be better for the window-frames?*). The meaning of the resultant noun is very often like that of a sequence of the adjective plus another noun: **friendly**$_N$ = "friendly match", **empty**$_N$ = "empty bottle/jar, etc.", **weekly**$_N$ = 'weekly magazine/newspaper" – and indeed the noun may have a variety of senses depending on what is incorporated in this way – **daily**$_N$ can mean "daily newspaper" or "daily help", **white**$_N$ can mean not only "white colour", as above, but "white wine", "person with white skin", "white part of eye", and so on.

We are not postulating conversion, by contrast, in examples like *The tallest (of them)* [*was only five foot*], *The more important (of the objections)* [*was the moral one*] (see 7.3), since any superlative or comparative, whether inflectional or analytic, can occur here. Such forms as *the tallest (of them)* and *the more important (of the objections)* then differ from prototypical NPs in that they do not have a noun head, but they have so much else in common with NPs that we shall want to include them as peripheral members of that class: for example, they have the potential to function as subject, or as complement in EVP and PP structure, they can be singular or plural (as evident from the verb agreement when they are subject), and they contain the determiner *the*. Instead of saying that they are NPs with adjective heads, which would be inconsistent with our account of the relation between word- and phrase-classes, we suggested that there is here no head present in the structure – that they involve a kind of ellipsis of the head.

The case for lexical conversion from adjective to noun is clearest when, on the one hand, the adjective is gradable and hence takes comparative/superlative inflections (*white* ~ *whiter* ~ *whitest*)[5] and/or adverbs of degree as

---

[5] In one or two cases it is the comparative rather than the absolute form that is converted – cf. *Don't speak to your betters/elders like that.*

modifier (*more extreme, very particular, extremely ancient*) and, on the other, the noun has contrasting singular and plural forms (*white ~ whites, [one] extreme ~ [the] extremes, [one] particular ~ [both] particulars*) – or at least an inflectional plural (*the ancients*). Gradability, however, is not a necessary property of adjectives in general and we will not regard it as necessary in particular for the adjective member of an adjective–noun pair. Thus the *weekly* of *her weekly outing*, for example, is not gradable but it is clearly an adjective: although we allow in principle for a noun to modify another noun (as in our *boy actor* example of 3.1), we shall not want to equate this *weekly* with that of the noun *weekly* in *another British weekly* because the meaning is not the same – and the meaning of **weekly**$_N$ is evidently less basic than that of **weekly**$_{Adj}$. Nor shall we regard the existence of a plural form as a necessary property of the resultant noun – though certainly the great majority of de-adjectival nouns inflect for plural. Among those that don't we may mention such a language name as *Swedish*.[6] In *He learnt Swedish, Swedish is closely related to Norwegian* and the like, the fact that *Swedish* stands alone as object or subject is sufficient to establish that it is here a noun – but the sense ("Swedish language") is obviously less basic than that of *Swedish cooking, a Swedish film, the Swedish language* so that (as with *weekly* above) the attributive function of *Swedish* in these examples establishes it as an adjective.

The case against the lexical conversion is clearest in the constructions cited above which involve a comparative or superlative together with an explicit or implicit partitive. But again we will handle certain other constructions in the same way – for example, the subject and object phrases of *The strong should help the weak*. We will not analyse *strong* and *weak* as nouns here: they differ too much from the prototype. They do not inflect for number – but the phrases *the strong* and *the weak* are syntactically plural. *The* is the only determiner they combine with – we cannot say for example, **These strong should help those weak*, **The two strong should help us*. And, most significantly, they retain the property that they have in straightforward adjectival constructions like *[They are] strong/weak* of being able to take degree adverbs like *very, extremely*, etc. as dependents: *The very strong should help the very weak*. This makes the construction quite unlike those involving standard instances of conversion. When the noun stem *bottle*, for example, is converted to a verb, it loses its nominal properties: we cannot say, for example, **I must the bottle it* because **bottle**$_V$, unlike **bottle**$_N$, cannot enter into construction with determiners – and similarly **white**$_N$ lacks the adjectival properties of **white**$_{Adj}$, so that we could not add *very, extremely*, etc. to

[6] In fact one linguistic change currently underway involves pluralising language names like this: *Englishes*, for example, is now established in the technical discourse of sociolinguistics. But the point remains that the status of *Swedish* as a noun is not dependent on *Swedishes* being recognised as a word.

the examples cited above: *There's too much extremely white in the picture,* *Which of these beautifully whites would be better for the window-frames?.* We will accordingly treat *strong* and *weak* as adjectives in *The strong should help the weak*; the phrases *the strong* and *the weak,* however, are not AdjPs and it is probably again best to treat them as peripheral members of the NP class, differing from normal NPs in that there is no head element present.

The construction is one whose analysis must remain problematic – and there is indeed a further complication we should note. Other adjectives that are semantically like **strong** and **weak**, in that they can be used to classify human beings, also figure freely in it[7] – but with some the degree of what we are informally calling 'nominalisation' seems to be marginally greater: **poor** and *dead,* for example, can certainly occur with PossP determiners: *today's/Britain's poor, They buried their dead.* The degree of nominalisation is somewhat greater again in certain adjectival past participles, like *accused* or *deceased.* While *the strong* applies to strong people in general, which is why it is syntactically plural, *the accused* and *the deceased* are normally used in definite reference to one or more accused or deceased persons, and hence can be singular or plural – cf. *Both accused/Three of the accused were convicted, The accused is doubtless aware of the seriousness of the charge.* *Unemployed* is always plural but, unlike **strong,** **poor** and the like, combines freely with numerals: *This town alone has three thousand unemployed.* It is arguable whether these latter items should still be regarded as adjectives: there is inevitably some fuzziness at the boundary between nouns and adjectives. Clearly the degree of nominalisation in *accused, unemployed* and the like is significantly less than in **married,** where the plural *marrieds* (as in *the young marrieds*) is sufficient to establish conversion.

9.3.2   *Adjectivalisation of nouns*

The most straightforward type of adjectivalisation involves affixation, as in the formation of *heroic* from *hero, faithful* from *faith,* and so on: as with the formation by affixation of de-adjectival nouns, there is no problem here for the distinction between the two classes, and we need not concern ourselves further with it.

We can also use the informal term adjectivalisation for the kind of construction discussed at some length in 3.1 in connection with the example *a boy actor,* where *boy* functions as modifier to the noun *actor,* a function that is most characteristically performed by adjectives. We have argued, however, that it would be inappropriate to postulate conversion here – that *boy* is a noun in *a boy actor* as well as in *A boy arrived.* Just about any common or proper noun can function as modifier in NP structure in this

---

[7] The construction is not however restricted to phrases applying to humans – cf. *the cool of the evening, on the defensive, out of the ordinary, from the ridiculous to the sublime,* etc.

way. The degree of adjectivalisation that we find with *boy* is arguably slightly less than with words like *gold* or *cotton* that denote the material out of which things can be made: *a gold watch, a cotton shirt*. One of the properties distinguishing the noun *boy* from an adjective like *great* in the pair *a boy actor*/*a great actor* is that we do not have a corresponding predicative use: *The actor is great* but not **The actor is boy*. But *gold* and *cotton* can be related to *watch* and *shirt* either attributively, as above, or predicatively as in *The watch is gold, The shirt is cotton*. The predicative complement position, however, can be filled by NPs as well as AdjPs just as the modifier position in NP structure can be filled by nouns as well as adjectives, so that the predicative use of *gold* and *cotton* does not suffice to show that there has been conversion from noun to adjective. And indeed there is again quite compelling evidence against a conversion analysis: the dependents that *gold* and *cotton* themselves take in either their attributive or their predicative use are those that characteristically modify nouns, not adjectives. Thus we may compare *It was made of pure gold/Egyptian cotton* (where the status of *gold* and *cotton* as nouns is not in dispute) with *a pure gold watch, an Egyptian cotton shirt* or *It is pure gold, It is Egyptian cotton*. Note also that the postpositive construction is barely possible: *?*I must put everything gold into the safe, ?*Buy something cotton*; if *gold* and *cotton* were adjectives we would expect such examples to be wholly acceptable, whereas we have noted that there are considerable restrictions on the postpositive use (restrictive apposition) of NPs.

There will then be very little occasion to postulate conversion from noun to adjective. Where we can add degree adverbs as dependents, as – for some speakers at least – in *a very fun party, an extremely Oxbridge accent*, we will certainly regard the degree of adjectivalisation such as to justify a conversion analysis, but there are not many examples of this kind.

9.3.3 Numerals

One final issue we should mention briefly here concerns the classification of numerals – or, more precisely, **cardinal numerals** like *one, two, five, eighteen*, etc. (as opposed to **ordinal numerals** like *first, second, fifth, eighteenth*). Some grammars treat them as a distinct part of speech, but very often they are treated as belonging to both adjective and noun classes. That there are nouns **one**, **two**, **five**, **eighteen**, etc. is evident from the fact that they exhibit inflectional contrasts of number – witness the plurals in *They left in ones and twos, Divide them into fives, Two eighteens are thirty-six*. What is a good deal less clear is how the cardinal numerals should be analysed in *one man, two bottles*, etc., where they have determiner function. They certainly differ quite sharply from prototypical adjectives – and even in determiner function they have some nominal properties, as we saw from examples like *another two candidates* discussed in 6.4. If we are right in assuming that the constituent structure is *another two* + *candidates* then there is reason for saying that *two* is a noun here, functioning as head to the dependent *another*. Whatever primary class they belong to, it is clear that the cardinal numerals must also be recognised as a distinctive subclass. For this reason there is little to be said for assigning them to two primary classes – noun and adjective or determinative; it would seem better to assign them to the noun class on the basis of their number inflection and to handle their determiner use in terms of statements concerning a special subclass of nouns.

FURTHER READING

For an account of the distinction between participles and gerunds in traditional grammar, see Sweet 1891–98, Pt II:120–7. For a more recent and detailed survey of words in *-ing*, see Quirk et al. 1971:§§ 4.9–12. On the particular problems raised by the hybrid nature of the *-ing* construction, see Horn 1975, Schachter 1976. On the construction with *un-* + past participle, see Hust 1977.

10
Adverbs, prepositions and conjunctions

10.1 **Adverbs and adverb phrases**

The last of the four open word-classes that we have to consider is the adverb. It is traditionally defined as a word that modifies a verb, an adjective or an adverb – and it will be helpful to begin with some explanation of this very broad definition.

We noted in 3.4 that of the four open classes noun, verb, adjective, and adverb, the first two have special status in that every kernel clause must contain at least one noun and one verb – and the most elementary kind of kernel clause will contain just these: *Dogs bark, Max disappeared, Rain fell.* One way of expanding such minimal constructions is to add one or more modifiers to the noun and/or verb. For nouns the most characteristic modifiers are adjectives, while for verbs they are adverbs – compare *Heavy rain fell* where the adjective *heavy* modifies the noun *rain*, and *Rain fell heavily*, where the adverb *heavily* modifies the verb *fell*. We can then increase the complexity further by modifying the modifiers, as in *Unusually heavy rain fell*, where *unusually* modifies *heavy*. Now to a significant extent the words that modify other modifiers, whether these latter be adjectives or adverbs, are the same as those which modify verbs and different from those which modify nouns – compare

(1)   i *She loved him sufficiently*
        ii *a sufficiently long delay*
        iii *She spoke sufficiently slowly*
        iv *a sufficient sum*

where *sufficiently* modifies the verb *loved* in (i), the adjective *long* in (ii), the adverb *slowly* in (iii), while *sufficient* modifies the noun *sum* in (iv). It is this fact, essentially, that provides the rationale for the very broad definition of adverb given in traditional grammars.

It will be clear at this stage, of course, that the definition will not serve satisfactorily as a language-particular definition. Not all adverbs occur with all three functions: we noted in 9.2.1, for example, that *very* modifies adjectives (and adverbs) but not verbs, and conversely such traditional adverbs as *ashore, downstairs, why*, etc., modify verbs[1] but not adjectives or adverbs. Furthermore, adverbs are not restricted to those three functions: in *The room downstairs is still vacant*, for example, *downstairs* is modifying *room*, which is a noun. Nevertheless, the essence of the traditional definition is undoubtedly relevant to a general definition of adverbs, and to a characterisation of what can reasonably be regarded as the most central type of adverb in English.

We should add at this point that the concept 'modifier of a verb' is in need of some clarification. We are working within a framework where sentences are assigned a constituent structure such that, in general, the functional positions within the structure of the clause will be realised by phrases rather than, immediately, by words. Moreover we have recognised three constructions whose immediate or ultimate head is a verb: the VP, EVP and clause (and we have raised, without resolving, the issue of whether others might be needed as well). Thus in

(2)   *Unfortunately he was talking too quickly*

talking is head of the VP and as such has the auxiliary *was* as dependent, *was talking* is head of the EVP and as such has *too quickly* as dependent, and *was talking too quickly* is head – more specifically, predicate – of the clause and as such has *unfortunately* as dependent (unless we assign a structure in which the immediate constituents are *unfortunately* and *he was talking too quickly* – see 5.7). Within this framework, therefore, an adverb will not generally enter immediately into construction with a verb: it will be head of a phrase functioning as dependent of a VP or of a larger phrase with a verb as ultimate head.

Notice, however, that *too quickly* in (2) could be replaced, without change of function, by such a phrase as *at too fast a rate*:

(3)   *Unfortunately he was talking at too fast a rate*

but *at* – unlike *quickly* – is not analysed as an adverb: it is a preposition. The reason for this as far as traditional grammar is concerned is that *at* is thought of as serving to relate the verb (phrase) *was talking* to the noun (phrase) *too fast a rate* rather than as having this noun (phrase) as its dependent, as *quickly* in (2) has *too* as its dependent. Within the analysis adopted here, where *at* is taken as head of *at too fast a rate* just as *quickly* is head of *too quickly*, there are two arguments for assigning *quickly* and *at* to different word-classes – adverb and preposition:

(a) In the first place, they differ sharply as to the kinds of dependent they take within their respective phrases – prepositions, for example, usually take NP complements, while adverbs never do.

---

[1] Or at least are traditionally regarded as modifying verbs: we shall look further into the implications of that formulation in the next paragraph.

(b) Secondly, there are differences in the functional potential of the phrases headed by *quickly* and *at*. As well as functioning as dependent in clause structure, a PP can normally function as dependent in NP structure, whereas the most central type of AdvP cannot: compare *delivery at too fast a rate* and **delivery too quickly*.

Before leaving the relation between (2) and (3), it is worth observing that although the word *at* is not analysed as an adverb, the phrase *at too fast a rate* is commonly said to be 'adverbial' – or indeed to be an adverb. Because the word-class adverb is traditionally defined with reference to syntagmatic relations, the term 'adverb' and its derivatives tend to be used for the corresponding function too. Since we are here making a consistent distinction between classes and functions we will not adopt that usage, but will use 'adverb' exclusively for a word/lexeme class and 'adverb phrase' for the class of phrase having an adverb as head.

One final point that we should make about the traditional concept 'modifier of a verb' is that 'modification' covers a somewhat broader range of dependent functions than in the usage adopted here – in particular it covers certain kinds of complement. For example, in *He went ashore* or *She took it downstairs* we are taking *ashore* and *downstairs* as complements, not modifiers (adjuncts), but they would traditionally be regarded as satisfying the cited definition of adverb. Nevertheless, modifier, in the narrower sense we are giving it, is the more usual function of adverbs, and words like *ashore, downstairs*, etc., are arguably less central members of the class than *quickly* and the like.

We observed in 3.1 that the traditional part-of-speech classification is commonly criticised for the heterogeneity of the adverb class: to say that a word is an adverb is to give less distinctive information about it than to say that it belongs to one of the other classes. There is not space here for a comprehensive examination of the class: I will rather confine myself to commenting briefly on the morphology of adverbs and then on a selection of the more important syntactic subclasses.

Morphologically we can classify adverbs according as their lexical stems are complex, compound or simple. The great majority have complex stems, and most of these are formed by the highly productive process of suffixing *-ly* to an adjective stem: *quickly* (from *quick*), *carefully* (from *careful*) and so on. As is characteristic of lexical morphology, we find considerable variation in the semantic relation between the adjective and adverb. Often, *X-ly* can be glossed as "in an X way", as with *beautifully, carefully, expertly*, etc., but we also find many where the adverb meaning has to be stated ad hoc – cf. *actually* ("in actual fact"); *frankly* [*it was horrible*] ("speaking with candour"); [*I'll see them*] *individually* ("one at a time"); *certainly* [*I'll help*] ("I assure you"), and so on. Although most words in *-ly* are adverbs, it should be noted that the suffix is also used, though very much less productively, to form adjectives – from nouns, as in *princely, husbandly*, etc., or from other adjectives, as in *goodly, kindly*, etc. (*kindly* is an adjective in *a kindly man*, an adverb in *He kindly helped me*). Two suffixes that form only adverbs are *-ward(s)* and *-wise*, as in *backward(s), onward(s), clockwise, money-wise*, etc.; adverbs so formed are clearly far fewer than those in *-ly* but the *-wise* suffix used with the meaning "as far as ... is concerned" is the source of a number of recent coinages, especially in US English. A handful of adverbs are formed with the prefix *a-*: *abroad, ashore, aside, apart, asunder* – but again this prefix is also found in adjectives like *ablaze, ashamed, asleep, awake*.

The number of compound adverbs is by contrast quite small: *downstairs, upside-down, nevertheless, furthermore*, etc. The only compounding processes with any significant degree of productivity involve joining *there* or *where* to a preposition stem, as in *thereby, therein, whereupon*, though many such items are either archaic or characteristic of formal styles. We noted in comparing (2) and (3) that, from a functional point of view, adverbs have much in common with PPs, and with some of these compounds the functional similarity is matched by a resemblance of internal structure – compare the adverbs *downstairs, thereafter* with the PPs *down the stairs, after that*, and so on.

Finally there are adverbs with simple lexical stems: *how, just* (as in *He's just arrived*), *so, soon, too, very, well, yet*, and so on. The number, however, is vastly smaller than is the case with the three other open word-classes. Quite a few stems, mainly though not exclusively simple, belong both to the adverb class and to either the preposition or adjective classes. Thus *in* and *on* are traditionally analysed as adverbs in *He went in, She carried on* but as prepositions in *It fell in the river, She was on the committee*, and similarly *fast* and *hard* are adverbs in *He drove fast, She tried hard* but adjectives in *a fast driver, a hard worker*. The justification for saying that *fast* is an adverb in *He drove fast* and an adjective in *a fast driver* is that only a small number of items occur in both constructions: for the most part we find contrasting forms, as in *He drove carefully* vs *a careful driver*; those that can occur in both have to be individually specified, and this is accordingly best done by specifying in their lexical entries that they belong to both adverb and adjective classes. The justification for treating *in* and *on* as both adverbs and prepositions is much less compelling, and I will return to this issue in §7 below. In addition, it will be recalled from 8.5 that a handful of words with simple stems belong to both adverb and determinative classes: *the, this, that, much, less*, etc.

As for inflectional morphology, a few adverbs inflect for comparison: *soon, sooner, soonest*, etc. This inflectional category applies much more extensively, of course, to adjectives – and indeed in the majority of cases where an adverb inflects the lexeme in question is one that belongs to the adjective as well as to the adverb class: ***fast, hard, early, late, long***, and so on. In particular, adverbs formed from adjectives by -*ly* suffixation do not inflect. *Rather* is a comparative with no absolute or superlative counterparts; it behaves syntactically like a comparative in constructions like *I'd rather die than do that* (witness the *than* clause), but not when functioning as a degree modifier with the sense "somewhat", as in *a rather questionable move*.

Let us turn now to the syntax of adverbs. There are two main dimensions of classification. One is concerned with the kinds of forms that they (or the phrases they head) can modify or otherwise enter into construction with. A prototypical adverb can modify a VP, an adjective or another adverb, but we have noted that not all adverbs have this property: we need not pursue this point further. The other dimension distinguishes various types of dependent function, such as degree modification, manner modification, and so on. To a considerable extent the distinctions made here will correspond to those proposed between various kinds of adjuncts (see 5.7), since almost all the latter can be realised by AdvPs. Thus we will have manner adverbs (*carefully*), means adverbs (*spectroscopically*, "using a spectroscope"), time adverbs (*now*), duration adverbs (**long**: *It lasted longer than we'd expected*), frequency adverbs (*often*), place or 'locative' adverbs (*here*), reason adverbs (*why*), degree adverbs (*much*), viewpoint adverbs (*philosophically*, "from a philosophical point of view"), modal adverbs (*perhaps*), connective adverbs (*however*), and so on. We will comment very briefly on just a few of these classes.

(a) Adverbs of degree. These include a significant number of the morphologically simple adverbs (*as, how, much, pretty, quite, so, this, that, too, very*), various -*ly* adverbs (*surprisingly, excessively, sufficiently*) and a few others (*almost, rather, somewhat*). Several of the simple ones cannot modify VPs: compare *He wasn't that tall* and **He didn't love her that* – the VP takes *that much*, etc. Some degree adverbs can themselves be modified by other degree adverbs: *almost too good, so very happy, quite sufficiently obvious*.

(b) Adverbs of manner. These typically have the -*ly* suffix (*carefully, quietly, smoothly*, etc.), though the class also includes *well, how* and sundry others. They normally modify VPs (*She spoke quietly*), but they are occasionally found with adjectives (*She seemed quietly confident*). Some adverbs that primarily indicate manner may acquire a degree or quasi-degree interpretation when modifying an adjective – cf. *her beautifully clear presentation*. It is adverbs of manner that are most freely modified by other adverbs (normally of degree): *She spoke very quietly*.

(c) Adverbs of time. A mixed bunch morphologically, with some simple (**late, soon,** *again, just, now, then, when*), some in -*ly* (*initially, immediately, presently, recently*), and a variety of others: *afterwards, nowadays, today, tomorrow, tonight, yesterday*, etc. The inclusion of these last four, however, is open to question. They are traditionally analysed as belonging to both noun and adverb classes – nouns when the phrase they head functions as subject, object or the like (*Tomorrow is his birthday*), adverbs when it functions as adjunct or temporal complement (*She's arriving tomorrow, The meeting is tomorrow*). However, there are certain NPs with the same distributional range: *this morning, last night, next Tuesday*, and the like; cf. *This morning was wasted, She arrived this morning, The meeting was this morning. Tomorrow* and the others belong semantically with these (they all refer deictically to a period of time: *tomorrow* refers to the day after that on which the utterance containing it takes place, *last night* to the night preceding the day on which it takes place, and so on), and there is no reason why we should not treat them all alike syntactically too: *tomorrow*, etc., would then be just nouns, like *night, Tuesday*, etc. and we would have a general rule that the class of deictic temporal NPs *last night, tomorrow* ..., can all function as subject, object, adjunct, temporal complement, or complement of a preposition. Note, in support of such a treatment, examples like *She's arriving tomorrow, which is his birthday*: *tomorrow* is here an adjunct, but is nevertheless like an NP in serving as antecedent to the pronoun *which*.

(d) Adverbs of place. *Here, there, where, upstairs, ashore, eastwards*, and the like: note that *-ly* does not derive adverbs of this class (except for *locally*). They function as modifiers (or complements) of VPs rather than of adjectives or adverbs: *He slept downstairs* (modifier), *He went ashore* (complement). We observed above that a number of words are traditionally analysed as members of both the adverb and preposition classes according as they lack or have an NP complement. Most of these belong in their adverbial use to the place subclass: *above, across, behind, below, between, in, off, on, to, through, under, up* and a number of others; we take up this issue in §7 below.

Finally we should note that there are two important closed classes which cut across the primary part-of-speech classification to include a few adverbs as well as certain pronouns and determinatives. Adverbs belonging to the class of '*wh*' words (covering interrogatives, relatives and exclamatives: see 11.4, 12.4, 11.5) are *how* (degree or manner/means), *when* (time), *where* (place), *why* (reason) – and complex or compound forms like *whence, whenever, whereby*, etc. Adverbs belonging to the class of negative words are *nowhere* (place), *never* (time) and *not* itself (a 'pure' negative without any additional component such as place or time).

There is little that needs to be said about the structure of AdvPs, which is much simpler than that of phrases headed by members of the other three open classes. Few adverbs take complements (as *independently*, say, can take a PP with *of*: *independently of such factors*) and modification is generally of the degree type, paralleling that discussed for AdjPs (compare *more careful than ever before* and *more carefully than ever before*). Quite a number of adverbs cannot take dependents and it is very doubtful whether there is any justification for talking of AdvPs at all in cases like *however, nevertheless, perhaps,* etc. (see 3.3).

10.2 **Prepositions**

It will be recalled that the preposition is traditionally defined in something like the following way: 'a word that indicates a relation between the noun or pronoun it governs and another word, which may be a verb, an adjective or another noun or pronoun' (the definition cited in 3.1 from Curme 1935:87). Thus in *She voted against us, She was dependent on us, Her opinion of us improved* the prepositions *against, on* and *of* are said to relate *us* to the verb *voted*, the adjective *dependent* and the noun *opinion* respectively. The concept of 'indicating a relationship', however, is very vague and such a definition is clearly in need of considerable refinement (whether construed at the general or language-particular level) to distinguish prepositions from, for example, verbs and 'coordinating conjunctions', which can also relate one NP to another, as *loves* and *and* do in *Ed loves Kim, Ed and Kim arrived.*

Central members of the closed class of prepositions in English have the following properties:

(a) Functional potential, I. They take NPs as complements – *for my uncle, with every care,* etc.

(b) Functional potential, II. The phrases they head have a considerable variety of functions in larger constructions, notably: in clause structure, complement ([*She relied*] *on Max*) or adjunct ([*She left*] *before the end*); in AdjP structure, complement ([*similar*] *to the other one*) or modifier ([*tall*] *for his age*); in NP structure, complement ([*the author*] *of the book*) or modifier ([*a man*] *without scruples*).

(c) Invariability. They show no inflectional variation.

Where the PP is a complement, rather than adjunct or modifier, the choice of preposition is often determined or severely limited by the verb, adjective or noun head to which the PP is complement and/or by the kind of complement it is. For instance, in the examples just given – *She relied on Max, similar to the other one, the author of the book* – the *on, to* and *of* are determined by **rely**, *similar*, and **author** respectively. In *This book was written by Max* – the passive counterpart of *Max wrote this book* – the *by* is determined by the passive construction: the rule is that the complement corresponding to the active subject takes the preposition *by*. In *Ed gave the key to Max* the *to* is attributable to a combination of factors: the verb **give**, which takes a *to* complement, the choice of the NP + PP construction rather than the double object construction of *Ed gave Max the key*, the fact that *Max* is associated with the semantic role of recipient. Where, as in these constructions, there is little or no possibility of paradigmatic variation of the preposition, so that it makes little or no independent contribution to the meaning, we have what is often called a 'grammatical' use of the preposition, as opposed to its 'lexical' use in examples like *He left before/towards/at/after midnight*, where it has its full lexical meaning. The grammatical uses are not found with all prepositions: they are characteristic of a handful of very short items like *of, on, in, by, for, from, to, with* – but not, say, *among, before, below, beside, beyond, despite, opposite, throughout, underneath* and the like. In some of their grammatical uses prepositions do the same kind of work as case inflections: as we noted in 2.3, for example, the *to* in a sentence like *Ed gave the key to Max* serves to show that Max was the recipient, while in Latin this would be shown by a dative case inflection. It does not follow, however, that prepositions should be considered case-markers. Languages like Latin have both prepositions and case inflections, with prepositions typically being like verbs in determining the case of their complements, so that in such languages one would still want to regard prepositions and case inflections as distinct phenomena. Thus the difference between English and Latin is not a matter of analytically versus inflectionally marked cases but of a quite different balance between cases and prepositions (and the linear order of elements) in showing syntactic functions and semantic roles.

10.3   The position of prepositions

Any satisfactory general definition of 'preposition' will include a reference to the fact that prepositions normally precede their complements. In some languages, such as Japanese, items which are otherwise like prepositions follow their complements and are accordingly called 'postpositions'; 'adposition' is then a more general term covering both. The position of adpositions relative to their complements in a given language normally correlates with various other aspects of the order of elements in that language: in English, for example, verbs also precede their complements, whereas in Japanese they follow. However, there may be some mixing of types within a single language: in English the great majority of adpositions are prepositions, but we find one or two items that might most appropriately be analysed as postpositions. Thus in *I saw it three weeks ago, these errors notwithstanding, my uncle's car*, for example, *ago, notwithstanding* and the possessive clitic are functionally analogous to prepositions yet follow their complements. They are so few and exceptional, however, that traditional grammars do not recognise a class of postpositions or treat prepositions as a special case of adpositions – *ago* in the above example would be an adjective, *notwithstanding* an adverb (it is a preposition in *notwithstanding these errors*), and the possessive element, an inflectional suffix, as we have noted.

The distinction between prepositions and postpositions is based on their position relative to their complements in constructions with an unmarked order of elements: it should not be confused with the contrast between constructions like *He was looking at something* and *What was he looking at?*. In the latter, the complement of *at*, namely *what*, occurs in initial position in what is, for this and other reasons, a non-kernel clause: we have suggested that such constructions can most conveniently be described in terms of a transformation that moves an element from the position it occupies in declarative clauses. The transformation does not affect the class of *at* (just as the fronting of the complement of the verb in *What had he bought?* does not affect the class of *bought*): *at* is a preposition in both the kernel and non-kernel constructions.

The fronting of elements in interrogatives, relatives, etc., may affect a complement of a preposition or else a whole PP, so that in general we have a choice between the following constructions:

(4)   i *Which door did he go through?*
       ii *Through which door did he go?*

The first belongs to a less formal style than the second. In the past, examples like (4i) have often been claimed to be grammatically incorrect, violating a putative rule that a sentence should not end with a preposition, but this 'rule' has so often been held up to ridicule that we may reasonably hope that not even the most prescriptively-minded schoolteacher would now subscribe to it. We should also note that with a few expressions only one or other construction is available. Thus *what ... for*, in the sense "why?" never has the preposition fronted (*What are you looking at me like that for?*, not **For what are you looking at me like that?*), conversely *what circumstances/conditions* always takes the preposition *under* along with it (*Under what circumstances would he agree?*, not **What circumstances would he agree under?*). In between these extremes there are differences of degree in the readiness or naturalness with which the various prepositions can be left 'stranded' through the fronting of their complements. In general it is those which are short, frequent and have 'grammatical uses' that are most easily stranded – *in, on, of, at, with*, etc., rather than *beside, throughout, despite, underneath*, and the like.

10.4 Conjunctions and their relation to prepositions

Central members of the closed class of conjunctions have the following properties:

(a) Functional potential. They serve to relate a tensed declarative clause to a larger construction containing it. Thus in *The car had broken down and it was raining, He said that it was raining, He stayed in because it was raining* the conjunctions *and, that* and *because* relate the tensed declarative clause *it was raining* to the construction forming the whole sentence.

(b) Invariability. Like prepositions, they show no inflectional variation.

Two major subclasses of conjunction are distinguished: coordinating and subordinating. The central **coordinating conjunctions** are *and* and *or*, with *but* not far from centre. The **subordinating conjunctions** are more numerous: *after, although, as, because, before, if, since, that, unless, until, while*, etc. The distinction depends of course on that between coordinate and subordinate constructions, which we shall be dealing with in 12.1.

Traditional definitions of the conjunction are often couched in quite general terms: for Curme, as we have seen, it is 'a word that joins together sentences or parts of sentences'. This would seem to subsume, rather than contrast with, the class of prepositions as he defines it. The distinction traditionally drawn can be seen in the following definitions from the *Concise Oxford Dictionary*: 'Preposition: indeclinable [i.e. uninflected] word serving to mark relation between the noun or pronoun it governs and another word'; 'Conjunction: uninflected word used to connect clauses or sentences, or to co-ordinate words in same clause'. In the light of what was said in 1.5, the *COD*'s 'clauses or sentences' can to all intents and purposes be simplified to just 'clauses', so that the traditional distinction between the two parts of speech is thus basically that a preposition enters into construction with a noun or pronoun (or, as we would put it, an NP), whereas a conjunction – except in certain cases of coordination – enters into construction with a clause:

(5)   i *I was there during the riots*
        ii *I was there while the riots were raging*

In (i) *during* is a preposition since it is in construction with the NP *the riots*; in (ii) *while* is a conjunction since it is in construction with the clause *the riots were raging*.[2]

The distinction is not, however, as straightforward or well-motivated as this might suggest. There are several points we should note.

(a) A number of words enter into construction with either an NP or a clause and are therefore traditionally analysed as belonging to both classes: *after, before, some, as*, etc. Compare *He left before the meeting* (with *before* a preposition) and *He left before the meeting began* (with *before* a conjunction).

---

[2] This account is slightly misleading in that *while* is traditionally analysed as being part of the subordinate clause, so that although *during the riots* is a PP, *while the riots were raging* is not analysed as, as it were, a 'conjunction phrase'. It will be convenient to continue using the expression 'enter into construction with' in a looser way than hitherto so that it covers not only the relation between *during* and *the riots* but also that between *while* and *the riots were raging*.

(b) As is clear from the *COD* definition, coordinating conjunctions can link smaller forms than clauses, such as NPs: *Ed and his uncle*. The conjunction–preposition distinction is thus based on two largely independent variables – coordination vs subordination on the one hand, construction with clause vs construction with NP on the other:

(6)

		Coordination	Subordination
With clause	(i)	*Bill left and Ed did too*	(ii) *Bill left before it began*
With NP	(iii)	*Bill and Ed left*	(iv) *Bill left before the meeting*

If *before* is a conjunction in (ii) and a preposition in (iv), one might ask why *and* is a conjunction in both (i) and (iii).

(c) Some of the words traditionally analysed as prepositions do in fact take clause complements of certain kinds. In *He was worrying about who he should confide in* or *He raised the question of why it had been concealed*, for example, the prepositions *about* and *of* take interrogative clauses as complement. In *He insisted on there being at least one student on the committee* or *He objected to being forced to vote*, the prepositions *on* and *to* take as complement *-ing* class constructions, which we are regarding as peripheral members of the category 'clause'. It was for this reason that my own initial account of the properties of conjunctions specified 'a tensed declarative clause', not simply a clause. But the question then arises as to why we should make a primary part-of-speech division on the basis of such a specific distinction in the kind of complement – tensed declarative clause vs NP or clause of some other kind. As we have seen, members of the three major parts of speech have to be subclassified according to what kinds of complements they take: **insist** takes, inter alia, a tensed declarative clause (*He insists he's innocent*) but not an NP (**He insisted his innocence*), **ask** takes an NP or an interrogative clause (*He asked a question, He asked who I was*) but not a tensed declarative clause (**He asked that she was tired*), and so on. There is much to be said for conflating prepositions and conjunctions into a single class, which would then similarly be subclassified according to the kind of complements permitted. Note that we would need more than two subclasses (just as we do with verbs), as can be seen from the following sample:

(7)

	Kind of complement			
	(i)	(ii)	(iii)	(iv)
	Tensed declarative clause	Interrogative clause	*-ing* construction	NP
after	√	×	√	√
behind	×	×	×	√
of	×	√	√	√
through	×	×	√	√
until	√	×	×	√

(8)   i   *after/*behind/*of/*through/until he had finished*
          ii **after/*behind/of* (e.g. *the question of*)/**through/*until who it was*
          iii *after/*behind/of* (e.g. *the importance of*)/*through/*until studying it*
          iv *after/behind/of/through/until the riot*

Many modern grammarians have argued for a revision of the part-of-speech classification along such lines, but with considerable differences of detail in their proposals. Thus it is arguable that not all the traditional conjunctions should be conflated with the preposition class in the above way. For example, *that* is significantly different from the other subordinating conjunctions in that in many constructions it is freely omissible: compare *He assumed that she was ready* and *He assumed she was ready*. For this reason we shall hardly want to treat *that* as head of the construction *that she was ready* – and we shall certainly not want to record in our lexical entry for a verb like **assume** that it can take two quite different kinds of complement with *that she was ready* being a PP, *she was ready* a clause. If we keep *that* distinct from our enlarged preposition class, we might do the same for *whether*, which is closely related paradigmatically to *that* inasmuch as the contrast between them reflects a contrast in the system of clause type as it applies to subordinate clauses, with [*He didn't know*] *that she was ready* being declarative, [*He didn't know*] *whether she was ready* being interrogative (see Ch. 11).[3] The coordinators might also be kept apart. We will not pursue the matter any further here: for our purposes it is sufficient to have presented the traditional analysis and to have suggested in very general terms how it might be improved; in the absence of any widespread agreement on any particular alternative classification, we will continue in what follows to use the traditional one in spite of its rather clear shortcomings.

10.5   **On so-called 'complex prepositions'**
          Many grammars make a distinction between 'simple prepositions', consisting of a single word, and 'complex prepositions', consisting of from two to four words including at least one simple preposition. Examples of complex prepositions are: *aside from, because of, by dint of, by means of, by virtue of, for the sake of, in accordance with, in addition to, in case of, in comparison with, in front of, in lieu of, in spite of, instead of, in view of, on account of, on behalf of, on the strength of, with reference to, with a view to*, etc. The structure of a PP headed by a complex preposition will be distinguished from that of a PP containing a smaller PP embedded within it. For example, *by dint of hard work* will have the structure shown in (9),

---

[3] One complicating factor here is that *if* can occur in most subordinate interrogative constructions as a variant of *whether* (cf. *He didn't know whether/if she was ready*), although its most frequent use is as an 'ordinary' subordinating conjunction (as in *He gets annoyed if/unless/because/although we try to help*).

whereas *after years of hard work* (where there is no complex preposition) will have that shown in (10):

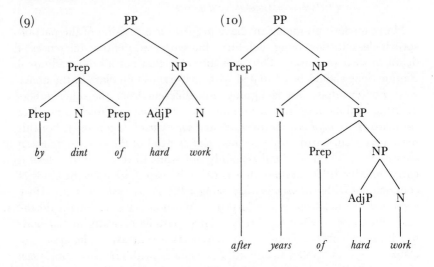

(9) ... (10)

There are, however, considerable difficulties with this analysis.

It is reasonable to regard (10) as a more basic or elementary syntactic construction than (9). *After* has an NP as complement, following the most frequent structure for PPs; the NP *years of hard work* contains a PP as post-head dependent, which again is a very frequent structure for NPs: putting these two standard structures together then yields (10), which thus represents a virtually fully productive construction. In (9), by contrast, there are very severe restrictions on the permitted combinations of words in the complex prepositions, such that the latter must be listed in the dictionary as wholes rather than being the output of general rules. We may think of complex prepositions as arising historically through the 'lexicalisation' – the fusion into a single lexical item – of the first words of some productive construction like (10). (The **dint** which survives in *by dint of* meant "stroke, blow".) Analysis (9) takes this lexicalisation to be accompanied by a syntactic regrouping such that the lexicalised sequence becomes a syntactic constituent.

(9) and (10) both contain the partial structure:

(11) $Prep_1 + N + Prep_2 + NP$

The fusion of the first three words in the case of the complex preposition is reflected in the failure of the $N + Prep_2 + NP$ sequence to exhibit the normal syntactic properties of an NP. Let us call this sequence 'X' (to avoid prejudging the question of its syntactic status) and consider the extent to which it behaves like an NP by asking such questions as the following:

(a) Can X occur in the normal range of NP functions – as subject or complement in clause structure, and so on? The distribution of *years of hard work* is governed by the ordinary NP rules (cf. *Years of hard work had taken their toll*; *He had wasted years of hard work*; etc.) but *dint of hard work* cannot occur in such positions – it cannot even occur after any other preposition than *by*.

(b) Does X enter into the usual paradigmatic contrast of definiteness? More generally, does it permit the usual range of determiners? Indefinite *years of hard work* contrasts with definite *the years of hard work*, and we could have other determiners such as definite *these*, indefinite *a few*, *several*, and so on, but no such variation is possible for *dint of hard work*. (In testing for variability we must of course require that the resulting change in meaning be predictable. Thus in moving from *in front of the car* to *in the front of the car* we change from "before" to "in the forward section of", which is not attributable to any variation in definiteness, and hence the answer to the present question for the X part of *in front of the car* would be 'no'. Compare similarly *in case of fire*, "in the event of fire", and *in the case of fire*, "as regards fire".)

(c) Does X enter into the usual paradigmatic contrast of number? Thus plural *years of hard work* can be replaced by singular *a year of hard work*, but singular *dint of hard work* has no plural counterpart. (Again such changes are relevant only when the meaning change is regular: *with references to* is perfectly grammatical – as in *He filled his paper with references to his earlier work* – but is not systemically related to *with reference to*, "as regards".)

(d) Does X allow variation between the *of* phrase and PossP constructions (see 6.13)? For example, *after the arrival of the prime minister* – which is like (10) except for irrelevant differences in the structure of the NPs – can be varied to *after the prime minister's arrival*, but *on the strength of his previous work* cannot be varied to **on his previous work's strength*.

It is this last property that raises the greatest problems for the analysis of complex prepositions along the lines of (9). For some of them do allow variation with the PossP construction – compare *on behalf of my father* and *on my father's behalf*, *for the sake of my father* and *for my father's sake*. The X sequence *behalf of my father* is just as fixed as *dint of hard work* with respect to properties (a)–(c) – except, trivially, that some speakers have it following *in* as well as *on* – but its paradigmatic relation to *my father's behalf* provides strong evidence for saying that it is an NP. Certainly it is difficult to see what other analysis we could assign to *on my father's behalf* than (12).

(12)

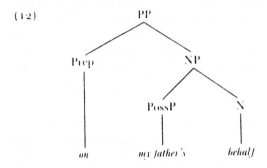

Our lexical entry for **behalf** would say that it is invariably singular and occurs only in the environments '*on/in* PossP ____' or '*on/in* ____ *of*'. Once we recognise that the dictionary must be able to include distributional statements of this degree of specificity, then there seems no reason why we should not assign *by dint of hard work* the same syntactic structure as *after years of hard work*, with a similarly restrictive lexical entry for **dint** (and traditional dictionaries, though not traditional grammars, in effect do this). Under such reanalysis, 'complex preposition' would be a misnomer, for *by dint of* would not be a syntactic constituent (any more than *on . . . 's behalf*) – it would be a (preposition-based) idiom.

In general the apparatus we have introduced for syntactic description is most useful and illuminating when we are dealing with highly productive constructions. To assign a structure like (10) to *by dint of hard work* is less helpful because we have to exclude so many of the normal paradigmatic contrasts. However, as we have just seen, there are good reasons to doubt whether we are any better off with a special structure like (9). The lack of productivity renders it inevitable that we make ad hoc statements, and these can be made within the framework of (10) as well as within that of (9). But it is a tricky area where it ill becomes us to be dogmatic, and the reader will find both analyses in the literature.

Two final points are worth noting. Firstly, there are undoubtedly some cases where lexicalisation has been accompanied, historically, by some syntactic restructuring. Thus *because of* derives from *by cause of* but there is no question of Modern English *because of hard work* having a structure like (10); similarly in *inside the box* we now have a syntactically simple preposition *inside* deriving from earlier *in + side + of*. Secondly, the phenomenon we have been looking at here has parallels in several other areas of the grammar, so that some writers will recognise (under various terms)

344

'complex conjunctions', such as *in that, in order that, so that, according as, insofar as, as if, in case*; 'complex verbs' like **take** *advantage of,* **take** *account of,* **make** *use of,* **have** *recourse to* or **give** *up,* **hold** *on,* **break** *down* (see 5.5.2 for these latter); 'complex determinatives' like *a lot of, a number of, a great deal of* (see 6.4); and so on.

10.6 Complementation and modification in PP structure

Prepositions take the following kinds of complement:

(a) NPs, as in *against the tree, of little value,* etc. These are much the most frequent kind of complement and, as we have seen, the preposition is in effect traditionally defined as taking an NP complement. But we must certainly allow for other kinds too.

(b) Clauses, as in [*the question*] *of why he had left,* including *-ing* constructions, as in *before going to bed.*

(c) PPs, as in *from under the car* or *until after the meeting.* Here one PP, *under the car,* is embedded as complement within a larger PP *from under the car.* Only a few prepositions take such complements, and the examples given illustrate what are probably the most productive cases: *from* + locative PP (cf. *from inside the building*) and *until* + temporal PP (cf. *until just before the meeting*). Note, however, that the most neutral locative and temporal preposition, *at,* does not occur in such complements: *from* (*at) *Sydney, until* (*at) *noon.* In addition there are a number where the second preposition is determined by the first, instead of being paradigmatically contrastive as in the above examples: *except for the spelling, apart from his uncle,* [*a decision*] *as to whether it would be cancelled, because of the rain,* etc. Again these Prep + Prep sequences are often analysed as 'complex prepositions' in the sense of §5 above, implying that the ICs are *except for* + *the spelling* rather than *except* + *for the spelling,* as assumed here.

(d) AdvPs, as in *from here, since then* and the like. The prepositions concerned are those that occur productively with PP complements, and the AdvPs are locative or temporal (see §7 below).

(e) AdjPs, as in [*He regarded it*] *as inefficient,* [*He took her*] *for dead,* [*It went*] *from bad to worse.* Of these, the construction with *as* is much the most productive, with virtually any AdjP being a potential complement. In the example given, the semantic relation between *inefficient* and *it* is the same as in *He considered it inefficient,* where *inefficient* is a (predicative) complement of the verb (see 5.5).

Normally prepositions take a single complement, but there are some constructions which are probably best analysed as PPs with two complements. In *He lives across the road from us,* for example, *from us* is dependent on *across* (*the road*) in that we could not have *He lives from us. The omissibility test must, of course, be applied with some care – the fact that we cannot omit *John* from *She congratulated John on his promotion* doesn't mean that *on his promotion* is a complement of *John*: it is rather, a complement of *congratulated*, but one which can occur (in active-voice clauses) only if the verb also has an object complement. To distinguish the two cases, we need to show that *across the road from us* behaves as a single constituent while *John on his promotion* does not: relevant evidence comes from thematic fronting (*Across the road from us lived a strange old woman from Glasgow*; cf. **John on his promotion everybody congratulated*), the cleft construction (*It was across the road from us that he lived* vs **It was John on his promotion that she congratulated*). As there is no reason to regard *the road from us* as a constituent (and note also the possibility of omitting *the road*, as in *across from us*) the only reasonable analysis will have *across* as head, the NP *the road* as first complement and the embedded PP *from us* as second complement. Another example cited in the literature is [*He sent it*] *to Bill in New York*, where similar evidence can be found. More difficult to handle are examples like [*He went*] *from Sydney to Brisbane*: either *from Sydney* or *to Brisbane* can be omitted, which argues against their forming a constituent, yet there are examples where they surely do: *From Sydney to Brisbane is over 600 miles* or *It is only from Sydney to Brisbane that you have to travel by train*.

A very limited amount of modification is found in PPs. For the most part it involves expressions indicating extent modifying locative or temporal prepositions: *five inches below the surface, a short distance beyond the church, two hours before the meeting, just after his arrival*.

10.7 Prepositions in relation to verbs, adjectives and adverbs

Prepositions are very clearly distinguished from central, i.e. tensed, verbs – unlike the latter, they do not have tense inflection, cannot be modified by auxiliaries, cannot function as ultimate head of a clause, and so on. With *-ing* and *-en* forms, however, the boundaries are not so sharp, and a few prepositions are lexically converted from such verb forms, e.g. *considering, excluding, regarding, given*, etc.

Let us use the first of these to illustrate the distinction between preposition and verb:

(13)
  i *Considering all these disadvantages, his performance was quite creditable*
  ii *The committee was considering some new proposals*
  iii *The committee considering the matter had met only once*
  iv *Considering all these disadvantages, Ed decided to abandon the project*

In (i) *considering* is generally analysed as a preposition; in (ii–iv) it is a verb. (ii) is the most obvious: *considering* is head of a VP, which is the progressive counterpart of *considered*, and ultimately head of the whole clause. In (iii)

346

considering the matter is a clause modifying *committee* – it can be compared to the kernel clause *The committee considered the matter* (see 6.9; 12.3). The modifier position in NP structure is, as we have seen, one that can be filled by PPs: it is then a measure of the marginal status of *considering* as a preposition that it cannot head a PP in this position – or indeed in any position save that illustrated in (i), where the PP is a peripheral dependent in clause structure. (iv) illustrates a use of an *-ing* construction that we have not yet introduced: it too is functioning as peripheral dependent in clause structure. The difference between (i) and (iv) is that in (iv) the understood subject-argument of the subordinate clause is derivable from the superordinate clause, an approximate paraphrase being "After Ed had considered all these disadvantages, he decided to abandon the project", whereas in (i) we do not derive a subject-argument for *considering all these disadvantages* from *his performance was quite creditable* – the meaning here is, rather, something like "If we consider all these disadvantages we will conclude that his performance was quite creditable". Thus in (i) *considering* has lost the verb-like property of having either an overt subject or an understood subject/subject-argument derivable from the clause or NP within which the constituent it heads is embedded. This loss makes it more like a preposition, and (i) is thus similar to *In view of all these disadvantages, his performance was quite creditable*, where the initial phrase is clearly a PP.

(13i) may be compared with examples like **Arriving late, there were no seats left* or **Being wet, the match was postponed* – the kind of example that many prescriptive grammars warn against. *Arriving* and *being* are said to be 'dangling' or 'unrelated' participles – they are not related to the superordinate clause subject as the *-ing* form in (iv) is. The unacceptability of such examples shows that the *considering* in (i) differs from standard *-ing* form verbs and hence supports its allocation to a different class. However, certain kinds of dangling participle are quite acceptable, as in *Strictly speaking, it's against the law*: as *speaking* is clearly not a candidate for the preposition class we cannot divide *-ing* words into verbs and prepositions simply by seeing whether there is an understood subject-argument derivable from the larger construction. In *Taking all these disadvantages into consideration, his performance was quite creditable*, the *taking* is again a verb rather than a preposition since its complementation (NP + PP) is characteristic of verbs, not prepositions; and although the example is perhaps not as completely acceptable as (i), it can hardly be dismissed as simply ungrammatical. I think we must conclude that the *considering* of (13i) lies on the borderline between prepositions and verbs and that its assignment to one or other class must inevitably involve a certain amount of arbitrariness.

Turning now to the preposition and adjective classes, we again find clear differences at the centres. Central adjectives, unlike central prepositions, can be used attributively, take analytic or inflectional comparatives and

347

modifiers like *very*, and do not take NP complements. Both PPs and AdjPs can function as complement in clause structure – and more specifically as complement to a copulative verb like **be**: *He was on the roof* (PP)/*in a bad temper* (PP)/*very angry* (AdjP). The adjunct position in clause structure is more characteristic of PPs – but we do find some constructions where an AdjP might be regarded as having this function, e.g. *Furious at his own incompetence, Ed abandoned the project* or *She left the rehearsal thoroughly demoralised* (see 5.2).

At the borderline between the two classes we find such items as **near** and *like* (or *unlike*) which have both prepositional and adjectival properties and are traditionally assigned to both parts of speech. We will consider just **near**. Its prepositional properties are evident in examples like *He buried it near the fence*, where it has an NP complement, heads a phrase functioning as adjunct and is in paradigmatic contrast with such central prepositions as *at, by, beside, under*, etc. Its adjectival properties are illustrated in *his near relatives, his nearest relative*, where it is gradable and is used attributively. But it is not simply a question of its having prepositional properties in some uses and adjectival ones in others: there are uses where it exhibits both kinds of property at once, as in *the one which he had buried nearest the fence* (or *nearest to the fence*, for it can take a *to* phrase complement instead of an NP). Its classification thus remains somewhat indeterminate, and however it is analysed we need to include some ad hoc account of its peculiarities.

Finally, let us consider the distinction between prepositions and adverbs. As usual, we find a very sharp contrast between a prototypical preposition like *of* and a prototypical adverb like *sufficiently*. Non-central cases presenting classificatory problems involve locative (and to a lesser extent, temporal) items. We noted in §1 that words like *above, across, behind, below, between, down, in, off, on, to, through, under, up*, etc., are traditionally analysed as belonging to both preposition and adverb classes, according to whether or not they have a complement:

(14) i *He came across the bridge*
      ii *He came across*
(15) i *He walked up the hill*
      ii *He stood up*

Where there is an NP complement, as in (14i) and (15i), *across* and *up* are central members of the preposition class: there is no dispute over the analysis of such cases. The problem lies in (14ii) and (15ii), where they are said to be adverbs (of the subclass that in 5.5.2 we called 'particles'): obviously they are not central members of the adverb class, for they cannot modify adjectives or adverbs. The reason for the dual analysis stems from the traditional idea of a preposition as a word relating a noun to a verb, adjective or another noun: *across* and *up* cannot then be prepositions in *He came across*, *He stood up* because they are not serving to relate any noun (NP) to *came* or *stood*. If, however, we take the view that prepositions occur as heads of phrases functioning as complement or adjunct in clause structure, complement or modifier in NP structure and so on, then there is no reason in principle why the above items should not simply be classified as prepositions which can occur either with or without a complement (just as many verbs, nouns and adjectives can occur with or without a complement) – and this is what a number of writers have proposed. In some cases, such as (14ii), we can add a complement, to give (14i) or the like, whereas in others, such as (15ii), we can't – but this is no different from the situation we find with verbs, where we can add an NP complement to *He was eating* (e.g. *his sandwiches*) but not to *He was disappearing*, and so on. *Across, up*, etc., without complements differ from central PPs in that they do not readily occur as post-head dependent in NP structure: we can have *the village across the river* or *the people down the road* but not **the village across*, **the people up*, etc. Nevertheless a few nouns do allow such dependents: *the way across, the journey up*. Moreover, pairs like (14) can be paralleled by such examples as

(16)   i   *He stood in front of the picture*
        ii *He stood in front*

where, if the analysis of §5 above is accepted, *in front* in (ii) will be a PP no less than *in front of the picture* in (i). The proposal to analyse *across* and *up* as belonging to the same part of speech in both members of pairs (14) and (15) thus has a good deal to commend it – but it would raise the question of whether 'preposition' was the best general term for the enlarged class.

FURTHER READING
On adverbs, see Quirk et al. 1971: Ch. 5, Bowers 1975. On prepositions, see Jespersen 1924: Ch. 6, Jackendoff 1973, Vestergaard 1977, Van Oosten 1977. On 'complex prepositions', see Quirk & Mulholland 1964.

11
Clause type

11.1 Clause type and illocutionary force

The major terms in the system of clause type were introduced in 1.4; they are illustrated again in (1):

(1)
    i *You made a good job of it*   Declarative
    ii *Did you make a good job of it?*   Interrogative
    iii *What a good job you made of it!*   Exclamative
    iv *Make a good job of it*   Imperative

The system is usually discussed under the heading 'sentence type' rather than 'clause type': I have preferred the latter in order to make the terminology consistent with the way I am differentiating between 'sentence' and 'clause' (see 1.5), for it is clear that the system applies in the first instance to what I am calling clauses. Thus in a sentence consisting of a sequence of clauses, as in (2):

(2)   *Come with us by all means but you may find it hard work*

it is the separate clauses that are classified for type: *come with us by all means* is imperative and *but you may find it hard work* declarative – the sentence as a whole cannot be assigned to any of the four types. Moreover, the system applies to certain kinds of subordinate clause as can be seen in (3), where the unbracketed parts – which, clearly, are not themselves sentences – are classified as shown:

(3)
    i [*They didn't tell me*] *that you made a good*   Declarative
       job of it
    ii [*They didn't tell me*] *whether you made a good* Interrogative
       job of it
    iii [*They didn't tell me*] *what a good job you made* Exclamative
       of it

Although there are certain differences of form between these and their main clause counterparts (note the *that* in (i), the *whether* and the different position of the subject in (ii)), the paradigmatic relation between the three classes is the same, so that we shall want to apply a single classification to subordinate and main clauses. The subordinate clauses to which the type contrasts apply are for the most part content clauses functioning as subject or complement of certain verbs, adjectives and nouns, and it is worth observing at this point that apart from classifying verbs, adjectives and nouns according as they can or cannot take content clauses as subject or complement, we must also classify them according to which clause type the content clause may belong to. **Tell**, as we see from (3), takes declarative, interrogative or exclamative clauses as complement; **believe**, by contrast, takes just a declarative (*They believed that/*whether you made a good job of it/*what a good job you made of it*); and so on. (Some verbs, adjectives and nouns, such as **insist,** *essential,* **requirement**, take a fourth type, which we shall call 'jussive': *It is essential that you/he make a good job of it*; the relationship between this type of subordinate clause and the imperative type of main clause is a matter we will take up in §3.)

Where a sentence has the form of a clause, we can of course talk, derivatively, of the sentence as being declarative, interrogative, or whatever, and it will in fact be convenient in the discussion below to use 'declarative sentence' in preference to the more cumbersome 'sentence having the form of a declarative clause', and so on. But this does not detract from the arguments just given for saying that the system applies primarily to the clause – and hence for adopting 'clause type' as the name of the system. It may be thought that 'type' is hardly a transparent term for the system, given that its everyday sense is so general that it might apply to any dimension of classification; as a technical term, however, its specialisation to the system of concern to us here is well-established, and 'clause type' is accordingly to be understood as applying to this particular set of contrasts.

A declarative sentence will typically be used to make a statement; an interrogative sentence will typically be used to pose a question; an exclamative sentence will typically be used to make an exclamation; and an imperative sentence will typically be used to issue what we shall call a 'directive' – a term that covers requests, commands, prohibitions, instructions and the like. It cannot be too strongly emphasised, however, that declarative, interrogative, exclamative and imperative are quite different kinds of concept from statement, question, exclamation and directive. Declarative, interrogative, exclamative and imperative are SYNTACTIC categories: they are terms in a system of clause classes distinguished from each other by certain features of syntactic structure (the position of the subject, the form of the VP, the presence or absence of the so-called '*wh* words' *who, when*, etc.), which we shall be looking at in more detail in §§2–5 below. Statement, question, exclamation and directive are, by contrast, SEMANTIC categories. Exclamation is in fact somewhat different in kind from the other three in that it involves an emotive element of meaning that can be overlaid on a statement, a question or a directive, as in:

(4) i *What a rogue he was!*
  ii *How on earth did you do it so quickly?*
  iii *Take that bloody grin off your face!*

That is, these would characteristically be used to make an exclamatory statement, put an exclamatory question and issue an exclamatory directive respectively. Syntactically, only (4i) is exclamative – (ii) is interrogative and (iii) imperative. For this reason we can amend slightly what was said at the beginning of this paragraph: an exclamative sentence will typically be used to make an exclamatory statement. And in the remainder of this section we will concentrate on the distinction and relationship between, on the one hand, the syntactic categories declarative, interrogative, imperative and on the other the semantic categories statement, question, directive.

Statement, question and directive apply in the first instance to utterances – hence my formulation 'a declarative sentence will typically be USED to make a statement', and so on. The terms 'statement', 'question' and 'directive' are in fact each used in two different but related senses: for a certain kind of act or for what we may call the 'product' of such an act – thus 'statement' may apply to the act of stating something or to what is stated, and so on. To utter a sentence is, clearly, to DO something, to perform an act – and in uttering (1i), (ii) and (iv) I would normally be, in one respect, performing different kinds of act: I would be stating that you made a good job of it, questioning whether you made a good job of it and directing you to make a good job of it. I say that the utterance acts would differ 'in one respect', for in another they would be alike: in each case I would be uttering a sequence of words, articulating a chain of sounds (or writing a sequence of letters). This is in itself of little interest to us here: I mention it only to explain why a more specific term, **illocutionary act**, is introduced for the kinds of act that we are here interested in, so that stating, questioning and directing are said to be different kinds of illocutionary act.

Precisely because they are semantic categories, the criteria that distinguish statement, question and directive from each other are of a quite different nature from those that distinguish the syntactic clause type categories. In performing the illocutionary act of stating, I express some proposition and commit myself to its truth: I tell my addressee(s) that such and such is the case. Statements, in the 'product' sense, are assessable as true or false: questions and directives are not.

A directive, in the central cases at least, identifies some future action or behaviour on the part of the addressee(s) (including refraining from doing something) and seeks to bring about that action or behaviour. Although we cannot ask whether a directive is true or false, we can ask whether it is (subsequently) complied with.

A question defines a set of (right or wrong) answers to it. For example, the set of answers to the question posed in a normal utterance of *Who broke the window?* consists of "I broke the window", "Tom broke the window", "The plumber broke the window", and so on. I give the answer in this format because they are defined by their propositional content (see 1.8) rather than by their linguistic form, so that *I broke the window, I broke it, I did, Me*, etc., would all express the same answer in this case. For the same reason I will represent questions, in the product sense, in double quotation marks. Again, then, for the question "Where were you last night?", *We were at home* uttered by one of the addressees, *You were at home* uttered by the questioner, *They were at home* uttered by someone else with *they* referring to the addressees of the question would all express the same answer. 'Answer' is to be understood in a technical sense, not to be identified with 'response' or 'reply'. You may respond to a question by giving an answer or you may respond in some other way. Thus if I say *Who broke the window?* and you reply *I did*, you have given an answer; but if you reply with *I don't know* or *Why ask me?*, you haven't. And conversely, *Yes* and *No* might be used in response to a statement, a directive or a question, but they would normally express answers only in the last of these three cases: said in response to a statement *Yes* typically indicates agreement with the statement, and said in response to a directive it typically indicates agreement to comply. For the majority of questions the answers are potential statements, as in the examples given so far. But with certain kinds of question the answers are potential directives: the most straightforward cases of this kind are expressed by interrogative clauses containing a first person subject and one of the modal auxiliaries **shall** and **will** (some dialects using **shall**, others **will**): *Shall/ Will we go now?, What shall/will I tell him?*. For example, if you reply to an utterance of the latter with *Tell him you can't afford it*, you have given a directive as answer.

In performing the illocutionary act of questioning, we usually intend that the addressee(s) should respond by providing the right answer. Here we 'ask' a question and 'ask for' the answer. But we do not invariably have this intention. We may, for example, intend to go on to give the answer ourselves: we are simply focusing our addressees' attention on the question, not asking for the answer – this is a not uncommon device in certain kinds of expository writing or speaking. Or I might be just raising a question without any suggestion that either of us could give the right answer or should even try to: *Where will we be in ten years' time, I wonder?*. Or the right answer may be deemed so obvious that it would be superfluous for you to give it – this is the so-called 'rhetorical question', as when I say *Who's going to notice it anyway?*, with the implication that no one is. For this reason, we shall not incorporate into our definition of the illocutionary category of question a condition that the speaker intends to elicit an answer from the addressee(s): we need a less specific intention, such as that of directing attention to the selection of the right answer – and we will speak of 'posing' or 'putting' a question, with 'asking' a question being a special case thereof.

Although the criteria for the semantic categories are so different from those for the syntactic ones, there is of course a very significant correlation between declarative and statement, interrogative and question, imperative and directive. This provides the basis for general definitions of the clause types: a declarative clause is one belonging to a syntactically distinguishable clause class whose members are characteristically used to make statements – and analogously for the others. But we cannot use the semantic categories to give language-particular definitions of the clause types, as we saw in our discussion of notional definitions in 2.1, for the correlation is far from being one-to-one. This is why I have emphasised the importance of keeping the two sets of categories conceptually and terminologically distinct.

In the first place, it should be borne in mind that the illocutionary categories apply initially to utterances, to uses of clauses rather than to clauses themselves – and they inevitably involve consideration of speaker/ writer intentions. Suppose, for example, I type out the sentence *The quick brown fox jumps over a lazy dog*. I might do this simply as a typewriting exercise (it contains all twenty-six letters of the alphabet), without having any particular fox or dog in mind and thus without the intention of expressing any proposition. In these circumstances I would not have made a statement (or performed any other kind of illocutionary act) – note how absurd it would be to ask whether what I had written was true or false. But it is still syntactically declarative. In what follows, we will exclude such cases by confining our attention to 'normal use', but this qualification is an important one.

Secondly, the correlation between the syntactic and semantic categories is significantly less direct with subordinate clauses than with main clauses. Consider again the first two examples in (3). It will be clear that in uttering the clause *that you made a good job of it* in (i) I do not make a statement, and that I do not pose a question by uttering *whether you made a good job of it* in (ii). The uttering of the subordinate clause does not in either case constitute an illocutionary act: it is only in uttering the main clause of which it is part that I would perform such an act – and it would be a statement in both (i) and (ii). This is not to deny that the category of question is highly relevant to the semantics of *whether you made a good job of it*: merely to say that the semantic categories apply, if at all, in a much more indirect way to subordinate clauses (and *whether you made a good job of it* is indeed traditionally analysed as an 'indirect question'). In what follows, we will

354

confine our attention, in discussing the correlation between syntactic form and meaning, to main clauses.

Thirdly, even when we confine our attention to the 'normal' use of main clauses, the correlation is by no means perfect – because clause type is not the only factor relevant to the determination of illocutionary 'force'. We will regard it, rather, as the initial determining factor, and say that an utterance of a declarative main clause will be a statement, an utterance of an interrogative main clause will be a question, an utterance of an imperative main clause will be a directive – unless there are special factors of form, meaning, prosody, paralinguistic accompaniment or of context to override this initial assignment of illocutionary function.

Let us consider some examples where such overriding factors would typically come into play:

(5)   i *Have a good holiday*
       ii *'B' Company will parade for muster at 0800 hours*
       iii *You must come in immediately*
       iv *Could you pass the salt (?)*
       v *I promise not to tell anyone*
       vi *It gives me great pleasure to declare this Exhibition open*

Sentence (5i) has the form of an imperative clause, but if I said it to you, you would not normally take me to be directing you to do something: rather I would be expressing a wish or hope. One reason is that whether one has a good holiday or not depends to a considerable extent on factors beyond one's control, whereas a directive will normally be to do something that does lie within the power of the addressee(s). (A second factor is the almost formulaic nature of the example: there is a rather limited range of wishes we can make using imperatives – we conventionally say *Sleep well, Get well soon*, etc., but we would hardly say, for example, *Have no pain at the dentist's* or *Receive the letter you're so eagerly awaiting by this morning's mail*.) (5ii) has the form of a declarative clause, but the sentence could well be used in a set of military orders, and in such a context the utterance of it would itself be an order, and hence a directive. (iii) is likewise a declarative whose most natural use would be to issue a directive – a father saying this to his children, for example, would be telling them to come in; **must**, as we have seen in 4.8, can express deontic modality, and this makes it highly appropriate for use in directives, especially where it has a second person subject. (iv) has the form of an interrogative clause, but it too would most naturally be used to issue a directive: in saying this I would normally be asking you to pass me the salt. A typical utterance of (v) would count as a promise – which doesn't belong to any of the categories statement, question, directive. One of the main themes of illocutionary theory is that there are indeed many things one can do in uttering sentences that cannot be subsumed

355

under our three initial categories.[1] Like a directive, a promise identifies some future action or behaviour – but this time it is action or behaviour not of the addressee(s) but of the speaker/writer, who commits him- or herself to doing the action or behaving in the specified way. The fact that an utterance of (v) would have the illocutionary force of a promise is obviously attributable to the fact that the sentence contains the verb ***promise*** itself (used in the present tense, with a first person subject, and so on). Similarly the presence of ***declare*** in (vi) is one of the factors that makes the sentence one that can be, and most typically would be, used to effect the opening of the exhibition. Opening an exhibition belongs to the illocutionary class of 'declarations' – acts where the state of affairs specified in the utterance (in this example the exhibition's being open) is brought about by the utterance itself. Other examples include placing someone under arrest, as when a police officer says *You are under arrest*, joining two people in matrimony, as when a minister of religion says (in the appropriate context) *I pronounce you man and wife*, and so on.

Besides showing again that there are illocutionary acts not covered by statements, questions and directives, (vi) also illustrates the important point that in uttering a single sentence one can simultaneously perform more than one illocutionary act. For in uttering this sentence I would normally not only be opening the exhibition, but also making a statement – true or false according as the ceremony is or is not pleasurable to me. The declaration would, we may assume, be much more important than the statement when the utterance is considered as a social act (the audience would probably be uninterested in the truth of the statement), but that doesn't affect the point that a statement would have been made. Indeed, it might be argued that in a standard utterance of (v) I would be making a statement as well as a promise (a statement that would be true by virtue of my making the promise), or again that a standard utterance of (iv) would be a question as well as a directive, and analogously in other (but not all other) cases. These, however, are matters of considerable controversy in illocutionary theory, and it would take us too far from our main concerns to pursue them here. We can avoid taking a stand on them providing it is understood that when we speak of factors 'overriding' clause type in the determination of illocutionary force we intend this to cover both cases where an utterance would not normally have the force generally associated with its clause type and also cases where it would have some other force in addition to (and typically more important than) that deriving from its clause type.

In the following sections we will examine the four clause types in turn,

---

[1] In the light of this observation we should note that the answers to questions are then not confined to potential statements and directives: (5v), or an elliptical version thereof, for example, could be used in answer to the question "Do you promise not to tell anyone?"

beginning with declaratives, the unmarked class. Of the remaining three
classes there are grounds for saying that imperatives differ more from
declaratives than do interrogatives and exclamatives: imperatives are non-
tensed while the others are tensed. Furthermore interrogatives arguably
differ more from declaratives than do exclamatives: the latter allow confirmatory tags to be added, just like declaratives (cf. *It was a shambles, wasn't
it?* and *What a shambles it was, wasn't it?*, with *wasn't it?* tagged to a declarative in the first, an exclamative in the second) and all verbs, adjectives and
nouns which are subclassified as allowing an exclamative content clause as
complement or subject also allow a declarative, whereas there are some –
such as *inquire* or *investigate* – that allow interrogatives but not declaratives. This then suggests the following classification:

(6)

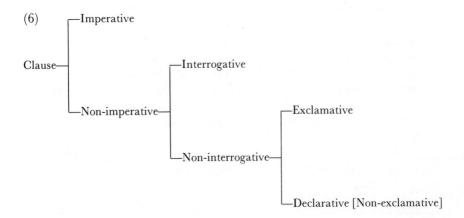

11.2   **Declaratives**

Declarative, as just observed, is the unmarked clause-type: all
kernel clauses are declarative. Subordinate declaratives belong to the
class of content clauses, the primary marker of subordination being the
conjunction *that*, as in (3i). *That*, however, is very often omissible (cf. [*They
didn't tell me*] *you made a good job of it*) – as a first approximation we can say
that it is optional when the content clause follows the predicator of the
superordinate clause (see 12.4.2). And when the *that* is omitted the subordinate clause will generally not differ in its internal structure from a
main clause (but cf. 12.3). Nothing further need be said here about the
syntactic structure of declaratives: rather, we shall describe the syntax of
the other classes in terms of the special properties that distinguish them
from the unmarked class.

Let us therefore turn to the semantics, confining our attention to main clauses. As we have said, a declarative will be used, other things being equal, to make a statement. Thus in uttering a declarative I normally commit myself to the truth of the proposition that it is used to express. The strength of the commitment will vary according as I am making a statement of fact based on solid evidence, expressing an opinion or merely making a conjecture, though the distinction between these different kinds of statement need not be encoded in the sentence.

Of the linguistic factors that can override declarative clause type in determining the illocutionary force of an utterance, we will mention just three (of which the first two were involved in (5) above).

(a) There are many verbs that denote a kind of illocutionary act – verbs such as ***promise, request, order, advise, thank, apologise***, etc. (as opposed to verbs like ***watch, like, anger, worry***, etc.). Most of them can be used **performatively**, i.e. in such a way as to bring about the performance of an illocutionary act of the kind they denote. Thus I can make a promise by saying (5v) – *I promise not to tell anyone* – or a request by saying *Passengers on flight 404 are requested to proceed to Gate 6*: the fact that these utterances would be respectively a promise and a request is attributable to the performative use of the illocutionary verbs ***promise*** and ***request***. Such verbs are of course not always used performatively: the above examples may be contrasted with, say, *Ed won't promise not to tell anyone* or *I had requested him to leave*, where the presence of ***promise*** and ***request*** is irrelevant to the illocutionary force, so that declaratives like these would normally be used as statements, as is characteristic of declaratives without such verbs.

(b) As is illustrated by (5ii–iii), a declarative containing such a modal auxiliary as ***will*** or ***must*** can be used with the illocutionary force of a directive. This represents a special case of what we have called the deontic use of the modals: recall the discussion in 4.8.

(c) A third factor that may override declarative clause type in determining illocutionary force is intonation – or punctuation. If a declarative is spoken with rising intonation (represented by ' ↑ '), or written with a question mark, the utterance will typically have the force of a question: *You're ready* ↑ , *You're ready?*. The intonation or punctuation here cancels my commitment to the truth of the proposition that you are ready; the effect is much like that of the interrogative *Are you ready* (which would of course also be punctuated with '?' or, very often, spoken with ' ↑ '), except that *You're ready* ↑ / ? more strongly suggests an expectation on my part that you are ready, or should be. Notice that the sharp distinction we have drawn between clause type and illocutionary force means that we can handle the question force of such utterances of *You're ready* whilst still analysing the clause itself as a declarative. And there are good syntactic reasons for not treating it as an interrogative. In the first place, there are certain words and expressions which can occur only in what we shall call 'non-affirmative' contexts (13.2) – approximately, interrogatives or negatives as opposed to positive declaratives: they include *ever*, the verbs **bother** or **care** (with following infinitival complement), the modal auxiliaries **dare** and **need**, and so on:

(7)
 i *Has he ever been to Paris?*
 ii *Did he bother to finish it?*
 iii *Need she know?*

(8)
 i **He has ever been to Paris*
 ii **He bothered to finish it*
 iii **She need know*

The examples in (8) can be saved by making them negative (*He hasn't ever been to Paris*) – but not by pronouncing them with rising intonation, or punctuating with a question mark. Thus as far as this syntactic constraint is concerned, ↑ intonation or *?* punctuation cannot be regarded as an alternative means of realising the interrogative category. In the second place, consider an example like (9), again spoken with ' ↑ ' or written with '*?*':

(9) *I suppose he's staying to lunch*

What is being questioned here is whether or not he's staying to lunch, not whether or not I suppose he is: it is thus not equivalent to (the pragmatically rather odd) interrogative *Do I suppose he's staying to lunch*, so that there is not even any semantic reason for treating the main clause in (9) as interrogative. Nor shall we want to say that the subordinate clause *he's staying to lunch* is interrogative. We noted above that verbs taking content clauses as complement must be subclassified according to the clause type of the complement – and what we find with **suppose** is that it belongs to the same class as **believe**, allowing only a declarative (*They supposed that/ *whether she had arrived*). Thus here again the intonation or punctuation doesn't result in a construction that behaves syntactically like an interrogative.

11.3   Imperatives and related constructions: jussives

The most central members of the imperative class are clauses like *Be careful!*, *Open the door!*, *Put it away!*. They differ structurally from declaratives in two respects: (i) they have as their first verb not a tensed form but a base form (with no preceding *to*); (ii) they have no subject. The first of these properties they share with a number of other clause constructions having varying degrees of semantic affinity with them: *You be careful*; *Everybody stand still*; *Let's go to the beach*; *If that is what the premier intends, let him say so; Heaven forbid!*; and the subordinate [*It is essential*] *that they be present*. It would stretch the term 'imperative' too far beyond its traditional and currently standard use to apply it to all of these, and I shall accordingly introduce the term **jussive** for a more general clause type which does embrace them all. This larger class may may then be divided into imperative and non-imperative, and into various other subtypes, as shown in (10):

(10)

	Imperative	Non-imperative
	I	III
−*let*^{gr}	IA −Subject *Be careful*	IIIA Main *Heaven forbid*
	IB +Subject *You be careful* *Everybody stand still*	IIIB Subordinate [*It is essential*] *that they be present*
+*let*^{gr}	II *Let's go to the beach*	IV *If that is what the premier intends, let him say so*

We will consider these various subtypes in turn.

IA is the central and much the most frequent type of imperative with which we began. Such clauses have no subject, but it is plausible to say that *you* is 'understood' as subject or "you" as subject-argument. Although the first verb is in the base form, the auxiliary ***do*** is introduced in the formation of negatives (more specifically those with a negative VP), as in *Don't/do not stay long* and emphatic positives, as in *Do take care* – ***do*** is added, moreover, even when the first verb of the positive is the base form of the operator ***be***: *Don't be long, Do be careful.*

Type IB differs in having a grammatical subject present: it can be second person, *you*, or third person, like *everybody*. In the negative the subject follows *don't*: *Don't you be so sure!*; *Don't anybody move!*.[2] Second person *you* can be overtly present (instead of being merely implicit, as in IA) when it is contrastive (*You be wicket-keeper and I'll bowl*) or when there is a somewhat bullying or aggressive tone (*Just you watch what you're doing!*). With all verbs other than ***be*** there is syncretism between the base form and the general present tense form so that there will be ambiguity when *you* is selected – at least in the verbal component: it would normally be resolved prosodically. Thus positive *You go with her* could be imperative or declarative, while negative *Don't you watch her* could be imperative or interrogative.

We should also note that *You go with her* (again considered in abstrac-

---

[2] The fact that there is no agreement here – we have *don't*, not *doesn't* – is a strong reason for taking *don't* as a base form, but the imperative construction is the only place where we find a non-tensed inflectional negative.

tion from the non-verbal component) has a third analysis and interpretation: besides being a declarative or a type IB imperative it can also be a type IA imperative with *you* a vocative (5.8) rather than a subject. Compare *Hey, you, watch what you're doing*, imperative (IA), with *Hey, you, you're trespassing*, declarative. Vocatives and subjects differ with respect to their positional possibilities – the *you* of *Shut up, you* cannot be subject while that of *Don't you speak to me like that* could hardly be vocative; in initial position the vocative will be distinguished from a subject prosodically (being spoken with a separate intonation contour) or by being marked off by punctuation.

The distinction between vocative and subject is relevant also with third person NPs – but is perhaps not so easy to draw in all instances. We can distinguish readily enough between *Kim, open the window please*, with *Kim* marked off prosodically or by punctuation from the rest, thus vocative + type IA imperative, and *Somebody open the window please*, with *somebody* integrated prosodically or by punctuation with the rest, thus type IB imperative, with *somebody* subject. But what have we in *Put your hands up all those who got it right* or *Stand up the boy who said that* spoken with a simple contour or written without an internal comma? My preference would be to give priority to the non-verbal criterion, analysing the final NPs as thematically postposed subjects, but others might opt for the vocative analysis: the distinction is somewhat blurred.

Normally the subject of an imperative will express a semantic argument representing the addressee(s) or some (specific or non-specific) member(s) of the set of addressees: *Everybody stand still*, for example, will be interpreted pragmatically as "All of you stand still". This is why **you** can generally be added in a tag (*Everybody stand still, will you*) or occur elsewhere in the clause (*Everybody close your eyes*).[3]

Type II imperatives are marked by the presence of *let* – more specifically of what I shall call *let*^{gr}, 'grammaticalised *let*', as opposed to *let*^{lex}, 'lexical *let*', the ordinary catenative verb with the meaning "allow" that we find in *He won't let us go to the beach*. *Let*^{lex} can occur in type I imperatives, and there is then a transparent structural similarity between type II *Let's go to the beach* and type IA *Let us come with you*. In the historical development of construction II, there has been a specialisation, a grammaticalisation of the base form of **let** such that we can distinguish *let*^{gr} from *let*^{lex} by the following properties:

(a) It is restricted to imperatives and (hence) to main clauses, whereas *let*^{lex} occurs in all clause types and in subordinate as well as main clauses.

[3] We could also have anaphoric *their* instead of deictic *your* here but not in *Put your hands up all those who got it right*, where the structural conditions for the marked order of anaphor followed by antecedent are not met (see 7.2). Some analysts might regard the choice between *your* and *their* (etc.) as criterial for the distinction between vocative and subject respectively.

(b) *Let*^{gr} cannot take *you* (or any other NP) as subject, witness **You let's go to the beach*; *let*^{lex} by contrast enters into imperatives of type IB as well as IA (cf. *You let your brother have a look* in its non-declarative interpretation).

(c) The difference in the 'scope' of the negation that we find with *let*^{lex} in, say, *Don't let him eat it* ("Prevent him . . .": *let* is inside the scope of the negative) vs the comparatively rare but perfectly grammatical *Let him not eat it* [*if he's not hungry*] ("Allow him not to . . .": *let* is outside the scope of the negation), is lost with *let*^{gr}: *Don't let's bother* and *Let's not bother* are equivalent.

(d) The *us* following *let*^{gr} may be – and generally is – contracted to *'s*, but such contraction is not possible in construction I: *Let us/ *'s come with you*.

(e) Whereas **we** can normally be interpreted 'inclusively' or 'exclusively' (i.e. as referring to a group including or excluding the addressee(s): see 7.4), the *us* following *let*^{gr} forces an inclusive interpretation – if I say *Let's go to the beach* I'm proposing that you go too. In the verbal component there will often be ambiguity (*Let us see the film* can be type II, roughly "I propose that we see the film" or type IA "Allow us to see the film"); I chose *Let us come with you* to exemplify IA because the following *you* effectively rules out an inclusive interpretation of *us*.

(f) *Let*^{gr} cannot of course be replaced by *allow* or *permit* without changing the construction.

As is often the case with constructions marked by some special grammaticalised word(s), the constituent structure analysis of type II imperatives is partially indeterminate or unilluminating. Some writers take the *let* as an auxiliary or 'particle' and *us* as the subject, but it is not clear that the specialisation just described provides valid grounds for assigning distinct constituent structures to, say, *Let us go*, according as it is interpreted as belonging to construction I or II.[4]

Consider now the type III jussive construction. It is more or less restricted to subordinate clauses: the only type III main clauses we find are fixed expressions or formulae like *Suffice it to say . . ., So help me God, Long live . . ., So be it, Come what may, Witness . . .* (their special status being reflected also in the fact that in most the subject is moved to the right of the VP and its complements – but cf. *Heaven forbid!*). Traditional grammar, as noted in 2.4, distinguishes I and III in terms of the inflectional form of the verb: the

---

[4] In some varieties of English, probably still non-standard, the specialisation has gone one step further in that *let's* may be followed by an NP: *Let's you and I do it*, which is evidence for saying that *'s* is no longer perceived as an element grammatically comparable to the NP that follows a catenative such as *your brother* in the above *Let your brother have a look*; at this stage in the development *let's* is probably to be analysed as a single word rather than verb + cliticised pronoun.

verbs in I are said to be in the imperative mood, those in III in the subjunctive mood. We argued, however, that as there is no verb lexeme in English with overtly distinct forms for I and III there is no justification for assigning different verbal inflections. In calling type I 'imperative' I am accordingly departing from the traditional usage of the term, allowing it to apply, like 'declarative' and 'interrogative', to a clause type not marked inflectionally in the verb; there are some dangers of misinterpretation in this, but since clauses like *Be careful* are called 'imperative' in virtually all modern grammatical studies (including the many which, like the present one, do not recognise an inflectional mood distinction between I and III) it seems better to accept that this usage is now firmly established. 'Subjunctive', on the other hand, continues to be used only for a verb mood (or for a clause whose verb is in that mood), and I will therefore not apply it to type III: instead I will resort to the negative nomenclature 'non-imperative jussives'.

It remains to be argued, however, that in spite of the identity of verb inflection there is a grammatical difference at the level of clause constructions between

(11)   i *(You) make a good job of it*   cf. (1iv)
        ii *[It is important] that you make a good job of it*

beyond that which can be accounted for in terms of the contrast between main and subordinate clauses. There are two reasons for saying that the paradigmatic relation between (ii) and (i) here is not the same as between (3i–iii) and (1i–iii) respectively – i.e. between subordinate *[They didn't tell me] that you made a good job of it* and main *You made a good job of it*, etc., and we will accordingly take the view that the imperative clause type is restricted to main clauses.[5]

(a) The first point is that there are severe constraints on the type I construction which do not apply to IIIA, so that a high proportion of IIIA clauses have no analogues of type I. For example, we have *[It is essential] that there be complete silence*, *[I insist] that no one be informed until tomorrow*, whereas *?There be complete silence* and *?No one be informed until tomorrow* will not be found in class IA. I will not pursue the question of how the constraints in type I are to be stated; they are clearly related to the fact that type I clauses are characteristically used as directives: the one(s) of whom compliance is sought must normally be identified in an overt subject or in a covert one reconstructible as *you*. How far the constraint is grammatical rather than merely

---

[5] A directive issued by means of an imperative clause like *Move the table* can of course be reported by a 'complex' sentence like *He told me to move the table* – but this doesn't provide any justification for saying that *to move the table* is imperative. This same clause occurs in sentences that wouldn't be used to report directives, such as *I tried to move the table*, *He helped me to move the table*, *It was foolish of me to move the table*, and so on: it is simply an infinitival clause.

pragmatic is difficult to say (hence my use of the '?' prefix), but it remains unilluminating to relate subordinate *that there be complete silence* to main *?There be complete silence.* In terms of the approach to the description of non-kernel clauses adopted here, it is clearly preferable to give priority to the dimension of subordination over that of clause type, and to relate *that there be complete silence* to main declarative *There is/was complete silence* via the subordinate declarative *that there is/was complete silence* rather than via the main imperative *?There be complete silence.*

(b) As we have noted, type I jussives take *do* and *don't* in the emphatic positive and negative, but type IIIB clauses do not: the negative of [*I insist*] *that he be told* is [*I insist*] *that he not be told* (not **that he don't be told*). Note that it is IIIB that is regular here: it follows the normal rule that in these constructions *do* is inserted only as a tensed operator.[6]

Because of the non-productive nature of IIIA, this latter test cannot really be applied to it: there is no negative of *Long live the Emperor*, etc. In the absence of clear grammatical evidence for deciding whether *Heaven forbid!* belongs in class I or class III, I have resolved the indeterminacy on historical and semantic grounds.

Finally construction IV. This is syntactically productive, but comparatively rare and largely restricted to rather formal, typically argumentative or debating styles. I have distinguished it from II by the *do* criterion: cf. *If that is what he said, let him not now deny it.* It is nevertheless like II in being confined to main clauses, and it may indeed be that some speakers do have *don't* here, which would imply a merging of II and IV.

Let us turn now to the semantics, confining our attention to the prototypical type IA imperative. We have said that imperatives are characteristically used in issuing directives, which identify some future action, mode of behaviour or the like on the part of the addressee(s); in the central cases, the great majority, issuing a directive counts as an attempt to get the addressee(s) to carry out the action, or whatever, that constitutes compliance with the directive.

The most obvious types of directive are perhaps requests and commands (or orders: I make no distinction between 'command' and 'order'). The difference is that a request acknowledges your right not to comply, whereas a command does not: one who issues a command has, or implicitly claims to have, the authority to require compliance. Invitations have much in

---

[6] Clauses of type IIIB, especially negatives perhaps, are not found in all dialects: some speakers use *should* instead, as in [*I insist*] *that he should (not) be told.* Given that *should* is a tensed verb it is arguable whether the subordinate clauses in these latter examples should be grouped with type III jussives, or indeed with the jussive clause type at all: the alternative is to treat them as declaratives, with the special use of *should* being handled in our account of analytic mood in the VP.

common with requests and should perhaps be subsumed under that category; their special property is that compliance is assumed to be pleasurable to you. Instructions are another very clear case of directive – instructions or directions for using materials (*Allow surface to dry thoroughly before applying a second coat*), cooking or washing instructions and the like. Less central members of the directive class are the giving of advice or the granting of permission – less central because it is not so clearly or necessarily the case that it is my will that you should comply (and indeed we would not in the everyday use of the term talk about 'complying' with permission). Nevertheless, imperatives can be used in the performance of these acts – as when you say *What do you advise?* and I reply *Don't sell your shares if you can possibly avoid it*, or you say *May I have some of these forms?* and I reply *Of course; take as many as you like*.

To the extent that the various types of directive mentioned above are performed by uttering an imperative (and it will be clear now that they can also be performed using non-imperatives), the distinction between them will be marked by linguistic features other than clause type, e.g. prosodic/paralinguistic features, or the use of *please*, which leads to a request interpretation. Indeed, the distinction may not be encoded at all, with the interpretation depending on such pragmatic factors as the relations between the speaker and addressee (have I the authority to command?), and assumptions about who is intended to benefit from compliance.

We have discussed one case where an imperative would standardly be used with non-directive force – the *Have a good holiday!*, *Sleep well!*, *Get well soon!* case. A second involves coordinations like *Speak to me like that again and I'll disinherit you*: in uttering this I would not normally be construed as performing a sequence of two illocutionary acts, the first a directive, the second a statement; instead, the illocutionary interpretation would apply to the utterance of the sentence as a whole, rather than the constituent clauses. It would be equivalent to the threat *If you speak to me like that again I'll disinherit you*. Again, such an interpretation clearly depends on pragmatic considerations – in particular the assumption that my disinheriting you is something you would rather avoid; compare *Mow the lawn for me and I'll give you five dollars*, which would normally be construed as a directive to mow the lawn.

11.4 Interrogatives

There are two major subtypes of interrogative clause, illustrated in

(12) i *What time is it?*   *Wh* interrogative
      ii *Is she ill?*   Non-*wh* interrogative

The type exemplified in (i) is marked by the presence of one or more of the interrogative words *who, whom, which, whose, what, where, when, why, how,* or their compounds in *-ever: whoever, whatever,* etc. These words are commonly called '*wh*' words (a term, however, which should be understood as covering *how* – but not of course *whiskey* and the like: the class is defined syntactically, with the orthographic property found in all but one of the members providing simply a convenient short label) – hence the term **wh interrogative** for the clause type. (ii) then belongs to the unmarked interrogative type, the **non-*wh* interrogative**, where there is no interrogative word.

There is a further division to be made within the non-*wh* class, but, before we introduce it, it will be helpful to pause briefly to look at the semantic correlate of our initial distinction. We have said that in the absence of overriding factors, an interrogative main clause will be used to pose a question, where each question defines a set of possible answers. We can now draw a distinction between two different kinds of question that correlates closely with the syntactic distinction between *wh* and non-*wh* interrogatives. Consider the sets of answers to the questions expressed in an utterance of

(13)   i *Who broke the window?*
          ii *Is he alive or dead?*

In the first case, as we noted earlier, the answers include "I broke the window", "Tom broke the window", "the plumber broke the window", and so on: they are all of the semantic form "x broke the window", supplying different values for the variable x. Such questions are commonly called **x-questions** and are of course the kind of question that *wh* interrogatives are normally used to express. Thus, to take a second example, the answers to the question expressed in uttering *Why did he resign?* have the form "He resigned for reason x" – "He resigned on account of ill health", "He resigned because he had become disillusioned" and so on. In the case of (13ii), by contrast, the answers are simply "He is alive" and "He is dead". Here the set of answers is derivable from the question itself: it is a matter of selecting from among a number of alternatives given in the question – and such questions are therefore commonly called **alternative questions**.

One special case of the alternative question is that where the alternatives differ as positive vs negative:

(14)   i *Is it genuine or isn't it?*
          ii *Is it genuine or not?*

The answers are positive "It is genuine" and negative "It is not genuine". A much more frequent form for such questions, however, is that where only one of the alternatives is overtly given:

(15)   i *Is it genuine?*
          ii *Isn't it genuine?*

The answers are still "It is genuine" and "It is not genuine", so that there is a sense in which (14i), (14ii), (15i) and (15ii) could all be used to express the same question. But this is not to say that they have the same meaning. Of the two types illustrated in (15), for example, the negative indicates that my previous expectation was that it was genuine, that present evidence suggests to me that it isn't (or may well not be) and that the question is directed to the issue of whether it is in fact the case that it isn't genuine; the positive, by contrast, is neutral: it encodes no information about my expectations or attitudes. The positive is thus the semantically unmarked member of the pair – and much the more frequent.

The simplest way of expressing the propositions "It is genuine" and "It is not genuine" in answer to (15) is by using the forms *Yes* and *No* respectively: for this reason such questions are generally called **yes/no questions**.[7] The label '*yes/no*' is also widely used in combination with 'interrogative' – the clauses in (15) are commonly analysed as '*yes/no* interrogative clauses'. The correspondence between the semantic and syntactic categories is, however, not perfect and it is therefore arguably preferable not to use '*yes/no*' for a subclass of interrogatives. In the first place, we have already observed that a clause like *It is genuine* is not interrogative at all but could be used, if spoken with rising intonation or written with a question mark, to pose a *yes/no* question. Secondly, a single question may be expressed by a coordination of clauses:

(16)   *Is it genuine or is it a hoax?*

There are two interrogative clauses here, but the sentence would normally be used to pose a single question. The first clause is identical with (15i) and the second is of the same syntactic type, but the question is not a *yes/no* one: the answers are "It is genuine" and "It is a hoax".[8]

In the light of these observations let us now resume the syntactic classification of interrogatives. The distinction we have drawn so far is

---

[7] *Yes* or *No* alone would hardly be a natural response to (14), particularly (14i), though *Yes, it is* and *No, it isn't* would be. Writers often do not explicitly say whether they intend the term '*yes/no* question' to cover (14) as well as (15); for simplicity I will assume that it does – given that I am using 'question' in such a way that utterances of (14) and (15) in the same context would express the same question (just as the responses *It is genuine, It is, Yes*, etc. would express the same answer, the same statement).

[8] Another case where what is arguably a sequence of two interrogative clauses would be used to put a single question is illustrated in *Who did it, John or Peter?* (spoken without a sharp break or pause after *did it*). The question would be an alternative one. Syntactically it is probably best to analyse *John or Peter* as an elliptical clause (deriving from *Did John or Peter do it?*), in which case the sentence will consist of a *wh* interrogative with a non-*wh* interrogative juxtaposed to it. Both cases provide further illustration of the importance of distinguishing interrogative clause and question.

between the *wh* and non-*wh* types. The latter covers clauses like *Is he alive or dead?* and also those like *Is it genuine(?)*, whether it stands alone as in (15i) or forms part of a coordination of clauses, as in (16). Within the non-*wh* class, we now distinguish the *Is it genuine(?)* type as unmarked and the *Is he alive or dead?* type as marked – we will call it 'marked disjunctive' (from 'disjunction', the term used for the logical relation expressed by *or*).

The presence of *or* is necessary but not sufficient for an interrogative clause to belong to the marked disjunctive type. Considered in abstraction from the intonation, examples like (17) are ambiguous:

(17)   *Is Ed trying for Oxford or Cambridge?*

Uttered with a rise on *Ox(ford)* and a fall on *Cam(bridge)*, it would express a question with the answers "He's trying for Oxford" and "He's trying for Cambridge" – i.e. a non-*yes/no* alternative question: I assume that Ed is trying for one of the two and the issue is which of them it is. In this case the clause belongs to the marked disjunctive class. Uttered with, say, a rise on *Cam(bridge)* it could be used as a *yes/no* question (with the answers "Ed is trying for Oxford or Cambridge" and "Ed is not trying for Oxford or Cambridge")[9] or it might be part of a sentence like (16), such as *Is he trying for Oxford or Cambridge or does he intend to stay in Scotland?*. In the second interpretation of (17) the *or* is irrelevant to the clause construction – it is just like *Is Ed trying for Oxbridge?*, or our earlier *Is it genuine?*, i.e. it is a non-*wh* interrogative of the unmarked subclass. The difference in interpretation is relevant not just to the intonation: the *or* of a marked disjunctive cannot be paired with *either*. Thus if we insert *either* before *Oxford* only the second interpretation is retained. That this is so can perhaps be more easily seen by observing the effect of adding *either* before *a boy* in *Is it going to be a boy or a girl?*, said to a pregnant woman. Without the *either* the clause has the same ambiguity as (17), but the first interpretation is for pragmatic reasons vastly more salient than the second: adding *either* then excludes the salient interpretation and forces the one which entertains the possibility that it isn't going to be either a boy or a girl.

Let us now look more carefully at the way interrogative clauses differ structurally from members of the unmarked term in the system, declaratives, considering in the first instance just main clauses: they differ with respect to one or both of two properties, one a matter of selection, the other of order.

The special property of selection is found in *wh* interrogatives, which contain one (or more) of the following interrogative words:

---

[9] You might of course reply with something like *Yes, Oxford*, but in that case you would be giving more information than is directly asked for, i.e. providing more than an answer – just as you would be in replying to *Has he arrived?* with *Yes, half an hour ago*.

(a) *who* and *whom* – nominative and accusative forms of the pronoun **who** (see 7.5). **Who** occurs as head of an NP functioning as subject (*Who said that?*), object (*Who(m) did you see?*), predicative complement (*Who is he?*), complement of a preposition (*Who did you give it to?/To whom did you give it?*). Interrogative *whose* stands in the same relation to *who* as *his* does to *he*, and raises the same problems of analysis (see 7.4). *Whose* occurs as determiner within an NP having any of the above functions (*Whose entry won the prize?*, *Whose car did they steal? . . .*); it also occurs alone as anaphoric NP (*Whose won?*) or a PossP in predicative complement function (*Whose was it?*).

(b) *what* – a pronoun or a determinative. As a pronoun it occurs as head of an NP with the same functional potential as **who** (*What happened?*, *What did you see? . . .*). Interrogative **who** and *what*[pro] contrast for the most part as "human" vs "non-human": in *Who/what caused that?* the *who* indicates that I assume that someone caused it, *what* that something caused it. In predicative complement function, however, the contrast is somewhat different, for we can have both *Who is he?* and *What is he?*. The first is used to ask about his identity (it could be answered with, for example, *He's my brother-in-law*), while the second is used to ask about certain kinds of property – profession, religion, race, nationality, political affiliation, etc. (so that it might be answered with *He's a social-worker/a Catholic/ . . .* – where the NPs *a social-worker, a Catholic* are not used referentially). Determinative *what* occurs as determiner in an NP with any of the above functions – or with the function of complement to the possessive clitic (*What schoolchild's imagination could fail to be stimulated by such a challenge?*); it enters into construction with both "human" and "non-human" nouns (*What child . . .?/What chance . . .?*).

(c) *which* – likewise a pronoun or a determinative. In either use it is neutral with respect to the "human"/"non-human" contrast; what distinguishes it from **who** and **what** is that it is explicitly or implicitly partitive (see 7.3): *Which (of the candidates) do you support?*, *Which (of the versions) shall we use?*.

(d) *when* and *where* – adverbs or pronouns. As an adverb, *when* occurs as head of a phrase functioning as complement or adjunct of time (*When is the concert?*, *When did he arrive?*), while *where* occurs as head of one functioning as complement of goal (*Where did he go?*) or complement/adjunct of place (*Where is he?*, *Where were they swimming?*). Their most obvious pronoun use is as head of NPs functioning as complement to a preposition (*Since when has he been a member?*, *Where does he come from?*), but they are also found under certain conditions in NPs functioning as subject (*When/where would suit you?*) or complement, especially of *be* in its identifying sense, where they are equivalent to *what* (*When/what is the best time to plant them?*, *Where/what is the best place for it?*).

(e) *why* – an adverb: it heads a phrase functioning as adjunct of reason (*Why did she leave?*).

(f) *how* – an adverb (of degree or manner) or an adjective. The degree adverb modifies adjectives, predicative or attributive (*How big is it?*, *How big a piece do you want?*), *many, much, few, little* in determiner or head function (*How many pieces are there?*, *How much do you want?*) or adverbs (*How quickly was it travelling?*). Adjectival *how* is used only predicatively (*How are you?*, *How was the film?*, *How do you like your coffee?*).

In addition the above may be compounded with *-ever* (*whoever, whatever*, etc.) or else be postmodified by *ever* (*who ever, what ever*): this is an area, reflected in variation in spelling, where there is uncertainty as to whether we have a single word or a sequence of two. The *ever* adds an emotive component of meaning: *Wherever/where ever did you find that?* poses the question "Where did you find that?" and at the same time expresses some element of surprise that you should have found it anywhere – it would be used as an exclamatory question (see §1 above).

The phrase containing the *wh* word may have a function within a declarative content clause or a non-finite clause embedded inside the interrogative clause itself:

(18)   i   *What did he think had happened?*
         ii *When do you suppose they'll arrive?*
         iii *Who did she say she expected them to invite?*

Thus in (i) *what* is subject of the clause *what . . . had happened* which is object of **think**. And as we see from (iii) there can be 'recursive' (repeated) embedding of this kind: *who* is object of the **invite** clause, which is complement in the **expect** clause, which is in turn complement of the **say** clause.

Most *wh* interrogatives contain a single *wh* phrase, but we also have 'multiple *wh* interrogatives', as in *What did he give to whom?*, *Who gave what to whom?*, and so on; we will not investigate the question of what combinations are permitted.

So much for the distinctive property of selection: consider now the matter of order. The first point to make here is that the *wh* phrase (or one of them, in the case of multiple *wh* interrogatives) generally occurs in initial position in the interrogative clause – as in all the examples cited so far. But it is not grammatically obligatory for it to do so – witness examples like

(19)   [*And then*] *you left the building at what time approximately?*

Here the time adjunct occupies the same position as it does in declarative clauses. Clauses like (19) – which should not be confused with the superficially similar '*wh* echo' (see §7 below) – are most characteristically used in contexts involving sustained interrogation, by an investigator, quizmaster or the like. One convenient way of handling the order in the usual type, such as *At what time approximately did you leave the building?*, is then to derive them from clauses like (19) by a transformation of *wh* phrase fronting. With a *wh* phrase that is complement of a preposition there is generally a choice between moving the *wh* phrase alone, leaving the preposition behind, as in *Which book did you take it from?* and taking the preposition along with the *wh* phrase, as in *From which book did you take it?*: recall the discussion of 10.3. Where the *wh* phrase is subject, it will already be in initial position, so that the transformation doesn't apply – or else we might say that it applies 'vacuously'.

A second non-kernel feature of order concerns the position of the subject. In non-*wh* interrogatives and in *wh* interrogatives in which the *wh* phrase is moved to pre-subject position, the subject follows the tensed verb, which must be an operator. We will again suggest a transformational treatment, so that (20ii), for example, will be derived from (i)

(20)   i *Pat has arrived*
         ii *Has Pat arrived?*

by a transformation of subject–operator inversion; if the version with the unmarked order has no operator, the dummy operator **do** is added – see 4.4 for details.

It remains now to consider the properties of interrogative subordinate clauses, as in

(21)   i [*I wonder*] *what time it is*   *Wh* interrogative
         ii [*I wonder*] *whether she is ill*   Non-*wh* interrogative

As far as order is concerned, they differ from interrogative main clauses in two respects. First, the fronting of the *wh* phrase is obligatory, not optional. Second, subject–operator inversion generally does not apply; the non-*wh* type is then marked as interrogative by the conjunction *whether* (or, in some but not all cases, *if*).

On another dimension we can distinguish two kinds of interrogative subordinate clause. One functions as complement (in the broad sense which includes subject as a special case – see 5.1) within a larger construction: the occurrence of such an interrogative is contingent on the presence in head position of a verb, adjective, noun or preposition allowing an interrogative clause complement (as **wonder** in (21) allows an interrogative clause as object, while **believe**, say, does not – see §1 above). I will call these 'interrogative clauses in complement function'. The compounds in *-ever* (or head + *ever* sequences) are permitted only where the governing verb, etc. is one of (roughly) "asking" as opposed to "telling": *He asked/*told her whoever could have dreamt up such an idea.* And besides tensed clauses like those of (21) we find also subjectless infinitival clauses: [*He wondered*] *what to do/whether to go.*

The second kind of interrogative subordinate clause is commonly called 'concessive':

(22)   i [*They'll sell it*] *whatever you say*   *Wh* interrogative
         ii [*They'll sell it*] *whether you approve or not*   Non-*wh* interrogative

The *wh* type always has an *-ever* compound (without the emotive component of meaning mentioned above), while the non-*wh* type always has *or* (within the clause or coordinating two clauses). The link with the first kind is that the construction is essentially equivalent to *It doesn't matter what you say/whether you approve or not, they'll (still) sell it* – where the interrogative clause is complement to **matter**. The interrogative clause in (22i) and the coordination of interrogative clauses in (22ii) are immediate constituents of the sentence, rather than being embedded within the superordinate clause: see 12.1 for discussion of such non-embedded subordination.

To conclude this section we will return to interrogative main clauses, mentioning briefly some cases where the clause type is overridden in the determination of illocutionary force.

(a) Example (5iv) – *Could you pass the salt?* – is illustrative of a rather large family of interrogatives whose most characteristic use is to issue directives, primarily requests: compare *Can you . . .?, Will you . . .?, Would you . . .?, Would you mind . . . ing . . .?, Would you like/care to . . .?, Would you be so kind as to . . .?*, and so on. Whether we say that when *Could you pass the salt?* is used to make a request it also expresses a question (so that the literal meaning is that of a question, with the request meaning implied or 'indirect') or that the sentence is ambiguous, having the meaning of a potential question or a potential directive (both of these views will be found in the literature), it is clear that *could you, can you*, etc., can all occur in sentences which would characteristically be used with question force: *Can you understand it?*, etc. What the various expressions have in common is that they can all be used to ask about the addressee's ability, wish or willingness to do something – and you will not comply with a request unless you are able and willing to do so. Thus the use of these expressions in directives is by no means arbitrary. At the same time we must recognise a certain amount of conventionalisation, for there are other expressions that can be used in questions about ability, etc., which are not, or only rarely, used in directives – cf. *Are you able to open the door?, Do you wish to take the cat out?*. In the absence of prosodic and/or paralinguistic features with contrary effect, requests of the form discussed here are regarded as more polite than those in the form of imperatives – compare *Pass the salt.*

(b) Certain types of *wh* interrogative are standardly used with non-question force. At the extreme of idiomatisation we have *How do you do?*, which is used as a greeting. *How dare you* is typically used in utterances with a force approximating that of a reprimand. *Why* + negative is used in directives of the suggestion subclass like *Why not give it to Peter?*, *Why don't you be more careful?* (note the exceptional occurrence here of the dummy operator *do* with *be*, a feature shared with the imperative construction). Whereas directive utterances of the kind exemplified in (a) can be reported by means of *ask* + embedded interrogative, perhaps with varying degrees of naturalness (cf. *I asked him whether he would mind turning his radio down*) this is virtually impossible with these *wh* interrogatives (**I asked how he did/how he dare come home so late/why he didn't be more careful*): the degree of specialisation to the non-question force is thus here appreciably greater.

(c) It may be that we should also include here the case where prosodic and paralinguistic features give utterances of non-*wh* interrogatives like *Isn't it a lovely day!*, *Was I furious!* the force of exclamatory statements ("It is indeed a lovely day", "I was extremely furious"). These have some affinity with rhetorical questions and represent another instance where it is debatable which of the two cases subsumed under our concept of 'overriding' the clause type is appropriate, i.e. whether they are both questions (literally) and exclamatory statements (indirectly) or just exclamatory statements.

11.5 **Exclamatives**

Exclamative clauses are marked by one or other of the *wh* words *how* and *what*. *How* is more characteristic of formal or careful style than *what* – compare

(23)   i *How well she sings!*
         ii *What a fine singer she is!*

Exclamative *what* is a determinative; it differs from interrogative *what* semantically in that it is concerned with degree not identity, and syntactically in that it occupies determiner position I not II (see 6.4). *How* generally functions as degree modifier to an adjective, adverb or to *many, much, few, little*, but it can also occur as head of an AdvP on its own: *How we laughed!*.

As with interrogatives, we posit a transformation moving the *wh* phrase to initial position – and here its application is obligatory. The subject normally remains in its basic position but – in the *how* type at least – subject–operator inversion may apply or (if the main verb is *be*) subject–VP inversion:

(24)   i *How often have I regretted not accepting his offer!*
         ii *How great had been her surprise when she read the will!*

Since there is also an interrogative *how* and *what*, there may be ambiguity (in the verbal component – it would be resolved prosodically) between the two clause types:

(25)   i *How much remains to be done!/?*
         ii *What foolish ideas filled his mind!/?*

If I use (25i) in its interrogative interpretation, I am asking about the amount of work or whatever remaining to be done; if I use it in its exclamative interpretation, I am exclaiming about it.

With exclamatives subordinate clauses are not differentiated from main clauses in their internal structure – except that the marked construction where the subject follows the operator or VP is normally found only in main clauses. Since interrogative subordinate clauses likewise normally have the subject positioned before the predicator there is somewhat greater overlap between the two clause types here than in main clauses. Thus [*He remembered*] *how long it had taken* is ambiguous: with an exclamative subordinate clause the meaning is "He remembered that it had taken a remarkably long time", with an interrogative it is, roughly, "He remembered the answer to the question, 'How long did it take?' ". Such ambiguities will occur, of course, only when the clause is in construction with a verb, etc., that – like **remember**, **know** and so on – allows both interrogative and exclamative complements. *He inquired how long it had taken* is not ambiguous because **inquire** takes only an interrogative complement, as we can establish from the ungrammaticality of examples like **He inquired what a long time it had taken*, where the occurrence of *what* in determiner position I makes the subordinate clause clearly exclamative.

Exclamative main clauses are normally used to make exclamatory statements – there do not appear to be any features of form that can override the clause type here (except for the general phenomena of 'echoes' discussed in §7 below). An exclamatory statement is one overlaid with some 'emotive', attitudinal meaning. More or less the same emotive effect can be achieved by other means – prosodic and paralinguistic features and various lexical items: cf. *It was incredibly hot!, She has just finished an absolutely marvellous play!, He was a complete bastard!.* There are two reasons for excluding these from the exclamative clause type. In the first place, subordinate counterparts of such clauses can occur as complements to verbs, etc. that are subclassified as allowing declarative but not exclamative content clauses as complement: *I believe that it was incredibly hot/that she has just finished an absolutely marvellous play/that he is a complete bastard/*how incredibly hot it was/*what a marvellous play she has just finished/*what a bastard he was.* And in the second place, the expressive devices concerned can occur equally in interrogative and imperative clauses: *Why is it so incredibly hot today?, Let's give her an absolutely marvellous reception!.* The appropriate way to handle the exclamatory component in these examples is thus not by assigning them to a special clause construction, but simply in terms of our semantic description of the lexical items and non-verbal signals concerned: it is only in the *how/what*

374

cases that the exclamatory component is grammaticalised in a distinct clause type, exclamative.

11.6   **Interrogative tags**

One special kind of non-*wh* interrogative is the interrogative tag, which may be attached to declarative, exclamative or imperative clauses. We will deal first with the case where the tag is attached to a declarative, as in

(26)   i *She has finished, hasn't she?*
         ii *She hasn't finished, has she?*
        iii *She has finished, has she?*
         iv *She hasn't finished, hasn't she?*

(Not all speakers – perhaps, indeed, only a minority – find the last of these acceptable.) *Hasn't she?* and *has she?* in (i) and (ii) are 'reversed polarity' tags: they have the opposite positive/negative polarity from that of the declarative clause to which they are attached; those in (iii) and (iv) are 'constant polarity' tags. The tag consists of an operator followed by a personal pronoun subject – and optionally *not* (*has she not?*), though inflectional negation (*hasn't she?*) is a good deal commoner in this construction than analytic negation. The personal pronoun is a repetition of, or else an anaphor for, the subject of the declarative (*The boss has finished, hasn't he/she?*). The operator is the same as that of the declarative clause (except for the polarity, which may be different, and for any person–number properties, which will be determined by agreement with its own subject: *Everyone has finished, haven't they?*) or – where the declarative has no operator – it will be the appropriate form of the auxiliary ***do*** (*She finished, did she?*). The tag is probably best regarded as involving a special case of ellipsis (so that there would be ellipsis of *finished* in (26), and so on), though we could not reinstate the elliptical material without breaking the close tie between the clauses that is characteristic of the construction.

In the reversed polarity construction, the tag may be accompanied by rising or falling intonation. With a rise on the tag, the construction indicates that I am inclined to believe or assume the proposition expressed in the declarative, but ask you to say whether it is in fact so. With a fall on the tag, it indicates my commitment to the truth of the proposition expressed in the declarative and seeks your confirmation. Thus the rising tag indicates doubt: I am prepared for an answer that accepts or one that rejects the proposition at issue; with the falling tag, on the other hand, I am prepared only for a confirmatory answer. The constant polarity construction is often used when there is in fact no doubt about the truth of the proposition encoded in the declarative: the inclusion of the tag commonly expresses some kind of disapproving attitude on the part of the speaker.

Exclamative clauses allow reversed polarity tags with falling intonation: *What a mess he made of it, didn't he?*. The tag would be used to seek confirmation of the exclamatory statement expressed in the exclamative.

Consider finally imperatives. With *let* imperatives, whether positive or negative, the only possible tag is *shall we?* or *will we?* (depending on dialect). With other imperatives it is selected from a small set including *will you?*, *won't you?*, *would you?*, *can you?*, *can't you?*, etc. The permitted tags are derivable by ellipsis from interrogative clauses of the form 'modal auxiliary + *you* + main verb' with a potential illocutionary force and propositional content matching that of the imperative to which they are attached. For example, interrogative *Will you open the door?* could be, and most characteristically would be, used as a directive to open the door (see §4 above), and accordingly *will you?* can be tagged to imperative *Open the door*. Likewise *Can't you open the door?* could be used as a directive to open the door, so we can have *Open the door, can't you?*. Of course, *Will you open the door?* and *Can't you open the door?* would be different kinds of directive, the second being less polite, more impatient than the first, and this difference carries over to the tags. Similarly, *Shall/will we go to the beach?* could be used as a proposal or suggestion that we go to the beach, so that elliptical *shall/will we?* can be tagged to *Let's go to the beach*. This principle accounts for the fact that a positive imperative like *Take a seat* can take either *will you?* or *won't you?* as tag, whereas negative *Don't touch the silver* can take *will you?* but not *won't you?*. *Will you take a seat?* and *Won't you take a seat?* can both be used to ask/invite you to take a seat, whereas a directive not to touch the silver could take the form *Will you not touch the silver?* but not *Won't you touch the silver?*.

11.7 Echoes

The clause types discussed in §§1–5 are mutually exclusive: a clause cannot be simultaneously exclamative and imperative (**Give them what a lot of support!*), and so on. The only point of clarification we need to make in this connection concerns 'echoes', as in

(27)	⟨A⟩	i *He gave it to Georgina*	Declarative
	⟨B⟩ {	ii *He gave it to Georgina?*	
		iii *He gave it to who?*	
(28)	⟨A⟩	i *When is Georgina coming?*	Interrogative
	⟨B⟩ {	ii *When is Georgina coming?*	
		iii *When is who coming?*	
(29)	⟨A⟩	i *What a bitch Georgina is!*	Exclamative
	⟨B⟩ {	ii *What a bitch Georgina is?*	
		iii *What a bitch who is?*	
(30)	⟨A⟩	i *Give it to Georgina*	Imperative

⟨B⟩ $\left\{\begin{array}{l}\text{ii} \;\; \textit{Give it to Georgina?} \\ \text{iii} \;\; \textit{Give it to who?}\end{array}\right.$

Here B echoes A's utterance in either of two ways. The examples numbered (ii) are *yes/no* echoes: B repeats A's words with an intonation indicating "Is that (really) what you said?". The examples numbered (iii) are *wh* echoes: B repeats A's words except for one (or perhaps more) that is replaced by the corresponding *wh* form, and asks for repetition of the word replaced (because he or she didn't catch it, or can't believe it). As the examples show, a clause of any type can be echoed, so that the echo phenomenon is independent of the type system. We will analyse the echoes as belonging to the same clause type as the corresponding examples numbered (i), differing from them by means of a property distinct from clause type; the echo property is, of course, another factor that overrides the clause type in the determination of illocutionary force.

FURTHER READING

On illocutionary force and the distinction between illocutionary categories and clause types, see Lyons 1977:§16.1, 1981a:134–41, 171–94. For the various categories of illocutionary act I have followed the terminology of Searle 1975b. On 'indirect speech acts', see Searle 1975a. On imperatives, see Bolinger 1967a, 1977:Chs. 8 & 9, Lyons 1977:§16.2 (p. 748 for the term 'jussive'). On interrogatives and questions, see Chafe 1970:Ch. 20, Quirk et al. 1971:§7.55–71, Langacker 1974, Hudson 1975, Lyons 1977:§16.3, Hiż 1978.

12

Coordination and subordination

12.1 Compound and complex sentences

Traditional grammars classify sentences as **simple**, **compound** or **complex**:

(1)   i   *Liz prepared the food*   Simple
       ii *Liz prepared the food and Ed bought the wine*   Compound
       iii *Liz prepared the food that they had ordered*   Complex

If we continue to use 'clause' in our sense, rather than the more restricted traditional sense, we can explain this classification very straightforwardly by reference to the distinction between subordinate and main (i.e. non-subordinate) clauses. A simple sentence contains only one clause, a main clause; a compound sentence contains two or more main clauses; a complex sentence contains two or more clauses at least one of which is subordinate. Thus *that they had ordered* is a subordinate clause, so that (iii) is complex, while *and Ed bought the wine* is a main clause, so that (ii) is compound.

It will be recalled that the same terms are used in the morphological analysis of words, the other basic unit of traditional grammar, and it is easy to see the similarity between the two sets of contrasts. A compound word consists of two (or occasionally more) stems, while a complex word consists of a stem plus an affix. Stem is thus the analogue of main clause, and affix of subordinate clause – a stem (in some languages, only an inflectional as opposed to a lexical stem, see 1.7) can generally stand alone as a word, just as a main clause can normally stand alone as a sentence. One difference between the two cases is that in a compound sentence the constituent main clauses are typically coordinated, whereas coordination is not a relation found (other than very exceptionally) in the structure of words – but note that although coordination figures in some modern definitions of a compound sentence, it does not generally figure in traditional definitions. A further limitation to the analogy is that whereas stems and affixes are rather sharply distinct, there is considerable overlap between main and subordinate clauses. For example, the clause *he is dying* is subordinate in

(2)   *He knows he is dying*

378

but it is a main clause in the simple sentence *He is dying*: subordination need not be reflected in the internal structure of the clause, though of course it very often is.

As I defined them in the first paragraph, the classes of compound and complex sentences are not mutually exclusive: an example like *Liz prepared the food that they had ordered and Ed bought the wine* would belong to both. It is an elementary matter to give more restrictive definitions that are contrastive and then introduce a further term, 'compound-complex' for examples like this last one – and indeed this is probably the most usual analysis in traditional grammars. Such differences are, however, of little importance: what is of interest is the syntagmatic relations between the constituent clauses of non-simple sentences.

In the most central cases of complex sentences, the subordinate clause is a constituent of the superordinate clause. In (1iii) for example, *that they had ordered* is modifier within the NP *the food that they had ordered* – and hence a constituent (non-immediate, of course) of the clause of which that NP is object. Similarly in (2) the subordinate *he is dying* is complement of **know** and hence a constituent of the superordinate *he knows he is dying*. In these examples the superordinate clause is a main clause, but of course this will not be the case for second or subsequent layers of subordination: in *I think he knows he's dying*, the clause *he knows he's dying* is superordinate to *he's dying* but at the same time it is subordinate to *I think he knows he's dying*.

Where a subordinate clause is a constituent of the superordinate clause, we say that it is *embedded*. This term is a relatively modern one, and so too is the concept, for in traditional grammar the main clause in (1iii), would be just *Liz prepared the food*, and in (2) it would be just *he knew*, and so on. However, contrary to what is assumed in many modern grammars, there is good reason to doubt whether all cases of clause subordination should be handled in terms of embedding. Thus in

(3)   *Ed liked it, whereas Max thought it appalling*

we shall want to say that *whereas Max thought it appalling* is subordinate (for reasons we shall go into in §2.2 below), but the superordinate clause here is *Ed liked it*: this – unlike *Liz prepared the food* in (1iii) or *he knew* in (2) – is a clause. The suggestion is that in (3) the subordinate clause is an immediate constituent of the sentence, and in that case it is not embedded, just as *and Ed bought the wine* is not embedded in (1ii). Let us represent the two kinds of constituent structure schematically as in (4), where X and Y are clauses:

(4) i 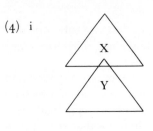 ii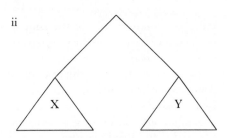

(i) represents embedding: clause Y is a constituent of clause X; in (ii) clause X and clause Y are each immediate constituents of the sentence. The point being made then is that although the clauses in (4i) are unequivocally related in subordination, structure (4ii) can cover a variety of relationships including subordination as well as coordination. It is true that the embedding kind of subordination is more clearly distinct from coordination than is that in (3), but this simply reflects the familiar phenomenon whereby the distinction is partially gradient rather than sharply polarised.

The most central kind of compound sentence has the constituent main clauses related by coordination, as in (1ii). In other cases the clauses are simply 'juxtaposed' – still with the constituent structure of (4ii); examples are:

(5)   i *He has finished, hasn't he?*
          ii *Will he do it, do you suppose?*
          iii *The more I listen to it, the more I like it*

(5i) is the tag construction discussed in 11.6. In (ii) the second clause is again elliptical (cf. *Do you suppose he will do it?*), but with a type of ellipsis more or less special to this construction, for *do you suppose?* would not normally occur elsewhere as a clause. (iii) illustrates what is commonly called a 'correlative' construction. Note that although main clauses can mostly stand alone as complete sentences, they cannot all do so, as we see from these examples; main clauses are defined by the property of not standing in the syntagmatic relation of subordination to any other clause, not by the property of being able to stand alone. We shall not have anything further to say about examples like (5), but the reader should bear in mind that coordination and subordination do not exhaust the types of syntagmatic relation to be found between clauses. And it should also be remembered that differences will be found among grammars with respect to how much they bring within the scope of the compound sentence. In a case like (6), for example,

(6)   *They had a miserable holiday: it rained every day*

I am here taking the view for reasons given in 1.5 that, grammatically, we have a sequence of two sentences, not a single compound sentence, but others (particularly those who give greater weight to the non-verbal component of the signal, to prosodic properties and punctuation) will take the contrary view.

Coordination and subordination, of course, hold between other classes of forms as well as between clauses. In the next section, therefore, we will deal with coordination more generally, rather than confining our attention to compound sentences. Subordination has already been extensively covered in the preceding chapters: we have analysed the structure of verb phrases, noun phrases and so on in terms of such relations as complementation and modification, which are special cases of subordination. In this chapter, therefore, we need only take up certain aspects of subordination that haven't been handled earlier because they cut across our primary organising dimension of clause vs NP vs AdjP, etc. Thus in §3 we will look briefly at the classification of subordinate clauses (which can function within the structure of clause, NP, AdjP, etc.), while §§4 and 5 deal respectively with relative and comparative constructions.

12.2   Coordination

We will take the view that coordination is always marked by the presence of one or more coordinating conjunctions: we thus exclude cases like the classic *I came, I saw, I conquered* (which some grammarians regard as a special type of coordination), relegating it to the fringe of, or beyond, sentence syntax, like (6) above. We will accordingly begin by discussing the various coordinating conjunctions; we will then consider the contrast between coordination and subordination, and finally we will draw attention to some difficulties in the syntactic analysis of coordination.

12.2.1   *Coordinating conjunctions*

The central coordinating conjunctions are *and* and *or*. There are two properties which together distinguish them from others. Firstly, they can enter into constructions with any number of coordinate terms. In *Ed and Max*, we have two, in *Ed, Max and Tom* three, in *Ed, Max, Tom and Bill* four, and so on without grammatical limit. Usually the conjunction introduces just the final term, but it is also possible for it to introduce all but the first – *Ed and Max and Tom*. Secondly, they can link the full range of coordinatable elements – *a black and white dress* (adjectives), *the conventions that they may or must observe* (modal auxiliaries), *with or without help* (prepositions), *the boss and his wife* (NPs), *She was intelligent and very conscientious* (AdjPs), *Give it to Tom or keep it yourself* (imperative clauses), *those that he had received from Bill and that had impressed him so much* (relative clauses), and so on.

Less central, but nevertheless standardly included among the coordinating conjunctions, is *but*. It differs from *and* and *or* in respect of both the above properties. It is effectively limited to two-term coordinations. (In an example like *He was intelligent and handsome but insufferably arrogant* we have not a three-term coordination, but one two-term coordination inside another: *intelligent* and *handsome* are first coordinated by *and*, and then the construction so formed is coordinated with *insufferably arrogant* by *but*.) As for the second property, *but* does not, for example, freely coordinate NPs – cf. *Tom and/or/*but Bill can do it*; we will not explore the restrictions in detail. Semantically *but* is like *and* plus some extra component of (arguably non-propositional) meaning: "and, however", "and, by contrast" or the like.

Two further coordinating conjunctions are *both* and *either*, which pair with *and* and *or* respectively in 'correlative' coordinations like *both John and Bill, either John or Bill*.[1] *Both* is appreciably more restricted in its distribution than *either*. It is strictly limited to two-term coordinations, whereas *either* – for many speakers at least – is not (cf. *either John or Bill or Ed*). And *both* cannot, for example, join main clauses, whereas *either* can: **Both Ed is a liar and Max is, Either Ed is a liar or Max is*. There are a few fairly specific restrictions with *either*: as we have seen (11.4), it cannot combine with an *or* that marks a disjunctive interrogative; and it cannot coordinate relative clauses, and so on.

We must also include the correlative pair *neither* and *nor*, which result from the morphologically rather transparent incorporation of a negative into *either . . . or*. Thus we can negate *He had either borrowed it or stolen it* as *He hadn't either borrowed it or stolen it* (with the negative in the auxiliary) or as *He had neither borrowed it nor stolen it* (with the negative in the coordination). For some speakers, *neither . . . nor* cannot coordinate main clauses, as in *Neither he had borrowed it nor had he stolen it*.

12.2.2 *Coordination vs subordination*

In coordination the terms in the relationship are of equal syntactic status, in subordination they are not – one is subordinate, the other superordinate. The contrast is clearest when the subordinate term is a constituent of the superordinate term, as in clause embedding. Thus we may contrast coordinative *Ed was rude to her parents and this annoyed her immensely* with subordinative *That Ed was rude to her parents annoyed her immensely* – in the latter the subordinate clause is subject of the superordinate.

Consider next a case of non-embedded subordination, such as (3) above – *Ed liked it, whereas Max found it appalling*. Semantically *whereas* is here quite similar to *but*; nevertheless there are at least two respects in which *whereas* can be distinguished from a coordinating conjunction. Firstly, the *whereas*

---

[1] Note that correlative and coordinative constructions may or may not combine: these examples are correlative and coordinative, while *John and Bill* is simply coordinative and (5iii) above is correlative but not coordinative.

clause can be shifted to front position: *Whereas Max found it appalling, Ed liked it* (compare *Ed liked it, but Max found it appalling*, where we cannot move the *but* clause to the front). (3) shares this property with prototypical subordinative constructions such as *Ed liked it when he got used to it*. Secondly, the difference in syntactic status of the terms related by *whereas* is evident from an example like *I'd send John, who has considerable overseas experience whereas the others have served only in this country*. Here the *whereas* clause enters into construction with a relative clause (*who has considerable overseas experience*) but the *whereas* clause itself is not a relative clause (or the functional equivalent of one) – note that *whereas* could not be replaced by *but* here, so that in this respect (3) differs from a coordinative construction.

Similar to *whereas* are *although* and *since* (in the causal sense: temporal *since* introduces an embedded clause). More problematical is *for*, as in

(7)   *He didn't pursue the matter, for his mind was now on other things*

This time we cannot move the *for* clause to the front (contrast the clearly subordinative *Because his mind was now on other things, he didn't pursue the matter*). A further respect in which *for* differs from clear subordinating conjunctions is that it seems just possible for it to introduce an imperative clause: *We should do it now, for remember that next week the boss is back*. On the other hand, the terms related by *for* can be of different syntactic status – as in *I'd send John, who seems the best of a poor bunch, for the others haven't had any overseas experience at all*. Not surprisingly, some grammars treat *for* as a coordinating, others as a subordinating conjunction: it falls at the borderline between the two and seems to lack the positive properties of both.

The equal syntactic status of the terms related in coordination may be reflected in the possibility of reversing their order without change of meaning. Thus *Ed was a solicitor and Tom was a barrister* is equivalent to *Tom was a barrister and Ed was a solicitor*. However, there are many cases where the terms cannot be reversed in this way. In the first place, it will not normally be possible if the second term contains an anaphor whose antecedent is in the first (*Three of them took the test this morning and three of them are taking it this afternoon* cannot be switched to *Three of them are taking it this afternoon and three of them took the test this morning*) – or, more generally, if the second term contains some element that makes it 'cohesive' with the first (as in *It was his first public speech and he was consequently somewhat nervous* – where connective *consequently* has the same effect as *in consequence of this*, with anaphoric *this*). Secondly, the order of the terms will often be of pragmatic significance. For example, in *She went to town and bought a new hat* it would normally be inferred that she went to town and there, then bought the hat, pragmatic implications that would be lost if the order were reversed. Or again, in *It was his first public speech and he was somewhat nervous* the normal pragmatic implication would be that the first clause gives the reason for his nervousness (an implication explicitly expressed in the earlier example with *consequently*), and this is dependent on the order of the clauses in the coordination. Thus although the possibility of reversing the terms is characteristic of the most prototypical coordination, it cannot be regarded as a defining property (at the level of language-particular definitions).[2]

12.2.3   Problems in the description of coordinative constructions

Let us now turn to the analysis of coordinative constructions. It raises, in fact, serious difficulties, which I cannot hope to resolve here: I shall instead simply attempt to draw attention to two problems, one concerning the classification of the coordinative construction as a whole, the other concerning the analysis of the separate terms.

We will begin, then, with cases where the coordinated terms are, or at least appear to be, unproblematic: they are main clauses, subordinate clauses, NPs, auxiliary verbs, and so on, as in

(8)   i *Liz prepared the food and Ed bought the wine*   (= 1ii)
        ii *[the advice] that Liz kept giving him and that he kept ignoring*
        iii *John and his brother [are coming for lunch]*
        iv *[You] can and must [help her]*

To what syntactic classes should we assign the unbracketed parts of these examples?

Traditional grammar would say that in (8i) the whole is a sentence and the coordinated terms are clauses. But this is not (and is not intended to be) a general solution to the problem, even for case (i) – for note that a coordination of main clauses can occur as one term in a larger coordinative construction:

(9)   *Liz prepared the food and Ed bought the wine, but neither received any thanks for their trouble*

Here, *Liz prepared the food and Ed bought the wine* would be neither a sentence nor a clause. Some modern linguists have reinterpreted the traditional distinction between sentence and clause so as to parallel that between clause and phrase or between phrase and word (in modern senses of these terms too): sentence would denote a syntactic class higher in the constituent hierarchy than clause. In this interpretation, saying that (8i) is a sentence consisting of two clauses is intended to provide an answer to the question of the classification of coordinative constructions, insofar as the

---

[2] Note that we have invoked two kinds of reversal of a structure X C Y, where C is a conjunction: in prototypical coordination we can switch to Y C X, in prototypical subordination to C Y X.

coordinate terms are clauses. But since it deals only with case (i) – or rather case (i) in the absence of layered coordination such as we have in (9) – this cannot be regarded as a satisfactory answer.

An alternative and now very widely accepted solution is to say that the whole belongs to the same class as its parts. Thus in (8iii), for example, *John and his brother* would be an NP, just like *John* and *his brother*.

The distributional equivalence of a (non-coordinative) NP and a coordination of NPs (it is virtually always possible to replace an instance of the former by one of the latter) lends considerable plausibility to this proposal. Those who adopt this solution generally use 'sentence' rather than 'clause' for the relevant syntactic class, so that (8i) and the unbracketed part of (ii) would be sentences each composed of two coordinate sentences, and so on. This of course represents a departure from the sense of 'sentence' in traditional grammar and much of the earlier work in structural linguistics, where a sentence cannot be part of any larger syntactic construction. A further terminological point to note is that if we say that *can and must* in (iv) is a verb (an auxiliary verb), our part-of-speech labels will have to be extended to cover not just words (or stems) but also groups of words.

The problem with this solution, however, is that although the terms in a coordinative construction are generally of the same class, they are not invariably so, witness

(10)   i *[He was] enormously wealthy and an obvious target for kidnappers*
        ii *[He was] unwell, very tired and in a terrible temper*
      iii *The purpose of the bill and how it had got passed [was something of a mystery]*
      iv *[I saw him] last week and on two earlier occasions*

In (10i) an AdjP is coordinated with an NP – the possibility of coordinating them derives not from any likeness of internal structure but from the fact that they could each occur alone with the same function: both *He was enormously wealthy* and *He was an obvious target for kidnappers* have the structure S–P–PC^s. Similarly in (ii) we have a coordination of two AdjPs and a PP, in (iii) of an NP and a (subordinate interrogative) clause, and in (iv) of an NP and a PP. The proposal to apply the same class label to the whole as to the parts is insufficiently general to handle mixed coordinations of this kind – and in the absence of any solution to this problem I will continue to avoid it by talking of 'a coordination of NPs', 'a coordination of an NP and a clause', and so on.

Our second problem concerns the relation between coordination and ellipsis. With one exception, all the examples given so far are such that each of the coordinated terms could occur as a constituent (and/or construction) in a sentence from which all the others had been removed. For example, if we retain just one of the coordinated terms in (10i) we get either

He was enormously wealthy, where *enormously wealthy* is a constituent, an AdjP, or *He was an obvious target for kidnappers*, where *an obvious target for kidnappers* is a constituent, an NP. The discussion above took this for granted. The one exception was *He had either borrowed it or stolen it*: in *He had borrowed it* we do not have *borrowed it* as a constituent – we have grouped *borrowed* with *had*. Similarly *a Welsh* is not a constituent of *He had found a Welsh version of the legend* but it can be coordinated, as in *He found both a Welsh and an Irish version of the legend*. More obviously still, the 'discontinuous' *John . . . an Australian* is not a constituent of *John was an Australian* but can be coordinated, as in *Ed was a Canadian, but John an Australian*. This last case we have met before and have analysed in terms of ellipsis: the second term is derived from *John was an Australian* by ellipsis of the VP (this particular kind of ellipsis is commonly called 'gapping' in the transformational literature). And we might analogously say that *a Welsh* was an elliptical NP, derived from *a Welsh version of the legend*, that *stolen it* is an elliptical EVP, derived from *had stolen it* (though note the position of *either* in the example makes the ellipsis of *had* virtually obligatory: *He had either borrowed it or had stolen it* will be rejected as ungrammatical by most speakers).

The question then arises as to how much ellipsis we should postulate. Should we say that in *Ed came in and sat down* we have a single clause with the predicate filled by a coordination of EVPs, or that we have a coordination of clauses, the second derived by ellipsis from *Ed sat down?*. Some grammars choose the second alternative, although given the analysis of clause structure presented here it postulates more ellipsis than is necessary – necessary for coordination to be described as a relation between independently established constituents.

If such an approach were carried to its extreme, all coordination would be of clauses – (8iv) would derive from *You can help her and you must help her*. However, this leads to considerable complexity and in many cases is also semantically unsatisfactory. In (8iii) *John and his brother* constitutes a single plural unit determining the selection of the verb form *are* (as opposed to *is*): *are* does not agree with either of the coordinate terms taken individually, so that we would not want to say that there is coordination of an elliptical clause *John* and a putative non-elliptical *his brother are coming to lunch* – to derive it from *John is coming to lunch and his brother is coming to lunch* would involve more than mere ellipsis, and take us into a form of analysis considerably more abstract than adopted elsewhere in this book. And think of the problems of knocking into shape the source of, say, *Ed, Jill and the kids are hoping to see both 'Hamlet' and 'Macbeth' when they are in London next June or July*. The analysis would be more semantic (a partial listing of entailments) than syntactic. Yet there are many cases where reducing all coordination to clause coordination fails on semantic grounds. The most obvious are those involving a semantic predicate that applies to a set rather than to an individual, as in a standard example like

(11)   *Ed and Liz are an amiable pair*

where "an amiable pair" can only be coherently predicated of a set containing two members, so that a clause coordination source *Ed is an amiable pair and Liz is an amiable pair* would be nonsensical. Other such predicates are those expressed by **meet**, **agree**, *similar*, *equal*, etc., when used with a single argument (as in *John and Mary met* rather than *John and Mary met the headmaster*). But it is not just with such predicates that these semantic problems arise. *I've got a black and white terrier* is not equivalent to *I've got a black terrier and I've got a white terrier*. A less obvious difficulty arises in an example like *The main beneficiaries were Tom and Ed*: the putative source *The main beneficiary was Tom and the main beneficiary was Ed* is pragmatically unacceptable, because each of the coordinated clauses implies – by virtue of the use of *the* plus a singular head (see 6.7) – that there was just one main beneficiary.

For such reasons no one would want to push the ellipsis analysis to the extreme of deriving all coordination from clause coordination. Here, by contrast, we shall make minimum use of ellipsis, resorting to it only when the actually present terms in the coordination are not independently identifiable as constituents (as, for example, in *He has either borrowed it or stolen it*, and the like). We adopt this as the apparently simplest solution, but without exploring the full range of alternatives – for which the reader is referred to the works cited under 'Further reading'.

12.3   Classification of subordinate clauses

We turn to subordination, where the first issue we will consider concerns the various subclasses of subordinate clause that need to be distinguished. One preliminary distinction it will be helpful to clarify is that between finite and non-finite clauses. With a very limited range of exceptions (such as *Not to worry!*, *Why bother?*, and so on) main clauses are finite, whereas subordinate clauses can be finite or non-finite: it is thus primarily with respect to subordinate constructions that the contrast is of significance.

The distinction between finite and non-finite constructions is traditionally based on the inflectional form of the first verb (see 2.4, 5.6), but given the analysis of verb inflection adopted here, the primary verb-based contrast is that between tensed and non-tensed constructions, which is not quite the same. All tensed clauses are finite, but certain non-tensed ones are traditionally classified as finite too. And there are good reasons for wanting to retain the traditional class of finite clauses. Consider the set of examples in (12):

(12)   i [*I hope*] *that they are moved*   Finite; tensed
        ii [*I insist*] *that they be moved*   Finite; non-tensed
        iii [*I wouldn't let them*] *be moved*   Non-finite; non-tensed

The verb inflection criterion groups (ii) with (iii) as non-tensed in contrast with (i), which is tensed, but when one takes account of other features of clause structure it is clear that (ii) is closer to (i) than to (iii), and this is the grouping that we have on the finiteness dimension: (i) and (ii) are finite while (iii) is non-finite. Non-finite subordinate clauses differ a good deal more radically from the structure of main clauses than do finite ones.

It is only the base form that can occur as the first verb in both finite and non-finite clauses; tensed forms, as noted above, are restricted to finites, while *-ing* and *-en* forms occur only in non-finites, so that the correlation between verb inflection and clause finiteness is as shown in (13):

(13)   Inflection of 1st verb   Finiteness of construction

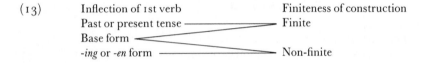

Past or present tense ———————— Finite
Base form
-ing or *-en* form ———————— Non-finite

The property that we take to be criterial for central members of the finite class is that when the subject is a case-variable pronoun a nominative form is required. Thus just as (12i) requires nominative *they*, so too does (12ii) – contrast the non-finite [*It would be inappropriate*] *for them/ *they to be moved* or (with an *-ing* class VP) [*I don't approve of*] *them/their/ *they being moved by the owner*. Imperative clauses do not readily take a case-variable pronoun as subject, so that our criterion is not directly applicable; we can, however, include them among the finites (which is where they traditionally belong) by the supplementary criterion that they occur regularly (indeed, more or less exclusively) as main clauses, whereas it is characteristic of non-finites to be subordinate. Our class of finite clauses thus coincides with the traditional class, although we have suggested a different account of their distinctive properties; given the contrast we have drawn between general and language-particular definitions it is of course appropriate for us to continue to use the general term 'finite' in spite of our revision of the language-particular definition, for the class will continue to contain among its members clauses where the first verb is 'limited' by properties of person, number and tense.

Let us now focus our attention on finite subordinate clauses. We observed in 3.3 that the major dimension of classification for such clauses in traditional grammar contrasts noun clauses, adjectival clauses and adverbial clauses, as in (14i–iii) respectively:

(14)   i *That he was a charlatan* [*was now undeniable*]
          ii [*The man*] *who came to dinner* [*stole the silver*]
         iii [*He stayed behind*] *because he couldn't speak French*

This classification is based on functional analogies with the corresponding parts of speech. In (i) the subordinate clause is subject of the superordinate clause and subject is a function characteristically filled by nouns (or NPs, as we would have it) – cf. *His guilt was now undeniable.* In (ii) it is modifier in the structure of the NP *the man who came to dinner*, and modifier in NP structure is a function characteristically realised by adjectives (AdjPs) – cf. *The old man stole the silver.* And, finally, in (iii) the subordinate clause *because he couldn't speak French* is adjunct in the structure of the superordinate clause, a function characteristically realised by adverbs (AdvPs) – cf. *He stayed at home therefore.* We argued, however, that given a framework where we systematically distinguish between functions and classes we shall not want to take over this traditional classification. We want our classification to complement, not duplicate, our functional analysis of the constructions in which they occur, and our concern will accordingly be with the different ways in which their form may differ from that of main clauses.

From this point of view we can initially distinguish four, or perhaps just three, major classes.

(a) relative clauses, as illustrated in:

(15)   i [*The man*] *who came to dinner* [*stole the silver*]   (= 14ii)
          ii [*They found the weapon*] *with which he had shot her*

Relative clauses of the most central kind, such as we have in (15), differ structurally from main clauses like

(16)   i *The man/he/. . . came to dinner*
          ii *He had shot her with the weapon/it/. . .*

in that they contain one of the relative *wh* words *who, whom, which,* etc. and the phrase containing it occurs initially in the clause irrespective of whether it is functioning as subject, object, adjunct, etc. We will look more carefully at their special properties in §4 and introduce a range of relative constructions besides the elementary one shown in (15).

(b) Comparative clauses, as illustrated provisionally in

(17)   i [*There have been far more strikes this year*] *than there were last year*
          ii [*He's about as old*] *as I am*

The most obvious respect in which comparative clauses differ from main clauses is that they are structurally 'incomplete' or elliptical: we will describe their structure by relating them to such structurally complete main clauses as

(18)   i *There were that/so/. . . many strikes last year*
         ii *I am that/so/. . . old*

– see §5 below.

(c) Clauses introduced by such subordinating conjunctions as *because, before, unless,* etc.:

(19)   i *[He stayed behind] because he couldn't speak French*   (= 14iii)
         ii *[I left] before the meeting was over*

Here the structural difference from main clauses is less: for the most part we can relate them to declarative main clauses differing only in the absence of the conjunction: *He couldn't speak French, The meeting was over.* Sometimes, however, the subordinate clause may contain an element that could not occur but for the subordination: thus we can have *I'll be surprised if he ever returns,* but not **He ever returns,* for *ever* is restricted to 'non-affirmative contexts' (see 13.2, where we will see that this same point applies to comparative clauses). It should also be borne in mind that subordination may affect the interpretation of tense: the main clause *Sue arrives tomorrow,* for example, will be interpreted with Sue's future arrival already scheduled in the present, but there is no such present time component in the interpretation of the subordinate *If Sue arrives tomorrow [we can take her along too].*

(d) Content clauses, as in

(20)   i *That he was a charlatan [was now undeniable]*   (= 14i)
         ii *[I wonder] whether he'll win*

Content clauses are subclassifiable in the system of clause type, *that he was a charlatan* being declarative, *whether he'll win* interrogative, and so on; very often, however, features of the superordinate construction will allow only the unmarked declarative type or otherwise restrict or determine the selection of clause type – as **wonder** in (20ii) selects an interrogative. These matters were discussed in Ch. 11, and we need not pursue the analysis of content clauses any further here.

The distinction between (c) and (d) is somewhat problematic. We raised in 10.4 the question of whether words like *because* and *before,* as used in (19), should be assimilated into the class of prepositions. If this solution is adopted, it will follow that *because he couldn't speak French* is not a clause: it will be a PP, with *because* as head and *he couldn't speak French* as complement; the subordinate clause, in other words, will be *he couldn't speak French,* not *because he couldn't speak French* – and *he couldn't speak French* can then be handled under our subclass of content clauses. Some members of our enlarged preposition class, such as *because, before, unless,* would take content clause complements without *that*; others, such as *except, in, in order* (arguably a single word), would take one with *that*; while others again, such as deverbal *granted, provided, seeing*, would take one with or without *that* – compare (19i) with

(21)   [*He was at a disadvantage*] *in that he couldn't speak French*
(22)   [*He didn't have much chance*] *seeing* (*that*) *he couldn't speak French*

If we adopt this solution we will of course also want to include the *than* and *as* of (17) among the preposition class – and they clearly belong to that class when occurring with such NP complements as they have in *Ed is taller than six feet, It may be as old as a hundred years*. This is why I spoke of *than there were last year* and *as I am* in (17) as 'provisionally' illustrating the class of comparative clauses. We would still of course need to recognise a distinct comparative class of subordinate clauses for constructions like *there were last year* and *I am*: comparative clauses would simply occur as complement to *than* or *as* instead of being introduced by them. (*As* would also allow a content clause as complement when its meaning is "since": *I had to leave as I had no more money*.)

Let us now turn briefly to non-finite subordinate clauses (assuming for present purposes that they are in fact to be accepted as clauses – see 3.3). Our first dimension of classification here derives from the kind of VP they contain. As base kind VPs can occur in finite clauses (more specifically in jussives), we are using the more specific term 'infinitival' for non-finite clauses with such a VP, distinguishing then between '*to*' and 'bare' according as they do or do not contain the infinitival marker *to*; the other classes correspond directly to the kind of VP (see 5.6.2):

(23)   Subclass of non-finite clause
         to-infinitival   [*He went to the pub*] *to get some lunch*
         bare-infinitival   [*The experiment helped*] *define the problem areas*
         -ing class   [*He ignored those*] *living on their own*
         -en class   [*He set aside those*] *considered too young*

Secondly we will distinguish between those that do and those that do not contain an overt subject. The examples in (23) are clearly subjectless. If sentences like *The experiment helped us* (*to*) *define the problem areas* are correctly analysed with the NP *us* a complement in the superordinate clause rather than subject in the subordinate one (see 5.6.3), then it is doubtful whether bare-infinitivals can contain a subject, while full-infinitivals will do so only in the construction with *for*:

(24)   *For such a thing to happen again* [*would be an absolute disaster*]

The problem of deciding on a satisfactory analysis of prepositions and conjunctions arises in a particularly acute form with this *for*; I am assuming that it is here a conjunction, like *that* – with *such a thing* accordingly the subject – but it is difficult to find convincing arguments for choosing between alternative constituent structure analyses of the construction. Non-finites of the *-ing* class may occur, under certain conditions (see 5.6.3 for some discussion), with a preceding NP or a preceding PossP:

(25)   *Ed resented your father('s) opening the mail*

though we drew attention in 9.1 to the somewhat problematic status of sequences like *your father('s) opening of the mail* as subject + predicate constructions. Finally *-en* class non-finites are generally subjectless (again given our assumption that in constructions like *He had his hair cut* the NP *his hair* belongs syntactically in the superordinate clause), but subjects can be found in *-en* class clauses functioning as peripheral dependents in clause structure or within a *with* PP having this function:

(26)   *With three of his companions already killed [his position looked grim]*

The interpretation of subjectless non-finites will involve supplying an understood subject or subject-argument, in ways that depend on the particular superordinate construction to which the non-finite is subordinate; we will not take the discussion of this matter beyond what was said in 5.6, although of course the account given there was restricted to constructions where the non-finite functions as complement within a larger clause.

A third dimension we need to recognise is according to whether or not the non-finite clause is structurally complete, relative to analogous main clause constructions, with respect to its non-subject NPs. The examples given above all belong to the unmarked class on this dimension; examples of the marked class, lacking a non-subject NP, complement (generally object) of the verb or complement of a preposition are shown in:

(27)   i *The food was too hot (for them) to eat*
         ii *She's the best person (for you) to talk to*

where the subordinate clauses may be compared to the structurally complete main clauses *They ate the food/it/*... and *You talk to the person/her/* ... Only *to*-infinitival clauses are found in the marked class; they occur in a variety of functions: modifier in AdjP structure (especially one with a degree modifier like *too* or *enough*), as in (27i), complement in AdjP structure, as in *The food is ready to eat* (see 8.4), modifier in NP structure, as in (27ii), complement of the verb **take**, as in *The programme took three years to make*, and certain others. A full account of these constructions will of course need to show where the missing non-subject argument is recovered from – from the subject of the superordinate clause in (27i), the head of the superordinate NP in (27ii), and so on.

For the rest, the two marked classes introduced above in our discussion of finite subordinate clauses include a very limited range of non-finites: the relative class includes subjectless *to*-infinitivals, as in (28), the comparative class subjectless bare-infinitivals, as in (29):

(28)   *I thought of a good place in which to hide it*
(29)   *I'd rather die than accept such terms*

Besides finite and non-finite constructions, it is arguable that we should include within the class of subordinate clauses certain verbless constructions such as

(30)   i [*He walked out of the restaurant*] *with a spoon in his pocket*
          ii *The meeting over,* [*she resumed work on her novel*]

The relation between *in his pocket* and *a spoon, over* and *the meeting* is like that between a predicate and a subject (cf. the main clauses *A spoon was in his pocket, The meeting was over*) rather than like that between a modifier and a head (+ determiner) in NP structure, which makes the constructions clause-like even though there is no VP present.

12.4 **Relative constructions**

There are a number of different kinds of relative clause – and some differences among grammarians as to just how much they subsume under this category. It is another case where it does not seem possible to give a set of defining properties shared by all relative clauses and distinguishing them from other kinds of syntactic construction; we will therefore proceed by examining first the most central kind of relative clause and then considering various other kinds in terms of their similarities and differences with respect to prototypical relative clauses.

12.4.1 'wh' restrictive relatives

The following are examples of prototypical relative clauses:

(31)   i [*I didn't like the guy*] *who spoke first*
          ii [*The books*] *which he had recommended* [*were unobtainable*]
          iii [*We will evacuate the village*] *whose water supply they have contaminated*
          iv [*He found a place*] *where he could spend the night*

We will call them '*wh* restrictive relatives' (contrasting them in due course with the 'non-*wh*' class and with 'non-restrictive relatives'), and we will initially confine our attention to those which are tensed.

Such clauses function as modifier in NP structure. What is distinctive about them as far as their own structure is concerned is that they have as or within their initial phrase one of the relative *wh* words, namely (ignoring the more or less archaic *whence, wherein*):

(a) **who** and *which* – these are pronouns functioning as full NPs: they cannot take dependents within the NP. **Who** subsumes nominative *who* and accusative *whom*: see 7.5 for the relation between them. **Who** and *which* function as subject, as in (31i); object, as in (ii); or complement of a preposition ([*It was an issue*] *about which she felt strongly*) – but hardly indirect object (*[*John wasn't the one*] *whom they had sent it*: see 5.4) or predicative complement (*[*He was no longer the kind and gentle person*] *who/which he had been when we first met him*). *Which*ʳᵉˡᵃᵗⁱᵛᵉ differs from *which*ⁱⁿᵗᵉʳʳᵒᵍᵃᵗⁱᵛᵉ in that it is not partitive and is confined to non-humans (or infants); **who** is normally used of humans – its application to animals is much less usual (in restrictive relatives) than is that of the personal pronouns **he** and **she**, and it is not normally applied to ships, etc.

(b) *whose* – this functions as determiner in NP structure, as in (iii), where it is determiner within the NP *whose water supply*. Thus unlike interrogative *whose* it cannot occur without a following noun head: not *[*They found the girl*] *whose the book was* (cf. interrogative (*Whose was the book?*), only [*They found the girl*] *whose book it was*. As this last example shows, the NP containing *whose* as determiner can occur as predicative complement; for the rest it occurs in the same range of functions as the **who** and *which* phrases of (a). A second respect in which *whose*ʳᵉˡᵃᵗⁱᵛᵉ differs from *whose*ⁱⁿᵗᵉʳʳᵒᵍᵃᵗⁱᵛᵉ is that it is the possessive analogue of *which* as well as **who**: cf. *the books whose spines were damaged*.

(c) *where, when* and *why* – these are adverbs functioning as full AdvPs: like **who** and *which*, they do not take dependents. The AdvPs themselves function respectively as complement/adjunct of place/goal, complement/adjunct of time, adjunct of reason.

The *wh* words are anaphoric to the part of the NP preceding the relative clause – to *the guy* in (31i), *the books* in (ii), and so on: they thus 'relate' the subordinate clause to the NP containing it. I will then use the term 'relative construction' to embrace both the antecedent and the subordinate clause, so that in (i), for example, *the guy who spoke first* will be a relative construction, *who spoke first* a relative clause.

We noted in our discussion of anaphora in 7.2 that anaphors are not always semantically equivalent to a copy of their antecedent, and the relative anaphors that are our present concern are a case in point. This is most obvious when the antecedent is negative or involves certain kinds of quantification, as in

(32)   i *Nobody who knows her could believe her capable of such an act*
        ii *Every vehicle which they had tested had some defect*

"Nobody knows her" is clearly not part of the meaning of (i), and (ii) does not entail that they had tested every vehicle. Even in a seemingly straightforward case like (31i), where the antecedent contains the definite article,

who spoke first is not pragmatically equivalent to *The guy spoke first*: the latter
would normally be used when it is assumed that the referent of *the guy* can
be picked out by virtue of the description *guy*, independently of the information that he spoke first, whereas in (31i) the property of having
spoken first is presented as crucial for picking out the person I didn't like
(see 6.7). Thus just as we cannot analyse (32i) semantically as "Nobody
knows her; nobody could believe her capable of such an act", so we cannot
analyse (31i) as "the guy spoke first; I didn't like the guy". We clearly
again need some more abstract form of analysis involving variables – very
crudely, "No person x such that x knows her could believe her capable of
such an act", "I didn't like the guy x such that x spoke first". The relative
clause itself does not express a complete proposition and hence the
meaning cannot be the same as that of any main clause.

For this reason we will not derive relative clauses from main clauses by
the transformational substitution of a relative anaphor for some non-
anaphoric NP: we will not regard *who knows her* in (32i) as a transform, the
relative clause counterpart, of *Nobody knows her*, nor *who spoke first* as a
transform of *The guy spoke first*, and so on. Thus the fact that the subject-
argument of "speak" in (31i) is understood as representing some guy will
be handled by a semantic account of the anaphoric interpretation of *who*,
not by deriving *who* syntactically by substitution for *the guy*. But it is again
useful to invoke the concept of transformation to account for the special
order of elements in relative clauses. Thus, just as we did with *wh* interrogative clauses, we will derive them by a transformation of *wh* phrase
fronting, moving the *wh* phrase to initial position from a position identical
to that occupied by a phrase with equivalent function in a declarative main
clause. This will involve postulating hypothetical underlying clauses (see
1.4), so that the relative clauses in (31i–ii), for example, will derive from

(33)   i †*who spoke first*
         ii †*he had recommended which*

Where the *wh* phrase is already initial, as in (i), the application of the
fronting rule will be vacuous. The advantage of this form of description is
again that it enables us to handle separately the various distinctive
properties that characterise relative clauses – in particular, to separate the
issue of the order of elements from the two other properties, one major and
one minor, that distinguish tensed *wh* restrictive relatives from declarative
main clauses, for at the underlying level the order will be the same as in the
latter.

The major respect in which our hypothetical relative clauses differ structurally from main clauses is that they have a relative *wh* word in one of the
functions outlined above: (33ii) will then be structurally like *He had recommended the books/the film/them/it/*. . . and the ungrammaticality of, say, *[the

395

book] which he disappeared will follow from that of *†*he disappeared which*, which is excluded by the intransitivity of ***disappear***, just like **He disappeared the book/it/...* As with *wh* interrogatives, the *wh* phrase need not be functioning directly within the relative clause itself, but may occur within a clause embedded within it:

(34)
  i   [*the books*] *which he had recommended that we buy*
  ii   †*he had recommended that we buy which*
  iii *He had recommended that we buy the books/the films/them/...*

The minor difference between relative and main clauses concerns subject–verb agreement. The relative pronouns ***who*** and *which* are inherently non-specific with respect to the grammatical categories of person and number: where they function as subject, any person–number properties in the verb will accordingly not be determined by agreement with the subject of the relative clause itself, but rather with the antecedent of the pronoun. Thus in *the woman who was talking* and *the women who were talking* the verbs *was* and *were* agree with *the woman* and *the women* respectively.

The order difference between relative and main clauses is then handled by our *wh* phrase fronting transformation. Except for the fact that the rule is obligatory, the rule works in the same way as with interrogative *wh* phrases. Thus in the case of determiner *whose* the *wh* phrase is the whole NP having *whose* as determiner, so that in (31iii), for example, underlying †*they had contaminated whose water supply* becomes *whose water supply they had contaminated*, not **whose they had contaminated water supply*. And in the case where the *wh* phrase is complement of a preposition, the latter may or may not accompany it (see 10.3) – thus hypothetical [*the chair*] †*he was standing on which* may become either [*the chair*] *on which he was standing* or [*the chair*] *which he was standing on*.

So much for the relative clause itself. As for the relative construction we need only add that the antecedent part of the NP must be consistent with the inherent properties of the *wh* word. In *the reason why he left*, for example, we cannot replace *reason* by *guy*, *place* or whatever because the semantic variable "x" expressed in *why* must range over reasons.

Before turning to the other main kinds of relative clause we should note that the *wh* class contains not only tensed clauses, as considered above, but also *to*-infinitival ones, as in (28) above – [*I thought of a good place*] *in which to hide*. They are obligatorily subjectless, the *wh* phrase can only be complement of a preposition, and the preposition must accompany the *wh* phrase in the movement to initial position; I will not pursue their description any further.

12.4.2   *Non-'wh' restrictive relatives*
Our second kind of relative clause is illustrated in

(35)
  i   [*I didn't like the guy*] *that spoke first*
  ii   [*The books*] (*that*) *he had recommended* [*were unobtainable*]
  iii [*One had to admire the way*] (*that*) *he handled the crisis*

These differ from the prototype in that they are not introduced by one of the relative *wh* words: instead they have *that* or no overt marker of subordination at all – the *that* is omissible in (ii) and (iii). The *that* is commonly analysed as a relative pronoun (or relative adverb in cases like (iii)), but an alternative analysis, which we shall adopt here, is to identify the *that* with the subordinating conjunction we find in content clauses like [*He said*] *that he was ill*. According to this second analysis the *that* of (35i), for example, will not be subject: rather it is simply a conjunction and the relative clause lacks a subject. Similarly the relative clause of (ii) lacks an object independently of whether the *that* is present.

The major differences in structure between 'non-*wh*' relatives and main clauses are then as follows:

(a) Such relative clauses are structurally incomplete in comparison with main clauses – (i) lacks a subject, (ii) an object, and so on. We will account for this by postulating hypothetical clauses like (36) underlying the actual relatives of (35):

(36)   i †*that Ø spoke first*
         ii †*that he had recommended Ø*
       iii †*that he handled the crisis Ø*

The incompleteness then arises through the transformational deletion of $Ø^{\text{relative}}$, an abstract anaphor, and the particular kinds of incompleteness found are determined by the functional potential of $Ø^{\text{relative}}$ in those hypothetical clauses. It can have the same functions as relative **who,** *which, when, where* and *why* – but not *whose* (cf. *[*the town*] (*that*) *they had contaminated water supply*). In addition it can be manner adjunct, as in (36iii), or predicative complement, as in [*He was no longer the kind and gentle person*] †(*that*) *he had been Ø when we first met him.*

(b) The relative clause may be introduced by the subordination marker *that*: we include *that* in our hypothetical clauses and allow for its optional deletion providing it does not immediately precede the Ø.

(c) As with *wh* relatives, there is also the difference that any person–number properties of the verb are determined by agreement with the antecedent of the relative anaphor: compare *the one that was ill* and *the ones that were ill*.

There are several arguments in favour of analysing *that* as a conjunction rather than a relative pronoun/adverb; no one of them would be conclusive by itself but cumulatively they do make a strong case. I will give three of them here: a fourth will be noted in 14.6 when we are dealing with a different kind of non-*wh* relative.

(a) Where the relativised element is complement of a preposition, the preposition cannot be fronted, so that we have [*the chair*] *that he was standing* *on* but not *[*the chair*] *on that he was standing*. According to our proposal, the underlying clause here would be †*that he was standing on* ∅, and since the transformation that applies is one of deletion not movement there is no way for the preposition *on* to be fronted. If *that* were a relative pronoun like *who*(*m*) or *which*, we would expect it to be able to function as complement to a preceding preposition.

(b) The *that* of relative clauses is like the *that* of content clauses in being omissible, under certain conditions. The conditions are not the same in the two cases, but in both cases they may be regarded as having their origin in the need to avoid having a subordinate clause misinterpreted as a main clause. If we omitted *that* from *That he was embarrassing her was only too obvious* the subordinate *he was embarrassing her* would initially be construed by the hearer as a main clause, and similarly if we omitted it from *The guy that spoke first was much the best* the subordinate *spoke first* would initially be construed as a main clause predicate with *the guy* as subject. I say that the restrictions on the omissibility 'have their origin' in such perceptual considerations because it is not a question of the omissibility depending in any given instance on whether or not there would be a risk of misconstrual: the restrictions are 'grammaticalised', i.e. built into a rule applying under grammatical conditions, with the perceptual factors providing the general motivation for such a rule rather than accounting for the details. Thus omitting *that* from (35i) would not create the same perceptual problems as in the above example, but the grammatical rule is that *that* cannot be omitted from restrictive relative clauses when the ∅^relative element is subject.

(c) As with content clauses, *that* is restricted to finite constructions. The *wh* class of relative can, as we have observed, be infinitival, as in [*He was looking for a box*] *in which to store her letters*; but there is no corresponding non-*wh* construction: *[. . . *a box*] *that to store her letters in*. This follows from the general properties of *that* as a conjunction, but would require special provision if *that* were a pronoun.

12.4.3   *Non-restrictive relatives*

We turn now to the contrast between restrictive and non-restrictive relative clauses, illustrated in the following examples (where they are labelled 'R' and 'N-R' respectively):

(37)   i [*She was wearing a dress*] *that I'd never seen before*   R
         ii [*She was wearing a beautifully-tailored ankle-length gown of cream silk,*] *which I had never seen before*   N-R
(38)   i [*She had three sons*] *who were still at school* [*and one*] *who had just completed a science degree*   R,R

ii [*She had three sons,*] *who were still at school,* [*and a
daughter,*] *who had just completed a science degree*   N-R,N-R

iii [*She had three sons*] *she could rely on for help,* [*so she wasn't
unduly worried*]   R

(39)   i [*Members of Parliament*] *who have no private income* [*find it
hard to make ends meet*]   R

ii [*Members of Parliament,*] *who are already grossly overpaid,*
[*should not vote themselves any further pay rise*]   N-R

(40)   i [*The necklace*] *which Elvis had given her* [*was in the safe*]   R

ii [*The necklace,*] *which Elvis had given her,* [*was in the safe*]   N-R

Non-restrictives differ from restrictives in phonology (or orthography), semantics and syntax – we will take these differences in turn.

First, the phonology and orthography. Non-restrictive relatives are spoken with a separate intonation contour: they are marked off prosodically from the remainder of the sentence, whereas restrictive relatives are prosodically bound to their antecedent. In writing, non-restrictives are typically separated off from the remainder by commas (or stronger punctuation, such as dashes or parentheses); punctuation is not a completely reliable guide, in that the commas are sometimes omitted, but here I shall consistently distinguish the two constructions by punctuation, as I have in (37)–(40).

Consider now the semantics. The most general account, I believe, involves initially a distinction of thematic meaning: in the non-restrictive construction, the information encoded in the relative clause is presented as separate from, and secondary to, that encoded in the remainder of the superordinate clause. In the restrictive construction on the other hand, the information contained in the relative clause forms an integral part of the message conveyed by the larger construction. As we shall see, certain differences in propositional meaning follow from this thematic distinction.

Let us consider first how it applies to (37). In (i) the reason for integrating the relative clause into the primary message is likely to be that the fact that she was wearing a dress is not in itself sufficiently newsworthy to be worth saying – it is something that would, in many contexts, 'go without saying': the significant part of what I have to say will then be that it was a dress I'd never seen before. In (ii), by contrast, the antecedent of the relative anaphor is specified in a much more detailed way, so that it is reasonable to present the bracketed part as an independent and self-sufficient piece of information.

In (38i) the restrictive relative clauses are clearly indispensable. Without them we would have *She had three sons and one* ("one son"), which is incoherent by itself, since the only reason for dividing the sons into the two groups is that they are differentiated by the properties given in the relative clauses. In (38ii), on the other hand, *She had three sons and one daughter* is coherent because the division of her children into the two groups is based on sex – it is quite independent of the properties given in the relative clauses. In (i) the relative clauses give distinctive, contrastive properties of the class denoted, so that *sons who were still at school* and *one who had just completed a science degree* denote distinct subsets of the set of sons: the relative clauses 'restrict' the application of the NP to these subsets. It is in cases like the contrast between (i) and (ii) that we have a clear difference in propositional meaning. But although (38i) illustrates a very frequent use of the restrictive relative – one, obviously, which gives it its standard name – this is not the only use. In (38iii), for example, there is no implication that she had other sons beside the three that she could rely on; the information that she could rely on the three sons might be put in a restrictive clause not in order to distinguish them from unreliable sons but because their reliability is an indispensable feature of the situation that causes her to be not unduly worried. It is for such reasons that I have distinguished the two constructions primarily in thematic terms, rather than in terms of sets and subsets: the reason for presenting the information contained in a relative clause as indispensable and integral to the message may be that it is needed to define a given subset of the set denoted by the noun it modifies – but it does not have to be.

(39i) exemplifies the case where the concept of subset applies in the most obvious and straightforward way. It is not the whole set of MPs, but just that subset without a private income, that are said to find it hard to make ends meet. The restrictive relative clause is clearly indispensable in that its omission would result in a proposition about MPs in general, quite a different matter. The non-restrictive relative clause in (39ii), by contrast, does not serve to select a subset: both clauses express propositions about the whole set of MPs, and omitting the relative would not change the proposition encoded in the remainder of the sentence.

(40) is the example used in our preliminary discussion of the restrictive/non-restrictive contrast in 6.11. The relative clause in (i) is indispensable in that the information it gives is necessary for determining which entity the speaker wants to refer to. (i) would be used in a situation where there was more than one necklace, but just one given by Elvis, so that the expression *necklace which Elvis had given her* serves to pick out a unique entity in the situation. (ii), on the other hand, would be appropriate in a situation containing a single necklace, so that the description *necklace* is sufficient to pick it out: the fact that Elvis had given it to her is separate, non-defining and hence dispensable information.

Let us turn now to the syntactic differences between the two kinds of relative clause. They involve (a) the range of relative constructions in which the clause can occur, and (b) the form of the relative clause itself.

(a) Restrictive relatives function only within NP structure, as modifier, whereas non-restrictives occur in a wider range of constructions. In the examples given so far they have been what we are calling peripheral dependents in NP structure. They can also be subordinated to a clause, as in [*John died the following year,*] *which made Max the sole heir*; this illustrates the non-embedded kind of subordination discussed earlier, having the constituent structure shown in (4ii). The relative anaphor, as well as having clauses and NPs as antecedent, can also have other classes of phrase, such as the AdjP *incompetent* in *She considered him incompetent, which indeed he was*. Within NP structure, proper nouns unaccompanied by a determiner can take only non-restrictives, as in *Liz, who knows him well, says he intends to resign* (cf. the restrictive relatives in *I meant the Liz who works for Tom* or *What has happened to the Liz who used to be so full of joy and vitality?*). Conversely, non-restrictives do not enter into construction with negative NPs or with NPs quantified by *every, each, all, any*. This limitation can be related to what we have said about the semantics – most clearly in the case of negatives. The semantic content of the non-restrictive clause is presented as a separate piece of information; the clause accordingly expresses a proposition and the relative pronoun will be a referring expression, rather like a personal pronoun in a main clause. Thus (37ii), for example, may be compared with *She was wearing a beautifully-tailored ankle-length gown of cream silk; I had never seen it before*: the *which* of (37ii), like the *it* of this last example, refers to the gown introduced into the context of discourse in the first clause. We cannot have **Nobody, who knows her, could believe her capable of such an act* because there is no referent for *who*: *nobody* does not introduce any person into the context of discourse; in restrictive *nobody who knows her* the relative pronoun does not serve as a referring expression, and the relative clause does not itself express a proposition.

(b) As for differences in the form of the relative clauses, the first point is that non-restrictives are more or less limited to the *wh* class.[3] Within the *wh* class *why* is limited to restrictives and **who** applies as readily as **he** and **she** to animals (*Fido, who was barking again, . . .*), but a more significant difference is that in non-restrictives *which* is not limited to head function: it can also occur as determiner, as in

---

[3] There is some variation in judgements on the acceptability of examples like *To her surprise there was a Christmas card from her father, that she hadn't seen or heard from for ten years*; they are certainly much less frequent than those with a *wh* word and limited to cases where the antecedent is an NP – and *that* is not omissible.

(41)   *He may have seen her yesterday, in which case he will certainly have told her the news*

Determiner *which* occurs most frequently in the expressions *in which case* and *by* (etc.) *which time*, but is certainly not limited to them. We will regard the full NP, *which case, which time*, as the anaphor, rather than the *which* alone – just as we would with demonstrative *in that case, by that time* (see 7.2). In (41) *which case* will be interpreted as "the case where he did see her yesterday"; such examples provide further reasons for not trying to derive relative clauses syntactically from a main clause containing a copy of the antecedent in place of the relative anaphor. Instead we derive the relative clause in (41) simply from †*he will certainly have told her the news in which case* (with the preposition being obligatorily fronted with the *wh* phrase) and the interpretation of the anaphor will be a matter of semantics, not syntax.

12.4.4 *The fused relative construction*
The final kind of relative we will consider in this section is what I shall call the 'fused relative construction', illustrated in:

(42)   i   *Whoever wrote the letter* [*must be insane*]
       ii   *What errors remained* [*were of a minor nature*]
      iii   *What money she gave him* [*was quickly spent*]
       iv   [*I didn't like*] *what I saw*
        v   [*Put it back*] *where you found it*
       vi   [*I could have died*] *when I saw the result*

How the unbracketed portions of such examples are to be analysed syntactically is quite unclear. They are very often taken to be clauses, and as far as their internal structure is concerned this has a good deal of plausibility: in (i) *whoever* would be subject, *wrote* predicator, *the letter* object, and so on. It would be a straightforward matter to describe such structures in the same kind of way as our *wh* restrictive or non-restrictive relative clauses, with (iii), for example, deriving from †*she gave him what money*: the only difference would be a matter of what *wh* phrases occurred. But when we consider their behaviour in larger constructions – and their meaning – it becomes apparent that they cannot be satisfactorily regarded as clauses: I shall take the view that (i–iv) are NPs, (v) and (vi) AdvPs. Examples like (i–iv) behave syntactically like NPs in at least the two following respects:

(a) Firstly, we see from (ii) and (iii) that there is a potential contrast of number: *what errors remained* is plural while *what money she gave him* is singular – witness the agreement of the following *were* and *was*. By contrast, when a clause is embedded as subject to a larger one it is invariably singular (cf.

Which books he had recommended was/*were unclear, where the subject is an interrogative content clause).

(b) Secondly, when the fused relative construction is subject, as in (i–iii), it cannot be moved to the right by the process of extraposition: **It must be insane whoever wrote the letter.* As we have seen (9.1), ordinary NPs likewise cannot normally be extraposed (**It must be insane the boss*), but embedded clauses, certainly finite and infinitival ones, can be, so that the process can be applied to examples like *Whether that is wise is debatable* to yield *It is debatable whether that is wise.*

Semantically (i–iv) are like NPs rather than clauses in that in (i) *whoever wrote the letter* is interpreted as some person, in (ii) the predicate expressed by *were of a minor nature* is predicated of certain errors, and so on, whereas when an argument of a semantic predicate is expressed by an embedded clause it can only represent a fact, a proposition, a state of affairs, an action or the like – never something concrete like a person.

If we attempt an analysis in terms of variables we arrive at something along the lines of "x wrote the letter; x must be insane" for *Whoever wrote the letter must be insane.* But we cannot find distinct parts of the sentence corresponding to the two occurrences of the variable – as we can in *the person who wrote the letter must be insane* (with *who wrote the letter* a *wh* restrictive relative clause), namely the antecedent *the person* and the anaphor *who. Whoever wrote the letter* corresponds not to the relative clause *who wrote the letter* but to the whole relative construction *the person who wrote the letter,* and that is why I am calling it a relative construction, not a relative clause. The term 'fused' is intended to suggest that the two occurrences of the x variable are incorporated into the meaning of the *wh* phrase, instead of having separate expression as in non-fused relative constructions.

One way of analysing (i) would be to say that *whoever* was a pronoun functioning as head of the NP, while *wrote the letter* was a relative clause deriving from †∅ *wrote the letter* and functioning as modifier. There would then not be any 'fusion' in the above sense inasmuch as *whoever* would be antecedent to the anaphor ∅^{relative}, and *whoever* would correspond to just one of the x's, ∅ to the other. The objection to this is that the so-called clause *wrote the letter* is not omissible, as one would expect it to be if *whoever* + *wrote the letter* were a head + modifier construction. Notice here the contrast between (iv) and [*I didn't like*] *those I saw,* where *I saw* (a non-*wh* relative clause) is modifier to the head *those* and is omissible. However, as I am not able to offer any more satisfactory analysis, I will simply leave the question of the internal structure of the fused relative construction unresolved.

The main *wh* words occurring in it are: *what, whatever, whichever* (all functioning as head or determiner) and *whoever, when, where* (head only). Note that **who** and *which* cannot normally occur in this construction: **Who* *was speaking suddenly switched off the microphone,* **Take care of which books she lent you.*[4] Leaving aside the 'pseudo-cleft construction' (see 14.6.2) the pronominal use of *what*[relative], like that of *what*[interrogative], implies non-human (except in predicative complement function – see 11.4).

12.4.5 Relatives contrasted with content clauses

There is some overlap between relative clauses (or the fused relative construction) and content clauses, as illustrated in the following examples, where 'Rel' indicates relative, 'Con' content.

(43)	i [*He quickly spent the money*] *that he had won*	Rel
	ii [*He was taken aback by the news*] *that he had won*	Con
	iii [*They told him*] *that he had won*	Con
(44)	i [*The place*] *where he had hidden it* [*wasn't very safe*]	Rel
	ii [*I wondered*] *where he had hidden it*	Con
(45)	i [*He spent*] *what they gave him*	Rel
	ii [*She told me*] *what they gave him*	Con

The non-*wh* relative partially overlaps with declarative content clauses, the *wh* class and the fused relative construction with interrogatives (or, occasionally, exclamatives). Restrictive and non-restrictive relatives can be distinguished from content clauses by the fact that they are in construction with the antecedent of the *wh* or $\emptyset$ anaphor. Thus *the money* is antecedent in (43i), whereas *the news* is not in (43ii). Using the crude type of representation introduced earlier we can give a partial analysis of (43i) as "He had won x; he quickly spent x", whereas (ii) is not understood as "He had won x; he was taken aback by x", nor (iii) as "He had won x; they told him x". Similarly in (44i) we have "He had hidden it at/in x; x wasn't very safe", whereas (ii) is not analysable as "He had hidden it at/in x; I wondered x". As observed above, with the fused relative construction we cannot readily identify an antecedent expression but can still give the same kind of semantic analysis, so that in (45i) we have "They gave him x; he spent x", whereas (ii) is again not similarly analysable as "They gave him x; she told me x".

Usually, as in these examples, the larger context will make clear which kind of construction we have, but it will not invariably do so. We can accordingly find ambiguities such as *The proposal that he was advancing was preposterous*. In the relative interpretation this may be represented partially as "He was advancing x; x was preposterous" (thus "He was advancing a preposterous proposal"), whereas with a content clause the meaning is

---

[4] The qualification 'normally' is required because they do occur (though with the sense "whoever" and "whichever") when the relative clause contains the verbs **please**, **choose**, **like**, etc.: *You can tell who you please*. *Who* also occurs after *that* + **be**, as indeed do *why* and *how*: *That's who I meant/why he left* (see 14.6.2).

"The proposal to the effect that he was making progress was preposterous". Similarly *I told them what she suggested I tell them* may be construed with a fused relative or an interrogative content clause as the second complement of *told*. In the former case we have "She suggested I tell them x; I told them x", in the latter "I told them the answer to the question, 'What did she suggest I tell them?' "; thus suppose she suggested I tell them I was ill: then in the relative interpretation I told them I was ill, while in the interrogative content clause interpretation I told them that she suggested I tell them that I was ill.

12.5   **Comparative constructions**

There is too great a range of comparative constructions for us to be able to hope to cover them all in this section. One initial limitation is that we will deal only with those involving what we are calling comparative clauses. This will include examples like (46) but exclude those like (47):

(46)   *The conference was more successful this year than it was last year*
(47)   i *Sue and Kim are equally reliable*
          ii *[Her first novel was very good] but the second was even better*
         iii *Any paper longer than twenty pages she automatically rejected*
          iv *She had just enough strength to press the emergency button*

I shall distinguish between 'comparative construction' and 'comparative clause' in such a way that in an example like (46) the superordinate clause – which is here coextensive with the sentence as a whole – is a comparative construction, while the subordinate clause is a comparative clause. For the purposes of the present discussion I will take *than* to be a preposition rather than a conjunction (see §3 above), so that the comparative clause here will be *it was last year*, not *than it was last year*, but nothing of significance will hinge on this decision. Semantically (46) involves a comparison between two terms: a 'primary' term, the degree to which the conference was successful this year, and a 'secondary' term or 'standard', the degree to which the conference was successful last year: the comparative clause expresses the standard. In (47i) the two terms under comparison – the degree to which Sue is reliable and the degree to which Kim is reliable – are of equal status instead of being distinguished as primary vs secondary, so that there is here no standard. In the unbracketed clause of (47ii) the standard – the degree to which the first novel was good – is not overtly expressed (being recoverable from the bracketed context). In (47iii) there is an explicit standard, but it is expressed by an NP – *twenty pages* – not by a comparative clause. And finally in (47iv) there is again an explicit standard but although it is expressed by a clause – *to press the emergency button* (the comparison is between the amount of strength she had and the amount she needed to press the emergency button) – it doesn't belong to the special class we are calling comparative: it is a subjectless *to*-infinitival clause which need not be syntactically distinguished in terms of its internal structure from that which figures in the non-comparative construction *She was eager to press the emergency button.*

Comparative constructions may be cross-classified along two major dimensions: one contrasts 'comparisons of equality' and 'comparisons of inequality' (I use the traditional terms, though they are not wholly satisfactory), while the other contrasts 'scalar comparisons' and 'non-scalar comparisons'. Insofar as the standard is expressed by a comparative clause, comparisons of equality have *as* as the preposition, while comparisons of inequality have *than*. Thus (46) is a comparison of inequality (the degree to which the conference was successful this year does not equal that to which it was successful last year), while the corresponding comparison of equality is *The conference was as successful this year as it was last year.* Elsewhere we often find *to* rather than *as* in comparisons of equality, *from* rather than *than* in comparisons of inequality: *This one is similar to that one, This one is different from that one.* As we shall see shortly, the comparison of equality is the syntactically and semantically unmarked term in this system – and indeed one rather minor reflection of this may be mentioned immediately as it relates to the example just given: many speakers use *to* instead of *from* with *different* (a usage condemned by some, though certainly not all, prescriptive grammarians), whereas we do not find any analogous extension of *from* into comparisons of equality.

The contrast between scalar and non-scalar comparison is illustrated in

(48)   i *He is as absent-minded as I am*   Scalar
        ii *He went to the same school as I did*   Non-scalar

With a scalar comparison we are concerned with degree or quantity: we have a scale which allows in principle for three different relations between the terms, as in

(49)   i *He is more absent-minded than I am*
        ii *He is as absent-minded as I am*   (= 48i)
        iii *He is less absent-minded than I am*

(49ii) is the comparison of equality but there are two possibilities for the comparison of inequality: in (i) the primary term is located at a higher position on the scale than the standard ('comparison of superiority'), in (iii) it is located at a lower position ('comparison of inferiority'). With a non-scalar comparison we are concerned with quality or identity and do not have the superior/inferior distinction within the comparison of inequality. Thus instead of the three-way contrast illustrated in (49) we have only a two-way contrast, as in

(50)   i *He went to the same school as I did*   (= 48ii)
         ii *He went to a different school than I did*

(or *He went to a different school from the one I went to*, for speakers who do not have *different* entering into construction with *than*).

I mentioned above that the terms 'comparison of equality' and 'comparison of inequality' are not wholly satisfactory. One reason is that they are more naturally applicable to scalar than to non-scalar comparison – 'likeness' is perhaps a more general concept than 'equality'. A second, more important, point is that in scalar comparisons the *as* construction indicates not equality but non-inferiority. Thus in (49), for example, (ii) is semantically inconsistent with (iii) but not with (i): it would be contradictory to add *indeed he's less so* to (ii), but it would not be contradictory to add *indeed he's more so*. It was for this reason that I said the so-called comparison of equality is the semantically unmarked member of the pair: it excludes one kind, but not both kinds, of scalar inequality.

In scalar comparisons of equality; the preposition *as* is paired with the degree adverb *as* (except that in negatives *so* is found as a somewhat more formal variant of the latter: *He is not as/so absent-minded as I am*). The degree adverb *as* functions as modifier in a range of constructions, as illustrated in (51):

(51)   i *She gave as clear an indication of her intentions as you could hope for*
         ii *The singing wasn't as good as it usually is*
         iii *I'll do it as quickly as I can*
         iv *She behaved with as much tact as she always does*
         v *You can take as much as you like*
         vi *She enjoyed it as much as we did*

In (i) the (first) *as* modifies an adjective used attributively: *as clear* modifies *indication* (this being one of the few constructions where a modifier precedes the determiner in NP structure). In (ii) *as* modifies an adjective used predicatively (and we could also have included an example where it is used postpositively, as in *Anyone as careful as you are will have no difficulty at all*, but as far as our subsequent discussion is concerned the distinction between the postpositive and predicative constructions is not significant). In (iii) *as* modifies an adverb. In the remaining examples *as* modifies *much*, which is a determinative in (iv), a pronoun in (v) and an adverb in (vi). Examples (i–iii) illustrate very general patterns in that there are a great many adjectives and adverbs that can occur in them, whereas (iv–vi) are highly restricted: (iv) and (v) allow only *much, many, little* and *few*, while (vi) allows only *much* and *little*. Strictly speaking (vi) is a special case of (iii), since *much* is here an adverb, like *quickly*: what makes it worth mentioning separately as a special case is that the contrast between comparisons of equality and comparisons of inequality is realised somewhat differently with *much, many, little* and *few* than elsewhere.

In scalar comparisons of inequality, the preposition *than* is paired with an inflectional comparative or with *more* (see 8.1) in the case of superiority and with *less* in the case of inferiority:

(52)   i   *He's older than I am*
         ii   *It was more elaborate than I had expected*
        iii   *It was less elaborate than I had expected*

All three of these involve the predicative use of a compared adjective and thus correspond to (51ii): similar trios can easily be constructed for an attributive adjective like that of (51i) or an adverb like that of (51iii). Notice that the 'orientation' of the scale, i.e. which end counts as 'high' and which as 'low', is determined by the semantic properties of the adjective or adverb – and one kind of oppositeness of meaning, known more specifically as 'antonymy', involves an oppositeness in the orientation of what is otherwise the same scale. Thus **old** and **young** are antonyms by virtue of the fact that *X is older than Y* entails and is entailed by *Y is younger than X*. It follows that although *He is less old than I am* entails *He is younger than I am*, the former is a comparison of inferiority, the latter a comparison of superiority. In a loose but intuitively fairly obvious sense of the terms 'positive' and 'negative' we might say that **old** has positive orientation, **young** negative orientation: *He is younger than I am* would thus be a comparison of superiority with negative orientation.

Consider now comparisons of inequality corresponding to comparisons of equality involving *much, little, many, few*. Here *than* is paired with *more, less* or *fewer*:

(53)   i   *She experienced more difficulty than he did*
         ii   *She experienced less difficulty than he did*
(54)   i   *She made more mistakes than he did*
         ii   *She made less mistakes than he did*
       iii   *She made fewer mistakes than he did*

With a singular NP, as in (53), the only possibilities are *more* and *less*, with a plural, as in (54), we have *more* and variation between *less* and *fewer*: some speakers have just *less*, others have both with *fewer* more formal, others only *fewer* (in accordance with a common prescriptive rule). In both sets we have the determinative construction comparable with (51iv): but again we can easily devise similar sets corresponding to (51v) and (with *more* and *less* but not *fewer*) to (51vi). How such constructions should be analysed is by no means clear. It is complicated by the fact that *much* and *little* on the one hand, *many* and *few* on the other, are antonyms. This means that we must consider whether (53ii) is the comparison of inferiority (with positive orientation) corresponding to (55i) or the comparison of superiority (with negative orientation) corresponding to (55ii):

(55)   i *She experienced as much difficulty as he did*
        ii *She experienced as little difficulty as he did*

Fewer is transparently the comparative form of *few*, with (54iii) clearly a comparison of superiority with negative orientation: in the variety of English which excludes (54ii) the relation of *less* to *little* matches that of *fewer* to *few* so that *less* might be regarded as an irregular (suppletive) comparative form of **little**, making (53ii) also a comparison of superiority with negative orientation. By further extension *more* could be taken as the comparative form of both **much** and **many** (compare *better*, which we have analysed as the comparative of both **good** and **well**). Since *less* does not function as modifier to *much, little, many* or *few* (cf. **She experienced less much difficulty than he did*, etc.) we would have no comparisons of inferiority in this area – only comparisons of superiority with positive or negative orientation. And if we pushed such an analysis to its extreme we would have *more* and *less* as the comparative forms of **much** and **little** respectively even in (52), which would effectively get rid of the category of comparison of inferiority altogether. But surely it would be a mistake to push it to that extreme. *Much* and *little* cannot in general modify adjectives (see 9.2.1): we must exclude **much/little elaborate* and the like. It would therefore be a pointless complication to analyse *more/less elaborate* by relating them to such non-existent constructions instead of to *elaborate* on its own – *more elaborate* is to *elaborate* as *older* is to *old*. This argues for recognising *more* and *less* as uninflected words, morphologically unrelated to *much* and *little*; and if that is how we analyse them in (52) there is little reason for handling them differently in (53)–(54). On this view *much, more, little* and *less* will all be uninflected determinatives. There will not then be any reason to regard (53ii) as a comparison of superiority. Instead we will take (53i) and (ii) as respectively comparisons of superiority and inferiority corresponding to the comparison of equality given in (55i) – and (51ii) will not have any corresponding comparisons of inequality. But this is another area where it would be foolish to be dogmatic: we cannot avoid some measure of indeterminacy, and the variation in the status of (54ii) is one reflection of this.

Let us turn now to non-scalar comparisons. In comparisons of equality, the preposition *as* is paired with *same* or *such*, or else occurs without any correlative item at all:

(56)   i *I made the same mistake this morning as I did last week*
        ii *He was keen not to forfeit such privileges as he still retained*
        iii *He won easily, as might have been expected*
(57)   i *My attitude remains the same as it has always been*
        ii *His behaviour was hardly such as we would have expected*
        iii *Everything is now as it was before*

In (56) the terms in the comparison in (i) are the mistake I made this morning and the mistake I made last week; in (ii) the privileges he was keen not to forfeit and the privileges he still retained; and in (iii) what happened (his winning easily) and what might have been expected to happen (likewise his winning easily). Analogously for (57). *Same* and *such* function attributively, as in (56), or predicatively, as in (57); I have taken the function of *such* in (56) to be determiner, though it doesn't occupy the central position II (see 6.4); *same* lies at the rather fuzzy boundary between determiners and modifiers. The immediate constituents of (56ii) would seem to be *he won easily* and *as we had all expected he would*, so that the sentence exhibits the kind of clause subordination shown in (4ii) above (adjusted to allow for the reanalysis of conjunctions as prepositions if necessary), whereas in (57iii) *as it was before* functions as predicative complement.

Non-scalar comparisons of inequality are grammatically more restricted, which is why I am regarding comparison of equality as the syntactically unmarked member of the pair. There is no analogue of (56iii)/(57iii): *than* does not occur without some correlative item. For some but not all speakers it occurs paired with *different*, as in (50ii) above; all have it paired with *other* but certainly when *other* is functioning attributively rather than predicatively *than* cannot then take a clause as its complement. Thus we do not have, for example, **He was keen to acquire other privileges than he already had*: instead of the comparative clause *he already had* we would normally find the NP *those he already had* (where *he already had* is a relative clause).

It remains now to look briefly at the structure of the comparative clause. We may begin with an elementary example like

(58)   *He's as old as I am*

The comparative clause *I am* is of course non-kernel and again it is helpful to approach the description of such clauses by considering how they differ structurally from kernel clauses – or, more generally, from non-elliptical main clauses, for we are not here concerned with departures from kernel patterns due to thematic marking or the like. It might at first appear as though the most appropriate such clause to which we should relate *I am* is simply *I am old*. There are, however, grounds for preferring one where *old* is modified by some adverb of degree, such as *that*. Evidence for this comes from examples like

(59)   i   *It was exactly twice as long as it was broad*
        ii **It was exactly twice as long as it was somewhat broad*

We cannot add a degree modifier like *somewhat* to the subordinate clause *it was broad* in (59i), just as we cannot add one to the main clause *It was that broad* – cf. **It was somewhat that broad*. In the latter case this is because the relevant structural position is already explicitly filled, whereas in the comparative clause case, we are suggesting, it is because it is implicitly filled.

Thus even in a case like (59) where, unlike (58), the adjective is retained (because it is distinct from the corresponding adjective in the superordinate clause) the subordinate clause is best regarded as in some way incomplete relative to the structure of main clauses. Similarly in [*He wrote as many comedies as*] *he wrote tragedies* the NP *tragedies* in the subordinate clause is implicitly quantified, so that we cannot add an explicit determiner such as *ten*: a comparable main clause is *He wrote that many tragedies* rather than simply *He wrote tragedies*.

The postulation of an implicit degree modifier in (58) also makes sense from a semantic point of view. For notice that (58) does not entail that I am old: it could be as appropriately uttered by a schoolchild as by an octogenarian. *I am old* implies that I am located in the upper region of the scale of oldness, whereas *I am x old*, where *x* is some degree modifier, does not: my location on the scale is specified by the particular value of *x* (so that *I am 5 years old*, for example, doesn't imply that I am old). This is not to suggest that the comparative clause *I am* should be derived transformationally from the main clause *I am that old*: there is no question of the understood degree modification having the particular properties of *that*. We can give a rough semantic analysis of (58) along the lines of:

(60)   "He is x old; I am y old; x = y"

The values of the variables x and y are not specified independently, but simply compared: we are given comparative values not absolute values. The comparative clause expresses the "I am y old" component of (60), which is not a proposition; thus we again have a subordinate clause that does not itself express a proposition and hence its meaning cannot be the same as that of any main clause. For this reason we will again resort to an abstract $\emptyset$ element – $\emptyset^{comparative}$ – and derive the *I am* of (58) from †*I am $\emptyset$ old*. Similarly we will derive the *I did* of *He went to the same school as I did*, (50i), from †*I went to $\emptyset$ school*; the *he did* of *She made more mistakes than he did*, (54i), from †*he made $\emptyset$ mistakes*; and so on.

This enables us to break down the task of accounting for the structural differences between comparative clauses and main clauses into two parts:

(a) At the level of our hypothetical underlying structures, comparative clauses are characterised by the selection of the $\emptyset^{comparative}$ element. It functions as: (i) degree modifier to an adjective; (ii) degree modifier to an adverb; (iii) degree modifier to *much, many, few* in any of their functions; (iv) determiner in NP structure; (v) predicative complement. These are exemplified respectively in

(61)   i [*He's as old as*] †*I am $\emptyset$ old*   (=58)
          ii [*I'll do it as quickly as*] †*I can do it $\emptyset$ quickly*   (=51iii)
         iii [*She enjoyed it as much as*] †*we enjoyed it $\emptyset$ much*   (=51vi)

    iv [*He went to the same school as*] †*I went to* Ø *school*   (=50i)
    v [*My attitude remains the same as*] †*it has always been* Ø   (=57i)

At this level comparative clauses are like declarative (normally positive) main clauses containing some actual form with the same function as the abstract $Ø^{comparative}$ element.[5]

(b) The actual comparative clause is then derived from the hypothetical underlying clause by various syntactic obligatory or optional processes, which include: (i) dropping the abstract $Ø^{comparative}$ element (obligatory); (ii) deleting recoverable material (in part obligatory, in part optional); (iii) substituting the anaphor **do** for the verb (optional);[6] (iv) replacing a nominative pronoun by the corresponding accusative (optional). Thus (61iv) may be reduced to any of *I went to, I did, I* and *me*. Process (iv) is generally condemned in prescriptive grammars but again there is no question of *me* being non-standard – both *I* and *me* are used by speakers of the standard dialect, with the nominative being more characteristic of formal style, the accusative of informal style. In what follows we will confine our attention to process (ii), the deletion of recoverable material; there are two main points to make.

The first point is that we need to speak of the deletion of 'recoverable' material rather than of 'repeated' material. Notice for example that in (61i) the *old* is repeated whereas the *am* is not: *am* is nevertheless recoverable in that the **be** and present tense components are repeated while the 1st person singular component is predictable from the subject *I*. Or to take a more elaborate example, consider

(62)   *He made more mistakes than usual*

where the comparative clause *usual* can be reconstructed as *it was usual for him to make* Ø *mistakes* ($Ø^{comparative}$ can occur within a clause embedded within the comparative clause, just as interrogative or relative elements can occur in clauses embedded within the interrogative or relative clause). The repeated material here is *mistakes*, **make**, **he** and the past tense component of *was*, while the rest is predictable from the properties of *usual*. *Usual* is an adjective and in the absence of any explicit or implicit noun head it will be taken as functioning predicatively; its lexical properties specify that it can take an infinitival clause as subject (which predicts the *for*, the accusative inflection on *him*, the *to* and the base form inflection on

---

[5] A further difference is that comparative clauses may contain items like *ever* that are restricted to 'non-affirmative contexts' (see 13.2): [*She worked harder than*] †*she had ever worked* Ø *hard before* (underlying [. . . *than*] *she had ever worked before*) but not **She had ever worked that hard before.*

[6] If the **do** of *He went to the same school as I did*, and the like, is an operator rather than an anaphor (see 4.4) there will be no substitution, only deletion.

make); the copulative construction requires a copulative verb and in the absence of any overt one we can supply the neutral *be*; and the *it* derives from the extraposition rule. In fact, it is not quite as simple as this. On semantic grounds there is no justification for reconstructing *was* rather than *is*: (62) is non-specific as to whether the comparison is with what was usual or with what is usual. Or take the case of the pronoun *him*. Suppose the *he* of (62) were replaced by *nobody*: clearly we shall not reconstruct as *it was usual for nobody to make Ø mistakes*, for this is another case where we need our concept of variable – "No person x made more mistakes than it was usual for x to make Ø mistakes." This problem cannot be overcome by using personal pronouns in our reconstructions rather than repeated NPs (e.g. *Nobody made more mistakes than it was usual for them to make*) because – as we saw in 7.2 – personal pronouns may encode information not expressed in the antecedent (so that *The boss made more mistakes than it was usual for her to make* specifies the sex while *The boss made more mistakes than usual* does not). It might also be argued that there is no valid reason for preferring the extrapositioned †*it was usual for him to make Ø mistakes* over the non-extrapositioned †*for him to make Ø mistakes was usual*. What emerges from these considerations is that the reconstruction is in the first instance a semantic matter. We observed above that the comparative clause itself does not express a proposition, so that there is no reason to expect its meaning to be expressible by any actual main clause: we made this point in connection with the $Ø^{comparative}$ element, but it has relevance to other features of the clause. What we find, therefore, is that our syntactic reconstruction cannot be complete. This doesn't mean that it is not worth carrying out: it merely provides further reason to allow a certain amount of abstractness in the syntactic structures from which we derive our non-kernel clauses.

The second matter we must look into concerning the deletion process involves the distinction between obligatory and optional deletion. This distinction is illustrated in (63):

(63)   i   *He had been more careful than you had been careful*
       ii   *He had been more careful than you had been*
      iii   *He had been more careful than you had*
       iv   *He had been more careful than you*

These examples show that the deletion of *careful* from †*you had been Ø careful* is obligatory, whereas progressively further reduction is optional. I will refer to the part of our underlying hypothetical clause where the deletion of recoverable material is obligatory as the 'C phrase'. This is a phrase containing $Ø^{comparative}$ whose more specific characterisation depends on the function of the latter: as a first approximation the C phrase can be found by moving as far up the constituent structure hierarchy from $Ø$ as one can before encountering a phrase headed (immediately or ultimately) by a verb or a preposition. Compare (63ii) with

(64)   *Kim had a bigger piece of cake than Ed had*
(65)   *He went to the same school as I went to*   (cf. 50i)
(66)   *He made an even more outrageously obscene suggestion than you had made*
(67)   *My attitude remains the same as it has always been*   (= 57i)

The underlying hypothetical clauses for (63) and (64) are respectively †*you had been ∅ careful* and †*Ed had a ∅ big piece of cake*, for which constituent structure representations (simplified by the omission of functional labels) are given in (68) and (69), with the C phrases boxed:

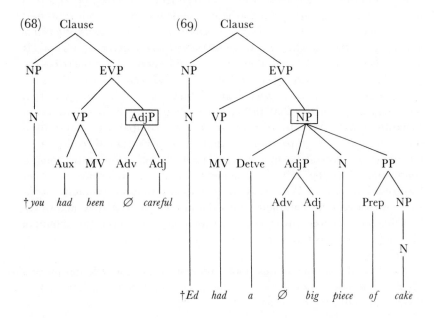

In (68) the AdjP headed by *careful* is an immediate constituent of the EVP, whose ultimate head is a verb, so that the AdjP is the C phrase; in (69) by contrast, the AdjP headed by *big* is an immediate constituent of an NP and hence is not itself the C phrase – witness the ungrammaticality of **Kim had a bigger piece of cake than Ed had a piece of cake*. In (65) the C phrase is the NP ∅ *school*: we stop at this point in the hierarchy because the next higher phrase is a PP – note that the *to* is not deleted. In (66) the C phrase is *a ∅ outrageously obscene suggestion*: we move from the AdvP ∅ *outrageously* to the AdjP headed by *obscene* to the NP headed by *suggestion* but stop here because the next phrase is an EVP. As for (67) the underlying hypothetical clause is

†*it has always been* Ø, where the C phrase is simply the Ø: again the next higher constituent is an EVP.

We can generalise the concept of C phrase so that it applies to the superordinate clause as well as to the subordinate (comparative) one. The C phrase of the superordinate clause will contain *more* (or the comparative inflection), *less, same, different*, etc. (i.e. the element with which *as* or *than* is correlated) – and it will stand in the same hierarchical relation to these elements as the subordinate C phrase does to Ø^{comparative}. We can then state the following condition on the comparative construction: the superordinate and subordinate clauses must be 'parallel' in structure up to the level of the C phrase. What is meant by this can be seen by considering a set of examples like

(70)   i   *This is a bigger car than that* (*is*)
          ii *This is a bigger car than the garage will take*
          iii **This is a bigger car than the garage* (*is*)
          iv *This car is bigger than the garage* (*is*)

In (i) the underlying hypothetical clause is †*that is a* Ø *big car*, which is parallel to the superordinate clause right up to the level of the clause. In (ii) it is †*the garage will take a* Ø *big car*, where the parallelism extends to the C phrase (*a* Ø *big car* is parallel to *a bigger car* if we accept the comparative inflection as the equivalent of a degree modifier) but not beyond (*a* Ø *big car* is object while *a bigger car* is predicative complement). (iii) is then ungrammatical under the interpretation where *the garage is* derives from †*the garage is* Ø *big*, for the C phrase here is an AdjP while that in the superordinate clause is the NP *a bigger car* – contrast (iv), where *the garage is* Ø *big* is permitted because in this case the superordinate C phrase is the AdjP *bigger*. (Of course (iii) is not ungrammatical if we take the underlying clause to be †*the garage is a* Ø *big car*, but in this case it is semantically anomalous.) The requirement of parallelism doesn't mean that the C phrases have to be identical (save of course for the contrast between Ø and *more, less*, etc.); in the great majority of cases they are, but we must also allow for examples like *It was as long as it was broad* or *He wrote as many comedies as he wrote tragedies*, where the two C phrases have contrasting heads.

It is where the parallelism extends beyond the C phrase that further omission of anaphorically recoverable material is optional. And such omission may result in ambiguity, as in

(71)   *Ed likes Sue more than Jill*

interpretable as "Ed likes Sue more than Jill does" or "Ed likes Sue more than he, Ed, likes Jill". In the first interpretation Jill is subject of the comparative clause, whose source will be approximately †*Jill likes her* Ø *much* and in the second *Jill* is object and the source approximately †*he likes*

Jill Ø much. (I say 'approximately' for the reason given above: we cannot syntactically reconstruct the missing object or subject as a personal pronoun. Strictly speaking the underlying clauses will be †*Jill likes Ø Ø much* with the first Ø an abstract anaphor with *Sue* as antecedent and †*Ø likes Jill Ø much* with the first Ø anaphoric to *Ed*, so that it is not a matter of optional deletion but of optional syntactic specification.) But constructions where the comparative clause is reduced to a single NP – whether it results in ambiguity, as here, or not, as *Ed can run faster than Pat* – are to be distinguished from those where *than/as* has simply an NP complement, as in *The death toll is expected to be as high as a thousand* or our earlier (47iii). Here *a thousand* is not the remnant of a clause but an NP expressing an explicit standard of comparison.

The discussion of comparative clause structure so far has been limited to constructions where *than* or *as* is paired with some correlative item – *more, as, same,* etc. – in the superordinate clause; how far can the account sketched above be extended to cover the non-correlative *as* construction of examples like (72)?

(72)   i *Everything is now as it should be*
        ii *Everything is spotlessly clean, as of course it should be*

Where *as* + comparative clause functions as predicative complement in the superordinate clause, as in (i), our analysis applies quite straightforwardly: we reconstruct *it should be* as †*it should be Ø* (with Ø in PC function) and take *as* as the superordinate C phrase – the meaning is roughly "Everything is now x; it should be y; x = y". But (ii) is different: the reconstruction of the comparative clause here is surely just †*of course it should be spotlessly clean.* What is special about this kind of non-correlative *as* construction is that we do not have to resort to our abstract $Ø^{\text{comparative}}$ element in reconstructing the comparative clause, and this is no doubt related to the fact that there is no grammatical item (a grammatical word like *such* or *more*, or an inflection) corresponding to the variable "x" in our semantic analyses. Thus for (72ii) we have "Everything is x; of course it should be y; x = y", where "x" is expressed by the lexical material *spotlessly clean.* Similarly in (56iii) above (*He won easily, as might have been expected*) the comparative clause can be reconstructed along the lines of †*that he would win easily might have been expected.* Where, as in this example, the missing material can be reconstructed as a clause (*that he would win easily*) a further special property of this kind of *as* construction is that we very often find the marked order of anaphor followed by antecedent: *As might have been expected, he won easily.*

There is not space to pursue the analysis of the structure of comparative clauses beyond this initial sketch. There are, however, two final points about the comparative construction that are worth making before we close this section.

The first is that there are certain affinities between comparative and relative constructions reflected in the possibility of having a relative either in place of or in combination with a comparative. In two kinds of non-scalar comparison of equality a relative clause can often be used instead of *as* + comparative clause – one is where *as* is correlated with *same*, the other is the non-predicative non-correlative *as* construction we have just been considering:

(73)   i *He likes the same things as I like*
          ii *He likes the same things that I like*
(74)   i *They finally tendered their resignations, as we hoped they would*
          ii *They finally tendered their resignations, which we had hoped they would*

In (73ii) we have a restrictive relative, in (74ii) a non-restrictive. The equivalence will be apparent from the kind of analysis we have given of the two constructions. Thus in (73i) we have "He likes x things; I like y things; x = y", where the nature of the equality expressed by *same* is such that this is equivalent to "I like x (things); he likes x (things)", which we have in (73ii) – the *same* in (73ii) is arguably redundant, so that the construction might be regarded as a 'blend' between (73i) and *He likes the things that I like*. The combination of comparative and relative constructions is illustrated in (75ii), which may be contrasted with the purely comparative (i):

(75)   i *She has more patience than I have*
          ii *She has more patience than what I have*

These of course belong to different varieties of the language: most if not all of the dialects that include (ii) are non-standard. Grammatically the difference is that in (i) *than* takes a comparative clause as complement, whereas in (ii) it takes an NP, a fused relative construction; in (i) we have "She has x patience; I have y patience; x exceeds y"; in (ii) "She has more patience than x; I have x". In the dialects which have it the fused relative NP replaces the comparative clause in a wide range of the comparative constructions we have introduced.

The second point is that we need to distinguish the comparative construction from another kind of construction which superficially looks very similar. Compare, for example:

(76)   i *I'll stay as long as I can*
          ii *I'll buy it as long as you're sure it's what she wants*

In (i) *I can* is a comparative clause, derivable from †*I can stay Ø long*, but (ii) is not interpreted as "I'll buy it x long; you're sure y long it's what she wants; x = y": *as long as* here means "provided that" and there is no ellipsis in *you're sure it's what she wants*. How this second *as long as* should be analysed raises again the issue of 'complex' units – it is commonly analysed as a 'complex subordinating conjunction'; I shall not pursue the question further here (see 10.5), but however we analyse *as long as* it is clear that *you're sure it's what she wants* is not a comparative clause: it is simply a content clause, not different in its own structure from a main clause. Similarly *as far as* is followed by a comparative clause in *He walked as far as we did* but not in *As far as I know, it's impossible* or *It's out of the question as far as I'm concerned*. *Insofar as* and *inasmuch as* take only content clauses as complement – and the grammaticalisation of these sequences is reflected in the inclusion of the first three components within a single graphological word. *As well as* takes a comparative clause complement in *She sang as well as he did*, but not in *As well as being a brilliant pianist she was very accomplished on the violin* (where it takes an *-ing* class non-finite clause), *We're spending some time in Paris as well as in London* (PP complement), *I saw Tom as well as Bill* (NP complement); these last two constructions fall in the borderline area between subordination and coordination. Less clearly distinct from a genuine comparative is that involving *as if*: *He ran as if his life depended on it*. This falls somewhere between (76i) and (ii): a comparative construal (cf. *He ran as he would run if his life depended on it*) is more plausible than for (76ii) but less clearly needed than for (76i) – note that we could substitute *though* for *if* in *as if his life depended on it* and the like, but not in *as he would run if his life depended on it*.

FURTHER READING

On coordination, see Dik 1968, Wierzbicka 1980: Ch. 7, Schachter 1977, Peterson 1981, Matthews 1981: Ch. 9, Quirk et al. 1971: Ch. 9. On the division between coordination and subordination, see Quirk et al. 1971: §§11.1–3, 8–12. On correlative constructions and non-embedded subordinate clauses, see Matthews 1981: 236–9. On relative clauses, see Thompson 1971, Bresnan & Grimshaw 1978, Bache & Jakobsen 1980, McCawley 1981, Comrie 1981: Ch. 7. 'Fused relative construction' is not a standard term – Quirk et al. 1971: §11.20 use 'nominal relative clause', while the most usual term in the transformational literature is probably 'free relative'; Sweet 1891–98: §112 talks of the *what* of *What you say is true* as a 'condensed relative pronoun' (but cf. Jespersen 1924: 104n.1). On the comparative construction, see Jespersen 1924: Ch. 18, Quirk et al. 1971: §§11.53–64, Bresnan 1973, 1975, Kuno 1981.

13
Negation

13.1 Clausal and subclausal negation
Of the three examples in (1):

(1)   i *She wasn't happy*
          ii *She was unhappy*
         iii *She was happy*

the third is straightforwardly positive, while (i) and (ii) are each in some sense negative. We noted in 2.1, however, that from a syntactic point of view there is a significant difference between (i) and (ii) – namely, that (i) takes a coordinate tag with *nor* (or *neither*) while (ii) takes one with *so*: *She wasn't happy and nor was Ed* vs *She was unhappy and so was Ed*. We noted that the tag for (ii) is just the same as for (iii): *She was happy and so was Ed*, and we accordingly group (ii) syntactically with (iii), analysing them both as positive clauses. (i) is the negative counterpart of (iii) while (ii) is the positive counterpart of *She wasn't unhappy*. There is of course something negative about (ii), the prefix *un-*, but in the light of the above syntactic contrast with (i) we will say that the negation in (i) is 'clausal' while that in (ii) is 'subclausal': it does not affect the polarity of the clause as a whole.

There are other ways in which the contrast between positive and negative clauses is reflected, besides the use of *so* vs *nor*/*neither* in coordinate tags. Very similar is the contrast between *too* and *either* in coordinated or juxtaposed clauses without the operator + subject order of the above tags:

(2)   i *She wasn't happy; (and) Ed wasn't (happy) either*
          ii *She was unhappy; (and) Ed was (unhappy) too*

We also find a distinction in the interrogative tags that can be added:

(3)   i *She wasn't happy, was she?*
          ii *She was unhappy, wasn't she?*

Here, however, it is necessary to distinguish these neutral tags which seek confirmation of what is expressed in the declarative from the more emotive tags of *She wasn't happy, wasn't she?* (for those speakers who allow a negative tag here) and *She was unhappy, was she?*: see 11.6. The point is that although *was she?* can be tagged to (ii) as well as to (i) the meaning is quite different in the two cases. Once this distinction between the neutral and emotive tags is recognised, we can say that with the former the tag reverses the polarity of the clause to which it is juxtaposed, while with the latter it keeps it constant.

The tests for clause polarity apply directly only to declarative (and, marginally, exclamative) main clauses: the classification of other clauses will be derivative from that of comparable declarative main clauses. Thus *Wasn't she happy?* is a negative clause, being the non-*wh* interrogative counterpart of (11), while *Was she unhappy?* is a positive clause with subclausal negation.

The most straightforward negative clauses are those with a negative VP – whether it is inflectionally negative like (11) or analytically negative like *She was not happy* (see 4.3). These are the most straightforward because, as a reasonably close first approximation, we can say that they can all be put in correspondence with positive clauses differing only in the form of the VP and that all positive clauses have negative counterparts of this kind. Thus *It won't rain* and *It will not rain* are respectively the inflectional and analytic negative counterparts of *It will rain*, and so on. It will be recalled that a negative VP requires an operator: if the corresponding positive has no operator, the 'dummy' ***do*** is used – the negative of *I like it* is *I don't like it* (4.4).

Less often the negative element in clausal negation is located elsewhere than in the VP. The principal such negative elements are as follows:

(a) *nothing, nobody, no one*, as heads of NPs, *never* as head of an AdvP and *nowhere* as head of an AdvP or NP: *It solves nothing, does it?, He never finished it, did he?, He could find peace nowhere, and neither could his wife.*

(b) *no* as determiner in NP structure or modifier in the structure of comparative AdjPs or AdvPs: *He had no patience, had/did he?, It's no better than the last one, is it?.*

(c) *none* as head in NP structure or modifier in a comparative AdjP or AdvP (preceding *the*): *I've got none left and nor has Ed, You're none the worse for it, are you?.*

(d) *neither* as determiner or (perhaps: see 7.3) head in NP structure, and *neither* and *nor* as coordinating conjunctions or cohesive adverbs: *neither (proposal) was satisfactory, was it?, [Ed wasn't there –] and neither was Jill, was she?.*

(e) *not* as modifier to such determinatives as *much, many, enough, one*, or in construction with *even*: *Not many people came, did they?, Not even John could do it, could he?.*

(f) *few* and *little* as determiners or (again perhaps) head in NP structure: *Few of them were perfect, were they?, There's little chance of improvement, is there?.*

(g) The adverbs *seldom, rarely, scarcely, hardly* and *barely*: *It is hardly worth bothering about, is it?.*

With a negative clause marked by one of the stems in (a)–(g) it is commonly impossible to find a positive clause that we would want to regard as differing from it purely in terms of polarity, i.e. to find a positive counterpart. There is, for instance no strict positive counterpart to the last example given, *It is hardly worth bothering about.* The same holds for *Few of them were perfect* and arguably *Nobody knew him* and the like – the concept 'clause A is the negative of clause B' is by no means as straightforward as one might at first think, as we shall see. But certainly negatives do not differ from positives simply by the addition of some negative marker: in the terms of 1.4 they often differ with respect to 'selection' and the phenomenon does not in general lend itself to an analysis where negatives are simply trans-formationally derived from positives.

Let us turn now briefly to subclausal negation. The most straightforward cases here are those lexemes derived in lexical morphology by adding one of a variety of negative prefixes – *un-, in-* (and the variants found in *illicit, impossible,* etc.), *non-, a-* (as in *amoral*), *dis-.* Thus *The bottle is non-returnable, She disinherited him,* and so on, are clearly positive clauses, like (iii). More interesting are those involving one or other of the items in (a)–(g) above, for in general the latter do not occur exclusively as markers of clausal negation. For example, *She had a not inconsiderable talent, They were talking in a barely audible whisper, He solved it in no time* are all clearly positive clauses, witness the confirmatory tags *didn't she?, weren't they?* and *didn't he?.*

It is a difficult matter to specify precisely the conditions under which these items yield subclausal negation, and the following remarks merely deal in a fragmentary way with a few cases.

(a) The clearest case is where the negative occurs with modifying function within an AdjP used attributively, normally with a preceding determiner. This is what we have in the first two of these last examples – *a not inconsider-able talent, a barely audible whisper*; compare also *They were arguing violently about a not really very important matter (weren't they?).*

(b) We may also regard as subclausal negation examples like *I hope not.* This might be used as a reply to, say, *Is Ed going?,* with *not* in paradigmatic contrast with *so: I hope so. So* and *not* are anaphors with clausal antecedents: *I hope not* is here interpreted as equivalent to *I hope Ed is not going.* The latter contains a negative clause inside a positive one; *I hope not* contains only one clause, a positive one (cf. *I hope not, and so, no doubt, do you*).

(c) In an example like *He prefers not to tell her* the *not* belongs in the non-finite construction: the complement of *prefers* is *not to tell her*. We have noted (3.3) that there are differing views on the question of whether the latter is to be regarded as a clause, but for present purposes it will be helpful to sidestep that issue by saying that the negation is subclausal as far as the **prefer** clause is concerned, for this clause is clearly positive. Now where a negative occurs within a non-finite construction, the negation is almost invariably subclausal. Thus *We told you to do nothing* will be interpreted positively as "We told you not to do anything", rather than negatively as "We didn't tell you to do anything". Some speakers, however, may allow both interpretations, and there are certainly some cases where a clausal negation interpretation is quite natural: *Unfortunately I was able to do nothing about it, and nor were my colleagues.*

(d) We have been distinguishing between the structure of, say, *He prefers to tell her*, where *to tell her* is complement (whether a clause or not) of the catenative main verb *prefers*, and that of *He will tell her*, where there is just one VP *will tell*, with *will* an auxiliary (see 4.4). And while *He prefers not to tell her* has subclausal negation, *He will not tell her* has clausal negation. However, we do find cases where auxiliaries are followed by subclausal negation of the kind we find with main verbs taking non-finite complements. Thus *We could do nothing* is ambiguous, having a subclausal negation interpretation ("One of the possibilities open to us would be to do nothing" – here the confirmatory tag would be *couldn't we?*) as well as the clausal negation one ("We wouldn't be able to do anything"). Subclausal negation of this kind after an auxiliary is most natural when the auxiliary is separated from the negative element by an adjunct, particularly *always, often* and the like. Thus *We could always do nothing* forces the first of the above interpretations. Similarly we have subclausal negation in *He will sometimes not speak to her for days on end, He has often not kept his promise in the past*, and so on.

(e) In 6.4 I contrasted negative *few* and *little* with positive *a few* and *a little*, and the latter do not of course result in either kind of negative, but even negative *few* and *little* yield clausal negation only under quite restrictive conditions. For example if we replace the *few* of our earlier example by *too few* or *fewer* – *Too few/fewer of them were perfect* – the *were they?* tag becomes inappropriate. And where the NP containing *few/little* is not subject (or the post-verbal NP of the *there* construction), the clause seems to be treated as positive: *He has few redeeming features and so/*neither has she, He's little better than a beast and so/*neither is she* (though just what the interrogative tags would be in such cases is uncertain – neither positive nor negative sounds wholly comfortable).

(f) So-called double negatives like *He doesn't know nothing about it* are of somewhat marginal status in Standard English: this example would only be used as a **denial** – i.e. a contradiction of a previous explicit or at least implicit negative assertion – in this case a denial of the proposition that he knows nothing about it. A less context-dependent example might be *No one has absolutely no redeeming features.* From the point of view of logic, the two negatives cancel each other out: they are logically equivalent to the positives *He knows something about it* and *Everyone has some redeeming feature(s)*. But from a syntactic point of view the negatives do not cancel each other: the clauses are negative, not positive. This is because the first negative is clausal, the second subclausal. And of course our earlier examples of subclausal negation can be combined with ordinary clausal negation, again most readily in the case of denials: *We couldn't do nothing, He hasn't often not kept his promise,* and so on.

Having surveyed in outline the range of negative elements, we can now, to conclude this section, introduce one final syntactic distinction between clausal and subclausal negation. It may be illustrated by reference to the following pair:

(4)   i *She had had complete faith in no man*   Clausal negation
        ii *She had solved the problem in no time*   Subclausal negation

If we apply the process of thematic fronting to the final PP we find that in (i) but not (ii) it requires the operator + subject order:

(5)   i *In no man had she had complete faith*
        ii *In no time she had solved the problem*

Note similarly the order in such clausal negatives as *Never had I seen such chaos, At no time had he intended to resign,* and so on. It should be borne in mind, however, that thematic fronting is accompanied by the operator + subject order in certain kinds of positive clauses too – those where the fronted phrase is introduced by *only,* the degree adverb *so,* etc. Thus *Only then did I realise my mistake, So persistent was he that we finally gave in,* and the like, are positive clauses.

13.2 **Affirmatives and non-affirmatives**

To a very large extent the systems of clause polarity and clause type are independent: in general we find the same positive/negative contrasts in different clause types, as illustrated in (6):

(6) | | | Positive | Negative |
|---|---|---|---|
| Declarative | | *He has read it* | *He hasn't read it* |
| Interrogative | *wh* | *Who has read it?* | *Who hasn't read it?* |
| | non-*wh* | *Has he read it?* | *Hasn't he read it?* |
| Exclamative | | *What a lot of people have read it!* | *What a lot of people haven't read it!* |
| Imperative | | *Read it* | *Don't read it* |

However, the qualifying phrases 'to a very large extent' and 'in general' are certainly needed, for the systems are by no means wholly independent. For example, exclamative *How tall she is!* and interrogative *How tall is she?* have no negative counterparts.

In this section we will consider just one aspect of the partial interdependence between the systems, for which (7) provides an initial example:

(7)		Positive	Negative
	Declarative	*He has ever been there*	*He hasn't ever been there*
	Interrogative	*Has he ever been there?*	*Hasn't he ever been there?*

What we find is that *ever*, in the sense "at any time", can occur in clauses that are negative or interrogative (or both), but it cannot occur (normally) in positive declaratives. Since the phenomenon involves quite a number of forms besides *ever*, it will be useful to have simple terms for the classes of contexts from which these forms are excluded or in which they are allowed: I shall call them **affirmative** and **non-affirmative** respectively. The central members of the affirmative class are (most) positive declarative main clauses, and it is for this reason that the term 'affirmative' seems an appropriate one: it is commonly used in contrast with 'negative' (cf. the expression *to answer in the affirmative*), while the verb ***affirm*** denotes a type of illocutionary act characteristically performed by uttering a declarative rather than an interrogative. The questions we need to consider – though again we cannot attempt full answers here – are: (i) What items occur only or characteristically in one or other of the two classes? and (ii) How is the class of affirmative contexts to be defined more carefully than our first approximation, namely positive declarative main clauses? We will take them in that order, continuing to work with our rough definition of affirmative contexts while discussing the first question.

Among the expressions which are strictly limited to non-affirmative contexts are *ever* ("at any time"), *at all*, ***can** help + ... ing*, ***bother** + to ...*, ***dare***$_{Mod}$ and ***need***$_{Mod}$ (i.e. the modal auxiliaries as opposed to the main verbs – see 4.8), *either* (as a cohesive adverb – though it is in fact more narrowly restricted, being almost limited to negative clauses) – compare *He liked it at all, *I can help laughing, *He dare/need go alone*, etc. There are others which characteristically occur in non-affirmatives, but which are found in affirmatives under certain conditions: *any* and its compounds *anyone, anything*, etc., *either* (as determinative or pronoun), *yet* (in its temporal sense).

Given the limited space available, let us confine our attention to *any* (and its compounds), beginning with the contrast in acceptability shown in (8):

(8)   i *As soon as she phoned this morning, I dashed out and bought any biscuits*
       ii *The shop was closed so I couldn't buy any biscuits*

Any confers what we have called a non-specific interpretation on the NP in which it is determiner or head – see 6.7. The non-affirmative context in (ii) creates an environment where we can have a non-specific NP, whereas (i) is anomalous because we are talking about a single act of buying that took place this morning, which means that there must be some specific biscuits that were bought.

Now while a non-affirmative context allows for a non-specific NP, an affirmative context does not always require a specific one, as it does in (8i). This will be apparent from the examples of 6.7, where we contrasted *Ed bought a house in Honour Avenue* (specific) and *Ed wants to buy a house in Honour Avenue* (non-specific – or ambiguous between non-specific and specific interpretations). Thus in affirmatives that do not involve such a requirement, *any* is possible, as in

(9)   i *Take any of them*
       ii *He'll buy any block meeting these requirements*
       iii *Anyone could do that*

Here we are in the realm of the future or the potential, rather than the actual, and hence it makes sense to have a non-specific NP. Notice that in such cases *any* may in effect be equivalent to *every* or *all. Everyone could do that* follows from (9iii), though (9i) is not equivalent to *Take all of them*; (9ii) could be interpreted either way – as saying that he'll buy every block meeting these requirements (every one, that is, within some pragmatically determined set, such as the set currently on the market) or that he'll buy one block meeting these requirements but doesn't mind which.

For convenience I will distinguish notationally between $any^{n/aff}$ and any^{neut}, with the former restricted to non-affirmative contexts, the latter being neutral as to which kind of context it can occur in (though affirmatives predominate). In non-affirmative contexts, therefore, there is a potential contrast between them, exemplified in, say:

(10)   *Can anyone do that?*

With $any^{n/aff}$ the meaning is "Is there anyone who can do that?"; with any^{neut} "Is it such that anyone can do it?" (i.e. "Can everyone do it?") – only in the latter case would *Yes, anyone can do it* be an appropriate answer. Similarly *I won't marry anyone* is ambiguous (in the verbal component): with $any^{n/aff}$ it means "I will remain unmarried" but with any^{neut} it says that I shall exercise some discrimination in the choice of marriage partner; inserting *just* before *anyone* would force this second interpretation. It is because of such contrasts that it is convenient to distinguish $any^{n/aff}$ and any^{neut}, but this is not to say that the appropriate way to handle them is in terms of different meanings for *any*. *Any*[neut] is always stressed; when it occurs in a non-affirmative context it is normally marked prosodically as contrastive.

(8i) can be corrected by replacing *any* by *some*, and it is worth looking briefly at the relationship between the *any*[n/aff] and the *some* series of forms. If it is false to say *He did something about it* then it is true to say *He didn't do anything about it*, and vice versa, and on the basis of this semantic relationship between such pairs it is tempting to think of *some* and *any*[n/aff] as alternative forms of a single syntactic element – affirmative and non-affirmative forms, let us say. And this view was quite widely adopted in the literature at one time. It cannot, however, be sustained, for there are undoubtedly places where they are in paradigmatic contrast:

(11) i *I didn't like some/any of her paintings*
      ii *Have you told somebody/anybody?*

Some, like most determinatives, is not inherently specific or non-specific: it can occur in NPs with either interpretation. For example in *I found someone who could repair it* the object NP is specific, while in *I'm looking for someone who can repair it* it would normally be taken as non-specific. After a negative, *some* tends to invite a specific interpretation, so that we have a very sharp contrast in (11i) between specific *some* ("there were some paintings I didn't like") and non-specific *any* ("there were no paintings that I liked"). However, a non-specific interpretation of *some* is not in general excluded after negatives: we could, for example, replace *any* by *some* in (8ii) without any change in specificity. The difference between *some* and *any* in (8ii) would be slight – *some* draws more attention to the intention that I had to buy some. With interrogatives the contrast in the non-specific interpretation can be sharper, as in (11ii): the use of *somebody* here suggests I think you may well have told somebody, or ought to have, whereas *anybody* is more neutral. Our conclusion must be, therefore, that *some* and *any*[n/aff] contrast in meaning and that the choice between them cannot be determined by any rule of syntax.

Never and *neither* are morphologically analysable as *n + ever* and *n + either* and semantically as "not + ever" and "not + either", as we see from the paraphrase relation between pairs like *Have you never been there?* and *Haven't you ever been there?* or *I liked neither of them* and *I didn't like either of them*. We find a somewhat similar relation between

(12) i *I saw no one*
      ii *I didn't see anyone*

But the relationship between *any* and *no* is not quite the same as that between *ever* and *never*, *either* and *neither*. In the first place, there is clearly no morphological connection (and note that the distinction between the determinative *no* and the pronoun *none* has no parallel in *any*). And secondly there are places where *no* is not naturally paraphrasable as *not/n't . . . any*: for example *He's no genius* would be more normally paraphrased as *He isn't a genius* than *He isn't any genius*. *No* is analysable semantically into a negative plus some other component, but the latter is not to be identified precisely with that expressed by *any*.

Let us turn now to the question of refining our initial characterisation of non-affirmative contexts. The first point to note is that they cannot be identified with clause-size units, as can be seen from the following:

(13) i   *He hasn't ever lied to anyone*
      ii **He has ever lied to no one*
(14) i   *No one lies to me with impunity*
      ii **Anyone doesn't lie to me with impunity*

(13ii) and (14ii) are negative clauses, yet the non-affirmative items *ever* and *anyone*[n/aff] are still out of order – because they precede the negative element: the non-affirmative context begins with the negative element.[1] Notice, nevertheless, that the negative elements which open a non-affirmative context are in general those that yield clausal rather than subclausal negation. Thus *in no time* or *a not inconsiderable number of people* and the like do not create non-affirmative contexts: **A not inconsiderable number of people had ever been there.*

For the rest it is a question of adding to the set of constructions that produce non-affirmative contexts: we will mention just a few.

(a) *Only*: *Only John had ever been there.* This entails that no one other than John had ever been there, and it is presumably this close semantic relationship with the negative that facilitates the creation of a non-affirmative context.

(b) Conditional clauses: *If he has ever been there, he may know her.* Notice the contrast between this and, say, an adverbial clause of reason: **Because he has ever been there, he may know her.* It is easy to see the semantic basis for this contrast: in saying *Because he has been there, he may know her* I commit myself to the truth of the proposition that he has been there, but in *If he has been there, he may know her* I clearly do not, and this makes the *if* clause like our other non-affirmatives.

(c) Comparative clauses: *He ran faster than/as fast as he had ever run before.* We might seek an explanation here in the fact that the comparative clause does not itself express a proposition, the standard of comparison being implicit rather than explicit (see 12.5): there is some affinity with an interrogative: the comparison is with how fast he had ever run before.

---

[1] It is questionable whether (14ii) is correctly classified as ungrammatical: it depends on whether restrictions on the distribution of *any*[neut] are also determined by a rule of grammar. The same point applies to (8ii).

(d) Infinitival constructions dependent on the degree adverb *too*: *He was too tired to do anything about it*. Here we find a closely related negative implication – that he didn't do anything about it.

(e) Content clauses or non-finite constructions functioning as complement to verbs and adjectives with a negative component inherent in their lexical meaning: **forget** ("come to a state of not knowing"), **deny** ("say that ... is not the case"), **reluctant** (roughly "not want"), **dissuade** *from* ("persuade not to") etc.: *He was reluctant to do anything about it*. Here too there are obvious negative implications deriving from the inherent negation: that he didn't want to do anything about it, and so on. The complements of other verbs/adjectives are non-affirmative if the verb/adjective itself is in a non-affirmative context – hence the possibility of saying *She doesn't know he has ever been there*.

13.3 The semantic scope of negation

In contrasting clausal and subclausal negation we were drawing a distinction concerning the syntactic domain of a negative; in turning now to the scope of negation the focus of attention is on its semantic domain – on the question of what it is that is being negated semantically. We will confine our attention to the scope of clausal negation.

Let us begin with two very simple examples:

(15)   *Ed hasn't read the book*
(16)   *Ed wasn't there, though he had said he would be*

What is negated in (15) is the proposition that Ed has read the book – we might analyse it as "not + {Ed has read the book}", with the braces enclosing a semantic unit. What is negated in (16) is the proposition that Ed was there – the proposition expressed in the *though* clause is not within the scope of the negative. Thus the analysis of (16) is "{not + {Ed was there}} + {though he said he would be (there)}" rather than "not + {Ed was there though he said he would be there}". This is evident from the fact that the contrast implied by the use of *though* is between Ed's saying he would be there and his not being there, rather than between his saying he would be there and his being there. Now although the *though* clause is subordinate, it is not embedded: (16) is a complex sentence consisting of a sequence of two clauses, rather than of one clause embedded inside another (see 12.1).

(15) and (16) are thus consistent with the elementary hypothesis that the scope of clausal negation is simply the clause or rather the semantic material encoded in the clause less the negative component itself. However, although this covers a large class of cases, so that it provides a useful starting point, there are many exceptions to it and it must accordingly be

refined. There are no cases where the scope extends beyond the clause into another clause that is not embedded within it: the refinements thus involve cases where some of the semantic material encoded in a negative clause is outside the scope of negation. We will here mention three kinds of case where this is so.

(a) Adjuncts. Many kinds of adjunct fall outside the scope of negation.[2] What we have called peripheral adjuncts (5.7) always do, and this could indeed be given as a further criterion for peripheral status. Thus in *He didn't finish it, however* the semantic bracketing is "however + {not + {he finished it}}": the *however* serves to link the negative proposition "he didn't finish it" to what precedes but does not correspond to part of the negative proposition: the example could not be used to say that "he finished it" doesn't stand in a "however" relation to what precedes. Adjuncts of reason or purpose characteristically fall outside the scope of the negation, but can be brought within its scope by prosodic means. Thus an example like

(17)   *He didn't do it because he was angry*

considered in abstraction from the intonation, is ambiguous. With the *because* clause outside the scope of negation, the (propositional) meaning is "Because he was angry, he didn't do it"; it might be said with a sequence of two intonation contours, one covering *He didn't do it*, the other the adjunct (this presents the fact that he didn't do it as a separate piece of information), or with a single unit, with a falling pitch on *angry* (with the whole content presented as a single piece of information). If spoken as a single intonation unit with a fall–rise on *angry*, the *because* clause is made contrastive and brought within the scope of negation, the meaning then being, essentially, "It is not the case that the reason why he did it was that he was angry"; in this reading I might coherently add *he did it because she'd asked him to*. Adjuncts like *intentionally, deliberately, accidentally* normally fall inside the scope of the negation if they follow the negative, but outside if they precede: compare *He didn't touch it intentionally* ("His touching it wasn't intentional") and *He intentionally didn't touch it* ("His not touching it was intentional"). Finally adjuncts of manner generally fall inside the scope: *She didn't sing well, He doesn't speak clearly*. Notice that where an adjunct falls outside the scope of negation, the sentence formed by omitting the adjunct is an entailment of the original: *He didn't finish, however* entails *He didn't finish*; (17) on the first reading entails *He didn't do it*; *He intentionally didn't touch it* entails *He didn't touch it*; and so on. But where the adjunct is inside, the sentence

---

[2] Strictly we should speak of the semantic material encoded in the adjunct as falling outside the scope of negation, but I will continue to use the simpler formulation where no difficulties arise: we will see in (c) below that the scope cannot always be identified in terms of syntactic constituents.

formed by dropping it is clearly not an entailment: (17) on the second reading doesn't entail *He didn't do it* and *He didn't touch it intentionally* doesn't entail *He didn't touch it*. On the contrary, they strongly imply respectively that he did do it and that he did touch it: I will return to this implication below.

(b) Modal auxiliaries. Certain of the modal auxiliaries normally fall outside the scope of negation in all or some of their senses, as noted in 4.8: most clearly **must** and **ought** (all senses) and **may** (in its epistemic sense). Thus *You mustn't do that* means "You are required not to do that" rather than "You aren't required to do that" (a meaning that can be expressed as *You needn't do that*, where **need** is inside the scope). Similarly *She may not have read it yet* means "It is possible that she hasn't read it yet" rather than "It is not possible that she has read it yet" (which again can be expressed as *She can't have read it yet*, with **can** inside the scope). By contrast, deontic **may** falls inside the scope, as in the permission interpretation of *You may not have any more*, "You are not permitted to have any more", as opposed to "You are permitted not to have any more".

(c) Quantification. More complex is the relation between negation and quantification. Consider first an example like

(18)   *They hadn't processed one of the applications*

This is ambiguous (again in abstraction from the prosodic properties), meaning either "There was one of the applications that they hadn't processed" or "There wasn't one of the applications that they had processed – they hadn't processed any". In the first, where *one of the applications* is specific, the quantification expressed in the *one* is outside the scope of negation, whereas in the second, with *one of the applications* non-specific, it is inside. The glosses with *there was* bring this out, and we can also see it by comparing (18) with the passive sentences

(19)   i *One of the applications hadn't been processed*
            ii *Not one of the applications had been processed*

The first meaning of (18) corresponds to (19i), where *one* precedes the negative element, the second meaning to (19ii), where it follows. If we replace *one* in (18) by *some*, the normal interpretation will have the quantification outside, corresponding to *Some of the applications hadn't been processed* – notice that we cannot substitute *some* for *one* in (19ii).[3] By contrast if we put *all* in place of *one* in (18), the quantification will normally be included in the scope of negation: "The set of applications they had processed was not equal to the total set of applications", i.e. "Not all of the

---

[3] This is not to say that *some* never falls within the scope of a negative: it does in examples like our earlier *The shop was closed so I couldn't buy some biscuits.*

applications had been processed." If we put *all* in (19i), both possibilities exist, in principle, but with the interpretations distinguished prosodically. With *all* outside the scope of negation ("The set of applications not processed was equal to the total set of applications"), the sentence is very much less natural than its logical equivalent *None of the applications had been processed*. To bring *all* inside the scope, we need to put contrastive stress on it, with fall on *all* and rise on *processed*, but this is also somewhat less natural than the equivalent *Not all of the applications had been processed*. The various examples discussed here show, therefore, that our description must take account of at least three factors: (i) the properties of particular quantifiers; (ii) the position of the quantifier relative to the negative element; and (iii) the intonation.

Quantification does not involve just NPs: it also covers various kinds of adverbs such as *very, always, often, sometimes, ever,* and so on. *Very* falls inside the scope of negation if, and only if, the element it modifies does – compare *He didn't behave very wisely* (inside) and *He very wisely didn't accept* (outside). *Ever* always falls inside the scope. *Always, often* and *sometimes* behave like *all, many* and *some* respectively, except that it is less usual for *sometimes* than for *some* to fall inside, and *always* falls inside only when it follows the negative element.

In discussing (non-quantificational) adjuncts in (a) above, we noted that where the element is outside the scope of negation, the sentence formed by omitting it is entailed by the one containing it. But this doesn't hold with quantification. Consider, for example, (18) on the interpretation where the quantification is outside the scope of negation. We cannot drop the quantified NP and say that (18) entails *They hadn't processed*: the latter is not a complete sentence, and certainly doesn't express a proposition that follows from (18). Scope is a matter of semantic structure, and what our consideration of quantification shows is that we cannot expect to be always able to pick out a syntactic constituent or sequence of forms corresponding to that part of the semantic structure which falls within the scope of the negation. Another type of example that serves to make the same point is *None of the applications had been processed*, where *none* expresses simultaneously a negative and a quantifier falling within its scope: they are not syntactically separable, so that we cannot identify the scope by means of any sequence of forms in the sentence. To bring out the scope of the negation in such cases we again need to make use of the concept of variable; thus very informally we could represent the two interpretations of (18) as

(20)   i "There is an x, x being one of the applications, such that {not + {they had processed x}}"

        ii "Not + {there is an x, x being one of the applications, such that {they had processed x}}"

In (i) the scope of the negation is "they had processed x", where x is a variable whose value is given in the material outside the scope of negation: the formula can be translated into stilted English as *There is one of the applications such that it is not the case that they had processed it* – a paraphrase of (18) in its first interpretation. In (ii) the scope of the "not" is everything that follows it, including therefore the quantification. We will not pursue this matter any further, and thus need not concern ourselves with the various notational conventions that permit more succinct and rigorous representations than I have given in (20): it is sufficient for our purposes to have made the point that the syntactic constituent structure does not provide a suitable basis for showing the scope of negation in clauses involving quantification.

13.4   The interpretation of negation

Let us turn now briefly to the meaning of clausal negation, beginning with cases like (21), which (we will assume) do not involve quantification – and where the negative has the maximum possible scope:

(21)   *John didn't open the door*

The corresponding positive, *John opened the door*, has a set of entailments which define the conditions under which it could be used to make a true statement. Thus if I am to make a true statement in uttering *John opened the door*, each of the following conditions must obtain:

(22)   i Someone opened something
         ii Someone opened the door
         iii John opened something
         iv John opened the door
         v At the time immediately prior to the time at issue, the door was closed
        etc.

The truth condition for the negative (21) is then simply that the set of conditions for the truth of the positive, namely (22) suitably completed, is not satisfied. And the set of conditions is not satisfied if any one or more of the individual conditions fails to obtain.

From a strictly semantic point of view a negative does not indicate just where the failure lies. (21), for example, doesn't say whether condition (ii) is satisfied: it could be that someone other than John opened the door or it could equally well be that no one opened the door. But pragmatic factors will often provide further specification, so that the utterance will convey more information than is actually encoded in the sentence used. For example, there will very often be a pragmatic implication that the failure does not lie with condition (v) – (v) will thus be an entailment of the positive and a potential pragmatic implication of the negative. (That (v) is not an entailment of (21) is evident from the logical consistency of my replying to your *How did John open the door?* with *John didn't open the door: incredible as it may seem, the guard had omitted to close it.*)

Where an adjunct falls within the scope of negation there will normally be a strong implication that the non-satisfaction of the truth conditions for the corresponding positive is associated specifically with the adjunct. For example *She didn't sing well* will normally imply that she did sing – for if she didn't sing at all the question of whether she sang well or badly can't arise. But, particularly in contexts where one is correcting a misapprehension, the implication can be cancelled, showing that it does not have the status of an entailment. Thus if you say *I suppose Sutherland sang well last night as usual* I could reply without contradicting myself: *Well, no, actually, she didn't sing well because she didn't sing at all: she had laryngitis and they had to bring in the understudy.*

Contrastive stress – which, as we have seen, may be used in bringing an adjunct within the scope of negation – is, more generally, a common source of such implications. Thus if I say (21) with contrastive stress on *John* you would normally take me to be implying that someone other than John opened the door: the most obvious reason for contrasting John with someone else with respect to opening the door is that while he didn't do it, they did. But that is not the only possible reason: it could also be that the contrast is a matter of my knowing whether John opened the door but not knowing whether anyone else did (cf. ⟨A⟩ *Did anyone open the door?* – ⟨B⟩ *Well, John didn't open the door; as for the others, I can't say*).

Let us turn now to the interpretation of a negative that has some quantification within its scope. Diagram (23) shows a selection of words expressing quantification ordered on a scale from low on the left to high on the right:

(23)

$$\begin{array}{l} \text{— } a \\ \text{— } some \longrightarrow \\ \text{'zero' } \text{— } any^{\text{n/aff}} \longrightarrow \qquad\qquad \ldots many \longrightarrow \qquad all \end{array}$$

$no, \longleftarrow\!\!\!\!\!\!\!\!\!\!\!\!\!\!—few \ldots$
$none$

Those below the line simultaneously express negation and quantification, those above just quantification. I put *zero* in scare quotes because sentences like *He received zero votes* are, to say the least, unusual and stylistically restricted: this level of quantification is not normally expressed positively.

Some and *any*$^{\text{n/aff}}$ cover a portion of the scale beginning minimally to the right of zero (i.e. they denote greater than zero quantification) and stretching rightwards. Where *some* occurs in an affirmative context, there will typically be an implication that the level of quantification is less than that expressed by *all*. Thus if you say *He has read some of the papers* I would normally infer that he hasn't read them all. But this is not an entailment. If he has read all the papers then he must have read some of them, so *He has read some of the papers* must be consistent with *He has read all of the papers* – which is why it is not contradictory to say *He has read some of the papers, indeed all of them, I think*. Note also that while we say *some or* (*indeed*) *all* we do not say *some or more*. The pragmatic implication stems from the fact that if you were in a position to say *He has read all of the papers* you would normally be expected to do so, and the most obvious reason for your not being in a position to do so would be that it wasn't true – where the 'normally' and 'most obvious reason' provide the loopholes that deprive the implication of the status of an entailment. Notice also that if you ask *He has read some of the papers, hasn't he?*, I would say *Yes*, not *No*, if he has read them all (*Yes, he has read them all*, rather than a simple *Yes*, no doubt, but the introductory word is still *yes*). The same goes for *any*$^{n/aff}$ in *Has he read any of the papers?*. Thus in effect the portion of the scale in (23) covered by *some* and *any*$^{n/aff}$ extends to the far right.[4] And this is why negating them yields quite straightforwardly the zero level of quantification, the only place on the scale not covered by them. In *He wouldn't buy some/any*, for example, the number or amount that he bought (or would buy) is zero.

Unlike *some* and *any*$^{n/aff}$, *a* covers not a portion of the scale, but just a point. Nevertheless its negation yields the zero level of quantification: *I haven't got a hat* means, as it were, "I have zero hats". The negation thus effectively means "less than", as it does with other expressions of numerical quantification – compare *I'm afraid I haven't got five dollars*, which implies that I have less.

As it stands this account is oversimplified. It is possible to indicate by prosodic means that *some* covers a portion of the scale falling short of the endpoint at the right – to make *some* contrast with *all* instead of subsuming it. And then it is possible for the negation of *some* to yield the 'all' level of quantification, as in *He hasn't read some of the papers – he's read them all* (with fall–rise intonation on the first clause). This is a quite general phenomenon in the area of quantification. For example, *It was excellent* implies *It was good*, yet it is possible to contrast *excellent* with *good* and say *It wasn't good – it was excellent*. Or again *He has read two of the papers* implies *He has read one of the papers* (thus suppose he has read paper x and paper y: it follows by the most elementary logic that he has read paper x and from this it follows that he has read one of the papers), yet we can say *He hasn't read one of the papers, he has read two*. We can hardly do the same with *a*, however: we would not say

---

[4] Recall, in this connection, that we have already noted that *any*^{neut} may be equivalent to *all/every*.

He hasn't a son, he has two: where *a* is made contrastive, the contrast is taken to be with the definite article *the* rather than with a determinative indicating plurality.

The negation of *all* yields a level of quantification covering the portion of the scale beginning minimally to the left of the 'all' level and extending to the far left. *He hasn't read all of the papers* will generally suggest that he has read some of them, but clearly it does not entail that he has.

No and *none* express the negation of a level of quantification covering the whole scale beyond the zero level (which is why there is some initial plausibility to their analysis as "not + any$^{n/aff}$": see above); the negation of this yields the zero level itself. *Few* covers a portion of the scale stretching leftwards from some not sharply defined position, as represented by the dots in (23). It is debatable whether it stretches as far left as the zero point. Does *He has read few of the papers* entail or just pragmatically imply *He has read at least one of the papers*? *He has read few of the papers, indeed he has read none of them* sounds appreciably less natural than *He has read some of them, indeed he has read them all*, which suggests that it is an entailment. On the other hand (changing the example) could one not truthfully say *Ed invariably makes few errors* if he sometimes makes two, sometimes one and sometimes none at all? I think we have to recognise some indeterminacy as to whether *few* is or is not consistent with *no/none*: to the extent that it is, we can analyse *few* as the negation of a level of quantification covering the portion of the scale to the right of the associated dots in (23).

Finally, *many*. This covers a portion of the scale stretching rightwards from a position which again is not sharply delineated. What was said above on the implication from *He has read some of the papers* to *He has not read all of the papers* still holds if we substitute *many* for *some*. *Not many* is generally pragmatically equivalent to *few*, but they are not fully equivalent from a strictly semantic point of view. In the first place, the negation of *many* can, under conditions of prosodically marked contrast, yield the 'all' level of quantification: *He hasn't read many of the papers, he's read them all*. In the second place, the left boundary of the portion covered by *many* is to the right of the right boundary of the portion covered by *few*, so that it is possible in principle to have a level of quantification that falls between them. One might therefore say *He didn't make many mistakes and he didn't make few mistakes: I'd put it somewhere in between*. But most of the time we treat *many* and *few* as complementary, jointly covering the whole of the scale (excluding the endpoints).

There are a number of important distinctions which I have ignored in this discussion – that between individuated and mass NPs (see 6.6) and, within the former, between singular and plural, and that between different kinds of quantification, especially the distinction between proportional and non-proportional quantification: compare the proportional *He has read few of the papers* and the non-proportional *He made few mistakes*. The account given here is thus intended only to draw attention to a selection of the issues involved in the interpretation of negated quantification.

FURTHER READING

On negation in general see Quirk et al. 1971: §§7.41–52, Klima 1964, Jackendoff 1972: Ch.8, Smith 1975, Lyons 1977: §16.4, Givón 1978. On the relation between *some* and *any*, see Lakoff 1969, Bolinger 1977: Ch. 2. One kind of negative construction I have not considered in this chapter but which has received a good deal of attention in the literature is illustrated in *He didn't think she'd met them*: this is semantically close to *He thought she hadn't met them* (whereas there is no analogous semantic relation between *He didn't know she'd met them* and *He knew she hadn't met them*), so that it has been suggested that the first derives from the second by 'raising' or 'transferring' the negative from the subordinate into the superordinate clause – see Horn 1978 for detailed discussion. The pragmatic implications discussed in §4 are instances of the phenomenon known as 'conversational implicatures' – see Lyons 1977: §14.3.

14

Thematic systems of the clause

The concept of a thematic system was introduced in 1.4: a thematic system is one where corresponding members of the contrasting terms normally have the same propositional meaning and the same illocutionary potential, as with an active–passive pair like

(1)   i *John shot the tiger*
        ii *The tiger was shot by John*

I say that they 'normally' have the same propositional meaning, because under certain more or less complex circumstances there may be differences with respect to this area of meaning. Thus, to take an often-cited example, the following active–passive pair do differ in their truth conditions, at least in the absence of special intonation:

(2)   i *Many arrows didn't hit the target*
        ii *The target wasn't hit by many arrows*

Suppose, for example, that six hundred arrows were fired, with three hundred hitting and three hundred missing. Then one would be inclined to say that the statement made in uttering (i) would be true (three hundred qualifies as many), while that made in uttering (ii) would be false (if the target was hit by three hundred, then it isn't true that it wasn't hit by many). The difference in meaning is attributable to the fact that *many* precedes the negative in (i) but follows it in (ii) – but such differences arise only where we have quantification + negation (or two separate cases of quantification). And given that we are concerned with a general definition of thematic system, not a language-particular one (see 2.3), such differences do not invalidate our account: (i) stands in the same syntactic relation to (ii) in (2) as in (1), and we take the system as thematic on the grounds that in the overwhelming majority of such pairs the semantic relation is as in (1).

In this chapter we will look at the five systems mentioned in 1.4, and at certain further syntactic contrasts of a similar kind; we will examine the syntactic relations between the various constructions and consider some of the semantic factors favouring the selection of one or another term in different contexts.

14.1   Voice: active and passive

We begin with the system of voice, illustrated in (1) and (2) above. The unmarked member of the pair, (i), is said to be in the **active** voice, the marked one, (ii), in the **passive** voice. As explained in 2.3, these names are based on the role of the subject-referent in clauses expressing an action: it will standardly be the actor, or active participant, in the unmarked version, and the patient, or passive participant, in the marked version. Thus in (1), John is the actor, the tiger the patient, with *John* subject in the active, *the tiger* subject in the passive. This distribution of roles provides, it will be recalled, the criterion for naming the classes, not for determining the classification of a given clause. The clauses in (3) do not express actions, but they are still classified as respectively active and passive because they exhibit the same structural relation as the pair in (1):

(3)   i *Everyone should know the answer*
         ii *The answer should be known by everyone*

'Voice', as a general linguistic term, is applied to systems yielding such variation in the semantic role associated with the subject, normally where there is, as here, concomitant variation in the form of the VP; it is applied both to the clause system and to the VP system (or verb system when the terms are differentiated inflectionally).

The structural relation between (i) and (ii) in the above pairs lends itself to description by means of our informal concept of transformation. Taking the unmarked term as basic, we can derive the passive via the following operations:

(4)   i Change the object of the active into the subject of the passive;
          ii Change the subject of the passive into the 'agent' of the passive, which involves adding the preposition *by*;
         iii Add *be* in the final auxiliary position in the VP – and adjust the verbal inflections so that they conform to the rules given in 4.2.

Agent is the name of the function filled by *by John* and *by everyone* in our examples: it is a syntactic function figuring only in passive constructions. ('Agent', a syntactic function, should thus be distinguished from what we shall call **agentive**, a semantic role implying some measure of control, responsibility, choice: thus the semantic role associated with *John* is agentive in both (1i) and (1ii), while that associated with *everyone* is non-agentive in both (3i) and (3ii), whereas *by John* in (1ii) and *by everyone* in (3ii) are agents.) I am treating the agent as a special kind of complement, but the fact that it is always omissible differentiates it from central cases of that

438

function, and it is commonly treated as an adjunct. The change of functions effected by (4i) and (ii) yields a change in transitivity: (1i) is transitive, while (1ii) is intransitive.

By virtue of (4iii) the main verb takes on the *-en* form, while **be** will carry the inflectional properties carried by the main verb of the active, except for any person–number properties, which are determined by agreement with the passive subject. Thus *shot* is an *-en* form in (1ii) but a past tense form in (1i) (compare *saw* and *was seen*); the *was* takes over the past tense inflection and the selection of *was* as opposed to *were* is determined by agreement with *the tiger*.

Most of the remainder of this section will be concerned with the restrictions and extensions that need to be added to the above quite traditional account of the relation between active and passive constructions. In the first place it should be noted that not all active transitive clauses have passive counterparts. Examples are *John has three sons, Her dress touched/ reached the ground, The French word 'maison' means "house"*, and so on. In general the restrictions are to be stated not by simply identifying the verbs concerned, but in terms of particular uses or senses of certain verbs: note for example that the verbs in the above examples can occur in such passives as *A good time was had by all, Nothing else had been touched, That isn't what was meant*. We will not examine the restrictions in detail, but will mention just three special cases:

(a) Where an object is obligatorily reflexive, passivisation is not possible. Thus in *Ed perjured himself, The topic lends itself well to seminar discussion, Max drank himself under the table, The door opened itself*, we could not substitute any other NP for the reflexives, and there are accordingly no passive counterparts. Where a reflexive is in paradigmatic opposition to other NPs, as in *John taught himself/ the first-year students*, passivisation is in general possible, though relatively rare. The form is, of course, *John was taught by himself*, not **Himself was taught by John*, for the reflexive must follow its antecedent (assuming for simplicity that 'antecedent' is the relevant concept – see 7.4). As the passive of *John taught himself*, it would normally only be used contrastively, i.e. to emphasise that the one who taught John was John himself, not somebody else.[1]

(b) We cannot passivise clauses like *Ed liked/wanted/hated Liz to accompany them*: **Liz was liked/wanted/hated by Ed to accompany them*; we have observed (5.6.3) that the constituent structure of the active is somewhat unclear, so that it is arguable whether *Liz* is in fact an object. However, there is no independent reason for assigning a different structure to these than to *Ed*

---

[1] It also has an interpretation where *by himself* is not an agent but an adjunct with the meaning "on his own"; in this case it belongs to the 'agentless passive' construction discussed below.

expected Liz to accompany them, Ed believed Liz to be right, and so on, where *Liz* can become subject under passivisation.

(c) Where a verb has a sense in which it is logically 'symmetrical' pass-ivisation is unlikely or excluded altogether for some speakers. For example, **marry** in the sense "enter into matrimony with" is logically symmetrical in that *X married Y* entails and is entailed by *Y married X*, for any value of *X* and *Y*; similarly **resemble** and **equal** (as in *3^2 equals 9*, but not *Ed equalled the record*). Thus examples like *Kim was married/resembled by Chris* are judged awkward or unacceptable: instead of passivising *Chris married/resembled Kim* we can achieve essentially the same thematic effect by simply switch-ing the NPs to give *Kim married/resembled Chris*.

Just as not all transitive actives have a passive counterpart, so there are passives with no active counterpart. For the most part they involve other kinds of passive construction than the central one exemplified above and hence will be introduced below; here, however, we may note that the verb **rumour** is wholly restricted to passive constructions, while **say** occurs only in passives when it has an infinitival complement, as in *He was said by his parents to have been a docile child*:[2] the transformation will thus apply to a hypothetical active †*His parents said him to have been a docile child*.

Let us turn to some of the extensions that are to be made to the above account of the passive. (1ii) and (3ii) represent only the most central kind of passive: there are various others which cannot be derived from an active counterpart by the operations given in (4) – they bear a less direct or systematic relation to actives. Just how far we should extend the category of passive constructions is a matter on which different views are taken, but for present purposes it will be helpful to cast the net rather widely, incor-porating all those containing a passive use of a past participle – in the sense explained in 9.2.2. The other kinds to be considered include the following:

(a) Passives of ditransitive actives. The formulation in (4i) implies that the active has a single object, but an active may have two objects (5.4) and in that case there may be two passive counterparts:

(5)			
	i	*Ed gave Liz the money*	Active
	ii	*Liz was given the money by Ed*	Passive – class I
	iii	*The money was given Liz by Ed*	Passive – class II

In the derivation of the class I passive the indirect object becomes subject while in that of the class II passive it is the direct object that becomes subject. The class I passive is the more frequent and the less marked of the two; class II is not possible at all for some speakers and for those who do

---

[2] More precisely we would have to distinguish this kind of complement from that in *He said not to tell her*, where **say** is used to report a directive.

have the construction there are still some cases where only class 1 is available: compare *She was saved a lot of worry* (*by his action*) and **A lot of worry was saved her* (*by his action*). Whereas in (1) and (3) passivisation changes a transitive clause into an intransitive, here it changes a 'ditransitive' (two objects) into a 'monotransitive'.

(b) Passives with a stranded preposition, as in *It was dealt with by the boss.* This is the passive counterpart of *The boss dealt with it*, where *it* is not object of the verb but complement of the preposition *with* – so that in the passive *with* is a PP that has lost its complement. Generally the preposition concerned does not have any readily identifiable independent meaning, but is simply required by the verb whose complement it heads (contrast *The boss travelled with her*, which cannot be passivised) – **deal** *with*, **rely** *on*, **depend** *on*, **account** *for*, **approve** *of*, and so on (see 5.5.1 for discussion of such verb–preposition combinations). But examples are found where the preposition does have its normal locative sense: *The bed had been slept in, Her hat had been sat on*, etc.; for the passive to be acceptable in such cases, the process must be one that affects in some significant way the referent of the subject. Thus *Her hat had been sat on* is more likely than *The stone bench had been sat on*, for sitting on a hat is likely to put it out of shape, whereas sitting on a stone bench will not normally have any effect on it – though one could not of course say that the latter violates any GRAMMATICAL rule, and indeed if one adds a *plainly* acceptability is improved: the *plainly* indicates that there was some visible effect produced by sitting on the bench. For the most part the PP whose complement becomes subject under passivisation is complement in an intransitive active clause (note the impossibility of **The design was congratulated Ed on*, and the like), but in a few cases it may be complement within an object NP: *He had been taken advantage of by the boss*: these involve expressions like **take** *advantage of*, **take** *account of*, etc. which from a lexical (though not syntactic) point of view are single units.

(c) Agentless passives. The agent is a freely omissible element of clause structure: there are no cases where the rules of syntax require an agent to be present. In this respect it is quite different from the subject of the active. Thus omitting the subject from (1i) leads to the ungrammatical **Shot the tiger*, whereas omitting the agent from (1i) leaves us with the perfectly well-formed passive *The tiger was shot*. This kind of construction we shall call the 'agentless passive': it is much more frequent than the one with an agent – textual studies show that some 75%–80% of passives are agentless.

Now an agentless passive like *The tiger was shot* cannot be satisfactorily derived from any actual active clause. It might be proposed that the corresponding active is *Someone shot the tiger*; such a pairing cannot be accepted, however, because the active encodes information that is not encoded in the passive. With this particular pair the difference is not communicatively significant, because a hearer would pragmatically infer from *The tiger was shot* that someone shot it. Consider, however, a case like *Max was killed instantly*. This is not equivalent to *Someone killed Max instantly*, for unlike the latter it does not entail that Max was killed by a person. Nor can we relate it to *Something killed Max instantly*, for *something* normally contrasts with *someone*, instead of subsuming it. Or consider a case like *The project was completed in four years*: this is not equivalent to *Someone completed the project in four years*, which implies that a single person did it.

What we can do here is invoke again the concept of a zero element and postulate hypothetical actives as source †∅ *killed Max instantly*, †∅ *completed the project in four years*. The ∅ would be pragmatically interpretable, but the subject of the active would not be syntactically reconstructible. This works satisfactorily enough for the most part, but there remain some problem cases. One arises with examples like *The rumour was widely believed*, for there is no syntactically well-formed sentence at all with the form 'NP *widely believed the rumour*'. The adjunct *widely* expresses much the same meaning as an agent like *by many people*, but it is clearly not syntactically derivable from an active subject. A different kind of problem arises with an example like *Max was drowned*. This could be used in a context where it is clear that someone drowned Max (so that one would be able to find an interpretation for the hypothetical ∅), but more often than not it will be used when there is no such pragmatic implication, as in, say, *The boat capsized in the storm and Max was drowned*. The same event could have been described with the active intransitive *Max drowned*; in such a context it is difficult to accept that the former presents the event as one involving two participants (one of them merely implicit) while the latter presents it as involving only one; the subject of the active is here not even semantically reconstructible. Notice, moreover, that there are certain expressions which occur exclusively in agentless passives: we could not, for example, add an agent to *She was taken ill*, *She expects to be confined next week* (in the sense related to pregnancy), *Her son was born on Christmas day*,[3] and these likewise do not lend themselves convincingly to derivation from an active source.

(d) Adjectival passives. In 9.2.2 we distinguished between the verbal passive *The vase was broken by Tim* and the adjectival passive *The vase was already broken*, with *The vase was broken* being ambiguous between the two. In the adjectival interpretation of *The vase was broken* ("It was in a broken state", as opposed to verbal "It got broken") **be** is not the passive auxiliary but a main verb, and in general other copulative verbs can replace it (e.g. *The vase*

---

[3] A very peripheral passive this; the verb **bear** as used elsewhere has a somewhat different meaning and its *-en* form is spelt *borne*. But *born* differs from adjectives in that it cannot occur with any other verb than **be**; it is also semantically unlike an adjective in that *Tom was born in 1914* expresses an event: it doesn't attribute some quality or the like to Tom.

appeared broken), and *broken* is an adjective derived by lexical–morphological conversion of the verbal *-en* form. The relationship with an active construction is less direct than with verbal passives, and cannot be plausibly mediated by any syntactic transformation.

With **break** it is very easy to distinguish between the verbal and adjectival passives (see our earlier discussion), but with certain others it can be rather less straightforward: we will here draw attention to two such cases. It will be recalled that we distinguished two kinds of adjectival past participle: those like *worried, surprised*, etc., which are gradable and central members of the adjective class, and those like *broken, paid, married*, which are not gradable and hence less central members of the class. One problem case for the adjectival/verbal contrast involves the *worried* class. *Ed was very worried by her illness* is clearly adjectival, by virtue of the *very* (and note that we could also substitute *seemed*, etc., for *was* and *about* for *by*); and since *very* is omissible we will also have (6) as adjectival:

(6)   *Ed was worried by her illness*

(compare *Ed seemed worried by her illness*). But (6) can also be derived by applying the processes given in (4) to the active clause *Her illness worried Ed*. We thus have two different analyses for (6), just as we do for *The vase was broken*, yet it does not exhibit the clear ambiguity that we find in the latter. With **break** we can sharply distinguish between the process (which might take only a fraction of a second) and the resultant state (which is of potentially unlimited duration), but with **worry** the process of causing the state and the state itself are not temporally separable in this way. There seems no reason why we shouldn't say that (6) has two syntactic structures, but since the meaning is effectively the same in both cases it will not make any semantic difference whether a given instance is taken as verbal or adjectival.

The second case, very similar, involves some of the past participles that are less central adjectives, such as *known, admired, feared*, etc. Their adjectival status is established by their ability to occur with such a copulative verb as **become**: *It became known* (contrast **It became believed*, with *believed* always verbal), *He became more and more feared by his parishioners*, and so on. But again there is no reason for excluding *known* and the like from the verbal passive: (4) will convert *His parishioners feared him* to *He was feared by his parishioners*, and so on. Thus we are led to recognise *It was known, He was feared*, etc. as either verbal or adjectival, although there is no semantic distinction. The verbs **know** and **fear** denote states, not actions or processes, and there can accordingly be no contrast of the kind we found with *broken*.

Most adjectival passives are obligatorily agentless: if we add *by Tim* to *The vase was broken*, for example, we make it unambiguously verbal. But

443

agents are not invariably excluded (extending the term 'agent' now to the corresponding kind of complement in AdjP structure), witness examples like *He was unmoved by their entreaties*. And, as the examples above have shown, we can often have an agent in those cases, like (6), where the semantic distinction between the adjectival and verbal constructions is neutralised.

A number of adjectival past participles have developed senses (and sometimes kinds of complementation) not found in the associated verbs: *bound* (*It's bound to be raining*), *engaged* (*They're engaged to be married*), *numbered* (*His days are numbered*), *related* (in the kinship sense: *I'm not related to her*), *supposed* (in the deontic sense: *You're supposed to be working*), and so on. The specialisation of meaning distances them from the verbs, so that they are hardly felt to be passive.

(e) *-en* form non-finite complements. A small number of verbs can take as complement a passive non-finite construction with an *-en* class VP: *He saw United beaten by Spurs*. This may be compared with *He saw Spurs beat United*, where the active non-finite complement is infinitival. We note then that in this construction the passive is not marked by the auxiliary **be**. Similar pairs can be found for **hear**, **watch** and **want**, except that with **want** the active has *to*: *I want them cooked by Angela* and *I want Angela to cook them*. Similarly with **have** and **get** except that here (at least with **get**) there is a difference in the propositional, not just the thematic, meaning between the passive and active constructions. With a passive complement, as in *Max got his hair singed*, the referent of the subject of **get** can have either an agentive or a non-agentive role (thus "Max brought it about that his hair was singed" or "Something happened to Max: his hair was singed"), but with an active the non-agentive interpretation is not available. Thus *Max got his nose broken by the intruder* (where the non-agentive interpretation is more likely) is not equivalent to *Max got the intruder to break his nose*.

(f) **Get** passives. The copulative verbs **become**, **look**, **remain**, **seem**, etc., take only adjectival passives: in *It looked broken*, for example, *broken* is an adjective, not a verb. **Get**, however, must be recognised as an alternative to **be** in the verbal passive construction because it occurs with past participles that we have seen (9.2.2) to be uniquely verbal – thus *I got blamed for*, *Tom got struck on the chin*, etc. We accordingly distinguish, for example, between such pairs as *It became magnetised* (adjectival: "It came to be in a magnetised state") and *It got magnetised* (verbal: "It underwent magnetisation").

Get can of course also be a copulative verb, taking AdjP complements, as in *He got wet/angry/cold*, etc. It is to be expected, therefore, that it will also take adjectival passives, as it does in *He got interested/annoyed*. Thus like **be**, **get** figures in both verbal and adjectival passive constructions. But there is nothing like the same overlap as we find with **be**. For example, whereas *It* *was magnetised* is ambiguously verbal or adjectival, *It got magnetised* is only verbal. There are considerable restrictions on the combination of copulative verbs with those past participles that are slightly marginal members of the adjective class (cf. *The gate looked/*became closed, The money remained/*seemed unspent*, and so on): it is not clear that copulative **get** combines with any of them. One difficulty in investigating this matter is that the semantic difference that is typically very clear with **be** would in principle be largely neutralised with **get** because as a copulative verb **get**, unlike **be**, involves a change of state. Thus the meaning difference between **get** + verbal passive ("undergo the process") and copulative **get** + adjectival passive ("come to be in the state resulting from undergoing the process") would be extremely elusive. One place where we do find an ambiguity is with a handful of past participles including *washed, dressed, shaved, married*, etc. In one interpretation *They got washed* is like the verbal **get** passives above: "They underwent the process of washing" (cf. *The clothes got washed*) – in this interpretation we could add an agent. In a second interpretation, excluded if an agent is added, it is equivalent to an intransitive or reflexive active, *They washed (themselves)* (reciprocal rather than reflexive in the case of *married*). It may be that on the second interpretation it should be regarded as adjectival, but the particular difference of meaning is not predictable in any general way from the verbal vs adjectival distinction.

Leaving aside this question, let us review briefly the differences between verbal passives with **be** and **get**. (i) The most obvious is doubtless the stylistic one: **get** tends to be avoided in more formal styles. (ii) There are a few cases where **be** cannot be replaced by **get**, most clearly with verbs taking a non-finite complement: *Ed was/*got heard to observe that ...; Jill was/*got rumoured to be in Moscow*. (iii) **Get** lends itself more readily than **be** to the imputation to the subject-referent of some measure of initiative or responsibility. Consider, for example, such a pair as *Ed got arrested* and *Ed was arrested*. Either could be used to report something that simply happened to Ed, but if I believe he deliberately sought arrest or was careless in allowing it to happen, I will be more likely to use **get**. This is why **get** is more likely than **be** (in styles that permit a choice) in imperatives and other constructions that associate an agentive role with the (explicit or understood) subject: *Don't get arrested; I'll try and get arrested; Do I need to get vaccinated?*. Such an element of initiative or responsibility is also explicitly associated with the subject in the reflexive construction *Ed got himself arrested*, where we could not substitute **be** for **get**.

We noted earlier (4.4) that **get** is not an operator (cf. *Did he get killed?*, not **Got he killed?*), and in this respect is not a central member of the class of auxiliary verbs. Moreover, it is clearly a main verb taking non-finite complementation in *He got himself arrested*. The question thus arises as to how we should distinguish structurally between the latter and *He got arrested*: shall we say that *get* is a main verb in each, taking different kinds of complementation (cf. *He sat himself down/He sat down, He kept himself busy/He kept busy*), or that *He got arrested* has the same constituent structure as *He was arrested*, with *get* an auxiliary? *Get* undoubtedly raises problems for the distinction we have drawn between auxiliaries and catenatives.

It will be clear that our original transformational analysis, deriving passives from actives by means of the operations informally given in (4), accounts directly only for the central core of passive constructions. It is perhaps most appealing with examples like *Close tabs were kept on her by the new management*, where the impossibility of having *close tabs* as subject of a passive with a verb other than *keep* would follow automatically from the impossibility of having it as object of an active with a verb other than *keep*. Our survey shows, however, that the grammar must cater for a range of passive constructions, some of them related only indirectly, or indeed only tenuously, to actives.

It remains to consider some of the semantic differences between active and passive constructions, some of the factors which favour the choice of one rather than the other. We will confine our attention to verbal passives since there are no adjectival actives standing in a comparable relation to our adjectival passives.

(a) We have noted that one important syntactic difference between the constructions is that the passive agent is freely omissible while its active analogue, the subject, is not. The semantic correlate of this, of course, is that in the passive one is free not to encode information that would have to be encoded in the active. There are a variety of reasons why one might wish to use an agentless passive, as can be seen from a small set of examples like the following:

(7)
    i *The house was built in 1964*
    ii *Nothing is known about its origin*
    iii *The enemy opened fire and five of our men were killed instantly*
    iv *The specimens were examined spectroscopically*
    v *The delay in attending to this matter is regretted*

(i) would mostly likely be used to say how old the house was: I might well not know who built it, but even if I did that information would generally not be relevant to the issue of how old it was. In (ii) the understood agent is something like *by anyone* ("anyone at all" or "anyone in the context of discourse"); *anyone* is indefinite and non-specific – the only real positive information it encodes ("human") is already pragmatically inferable from the rest of the sentence. In (iii) the understood agent of the second clause is recoverable from the first (*by the enemy*). (iv) might occur in a report of some scientific investigation, and in such a context it will be readily inferable that the specimens were examined by the writer(s) of the report: the passive enables writers of such reports to avoid constantly referring explicitly to themselves. But it is not only in scientific writing that the passive is used to avoid self-reference: this kind of agentless passive is common in many other contexts, such as letters from government departments and the like, where the identity of the public servant who actually drafts the letter will typically not be revealed. (v), for example, is from a letter I received from the Taxation Office: the active *I/we regret* . . . would be out of place because it would involve the nominal signatory too directly and personally. (Notice in passing that (v) illustrates two other devices that permit the avoidance of self-reference: the use of an NP rather than a clause – *the delay* . . . rather than *x delayed* . . . – and the use of a subjectless non-finite construction, *in attending* . . .)

(b) Although the subject is not freely omissible, there are certain constructions where it may or must be omitted – imperatives and various non-finite constructions, as in [*Ed wanted*] *to go*, [*Jill tried*] *to find it*, and so on. In such cases, the missing argument of the subjectless verb may be derivable from the situation (in imperatives, where it is the person or persons that could be referred to as *you*) or from the larger construction (thus Ed and Jill respectively in the non-finite examples). The system of voice provides for variation in the association of arguments with syntactic functions; in the subjectless constructions under consideration here, that term in the voice system will be selected which allows the right argument to be left unexpressed. Compare, for example, *Open the door* and *Don't be intimidated by him*; the former has no passive counterpart, the latter no active counterpart: given that the unexpressed argument has the semantic role associated with the subject of **open** in active clauses and of **intimidate** in passive clauses, we need respectively active and passive for the subjectless imperatives. The same goes for *Jill tried to open the door* and *Jill tried not to be intimidated by him*, where the unexpressed argument of **open** and **intimidate** – unexpressed within the non-finite construction itself, that is – is "Jill".

(c) Although we argued in 2.2.1 that the subject cannot be defined as the element identifying the topic, it is nevertheless more closely correlated with the topic than are other elements of clause structure. Thus given an active–passive pair like *Kim interviewed Robin* and *Robin was interviewed by Kim* (spoken with the main stress on the last word), then the first is likely to be construed as being primarily about Kim, the second about Robin. Or compare (7iii) above with *The enemy opened fire and killed five of our men instantly* (which also avoids explicit reference to the enemy in the second term of the coordination); this second version suggests that the enemy is viewed as the main topic (*the enemy* is subject of a coordination of EVPs) whereas (7iii)

447

suggests that the topic of the second clause is five of our men (or perhaps our men) – the speaker appears to be presenting the event from the point of view of what happened to (five of) our men rather than of what the enemy did.

(d) There is a tendency for definite NPs to precede indefinites, for NPs expressing 'given' material to precede those expressing 'new' material. Thus other things being equal, one is likely to prefer the passive member of a pair like *Vandals wrecked the shop/The shop was wrecked by vandals*, but the active member of one like *I heard a loud scream/A loud scream was heard by me*. The referents of *the shop* and *I* will here be 'given' in the sense of being present and relatively salient in the context of discourse, while *vandals* and *a loud scream* introduce new elements into the discourse. This factor is related to the last inasmuch as if there is one definite and one indefinite NP in a clause, the former is likely to refer to the topic. Similarly the normal preference for, say, *Jill ran into the street and was knocked down by a passing car* over *Jill ran into the street and a passing car knocked her down* illustrates factors (b), (c) and (d) all working together.

(e) There is a related tendency for long, or 'heavy', phrases to come late in the clause, so that the predicator comes relatively early. Thus instead of the active *The woman who gave that excellent paper on the French tense system at last year's conference will open the discussion* one would generally prefer the passive *The discussion will be opened by the woman who gave that excellent paper on the French tense system at last year's conference*. This point is related to the last in that entities which are already in the context of discourse can typically be referred to by simpler NPs than entities which are new or less salient. Note, for example, the greater naturalness of *The novel must have been written by someone who knows the area well* in comparison with its active counterpart. And even in our first example, where both NPs are definite, the context is likely to be one where the discussion is more salient than the woman – if the latter were of high salience it wouldn't be necessary to use such a detailed description to refer to her.

(f) We have noted that the relative order of a negative and a quantified NP may be one factor in determining whether the quantification falls within the scope of negation (13.3). Since this order may be different in corresponding actives and passives, they may differ with respect to the scope of negation – cf. (2) above. In such cases the active and passive members of the pair differ in their propositional meaning, not just thematically.

14.2 The indirect object transformation

Grammars commonly posit a transformational relation between pairs of clauses like

(8)   i *Ed gave the key to Liz*
         ii *Ed gave Liz the key*
(9)   i *Ed bought some flowers for his secretary*
         ii *Ed bought his secretary some flowers*

The transformation involves dropping the preposition *to* or *for* and moving its complement to the left of the direct object. Like passivisation it effects a change in the grammatical functions: in (8i) *Liz* is complement within a PP that is itself complement, but not object, to the verb, whereas in (8ii) *Liz* is indirect object of the verb (see 5.4).

It is, however, questionable whether the relationship between the two constructions is regular and systematic enough to justify treating them in this way, treating them as terms in a system. In the first place, there are a significant number of verbs which enter into the ditransitive construction without there being a counterpart like (i): **allow/permit** (*I'll allow you one more try*); **bet/wager**; **bid**, **charge**, **fine**; **begrudge/envy**; **forgive/pardon**; **hit/strike** (*He hit me a mighty blow*); **reach** (*Just reach me my gloves*); **refuse**; **save/spare** (in the sense they have in *I'll save/spare you the bother*); and so on.

In the second place the transformation would not be able to apply to all clauses with an object followed by a PP with *to* or *for* – and only to a limited extent is it possible to state the restrictions in general terms. Take *to* first. We can distinguish (8i) from, say, *He took the rubbish to the tip* in terms of the semantic role associated with the complement of *to*: in (8i) *Liz* is 'recipient', while here *the tip* is 'goal'. The recipient will be a person (or animal) or a set/body of persons, while the goal is simply the place to which someone or something goes. Thus with a single verb we may contrast *He took his son to the zoo* (with *the zoo* as goal and no ditransitive counterpart) and *He took some flowers to his wife* (with *his wife* as recipient and the ditransitive counterpart *He took his wife some flowers*). Or again *He sent his son to Washington* (*to study law*) vs *He sent a stiff note to Washington/He sent Washington a stiff note* (where *Washington* is used to refer to the US government, which has a recipient role). With such verbs as **say** and **tell**, **explain** and **teach**, **reveal** and **show**, the role associated with the complement of *to* is recipient only in an extended or metaphorical sense, and here it seems there is no alternative to simply stating for particular verbs whether or not the ditransitive construction is possible – **tell**, **teach** and **show** allow it, while the other three do not.

With *for* we can again make a semantic distinction between, say, *Will you get some milk for Liz?* and *Will you iron this dress for Liz?*. In the first *Liz* is (potential) recipient: the milk is for her, whereas in the second she is the beneficiary of the whole action: it is your ironing the dress, rather than the dress itself, that is for Liz. (There is in general a difference with respect to immediacy or directness between recipients in the *to* and *for* constructions: when you have got some milk for Liz it still remains, as it were, to give it to

449

her – but note the non-immediacy in **bequeathe**/**leave** *to*.) The two kinds of *for* phrase combine in *Will you get some milk for Liz for me?*. In general it is the first kind that alternates with an indirect object: *Will you get Liz some milk?* but not **Will you iron Liz this dress?* (though some speakers find the latter construction acceptable with a pronoun like *me* as indirect object). However, as we have noted earlier, there is some variation in the precise semantic role associated with these indirect objects and complements of *for*: cf. *He lost us the match/lost the match for us*; *He sang us a song/sang a song for us* (the song is for us in a somewhat different sense from that in which the milk was for Liz in the above example); *Will you cash me this cheque/cash this cheque for me?* (where I receive the proceeds of the cheque, not the cheque itself), and so on. And again there are some *for* phrase complements of the 'recipient' kind that do not alternate with indirect objects: *They provided/ supplied clothing for the refugees* but not **They provided/supplied the refugees clothing*.

These last examples can be corrected by adding *with* before *clothing*: *They provided/supplied the refugees with clothing*, where *the refugees* is direct object, not indirect. This brings us to the point that there are a variety of other patterns of alternation between different combinations of complements than that illustrated in (8) and (9). Compare:

(10) i **blame** X *for* Y / **blame** Y *on* X
ii **present** X *with* Y / **present** Y *to* X
iii **envy** X Y / **envy** X *for* Y
iv **ask** X Y / **ask** Y *of* X
v **play** X Y / **play** Y *against* X

These patterns apply over an extremely small domain, being limited to from one to a handful of verbs (and with restrictions too on the value of Y in (iv) and (v): compare *I asked a question/complete loyalty of him* vs *I asked him a question/*complete loyalty*). There can be no question of deriving one from the other by means of a syntactic transformation: we simply have to specify the two patterns of complementation in the lexical entries for the particular verbs concerned. The domain over which the alternations in (8) and (9) hold is significantly greater than for those of (10), but much smaller than for the active/passive alternation – and hence there are those who wish to handle them like (10), in the lexical entries for the particular verbs, and others who will handle them like the voice system, by syntactic transformation.

From a semantic point of view the difference between (i) and (ii) in (8) and (9) involves thematic rather than propositional meaning. The fact that the order of the post-verbal NPs is different means that the two constructions may reflect different divisions between given and new material. Thus in a context where it is given, i.e. already established or able to be taken for granted, that Ed gave the key to someone and new that the someone was Liz, (8i) is likely to be preferred and conversely if it is given that Ed gave Liz something and new that it was the key then (8ii) is likely to be preferred – assuming in both cases that we have neutral intonation, i.e. the main pitch movement falling on the last word. (9i) and (ii) sound equally natural in abstraction from their context, but if we replace indefinite *some flowers* by definite *the flowers*, (i) becomes the more likely: if the identity of the flowers is assumed to be known, then it is quite likely also to be given that Ed bought them – the new information will typically be that they were for his secretary. And if instead of a definite description like *the flowers* we had a personal pronoun like *them*, then construction (i) becomes virtually obligatory. This correlation with the given–new distinction has some relevance to the fact that an indirect object cannot be an initial interrogative *wh* phrase (see 5.4): we can have *Who did Ed give the key to?*, an interrogative of structure (i), but not **Who did Ed give the key?*. If I am asking about the identity of the recipient then I will normally be taking it as given that Ed gave the key to someone – and we have just noted that where this is given (8i) is more natural than (8ii) (assuming, again, that the intonation is neutral): it is not surprising, therefore, that the interrogative used to find out who the someone is should follow the pattern of (8i) rather than (8ii). This is not to suggest that the deviance of **Who did Ed give the key?* could be predicted on thematic grounds: it is a syntactic not a semantic constraint; nevertheless if we were told that the recipient could be questioned in only one of the constructions in (8) we would expect it to be (i) rather than (ii).

14.3 **Extraposition**

We have posited a transformational relation between pairs of clauses like

(11)   i *That he was angry was obvious*
       ii *It was obvious that he was angry*

Although construction (ii) is much more frequent, we take (i) as basic since it conforms to the kernel clause structure S–P–PC; in (ii) *it* has replaced the embedded clause as subject, but *that he was angry* hasn't taken on the positive properties of any other kernel clause function.

Extraposition shifts a unit to the end of the clause (except that certain peripheral adjuncts may still follow it) and inserts *it* into the vacated position. The construction is to be distinguished from that exemplified in

(12)   *They're excellent company, the Smiths*

Here *the Smiths* has something of the character of an afterthought; its function is to clarify the reference of the personal pronoun *they*. But it could never provide the sole or primary indication of what *they* refers to – the

Smiths will have to have been mentioned earlier in the discourse (or at least to have been sufficiently salient in the context of discourse to be referred to simply as *they*). Compare also *I've not seen them for ages, the Smiths*, where the pronoun is object. The pronoun may of course be *it*, as in *It's a marvellous work, his latest novel*, but there is no difficulty in distinguishing this 'clarification of reference' construction from extraposition: apart from the semantic difference just noted, there is a clear prosodic difference – (12) will have a fall on *excellent company* and a rise on *the Smiths*. There is no reason to analyse (12) in an analogous way to (11ii): it is an amplification of *They're excellent company*, not a transformation of *The Smiths are excellent company*. Henceforth we will confine our attention to the extraposition construction.

(11) illustrates the most central case of extraposition, that where the extraposed element is a finite clause functioning – prior to extraposition – as subject of a larger clause. What are the other possibilities? We noted in 9.1 that NPs cannot normally be extraposed: we cannot transform *His anger was obvious* to **It was obvious his anger* (*It was obvious, his anger* is possible in the clarification of reference construction, but that is beside the point). Exceptions are found in examples like *It's extraordinary the amount of beer he puts away, It impressed me the way she disarmed him, It was amazing the number of times she got it right*, but they are highly restricted with respect both to the kind of NP that can be moved and to the kind of EVP over which it can be moved: the NPs, for example, are of the form 'the + N ... + relative clause' and are semantically close to subordinate interrogative clauses – *how much beer he puts away, how she disarmed him, how many times she got it right*. As for non-finites, we also saw that infinitivals extrapose as freely as finite clauses, *-ing* class non-finites very much less so: *It had caused many of us great distress to see him treat her like that* is completely grammatical whereas *It had caused many of us great distress seeing him treat her like that* is ungrammatical or at best marginal for many speakers. Nevertheless, contrary to what is sometimes said, extraposition of *-ing* class non-finites is not wholly excluded, and in general is more acceptable when both the non-finite construction and the one containing it are relatively short: *It's been nice meeting you, It was useful having her with us*, etc. Extraposition from subject position is obligatory with such verbs as **appear, seem, chance, happen** (finite clause subjects), **remain** and the passive of **hope, intend**, etc. (infinitival subjects): *It appears that he left/*That he left appears; It remains to consider the possible causes/*To consider the possible causes remains; It is hoped to follow this up in a later paper/*To follow this up in a later paper is hoped* – in such cases we shall need to have the transformation apply to hypothetical clauses. It is also obligatory – with finite clauses and infinitivals – when the larger construction has the operator + subject order: *Why is it necessary to tell her?/*Why is to tell her necessary*. Notice that *-ing* class non-finites can follow the operator: *Would recalling Smith serve any real purpose?*; the construction may sound somewhat clumsy, but it is not ungrammatical.

There are, conversely, conditions under which extraposition is not possible: restrictions must be placed on the kind of material across which a finite clause or infinitival would be moved. The most obvious case is illustrated in *That he survived at all shows that he must have been remarkably fit*: the first embedded clause cannot be extraposed across the second. Another restriction is found in *How he escaped is the really important question*: extraposition is excluded in the 'identifying' **be** construction that we shall be considering in §5 below.

Extraposition is also possible from direct object position under certain conditions. It occurs mainly when the object is accompanied by an objective predicative complement: *He considered it important to explain his reasons*. With finite clauses and infinitival constructions such extraposition is obligatory – except that in some cases it is possible just to shift the object to the right instead of inserting *it* as a new object: *He made (it) clear that he would not tolerate any dissent*. Again, *-ing* class non-finites do not readily undergo extraposition from object, and when they do the rule is optional: *He found it very frustrating having to wait so long / He found having to wait so long very frustrating*. A finite clause or infinitival construction can be extraposed around certain other elements than predicative complements, as in *I put it to you that you are lying*. This, however, applies with only a small number of verbs; much more frequent is the case where the clause or infinitival construction is simply moved to the right from the normal object position: *He explained to them why it was impossible*.

The main thematic effect of extraposition is that a 'heavy' unit appears at the end of the clause, which makes for easier processing, whether by speaker or hearer – and the longer the embedded clause or non-finite construction, the more likely it is that the extraposed construction will be selected. The greater ease of processing the latter is particularly evident in cases where we have one layer of embedding within another, as in

(13)   i *That for him to resign now would be a mistake is quite obvious*
          ii *It is quite obvious that it would be a mistake for him to resign now*

where, in (ii), the subjects of both the main clause and the finite subordinate clause are extraposed; where both layers of embedding are of the same kind, the version without any extraposition at all is scarcely acceptable: *?*That that he was angry was so obvious embarrassed her*. In examples like *It is assumed that he was trapped inside the mine*, extraposition allows us to achieve one result of passivisation (we avoid saying who is making the assumption) without as it were paying the normal price of having the *that* clause in subject position.

A second thematic factor relevant to the choice between the unmarked and extraposed constructions is that a context where the content of an embedded finite clause or infinitival is given may favour the unmarked construction. For example, in a context where it is given that a certain signature is, or might be, a forgery, we might prefer *That it might be a forgery was suggested several years ago by my uncle* over *It was suggested several years ago by my uncle that it might be a forgery*. There is of course no absolute correspondence between given and non-extraposed, new and extraposed, but there does appear to be some measure of correlation between them. Notice in this connection that with the verbs **appear**, **seem**, **chance** and **happen**, mentioned above as taking obligatory extraposition, the content of the extraposed clause will never be fully given.

14.4 Thematic reordering

Most elements of clause structure, certainly the more nuclear elements, have an 'unmarked' position – the position they occupy in kernel clauses. Departures from the unmarked order may be triggered by the selection of marked clause type, such as interrogative, or by various kinds of subordination, as in relative clauses, where the *wh* phrase comes first, irrespective of its function. There are other departures from the basic order that are motivated solely by thematic factors: in this section we will survey briefly a number of these, proposing various transformations that move an element from an unmarked to a marked position.

14.4.1 Thematic fronting

Here some element is moved to the front of the clause, into pre-subject position:

(14)   i   *The revised edition I haven't yet read*
         ii [*His humility must have been been invented by the ad man,*] *for humble, Mr Brown is not*
         iii *With this model you could do it a lot more quickly*

The fronted element may be a complement – object, as in (i), PC, as in (ii), or various other kinds; or an adjunct, as in (iii); or it can be just part of a clause element: part of a PP (*The others we're still looking into*) or part of an embedded clause (*The others I told him he could keep*). It can also be a sequence that – on the analysis we have adopted – does not form a constituent: a main verb plus its complements but less its auxiliaries ([*I promised to finish it*] *and finish it I shall*).

Thematic fronting may be accompanied by the displacement of the subject to post-operator position or to post-VP, generally clause-final, position (§4.2 below):

(15)   i   *Only then did I realise my mistake*
         ii *More important had been the moral objections*

The effect of thematic fronting is to assign greater prominence to the element concerned than it would typically have in an unmarked construction. The rule is commonly called 'topicalisation' and in many cases, certainly, the fronted element can be thought of as corresponding to the topic: it is very plausible to interpret (14i) as being about the revised edition, (iii) as being about 'this' model and perhaps even (ii) as being about the property 'humble'. But just as there is no one-to-one correlation between subject and topic, so there is none between initial element and topic. It doesn't seem to me at all plausible to suggest that the difference between (15ii) and the thematically unmarked *The moral objections had been more important* is that I would use the latter to say something about the moral objections while I would use (ii) to say something about the concept 'greater importance' or even, necessarily, about what is more important – the fronting of *more important* cannot be considered in isolation from the postponement of *the moral objections*, which serves to bring the latter into a position of greater phonological prominence.

Thematic fronting very often, though not invariably, serves as a cohesive device, linking the clause to the preceding (or sometimes following) one. One fairly common special case is that where we have a contrast between the clauses: the contrastive item may then be fronted in the second or in both clauses. (14i) and (iii) would most likely be of this kind. An example where both clauses have contrastive thematic fronting might be *This morning he was too ill to go to school but now he's well enough to go and play football* – where again an account in terms of topic seems very questionable. Is the first clause about 'this morning', the second about 'now'? I would prefer to say that the fronting serves simply to highlight the contrast between the two clauses. Where the fronted element is not contrastive, the cohesive effect will generally be due to anaphora: *then* in (15i) is straightforwardly anaphoric, while in (15ii) *more important* is implicitly anaphoric, for we understand it as "more important than x" with the value of x being derivable from the preceding text.

There are obvious similarities between the thematic effect of fronting and that of passivisation – compare, for example, *This question we will take up in Chapter 5* and *This question will be taken up in Chapter 5*. Thematic fronting applies to a wider range of elements than passivisation, where only NPs, generally objects, can be made subject. On the other hand it is more restricted than passivisation with respect to the kind of clause in which it can apply. It occurs most freely in declarative main clauses; in subordinate or non-declarative clauses it may be restricted to non-nuclear elements. Thus *The revised edition have you read?* is much less natural than (14i) and arguably ungrammatical, and similarly we shall reject *They deplored the fact that the revised edition he hadn't yet read*. In general, fronting is more acceptable in subordinate clauses when their content is part of the new information that the speaker is asserting, suggesting or the like, so that *I suspect that the revised edition he hasn't yet read*, say, sounds appreciably better than the last example.

14.4.2   *Thematic postponement*

Here an element is moved to the right of its basic position, rather than to the left. The main cases are as follows:

(a) Postponement of the subject. This is illustrated in (15), where the subject follows the operator or the VP. If the VP consists of just a main verb belonging to the operator class – i.e. a form of *be* or, under the conditions given in 4.4, of ***have*** – the distinction between post-operator and post-VP position is not immediately obvious, but is nevertheless easy to draw on the basis of a comparison with two-word VPs. Thus *At no time was she really happy* has the subject in post-operator position (compare *At no time had she been really happy*) while *More important are the moral objections* is like (15ii).

Postponement of subject to post-operator position is obligatorily triggered by the thematic fronting of certain types of element (see 13.1) or by the omission, with certain kinds of VP, of the conjunction in a conditional clause (*If I had known / Had I known, I would have gone too*). As it is not an independently variable aspect of structure, we cannot attribute any thematic effect specifically to it.

Postponement to post-VP position likewise generally accompanies thematic fronting – typically of a predicative complement, as above, or a locative, as in *Over the hill appeared a convoy of enemy troops, Away ran the dog*, and so on.[4] It is not, however, an obligatory accompaniment of such fronting: cf. *Over the hill a convoy of enemy troops appeared*, and also (14ii), which illustrates the fronting of PC without subject postponement. The effect of the postponement is to give greater prominence to the subject than it would have if it were sandwiched between the fronted element and the VP, or to put it another way, to give greater prominence to the subject than to the VP (it occurs with a quite small set of verbs: of position or motion with rather general meanings, e.g. ***be***, ***come***, ***go***, ***stand***, ***lie***, etc.). Thus it doesn't occur in (14ii) because the element that needs to attract the main stress there is *not*; similarly it is virtually impossible if the subject is a personal pronoun, whose referent will be given – compare the above with *Away he ran*. Often the subject will be the locus of new information – and hence in an example like *Closely related to the latter are certain species found in Indonesia*, with the fronted PC containing the anaphorically cohesive *the latter*, the reversal of the syntactically basic order yields the informationally unmarked order of given followed by new.

(b) Postponement of an object:

(16)   i *He considers quite stupid anyone who doesn't immediately grasp his most abstruse ideas*
           ii *They brought in the second suspect*

---

[4] It also occurs in parenthetic reporting clauses: '*It was*', *observed her father*, '*a simple case of mistaken identity*'.

An object may be moved to final position over various kinds of complement or adjunct. The main principle operating here is that which places heavy elements at the end: it is generally only long and complex objects that are postponed. Shorter phrases can be moved over a 'particle' complement, as in (16ii) – which we take to derive from *They brought the second suspect in* (see 5.5) – but even here there are restrictions: a personal pronoun cannot be so moved unless it is contrastively stressed.

(c) Postponement of part of a phrase:

(17) i *The fact remains that you stole it*
      ii *A difficulty arose that no one had foreseen*

Here the content clause complement of *fact* and the relative clause modifier of *difficulty* are moved to final position: again this moves heavy material to the end, and in so doing it avoids ending the clause with a short predicate of relatively little information value. We will not look in detail at the way phrases can be broken up in this way.

14.5   Subject–complement switch in the identifying construction

Compare the following pairs of thematic variants:

(18) i *The key he'd been looking for was inside the clock*
      ii *Inside the clock was the key he'd been looking for*
(19) i *The best place for it was inside the clock*
      ii *Inside the clock was the best place for it*

The first pair illustrates the thematic reordering that we have been considering: (i) represents the unmarked variant, while (ii) derives by fronting the locative complement and moving the subject to post-VP position. (19) may at first glance appear to be the same, but in fact the structural relationship is quite different. This can be seen by looking at the non-*wh* interrogative versions. (18ii) has no direct interrogative counterpart because the kind of thematic reordering it exhibits is restricted to declaratives: the only interrogative for (18) is thus *Was the key he was looking for inside the clock?*, which corresponds to (i). But for (19) there are two interrogatives: *Was the best place for it inside the clock?*, corresponding to (i), and *Was inside the clock the best place for it?*, corresponding to (ii). This shows that (19ii) does not derive from (i) by a reordering of the functions: there is a reassignment of functions, with *inside the clock* taking over as subject (see 2.2.2). Correlating with the syntactic difference is a semantic one. (18i) gives the location of the key, whereas (19i) IDENTIFIES the best place: I could use (18i) to give the answer to a question expressed by an interrogative with *where*, *Where was the key he'd been looking for?*, whereas for (19i) *what* would be an alternative to *where*: *What was the best place for it?*. Note also that while (19i) and (ii) could be negated with equal freedom, in (18) there is a sharp

457

difference, with (ii) virtually impossible to negate (except perhaps under conditions of contrast between the key and something else); more particularly we can say *Inside the clock wasn't the best place for it: it was perhaps the worst place*, with the second *it* anaphoric to *inside the clock*, but there is no matching construction for (18ii).

We will call (19) the identifying construction, with *the best place for it* associated with the semantic role 'identified term', *inside the clock* with the role 'identifier'. The main stress will normally be associated with the identifier, generally the locus of new information; we will accordingly regard (i) as the thematically basic or unmarked version, with (ii) deriving from it by switching the syntactic functions of subject and complement. The expression referring to the identified term is always an NP, whereas we find considerable variety in what can express the identifier. It can be a PP, as in (19); a content clause, as in *The point I want to emphasise is that they went separately* (declarative) or *The question we should focus on is how he got out* (interrogative); an AdvP, as in *The only way to proceed in such cases is very cautiously*, and so on – or, the most usual case, another NP. Contrasting pairs like (18) and (19) can thus be constructed with an NP rather than PP complement:

(20) i *James Bacharach was a thorough rogue*
  ii *A thorough rogue was James Bacharach*
(21) i *The second victim was a postgraduate student from King's College*
  ii *A postgraduate student from King's College was the second victim*

The issue is complicated by the fact that where both subject and complement are NPs there is very considerable potential for ambiguity between identifying and non-identifying uses of **be**. For example, *Hydrogen is the most abundant element in the universe* could be used to identify the most abundant element in the universe (answering the explicit or implicit question "What is the most abundant element in the universe?"), or it could simply be used to give a property of hydrogen. However, (20) hardly lends itself to an identifying interpretation, while that is probably the most salient interpretation for (21). Thus in (20) we would normally be saying what sort of a person Bacharach was, not identifying who he was, and with this understanding (ii) derives from (i) by thematic reordering and like (18ii) has no direct non-*wh* interrogative counterpart; with (21) we would be identifying the second victim and both versions have interrogative counterparts.[5]

---

[5] A further respect in which the rules of syntax are sensitive to the contrast between identifying and non-identifying **be** constructions concerns extrapositions: we noted in §3 above that a clause cannot be extraposed over a PC with identifying role (*That he knew her was the important point* cannot be transformed to **It was the important point that he knew her*) but it can be over a PC in a non-identifying clause (*That he knew her was a coincidence* → *It was a coincidence that he knew her*).

I will not pursue the matter of the range of interpretations of clauses containing the main verb **be**, which is a good deal more complex than might be suggested by the few examples given here. I have nevertheless thought it worth introducing the distinction between identifying and non-identifying **be** partly because the former is crucially involved in the 'cleft' constructions we shall be dealing with in the next section, partly because the contrast in our analyses of (18) and (19) clearly illustrates the structural methodology described in Ch. 2: it is worth noting that traditional grammars do not recognise the distinction.

14.6   The cleft and pseudo-cleft constructions

These constructions are illustrated in (22ii) and (iii) respectively, thematic variants of the non-cleft clause (i):

(22)   i *A faulty switch caused the trouble*
         ii *It was a faulty switch that caused the trouble*
       iii *What caused the trouble was a faulty switch*

What is a single unit (a clause) in (i) is divided up into two distinct parts (assigned to different clauses) in (ii) and (iii) – hence the term 'cleft'. (Why (iii) is called a 'pseudo'-cleft will be explained below.) One of the two parts is put in a superordinate clause, the other in a subordinate clause, more particularly a relative clause; the general effect is to give added prominence to the former – *a faulty switch* in our examples – and we will refer to it informally as 'the highlighted element'. We will look in turn at the syntax of the cleft and pseudo-cleft constructions, and then compare them briefly with respect to their thematic meaning.

14.6.1   The cleft construction

Here the highlighted element is complement of the verb **be**, with *it* the subject. The relative clause can be of either the non-*wh* class, as in (22ii), or the *wh* class, as in *It was John who did it*. The relative clause thus contains a relative element – ∅ in the first case, a *wh* phrase in the second – having the same function as the highlighted element in the non-cleft version. Thus in (22ii) ∅ is subject, as is *a faulty switch* in (22i), and similarly in *It was John who did it* the *who* is subject, as is *John* in the corresponding non-cleft *John did it*. The range of syntactic functions that can be occupied by the relative element is somewhat greater than in other relative constructions. It can be subject, direct object, complement of a preposition, neutral PP complement, complement or adjunct of time or place, various other kinds of adjunct – or, under conditions that we cannot here go into, any of the above from an embedded finite or non-finite construction. A selection of examples is given in (23):

(23)	i *It is Tom who is responsible*	Subject
	ii *It is Tom I blame*	Direct object
	iii *It was Ed that she was referring to*	Comp. of prep.
	iv *It was to Ed that she was referring*	Neutral PP comp.
	v *It is tomorrow that he's coming*	Time adjunct
	vi *It is tomorrow that she says he's coming*	Time adjunct within embedded clause
	vii *It is because he lied that he was dismissed*	Reason adjunct

However, the relative element cannot readily occur in predicative complement function (**It was highly inconsiderate/a lawyer that he was*) nor, as in other relative constructions, an indirect object (**It was Liz I bought the flowers*). Except where the *wh* word is *who* (and perhaps *whose* and *whom*), there is a fairly strong preference for the non-*wh* class of relative. The *wh* word cannot, or can scarcely, follow a preposition or longer sequence: we would use (23iii) or (iv) rather than *?It was Ed to whom she was referring*. In the non-*wh* class the *that* can be omitted even when the relative element ∅ is subject, at least in informal styles: *It was Tom did it*. Where a case-variable pronoun is the highlighted element, it may appear in the nominative or accusative form. We have noted that one factor influencing the choice of case is style, with nominative more formal than accusative; another relevant factor, for some speakers, is the function of the relative element – if **Tom** were replaced by **he** in the above, for example, one might use *he* in (i) but *him* in (ii).

All the examples given so far have consisted of *it* + *is/was* + the highlighted element + the relative clause: there are, however, a number of other possibilities. In deriving a cleft from a non-cleft we have a choice, with certain non-highlighted elements, between putting them in the superordinate clause and putting them in the subordinate clause; compare, for example, *It is usually Tom who mows the lawn* and *It is Tom who usually mows the lawn*. Apart from a few kinds of adjunct like *usually*, the main cases where we have this choice involve modal auxiliaries, perhaps with an associated perfect, and negatives: *It'll be Tom who wins/It's Tom who'll win*; *It wasn't Ed who read it/It was Ed who didn't read it*; we will return briefly to this choice in the discussion of the semantics. Notice, in addition, that the superordinate clause exhibits some of the syntagmatic and paradigmatic variation of ordinary clauses. Thus it can be subordinated (*I'll be surprised if it was Ed who wrote it*) or made interrogative or exclamative (*Was it you who did it?*; *What an excellent idea it was that she put forward!*); the complement can be thematically fronted (*John it was who broke it*); and so on.

Let us consider now the structure of the cleft construction. If we look for an analysis in terms of categories that have already been established on independent grounds, the most plausible is to take the subordinate clause as a restrictive relative clause functioning as postponed modifier to *it*, with the superordinate clause belonging to the identifying **be** construction. Thus in (22ii) the 'discontinuous' NP *it + that caused the trouble* would be associated with the identified role and the highlighted NP *a faulty switch* with the identifier role. A rough semantic analysis deriving quite straight-forwardly from this structure would be "The x (such that) x caused the trouble was (identifiable as) a faulty switch". We have already seen that a restrictive relative clause can be postponed – see (17ii) above: the cleft construction would thus be special only by virtue of the postponement here being obligatory. On the assumption that the subordinate clause is a re-strictive modifier, there are two reasons for saying that it modifies *it* rather than the highlighted element. In the first place it can occur with a proper noun unaccompanied by any determiner, as in (23i–iii): such expressions, we have noted (12.4.3), cannot take restrictive modifiers. Secondly, we need to account for the ambiguity of examples like

(24)   *It was the vase that Agatha gave us*

In one interpretation (with the main stress normally falling on *vase*) this is the cleft counterpart – thus a thematic variant – of *Agatha gave us the vase*. In a second interpretation (with the main stress typically on *Agatha*) *it* will refer anaphorically or deictically to some vase, which is identified as the one Agatha gave us – compare *The vase you broke was the vase that Agatha gave us*. It is in this second interpretation that the relative clause modifies *vase*: it serves to give defining information about it in the way discussed in 6.7 and 12.4. But this is not the role of the relative in the cleft construction: here the description *vase* is presented as sufficient to pick out the referent, just as in the non-cleft version.

The postponed restrictive relative analysis is adopted by a number of writers in this area, but it is open to objection on two counts.

(a) The first stems from the fact that there is only partial overlap between the subordinate clauses of the cleft construction and ordinary restrictive relatives. The problem lies not in the somewhat narrower range of *wh* relatives but in the significantly wider range of non-*wh* relatives – examples like (23iv) and (vii) or *It was out of sheer malice that he did it*, and so on. The structure proposed for (22ii) cannot be readily extended to these: it is not easy, to say the least, to make sense of an analysis like '*It + that she was referring* ("the x such that she was referring x") *was* ("was identifiable as") *to Ed*'.[6]

(b) The second objection is that the analysis does not account for the agreement properties of the verb in the relative clause. In *It's her parents who*

---

[6] Notice in passing that examples like these provide some further support for the suggestion that in the non-*wh* type of relative the *that* is better treated as a subordinating conjunction than as a relative pronoun, or anaphor (cf. 12.4.2): what kind of anaphor would *that* be here?

are to blame and *It is I who am to blame*, for example, the verb clearly agrees with *her parents* and *I* respectively, not with *it*.[7]

These points require us, I believe, to abandon the assumption that the relative clause functions as a restrictive modifier within NP structure. The alternative is to regard the cleft construction as exhibiting the non-embedded kind of subordination (12.1), with the immediate constituents of (22ii) thus *it was a faulty switch* and *that caused the trouble*. The antecedent for the relative element is the highlighted element, but the relative clause does not form a constituent with its antecedent. This avoids the difficulties encountered by the first analysis, but it is very largely ad hoc – the relative clause is of a kind that is sui generis, unique to this construction, while the *it* and **be** of the superordinate clause are treated as fully grammaticalised features of the construction whose contribution to the meaning is not directly predictable from their use in other kinds of clause. The construction is thus described indirectly, in terms of the non-cleft counterpart in conjunction with the cleaving operation.

We have so far considered only cases where what follows the highlighted element is a relative clause, but it can also be a non-finite construction with an *-ing* class VP, perhaps an *-en* class: *It was John causing all the trouble, It was Max caught trying to force open the door*. There are several other places where a relative clause is in paradigmatic opposition with a non-finite in this way (compare *I didn't know the guy who was causing all the trouble* and *I didn't know the guy causing all the trouble*), and we need not pursue the non-finite class further here.

14.6.2   The 'pseudo-cleft' construction

The pseudo-cleft construction, by contrast, can be described directly in terms of categories established independently and – as we shall see – is more appropriately so described than in terms of a cleaving operation performed on a more elementary clause. This provides the justification for the terminological distinction between 'cleft' and 'pseudo-cleft': in spite of the similarities between them, only the former is satisfactorily described in terms of cleaving.

The pseudo-cleft is a special case of the identifying **be** construction – the case where the identified role is associated with a fused relative construction. As in a prototypical identifying **be** clause, we can reverse the subject and complement to give, as a variant of (22iii), *A faulty switch was what caused the trouble*. Following the analysis of §5, we will refer to the construction where the fused relative is subject as the basic pseudo-cleft, and to that where it is complement as the reversed pseudo-cleft.

---

[7] An informal variant of the second example, however, is *It's me who is to blame*. There is some similarity here to the agreement pattern in the *there* construction (2.2.2).

It may be helpful at this point to contrast the pseudo-cleft with certain superficially similar constructions:

(25) i *What he wanted was unclear*
     ii *What he wanted was unobtainable*
    iii *The evening was what I would regard as a partial success*
    iv *The easiest such object to analyse is what we shall call a 'rigid body'*

The subject of (i) is an interrogative clause, not a fused relative: recall the distinction drawn in 12.4.5. In (ii) *what he wanted* is a fused relative, but *be* is not here used in its identifying sense. In (iii) the fused relative is complement rather than subject but otherwise it is like (ii) in that *be* is not identifying – the sentence would not be used to identify the evening but to describe it; note that in neither (ii) nor (iii) can subject and complement be reversed, in the sense of §5. Finally in (iv) *be* does have the identifying sense and *what we shall call a 'rigid body'* is again a fused relative, but it is associated (at least in the more salient and natural interpretation) with the identifier rather than the identified role – it is the easiest object of the relevant kind to analyse, not the thing that we shall call a 'rigid body', that is being identified, i.e. the implicit question that is being answered is "What is the easiest such object to analyse?", not "What shall we call a 'rigid body'?". Many sentences will be ambiguous between two or more of these constructions, and the reader is advised to treat the analysis of complex sentences containing *what* with some caution.

Let us now consider briefly the kinds of function that the relative element can have in the pseudo-cleft construction and the kinds of element that can occur as complement of identifying *be* (or subject, in the reversed version). The simplest case has the relative element as subject, object or complement of a preposition, with a non-human NP as complement of *be*: *What annoyed me was the delay, What she needs is a complete rest, What he's looking for is a small bungalow*. Unlike the cleft construction, the pseudo-cleft readily takes a finite clause as complement: *What annoyed me was that she was so slow, What he said was that it was illegal, What I object to in the proposal is that it makes no provision for serious consultation*. Conversely, only the cleft readily allows a human NP as complement – because the fused relative does not normally allow *who*: compare *It was Max who wrote it* and **Who wrote it was Max*. There are two cases where we can have a human NP. In the reversed pseudo-cleft, *who* (more specifically, *who*) is possible, generally when the subject is *that*: *That's who I meant*. And we can have a human NP used non-referentially, where the fused relative has *what* and the relative element as predicative complement: *What your brother is is an unmitigated scoundrel*. One frequent kind of pseudo-cleft involves relativising the complement of *do*: *What John had done was (to) obtain the data, What they were doing to the poor creatures was pulling their feathers out*; the complement in such cases is a non-finite construction, of the *-ing* class if *do* is in the *-ing* form, otherwise infinitival. There is of course no analogous cleft construction: **It was (to) obtain the data that John had done*.

In our original example, *What caused the trouble was a faulty switch*, we could easily devise a transformation which would straightforwardly derive the pseudo-cleft from the non-cleft *A faulty switch caused the trouble* – and it would generalise to most of the other examples given also. Those with *do* would require some special provision, for we would want the source to be, not **John had done obtain the data*, but *John had obtained the data*: the transformation would be required to insert *do* when the main verb is part of the highlighted element. But there are many cases where there is no non-cleft counterpart to serve as source. One has already been given: *What I object to in the proposal is that it makes no provision for serious consultation*; cf. also *What went wrong was that the valve overheated, What is unique about milk is its richness in minerals and vitamins*, and so on. These are not like the examples of (25): they are all instances of the construction with identifying *be* and the fused relative associated with the identified term. Such examples provide a strong reason for describing this latter construction directly rather than in terms of a transformational derivation from a non-cleft source. A second reason is that the direct description enables us to relate the pseudo-cleft to other cases of the identifying *be* construction. Compare, for example, *What I need is another hour* and *All I need is another hour*: where the former has a fused relative, the latter has *all* plus a restrictive relative; there is no plausible way of deriving the latter by cleaving, and thus deriving the former in such a way would mean giving them quite different treatments. The pseudo-cleft is thus appropriately so called: although it appears to be similar to the cleft construction proper, it cannot be satisfactorily derived in an analogous way by cleaving a more elementary clause. (22iii) may still be regarded, semantically, as a thematic variant of (i), but the suggestion is that while (i) and (ii) are syntactically related as opposing terms in a system, (i) and (iii) are not.

14.6.3 The thematic meaning of the cleft and pseudo-cleft constructions

We will not attempt a detailed account of the semantics of these constructions, but will simply draw attention to some of their main uses. For the cleft construction we will distinguish two. In the first the content of the relative clause is given, while the new information is associated with the highlighted element, which carries the main stress. For example, *It was Ed who broke it* is likely to be used in a context where it is given that someone broke it (the window, say) and the new information is that the someone was Ed. In this use the superordinate clause selects freely for polarity, so that we might have instead *It wasn't Ed who broke it*: again it is given that someone broke it, while the new information is negative – the someone wasn't Ed. We earlier contrasted *It wasn't Ed who read it*, which is just like this last example, and *It was Ed who didn't read it*, where the negative is part of the given information, namely that someone didn't read it. When the information in the relative clause has been established as given more or less immediately before, the relative can be ellipted: ⟨A⟩ *Who broke it?* – ⟨B⟩ *I don't know, but it wasn't me (who broke it)*.

However, the content of the relative clause is by no means always given. Thus in *It is only since he died that she has come to appreciate the importance of what he was trying to achieve*, it is likely that the relative clause will contain new information. Where this is so, the superordinate clause will not normally be negative, though negation is possible under certain conditions when there is an easily derivable positive implication, as in *It wasn't until he died that she came to appreciate* ..., which implies *It was when he died that she came to appreciate* .... Although the information contained in the relative clause is new, the fact that it is expressed in a subordinate rather than a main clause means that it is presented as something which is not at issue, something on which doubt or disagreement is not countenanced.[8] In the above, for example, what is at issue is not whether she has come to appreciate the importance of what he was trying to achieve, but merely when. Of course, the information expressed in the relative clause is presented as being not at issue in the first use of the cleft construction – there it is not at issue because it is given; what the second use shows is that it doesn't have to be given to be presented in this way.

When the information in the relative clause is new, the highlighted element will often be anaphoric or its referent otherwise given, especially when the relative element is a part of the nucleus, rather than an adjunct of time, place or the like. Thus *It was my brother who was largely responsible for the improvements in the company's security arrangements over the next two years* is unlikely to be used with the content of the relative clause new, unless there has been previous mention of my brother; in this case my brother would rather clearly be the topic and the cleaving would also have a cohesive effect similar to that achieved by thematic fronting (though the latter is of course not possible with subjects) – see §4 above.

Consider now the pseudo-cleft. The content of the relative clause is again presented as not being at issue. It may be given (⟨A⟩ *He said it was impossible, didn't he?* – ⟨B⟩ *Well not quite: what he said was that it was illegal*), but doesn't have to be, and in the majority of cases probably is not given in

---

[8] It is a slight oversimplification to relate this to the subordinate nature of the clause, for although subordinate clauses typically have this property there are certain cases where they don't. For example with *I think he'll reject it* the issue would generally be whether he'll reject it, with *I think* serving to qualify my commitment to the proposition that he will; these are the cases referred to in §4 as accepting thematic fronting more readily than the general run of subordinate clauses.

the strict sense. However, the kind of non-given information that we get in the relative clause of the basic pseudo-cleft is somewhat different from that in the cleft construction – it is very much lower in communicative significance, in 'communicative dynamism' as the Prague School linguists would put it. Suppose, for example, that after some energetic exercise I say *What I need now is a long cool drink*: that I need something is not given in the sense of having been mentioned or established, but it is very easy to accept and hence is presented, in the thematic organisation of the message, as subordinate to the identification of the thing needed. I would be unlikely to say *It's a long cool drink that I need* if it were not given that I need something. Or again I might say *What worries me is that he may not have sufficient will-power to carry it through* without it being given that something worries me: the fact that something worries me is nevertheless presented as being of minor significance in relation to the cause of the worry (and note that the content of the highlighted element is such that it is easy to accept it as a source of worry). The same considerations apply to the earlier examples, *What annoyed me was that she was so slow, What I object to in the proposal is that it makes no provision for serious consultation*, and so on. This difference between the basic pseudo-cleft and the cleft is related to the linear sequence of elements. In the former, the fused relative comes first and the construction thus conforms to the general tendency for communicatively more important elements to come later. In the cleft construction the highlighted element comes before the relative clause, and when the latter does not express given information it is thus also in conformity with this general tendency that it should be communicatively more significant than the fused relative. And notice that in the reversed pseudo-cleft the fused relative may contain more significant material. For example, in the English translation of Ibsen's *A Doll's House* Nora announces to her husband in the last act that she is leaving him with the words *That's why I'm leaving you*; that she is leaving him is clearly the major information, but as it is encoded within the fused relative it is presented – in accordance with what we said above – as information that is not at issue: it is settled, non-negotiable.

A further difference between the pseudo-cleft and the cleft is related to the fact that the fused relative is an NP, while the relative in the cleft construction is neither an NP nor part of one. NPs are well suited to picking out topics especially when, as in the basic pseudo-cleft, they come first in the clause. Thus the basic pseudo-cleft lends itself readily to interpretation as being about the referent of the fused relative, whereas the cleft lends itself more to an interpretation where it is about the referent of the highlighted element, especially in the second of the uses mentioned above.

One final point is that both cleft and pseudo-cleft contain a definite NP – *it* and the fused relative – which introduces a component of uniqueness or exhaustiveness that will be lacking or merely pragmatically implied in the corresponding non-cleft. For example, *It was Ed who didn't read it,* unlike *Ed didn't read it,* implies that only Ed didn't read it, and we have the same difference between *What they found in the safe was the unfinished manuscript of a novel* and *They found the unfinished manuscript of a novel in the safe.*

14.7 The *there* construction

The final kind of thematic variation we shall consider is exemplified in

(26)   i *A couple of Alsatians were in the garden*
        ii *There were a couple of Alsatians in the garden*

We take (i) as the syntactically unmarked member of the pair, structurally more elementary than (ii). (ii) is then commonly analysed as deriving transformationally from (i): we move the subject (*a couple of Alsatians*) to the right of the VP and insert *there* as a 'dummy' subject in its place. (See 2.2.2 for justification for analysing *there* as subject of (ii) – and for the distinction between the locative adverb *there* and dummy *there,* which we subsequently suggested is a pronoun; in this section, we shall be concerned solely with dummy *there.*)

There is a considerable variety of clause constructions containing pronominal *there* as subject; we will begin with what may be regarded as the most central kind, illustrated in (26ii), and then introduce some of the others in turn.

(a) The central case: *be* + locative. Our central *there* clause has *be* as main verb and a locative complement. Not all clauses containing *be* + locative allow the two variants illustrated in (26) – both are subject to certain restrictions, though they cannot be stated in purely syntactic terms. In the first place, the post-verbal NP in the *there* construction cannot normally be definite. For example, if we replace indefinite *a couple of Alsatians* by definite *Fido and Rex,* (26ii) becomes much less natural and acceptable. Definites are not excluded altogether, but seem to occur only in listing or answering implicit or explicit *there* questions: ⟨A⟩ *What's on at the cinema this week?* – ⟨B⟩ *Well, there's 'My Fair Lady' at the Odeon and 'Goldfinger' at the Regal;* ⟨A⟩ *Was there anyone you knew at the meeting?* – ⟨B⟩ *Yes, there was Harry* ("at the meeting"). In fact the restriction applies equally to certain kinds of indefinites: compare *There were many/some/three professors on the Board* with ?* *There were all/most professors on the Board.*[9] *Many, some, three,* etc. are concerned with number (or 'cardinality'), *all, most* and the like with proportion, and definiteness may be subsumed under this second kind of quantification inasmuch as *the chairs,* say, is interpreted roughly as "all things (in the context

---

[9] The version with *all* is acceptable to some speakers with *all* construed as "only", rather than determiner in NP structure.

of discourse) satisfying the description 'chair'". With mass NPs, the analogue of number is amount, which likewise contrasts with proportion, so that *There was some sugar on the floor* is perfectly acceptable, while *?*There was most of the sugar on the floor* is not.

In the second place, under certain conditions only the *there* version is acceptable: *There was an accident at the factory* but not *An accident was at the factory*, *There's a mistake in the last line* but not *A mistake is in the last line*. In the first pair *be* means "occur, take place", and with this meaning the *there* construction is always mandatory. The second pair is less easy to distinguish from (26). One very promising hypothesis that has been proposed is that *there* is required unless the clause describes a scene having 'visual impact' – clearly a pragmatic rather than a syntactic concept.

Consider now the thematic motivation for the *there* construction. What it does is to place in postverbal position an NP which would otherwise be subject; the NP concerned will normally be associated with a referent that is new rather than given – this follows from the above constraints on the permitted kinds of NP – and the construction thus fits in better with the general tendency for new material to be introduced later rather than earlier within the linear progression of the clause. Very often *there* is used to introduce new entities into the universe of discourse.

(b) *be* + predicative complement. A second construction is exemplified in *There were some non-members present*, corresponding to unmarked *Some non-members were present*. These differ from construction (a) above only in having a predicative complement instead of a locative. There are, however, severe constraints on the kind of PC that can occur: it normally denotes a state (*present, absent, eligible, ill, open, confused*, etc.) rather than a property (*tall, fat, intelligent, naïve, French* – or NPs like *a scientist, a genius*); compare *There were some people ill/*French*; *There was a door open/*wooden*.

(c) The 'bare' *there* construction. In our third case, there is no complement at all following the NP displaced by *there*: *There are many different kinds of jelly-fish*; *There's no such word as 'personhood'*. These have no counterparts without *there* (**Many different kinds of jelly-fish are*): in kernel clauses *be* can hardly constitute the whole of the predicate. We can again distinguish between the dynamic *be* ("occur, take place"), as in *There was an accident/a strike* and the static *be*; the latter can often be glossed as "exist" (as in the jelly-fish and 'personhood' examples) – but not always: cf. *There must be some mistake*. From a semantic point of view, some locative element will typically be implied – either quite particular (*There must be some mistake*: "here") or general (*There are many different kinds of jelly-fish*: "on earth"). The kinds of NP we find are thus in general like those in the central construction – but certain abstract NPs, with heads like *possibility, reason*, etc., perhaps occur here more readily with determiners like *the* or *every*, which we have noted are in general rare in the *there* construction: *There's always the possibility that he will refuse; There is every reason to think it'll work.*

(d) Verbs other than **be**. A small range of intransitive VPs can also occur in the *there* construction: *There remain many problems; There followed a long digression on dreams.* It is difficult to define precisely what kinds of intransitives can occur; a considerable number involve verbs of motion and here we find a restriction to verbs denoting arrival, appearance, rather than their opposites, departure, disappearance – compare *There appeared a giant oil-tanker on the horizon* and **There disappeared a giant oil-tanker over the horizon.* The VPs *remain, followed* and *appeared* are intransitive by virtue of having an intransitive verb as head, but we can also have VPs that are intransitive by virtue of being passive: *There are now being advertised as many as seven different brands of toothpaste on just this one channel.*

(e) **be** + NP + relative clause. Consider the following examples:

(27)   i *There are people that have an IQ far greater than that*
        ii *There was one man that kept interrupting*

The first can be handled quite straightforwardly under our construction (d): we simply have an NP containing a restrictive relative clause as modifier, so that (i) is analogous to, say, *There are far cleverer people than that.* But (ii) is arguably different in its structure; for some speakers at least the *that* can be omitted from (ii) but not (i), which suggests that (ii) is a kind of cleft construction (compare *It was John (that) kept interrupting*), and indeed it is a thematic variant of *One man kept interrupting.* There would seem to be a semantic distinction correlating with the syntactic one: (i) predicates existence of people of a certain type, while (ii) is, rather, descriptive of an event that took place. If this proposal is correct we shall have to recognise two subclasses of cleft construction, *it* clefts and *there* clefts, and to allow for another kind of transformational derivation of *there* clauses than that adopted for (a)–(d) above.

(f) **be** + NP + *-ing/-en* class non-finite. Here we have thematic variants like

(28)   i *Some students were playing cricket*
        ii *There were some students playing cricket*

– or, with an *-en* class non-finite, *Several people were killed* and *There were several people killed.* It is commonly assumed that (ii) derives from (i) by moving *some students* around the auxiliary **be** and replacing it as subject by *there* – in other words, by the same rule as applies in our central *there* construction, formulated so that the NP is moved around **be** independently of whether it is a main verb or an auxiliary. If the analysis suggested for

(27ii) is sound, however, then we can likewise handle (28ii) as a cleft construction – compare the *it* cleft *It was John causing all the trouble*, cited above. We would have two transformations involving *there*: one, applying in constructions (a)–(d), moves a subject NP around a VP (whose head may or may not be **be**) and inserts *there* as the new subject, the other, applying in (27ii) and (28ii), introduces both *there* and **be** in forming a cleft clause. Notice that (28ii) differs from (29) in a way which closely parallels the difference between (27ii) and (i):

(29)   *There were specimens measuring over twelve inches in length*

Like (27i) this belongs to construction (b), with *specimens measuring over twelve inches in length* constituting a single unit, an NP: (29) does not derive from *?Specimens were measuring over twelve inches in length*; semantically, (29) predicates existence of a certain type of specimen, whereas (28ii) is descriptive of an event in progress.

(g) **be** (etc.) + NP + infinitival. The final construction we will mention is illustrated in *There is/remains John to consider/to be considered*. Infinitivals of this form can function as modifier (*The next option to consider/to be considered involves combining the two offices into one*), but the fact that in our example they follow the proper name *John* shows that they cannot here have modifying function: *John to consider/to be considered* is not an NP. Just how the example should be analysed, however, remains unclear. It cannot belong to the *there* cleft constructions; perhaps it should be assimilated to constructions (c) and (d) above, with the infinitival an adjunct of some kind – but a kind unique, it would seem, to this construction.

FURTHER READING

On thematic systems generally, see Quirk et al. 1971: Ch. 14, Halliday 1967–68, 1984: Ch. 3, and for the semantic concepts involved, Lyons 1977: §12.7. On passives, see Freidin 1975, Langacker & Munro 1975, Davison 1980, Stein 1980 – and on the passive with a stranded preposition, Couper-Kuhlen 1979, Ziv & Sheintuch 1981. For the indirect object construction, see references to Ch. 5. In pairs like *That he was angry was obvious* and *It was obvious that he was angry* we have taken the former as unmarked with the latter derived by extraposition; an alternative analysis adopted by some writers is to take the second as unmarked with the first derived by 'intraposition': see Jackendoff 1977: §4.8. On the concepts 'given' and 'new', see Prince 1981a. On thematic fronting and the order of elements, see Firbas 1964, Prince 1981b; on the distributional restrictions on clauses with marked order, see Hooper & Thompson 1973. On the identification construction, see the above works of Halliday, and Lyons 1977: §12.2. On clefts and pseudo-clefts, see Gundel 1977, Prince 1978, Wirth 1978, Higgins 1979, Atlas & Levinson 1981. On the *there* construction, see Jenkins 1975, Erdmann 1976, Bolinger 1977: Ch. 5, Rando & Napoli 1978, Milsark 1977, 1979a, b, Breivik 1981.

References

Note: titles of journals and periodicals are abbreviated in accordance with the following conventions, taken (where available) from the permanent International Committee of Linguists' annual *Linguistic Bibliography* (The Hague: Martinus Nijhoff):

AJL	*Australian Journal of Linguistics*. University of Queensland: Australian Linguistic Society.
ArchL	*Archivum Linguisticum*. Menston: Scolar Press.
ES	*English Studies*. Amsterdam: Swets & Zeitlinger.
FL	*Foundations of Language*. Dordrecht: Reidel.
Glossa	*Glossa*. Simon Fraser University, British Columbia: Glossa Society.
JL	*Journal of Linguistics*. Cambridge: University Press (for the Linguistics Association of Great Britain).
LAn	*Linguistic Analysis*. New York: Elsevier.
Lg	*Language*. Baltimore: Waverly Press (for the Linguistic Society of America).
LIn	*Linguistic Inquiry*. Cambridge MA: MIT Press.
Lingua	*Lingua*. Amsterdam: North-Holland.
Linguistics	*Linguistics*. The Hague: Mouton.
LiS	*Language in Society*. Cambridge: University Press.
NS	*Die Neueren Sprachen*. Frankfurt: Diesterweg.
PBLS	*Proceedings of the Annual Meeting of the Berkeley Linguistics Society*. University of California: Berkeley Linguistics Society.
PCLS	*Papers from the Regional Meeting of the Chicago Linguistic Society*. University of Chicago: Chicago Linguistic Society.
SLang	*Studies in Language*. Amsterdam: Benjamins.
SynS	*Syntax and Semantics*. New York: Academic Press.
TLP	*Travaux Linguistiques de Prague*. Paris: Klincksieck.
TPhS	*Transactions of the Philological Society*. Oxford: Blackwell.

Adams, V. 1973. *An introduction to English word-formation*. London: Longman.
Akmajian, A. 1977. The complement structure of perception verbs in an autonomous syntax framework. In Culicover et al. 1977. 427–60.
Akmajian, A. & Lehrer, A. 1976. NP-like quantifiers and the problem of determining the head of an NP. *LAn* 2. 395–413.
Allan, K. 1976. Collectivising. *ArchL* 7. 99–117.
    1980. Nouns and countability. *Lg* 56. 541–67.
    1981. Interpreting from context. *Lingua* 53. 151–73.
Allerton, D. J. 1978. Generating indirect objects in English. *JL* 14. 21–34.
    1982. *Valency and the English verb*. London: Academic Press.
Atlas, J. D. & Levinson, S. C. 1981. *It*-clefts, informativeness and logical form: radical pragmatics (Revised Standard Version). In Cole. 1981. 1–61.

References

Bache, C. & Jakobsen, L. K. 1980. On the distinction between restrictive and non-restrictive relative clauses in Modern English. *Lingua* 52. 243–67.

Bodine, A. 1975. Androcentrism in prescriptive grammar. *LiS* 4. 129–46.

Bolinger, D. L. 1961. Syntactic blends and other matters. *Lg* 37. 366–81.

    1967a. The imperative in English. In *To Honor Roman Jakobson*. The Hague: Mouton. 335–63.

    1967b. Adjectives in English: attribution and predication. *Lingua* 18. 1–34.

    1977. *Meaning and form*. London: Longman.

Bowers, J. S. 1975. Adjectives and adverbs in English. *FL* 13. 529–62.

Breivik, L. E. 1981. On the interpretation of existential *there*. *Lg* 57. 1–25.

Bresnan, J. W. 1973. Syntax of the comparative clause construction in English. *LIn* 4. 275–343.

    1975. Comparative deletion and constraints on transformations. *LAn* 1. 25–74.

Bresnan, J. W. & Grimshaw, J. 1978. The syntax of free relatives in English. *LIn* 9. 331–91.

Burton-Roberts, N. 1975. Nominal apposition. *FL* 13. 391–419.

    1976. On the generic definite article. *Lg* 52. 427–48.

Carden, G. 1982. Backwards anaphora in discourse context. *JL* 18. 361–87.

Chafe, W. L. 1970. *Meaning and the structure of language*. Chicago: University of Chicago Press.

Chomsky, N. A. 1957. *Syntactic structures*. The Hague: Mouton.

Cole, P. (ed.) 1981. *Radical pragmatics*. New York: Academic Press.

Comrie, B. 1976. *Aspect*. Cambridge: University Press.

    1981. *Language universals and language typology*. Oxford: Blackwell.

    1982. Future time reference in the conditional protasis. *AJL* 2. 143–52.

Couper-Kuhlen, E. 1979. *The prepositional passive in English*. Tübingen: Niemeyer.

Crystal, D. 1967. Word classes in English. *Lingua* 17. 24–56.

Crystal, D. & Davy, D. 1969. *Investigating English style*. London: Longmans.

Culicover, P. W., Wasow, T. & Akmajian, A. (eds.) 1977. *Formal syntax*. New York: Academic Press.

Curme, G. O. 1931 *Syntax*. Boston: Heath.

    1935. *Parts of speech and accidence*. Boston: Heath.

    1947. *English grammar*. New York: Barnes & Noble.

Davison, A. 1980. Peculiar passives. *Lg* 56. 42–66.

DeArmond, R. C. 1977. On *decide on* and similar constructions in English. *Glossa* 11. 20–47.

Declerck, R. 1981. On the role of progressive aspect in non-finite perception verb complements. *Glossa* 15. 83–114.

Dik, S. C. 1968. *Coordination: its implications for the theory of general linguistics*. Amsterdam: North-Holland.

Dinsmore, J. 1981. Tense choice and time specification in English. *Linguistics* 19. 475–94.

Dixon, R. M. W. 1982. The grammar of English phrasal verbs. *AJL* 2. 1–42.

Dougherty, R. C. 1974. The syntax and semantics of *each other* constructions. *FL* 12. 1–47.

Dudman, V. H. 1983. Tense and time in English verb clusters of the primary pattern. *AJL* 3. 25–44.

Elliott, D. E. 1974. Toward a grammar of exclamations. *FL* 11. 231–46.

Erdmann, P. 1976. *'There' sentences in English: a relational study based on a corpus of written texts*. Munich: Tuduv.

Evans, G. 1980. Pronouns. *LIn* 11. 337–62.

Firbas, J. 1964. On defining theme in functional sentence analysis. *TLP* 1. 267–80.

Foley, W. A. & Van Valin, R. D. 1977. On the organisation of 'subject' properties in universal grammar. *PBLS* 3. 293–320.

Fowler, H. W. 1926. *A dictionary of modern English usage*. Oxford: Clarendon Press.

Freidin, R. 1975. The analysis of passives. *Lg* 51. 384–405.

Givón, T. 1978. Negation in language: pragmatics, function, ontology. *SynS* 9. 69–112.

References

Gleason, H. A. 1965. *Linguistics and English grammar*. New York: Holt, Rinehart & Winston.

Green, G. 1974. *Semantics and syntactic regularity*. Bloomington: Indiana University Press.

Greenbaum, S., Leech, G. & Svartvik, J. (eds.) 1980. *Studies in English linguistics for Randolph Quirk*. London: Longman.

Gundel, J. K. 1977. Where do cleft sentences come from? *Lg* 53. 543–59.

Halliday, M. A. K. 1967–68. Notes on transitivity and theme in English, Parts 1–3. *JL* 3. 37–81, 199–244 & 4. 179– 215.

1984. *A short introduction to functional grammar*. London: Arnold.

Halliday, M. A. K. & Hasan, R. 1976. *Cohesion in English*. London: Longman.

Hankamer, J. & Sag, I. 1976. Deep and surface anaphora. *LIn* 7. 391–428.

Hawkins, J. A. 1978. *Definiteness and indefiniteness: a study in reference and grammaticality prediction*. London: Croom Helm.

Hawkins, R. 1981. Towards an account of the possessive constructions *NP's N* and *the N of NP*. *JL* 17. 247–69.

Higgins, F. R. 1979. *The pseudo-cleft construction in English*. New York: Garland.

Hirschbühler, P. 1981. The ambiguity of iterated multiple questions. *LIn* 12. 135–46.

Hiż, H. (ed.) 1978. *Questions*. Dordrecht: Reidel.

Hooper, J. B. & Thompson, S. A. 1973. On the applicability of root transformations. *LIn* 4. 465–97.

Horn, G. M. 1975. On the non-sentential nature of the POSS-ING construction. *LAn* 1. 331–87.

Horn, L. R. 1978. Remarks on Neg-Raising. *SynS* 9. 129–220.

Huddleston, R. D. 1980. Criteria for auxiliaries and modals. In Greenbaum, Leech & Svartvik. 1980. 65–78.

Hudson, R. A. 1975. *The meaning of questions*. *Lg* 51. 1–31.

Hust, J. R. 1977. The syntax of the unpassive construction in English. *LAn* 3. 31–63.

Jackendoff, R. S. 1972. *Semantic interpretation in generative grammar*. Cambridge, MA: MIT Press.

1973. The base rules for prepositional phrases. In Anderson, S. & Kiparsky, P. (eds.), *A Festschrift for Morris Halle*. New York: Holt, Rinehart & Winston. 345–56.

1977. *X̄ syntax: a study of phrase structure*. Cambridge, MA: MIT Press.

Jenkins, L. 1975. *The English existential*. Tübingen: Niemeyer.

Jespersen, O. 1924. *The philosophy of grammar*. London: Allen & Unwin.

1909–49. *A Modern English grammar on historical principles*. Copenhagen: Munksgaard and London: Allen & Unwin.

Joos, M. 1964. *The English verb*. Madison: University of Wisconsin Press.

Kirsner, R. & Thompson, S. 1976. The role of pragmatic inference in semantics: a study of sensory verb complements in English. *Glossa* 10. 200–40.

Klima, E. S. 1964. Negation in English. In Fodor, J. A. & Katz, J. J. (eds.), *The structure of language: readings in the philosophy of language*. Englewood Cliffs, NJ: Prentice-Hall. 246–323.

Koster, J. & May, R. 1982. On the constituency of infinitives. *Lg* 58. 116–43.

Kruisinga, E. 1925. *A handbook of present-day English*. Utrecht: Kemink en Zoon.

Kuno, S. 1981. The syntax of comparative clauses. *PCLS* 17. 136–55.

Lakoff, R. 1969. Some reasons why there can't be any *some–any* rule. *Lg* 45. 608–15.

Langacker, R. W. 1974. The question of Q. *FL* 11. 1–37.

1978. The form and meaning of the English auxiliary. *Lg* 54. 853–82.

Langacker, R. W. & Munro, P. 1975. Passives and their meaning. *Lg* 51. 789–830.

Leech, G. N. 1971. *Meaning and the English verb*. London: Longman.

Li, C. N. (ed.) 1976. *Subject and topic*. New York: Academic Press.

Lightfoot, D. 1976 . The theoretical implications of subject raising. *FL* 14. 257–85.

Lyons, J. 1968. *Introduction to theoretical linguistics*. Cambridge: University Press.

1977. *Semantics*. Cambridge: University Press.

References

1981a. *Language, meaning and context*. London: Fontana.

1981b. *Language and linguistics*. Cambridge: University Press.

McCawley, J. D. 1981. The syntax and semantics of English relative clauses. *Lingua* 53. 99–149.

McCoard, R. W. 1978. *The English perfect: tense-choice and pragmatic inferences*. Amsterdam: North-Holland.

Makkai, A. 1972. *Idiom structure in English*. The Hague: Mouton.

Marchand, H. 1969. *The categories and types of present-day English word-formation*. (2nd edn) Munich: Beck.

Matthews, P. H. 1967. Word classes in Latin. *Lingua* 17. 153–81.

1974. *Morphology: an introduction to the theory of word-structure*. Cambridge: University Press.

1980. Complex intransitive constructions. In Greenbaum, Leech & Svartvik. 1980. 41–9.

1981. *Syntax*. Cambridge: University Press.

Milsark, G. L. 1977. Toward an explanation of certain peculiarities of the existential construction in English. *LAn* 3. 1–29.

1979a. *Existential sentences in English*. New York: Garland.

1979b. Review article on Jenkins 1975. *SLang* 3. 99–108.

Mufwene, S. S. 1981. Non-individuation and the count/mass distinction. *PCLS* 17. 221–38.

Mühlhaüsler, P. 1983. *Stinkiepoos, cuddles* and related matters. *AJL* 3. 75–91.

Nanni, D. L. 1980. On the surface syntax of constructions with *easy*-type adjectives. *Lg* 56. 568–81.

Palmer, F. R. 1971. *Grammar*. Harmondsworth: Penguin.

1974. *The English verb*. London: Longman.

1979. *Modality and the English modals*. London: Longman.

Perlmutter, D. 1980. Relational grammar. *SynS* 13. 195–229.

Peterson, P. G. 1981. Problems with constraints on coordination. *LAn* 8. 449–60.

Phythian, B. A. 1980. *English grammar*. (Teach Yourself Books.) London: Hodder & Stoughton.

Postal, P. M. 1974. *On raising: one rule of English grammar and its theoretical implications*. Cambridge, MA: MIT Press.

Poutsma, H. 1926–29. *A grammar of Late Modern English*. Groningen: Noordhoff.

Prince, E. F. 1978. A comparison of WH-clefts and *it*-clefts in discourse. *Lg* 54. 883–906.

1981a. Toward a taxonomy of given–new information. In Cole 1981. 223–55.

1981b. Topicalization, focus-movement and yiddish-movement: a pragmatic differentiation. *PBLS* 7. 249–64.

1982. The simple futurate: not simply progressive futurate minus progressive. *PCLS* 18. 453–65.

Quirk, R. 1965. Descriptive statement and serial relationship. *Lg* 41. 205–17. Reprinted in Quirk 1968. 167–83.

1968. *Essays on the English language: Medieval and Modern*. London: Longmans.

1978. Grammatical and pragmatic aspects of countability. *NS* 77. 317–25. Reprinted in Quirk, R., *Style and communication in the English Language*. London: Arnold, 1982. 110–20.

Quirk, R., Greenbaum, S., Leech, G. & Svartvik, J. 1971. *A grammar of contemporary English*. London: Longman.

Quirk, R. & Mulholland, J. 1964. Complex prepositions and related sequences. *ES* 45. 64–73. Reprinted in Quirk 1968. 148–60.

Rando, E. & Napoli, D. J. 1978. Definites in *there*-sentences. *Lg* 54. 300–13.

Reinhart, T. 1983. *Anaphora and semantic interpretation*. London: Croom Helm.

Sag, I. A. 1979. The nonunity of anaphora. *LIn* 10. 152–64.

Schachter, P. 1976. A nontransformational account of gerundive nominals in English. *LIn* 7. 205–41.

1977. Constraints on coordination. *Lg* 53. 86–103.

Scheurweghs, G. 1959. *Present-day English syntax: a survey of sentence patterns.* London: Longmans.

Searle, J. R. 1975a. Indirect speech acts. *SynS* 3. 59–82.

1975b. A classification of illocutionary acts. *LiS* 5. 1–23.

Selkirk, E. 1977. Some remarks on noun phrase structure. In Culicover et al. 1977. 285–316.

Silva, G. & Thompson, S. A. 1977. On the syntax and semantics of adjectives with 'it' subjects and infinitival complements in English. *SLang* 1. 109–26.

Smith, N. V. 1977. On generics. *TPhS* 1975. 27–48.

Smith, S. B. 1975. Meaning and negation. The Hague: Mouton.

Stein, G. 1980. *Studies in the function of the passive.* Tübingen: Narr.

Strang, B. M. H. 1968. *Modern English structure.* (2nd edn) London: Arnold.

Svartvik, J. 1966. *On voice in the English verb.* The Hague: Mouton.

Sweet, H. 1891–98. *A new English grammar.* Oxford: Clarendon Press.

Sweetser, E. E. 1982. Root and epistemic modals: causality in two worlds. *PBLS* 8. 484–507.

Tedeschi, P. J. & Zaenen, A. (eds.) 1981. *Tense and aspect* (= *SynS* 14).

Thompson, S. A. 1971. The deep structure of relative clauses. In Fillmore, C. J. & Langendoen, D. T. (eds.), *Studies in linguistic semantics.* New York: Holt, Rinehart & Winston. 79–84.

Trudgill, P. & Hannah, J. 1982. *International English: a guide to varieties of Standard English.* London: Arnold.

Van Oosten, J. 1977. On defining prepositions. *PBLS* 3. 454–64.

Vestergaard, T. 1977. *Prepositional phrases and prepositional verbs: a study in grammatical function.* The Hague: Mouton.

Visser, F. T. 1963–73. *An historical syntax of the English language.* Leiden: Brill.

Wasow, T. 1979. *Anaphora in generative grammar.* Ghent: Story-Scientia.

Wekker, H. C. 1976. *The expression of future time in contemporary British English: an investigation into the syntax and semantics of five verbal constructions expressing futurity.* Amsterdam: North-Holland.

Wierzbicka, A. 1980. *Lingua mentalis.* Sydney: Academic Press.

Wirth, J. R. 1978. The derivation of cleft sentences in English. *Glossa* 12. 58–82.

Woisetschlaeger, E. 1983. On the question of definiteness in 'an old man's book'. *LIn* 14. 137–54.

Wunderlich, D. 1981. Questions about questions. In Klein, W. & Levelt, W. (eds.), *Crossing the boundaries in linguistics: studies presented to Manfred Bierwisch.* Dordrecht: Reidel. 131–58.

Zandvoort, R. W. 1972. *A handbook of English grammar.* (2nd edn) London: Longmans.

Ziv, Y. & Sheintuch, G. 1979. Indirect objects – reconsidered. *PCLS* 15. 390–403.

1981. Passives of obliques over direct objects. *Lingua* 54. 1–17.

INDEX

477